Lavery Library
EX LIBRIS
ST. JOHN FISHER COLLEGE

Aspirations and Anxieties

ASPIRATIONS AND ANXIETIES

New England Workers and the Mechanized Factory System 1815–1850

DAVID A. ZONDERMAN

New York Oxford
OXFORD UNIVERSITY PRESS
1992

Oxford University Press

Oxford New York Toronto
Delhi Bombay Calcutta Madras Karachi
Petaling Jaya Singapore Hong Kong Tokyo
Nairobi Dar es Salaam Cape Town
Melbourne Auckland

and associated companies in
Berlin Ibadan

Published by Oxford University Press, Inc.,
200 Madison Avenue, New York, New York 10016

Library of Congress Cataloging-in-Publication Data
Zonderman, David A.
Aspirations and anxieties: New England workers and the mechanized
factory system, 1815–1850 / David A. Zonderman,
p. cm.
Includes bibliographical references (p.) and index.
ISBN 0-19-505747-3
1. Labor—New England—History—19th century.
2. Working class—New England—History—19th century.
3. Factory system—New England—History—19th century.
4. Industrial sociology—New England—History—19th century.
5. Machinery in industry—New England—History—19th century.
6. Labor movement—New England—History—19th century.
I. Title.
HD8083.A11Z66 1992
331.25—dc20 91-8192 CIP

2 4 6 8 9 7 5 3 1

Printed in the United States of America
on acid-free paper

For Patty and Andrew

Acknowledgements

This book has been many years in the making. During these years, I have received generous assistance from a number of institutions and individuals for my research and writing. Without their support, this book would not have been possible.

A Sullivan Fellowship from the Museum of American Textile History and several graduate student travel grants from the American Studies Program at Yale University supported the research for this project. Salary support from the Research Committee of the Graduate School at the University of Wisconsin–Madison enabled me to devote time to revising the manuscript.

The staffs of the Yale University libraries and the library at the State Historical Society of Wisconsin were always considerate and helpful in assisting me. The following archives and libraries also gave me permission to publish materials in their collections: American Antiquarian Society, Andover (Mass.) Historical Society, Bailey/Howe Library—University of Vermont, Baker Library—Harvard University, Canfield Library (Arlington, Vt.), Canton (Conn.) Historical Museum, Connecticut Historical Society, Connecticut State Library–Archives, University of Connecticut Library, Fall River (Mass.) Historical Society, Lancaster (Mass.) Town Library, Manchester (N.H.) Historic Association, Massachusetts State Archives, Museum of American Textile History (North Andover, Mass.), New Hampshire Historical Society, New Hampshire State Archives, Old Sturbridge Village (Mass.) Research Library, Rhode Island Historical Society, Schlesinger Library—Radcliffe College, Sheldon Museum (Middlebury, Vt.), Slater Mill Historic Site (Pawtucket, R.I.), State Historical Society of Wisconsin, Stowe–Day Library (Hartford, Conn.), and Yale University Library.

This book began as a doctoral dissertation in the American Studies Program at Yale University. David Montgomery was my advisor, and his meticulous reading of the original manuscript guided many of my subsequent revisions. David Brion Davis and Alan Trachtenberg also read the dissertation and provided valuable comments. Thomas Dublin, Jonathan Prude, and Sean Wilentz all read the manuscript at various stages in the revision process—each made rigorous and generous remarks that helped me reshape the project.

Portions of this study were also previously presented in several conference papers, and I am grateful to the following commentators for their remarks, which also helped me sharpen my arguments: James Barrett, Iver Bernstein, Mary Blewett, Michael Folsom, Ken Fones-Wolf, Bruce Laurie, and Kathy Peiss. My colleagues in the History Department and the Industrial Relations Research Institute at the University of Wisconsin–Madison have also listened to my ideas at various colloquia and lunchtime discussion groups. In particular, Stan Schultz has answered many questions about writing and rewriting, and Diane Lindstrom gave the last draft of the manuscript a very vigorous reading that challenged me to rethink several of my ideas.

At Oxford University Press, Sheldon Meyer, Rachel Toor, Karen Wolny, and Gail Cooper have all guided this project from manuscript to book with patience and generosity.

Finally, this book is dedicated to my wife, Patty Williams, and my son, Andrew. They have supported me through the all the trials and tribulations of publishing my first book. Most important of all, they have nurtured my love of knowledge and my knowledge of love.

Contents

Aspirations and Anxieties

Introduction

— I —

This book is based on a series of simple, yet vital, questions in American labor history: what did the first American factory workers think about the origins of the industrial system? What did these men and women have to say, in their own words, about their experiences as technological pioneers? What was it like to be part of that first wave of workers moving from farms to factories? Did the perceptions and actions of the first operatives, at the cutting edge of a massive economic change that would spread across the nation over the nineteenth century, shape the attitudes of industrial workers in succeeding generations?

In seeking to answer these basic questions, I have conducted an intensive and extensive analysis of the working lives of factory operatives in antebellum New England. These workers were a significant part of the first generation of Americans to face a mechanized, integrated system of factory production. And their perceptions of technological and socioeconomic change shed much light on how working Americans first responded to the beginnings of the mechanized factory system.

A definition of "a mechanized factory system" is certainly in order at the outset of this study, since these mechanized workplaces are the principal setting for this investigation. I have determined mechanized factory systems to be those work sites where machines, driven by external sources of power, performed a substantial number of steps in the production process. The production process itself was divided into a number of discrete tasks and then integrated within factory buildings. The work force was often sizeable in number, and usually organized in some hierarchical fashion. Wages, working hours, and regulations were also frequently defined in a precise manner. It was the combination of these factors that gave the mechanized factory system its basic form, while each factory had its own unique variations on this fundamental structure.

The industries examined in this study—textile mills, paper mills, armories, clock factories, ropewalks, metalworking and machine shops—were the first ones to bring these factors together to create mechanized manufacturing systems. Yet these industries were not all absolutely comparable in every respect; each one had its own unique pattern of growth and change. It is both their similarities and their differences that delineate so many facets of what goes into making a mechanized workplace and what goes into the different responses of the various workers. And those men and women (both skilled and unskilled) who worked directly with the new manufacturing technology in the new industrial system are the subjects of this study—they were among the first industrial workers in America, the factory operatives of antebellum New England.

Historians have often turned to these industries of antebellum New England in their search for the roots of the modern industrial working class. Many of the most recent studies have focused on a single community and the impact of industrialization on that community's social structure. These studies have told us a great deal about the dynamics of socioeconomic change under the system of early industrial capitalism. But we still need to know more about what mechanization and industrialization meant to the working people themselves, who were most directly affected by the new mode of production.

We need to know what the factory system did to workers, but also how workers understood for themselves what this system was all about. We need to understand these workers as more than historical aggregates; we need to recognize them as individuals struggling to come to terms with changes in their lives. Therefore, what is needed now in antebellum American labor history is to expand the field of vision beyond the individual community and, at the same time, to pay careful attention to the words and deeds of the workers who actually worked with the new machines.

This study, then, is a direct probe into the world of workers' ideas and actions—an exercise in what I call "working-class intellectual history." First and foremost, this book is an effort to let these working people speak for themselves, to bring what they said about their own lives to the attention of present-day readers. I want my work to capture the first generation of American factory workers as they were, men and women who often struggled to articulate their own hopes and fears about socioeconomic change. This study strives to convey the depth and subtlety of these workers' ideas about labor in a new workplace, and to analyze their attitudes in a coherent and nonreductive manner. These workers were not an inarticulate mass, understandable only through analysis in the aggregate, but thoughtful individuals with their own insights into the early industrial system and the transformation of their working lives. Working-class intellectual history is a way to comprehend even relatively unknown historical actors—such as these operatives—both on their own terms and through the lens of historical analysis. It is a way for present-day observers to understand how these antebellum operatives understood their own experiences.

While this book is unashamedly qualitative, literary, and intellectually historical in its approach, it is in no way an attack on previous studies in labor history that have emphasized quantitative social history. This monograph is still history from the bottom up—in this case, a history of ideas and actions surrounding the changing nature of work, from the working people themselves, who were often thought of as not having any important ideas (much less leaving a record of them for historians to study). I see this study, not as a refutation of the decades of scholarship that have already explored the antebellum New England factories—from Caroline Ware's pioneering study of the textile industry, to Thomas Dublin's meticulous statistical examination of the working women in Lowell, to Jonathan Prude's exploration of industrialization in rural Massachusetts—but as an extention of these previous historical inquiries. (See the bibliography for complete references to these and other works cited in this introduction.) I seek to build on the foundations laid by these historians in the realms of technology, work, community, and social structure.

I see my work as an attempt to create bridges between the new social/labor history and more traditional historical sources. To move labor history beyond the quantitative community studies, I am returning to some of the classic tools of intellectual history within a new working-class framework. I maintain my focus on the writings by and for the operatives themselves—which no one has examined previously in a complete historical monograph devoted to questions of working-class attitudes and perceptions—and I analyze the thoughts and actions of these factory workers in the light of these previous studies of early industrialization. I want to carefully examine workers' attitudes toward the socioeconomic changes these previous studies have already delineated. I want to bring individual human figures back out of the aggregate numerical figures and analysis. Where others have touched on the subject of work and workers in a page or a chapter, or examined operatives' ideas and behavior in conjunction with quantitative analysis, I have devoted an entire book to understanding these men's and women's thoughts on labor in a changing society. No other scholarly work has examined such historical issues from across the entire New England region, and placed those sources and those earlier studies in a new and wider context through a variety of comparative frameworks.

This book is therefore built around an organizational structure that is deliberately broad in its geographic scope—encompassing the entire New England region—yet constantly focused on workers' ideas about the workplace itself. The combination of breadth and in-depth focus has allowed me to find a wealth of sources in working-class intellectual history, which might not be available in any one single community, and to subject those sources to a rigorous and close reading. The operatives of antebellum New England were generally a literate population, and they have left behind an extensive written record of their own thoughts and actions. But this record is scattered in bits and pieces across the towns and cities of New England. Thus, a regionwide study of these literary sources—rather than another community study based on quantitative analysis—proved to be the most fruitful way of analyzing what workers themselves thought about the new industrial mode of production.

— II —

What this study reveals is that from the beginning of the Industrial Revolution in America, factory operatives in New England had a divided—and at times fragmented—consciousness of their own identity as workers and of the opportunities and dangers in the factory system. Workers' ideas about their changing workplaces fell across a broad spectrum, ranging from enthusiastic support, to profound ambivalence, to outright condemnation. It is clear that many operatives were neither ingenious Yankees fascinated by the advantages of the machine, nor would-be revolutionaries intent on destroying the entire factory system. Rather, workers were constantly weighing the costs and the benefits of industrial labor and trying to make sense of the changes engulfing their workplaces—changes that could create opportunities and problems at the same time.

What emerges from this broad survey of the operatives' own ideas is not a unified history of an undifferentiated mass of workers, but a complex portrait of many individuals and groups of workers, each with their own experiences and values. Yet this spectrum of ideas was not entirely without form; certain common themes about the promises or perils of the factory did emerge from more than one worker. At times, two basic schools of thought developed within the workers' own debate over the factory system. One group of operatives argued in support of the factories and their opportunities for new work and advancement. Others warned that the factory was a growing threat to workers' livelihoods and lives, and that any potential opportunities paled in comparison with the specter of oppressive discipline and a monotonous division of labor.

The two sides in this debate, however, were never fixed or precisely predictable. They were fluid and constantly shifting—some workers changed sides over the course of their years working in the factories, others held onto apparently contradictory elements from both arguments at the same time. In effect, the debate among these workers often returned to being more of a broad continuum of ideas between and even within individual operatives. What finally comes out of this range of ideas, and from this study itself, is not a narrative with a single explanation or theme. The historical and intellectual picture is far too complex to be reduced to any one argument. Rather, what can be discerned is a constellation of ideas various workers gravitated around, taking parts of different arguments and incorporating them into their own understanding of the factory system.

— III —

The crucial task for this study, then, is to understand how and why workers developed so many different perspectives on the factory system. This is not an easy job, for the ideas of these women and men do not fall into easily defined catagories. And the workers themselves did not fit into any ideal types.

Antebellum factory workers were a surprisingly diverse population of men and women, children and adults, native-born and a small but often crucial group of immigrants. These operatives were not all "deskilled" laborers; they ranged in skill from the most rudimentary machine-tenders to highly trained machine-builders. They worked in a wide variety of industries and factories, each undergoing its own distinct and complex pattern of mechanization. They entered factory work for many different reasons. Some women went to the mills of Lowell in search of independence and personal opportunity before marriage; others lamented that they felt forced into the industrial cities. Some families worked in the mills of rural New England as a way to keep their households intact and economically viable; others saw themselves as trapped in a cycle of industrial poverty that doomed them and their children to a lifetime of grinding factory labor. Some men looked on their factory jobs as a steppingstone toward running their own businesses; others warned that factory work—no matter what its level of skill—locked operatives into a life of dependency. The diversity of the factory work force, the range of their skills, the variety of work sites, and the many reasons for taking a factory job, are all part of the explanation for why these early operatives had so many different ideas about the mechanized factory. A closer look at the sources and methodology of this study is necessary in order to appreciate further the complex nature of this historical puzzle and each piece of its explanation.

This is a study that is based essentially on traditional historical sources from nontraditional historical actors. The private writings of workers—their letters and diaries—are a key component; so are their public writings—such as labor newspapers, pamphlets, strike proclamations, and legislative petitions. The personal testimony of operatives about their working lives—as evidenced in these letters and pamphlets and other documents—helps restore a sense of agency and human individuality to the history of these operatives. And, by paying attention to the commonalities and the disjunctions between workers' private and public voices and linking their words with their deeds in the workplace wherever possible, I have tried to present an accurate portrait of the antebellum New England industrial workers and their world views. (It should also be noted that corporate and public records have also been used, especially where they yield information on the workers' thoughts and actions.)

There is no way to determine with any certainty whether this rich variety of material is precisely representative of all factory workers. In some instances, individual workers did speak as representatives of particular groups and viewpoints; at other times, individual workers spoke only their own minds. But, given the large number of operatives who could and did write and the sheer diversity of opinions and actions discussed, it is clear that a broad spectrum of ideas about the factory is presented.

This book is an intellectual portrait, not only of those workers who chose to speak out in public—through published criticism or defense of the factory system, or through protest demonstrations or legislative petition campaigns. It is also a study of those operatives who spoke more quietly about their working experiences in private correspondence or in fleeting actions that may have been recorded for posterity. Obviously, no historical record, written or otherwise, is complete, and not every worker's opinion is recorded. But I have tried to avoid, wherever possible, tilting this study toward any one kind of source or any one viewpoint of the workers. I have tried to capture the opinions of both leaders and the "rank and file." Since a wide range of materials from these antebellum operatives has survived and is available for research, I have deliberately chosen to examine the whole breadth of these sources. A single historical document or record has its limitations, but when a large corpus of documentation is taken together, a fuller and more dynamic picture of these workers' lives does emerge.

To make this picture even more challenging to interpret, the material from these workers was sometimes descriptive and sometimes proscriptive. Workers discussed what the mechanized factories were like, and they reflected on what they wanted their workplaces to be. This study thus becomes an exploration of both how workers saw their personal reality and what they hoped for their future (as well as remembered about their past).

Workers' words and deeds, their rhetoric and symbols, are the very bedrock of this study; yet they often had many layers of meaning. Even when the operatives' writing was not consciously literary or their actions were not deliberately symbolic, their thoughts and ideas resonated with keen perceptions of their material condition as well as their visions of an ideal workplace. One essential goal of this study is to carefully peel away each layer of meaning, understanding each one in its proper context while probing for ever deeper levels of explanation.

This book makes every effort to capture the words and deeds of workers in a wide variety of mechanized factories in antebellum New England. Yet it is quite clear that the bulk of material comes from workers in the textile industry, and particularly from young women in the mills of the emerging industrial cities—Lowell, Massachusetts, being the most famous of these locales. It is not surprising that so many sources come from textile operatives, especially from the "mill girls" of Lowell (and other cities, such as Manchester, New Hampshire). After all, the textile industry was by far the largest mechanized industry in antebellum New England in terms of capital invested and workers employed. And the industrial cities, such as Lowell, often attracted literally thousands of young women into the burgeoning mills. These young women, in turn, often wrote home to the families they left behind in rural New England or contributed articles to the labor newspapers and factory girls' magazines of the period. It is these private and public writings that have often survived until the present day, sometimes scattered in libraries and archives and private holdings across the region. Some of these cities and some of these sources are already familiar to historians, but I have not hesitated to reexamine them. I have found them to be filled with insights and nuances that have never been fully explored and that become all the richer when combined with newly discovered materials.

Even though the voices of the Lowell mill girls ring out especially clearly in this study, along with their fellow female textile operatives in other industrial cities, the words of other New England factory operatives are not forgotten. Wherever possible (that is, wherever the sources have permitted it), I have tried to set the words of these urban textile workers in a broader context of ideas of other laborers. I have discussed the attitudes of operatives in rural textile mills as a counterpoint to their urban co-workers. I have also analyzed what evidence remains regarding the ideas of workers in other mechanized industries so that the thoughts of the more prevalent textile operatives can be seen in an even wider perspective. In some chapters, I have blended the ideas of textile and nontextile workers to show some of the common attitudes operatives shared from one industrial setting to another. In other chapters, I have made a clear distinction between the writings of textile operatives and the opinions of other factory workers to show that differences in occupations and in the workplace can also sometimes lead workers' thoughts in different directions, and to demonstrate that the views of the textile operatives do not always tell the whole story of the early factory workers. It is certainly a challenge to analyze a wide range of industrial sites scattered across a broad geographic region, but I believe that such an extensive analysis provides important comparative dimensions and is essential for developing a more complete portrait of the working-class experiences in these early factories.

It is evident by comparing these various industrial sites that the emergence of the mechanized factory system was a complex phenomenon in itself; it did not always flow smoothly and steadily across all of New England. And the diverse attitudes of factory workers were both a cause and a reflection of this intricate process of uneven industrial development in the region, from industry to industry, and from rural to urban industrial sites.

This study also makes extensive use of reminiscences written by former factory operatives, as well as material written by workers during their employment. Autobiographical recollections, particularly those written by older women and men decades after their years in the factories, must be used with great care. Memories of events in the distant past can be colored by the haze of fond, but inaccurate, associations with one's youth. In fact, two of the most famous recountings of the Lowell mill-girl experience—Lucy Larcom's *A New England Girlhood* and Harriet H. Robinson's *Loom and Spindle*—can both strike any cursory reader as just such glowingly ahistorical visions of happy childhoods spent in the factories. Yet my close reading of these autobiographies, along with other reminiscences, reveals that these books are far more complex and thought-provoking than the first impression might suggest.

These women, Larcom especially, displayed a divided and problematic relationship with their memories of work in the Lowell mills. In the midst of praise of the factory system, there are often brief but telling criticisms of industrial labor. Whether they intended to or not, these authors (and others) revealed significant tensions and ambivalences at the heart of their industrial work experiences. And many of these same hopes and fears are found in operatives' writings from the antebellum period itself. Thus the reminiscences of factory operatives, if used with care, prove to be far more than faded memory books to be easily dismissed by historians. They are sensitive and sensible recollections of changing workplaces; recollections that are surprisingly fresh and vivid and accurate reflections of what workers were actually thinking at the time. Positive images of the factories were not merely fond memories, nor were critical appraisals simply the product of bitter recollections; they were both part of the real working experiences of antebellum operatives.

The specific time frame of this study—1815 to 1850—was also chosen with deliberate care. The year 1815 is a logical starting point because that was when the first fully integrated textile mill in America began operations in Waltham, Massachusetts. This was the first factory to mechanize all the basic processes of cotton textile production—from picking and carding the raw cotton, to spinning, dressing, and weaving the finished cloth—and integrate them all in one industrial complex.

There were numerous smaller textile operations, such as spinning and fulling mills, in previous decades. But the first fully operational and integrated mechanized factory system began in America at Waltham. Over the next three and a half decades, the textile industry itself would expand and develop throughout the region, while other industries would also go through their own process of creating mechanized factories.

As for the end point of this study, 1850 was not a year for any single momentous event in the history of the mechanized factory system. Rather, 1850 is an approximate point in time when the New England factory labor force began to shift significantly in its composition. Beginning in the late 1840s, and increasingly after 1850, large numbers of Irish immigrants moved into the textile mills of New England, while many native-born operatives began their exodus from these workplaces. While this is certainly a significant event deserving of historical investigation, it adds major new questions of immigration history and ethnicity that go beyond much of the scope of this study (although this book does discuss the small, but crucial, population of industrial immigrants in the factories before 1850). These workers, in effect, constituted a whole new first generation of foreign-born operatives, with their own particular problems of adjusting to a new culture as well as to a new mode of production. Moreover, the literacy rate among the Irish operatives was far lower than that of the previous native-born workers. Thus, the Irish workers left behind far fewer of the literary sources that make up the backbone of this book.

By keeping this study within the time frame of 1815 to 1850, therefore, I have been able to focus my research on a population of mostly native-born, literate workers who were writing about their experiences in a variety of industries undergoing technological change. The history of the mechanized factory system in New England did not absolutely begin and end during the years encompassed by this monograph. But the years from 1815 to 1850 are crucial to any understanding of the origins of industrial manufacturing and industrial labor in America.

Yet within the period of this study, there is no one overarching chronological pattern that can explain the response of workers to the factory system. Workers argued about that system all the way from 1815 to 1850. As early as the 1820s, a time which some saw as a golden age when factory labor was more leisurely and harmonious, there were also numerous strikes in factories across New England. There is evidence that the debate then intensified in the mid-1840s as the pace of labor quickened in many factories, criticism of deteriorating working conditions mounted, labor organizations formed, and the ten-hour movement flourished. But, in these same years, ringing defenses of the factory system were still published in some factory worker magazines. In 1850, workers were still debating the merits of industrial labor. The voices of criticism seemed louder than in previous decades, but they had by no means silenced the workers who supported the factory.

Certainly, then, there were some chronological dimensions to this debate—I am by no means saying that all the years between 1815 and 1850 looked alike. There were shifts over time in the technology itself, the composition of the work force, and the rhetoric and tactics of protest. But a simple explanation of decline or improvement over the course of these decades is not an accurate reflection of the reality of these workers' lives. Workers certainly debated whether there was a deterioration or an improvement in the quality of their lives, but the debate itself endured throughout the antebellum years.

There are also no demographic correlations that can satisfactorily explain or predict the response of operatives to the factory. Moreover, quantitative analysis linking demographic data on an operative with her ideas is often impossible to perform. Since workers often wrote publicly under pseudonyms or anonymously, it is not possible to trace many authors through census records or other sources. The literary evidence itself can indicate whether the writer was actually a factory worker, and when and where she worked, but other personal details are often harder to come by. What the written record does show is that workers did not become factory supporters or critics solely on the basis of their age, gender, ethnicity, occupation, or any other single factor. In fact, workers with similar backgrounds, working similar jobs at similar times, could come to different conclusions about the nature of industrial labor. Yet the above factors should not be dismissed entirely. While no single one of them (or any combination) was an entirely accurate predictor of a worker's beliefs, it is also true that a worker's age, gender, ethnicity, and occupation all exerted some influence on her response to the factory system.

Since this study makes a determined effort to analyze the ideas of operatives throughout antebellum New England, it provides an unparalled opportunity to compare the attitudes of female and male factory workers. And this cross-gender comparison—one of the unique facets of this book—indicates that gender did have a significant impact on workers' attitudes. Men and women often saw factory labor from different perspectives, but this does not mean that all men or women had identical attitudes based solely on their gender. Men and women were found among both the factory critics and the supporters, but their criticism or praise tended to be shaped, at least in part, by their gender. Thus, the male and female identity of these early factory operatives is an important analytical tool, though it is by no means the only explanation for this debate.

It is important, however, to realize that the differences among male and female operatives, in their responses to the factory system, were related not to biology but to gender roles in society. In antebellum American society, a woman's sex was inextricably linked with expectations about what work she could or could not do. Therefore, gender was connected with previous work experience and occupational status, and the conjunction of these factors was often an important influence on how men and women saw factory labor. For workers who were entering the wage-labor force for the first time (among them many female operatives), factory work often gave them opportunities they never had before—steady employment, cash wages, the chance to live on their own. For workers who already had established occupations (among them many men), industrial development could have been seen as a destructive force stripping away their skill, status, and wages.

Previous work experience, occupational status, and skill level also had some connections with an operative's age (particularly child versus adult workers) and sometimes with an operative's ethnicity. These factors are also examined in this study as potential influences on the workers' perceptions of the factory system. Again, no one of these variables was always directly linked with a particular response. Rather, a whole network of factors that made up each operative's personal identity helped to determine where she stood in relation to the emerging industrial order. It is essential to remember that no one single explanation lies at the root of this complex debate among early factory operatives. The variegated composition of the work force itself, in terms of personal background and range of skills; the great variety of mechanized workplaces; and the many reasons for entering industrial labor are all part of the reason why so many different attitudes toward the factory flourished in antebellum New England.

— IV —

While this book does provide an in-depth examination of antebellum New England factory operatives and their attitudes toward changes in their workplaces, it must also of necessity have certain limitations. First, this monograph remains focused on those industries undergoing the crucial process of mechanization in the period from 1815 to 1850. It should be noted that, during this antebellum period, other industries (such as shoemaking and the needle trades) were centralizing production and dividing labor, and subjecting workers to other aspects of a factory system. But these industries did not use power machinery in their work sites until after 1850. Therefore, these industries remain outside the scope of this study on the mechanized factory system in its totality.

A second limitation of this study is its sustained emphasis on the operatives themselves and their ideas about the mechanized factory system. Yet these workers are not studied in a historical vacuum. Where appropriate, the operatives are set in the context of their relationship with factory managers and owners. Moreover, in order to understand the workers' attitudes toward their labor, issues such as family dynamics, religious values, and political culture are also brought to bear on the workers' lives.

Nevertheless, this study makes no pretense of examining the attitudes of all antebellum New England workers toward the factory; the emphasis remains on those women and men who actually worked with the machines, for they had the most immediate experience with the new mode of production. These operatives, though they were only one part of the antebellum labor force, were crucial participants in the beginning of the modern American factory. Other antebellum workers were also experiencing wrenching changes in their workplaces. But the demands of the machine, within the confines of the integrated factory, made these transformations especially challenging for many industrial operatives. Some of them had to transfer their skills from handicraft to mechanized production; others had to learn entirely new industrial skills.

And while social, economic, political, and cultural factors all helped shape the ideas of workers and are certainly discussed where appropriate, this study does not delve deeply into the operatives' lives beyond the workplace. Not that workers' boardinghouses, cottages, communities, churches, schools, and other institutions were not as important as the factories they worked in. But the sheer wealth of material left behind by these operatives demands some analytical focus and framework, and I have chosen to concentrate on the issues most central to work life itself in the mechanized factories.

By focusing this investigation on the workplace, I am not arguing that workers were interested only in their jobs and said nothing about other facets of their lives. I am saying that technological and socioeconomic change were central features of work life for antebellum factory operatives, that workers thought a great deal about these changes in the emerging industrial order, and that what workers said and did in these early factories is crucial for an understanding of the roots of the American industrial working class. It is also important to realize, however, that while this study is most concerned with the worker and the job, and particularly with reconstructing working people's own ideas about labor, these techniques of working-class intellectual history can certainly be applied to workers' perceptions of their homes, families, and communities as well.

— V —

This study is concerned with both the physical reality of these operatives' working lives—the machines, buildings, people, and regulations they worked with—and the perceptions working men and women had of the objects and events in their work lives. These workers were shaped by the forces of technological and social change, even as they strove to shape those forces by carving out some space for themselves in their workplaces. Daily life, for these people, was a struggle both to survive in a world of real material constraints and to understand that world in terms of their own experiences. History for these working men and women, as for everyone, was a web of relationships between people and events and perceptions. What these people believed about their lives was just as important as the events that happened in their lives; and the two together—perception and event—are what consciousness comprises. This study tries to understand both the working experience of antebellum factory workers and the language those workers used to convey their own experience. There is no simple right or wrong in such a study; workers' perceptions and their material reality are considered together rather than weighed against each other. What matters is both the content of workers' texts and their historical context in the emerging factory system.

What workers thought about the factory system is as important as the components of that system. And the components of that system were more than an aggregation of machines. Factories encompassed a complex network of both technological concepts and human relationships. Therefore, this book is organized, chapter by chapter, around the perceptions factory operatives had of each facet of the factory system. Each section, each chapter, and therefore the book as a whole, is structured by topic and theme. These topics, rather than a simple chronology, provide the organizational framework for the study.

I have divided the book into two parts. Part I, comprising Chapters 1 through 6, is concerned with workers' ideas on the basic physical and socioeconomic components of the mechanized factory system. The first chapter discusses the operatives' relationship to the most distinctive feature of the mechanized factory—the machines themselves. Many operatives wrote of their first encounter with a machine in a tone filled with both wonder and terror. Fear of the new devices sometimes yielded, over time, to a sense of mastery—a kind of working partnership between the operative and her mechanical servant. At other times, the excitement of a new job soon devolved into boredom with routine tasks. The machines themselves were described as everything from precocious children, to magical creations, to uncontrollable fiends. The machine could be seen as a sophisticated tool, an extension of the operative, with tremendous potential for productive labor. Or it could be feared as an almost living being, capable of defying its supposed master. Underlying all this imagery were issues of human control, discretion, independence, and power over these inventions. A machine could perform certain tasks even as it demanded more exertion from the operative, or it could be a source of new skills even as it replaced old craft practices. Yet the question persisted: who was running whom? Machines could produce a multitude of goods, but would they eventually manufacture operatives in their own image?

The second chapter turns to a consideration of the factory buildings. The central issue regarding these new structures was how to reconcile them with images and ideals of nature and community. Given the agrarian character of many operatives, and of antebellum America as a whole, it is not surprising that workers pondered the place of the factory in the natural environment. The debate focused not only on particular sites and plans, but also on the larger question of whether factories enhanced or destroyed natural beauty, both inside and outside their walls. The impact of both industrial cities and small mills in isolated villages is also considered—for each kind of factory reshaped the landscape in its own particular way.

Workers saw that technological change involved more than mechanical invention and building construction. New machines did not inevitably follow a predetermined pattern of development, nor did they automatically dictate specific changes in work processes. People built machines, and people (usually managers or owners) planned how to use machines. Technological innovation and social choice were inextricably linked—there were certainly patterns to such changes, but they did not travel along one single, preordained path.

Therefore, Chapter 3 shifts the focus away from physical structures and toward social relations within the factory system—in particular, the dynamics between labor and management. Workers entering the factories often encountered a far more intricate and hierarchical social organization than they had ever known before. For some operatives, the relations between themselves and their supervisors were characterized by harmony, mutual interests, and kindly paternalism (especially between female operatives and male managers). Other workers took a much dimmer view of these relationships. Since only men could ever become managers, some female workers spoke of the sexual exploitation embedded in the factory hierarchy. Others warned of the specter of tyranny and slavery looming over the industrial system. The entire discussion was based, once again, on the fundamental questions of power, control, autonomy, and authority in the workplace.

Chapter 4 continues this examination of social dynamics by looking specifically at relations among the workers themselves. Factory work forces were never entirely homogeneous entities; operatives differed in regard to their jobs, their ages, their gender, and their ethnicity. The whole social milieu of the factory was filled with crosscurrents of cooperation and antagonism based on shared working experiences and divergent personal characteristics. This chapter argues that the workers' sense of their common experiences was sometimes fragmented by the differences that remained between them.

Chapter 5 discusses how the system of factory rules and regulations was used to try to bind the physical and social components of the factory system into a single unit of efficient production. Managers used legalistic procedures and religious inculcation to try and create a system of both labor and social control. Some workers felt reassured by the regularity of this system and the flexibility of many overseers in enforcing the rules—they spoke of the factory as something akin to a school where they learned proper discipline. Others were troubled by the regimentation of the rules, and they saw managers as being harsh and unyielding—they spoke of the factory as something akin to a prison.

Chapter 6 closes the first section by analyzing the links between wage labor and the factory system. In this chapter I focus on the concept of wage labor, not on quantifying wages. Wage labor was certainly not unique to mechanized factories, but it was an inextricable part of these workplaces. Wage labor was also a complex system that raised a series of questions about how and when workers were to be paid—in cash or in kind, by the day or by the piece, through monthly or annual payrolls. The fundamental questions were how much workers would earn and who would control the purse strings. Many women saw wage labor as an avenue to greater independence in their social and economic affairs. But other women, and many men, thought that working for others for wages was a retreat into dependency and slavery.

The second section of the book, comprising Chapters 7 through 9, looks at broader questions concerning workers' perceptions of the mechanized factory system. Chapter 7 focuses on those workers who protested against the factories, and the changing character of their protests in the antebellum decades. Factory operatives' protest showed some surprising and even ironic shifts during those years. The 1820s and 1830s were the era of the great strikes, when workers in numerous cities and towns directly confronted the manufacturers, but they usually confined their agitation to the problems of wage cuts and working conditions. The 1840s saw the rise of the labor organizations that often launched critiques of the factory system as a whole (in addition to working on particular issues, such as the hours of labor), yet these same associations were often less confrontational in tactics than their predecessors in the earlier strike waves.

Chapter 8 looks at the hours of labor in the factories, and particularly at the 1840s movement for legislation making ten hours a legal day's work. Managers were constantly concerned with measuring precisely and controlling exactly how many hours each operative labored. Workers, struggling to achieve some control of their workdays, launched a massive legislative petition drive for a legal ten-hour day. Their campaign produced few results by the close of the 1840s. By appealing directly to the government to control corporate excesses and vindicate the rights of the worker citizens, however, the operatives who joined the ten-hour movement reshaped the terms of political discourse in antebellum New England for working-class voters and even for disenfranchised women.

The final chapter of the book, Chapter 9, reflects on the constant dialogue among workers about the advantages and drawbacks of the factory system, and explores how these divergent attitudes often were rooted in deeper divisions over the economic and ethical value of work itself in a changing society. When workers debated the merits of the factory, they were also debating the value of their previous working experiences, the meaning of labor in their present-day lives, and their future in the industrial system. Workers who supported the factory saw it as a distinct improvement over most forms of preindustrial labor, a sensible means of improving their occupational and economic status, and an important stage in their own and the nation's continued progress and material advancement. Operatives who criticized the factory saw industrial labor as inferior to most agricultural and artisanal work. Furthermore, they believed that labor should have meaning in and of itself in a worker's daily life, and not serve merely as a means to other ends. They feared that the factory was creating a permanent industrial underclass that would drag all workers, and the nation as a whole, into a downward spiral that would make a mockery of all notions of progress. There was potential for advancement in industrial development, the critics said, but only if the factory was reformed so as not to exploit and impoverish the workers.

I place this chapter at the end of my study because I believe that these attitudes toward labor as a whole may help explain, even as they are explained by, the workers' diverse perceptions of the mechanized factory. Those who saw work as merely a means of earning money and gaining some training and discipline were prepared to endure any inconveniences in the factory as long as they thought that the material benefits outweighed the disadvantages. These operatives remained confident that their factory labor was a voluntary and temporary stage in a continuing process of social and economic advancement beyond the drudgery of agricultural, domestic, and handicraft work. And those who saw work as an end in itself, who recalled with affection and pride the labor of the farm or workshop, were more likely to resist what they saw as unfair working conditions. An entire class of men and women was said to be locked into a factory system of surplus labor, frequent layoffs, low wages, and declining skills; a system where the means of subsistence—employment—lay beyond the operatives' control. But where was the way out of this dilemma—a return to the agrarian life, or a modification of the mechanized factory system? The critics considered both ideas to be viable alternatives, even as many of their fellow operatives continued to enter confidently the factories of antebellum New England. And so the debate continued; within the factory gates, among the workers, and sometimes even inside the minds of individual operatives.

— VI —

Once again, the answers to this continuing riddle of why some operatives supported the factory and some criticized it lie not in any one category of analysis or any one factor, but in an appreciation of the whole complex struggle of antebellum workers to make sense of technological and social change. Therefore, much of this book's discussion does not pivot around merely the fact that workers persistently disagreed over the merits of factory labor and ultimately over the meaning of work itself. Instead, this study describes how workers tried to steer their way through a new and uncharted workplace (one made all the more mysterious and difficult by management's constant efforts to tinker with such components as wage rates, working hours, and machine speeds). In response to the challenges they faced, operatives sought to establish norms and standards in the workplace that were worthy of being defended.

In the midst of this struggle to define and comprehend new forms of work, no single worker or group of workers could be easily classified as conservative, progressive, or radical. Workers were seeking to reconcile the new forms of work with established social values, and both supporters and critics of the factory system ended up sounding progressive and conservative at the same time. Workers approached their new tasks with a complex mixture of confusion and confidence, exhaustion and exhilaration. The possibilities of exploitation or emancipation seemed to hang in the balance as operatives struggled to reconcile traditional values with new demands. These machine-tenders both confronted and cooperated with the emerging system; they learned the rules of the factory game, but many tried to play it to their own advantage. Workers knew that they could not design the factory system entirely to their own specifications, but neither did they always conform entirely to the demands of the managers and the owners.

Thus, throughout the antebellum decades, workers were shaping the factory system even as the system shaped them. Social and economic conditions certainly exerted a profound influence on workers' consciousness of themselves and their work, but the operatives' consciousness also impinged on the social and economic conditions. Throughout this study, a recurring theme is that of workers' always striving to carve out their own work lives, in spite of whatever managerial rules and strategies may have been working against them.

This study, in attempting to elucidate the mind of the New England factory worker, has uncovered many minds at work. All of these minds were striving to understand their changing workplaces. Among these minds, each individual had her own understanding, even as common terms and themes linked the thoughts of many workers. For some of these early operatives, a sense of class identity and consciousness was just beginning to emerge. Since this class consciousness was in its nascent stage, it was often expressed haltingly—in words, gestures, symbolic expression, and physical actions—as workers labored to define their own identity in relation to others in society and to the new means of production.

Factory supporters held to a middle-class world view of opportunity and freedom and equality in the new mechanized workplaces. They were steeped in the ideals of individualism. Any problems that might arise—poor health, moral degradation, overwork—were blamed squarely on the individual operative and not on the factory system itself. Factory critics began to develop a distinctly working-class perspective; they spoke of corruption, degradation, decline, and slavery in the midst of the factory system. These critics blamed the system itself, and not the individual workers, for these problems. They saw these problems as rooted in the industrial capitalist economy, and warned that the individual worker was nearly powerless to stop the oppressive forces of that industrial system. Yet these workers also asserted an ideal of equality at the same time that they were condemning the growing specter of their own proletarianization. And they appealed to workers to join in labor associations and collective action in order to reclaim their rights to equality and justice—as individuals and as a class—from the hands of the greedy owners.

What this rich and fascinating dialogue among America's earliest factory workers finally comes down to is not an orderly debate with clear and predictable sides. Rather, this is a study of the struggle to define the workplace—actually, the many struggles to determine the terms of labor. It was a struggle between the different ideas, values, and experiences of these factory operatives as individuals and in groups. Workers often debated not only among themselves, but within themselves, to make sense of the changes engulfing their workplaces. For some workers, the contest revolved around a fundamental confrontation between labor and capital. It was a fight for power and control over the new means of production. These were the workers who were beginning to grope toward an understanding of working-class consciousness. They believed that they were locked into an unjust and inequitable system based on the exploitation of a permanent working class. For other workers, the struggle centered on convincing themselves, their fellow operatives, and the surrounding society that factory labor opened up new opportunities for present and future advancement.

The dialogue among factory workers was thus spoken on many levels—between the workers themselves, between workers and managers, and between workers and a larger public. Workers were striving to convince each other of the rightness of their cause, even as they were still trying to make sense for themselves of their changing workplaces. The richness of their dialogue, and their continuing disagreements with each other about the role of the factory, demonstrate that they were well aware of the complexities and challenges of the new system of production. Their hopes, fears, and doubts also reflect some of our own mixed emotions about the ongoing process of technological and social change.

PART I

CHAPTER 1

Terror and Wonder: Workers and Machines

The mechanized factory system was a new way of earning a living for workers in antebellum New England. But what made these factories different from other workplaces such as the farm or the artisan's shop? The presence of power-driven machinery was certainly one of the most distinctive features of the new work sites. Consequently, these machines were the subject of much discussion among the first factory workers. As with so many other facets of the factory system, the workers' perceptions of the machines were dynamic and multifaceted.

Workers who tended the same kind of machinery side-by-side in a factory, on any given day, might express divergent opinions about those machines. Mrs. Ephrain Holt remembered many different attitudes in her recollections of Peterborough, New Hampshire, textile factory workers in the 1820s.

> Some work in perfect harmony with their machinery which seems to quietly respond to their requirements and accomplish all their mechanism has fitted them to perform, while other machines seem controlled by the spirit of mischief, and bother their tenders in every imaginable manner. if something wants tightening and she turns a screw often a vexatious snap follows and something is thrown out of gear. a shuttle bounds away from a loom, or a section of spindles refuses to operate, or indulge in provoking antics, and the harder the tender workes and the more weary she is the more exasperating the entire machinery becomes. had our ancestral grandmother's witnessed the antagonism sometimes manifested by machinery they would have pronounced it bewitched and punched it with red hot irons.[1]

Why some workers appeared to be in harmony with their machines while other operatives wrestled with what seemed to be a demonically inspired contraption is a social and technological puzzle with many pieces. These pieces begin to fall into place with workers' first contacts with the machines. The picture becomes even clearer when elements of experience and skill and the dynamics of gender and power are all taken into account. For workers' responses to these new machines were more than a matter of technological knowledge, they were part of the struggle for control of the labor process and the workplace.

— I —

The first encounter between workers and machines was often a memorable one, as many operatives recounted these experiences in letters, stories, and reminiscences. Abigail Mussey, for example, left her New Hampshire home in 1827, at the age of sixteen, to live with her brother in Methuen, Massachusetts. After her arrival in Methuen, she recalled, she went to see the nearby cotton mill. Such mills were a common sight in antebellum New England, but Mussey had never been inside one of these factories. Mussey remembered vividly her first impressions.

> How was I filled with surprise at the sight presented to my view! Thousands of spindles and wheels were revolving, the shuttles flying, the looms clattering, and hundreds of girls overseeing the buzzing and rattling machinery! I looked into the various rooms, and saw all I wished for that time, and turned away, thinking for a moment I was deaf, and would never hear again. I thought I should never want to work in such a dangerous place as that.

In subsequent years, however, Mussey changed her mind and twice tried her hand at work in a textile mill. But she left both jobs when her initial repugnance for the machinery's noise and confusion developed into a permanent distaste for factory labor.[2]

Abigail Mussey was one of the thousands of men and women who worked in the mechanized factories of antebellum New England. Many of these workers were like Mussey in that their first factory jobs were also their first contacts with the new power-driven technology of early American manufacturing. And some workers shared Mussey's confusion and concern on first confronting the machines in the factories. Lucy Davis wrote to a friend about her own unsuccessful attempts to come to terms with mill work. Her initial anticipation—a feeling workers often called "mill fever"—quickly developed into a real sense of unease.

> I could not get a chance to suit me, so I came here to work in the Mill. The work was much harder than I expected and quite new to me. After I had been there a number of days I was obliged to stay out sick but I did not mean to give it up so and tried again but was obliged to give it up altogether. I have now been out about one week and am some better than when I left but not verry well. I think myself cured of my Mill fever as I cannot stand it to work there.[3]

Other workers showed more determination to overcome their initial problems with machines. Mary Cowles began work in the spinning room of Lowell's Prescott mill during the fall of 1847. She wrote to her sister that learning to tend a spinning frame "requires some patience to lern when you first begin. I almost gave up in despair the first day, it made my fingers so sore. but I thought if the other girls could learn I could and now the work seames quite easy to me." In many spinning rooms, there were also children employed as bobbin-doffers to assist the spinners in removing bobbins filled with freshly spun yarn and replacing them with empty bobbins. Lucy Larcom, one of the most famous Lowell operatives, whose poetry and reminiscences were nationally known in later years, recalled her first day as a young doffer with great fondness. She found her new working experience to be far more intriguing than frightening.

> I went to my first day's work in the mill with a light heart. The novelty of it made it seem easy, and it really was not hard, just to change the bobbins on the spinning-frames every three quarters of an hour or so, with half a dozen other little girls who were doing the same thing. When I came back at night, the family began to pity me for my long, tiresome day's work, but I laughed and said,—
>
> "Why, it is nothing but fun. It is just like play." And for a while it was only a new amusement, I liked it better than going to school and "making believe" I was learning when I was not.

Larcom's memories of being a bobbin-doffer were filled with a child's sense of excitement in facing new experiences. Helping to tend a spinning frame was like playing with a newfound toy—or so it seemed during those first few days in the factory.[4]

In the weaving rooms of many mills, where the workers were often young women, the initial reactions to the power looms were as complex as the mechanisms themselves. One operative clearly conveyed the challenge of learning how to run a power loom in a story she wrote for the *Lowell Offering,* a magazine written by women workers and noted for its generally positive portrayal of industrial labor. This story of "Susan Miller" may have been based on the author's own experiences when she first entered the mill.

> . . . [S]he went into the Mill; and at first, the sight of so many bands, and wheels, and springs, in constant motion, was very frightful. She felt afraid to touch the loom, and she was almost sure that she could never learn to weave; the harness puzzled, and the reed perplexed her; the shuttle flew out, and made a new bump upon her head; and the first time she tried to spring the lathe, she broke out a quarter of the treads . . . the day appeared as long as a month had been at home. . . . There was a dull pain in her head, and a sharp pain in her ankles; every bone was aching, and there was in her ears a strange noise, as of crickets, frogs, and jewsharps, all mingling together; and she felt gloomy and sick at heart.

The story goes on to show how Susan Miller adapted to mechanized factory work and eventually achieved a kind of mastery over her machine. Her initial fear, frustration, and exhaustion were replaced by a sense of familiarity and confidence. "Every succeeding day seemed shorter and pleasanter than the last; and when she was accustomed to the work, and had become interested in it, the hours seemed shorter, and the days, weeks and months flew more swiftly by, than they had ever done before. She was healthy, active and ambitious. . . ."[5]

Other operatives also wrote about this pattern whereby they went from an initial fear of the machine to a feeling of expertise—workers like Susan Miller were not merely the stuff of fiction. Women workers may have needed some time to learn how to tend machinery because of their past unfamiliarity with many craft tools and shop practices. They may have found that mechanization was quite a new experience for them, one that was hard to pick up initially but also hard for many of them to resist. And many women did stick to their machines and they became quite proficient at their tasks.

Mary Paul was quite enthusiastic about her progress in a spinning room of the Lawrence Corporation in Lowell. She wrote proudly to her father in December

1845: "I get along very well with my work. I can doff as fast as any girl in our room. I think I shall have frames before long. The usual time allowed for learning is six months but I think I shall have frames before I have been in three as I get along so fast. I think that the factory is the best place for me and if any girl wants employment I advise them to come to Lowell."[6]

Mary Paul, and other workers who shared her ideas of achieving mastery over machines, knew how important it was to gain some command of a mechanism whose power source and speed were beyond the workers' control. Mastery often brought a sense of accomplishment and direction to the operatives' work lives. Increased proficiency could also mean increased earnings for workers who were paid a piece rate for what they produced, not to mention the fact that increased production from each worker usually meant increased profitability for the factory owner.

Beneath this portrait of an increasingly capable mill worker, however, there was an underlying warning that familiarity could breed contempt. A proficient worker was able to block out her initial sense of the factory's human and mechanical pandemonium and concentrate her efforts on her own machine and her own job. But the narrowing focus of the worker's attention could lead to a constricting sense of her own potential. Even the optimistic author of "Susan Miller" warned that the longer an operative tended her machine, the more she felt "the wearing influences of a life of unvarying toil. Though the days seemed shorter than at first, yet there was a tiresome monotony about them, Every morning the bells pealed forth the same clangor, and every night brought the same feeling of fatigue." Machine-tending required a modicum of skill to learn and master, yet the tasks quickly became familiar to operatives who were required to perform the same monotonous motions over and over with little variation in their workday. Many operatives quickly discovered that learning to operate a machine depended very little on their own independent judgement.[7]

Lucy Larcom, despite her fond childhood memories of her first day on the job as a bobbin-doffer, also saw that there could be a far drearier side to her work—particularly if there were no immediate prospects for advancing to other positions in the mill. In her poetical reminiscence of labor in the mills, "An Idyl of Work," one of her characters observed: ". . . When I first / Learned to doff bobbins, I just thought it play. / But when you do the same thing twenty times,— / A hundred times a day,—it is so dull!" The specter of monotony was always lurking in the factory: a job that was confidently mastered could deteriorate into a boring and arduous task.[8]

Operatives who discussed, either directly or indirectly, the monotony of working with machines often struggled to convey the reality of their unvarying labor to those outside the factory system. There seemed to be a kind of cultural or conceptual lag in the language; that is, there were no terms of reference readily available to describe labor that produced no sweat but was nonetheless exhausting. How could one explain a job that was ennervating, yet not arduous, to a working population who usually saw a clear distinction between real physical toil and lighter burdens? The very nature of mechanized labor—its form, content, and pace—was a new phenomenon for workers in antebellum New England. They were struggling to define its terms and meanings, and words like "monotony" became important rhetorical symbols for larger questions about the transformation of labor itself.

Many operatives used words like "monotony" to express their concern that machines were defining the conditions of factory labor. Each worker was performing relatively simple tasks innumerable times each day at increasing speeds, and there were few skilled workers with any power to regulate the pace of production. Tasks were constantly being broken down into simple, discrete, repetitive motions to maximize efficiency and output and management's control over production, while decreasing workers' knowledge of, and ability to control, the productive process. Machines, and often premade patterns and fixtures, directed the work and the workers. There was little need for human judgement or creativity in these mechanized factories, only stamina and speed. Workers were losing whatever control they might have had over their daily tasks as they were being harnessed to their machines. The Poignand and Plant mill in Lancaster, Massachusetts, made no attempt to hide the fact that the operatives' first priority was to attend to the machinery. An 1828 memorandum stated: "When the machines are going they require constant watching & if a persons attention is drawn away by talking or the machines are left by the tender something will be going on wrong or the machines must be stopped." The company required that all operatives remain on their feet by their machines; there was to be no sitting down on the job. To put the matter simply: the constant movements of the machinery demanded that workers maintain a machinelike pace themselves. Management set the speed of the machines, and the machines set the pace of the workers' daily labors.[9]

Those workers who tried to free themselves from the grip of the machine, at least in their thoughts, often found that a momentary distraction could lead to many problems. One operative wrote, in her story "Eleanor Mallows," that the title character

> was often completely abstracted from her present employments—lost, as it were, in a deep reverie. Her work often went wrong—the shuttles continued to run long after the yarn was exhausted—the looms got out of order, and the overseer reprimanded her, in the rudest manner, for these repeated instances of neglect. She bore these rebukes, so severe to her sensitive mind, without complaint; but she longed to break away from this restraint. . . .

Even when work seemed to be going well, an operative still had to remain constantly alert to any signs of malfunction. Lucy Larcom wrote, in "An Idyl of Work," that

> . . . one broken thread
> Can make such mischief with the web! I've seen
> One thread drop down through the long films of warp
> Winding themselves around the dresser's beam
> And catch, and tangle, and make such a snarl
> As hours could not undo. And after all
> Mending attempted, with the woof filled in,
> 'T was marked "Imperfect"; doomed to some cheap use.

The most attentive operatives were sometimes powerless to prevent such snafus—some machines seemed to demand more than a worker's total concentration. Yet machine-tending provided little mental stimulation in itself for these workers. Some workers felt trapped between both the monotony and the unpredictability of machines. A machine running well could become an exercise in boredom for the operative, while a problematic machine was less an exciting challenge than a frustrating loss of time and money.[10]

The result, for at least one young woman in the Lowell mills, was a sense of drudgery and ennui. She and her machine were caught up in a web of mindless repetition and boredom. H. E. Back wrote to Harriet Hanson (later Harriet Robinson), who also worked in Lowell at one time and later published her reminiscences of factory labor.

> You remember perhaps how I used to tell you I spent my hours in the mill—viz, in imagining myself rich and that the rattle of machinery was the rumbling of my chariot wheels, but now alas; that happy fact has fled from me and my mind no longer takes such airy and visionary flights for the wings of my imagination have folded themselves to rest; in vain do I try to soar in fancy and imagination above the dull reality around me but beyond the roof of the factory I can not rise. . . .

This letter conveys a constant thread of tension running through Back's work life—in the midst of monotony she could not let her mind truly run free; she still had to be constantly alert for the momentary problem that could ruin a day's work. Back saw the machine, not as a labor-saving device relieving her from physical exertion, but as a mechanism that merely made her work tedious. The supposed challenge of industrial labor did not stimulate this worker's higher faculties; rather, she felt that workers were required only to be willing drones. Thus, when operatives spoke out against monotony, they were often complaining about something more than boredom alone. They were speaking out against jobs that squeezed workers between mindless monotony and the necessity of paying constant attention to their boring tasks all day.[11]

Other workers held a more sanguine view of the pace of mechanized labor. These operatives did not believe that they were physically or mentally submerged by the machines. They welcomed new inventions that took on the burden of arduous, and sometimes dangerous, labor. Harriet Farley, an editor of the *Lowell Offering* and one of the leading supporters of the mechanized factories, spoke for many textile operatives when she said that "as new inventions are constantly announced, as new complications of machinery are rapidly and faithfully assuming the laborer's office . . . all that prevents [labor] from being an unmingled blessing, is taken away." Many mill workers thought that most machines made few unnecessary demands on their physical strength and coordination. Some operatives argued that while machine-tending itself was not always the most rewarding occupation, it did not monopolize every bit of their time and energy.[12]

Harriet Hanson Robinson admitted that her labor was often "monotonous and done almost mechanically, but [her] thoughts were free." The very fact that the work required so little mental effort was a positive benefit to some operatives. They did not pause to reflect on the lack of meaning in their tasks; instead, they chose to think as little as possible about their boring jobs. It is even quite possible that some workers deliberately stayed with particular jobs, even after they became almost a matter of mindless repetition, precisely because they believed that such absolute familiarity actually opened up more possibilities for them in the course of the workday. Familiar tasks could be valuable because they included familiar surroundings and friends to share moments of respite with. Some workers insisted that knowing a job inside-out could permit a worker to free her mind from the task at hand—there were ways to watch a familiar machine without giving all your attention to the work in front of you. These workers believed that they could gain a sense of personal space in the midst of the factory, and actually expand their intellectual horizons in the midst of routine manual labor. In effect, factory labor could be a positive experience, if not always in and of itself, then in some ways beyond itself. The danger of monotony lay in not making the effort to keep one's mind active.[13]

Bobbin-doffers were one group of textile operatives who were not required to constantly watch any one machine. Consequently, their labor was usually less regimented by the continuous operation of the machinery. Lucy Larcom began her work in the mills as a bobbin-doffer in the company of other children—their workday was a mix of labor and sport. Some older operatives might have been disturbed that these youngsters had to spend their playtime in the factory, but Larcom thought that such youthful entertainment lightened their tasks.

> . . . [T]he work given us was light and for a few weeks it seemed like beginning a new game with a new set of playmates. Replacing the full spools or bobbins with empty ones on the spinning frames was the usual employment given to children. It was a process which required quickness, but left unoccupied intervals of a half or three quarters of an hour, sometimes of a whole hour, during which we were frequently allowed to run home; or if that was not permitted, we gathered around a merry gray-haired waste-picker in the corner,—an Irish-woman was a rare sight in the mills at that time,—to listen to her funny brogue stories of old Erin; or we climbed into a wide window-seat, and repeated verses and sang songs and told fairy-tales; or some piously-disposed elder girl ranged us in a class, and heard us recite the Shorter Catechism . . . or [we] explor[ed], with the overseer's permission, the mysteries of the carding-room, the dressing-room, and the weaving-room.

Larcom's memories of work as a bobbin-doffer, and similar accounts from Harriet Hanson Robinson, are filled with this sense of the leisurely pace and sociability in the factory. Working with machinery meant free time for entertainment with friends, not oppressive regimentation inflicted on children.[14]

Both Larcom and Robinson, as they matured, took on new jobs in the mill. Nevertheless, Robinson insisted, "though their hours of labor were long, yet they were not overworked. They were obliged to tend no more looms and frames than they could easily take care of, and they had plenty of time to sit and rest. I have known a girl to sit twenty or thirty minutes at a time. They were not driven. They took their work-a-day life easy." Many older workers also did not make any absolute distinctions between the worlds of work and play. They thought that the speed of the machinery was managable, and that they were not bound to watch the equipment at every moment. If a problem arose, they were prepared to act quickly to solve it. Most days, however, many operatives stepped back, let their machines run on, and searched for other ways to occupy their time.[15]

One of the finest accounts of the intermingling of work and play in the mechanized factory is found in Eliza Jane Cate's story, "Lights and Shadows of Factory Life." Cate probably based her story on her own work in the mills of Manchester, New Hampshire. In one chapter, she wrote extensively on how operatives tried to break down the "mechanical listlessness of manner" in the mills. One character, Fanny, "hastily puts her work in such order that she can be absent from it some time in safety." She then proceeds to surprise those still at work by prodding them with sticks and chasing them around the room. These "victims" then "retaliate" against Fanny

> by stopping her looms and carrying her shuttles to the farther corner of the room; and while she is in quest of them, by filling her alley with her own and her neighbor's seats. Others are drawn in; and those not actually engaged, look on and laugh. They are interrupted at length, it may be, by the entrance of . . . their first overseer. They do not fear him. They would not hesitate to tell him all about it. But it is understood that he shall not witness such sports. He has no objections to them, and he has no reason for none. Their work may be somewhat neglected for the time, yet not much; for there are non participants all about—kind-hearted, but serious girls, who ever and anon pay the neglected looms a visit.
>
> And all feel better after such recreations. They give their nerves and their whole system a healthy spring. . . . All love Fanny . . . because [she] broke up the monotony that was so oppressive to them.

Though Fanny was the ringleader for these escapades, other workers were also involved in this intertwining of work and play. In fact, this story clearly shows that workers who wanted to engage in active amusements on the job usually had to depend on the cooperation of others—someone had to at least keep an eye on the machines so that others could carouse. It was simply not possible for operatives to shut down the machines for uninterrupted amusement, so they had to maintain a minimum of vigilance at their work or incorporate the machines into some of their games.

There were two particular gestures of Fanny's that were especially intriguing. In one instance, she mischievously tied a girl to her loom—this was a humorous yet perceptive play on the notion of workers' being obligated to tend their machines at all times. The girl in question resisted being tied down, just as Fanny's pranks defied any idea that she was trapped by her machine. As another diversion, Fanny "makes a 'rag baby' of her handkerchief and bits of cloth; and while a neighbor is busy with one loom, she ties it to some part of the other that is constantly in motion; and when the owner turns about, the puppet is swinging or dancing before her." This little prank is also rich with possible symbolic meanings. It could have been a way for workers to turn the machines themselves into instruments of entertainment, without interfering with their productive capabilities. The operatives could use the machine for themselves and, at the same time, tend it for their employers. On a more somber note, the puppet attached to the looms could have been representative of the workers' own relation to the machine. It may have been an expression of both humor and protest, a warning to workers not to become like that figure being thrown about by the machinery's moving parts.[16]

Many workers found other ways to keep their minds active during the workday. When the machines ran well and the pace was not frenzied, these operatives tried to fight off monotony through mental exercise. Unlike H. E. Back, they believed that they could let their minds and imaginations expand beyond the factory. One woman remembered her job in a Lowell mill's carding room (where cotton was cleaned and the fibers were straightened out for further processing): "My work was easy; I could sit down part of the time. . . . Being fond of reverie, and in the habit of constructing scenes and building castles in the air, I enjoyed factory life very well."[17]

Various "reveries" also appeared in the *Lowell Offering*—in essays the women wrote about how they drifted off into dreamscapes of almost mythical natural beauty, only to be called back to reality by their overseers' reminding them to tend to their machines. These essays showed how workers' imaginations were not destroyed by factory labor, but they also demonstrated that the demands of the machine could not be ignored entirely. Moreover, when these women dreamed, they traveled to places far removed from the factory. Although they said that their work was not onerous, they did not want to spend their free moments thinking about it. They relished the time when they could let their minds wander; sometimes it was almost painful to return to real life. One poem, entitled "Fancy," captured that tension between pleasure and pain in a worker's dreams.

O swiftly flies the shuttle now,
Swift as an arrow from the bow;
But swifter than the thread is wrought,
Is soon the flight of busy thought;
For Fancy leaves the mill behind,
And seeks some novel scenes to find.
And now away she quickly hies—
O'er hill and dale the truent flies.
Stop, silly maid! where dost thou go?
Thy road may be a road of wo:
Some hand may crush thy fairy form,
And chill thy heart so lately warm.
"O no," she cries in merry tone,
"I go to lands before unknown;
I go in scenes of bliss to dwell,
Where ne'er is heard a factory bell" . . .

O Fancy! now remain at home,
And be content no more to roam;
For visions such as thine are vain,
And bring out but discontent and pain.
Remember, in thy giddy whirl,

> That I am but a factory girl;
> And be content at home to dwell,
> Though governed by a "factory bell."[18]

Some operatives wanted a more rigorous mental regimen than merely daydreaming in the mills. If the machine separated their head from their hands, then they would reassert the primacy of mind over machine. As operatives became proficient in tending their machinery, many of them actually read books and worked out academic problems right on the job. Harriet Hanson Robinson wrote that "many of the pieces that were printed in the *Lowell Offering* were thought out amid the hum of the wheels, while the skillful fingers and well-trained eyes of the writers tended the loom or the frame." Some essays were even written down in the factory "on scraps of paper which we hid 'between whiles' in the waste boxes upon which we sat while waiting for the looms or frames to need attention." Robinson's remarks indicate that the operatives' desire to improve their minds in the midst of the factory was not always supported by management. Many workers saw machine-tending as a form of labor requiring little concentration and generous portions of free time—both of which were conducive to reading and reflection on the job. But managers wanted a work force that was constantly active and attentive in watching their machines.[19]

Lucy Larcom wrote about how operatives adapted their educational activities to try to evade regulations prohibiting such distractions as reading in the mill. Poems and essays were often posted on machinery and window frames, "where a girl sat watching her work between thinking and dreaming." Workers could go through the motions of tending their machines and still read and think about these literary works. Sometimes they would quote favorite passages to each other. When books were prohibited on the shop floor, Larcom's sister tore out pages from an old text and carried them with her to memorize. "It was [also] a common thing for a girl to have a page or two of the Bible beside her thus, committing its verses to memory while her hands went on with their mechanical occupation. Sometimes it was the fragment of a delapidated hymn-book, from which she learned a hymn to sing to herself, unheard within the deep solitude of unceasing sound." These religious books, however, were also in violation of factory regulations.

> Some of the girls could not believe that the Bible was meant to be counted among forbidden books. We all thought that the Scriptures had a right to go wherever we went, and that if we needed them anywhere, it was at our work. I evaded the law by carrying some leaves from a torn Testament in my pocket.
>
> The overseer, caring more for law than gospel, confiscated all he found. He had his desk full of Bibles. It sounded oddly to hear him say to the most religious girl in the room, when he took hers away, "I did think you had more conscience than to bring that book here."

Larcom asserted that reading and other "improvised escapes of the imagination" did not harm productivity, but actually improved the workers' attitudes and made their tasks seem easier. Nevertheless, managers usually frowned on such diversions.[20]

Magazines such as the *Lowell Offering* constantly reiterated this theme—that the factory was a place where plain living and high thinking could coexist. Even Sarah Bagley, who in the mid-1840s was a noted critic of the Lowell mills, published an early essay, "Pleasures of Factory Life."

> . . . [W]here can you find a more pleasant place for contemplation? There all the powers of the mind are made active by our animating exercise; and having but one kind of labor to perform, we need not give all our thoughts to that, but leave them measurably free for reflection on other matters. . . . In the mill we see displays of the wonderful power of the mind. Who can closely examine all the movements of the complicated, curious machinery, and not be led to the reflection, that the mind is boundless, and is destined to rise higher and still higher. . . .

The youthful Bagley believed that workers think great thoughts, not in spite of the machine, but because of it. The joy of tending machines was not only that they permitted operatives to have free moments for flights of fancy, but that these mechanisms stood as testimony to man's inventive powers. Bagley argued that factory workers did need a higher level of intelligence to run these new machines; thus industrial labor could be an opportunity for expanding an operative's mental horizon. The machines first stimulated workers' physical and mental capabilities, but in a way that would not overwhelm or exhaust them. Then, once the operatives were motivated, the machine lightened their burdens and set them free to contemplate larger questions.[21]

The very nature and pace of industrial labor—whether it was monotonous and whether monotony was necessarily detrimental to the workers—was a constant topic of discussion among antebellum New England factory operatives. But beneath all this attention focused on the question of monotony lay even deeper concerns about the root causes of monotony itself. Workers talked so much about monotony because the tempo of factory labor was intimately linked with basic issues of skill, control, and power in the mechanized workplace. These issues also had many different meanings far beyond the machine and the operative. But in order to begin to understand them as they related to mechanization, it is necessary to look even closer at how operatives perceived the physical operation of machines on the factory floor.

— II —

Some workers began their examination of machines by looking at their power sources. Water wheels (and some steam engines) were the primary sources of power for most antebellum mechanized factories. The operatives had little control over these mechanisms—this was one of the basic facts of tending power-driven machinery. Although some workers were troubled by the idea of working with power sources beyond their immediate control, others were fascinated by the great water wheels and engines that ran the factories. Julia Dutton wrote to her mother that "all this machinery carried by one great wheel, it seems all most miraculous to think of it." Lucy Larcom recalled that she was

> sometimes allowed to peer in through a sort of blind door at the great waterwheel that carried the works of the whole mill. It was so huge we could only watch a few of its spokes at a time, and part of its dripping rim, moving with a slow, measured strength through the darkness that shut it in. It impressed me with something of the awe which comes to us in thinking of the great Power which keeps the mechanism of the universe in motion.[22]

The speed of machinery was another basic aspect of the new technology that shaped workers' attitudes towards mechanized labor. Most operatives also had no control over the machinery's speed. Overhead shafts, connected with the central power source, ran constantly throughout the workday. The speed of that shafting, and consequently of the machinery, was usually not under the operatives' direction. Most workers had the power to stop and start their own machines, however. These machines had a clutch that acted as a primitive form of on–off switch. Workers pushed on a lever that slid a leather belt from an idle pulley to a pulley that turned with the shaft. This lever joined the machine and the central power source, and could be used to disconnect the motive power when the machine needed to be stopped.[23]

Machinery speeds became a topic of particular concern for many textile workers in the 1840s, as many mills underwent a process called a "speedup," whereby each machine's running speed was increased. One manager from Lawrence, Massachusetts, remembered: "In 1835 a girl tended two or three looms, weaving cotton goods, running 108 picks a minute, equal to 216 or 324 picks a minute as the aggregate result of her work upon the looms. In 1849, which was the first year that the Atlantic mills began to run, a girl tended four looms, running 120 picks each per minute, making 480 picks against the 216 or 324, 14 years before." The recollections of this manager reveal that the mills were also combining the speedup with another procedure, called a "stretch-out," to increase the number of machines each operative tended. Textile mill owners were constantly looking for ways to increase the productivity of each machine and each worker, because there were few major technical improvements in the industry during the 1840s. Increased production became dependent on increased output from each worker.[24]

The *Voice of Industry,* one of the leading labor newspapers and a frequent critic of New England factories, reported in February 1848 that managers often resorted to outright subterfuge in manipulating machine speeds. The editors traced an elaborate scheme to deceive the workers about the pace of their labor and their piece-wage rates.

> The corporation nearly doubled the number of their mills up to 1842 . . . these new mills were to be started. How? By doubling the number of operatives? No. But by doubling the work of those already employed. Accordingly, the Agents sent men into the mill night after night, to reduce the speed of the looms, unbeknown to the girls. Soon the girls found their looms going at a rate of seventy instead of one hundred and thirty strokes per minute. They, as was expected, asked an explanation of the Agents. They told them that the corporations could not sell their cloth, and therefore were obliged to manufacture less or else reduce the wages of the girls. They finally told them, that if they would consent to do double work, and thus spare hands enough to fill up the new mills, they would continue to employ them. The

> operatives were obliged to comply, as the only condition of being able to pay their board. No sooner, however, were the new mills in operation and all hands performing double work, than men were employed to go into the mills, as before, and night by night, increase the speed of the machinery, until within less than two months, every loom was running at a rate of one hundred and thirty strokes per minute. Then were the operatives informed that they were making too much. Why they were making more than their employers! That would not do. The poor girl who does all the work and endures all the disease attendant upon it, must not be paid as well as her intriguing overseer and agent. The next step was to lengthen their pieces, called "cuts," from twenty-eight to thirty-five yards each, and to reduce the price for weaving from 15 cents to 11 cents the cut. In 1840, a day's work was 120 yards—the wages for the same, 75 cents. Now a day's work is 140 yards—the wages 44 cents.

The *Voice* saw this whole plan as a kind of managerial conspiracy to deceive workers into accepting an inherently unfair system.[25]

This report summed up many of the problems workers saw in the speedup and stretch-out—the physical toll of the intense labor, the constant reduction of piece rates, and the knowledge that their extra efforts were being exploited by the owners. Sarah Bagley, once she became a leading critic of the factory system, also voiced her qualms about the increased speed of labor in the mills. She saw everyone working harder just to stay even; if an operative was lucky enough to make a few extra cents, she did so only through exhausting effort. "The companies do not pay more for the *same amount* of work; but the operatives do more work than formerly. A few years ago, no girl was required to tend more than two looms. Now they tend four, and some five; and because they make a few cents more than they did on two, it is trumpeted all over the country, that their wages have been raised." The entire system was based on constant increments in work and output, and continuing decreases in piece rates, so that workers' earnings could rise only slightly (if at all), while their production increased dramatically. Moreover, with each increase in speed, the operatives' earnings often dropped until they became accustomed to the quicker pace at the reduced rates. Factory owners saw the speedup and the stretch-out as simple means of increasing the productivity of their plant and their work force; workers saw these tactics as a means of increasing their exploitation.[26]

The weavers at the Massachusetts Corporation of Lowell, in the spring of 1846, tried to stop this cycle of increasing workloads and decreasing wage rates by confronting directly the problem of the stretch-out. The company proposed that weavers tend four looms and reduce their piece rate by one cent. The weavers unanimously adopted a pledge not to abide by the company's new work rules.

> In view of the rapid increase of labor without a corresponding renumeration, therefore, we the weavers of No. 2, Massachusetts Corporation, resolve, that we will not allow ourselves to be physically taxed again, to add to the already overflowing coffers of our employers,—that we will not work under the proposed reduction, embracing a fourth loom and receive a cent less per piece.
>
> *Resolved,* That we will not tend a fourth loom, (except to oblige each other) unless we receive the same pay per piece as on three, and that we will use our influence to prevent others from pursuing a course which has *always* had a tendency to reduce our wages.

Nearly every weaver in the corporation signed the pledge, and for at least two months they held to their word. So strong was their determination to maintain their ranks and their resistance to this stretch-out, they included in their resolution the following provision: "That any one giving her name, and violating this pledge, shall be published in the 'Voice of Industry,' as a traitor, and receive the scorn and reproach of her associates." These women made it clear that they were willing to deny their support and fellowship to any operative who went back on her promise of solidarity in defying the stretch-out.[27]

Other operatives remained unconcerned, and even quite satisfied, with their workload, even as the pace of their labor increased under the speedup and the stretch-out. As late as 1844, when criticism of the speedup and stretch-out was on the rise, a "Lowell Factory Girl" wrote to a Boston newspaper and praised the opportunities she had under the system of increasing work and decreasing piece rates. She saw her work as a challenge, and she took pride in her mastery of ever-more-demanding tasks and her increasing earnings. She simply did not mind the fact that she was working more just to stay a little ahead.

> In May, 1842, the last month before the reduction of wages, I tended two looms. . . . In the next month, June, when speed and prices had both been reduced, I tended four looms . . . and I certainly, after the first few days, had an easier task than with two looms at the high speed. I increased my earnings every month a little, by the gradual increase of the speed, as I grew accustomed to it. In January, 1843, the speed was raised . . . and the price reduced still lower . . . my work was in no degree harder . . . on three looms. . . . The speed was raised just as we could bear it, and often, almost always, at our own request, because with the increase of speed our pay increased. In June, 1843, I still tended three looms . . . and in June, 1844, feeling able to tend four looms . . . I affirm that I have not in any of these, or other months, overworked myself. I have kept gaining in ability and skill, and as fast as I did so I was allowed to make more and more money, by the accommodation of the speed of the looms to my capacity. I am by no means the best weaver in the room where I work, though perhaps better than the average.

This woman saw the constant adjustment of speed and wage rates as a pattern of labor that was shaped by the workers themselves to meet their goals.[28]

The sound of the machines was yet another fundamental component of mechanized labor that workers discussed in great detail. The harsh sounds of the mill were especially hard on new employees, as some of their first impressions have already indicated. One operative added that on her "second day's experience of mill life," she was still " 'sick and sorry.' The noise makes my head ache, and I feel almost deaf. I can hear the humming of the mill in my ears when I am here in my room." For some operatives, the start of every workday brought a crescendo of noise down on their ears. The short story "Eleanor Mallows," in the *Olive Leaf and New England Operative,* captured this cacophony quite clearly: "Soon the heavy wheels began to turn, the sound deepening at every revolution, until the confused hum of spindles and the discordant clang of looms filled the air, and the very earth seemed to tremble under the combined operations of these giant powers." At least one operative, writing in the *Voice of Industry,* hinted at possible problems resulting from exposure to such noise. "Can any one cultivate their auditory organs, where thousands of shuttles are flying at their utmost speed, and the clatter is as if ten thousand wind mills were set in motion by a hurricane?"[29]

Harriet Farley thought that long-term exposure to the noise of the cotton mills would have the opposite effect on operatives—they would become accustomed to the sounds, without any physical or mental harm. She wrote, in "Letters from Susan," that at first "it seemed as though cotton-wool was in my ears, but now I do not mind it at all. You know that people learn to sleep with the thunder of Niagara in their ears, and a cotton mill is no worse, though you wonder that we do not have to hold our breath in such a noise." Another operative wrote: "I have become acquainted with a very pretty sociable girl in the mill, who comes and screams in my ear to tell me funny things, but I cannot understand her half the time." With time and practice, however, workers usually made their needs known to each other with less difficulty. Experienced operatives learned how to communicate with each other through signs and words above the machinery's din. One former bobbin boy said that an important part of his childhood education had come from listening to the women weavers talk over their looms.[30]

Some operatives, such as Lucy Larcom, had no single, fixed opinion about working with such noisy machinery. The sound of mechanical production disturbed her at times, yet comforted her at other moments—the voice of the machine spoke to her in many different ways. She recalled at one point,

> I loved quietness. The noise of machinery was particularly distasteful to me. . . . I know that sometimes the confinement of the mill became very wearisome to me. In the sweet June weather I would lean far out of the window, and try not to hear the unceasing clash of sound inside. Looking away to the hills, my whole stifled being would cry out.

Larcom wanted to escape from the noise of the factory into the quiet of nature. Yet she also understood the ironic fact that "hours passed in the midst of monotonous noise, which drowned the sound of human voices, brought with them a sense of isolation such as one feels in the loneliest wilderness." But Larcom did not always see such solitude in a negative light. She sometimes welcomed the opportunity to be alone with her thoughts in the middle of the mill's "continuous moan and clatter." She wrote: "I discovered, too, that I could so accustom myself to the noise that it became like a silence to me. . . . Its incessent discords could not drown the music of my thoughts if I could let them fly high enough." Larcom did not want to feel, however, that this sense of isolation was being imposed upon her by a machine. At one point she left the mill, only to return with a new appreciation for those noisy machines. "When I returned I found that I enjoyed even the familiar, unremitting clatter of the mill, because it indicated that something was going on." Thus the noise of the machine meant many different things to Larcom—it could mean discord, or isolation and loneliness, or a curious kind of meditative silence in the midst of sound, or even a welcome sign of human activity.[31]

Many workers argued that real insights into the nature of industrial labor could be gained only by looking even closer at the demands of particular machines in the factories. In textile mills, the machine that lay at the heart of the integrated system of production was the power loom. These looms were first developed in the cotton textile industry during the decade from 1810 to 1820. The power looms were designed to perform all the tasks for weaving cloth that a skilled handloom weaver did, through mechanical components that mimicked, as much as possible, human motion. Power looms regularly wound up the woven material, evenly beat the threads into place, and maintained a constant tension on the warp of the cloth—all of which were the essential operations for the continuous weaving of cloth. Beams of warp threads (running vertically) were mounted on the looms, and each piece of yarn was drawn through harnesses onto a front roller. Filling yarn, already spun onto bobbins, was put into shuttles and placed into the loom. When the looms were in motion, hammers knocked the shuttle back and forth across the opening (the "shed") formed by the warp threads. The beams rotated to unwind the warp and wind up the woven cloth, and a reed moved back and forth to push up new strands of filling into the cloth.[32]

Power looms were first used primarily in an effort to cut production costs during a period of declining prices for finished cotton goods. There was no acute labor shortage to be alleviated by mechanization; many handloom weavers were eventually displaced by these machines. The handicraft workers were replaced, not so much because of their power and control over production, but because of their relatively high wages and low productivity. The handloom weavers were usually scattered across the countryside, not concentrated in or near a factory. Nevertheless, there were some reports of these workers' mobilizing to protest the later appearance of the power looms in woolen mills in towns such as Webster and Southbridge in Massachusetts.[33]

Jabez Hollingworth, working in a mill in South Leicester, Massachusetts, wrote to his uncle, William Rawcliff, in 1830 about the impact of power looms in the factory where his family worked. The Hollingworth family was already familiar with many forms of textile machinery, but they were troubled by the installation of those power looms. Jabez wrote: "Yesterday morning Father had Notice to Quit as they are going to have all their work done by Girls. . . . Now you see the Fruits of Large Factorys. Here we are supplanted by Females that is expected to perform the same quantity of work for one half the wages the quality being out of the question."[34]

Jabez Hollingworth's brief observations show how skilled male workers sometimes linked mechanization with feminization of the labor force, declining wages, and deteriorating workmanship. Power looms, women workers, poor pay, and inferior products were all part of a constellation of problems which the Hollingworths faced and tried to resist. They blamed the factory owners for installing machinery that brought this host of troubles in its wake. But there also seemed to be a tone of resentment of the women who took advantage of the new opportunities open to them for tending power looms and thereby displaced the male workers. These men saw the women workers as the "Fruits of Large Factorys"; the influx of lower-paid, less-skilled female labor was a harbinger of what awaited all labor as the mechanized factory system engulfed more workplaces. As for the question of quality, the letter is unclear whether the blame for the decline in workmanship rested with the machines—which pushed workers so fast or alienated them so much that they lost all interest in quality—or with women, who were seen as less talented and knowledgeable than craftsmen. The final product of mechanization, in the eyes of the Hollingworths, was a labor market in which they were becoming readily dispensable. They were craftsmen in the midst of a factory system predicated on fewer skills.

Jabez Hollingworth's skepticism about the quality of power-loom production was not entirely a case of sour grapes. Many of the early mechanical looms were notoriously cantankerous and inefficient; they seemed to save little in labor or money. The early power looms were such curiousities that they even attracted the attention of some mill owners' children. Such children, especially of wealthy manufacturers, would usually never run machinery in their fathers' establishments. However, Hannah Borden, the fourteen-year-old daughter of a Fall River mill stockholder named Richard Borden, badgered her father into letting her tend the third power loom ever to run in Fall River's Yellow Mill in 1817. Over sixty years later, Borden recalled the challenges of operating that pioneering machine.

> The looms went so wretchedly poor that they were constantly being tinkered. When they became too troublesome Mr. Anthony took them to pieces and carried them to Pawtucket to be changed. Yarn was dressed by being run through a trough of sizing while an arrangement of fans dried it as well as possible after it left the trough. . . . Damp weather and the failure of the fanning process to properly dry the yarn ended in an immense amount of waste, the yarn frequently rotting on the beams. . . . Up to that time the yarn used was on bobbins which we stuck on the spindles. When the loom was started the yarn flew off into a trough thus wasting more than one half. They tried hard to fix this by putting beeswax on the spindles or sticking knitting needles through the bobbins. During the three years I worked there was very little improvement.

Given this litany of mechanical problems, it is not surprising that none of the early Fall River weavers tended more than two looms. On many days, one machine was more than a handful when it "required constant watching."[35]

There was one component of the power looms that caused the most consternation among weavers—that was the shuttle that carried the filling thread (weft) across the warp threads to create woven cloth. Most early power looms had no mechanism to stop the weaving process if a shuttle failed to pass completely through the warp threads. If a shuttle remained inside the shed, it could break the threads or even the machine itself. Shuttles could also fly out of the looms and knock down the nearby operatives. As late as 1845, Josephine Baker wrote in the *Lowell Offering* about the continuing problems of errant shuttles. "Just see how lazily the lathe drags backward and forward, and the shuttle—how spitefully it hops from one end of it to the other. But we must not stop longer, or perchance it will hop at us." Baker's description nearly personifies the shuttle as an impish, mischievous character not always subject to the will of the operative.[36]

Textile-machine builders, throughout the antebellum period, tried to develop new devices to solve the problems of their early power looms. They believed that these problems were due, not only to clumsy machinery, but to inexperienced and inattentive operatives who could not be relied upon to regulate the looms. More and more machines were being built on the premise that the worker did not have the skill or intelligence to be entrusted with anything but the most simple-to-operate machinery. Machinery manufacturers added perpetual loom temples, which constantly rolled up the finished cloth and kept the remaining work secure. They also developed automatic fault detectors that stopped the loom whenever threads broke. Their goal was to make the looms as automatic as possible, so that weavers could tend more machines running at faster rates. These technical developments did alleviate many of the initial frustrations weavers faced with unproductive machines. But a machine that regulated itself could pose new problems for workers. Machines that left less and less room for human error also allowed even less room for human judgement. Such automatic machinery could turn weaving into an extremely monotonous task of merely glancing over rows of swiftly moving machinery. Each machine would make few demands on the operative, but the overall job could quickly become frenetic yet uninteresting, and workers would end up bored and nervous at the same time. They might feel caught between jobs that were uninteresting and a factory as a whole that seemed to be confusing and taking on a life of its own.[37]

The irony was that manufacturers were installing more technically complex machines that were actually intended to simplify more physical tasks for workers who had less skill and experience. More and more skill was being taken away from operatives and built into the machines, which could then be run by less-knowledgeable workers. But this process eventually proved to be a kind of zero-sum game, because workers without any skills could not run complex machinery, no matter how automatic the mechanical operations seemed to be. Some modicum of skill was still needed in spite of such technological development; workers without any knowledge or incentive to run machinery properly were of no value in the factory.

In at least one instance, weavers resisted a mechanical innovation, perhaps because they thought that it would undermine their control over their work. Workers at the mills in Waltham, Massachusetts, did not want to try Ira Draper's self-acting temple when it was introduced around 1820. These operatives preferred to use the old temples, which were adjusted by hand every few minutes when the looms were stopped. Draper's temples eliminated the need for such constant stopping and starting—this was a welcome idea to the managers, but a more problematic one for workers. These early weavers may have been paid by the hour, and thus saw no advantage for themselves in a faster rate of production. (Workers paid by the piece often did favor technical improvements in their machines if they were able to produce more goods per hour without more exertion and without having their piece rates cut.) Patrick Jackson, the mills' superintendent, had to use some creative bargaining to get the new device accepted. He finally persuaded one weaver to try the invention; then he turned to his overseer and said: " 'John, the weaver makes the self-acting temple work, and you mustn't be beaten by a common hand.' " Jackson thus triggered a rivalry between the overseer and weaver; the overseer rose quickly to the challenge, and saw to it that the self-acting temple was installed on every loom. Why the overseer himself needed such prodding is not known; perhaps he was slow to install the new devices because he did not want to stir up the weavers under his direction. Managers and workers both quickly discovered that each innovation reduced some of the power loom's idiosyncracies and complexities and eliminated some of the skills necessary to be a weaver.[38]

Other weavers saw their mechanized labor in a more positive light; they emphasized the remaining skill and spirit of cooperation among themselves. Lucy Larcom saw a room full of power-loom weavers as, literally, poetry in motion.

> A hundred girls who hurried to and fro,
> With hands and eyes following the shuttle's flight,
> Threading it, watching for the scarlet mark
> That came up in the web, to show how fast
> Their work was speeding. Clatter went the looms,
> Click-clack the shuttles. Gossamery motes
> Thickened the sunbeams into golden bars,
> And in a misty maze those girlish forms,
> Arms, hands, and heads, moved with the moving looms,
> That closed them in as if all were one shape,
> One motion. . . .

Some power-loom weavers insisted that they still had to maintain a relatively high degree of skill and dexterity compared with most other workers in the mills. They had to be alert and act quickly to repair broken warp threads, and constantly replace the shuttle bobbins when they ran out of weft thread. Weavers often watched the looms of an absent co-worker; they trained new employees; they frequently discussed common experiences in and out of the factory. Many weavers did not feel isolated and overwhelmed by their power looms—they saw their work as a collective experience.[39]

Harriet Farley also surveyed an entire room of looms in one of her semifictitious "Letters from Susan":

> The machinery is very handsomely made and painted, and is placed in regular rows; thus, in a large mill, presenting a beautiful and uniform appearance. I have sometimes stood at one end of a row of green looms, when the girls were gone from between them, and seen the lathes moving back and forth, the harnesses up and down, the white cloth winding over the rollers, through the long perspective; and I have thought it beautiful.

Farley saw beauty in the machine's physical appearance and in its working motions even without any operatives around. The beauty of the machinery was linked, in Farley's mind, with the utility, simplicity, and efficiency of mechanical operations.[40]

Spinning machines also elicited a variety of reactions from the operatives tending them. In the Lowell mills, the machines were called "throstle frames," and they were watched by relatively unskilled young women. These workers' major task was to piece together threads when they broke. These machines also had automatic stop motions, so the operative needed only to find the broken yarn, tie it back together, and restart the machine. Though this work was rather repetitive and mundane, Mary Cowles asserted: "I like it very much indeed it is very easy pretty work after you once get learned." Lucy Larcom also recalled: "I could look across the room and see girls moving backwards and forwards among the spinning-frames, sometimes stooping, sometimes reaching up their arms, as their work required, with easy and not ungraceful movements." Larcom saw a balletlike quality to the tending of these throstle frames, she thought that these machines brought out the traditional feminine attributes of beauty and grace in the operatives.[41]

When Josephine Baker looked at spinning mules, the province of skilled male workers, she had a more mixed reaction. She saw a fascination in their movements, but also had a sense of their power and danger. "We have spinning jacks or jennies," she wrote in the *Lowell Offering,* "that dance merrily along whizzing and singing, as they spin out their 'long yarns,' and it seems but pleasure to watch their movements; but it is hard work, and requires good health and much strength. Do not go too near, as we shall find that they do not understand the established rules of *etiquette,* and might unceremoniously knock us over." Baker seemed content to remain on the outside looking in on this world of male workers using their strength to control strong-willed machines.[42]

The dressing machine filled the crucial step between power spinning and power weaving. This device was a complex array of beams and fans that coated warp threads with a starch preparation (sizing) so that they would resist breakage in the loom. The dressing frame was one of those inventions that raised questions about the concept of labor-saving machinery—whose labor, if any, was really being saved? It certainly benefited the manufacturers, because it evenly coated large quantities of thread at a steady rate; but it could be a difficult machine for operatives to manage. Dresser-tenders had to make sure that the temperature of the sizing was correct, the level of sizing was not too low, the broken yarns were pieced together, and the sizing was completely dry before the warp threads were wound onto the beam.[43]

The dresser was also one of those machines that defied the simple equation of mechanization with the "de-skilling" of labor. Here was a machine that demanded more dexterity and attention than many handicraft processes. But it was still a machine governed by an external power source beyond the worker's control. Workers had to ask themselves whether a power-driven machine, which also demanded a high level of skill, was to be welcomed as a positive challenge in the workplace. Or whether tending such machinery would be a doubly frustrating experience—demanding that operatives be as skilled as craftsmen, while forcing them to keep pace with the machine. Was skill without control ultimately a forced and unhappy marriage between craft and industrial labor?

Many operatives regarded dresser-tending as very hard work, and the turnover rate in this department was often high. The agent of the Ware (Massachusetts) Manufacturing Company observed in 1827:

> There is no work in the factory considered so laborious for females as that of attending the Dresser. We have already had upwards of 20 Girls in our new Dressing Room, out of which not more than four have become sufficiently case hardened to remain there. The others either discouraged before they got experience or worn out after they had become efficient, & were obliged to quit. This keeps us more or less in raw hands which can only be remedied by time.

In the Lowell mills, the dresser-tenders were also women who approached their work with mixed emotions. Harriet Farley observed that the dressing frames moved "with a gentle undulating motion which is really graceful." But Farley added: "The dressers are generally quite tall girls, and must have pretty tall minds too, as their work requires much care and attention."[44]

Lucy Larcom also tried her hand briefly at dresser-tending in the Lowell mills. At one point, she said that all machinery seemed to be distant and foreign to her. "I never cared much for machinery," she recalled; "the buzzing and hissing and whizzing of pulleys and rollers and spindles and flyers around me often grew tiresome. I could not see into their complications, or feel interested in them." Despite her sense of alienation, however, Larcom left behind a fascinating description of her encounter with a dressing machine. Though it was written many years after she left the mills, it portrays in vivid detail how the machine nearly came alive and overwhelmed her. She had gone into the dressing room because it "was liked for its cleanly quietness; and . . . [its] wider spaces of leisure." She was captivated by these reports of a slower pace of work, and she did discover immediately that the dressing room was less crowded than the spinning room where she had worked previously. But part of the reason for this extra room was "the dressing-frame itself [which] was a large, clumsy affair, that occupied a great deal of space."

Larcom's machine quickly proved to be more than she had bargained for.

> Mine seemed to me as unmanageable as an overgrown spoilt child. It had to be watched in a dozen different directions every minute, and even then it was always getting itself and me into trouble. I felt as if the half-live creature, with its great, groaning joints and whizzing fan, was aware of my incapacity to manage it, and had a fiendish spite against me. I contracted an unconquerable dislike to it; indeed, I have never liked, and never could learn to like, any kind of machinery. And this machine finally conquered me. It was humiliating, but I had to acknowledge that there were some things I could not do, and I retired from the field, vanquished.

Larcom's memories of this dressing machine are rich and provocative; she was expressing more than mere frustration at not being able to tend her machine. The dressing frame seemed to be transformed in front of her eyes, growing ever more sinister as she tried to master it. What began as something like an "overgrown spoilt child"—a mischievous but essentially benign character—eventually became a "half-live creature" with a "fiendish spite against" Larcom. Larcom, like the sorcerer's apprentice, was battling an animated object that was supposed to serve her, but that developed a mind of its own and sought to dominate its master. Of course, Larcom never believed that her machine really possessed such supernatural powers. Nevertheless, she finally had to admit that this contraption had effectively mastered her; and that proved to be a rather "humiliating" confession for her to make. It was very disturbing for an operative to realize that the machine was running her, instead of her running the machine.[45]

Larcom's battle with the dressing frame soured her on all machinery. Up until that point she had never felt any real interest in mechanical inventions, but she always believed that she could learn how to run a machine for her own advantage. She thought that machine-tending was a good way to earn a living and still leave her mind free for higher thoughts. There always seemed to be time in the mechanized mill for dreams and reveries. In the dressing room, however, she discovered that the "huge creaking framework beside us [Larcom and her sister Emilie] would continually intrude upon our meditations and break up our discussions, and silence all poetry for us with its dull prose." Larcom eventually sought a place where she could still earn wages from the corporation, but where she could also be free from "the bondage of machinery." She found such a place in the mill's cloth room, where she measured and recorded the amount of cloth to be shipped. Larcom valued her new job because it maximized her sense of freedom and responsibility. There was almost no machinery in the room to influence the pace of labor, and even the managers were more lenient because they did not have to keep rows of machinery running constantly. "We were allowed to have books in the cloth room," Larcom remembered. "The absence of machinery permitted that privilege." Larcom, once she began working in the cloth room, never again changed jobs until she left Lowell in 1845.[46]

— III —

Larcom's means of resisting the machine was to escape from it, while still working on the corporation payroll. Though she and many other workers grew increasingly dissatisfied with their mechanized tasks, Larcom—like most textile operatives—saw little chance for stopping the introduction of more machinery into the workplace. Most textile workers who criticized the machine rarely contemplated blocking the process of mechanization itself. Even the critics usually accepted mechanization as an inextricable part of the mill because they had no real craft experience to compare with textile labor. In particular, most female textile workers entered mills, which had already installed machinery, without strong artisanal backgrounds. Young women were often familiar with spinning and weaving in their homes, but they were usually not skilled craft workers with a strong tradition of independent labor in their own shops. Rather, they often came to the mills looking for their first full-time wage-earning job. These women were not struggling to preserve a craft in the midst of technological change; they were trying to make sense of the total mechanized system of manufacturing in which they found themselves immersed. These workers rarely spoke about tearing down the entire mill structure; their debate focused on how workers could win a decent life from a mechanized system that was already established.

One of the key points underlying many workers' concerns with machinery was the physical toll such machines exacted from the operatives. Many workers said that mechanized labor was exhausting—sometimes because of real physical exertion, but more often because of the constant tedium of tending machines. One former Lowell operative recalled: "The habit of standing on the feet frequently produces varicose veins; and though the girls seldom complain, for they know it is useless, yet it is a fact that factory girls are great sufferers in this respect." Even Harriet Farley admitted, in "Letters from Susan," that the aches and pains of tending machinery did not disappear after the first few days on the job. Some operatives had chronically swollen feet, and after a year or two in the mills, they had to "procure shoes a size or two larger than before they came." Farley also observed that "the right hand, which is the one used in stopping and starting the loom, becomes larger than the left." Yet, she concluded, "in other aspects the factory is not detrimental to a young girl's appearance." Farley was probably correct in arguing that many operatives adapted themselves to the daily discomforts of their work, but she failed to recognize their concern about more serious industrial accidents.[47]

Letters from workers, and the labor press, were filled with reports of men and women injured by machinery. In some cases, workers were fortunate enough to escape with relatively minor injuries. Aaron Jewett wrote to his father that his sister Sally caught two fingers "in the gears and hurt them so that she staid out of the Mill 2 weeks." Julia Dutton wrote to her mother: "I have had a very bad hand I caught it in the temples braised it very badly it was bad sore and painful for a long time it was over three months before it got well." Some machine-builders praised their new devices because they were so automatic that they reduced the danger of workers' having to risk interfering with moving parts. But many operatives were fearful of these inventions because all the automatic mechanisms seemed ready to pounce on an inexperienced and unsuspecting machine-tender. Joseph Hollingworth observed rather critically that the women weavers who displaced his father could pay a high price for their unfamiliarity with the power looms. "Mary Kenyon has had the misfortun to lose the forefinger of the right Hand. She was weaving on a power loom. She put her finger where it had no business, and so the loom in return snapped it of between the first and second Joints." Of course, experienced operatives were not immune to industrial accidents. They were less likely to be injured through ignorance, but perhaps more prone to be hurt by careless indifference to the danger in routine machine operations.[48]

Some workers were seriously maimed by power-driven machinery. One great danger was the many shafts, bands, and belts that made up the power transmission systems in the factories. The *Voice of Industry* reported on a man named Sullivan, who worked in a Lowell cotton-batting mill and was caught in a band and carried several times over the main shafting. He fractured his knee severely and tore his arm so badly that it had to be amputated. One veteran operative, in testimony before the Massachusetts Bureau of Statistics of Labor in 1872, recalled the danger of adjusting the power systems in Lowell around 1850.

> In Lowell, we used to have drums about 30 inches in diameter, as well as I can estimate. They revolved very rapidly. I don't recollect the number of revolutions, but I know that I have frequently had to hold the belts while they were being laced. There would be nowhere to shift on either side, and when I held one, I had to have my hand up above the drum, to keep it from being caught. I must keep it so that it wouldn't touch the shaft, and when I was a good, strong, able-bodied man,—as I was 20 or 25 years ago,—my arm has ached until it trembled, and I have had to give warning to run, because I could not hold it; and I have seen the belt snatched and struck against the ceiling with the greatest force. That never occurred but once, and that was in season for me to give warning, and we ran off. . . . We have had to hold these belts, sometimes, in very dangerous positions in order to lace them, which could be remedied only by stopping a little more machinery. So far as I have had experience in this country the machinery and belts and shafting are not generally protected, and, therefore, many accidents occur in the mills to the fingers and hands of the young persons and women, and to their bodies. I remember a great many instances. . . . Shuttles sometimes fly out and make black eyes, and cut holes in the neck. Have not known of many instances of persons being caught by belts,

> thrown round the shafting, or injured by the shafting or belt; but I have seen the clothes rubbed off of a girl, and I grabbed another girl's dress and ran to her with it. That was in Lowell. Her clothes caught in the belt and were torn off.[49]

Some workers tried to dismiss these reports of industrial accidents as sensational exaggerations. A published collection, "Extracts from a Journal," in the *New England Offering,* said of one mill girl: "If she hears of an injury happening to any one, a smashed finger, or a shuttle bruise on the head, why we are straightaway sent to our graves by some mis-stroke of the machinery, or carelessness of our own." Other operatives insisted that machinery posed a danger to workers' lives, limbs, and livelihood. Moreover, as workers were often pushed by managers to run their machines faster, the fatigued operatives ran a greater risk of being injured by the rapidly whirring mechanisms. An industrial accident could mean, not only pain and potential disfigurement or death; it meant lost time and wages, and the possibility that the injured party would never work again.[50]

Many of the industrial accident reports in the *Voice of Industry* included the demand that manufacturing corporations develop some system of workmen's compensation. One article concerned a young man named Pierce whose arm was crippled in a carpet mill. Individual donors raised money to help pay the doctor's bills and support the youngster and his impoverished mother. But the company had failed to contribute anything for medical care or other expenses. Another issue of the newspaper reported that Elvira Rumrill, whose sister Sarah was very active in labor-reform organizations, was caught by the hand and dragged into the machinery at a mill in Manchester, New Hampshire. Her arm was broken in several places and her chest was crushed, causing severe pain. The newspaper used this incident to call again on the corporations to provide lifelong disability payments for workers injured in their service. A Manchester operative, perhaps referring to this tragic accident, wrote in a January 1847 issue of the *Voice:*

> I should like to see liberality and generosity from the directors of the Stark mills, toward my sister operatives—should like to see it extended to some subjects of misfortune crushed by their machinery; for instance to the girl who but a few months ago, broke her arm in two places, in one of their weaving rooms; and I am told this day . . . that "the poor girl never had received a mill [one-tenth of a cent] from the Corporation."[51]

The Ware Manufacturing Company was one establishment that made some effort to provide for disabled workers. This company did not pay cash, but it did make some unusual arrangements to assist one injured operative in making a new living for himself. On July 27, 1826, the company's board of directors voted

> that in consideration of Benjamin Pepper having lost his right hand in the employment of the Ware Mang. Co. & the Directors being desirous to alleviate in some degree his unfortunate situation, that the agent S.V.S. Wilder be authorized to appropriate for his use gratuitously a spot on the River at the South east part of the Common sufficiently large to erect a shop for the sale of small beer—fruit, vegetables, &c &c & to present to said Pepper the necessary timber–boards–clapboards shingles–paint & lime for building the same. The said lot to be held by said Pepper during the pleasure of the Corporation—he obliging himself to remove his building from the premises whenever they shall require it.

The directors probably thought that they were being very charitable in helping this man help himself. But the company's generosity was also orchestrated in a single gift of land and building supplies, with no mention of any additional aid. This gift contained the further stipulation that the corporation retain control of the land, and that Pepper's store could be removed whenever the company wanted that property back.[52]

Some victims of industrial accidents never had the opportunity to petition for any kind of assistance—their injuries proved to be fatal. The commonest cause of accidental death in textile mills appears to have been those same belts and drums of the power system. In the mill village of Southbridge, Massachusetts, during the 1820s, both an operative named Asenath Maria Townsley and a superintendent named Samuel Louis Newell died in the factories. Townsley's tombstone says that she was "caught in the machinery of a factory," and Newell was caught in a belt and drawn through the shafting overhead. The *Manchester Operative* of February 10, 1844, reported that an Irish immigrant named Smith was killed the week before in the Hamilton Corporation in Lowell. He became tangled in a belt and was carried over a drum. His body was crushed by being forced through an opening only eight inches wide, and he lived for only two hours after the accident. In the summer of 1845, the *Voice of Industry* reported on a similar incident. William Cline, a worker in a West Windham, New Hampshire, factory, was killed instantly when he was caught by a belt and carried through the main drum and flooring.[53]

Workers were troubled, not only by the physical dangers of tending machinery, but also by the specter of operatives mentally deteriorating into mindless drones and drudges. Some workers feared that their stultifying labor, coupled with increasing powerlessness on the job, would take over their lives—they would become like the very machines they tended. One operative warned: "They are confined so long in close, unhealthy rooms that it is a great wonder that they possess any life or animation, more than the machines which they have watched so unceasingly!" Another worker wrote to the *Voice of Industry* about men and women becoming unthinking automatons, and how tragic it was that few would raise their own voices to stop the degenerative process.

> It requires some moral courage to speak and act independently in Lowell, . . . There are many, *very many* here, who are prepared to allow others to think and act for them; and themselves be only the machines to give expression to the will and opinions of others.
>
> If there is a state of servitude more servile than slavery itself, it is that to which I have alluded. A man who in addition to being a servant *physically* will be one *mentally;* has descended a little lower than any man could possibly descend who has a decent amount of self-respect.

This operative asserted that the machines and the corporations who controlled them were the masters. The operatives had become the slaves; or worse, machines encased in hollow human forms.[54]

The very word "machine" began to take on ominous meaning for some operatives. It did not stand for wondrous human inventions, but for unfeeling and unthinking human beings. To call a man "a corporation machine," as the Lowell Female Labor Reform Association did in 1845 when it condemned the politician

William Schouler, was to denigrate that person for his lack of independence and integrity. These workers also declared, with growing anger, that they were "regarded as living machines" by their employers. The image of workers' becoming machines was a stark symbol for the loss of all control in the workplace. Women operatives especially did not tolerate that insult, however, although they might heap such scorn on others. Harriet Putnam declared: "Let us then heartily and with one voice respond against the libel that is upon the female; that would render her incapable of thinking . . . and reduce her to a mere machine, moved only by the operating power of a monied aristocracy. . . ."[55]

Other women answered this call to break the bonds of female modesty that yoked them to the machine. Sarah Bagley, when she became a leader of the labor reform movement, said that she wrote not "to evince that there is 'mind among the spindles,' but to show that the minds here are not *all spindles.*" Another contributor to the *Voice of Industry* wrote of her "earnest desire . . . that the operatives may no longer be recounted a mere cipher, or at most, a living, moving machine, with just intelligence enough to obey the orders of the overseer; but not sufficient to make it possible to allow them any degree of liberty, least they should not make a proper use of it." One writer summed up this protest with her pseudonym. She called herself "A MACHINE THAT THINKS," thereby serving notice to the corporations that no matter how deadening the work was, the worker would always retain her humanity. This operative proclaimed by her pen name that even if management regarded workers as mere cogs in the machinery of their establishments—simply another factor of production to be calculated into the accounts—the workers would have to make certain that they did not fall into the same trap of thinking of themselves as mere machines. They would have to continue the struggle to think for themselves.[56]

Many workers heard the warning in the *Voice of Industry* that operatives were becoming machines, and they joined in resisting that process of degradation. But it was not easy to stand up against the dehumanizing effects of mechanization. Operatives saw their work lives being fragmented into narrowly constrained tasks in the mechanized factory. Ironically, as the machines became more specialized and complex, the operatives' roles became more routine and removed from the completed, standardized product. Workers usually saw only a fraction of that finished product, and consequently they had little of the craftman's pride in knowing that he had made something from start to finish with his own hands. They felt, in effect, broken down by the division of labor in the workplace. They worried that mechanization was turning workers into interchangeable parts, easily transposed, replaced, or removed. They feared the machine, not only because of its power to physically harm workers, but also because of its potential to deaden the operatives' mental acuity.

Lucy Larcom, as she so often did, saw herself as somewhere in the middle of this battle for the minds of the operatives. She acknowledged "that there was some danger of our becoming drudges." Yet she "defied the machinery to make [her] its slave." She also noted: "Most of the work in factories is too mechanical to be really enjoyed by an intelligent person. And the stolid native is in danger of becoming more stolid in tending machinery which requires little thought, and of which the operator comes to be regarded, and to regard himself, merely as an adjunct. So employed, the toiler's only hope of elevation is in keeping his mind above his work." Larcom saw factory work as relatively uninteresting in itself, yet she did recall all those moments of free time when she could let her thoughts soar above the mundane labor. But, even in her most poetic moments, she always remembered the problematic nature of the mechanized factory.

> But this was waste,—this woman-faculty
> Tied to machinery, part of the machine.
> That wove cloth when it might be clothing hearts
> And minds with queenly raiment. She foresaw
> The time must come when mind itself would yield
> To the machine, or leave the work to hands
> Which were hands only.
> . . . These [women] counted but as "hands!" named such! . . .
> It must not be at all, or else their toil
> Must be made easier, larger its reward! . . .
> Here was a problem, then,
> For the political theorist: how to save
> Mind from machinery's clutches.[57]

At least a few workers in antebellum New England were so troubled by the power of the machine that they engaged in acts of sabotage and physical destruction in the factories. Although there were no organized Luddite attacks on machinery like those that occurred in England, there were scattered reports of individual operatives' destroying parts of their machines. N. B. Gordon, the manager of a small textile mill in Mansfield, Massachusetts, reported on June 8, 1829: "Since last Wednesday the mules have been very troublesome, by the bands running off as was supposed.—The real cause has this P.M. been found to be done by the back Piecer Lewis Kingman, throwing them off & at last cuting the spindle & one of the main bands.—The weavers from the above cause have not had fillg. for more than ½ the day For Boldness & Cunning the above tricks surpass all description." Gordon's diary provides no reasons why Kingman surreptitiously sabotaged the mule frames. He may have been expressing his anger and frustration at tending the machine, or he may have been trying to control the tempo of his labor by forcing the machine to stop and thereby giving himself a respite. Kingman, as a back piecer, worked under the mule spinner himself. It is also possible, therefore, that he was tampering with the machine at the mule spinner's request or to harm the spinner's work. Whatever the cause of this machine's breaking, Gordon quickly solved it and said that by the following day the mules were running smoothly.[58]

Another mill agent, in Valley Falls, Rhode Island, ran into similar problems with some of his mule spinners in the same year. The spinners had walked off the job to protest their wage rates, and then returned to the mill to try to get the remaining workers to leave. They found new workers at the mules, so they proceeded to break the threads in a dresser, throw belts off, and throw one mule frame out of gear. They were finally driven forcibly out of the mill by the agent. Their efforts at machine-breaking were not a protest against the use of machinery, but an action to shut down the factory and make their strike more effective.[59]

The impulse to tamper with machinery even spread to machine shops. A. and J.

Spaulding, textile-machine builders in Greenfield, Massachusetts, received complaints about their yarn beams from the Merino/Dudley Wool Companies in Sturbridge, Massachusetts. The Spauldings discovered the source of the problem and wrote to the Merino/Dudley agent:

> this was an absolute intrigue put upon us by our good for nothing and unfaithful workmen as my brother was sick & my self from home. I long since knew that a beam made without a shaft threw it would not answer but a few days. . . . I told Mr. Pratt for an absolute fact that the shaft ran clear threw the beams and would at that time forfeited the Looms that it was so but on enquiring since your letter find them to be without shafts. . . . I pledge my self that the beams will be made to the purpose in future and the rest of the work superior to that—I hope Mr. Pratt has made some good beams for with a beam that will spring in the middle no power Loom will make good work.[60]

Some manufacturers tried to take decisive steps to check any destruction of machinery. George Hollingworth wrote that the factory in South Leicester, at the beginning of 1830, was "posting up a new string of Rules more objectionable than the Old ones. In one of them there is the following 'That if any Workman damage any Work or Machinery he shall be liable to pay damage the damage to be assessed by the Superintendent or Agent.'" Another firm charged an employee for "damage to a Long Shear by a Stone or Something thrown against it which broke one of the long shear blades." Other companies took severer disciplinary actions against those caught breaking machinery. Sarah Maria Cornell was discharged from a mill in Norwich, Connecticut, for breaking parts of her loom. And children in Newburyport and Salem, Massachusetts, were brought up on criminal charges for breaking machinery.[61]

These incidents of workers' supposed unreliability, carelessness, laziness, or obstinacy can be seen as deliberate (sometimes organized, sometimes individual) attempts to resist the domination of a machine-based system of production that left little room for personal autonomy or craft pride, and put a premium on speed and productivity. But these acts of sabotage, if they may be called that, were not necessarily acts of political protest. Some may have been simply individual efforts to stop the incessant strain of machine-tending, a way of expressing exhaustion and pent-up emotion. These acts were a kind of underground protest whereby workers tried to relieve their stress and regain a margin of control over their work lives, without assuming a posture of open defiance.

Some workers may have abused their machines to show that they had little traditional pride in or attachment to their machines or to the products they made. Craftsmen often owned their tools and treated them with care as their working partners; operatives had little loyalty to monotonous machines someone else owned and made the profits on. But underneath many of these acts, organized or not, was an effort by workers to reassert the primacy of human beings over machines—ultimately, and literally, people could make or break machines.

Some workers brushed aside doubts and criticisms of mechanized labor and maintained a positive attitude toward the machine—it was a fascinating novelty, an engine of progress opening up new opportunities, particularly for women. Harriet Hanson Robinson praised "the genius of mechanical industry, which would build the cotton factory, set in motion the loom and the spinning-frame, call together an army of useful people, open wider fields of industry for men and (which was quite as important at that time) for women also." Machines were seen as implements that extracted women from the confinement of rural life and helped them forge their own opportunities for independent and productive labor.[62]

Harriet Farley also continued to espouse an enthusiastically positive attitude about the future of workers and machines. New inventions would not control workers, but would extend human control over the physical world. Machinery, "with magical strength and precision, [would perform] feats impossible to them—shaming human power, but for this, that man creates, guides, and governs it." The magic of the machine, therefore, was never sinister; it was all for man's benefit. There was no need to break the machine in order to assert human authority; machines were always under the power of people. New technology, Farley insisted, would never overshadow, but rather would enhance, the abilities and opportunities of workers. Farley continually reiterated the primacy of human control over machines. She dismissed any fears of the machine as foolish superstitions that blinded people to the benefits of technological progress.

> Each substitute for manual labor was looked upon, by those it supplanted, as a patent from the Evil One, for their destruction—the inventor was an enemy, and persecuted as an emissary from the region of woe. . . . [But] think of the toil which would devolve upon men, women, and children were it left for them to clothe again the nations without the aid of machinery . . . slavery seems to be the least concomitant of machinery. . . . The machine is the slave, and its overseer is master.[63]

Farley believed that, no matter what the demands of machinery or managers, workers were not driven beyond their endurance. After assuming the post of editor of the *Lowell Offering,* Farley saw that magazine as a shining example of human achievement in the midst of the mechanized factory. She stated proudly: "The din and clatter of the Mill had not confused the brains of the workers, and no cotton fuzz had obscured the brightness of their ideas." Some operatives felt that machinery offered new challenges; they were called on to use their hands and head in new ways. Others praised machinery for the opposite reason—automatic machines made work less burdensome and difficult. When labor was divided up among various devices, some operatives found their tasks simple and pleasant and not overwhelming. If machines sometimes seemed to have a mind of their own, that was nothing to be afraid of. These seemingly intelligent machines still served workers as helpmates and as monuments to human talent. Josephine Baker, in a letter to the *Lowell Offering* from the ropewalks at the Charlestown Navy Yard, showed that a mill worker's enthusiasm for machinery could extend to other industries. She remarked, upon seeing the mechanized manufacture of rope, that she "admire[d] the exquisite finish of the ponderous machine, and the genius that joined its parts in one grand whole." People made machines, and people mastered machines. Workers were not becoming drudges; rather, the new inventions were in harmony with operatives, as both became part of a productive partnership.[64]

One worker went so far as to pen a poem lauding the factory and its constituent machines. She felt inspired by the speed and coordination of all this machinery.

The rumbling wheels, and rattling bands
All in succession roll,
The regulator swiftly moves;
And regulates the whole . . .

The bales of cotton soon are brought,
And from the Picker flows
Swift through the cards and breakers come,
And to the Speeder goes.

With rapid flight the Speeder flies,
T'is pleasing to behold,
The ropeing round the bobins wind,
One half can near be told.

The next we know the spinners call
For ropeing to be brought,
It's carried from the carding room,
And on their spindles caught.

Come, listen friends, and you, I tell
What spinners, they can do,
The roping they will quick convert,
To warp and filling to.

Another sight I now behold,
It is a pleasing scene,
The warp is taken soon as spun,
And wound around the beam.

Then soon it's carried out of sight,
Into the dressing room,
It's warped and dressed all complete,
And fitted for the loom.

The slaie and harness is prepared,
Each thread for to convene,
The looms are placed in rows throughout,
The weavers stand between.

The shuttle now is swiftly thrown,
It flies from end to end.
And they stand ready all the while,
Each broken thread to mend. . . .

This worker-poet saw the mill as a single, vast machine connected by its complex system of shafts, pulleys, and belts. It worked properly as a whole when each part—each worker and each device—was functioning in a harmonious and coordinated way.[65]

— IV —

While textile mills and their employees made up the majority of mechanized factories and operatives in antebellum New England, the world of the factory worker did not end in these mills. There were other important mechanized workplaces in pre–Civil War New England—armories, metalworking factories, machine shops, and other sites. While the workers in these factories usually wrote less about their encounters with machinery, they were by no means entirely silent on the matter. And their attitudes provide a crucial counterpoint to the ideas of the textile mill workers.

In particular, while so many textile operatives were women, virtually all armorers and machinists were men. Throughout antebellum New England, many male factory operatives found themselves in different occupations and sometimes entirely different industries than female operatives. Therefore, these women and men often experienced mechanization in different ways, even though attitudes toward the machine did not cleave simply along the lines of gender. Men and women both praised and criticized mechanization, but often their praise and criticism came from different work experiences. Thus, if one explores the perceptions of mechanized-factory operatives outside the textile industry, more crucial questions regarding mechanization, skill, and particularly gender, can be brought to the fore.

The sound of power-driven machinery was one aspect of the mechanized factory that frequently captured these operatives' attention also. Metalworking machines, such as trip hammers, were often reported to produce deafening noises. In Torrington, Connecticut, brass kettles were hammered into shape with a long wooden beam sheathed in iron. The noise produced by this process was so loud that workmen stuffed their ears with cotton. William J. Clark vividly recalled an early nail-making machine that struck his young eyes and ears with a unique blend of terror and wonder. The new device,

> a massive machine of cast iron, with large wrought shafts and huge cast fly wheel, was built and brought in, in pieces, being too heavy to move in whole; it was set up with much labor and effort. A new Tyler turbine water wheel was put in also to propel the nail machine; suitable dies were made and set in place, and the rotary machine started; the fires of Vulcan flamed up on the forge; the heated rod of iron fed in was quickly chewed up in the intricate insides of the machine, and headed, tapered, and pointed, the nails flew out. . . . The noise was terrific to my youthful ears, but the broad smile of Mr. Andrus' thin face then has a distinct place in my memory, lasting beyond the clatter of the wonderful machine.[66]

One of the most positive responses to power-driven machinery in metalworking came (rather surprisingly) from an English immigrant named James Roberts. Roberts was a skilled cutler from Sheffield who emigrated to the large Sheffield immigrant colony in Waterbury, Connecticut, in 1849. Though English immigrants often expressed strong reservations about mechanization, Roberts welcomed the new technology as a constructive aid to his work. He did admit that his son "hapend a bad misfortune. We hammer our springs at one stroke under a stamp and he was hammering and got fore finger in the left hand crushed under the stamp, but I hope that will soon be better." In spite of these occupational hazards, Roberts concluded that the Waterville Company was "the largest spring knife manufactury in America and the best & convenientist shops I ever saw in my life. They have all their scales and springs made by machienry. The drilling is done by machienry except boring on, and we have power to do all the work we want to do by power." Roberts entered this highly mechanized factory without reservations because he thought that he could produce more knives, and earn more money, than he would under a handicraft system.[67]

Other metalworkers were more troubled by the dangers in mechanized labor. Water-powered grinding wheels attracted a large amount of attention because they were known to overheat and burst at high speeds, often with disastrous consequences. Cheney Kenney, a grinder at the John Russell Cutlery Company in Greenfield, Massachusetts, was killed when a new grindstone weighing about a ton exploded. One piece of the stone nearly went through the floor of the second story, and Kenney himself was struck under the chin by the iron housing over the stone. His jaw was instantly shattered, and he died after five days in a coma. When Luke Kendall was killed by an exploding grindstone in Fitchburg, Massachusetts, his friend wrote a poem in his memory, which was published in the *Voice of Industry.*

The tide of business as was usual sped,
And cheerful labor buoyant spirits bred;
There sat the victim on destruction's brink,
But still unknowing could not from it shrink,
Nought of a warning sick'ning pang did feel;
With vigorous hand, and undiminished zeal,
He pressed the blade upon the ponderous stone,
Which still revolved with tireless swiftness on,
Urged by the hurrying water's potent sway,—
When suddenly, conveying wild dismay,
A loud and fearful sound salutes the ear!
It speaks of danger to companions near,
And oh! How were they stung with anguish keen,
When on the ground his senseless form was seen,
And when they saw his wounded bleeding head,
And knew from when the death-winged blow had sped.

The sheer power of these grinding wheels, and their unpredictable and dangerous nature, were constant sources of anxiety to those literally keeping their noses to the grindstone. Those who were not decapitated or maimed were likely to find their respiratory systems chronically impaired from breathing the particles of stone and metal thrown off by the wheels.[68]

At the Collins Axe Company in the late 1840s, grinding wheels began to be replaced by shaving machines. These shaving machines were designed by the company's head overseer, Elisha K. Root, to alleviate the production problems and hazards of grinding. Root was a brilliant inventor who developed a sequence of machines for automating the production of axes during the 1830s and 1840s. These machines forged the axe head, cut out the hole for the handle, and sharpened the blade: all at a much faster rate than handicraft workers. These new inventions supplanted much of the skill, judgement, and strength of the blacksmiths and axemakers with a series of discretely divided and mechanized tasks. Each machine could now be tended by a relatively unskilled operative: here was a clear example of machinery's being used to replace autonomous, well-paid craftsmen.

The veteran axemakers at the Collins Company often objected to the introduction of these new machines. The foreman B. T. Wingate was the leader of this opposition, and he insisted that machines were compromising the final product. Samuel Collins himself noted, throughout 1847 and 1848, that "many axes [were] shaved too thin and flat on the steel and failed in consequence." He also was concerned about the "*trouble of rust* [which] was caused by the change from grinding to shaving, and grinding and shaving before they are tempered, not washing the tempering salt all out of the eyes of the axes." Wingate stated that the reason for the "large number of cracked axes" was "*bad uneven* shaving." He put the blame squarely on Root's new shaving machines. Root countered by attributing the problem "to bad heating of the steel." This was a process Root had not mechanized yet, and he thought that the workers in that department were at fault. He believed that his machines were resented merely because they showed up the poor workmanship of other employees. Root's never-ending quest to develop more productive machinery, and his determination to prove his inventions' worth despite opposition from handicraft workers, paralleled the efforts of Thomas Blanchard at the federal armory in Springfield, Massachusetts.[69]

What exactly was going on at the Springfield Armory? Throughout the decades before the Civil War, an increasing number of specialized machines were installed that transformed but never eliminated the work of the skilled armorers. These workers were machine-tenders, but they also retained important manual skills in working with their machines. Some of the most perceptive contemporary accounts of the impact of mechanization in Springfield came, not from the armorers, but from government and military inspectors' reports on this federal installation.

James Dalliba's report of 1819, for example, may have been the most honest appraisal of the conflict between the management's and the workers' interests at the Springfield Armory. Dalliba stated bluntly that the division of labor served the government's need for a productive work force. But this same organization of work robbed the operatives of their status as independent craftsmen. Occupational specialization undermined the future employment prospects of armorers.

> The general arrangement of the workmen to their work is the best that can be adopted for the United States, but not so for the interest of the workmen; that is, each man is kept at one particular kind of work, and is not shifted. . . . By this arrangement, it will readily be perceived that each workman becomes as adept at his part. He works with greater facility, and *does the work much better* than one *could* who worked all the parts. This is undoubtedly the best method for Government. The consequence, however, to the workmen is, that not one of them becomes a finished armorer. If he is always employed at the Government factories, it is no matter for him; he is, in fact, the better for it, for he does more work, and gets more money; but if he wishes to set up business for himself, he has got no trade, he cannot make a fire-arm.

Once workers became machine-tenders, they found themselves with less power over the whole manufacturing process. When the labor of making a gun was divided among many different departments and then subdivided into a multitude of tasks within each workroom, no single worker could control how those guns were made.[70]

In 1841, G. Talcott of the Army's Ordnance Department reported that the increased use of machinery should theoretically have continued to diminish the power of the operatives as more skill was supposedly transferred from workers to machines.

> Machines for performing work (that was formerly done by the skill of the eye and the hand) have been gradually introduced from time to time, until at length the machines perform nearly all the work, leaving the workmen nothing to do but to fix the article in a proper position, apply the necessary oil, and set the machine in motion. A great portion of the severe hand labor is thus dispensed with. The machines are usually so constructed as to stop when the work is done without the aid of the overseer. In this way, a man can attend two or more machines. . . . The difficulty of finding good armorers no longer exists; they abound in every machine-shop and manufactory throughout the country. The skill of the eye and the hand, acquired by practice alone, is no longer indespensable; and if every operative was at once discharged from the Springfield armory, their places could be supplied with competent hands in a week.[71]

A full inspection board, however, found in that same year that many armorers clung to their own shop practices wherever possible. The board found workers laboring at virtually whatever schedule they chose for themselves. Some shops were nearly deserted in the middle of the day, and often an entire room of machinery was kept running for a single worker. "The reading of newspapers during the ordinary hours of labor appear[ed] to be so common a practice as not to be deemed improper; for, in several instances, the reading was continued even during the inspection of the board." The inspectors also argued that armorers often rushed through their work to give themselves even more free time. This practice was said to lead to poor quality-control and damage to the machines, which were "often suffered to run beyond [their] proper speed." These armorers were determined, wherever possible, to retain the maximum discretionary power over the pace of their labor. They kept their own standards and refused to let anyone else—not even a government board of inspectors—intimidate them into changing their ways.[72]

On at least one occasion the armorers themselves did voice their opinions about a new machine. An oft-repeated story told of how operatives criticized Thomas Blanchard's invention for turning gun barrels, and how that criticism prompted Blanchard to develop his revolutionary machine for producing gun stocks. Blanchard's barrel-turning machine shaped the entire barrel, in all its varying dimensions, with one single, continuous mechanical operation. When this new device was demonstrated at the Springfield Armory in 1819,

> the workmen were gathered around to witness its operation, [and] an incident occurred which finally led to the truly wonderful invention for turning irregular forms. One of the men, addressing himself to a companion, says, "Well, John, he has spoiled your job!" "I care not for that," was the reply, "as long as I can get a better." One of the musket-stockers, with a confident shake of the head, then boastingly exclaimed, "that he [Blanchard] could not spoil his, for he could not turn a

> gun stock!" This remark struck Blanchard very forcibly, and in answer he observed, "I am not so sure of that, but will think of it for a while."

The armorers laughed at the thought of Blanchard's building such a complex machine to produce such irregular wooden forms. But their laughter may have been rather nervous—for even as they taunted Blanchard and challenged him to try to match their skills with his machinery, they already saw how one of his inventions could replace certain workers. Blanchard himself had his own laugh, about two years later, when he returned to Springfield with a machine that used wooden patterns to guide a set of revolving cutters and create a variety of irregular wooden forms, including gun stocks.

Blanchard was put in charge of gun-stocking operations, where he quickly ran into opposition from many workers. He wrote: "if I cut the inside of the lock the stockers say that is no help to them, and theay still say that turning the stock is of little or no saving and they are determined if possible to run the machine down, but I am determined they shal not." Blanchard's letter indicates that these workers were skeptical that the lathes would ever prove efficient enough to replace them. As for Blanchard, he claimed that his machine could "make a closer point in one minute than a stocker can in one hour," and that he would "soon be prepared to combat a whole battallion of stockers." When Blanchard hired outside men and boys to help tend his new inventions—operatives who were paid low wages, taught very little about gunsmithing except for their specialized tasks, and shuttled in and out of the factory on short notice—the armory workers became even angrier. Blanchard remained at the armory for five years to see that his equipment was run properly and to prove its worth technically and economically. The armorers' opposition to Blanchard's machines may have slowed down their initial acceptance into the factory, but this resistance may also have stimulated Blanchard to develop his fifteen different gun-stocking machines to challenge these recalcitrant workers. In practice, however, Blanchard's machines also did not completely "de-skill" the stockers. Most of the lathes were not fully self-acting; the machine-tenders had to use their hands (and sometimes their feet) to adjust levers, wheels, cutters, and the object being worked on. These actions required coordination, speed, and judgement from the workers. The system of gun-stocking lathes also required additional hand labor to finish each stock; therefore the hand-stockers were not all suddenly displaced by these machines. In 1845 and 1846, Cyrus Buckland's second-generation stocking machines were installed in a steam-powered shop where machines, machine-tenders, and hand-stockers all worked under the same roof for the first time. In the shop, stocking-machine operators often worked with more than one machine over the course of a week or month. But hand-stockers and machine operators rarely shifted between each other's jobs. Though each retained certain skills, there remained a sharp distinction between machine- and hand-stockers.[73]

Mechanization did narrow the skills of armory workers, but it did not eliminate them altogether. The work force in many armories contained both machine-tenders and highly skilled machinists and pattern-makers. Managers never attained their goal of a work force composed entirely of unskilled laborers; even the machine-tenders retained significant amounts of skill and control over their work.

Some machinery, in fact, required that workers become adept at both tending rather complex machinery and meticulous handwork to make parts fit after machining. The skill to make gun parts was not built completely into the machines, despite the observations of the government inspectors. Skill often remained in the hands of the workers, and they tried to preserve it wherever possible.

Some armory owners, and other manufacturers, found themselves in the paradoxical situation of building machinery to replace skilled workers with unskilled operatives, only to find that their new machines created an immediate shortage of workers trained to build and run these devices. Thus the early history of mechanization in antebellum New England was not always a simple story of how machines automatically "de-skilled" and displaced workers. Sometimes new technologies demanded new skills, at least in the initial stages of development when machines were often difficult to operate. The long-range goal for factory owners, then, was to perfect the technical operations of this machinery and thereby replace higher-skilled machine operators with a more tractable labor force of semiskilled workers.[74]

This process of constant innovation in the armories caused a great deal of consternation among the workers. Nathan Starr, who owned a private armory in Middletown, Connecticut, complained to the Army's Ordnance Department about the decision to discontinue the production of a particular rifle pattern. One reason for his concern was that "it is the bane of mechanics to be often shifting from one article to another." Armory workers also knew that retooling a plant to make a new model could cause problems. The Springfield Armory spent nearly eighteen months preparing to manufacture a new musket in 1840 and 1841. The superintendent declared that workers would need to learn, in effect, a new trade in order to produce the new gun. And, while the retooling was in process, many production workers had no jobs. Only the skilled pattern-makers and machinists had steady employment at that time.[75]

Many metalworkers and armorers, therefore, scrutinized the multitude of new machines that entered their workshops. These workers, however, judged the machinery from a somewhat different perspective than did most textile operatives. In textile mills, mechanization was used to create virtually a whole new industry, where most workers started out and continued as machine-tenders. In metalworking shops and armories, mechanization was more likely to be seen as an attempt (not always successful) to replace high-priced skilled labor, which was in short supply, or seemingly in control of the shop floor. Mechanization, in textile mills, often brought women into the workplace and created opportunities (and problems) that female workers did not have before. For women, machine-tending could be a step up from domestic labor. Mechanization, outside the textile industry, often threatened the jobs of skilled men and tried to take away some of their control over the production process. For men, machine-tending could be a step down from craft labor.

Metalworkers were often skilled craftsmen who saw their trade becoming mechanized around them, even though they retained some handicraft traditions. They usually did not enter a fully mechanized factory, but often found themselves working in the midst of an ongoing process of increasing mechanization. Thus, these workers often greeted mechanical innovations with even more resistance than did many textile operatives. Metalworkers often saw technological change as a disconcerting transformation of their livelihood, and they frequently struggled to preserve their established patterns of work, while textile operatives usually had fewer means of stopping their quick, total immersion in a mechanized environment.

Mill workers, if they criticized machines at all, were more likely to speak out against problems that already existed on the shop floor. Metalworkers often complained about new machinery before it was even installed. These workers rooted their criticism in their knowledge of their established work habits and their reluctance to see those patterns change with the introduction of more and more machinery. The textile mill was presented as a *fait accompli* to newcomers, but many metal-working shops were seen as places where mechanization was still an evolving process. Mechanization itself was a new phenomenon for many male factory workers; yet they often saw how the process was both related to previous shop practices and transformed those work standards. These men may have been slow to learn new machines, not because of their unfamiliarity with all manufacturing, but because of their resentment of and resistance to changes in established working procedures.

The workers with the most complex relationship to machinery were the men who actually built these new devices. The machinists of antebellum New England played a crucial role in the process of mechanization, even as they strove to remain above the occupational status of semiskilled machine-tender. Machinists were, quite simply, the quintessential combination of machine-maker and machine-user. They worked with both handicraft tools and power-driven machinery to create more machines for other industries as well as for their own shops. They saw their own trade being transformed by the very machines they built, but they tried to retain their skills in the face of mechanization.

Unlike most factory operatives, who tended specialized machines designed for one specific task, machinists often used more universal machine tools to perform a number of the basic mechanical operations needed to build a variety of new machines. These power-driven machine tools—such as millers, grinders, and lathes—were gradually developed and introduced in antebellum machine shops. These machines were designed to hold material in place, guide drills and milling wheels, and stop automatically when the proper cuts and shapes were made.

Some machinists saw great advantages in these new machine tools. William Worthen remembered "when the first Whitworth planer was introduced at the [Lowell] machine-shop, [he] went to see it work, and could appreciate the amount of chipping it would save." Where previously workers had finished flat pieces of metal by hand with chisels, scrapers, and files, material was now fastened directly to the planer's bed, which moved back and forth beneath a cutting blade. An automatic mechanism moved the blade slightly with each cycle of the bed to remove small scrapings of metal until the item was planed to the proper thickness and smoothness.[76]

Many machine tools were self-acting, but they were still carefully monitored by machinists. These workers, in fact, usually did much more than simply watch the machines; they were constantly interacting with the machines to shape the proper wooden or metal parts. They still needed substantial dexterity and knowledge to run machine tools. Machinists had to set up and change cutting tools, place the work in its proper position, set the cutting speed and the depth of the cut, keep the tool lubricated at the point where it cut the metal, and measure the finished work to make sure that the part was machined to its proper dimensions. Machinists, where they could, tried to control the pace of their labor with these machines by regulating the time they spent on setting up and measuring the work they produced. But it was the machines themselves—through a system of moving parts connected to set screws and chains that guided the blades and cutting wheels over the work at the correct rate and shape—that directed the pattern of production.[77]

As the demand for machinery increased, so did the need for machinists skilled in the craft of constructing new machines. In some highly mechanized factories, there were almost as many machine-builders as there were machine-watchers on the payroll. Men were always the ones who built and maintained the machinery, for only men were thought to have the skill and strength required for these jobs. Women, on the other hand, often tended the machines that required less skill and strength.

Thus, the operation of machines was usually kept separate from the building and maintenance of those machines. Operatives were supposed to have only enough knowledge to ensure that they kept the machinery running smoothly. Textile workers, for example, were not taught how to repair their machines; they were only shown how to splice broken threads, and do other routine procedures. An operative who knew how to fix her own machine was a dangerous prospect to management, because she might also learn how to adjust that machine to suit her pace of production. Separating the work of female machine-tenders from male machine-builders was one way of keeping the women workers more dependent and submerged in the hierarchy of the factory. Linking skill with the male workers helped divide the work force along the lines of knowledge, power, and gender. Women operatives were supposed to know only enough to work efficiently without challenging the position of skilled male workers and male managers.[78]

New machine tools were being developed constantly to alleviate production bottlenecks caused by shortages of machinists. Skilled workers were needed, however, to build these machines to take the place of other skilled workers. So it was the men skilled in the use of machine tools, not the machines themselves, that often remained the most important component of the machine shops. If enough machinists could be found, they seemed to have had few qualms about using their skills to build machines for "de-skilling" someone else's job. Many machinists profited from the introduction and construction of machinery that adversely affected the livelihood of other workers. They probably saw how many machines, even some in their own shops, were tended by unskilled youngsters performing the same simple task over and over. These operatives were quite proficient and profitable to their employers, but they had little knowledge of the machinist's trade. The machine-builders knew that they had to produce more of these machines for their livelihood. They also realized, however, that they could not dictate how these machines would be used. They could only hope that their creations would not turn around and render them obsolete.[79]

Some machinists approached their work with profound ambivalence. They built machines they could not always control; their skills underlay the process of industrialization, yet that transformation was sometimes a troubling one. Jabez Hollingworth found himself to be one of those machine-shop workers displaced by the technological changes that surrounded him. In the fall of 1829, his father George wrote that "Son Jabez . . . almoste expects to be at liberty soon. He is told that the Company intends to employ only one Machinist. This must be a man that can work boath in Wood and Iron. This rarely to be found except in a Yankee who professes to do every thing." Jabez was primarily a carpenter with little metalworking experience. As iron machines began replacing wooden ones, he found himself out of his job in the machine shop, and he drifted back into carpentry.[80]

The changing technology of machine tools brought both "de-skilling" and the demand for new skills in its wake. Some skilled machinists might have found themselves out of work when their employers discovered that it took less skill to shape metal parts by machine than by using hammer and chisel and file. When the parts made by machine tools became more complex, however, then more-skilled machinists were in demand, and those with limited training might find themselves unemployed.[81]

Some workers sought out positions in machine shops, often in preference to employment in a textile mill. In some cases, textile corporations owned the machine shops, but working conditions were different in the machine shops than in the mills themselves. Charles Metcalf wrote to his parents from Lowell, in April 1844, that he found bobbin-doffing to be hard work (in contrast to what Lucy Larcom may have remembered). He welcomed the opportunity to look for a post in the machine shop.

> [I]t is rather hard work and I get very tired by night and feel thankful when Saturday night comes so that I can have a short. I have to carry out and lay on the top of the frames 5000 or more bobbins every day, and the same number of empty ones back again so you see I have to be pretty lively my fingers are so tired tonight that I can scarcely hold on to my pen much less write a legible hand, and this must be my apology for poor writing . . . my nose bleeds every day more or less not much however owing probably in part to the irritation arising from the cotton flying about and partly from the temperature of the room and fatigue, think I shall go into the big machine shop the first good chance, unless I get a better place in the mill soon. That Shubuel's advice and he is on the lookout for a place.

The "Shubuel" whom Charles Metcalf mentioned was Shubal Adams, a cousin of the Metcalfs. And, two days after Charles' letter, Adams wrote to his cousins about his own efforts on Charles' behalf.

> At the time of Charles coming here there was no opportunity to get into the shop and after waiting some time he got a situation in the mill as he probably informed you. . . . His work at present is hard and pay low, and the prospect of promotion not immediate, and I think I shall advice him when a good opportunity offers itself in the shop to accept and leave the mill.
>
> Albion Benjamin is in the shop has got a first rate chance to learn I should think, and will undoubtedly do well—He will make a first rate mechanic—

In July of 1844, Charles had finally left the mill and was ready to go into the machine shop. He wrote to his mother:

> I finished in the mill the last Sat. in June, as it was too hard for me in hot weather, have not done much since, expect to go into the machine shop with Shubael soon, Mr. Johnson the man he works for, says he will give me 60 cts per day for the first year, and 70 the *2nd* perhaps more, and as 60 was only three cts per diem less than I had in the mill, and considerable easier work I thought on the whole it would be better for me to go there I have hardly known what to do, but this seemed to be the most feasible plan.[82]

Many workers probably shared Charles Metcalf's preference for the machine shop over the textile mill, if they had the chance to choose between them. Machinists often had more bargaining power with their employers, because of their higher skill level, than most mill workers. Machine-builders were part of the mechanized factory system, yet they remained aloof from some of its more deleterious effects. Machinists often had more freedom of movement in their shops than most operatives; in some cases they could even determine the overall pace of their work. They thought of themselves more as independent artisans than as operatives employed by a corporation. In reality, the skill and power of machinists was quite varied in antebellum factories. The most skilled among them—pattern-makers and die-sinkers, for example—were a kind of craft aristocracy in the midst of machinery. Those workers, however, who manned the increasing number of machine tools—lathes, millers, grinders, etc.—were beginning to look more like other operatives. Nevertheless, many machinists still looked with favorable eyes on the process of mechanization. They believed that the machine did not destroy the traditional practices of wood- and metalworking, it added new dimensions to these trades.[83]

John Rogers, an employee of the Amoskeag Machine Shop in Manchester, was one such enthusiastic machinist. His letters to his family during the summer of 1850 first spoke of his difficulties adjusting to the new work. He said that "my neck is suffering martyrdom while I am writing this, for leaning over a bench all day has made it ache." But three days later, he wrote: "I shall persevere, knowing that it will become less fatiguing and more interesting as I proceed." One week later, at the end of July, Rogers did find the work more interesting, because he was using machinery to build more machines. He wrote to his mother: "I told you I had been put on finer work but now I have got on to the machinery which is more interesting yet. It appears singular but nearly all the work in iron is done or assisted by machinery. If a bar is to be turned perfectly straight, all that is to be done is to put it in the lathe and wait till it is done. And iron can be planed as well as wood."

Rogers remained enthusiastic about his work because, for him, the machine did not mean drudgery. He said that his duties varied "constantly so I rarely have a job last over a day or two which makes it less monotonous. We have just finished ten *cardheads* and are now at work on some *Gills.* They are all going into the woolen mill now erecting. I have nearly all the finishing to do on the card heads & Mr. Buxton said I did my work as well as hands he had that had been with him a year or two." Rogers took great pleasure in receiving such praise from an experienced machinist; it reinforced the concept of craft pride in the shop. He also seemed to enjoy the fact that some finer hand labor was interspersed with his machine work. The intermingling of hand and mechanized labor broke the monotony of constant machine-tending and helped preserve handicraft skills among machinists. Rogers told his father: "All finished work has to be turned on the engines . . . then filed & polished in the lathes, but then there are nice joints to fit & a great deal of work which has to be filed in the vice. . . ."

Rogers added one negative note to his correspondence when he mentioned an accident he had on the job. Machine-builders were not immune to the dangers of working with machinery. Rogers wrote to his mother in mid-November: "I burnt my tongue rather singularly the other day. The chips of iron that are cut by the turning engines are as hot as a cinder, & as I was leaning over my work whistling one of these chips flew into my mouth & it was some time before I could sputter it out. We have to look out for our eyes. Some of the boys have scars on their eyes caused by hot chips. I never got any bad ones in yet. . . ." Rogers' injury was minor, but other machinists were more seriously harmed by their machinery. There were numerous reports from the shops of Taunton, Massachusetts, about fingers and limbs being caught and crushed in belts and gears and moving machine parts.[84]

Many machinists echoed Rogers' overall enthusiasm for his work. They saw their trade as something more than a way to make a living—it was a way of life. The machinist was a kind of industrial artisan—a human link between the two worlds of mechanized industry and craft labor—striving to balance his work life between the demands of traditional skills and the new possibilities of mechanized production. Machinists relished the element of creativity and imagination in building machines; not just the same models over and over again, but constantly searching for improved designs. Machinists were often a key source of technological innovation as they saw problems in production and tried to develop new devices for solving those difficulties. The most skilled machine-builders were often inventors trained through careful observation and constant tinkering rather than theoretical education. And worker-inventors, if they were fortunate enough to retain legal control and patent rights over their new ideas and inventions, could use the new machines they devised as a means of upward mobility from employee to entrepreneur.[85]

From machine-builders, to machine-users, to machine-breakers, the debate about mechanization continued in factories throughout antebellum New England. The issue was usually not whether to smash the machine, but how to control it. Operatives in the same workroom could disagree on that fundamental question. Some felt increasingly powerless as manufacturers constantly added new devices to the shop floor. They saw the machines as engines of destruction, breaking down traditional patterns of work. Yet, often their opposition was not focused on the technology itself, but on what they saw as management's misuse of that technology. They believed that machinery would benefit them only if they could retain some authority over when and where and how these machines were used. They wanted some say in the course of technological development—both in its mechanical operations and in its human decisions. Other workers confidently asserted that they were already in control of their machines. They saw the machine as the best of both worlds—it was an engine of constructive change moving society forward toward a future of material abundance, yet it also remained a tool in the hands of the worker.

Workers' responses to machines were more than simple reactions to the nuts and bolts of new technology. The operatives' attitudes were also shaped by their understanding of technological change as a social process. Workers were responding not only to mechanization, but also to the fundamental question of how that new technology was used by management and labor. Machines did not determine for themselves how they were to be used; aside from some basic mechanical requirements, it was management that sought to determine who, when, where, and how to run those machines. Yet the power of managers to shape the social uses of new technology was not absolute. Workers also exerted their influence to help construct the social dimensions of technological change, even as they were in turn shaped by other mechanical and human constraints.

Operatives disagreed with each other about whether the result of this interaction between machines, workers, and managers was a net gain or loss for themselves and their future prospects. But all workers knew that machinery had to be seen as only one part of the mechanized factory system—a system that also encompassed new forms of buildings, new working relationships within those buildings, and new ideas about time, money, and the meaning of work itself. And this factory system was part of the even larger changes associated with the emergence of industrial capitalism in antebellum New England. All workers, regardless of their ideas about machinery, would also have to address these other dimensions of factory life. And often, when they looked beyond the machines, the next challenge they confronted was the factory buildings themselves.

CHAPTER 2

The Quest for the Middle Ground: Workers and Factory Buildings

There was cause for celebration at the Lowell Manufacturing Company in the spring of 1848. The firm had recently completed a new carpet mill capable of containing 250 Bigelow power looms. But before the machinery arrived, the management decided to put on one of the biggest public demonstrations in the history of Lowell, Massachusetts. Some 5,000 operatives, overseers, and townspeople filled the new mill. They were serenaded by two bands and feasted on corned beef, cold ham, bread, cheese, pies, tarts, apples, oranges, and raisins. One hundred sets of dancers took over the mill floor for an evening of entertainment. Harriet Farley, then editor of the *New England Offering,* was captivated by the entire scene and remarked:

> we can only say, that when we entered the room, brilliantly lighted as it was, ornamented with the bright productions of the rug and carpet weavers, and filled, though not crowded, with a happy multitude of all ages and conditions, moving to and fro, and sending forth a low, pleasant murmur,—when we first entered, a soft, subduing influence fell upon us, for we were reminded of our childhood ideas of heaven.[1]

The Lowell Company's festivities were not the first of their kind in New England, though they were probably the grandest. Back in 1825, a woolen mill "raising" in Uxbridge, Massachusetts, brought forth a grand meal, including shankbone soup; and the name "Shankbone" was linked with that mill for many years after. In another part of the same town lay the mill village of "Crackerville," where less fortunate workers had been plied with mere crackers for their help in "raising" another factory. The Pomfret, Connecticut, Cotton Factory opened its mill with a celebration and punch for the whole community. And in Central Falls, Rhode Island, a factory opening was marked with speeches and toasts.[2]

These occasions were all intended to show off the new buildings in a favorable light. Factory owners were intent on rounding up support for these new enterprises from overseers, operatives, and townspeople. The owners wanted all these groups to perceive the factory as part of a common good in which each one had a stake:

success depended on everyone's working together. But did those who worked within the factory walls come to see these new buildings in such a favorable light?

The operatives' perceptions of the factory buildings, like their attitudes towards machinery, were varied and complex. The variety of factory shapes and sizes was as great as that of the machines they housed. But as was so often the case in antebellum New England, textile mills attracted the most attention from factory operatives. The textile mills were usually built according to specific technical requirements and constraints. The mills could not be more than a few hundred feet long, because the shafting would not be able to transmit power efficiently over longer distances. The building also had to be narrow enough to allow daylight to penetrate effectively from the peripheral windows into the mill's interior. And these mills needed deep foundations to withstand vibrations from the machines and to resist high floodwaters. All of these structural constraints were satisfied by the long, narrow, rectangular, multistoried block design typical of most antebellum textile mills. This layout ensured that the machinery would be close to both the power source and the windows, and it minimized the area necessary for those costly deep foundations. Subsequent improvements in shafting design and construction techniques enabled millwrights to build longer and taller mills. But the constant need for sunlight prevented any great increase in width without darkening portions of the interior, and the basic rectangular form remained intact.[3]

Within the confines of this general form there was room for substantial variation in these textile factories. Stone was used for some exteriors because it reduced the risk of fire and withstood the vibrations of machinery better than wood. The stone could have come from blasting out millraces and canals, or it may have come from the stone fences of abandoned farms. Stone, or a combination of wood and stone, was particularly popular in Rhode Island mills. Bricks were used quite frequently in constructing the larger mills of Massachusetts and northern New England. The mills of the Boston Manufacturing Company in Waltham, Massachusetts, were the largest brick buildings of their kind when they were built between 1813 and 1820. The uniformity of the bricks, and the sense of continuity they and the windows conveyed, may have served to reinforce the new demands for regularity and order within their walls.[4]

The quintessential brick factories were found in Lowell. Their physical appearance, like that of the mills at Waltham, reinforced the principles of order and regularity. Each corporation usually erected several mills, four to six stories high, and each building incorporated all the facets of production (except for a separate picking house). The arrangement of each of these units into a whole complex—which was itself an innovative concept—also conveyed that sense of discipline. The Reverend Henry Miles' description of the Lowell mills in 1845 captured that feeling of control, and hinted at the motives of the management in designing these complexes. Between the mills on the canal and the boardinghouses sat "a line of a one story brick building, containing the counting room, superintendent's room, clerk's and store rooms." The entire mill yard was

> so surrounded by enclosures, that the only access is through the counting room, in full view of those whose business it is to see that no improper persons intrude themselves upon the premises. Thus the superintendent, from his room, has the whole

> of the Corporation under his eye. On the one side are the boardinghouses, all of which are under his care . . . on the other side are the mills. . . .

The total physical structure of the Lowell mills—both individually and grouped together in the mill yards—supported the social structure of production within those factories. The factories were built so that people and machines could be brought together in one location where they could be supervised most effectively. Technological and managerial considerations were thus both embodied in these factories.[5]

The overall appearance of the New England textile mills was deliberately austere, even bordering on the monotonous. The essential simplicity of their structure was a counterpoint to the growing complexity of the mechanized production housed within. Yet these buildings were not entirely devoid of decorative detail. In Rhode Island, artistic touches were applied to the physical perimeters of the building: the cornices, eaves, stairs, tower, belfry, cupola. These embellishments were usually subdued, however, because the fundamental order and practicality of the mills was thought of as visually satisfying in itself. Any elaborate motif that engulfed the entire structure would have been seen as unnecessary, unproductive, and wasteful.[6]

The question remains, however, as to how factory operatives perceived these industrial structures. Most workers who discussed these buildings talked about more than basic physical dimensions. These workers focused much of their debate on three central issues: the relationship between the factory and nature, the links between factory interior spaces and working conditions, and the role of the factory in the community. Workers were striving to reconcile these new workplaces with their own ideals about the natural world, human nature, and the notion of community. Everyone was trying to find the proper physical and social niche for the factories. Some were quite confident that these buildings could be easily put in their proper place in a dynamic and prosperous region. Others were less sanguine, and urged more flexibility in adapting the physical components of the factory system to the needs of nature, people, and the surrounding society. They feared that an unreconstructed factory system would do great harm if it were forced into an unnatural place in the region.

— I —

The operatives' thoughts often first turned to the place of the factory in the surrounding environment. Given the fact that so many operatives came from rural, agrarian backgrounds, it is not surprising that they were concerned about whether the factory could coexist harmoniously with nature. The answers they gave demonstrate that these men and women were themselves divided about the impact of the factory on their lives.

Many operatives confidently claimed that the factory and nature complemented each other. The factory enhanced the bounties of nature, while the surrounding environment checked the excesses of industrialization. Harriet Farley toured some New Hampshire factory towns in her capacity as editor of the *New England Offering,* and she commented on "the romantic scenery amidst which our factories are located. The Merrimack and Nashua are beautiful streams; and, where they rush rapidly along some rocky declivity, or leap some rugged ledge, are wildly beautiful." A mill girl from Hopkinton, Rhode Island, also praised the setting of her factory in the midst of nature. "And then around our little mill, / Wild pleasant walks abound; / Where in this world of beauty, / Can a brighter place be found?" The factory, in the eyes of this operative, did not disturb the beauty, the tranquillity, or even the untamed characteristics of nature.[7]

The operatives of Lowell were also quick to point out the enduring presence of nature in and around their mills. Speaking at the Lowell semicentennial in 1876, Lucy Larcom reminisced:

> it seems to me as if Lowell must have been a picturesque and beautiful town in its youth. What if its corporation-enclosures did wear an arid newness of sand brick? They were in the midst of open fields, and in sight of the tree-bordered river . . . the swift Merrimack—the busy, beautiful stream that rippled an accompaniment to the young city's manifold song of labor. . . .

Larcom saw the river as both the basic source of industrial power and a force of great natural beauty. She also remembered how nature not only surrounded the burgeoning mills, but also came "very close to the mill-gates. . . . There was green grass all around them; violets and wild geraniums grew by the canals. . . ." Harriet Hanson Robinson also recalled that "sometimes we rambled by the 'race-way' or mill-race, which carried the water into the flume of the mill, along whose inclining sides grew wild roses, and the 'rock-loving columbine.'"[8]

In Lowell, however, the environment was not always a purely natural phenomenon. Many of the mills took pains to plant trees and shrubs in and around their yards. Larcom, again, said that the "slope behind our mills (the 'Lawrence' mills) was a green lawn; and in front of some of them the overseers had gay flower gardens; we passed into our work through a splendor of dahlias and hollyhocks." The long rows of these flowers were a kind of second mill gate for Larcom, but these "gates" seemed to mitigate the confinement of the real iron ones. There was a similar landscaping plan at Great Falls, New Hampshire, where rows of young trees were planted on the sides of the canal to form a promenade in front of the mills. And in Peterborough, New Hampshire, the factory agent Sam G. Smith "adorned the factory yard with rare and beautiful trees shrubs and flowers. He allowed any employee to have a small flowerbed arranged according to their tastes."[9]

All of these deliberate attempts at landscaping furthered the belief that the factory could coexist harmoniously with nature. While farmers cleared away natural growth to till their fields, industrialists carefully replanted their mill yards to give them a rustic appearance. Factory owners tried to reassure operatives and townspeople that the transition from farm to factory would not be a wrenching one. The continuing presence of trees and flowers and fields would tame the forces of industry, and perhaps ease the qualms of workers.

The influence of nature was felt, according to some operatives, even inside the factory walls. Most industrial buildings in the antebellum period had large numbers of windows to admit the maximum amount of sunlight. Josephine Baker wrote that "the almost innumerable windows glitter, like gems, in the morning sunlight."

Thus, operatives had a multitude of vantage points on the surrounding scenery. Lucy Larcom said that an "atmosphere" of natural freedom and expansiveness "poured in at the mill-windows." Though they were physically cut off from the outside environment during the workday, operatives could still catch glimpses of the fields and trees and the industrial community itself. The factory was a kind of idealized watchtower from which workers could observe the interaction between industry and nature, even as they were participating in it. A contributor to the *Lowell Offering,* in "The Prospect from My Window in My Mill," saw very clearly this "combination of nature, and human invention" in the canal, machine shops, mill yard, cottages, and hills. "True, it exhibits no mountains towering high, with 'ravines deep,' or 'reposing lakes,' nor splendid castles, and magnificance of art . . . but it has enough of beauty in nature and art, to call into exercise a perception of the beautiful and sublime, and to cause me often to wish a poet's eye, or a painter's skill." This operative saw a sublime and poetic balance between nature and art from her factory window. The mill was not an intrusive force for her; it added a human touch to the natural surroundings and heightened their beauty.[10]

There was another important way workers maintained contact with nature inside the factories. They often grew plants and flowers right on the windowsills. The warm and humid conditions inside the mills, which frequently made work uncomfortable, were ideal for growing such greenery. Lucy Larcom's poetry spoke of "geranium leaves / Grown lush and fragrant to the window-tops, / Bringing a hint of gardens and thick woods." Female workers often traded cuttings with each other, or helped a new arrival start her own window garden. And Harriet Farley wrote about an overseer's giving an operative a bouquet from the factory gardens. Flowers became a medium of social exchange among workers, and perhaps between them and management. These tokens of natural beauty, with all their pastoral and traditionally feminine symbolism, may have helped defuse latent antagonisms in the factory system.[11]

The flowers in the mills were an uplifting sight for many workers. Lucy Larcom recalled that her "pet window plant"—a constantly blooming red rosebush—remained beside her work for many years, "for it had been to me like a human little friend." Larcom also recognized that flowers were like poetry in their ability to inspire workers in their daily tasks. She remembered reciting Horace Smith's "Hymn to the Flowers": "[it] seemed as if all the wild blossoms of the woods had wandered in and were twining themselves around the whirring spindles, as I repeated it, verse after verse." The flowers' actual sight and smell, when combined with those stanzas, were a powerful elixir for Larcom. The presence of nature in the factory became a physical and psychological refreshment for her and other toilers.[12]

Even as Larcom was literally waxing poetic about the factory and nature, her writings also reveal that she was not always so confident about the relationship. She once admitted that the "picturesqueness" of Pawtucket Falls in Lowell "was sacrificed to manufacturing exigencies." Larcom also realized that the flowers in the mills could have been more than an expression of the factory's harmony with nature. "The sweet air of the woodland which lingered about them would scent our thoughts all day, and make us forget the oily smell of the machinery." Moreover, she confessed that she preferred wildflowers to those grown in the mills; but "there came summers when I could only look out of the mill window and dream about them . . . and when I could not see them, I wrote about them." Near the close of her mill career in 1845, she penned the poem "Idle Wishes" for the *Lowell Offering.* While the subject is not flowers, these lines certainly convey Larcom's concern that the factory's development could be at the expense of nature. Her ideas about harmony and balance are swept aside; the magical quality of nature—in the guise of mythical fairies—has taken flight in the face of the factory.

And 't is no wonder they have sped;—
The bright and happy creatures:
For from their ancient haunts have fled,
The old, endearing features.
On fairy circle, madly broke,
A factory's wheels are whirling.
Oak of the dryad! see the smoke
From yon black engine curling![13]

Larcom did not write frequently about this darker side of factory life; she preferred to emphasize the sunnier aspects of her mill experience. Yet that undercurrent of unease, the sense that there could be tension as well as harmony between the factory and nature, was also present in her work. Even as she spoke about Lowell being in close proximity to nature, she recognized that the search for natural beauty sometimes had to be pursued outside the mills. When the factories stopped for repairs or because of water problems, that was the time to go into the fields and gather the wildflowers she loved so much. Before the mills started up in the morning was the time to view the sunrise "down the rocky bend of the river at Belvedere Village." These excursions into nature were yet another source of mental and physical regeneration. No one could "feel more gratefully the charm of noble scenery, or the refreshment of escape into the unspoiled solitudes of nature, than the laborer at some close in-door employment." The worker could at least take the memories of hills and fields back into the mill to make the work more tolerable. " '. . . That mountain range is now / Woven, dyed into the texture of my mind; / And, standing at my loom, I shall behold / Its changes making tapestry of the web / My shuttle flies across, so beautiful!' " These memories were especially important to a manufacturing population in which the majority of operatives were born and raised amidst such rural scenery. Workers constantly thought about their homesteads, and many returned to their homes as often as possible. In between these trips, they still searched for new ways to remain in touch with nature while they continued their factory labors.[14]

Lucy Larcom was not the only operative with a dual vision of the factory and nature. Harriet Farley was another woman whose praise of the factory in harmony with its surroundings was sometimes colored with a darker side. In one of her editorials in the *New England Offering,* she devoted a good deal of print to a discussion of flowers in the mill. While she certainly praised the benefits of these companions, she also pointed out some problems associated with them. One operative grew a rare plant, only to see its flower torn from the stalk by the "third hand," a jealous, "rough, uncultivated fellow." The flower thus became, not a means of social exchange, but a source of social friction and antagonism. The woman felt an intense sense of personal violation; she "felt as though her rarest treasure had been ravished from her."

In another instance, a morning glory appeared mysteriously out of a geranium pot and proceeded to grow around an entire window, "forming a beautiful arch of leaf and blossom around the casement." Farley recalled that

> its wealth of foliage was astonishing, and every morn its purple blossoms, of every shade, greeted us as we came to our place of labor . . . we had never felt so deep an interest in a plant. But when the days shortened, and the late and early twilight darkened, we found that 'rosenglory' was a great obstacle to the light and our labor. So, before its beauty and the rigor had departed, it was cut down, not without many regrets, and cast into the mill stream. Never to be forgotten the look of sorrow and surprise with which the overseer first witnessed our work of destruction.

The overseer had good reason to be surprised; the operatives were sacrificing their own heartfelt interest in nature to the exigencies of the factory, even before being ordered to do so. Flowers in the mill were welcomed by the workers; but when they interfered with the ability to earn their wages, then the operatives took matters into their own hands and removed the impediments of nature.[15]

The very fact that much of this writing contemplating factories and nature was published in the 1840s, or in subsequent reminiscences, may reveal another tension in these workers' minds. That is, they were arguing most vociferously for the harmony of factory and nature at the time when factories were actually becoming increasingly distanced from the surrounding environment. By the late 1840s, industry had become so physically and economically dominant in places like Lowell that the corporations seemed to care far less about reconciling themselves with nature.

Throughout the 1840s, many mills expanded their physical plants by linking their existing buildings with new additions. This was done at Waltham in 1843; and by 1848, the Hamilton, Appleton, and Suffolk companies in Lowell had each joined their respective mills. The entire riverfront was crowded with new construction and the solid walls of factory buildings. The original detached mills, with their open spaces permitting those cherished views of the surrounding countryside and town, were now unbroken lines of brick blocking out any perspective on the environment. The factory stood as a barrier between the city and the river and whatever lay beyond.[16]

Harriet Farley discussed this transformation in an essay entitled "The Window Darkened" in the *Lowell Offering* of December 1845. Writing during the height of these physical changes at Lowell, for once she dropped all pretense about the harmony of factories and nature. Instead she lamented the closing of opportunities to remain in contact with people and nature. The view from her window had been "like a beautiful picture" encompassing both city and country, everything in balance. Sunlight streamed in through the window to give her "light for constant occupations . . . [and] a ticket to that picture gallery, where my eye wandered on an involuntary, though oft-repeated, tour of pleasure." But soon a foundation was dug on a parcel of land in front of the window.

> The red walls arose—*red,* the color of the conquerer—and they proclaimed a victory over my pleasures. With one story of the great fabric was screened from me whole streets of pleasant dwellings. The early sunrise was gone. . . . The first soft glance of moonlight was forever hid, and it seemed as though my best treasures were taken from me. But I clung more fervently to those which were left, and the more tenaciously as I saw them departing. This beautiful dwelling, and that majestic tree, were never to me so lovely as when they were shut from my window's view. . . . The church spire—that I should always have—and those highest houses, and the brow of the hill. But no! I had not calculated wisely. They began to recede from me—for the huge building rose still higher and higher. . . . Higher, higher still, arose the fabric. The mansions were gone—the church—the brow of the hill—and at last the very tip of the spire was taken from me. Oh! how was my window darkened!—but not quite dark, for there still was light from the skies above.[17]

Farley managed to blunt the criticism implied in her description of the factory's growing intrusion in the environment by turning the entire essay into a homily on spiritual values. But there were other workers who also saw the factory in conflict with nature. They were not so cautious in their critiques. They were not willing to write off or balance out the contradictions, as Larcom and Farley frequently did. They saw the tension as something embedded deep in the factory system, something not easily resolved by potted plants or a brief rural excursion.

These other workers saw a growing gap between the factory and nature. There were two separate landscapes forming—the industrial and the natural—and the transition between them was becoming more abrupt and disjointed. The natural beauties of "sunshine and flowers—the blue sky and green grass" always remained outside the confines of the factory. Even if an operative could steal a moment to look out upon "the fields, and hills, and woods, which lie beyond the Merrimack, steeped in golden sunlight and radiant with beauty," those views were not inspirational; they served only to heighten the feeling of separation. They could look out onto a "Land of Promise," as Moses did in the Old Testament, but they could never find the time to leave the factory and walk among those fields. The opening stanzas of "The Factory Bell" convey very clearly how the factory distanced the worker from the pace and rhythm of nature. Workers were herded quickly into a building that shut them away from natural sights and sounds and smells. There is no harmonious balance in this poem, but a clearcut victory for the factory system.

> Loud the morning bell is ringing,
> Up, up sleepers, haste away;
> Yonder sits the redbreast singing,
> But to list we must not stay.
>
> Not for us is morning breaking,
> Though we with Aurora rise;
> Not for us is Nature waking,
> All her smiles through earth and skies.[18]

The factory, for these workers, was opposed to nature—these buildings could be seen only as an intrusive force in the surrounding environment. The mills were something to escape from; nature was a refuge to run towards. Lydia Hall, in an early issue of the *Lowell Offering,* wrote:

> Wearied with the dull monotony of a factory life, I sought relief from the flying machinery in the many-toned sweetness of nature's melody. And a happy change to the pent up spirit it was, from the walled enclosure to the glad, fresh air. . . . Like a long-caged bird once more on the wing, I wandered from sweet to sweet, enjoying in each a livelier satisfaction than I had ever known until deprived of them.

There is a clear passage in Hall's essay from the confinement and deprivation in the mill to the expansiveness and bounty of nature. Many mill girls lavished praise and poetry on the concept of nature because it appeared to them in an ideal state, outside the gates and far beyond their grasp. Once separated from their rural inheritance, these workers longed for the physical presence of nature with increasing intensity.[19]

It was the absence of nature in the factories, not its presence, that inspired many writers. Even Harriet Farley admitted that factory operatives wrote constantly "about the beauties of nature" just as the hungry dream about food and the desert wanderer sees the mirage of an oasis. This outpouring of poems and essays about nature was not merely a sentimental convention for mill girls; it expressed a deeper need. The "love and longing" for nature, whether in workers' dreams or actions, was a yearning for something "not of the crowded, clattering mill, nor of the noisy tenement . . . nor of the thronged and busy street." Farley recognized that many workers were not satisfied with a window view or a flower by their loom. These operatives felt that they were moving farther from rural life and values. They feared that the expanding industrial structures were driving the factories farther away from any meaningful contact with nature.[20]

— II —

When operatives turned their attention away from the factory's overall relationship with nature, they often turned it to the interior of these buildings and the working conditions inside. The internal design of these factories was usually governed by two primary factors: management's desire to maximize the use of open spaces, and the need to combat the ever-present danger of fire.

The interiors of nearly all antebellum New England factories were wood-framed. Because of the emphasis on maximizing the open interior space, each floor of the factory was often a series of undivided rooms some ten feet high. These wide open spaces allowed for great flexibility in arranging the machinery, and there were few pillars and walls to block the view of supervisors. In effect, management could dictate where machines would be placed and where operatives would stand; the workers would have few places to hide from the overseers' scrutiny.[21]

The one major drawback to these wooden interiors was their vulnerability to fire. Textile mills in particular were filled with flammable materials. Fibers and lint filled the air and stuck to the walls and ceilings. Floors were often oily from machinery lubrication. The machines themselves often overheated or threw off sparks. And the artificial lighting inside was usually candles or oil lamps. All these factors combined to create serious fire hazards. Sometimes the result was a minor fire. John Haines, an overseer in a mill at Great Falls, remarked in his diary entry of December 27, 1845: "had a fire this fore noon a bearing of a frame caught Fire & frightened the girls a Little . . . no damage." The operatives' fear, however, was certainly justified in light of what Haines himself had written barely a month before. On the evening of November 18, a neighboring mill had been completely consumed by flames. The fire started when someone dropped a lamp into some loose cotton, and it soon engulfed the entire structure. A night watchman, sleeping in the attic at the end of his watch, was killed. Haines reported that "there were many about the mill who were aware that this young man sleeped in the attic but were so much excited by the fire that it did not occur to them until it was too late to save him." Exactly one week later, fire broke out in one of the picker houses at the company where Haines was employed. The fire spread to the carding room, where it was doused with water, but it broke out again and reached the spinning and dressing rooms before it was finally extinguished.[22]

Factory workers often regarded industrial fires with a mixture of awe at the physical spectacle and concern for their personal safety and the future of their jobs. Sarah Maria Cornell witnessed one of the five-story Lowell factories burning on a Saturday night in early January 1829. She saw the firefighters struggle in the bitter cold to save the other five mills in the yard. "The middle one caught at the furnace," she wrote:

> and in less than three hours it was burned to the ground. I expected to have seen the whole thirteen, with the whole Corporation swept by the flames. But through the goodness of that God who rules the elements although the air was keen and cold—it was still as in midsummer. The damage is great, but the distress is nothing to what it was in Slaterville—as each factory supported itself.—No one was personally injured.

Reflecting on the entire scene of danger and destruction, Cornell concluded that she was "a stranger in a strange land, exposed to sickness and death." The fire heightened her sense of alienation and uncertainty in the factory.[23]

Another factory worker wrote about how fires, in a curious way, could be a sign of constructive change and progress. Fires were a symbol of the passing of the old order and the opening of opportunities for new advances. Out of the ashes of a burned-out mill could arise—phoenixlike—a new and sturdier structure. A sense of regeneration was captured by this factory-girl poet from Hopkinton, Rhode Island.

> In eighteen hundred forty-eight,
> A rustic mill there stood;
> 'T was rather old and out of date,
> And did but little good.
>
> So fate ordained this mill should fall
> And a better one be raised;
> The fiery flames consumed it all,
> And all its contents blazed.
>
> And now we have a pretty one
> Erected in its stead,

Wherein to work we have begun,
To earn our daily bread.

The fire that consumed the old mill was welcomed by this worker, not as an act of destruction, but as an act of God leading to more material progress. The flames cleared away the old undergrowth, as they do in a forest, and made way for new and "pretty" buildings. But the most significant changes in factory construction were more than just pretty; they were a direct response to the problem of fire, and they had a profound effect on working conditions inside.[24]

A number of structural changes in and around factory buildings were instituted to combat the chronic problem of fires. Many textile mills, by the 1830s, had moved the highly flammable process of picking cotton to a building separate from the main mill. Also during this period, many mills installed force pumps to supply water throughout their buildings. Millwrights also began to consider using iron in their construction designs. Using iron in the frames, however, was not a satisfactory solution. The iron often melted and collapsed due to heat from the flames. Cast-iron frames also conducted machine vibrations throughout the buildings. Therefore, most millwrights continued to work with wood; but by the 1820s and 1830s they were trying new designs to control the speed at which a fire would spread (as opposed to developing fireproof materials). They moved stairwells from the main block of the buildings, and they relied more and more on brick and stone walls. But the critical problem was the rapidity with which floors burned and collapsed. Eventually, by increasing the thickness of the construction components and eliminating hollow fire-traps and excess exposed wood surfaces, new interior designs actually did retard the spread of fire.[25]

Of course, the proponents of this new scheme could not claim that the number of fires would be reduced, because the material used in construction was still wood. But when slow-burning building techniques were combined with fire doors, sprinklers, hoses, hydrants, and pumps, there was a better chance of stopping a fire before it turned into a conflagration. Ironically, Zachariah Allen's pioneering, slow-burning textile mill at Centerdale, Rhode Island, was the scene of a number of fires. Nevertheless, the construction techniques proved effective enough to preserve the mill up to the present day. These techniques also spread throughout New England factories by the 1840s. Some of the mills in Lowell added iron shutters "to prevent the communication of fire from one Mill to another . . . and platforms outside, with ladders extending right over the top of the building." In Fall River, Massachusetts, the Granite Mill fire of 1843 highlighted the danger of trapping people in the attic. Afterwards, the city's mills were built with flat roofs, which eliminated the enclosed spaces where fires could burn undetected. These mills also provided access to fire escapes at several points.[26]

Factories built with slow-burning construction techniques had solid and massive interiors. Any extraneous details were frowned on severely; they only created more exposed surfaces for fires to feed on. The Lowell Manufacturing Company went so far as to build the framework of its new carpet looms right into the pillars of the new mill to prevent any settling that might interfere with the machinery's proper operation. Thus the machinery and the factory physically merged in this case to present the workers with a total interior environment emphasizing stability, permanence, and rigidity.[27]

Workers' perceptions of these factory interiors were often shaped by the specific room they worked in. Different stages of production were frequently housed in different parts of a factory complex. In cotton textile mills, for example, the water wheel was generally in the basement along with mechanics' shops and the cloth room; the carding room was on the first floor; the spinning room was on the second floor; and the weaving and dressing rooms were located on the upper floor and the attic. In woolen mills, the raw wool was sometimes stored in the attic; the carding and spinning rooms were usually in the upper floors because the machinery was light and nonvibrating; and the heavier power looms for woolen weaving were located on the lower floors.[28]

The operatives in these mills knew that each room had its own particular character. Harriet Farley wrote that the carding room of a cotton mill was where "the cotton flies most, and the girls get the dirtiest." Lucy Larcom noted that this room was filled with "mingled smells / Of oily suffocation." Both of these women observed that the spinning room was an improvement. Farley called it "very neat and pretty"; while Larcom spoke of the "room's cool spaciousness / Of long clean alleys." The dressing rooms received mixed reviews from these women. Farley said they were "very neat . . . but these rooms are kept very warm, and are disagreeably scented with the 'sizing'" used in preparing the warp threads. Larcom recalled that this room was "more airy" than the spinning room, but she also remembered the "breathless heat" inside.[29]

Both of these women raised particular issues about their working conditions—cleanliness, ventilation, heating—that were also reflected in other workers' writings. Just as these operatives debated the relationship between the factory building and nature, they also discussed the impact of internal conditions on their own natures. This was more than the difference between particular departments; it was a deep-seated conflict over the basic issue of occupational health.

Some workers saw in the factory interiors the same sense of order that management deliberately built into the mill yards. Eliza Jane Cate, writing from Fisherville, Rhode Island, where she had gone as an agent for the *New England Offering,* observed that the mill's "entrance, the passages, and staircases are broad, well-lighted, well-aired, and tidy. . . . It is kept free from cotton and every kind of clutter . . . to make *their* mill-home fresher and more agreeable." Harriet Farley, when she wrote her semi-fictitious "Letters from Susan" for the *Lowell Offering,* also stressed the physical spaciousness of the mills. Farley's rhetoric dismissed any notion of "dark Satanic mills" closing in on workers and crushing their spirits. The "rooms were so light, spacious, and clean"; they were "kept nicely whitewashed . . . [with] white cotton curtains to the windows." These factory interiors, with the pillars painted bright green (like the wooden frames of the machinery), the floor under the machines often painted "a high cream colour," and the curtains on the windows, evoked images of nature and home in the mill. They served to reassure workers that the factory would not destroy the cherished values of the rural homestead. The operatives' lives would emulate the mills' appearance—everything would be "well-ordered" and "systematic" without being monotonous or oppressive.[30]

Farley also argued that the systematic nature of factory work ensured that heat and ventilation were always well regulated. She stated confidently: "we know that the mills are not too warm for comfort in Winter, and that few places are cooler in the middle of Summer." Once again, the factory did not destroy nature, but controlled the effects of seasonal cycles just enough for comfortable year-round labor, removed from the harshness of the elements outside. Farley also tried to refute charges of improper ventilation by stating: "We know that the rooms are spacious and high—we know that the air is not dead and stagnant—the constant motion of bands and drums keeps it continually changing." Yet, in one of her "Letters from Susan," Farley admitted that the warm weather could make mill labor fatiguing. Harriet Robinson also recalled that "cotton-factories . . . were light, well-ventilated, and moderately heated; each factory-building stood detached, with pleasant sunlit windows, cheerful views, and fresh air from all points of the compass." Robinson's description was becoming anachronistic by the 1840s, however, as many factories expanded and closed off their open spaces. Not only was nature being shut out aesthetically, but the free circulation of fresh air was also being cut off.[31]

Other workers stated that paint and curtains could not dispel the overwhelming sense of confinement they felt. Once the worker entered "that large gloomy looking building," she was drawn into "the confines of that close noisy apartment" where she had to labor day in and day out. The worker's physical movement and her future opportunities were constricted within the factory walls. Sometimes operatives blurted out their frustration in a brief remark in a diary or letter. Susan Forbes, after recording countless uneventful days in the Middlesex Corporation's woolen mill in Lowell, suddenly confessed on May 20, 1843, that she was "still immersed within the Busy Brick walls of a hateful Factory." And Caroline Ford, tending looms in a Middlebury, Vermont, woolen mill, wrote to her brother William in 1845 that she would "like to [k]now what is going around us if I am shut up in the old black mill." These women did not notice any brightly painted interiors; they colored their workplaces in rather somber hues. Their mills were dark and isolated from any contact with the outside world.[32]

Some workers found the mills, particularly those constructed early in the nineteenth century, to be cold as well as gloomy places. Hannah Borden, coming from her father's home to try her hand at the first Fall River power looms in 1817, remembered the difficult conditions in her factory.

> There was something over twenty looms in the room which was a great unplastered place with a big double door at one end that was kept stuffed up with cotton waste in winter. The only heat was furnished by a small sheet iron stove while a big pipe ran partly around the top of the room. It was terrible cold and many's the time when I couldn't feel the yarn, my fingers were so icy. When the yarn was touched, it snapped and this was another source of waste.

Borden was not the only worker to complain about cold factories. Operatives in the basement of the Lawrence Company in Lowell also spoke out about their cold rooms and succeeded in having more heat supplied.[33]

Workers in other mechanized industries also suffered similar problems during the winter months. Employees at the Reed and Barton britannia-ware plant in

Taunton, Massachusetts, had to be sent home during especially cold weather because the small wood stoves could not provide enough heat. Ropewalks were another industry particularly prone to problems with cold weather. They were left open, even on the coldest days, because of the need for light to penetrate throughout these immensely long buildings. In addition, it was practically impossible to heat all the interior space, so the temperature could plummet to near zero. At the Plymouth (Massachusetts) Cordage Company, when the temperature fell below ten degrees, work was cancelled. This was not done, however, for the comfort of the ropemakers. Rather, the tarred yarns became too stiff to work with at those low temperatures.[34]

In many larger factories with more sophisticated heating systems, some workers noted the opposite problem. These operatives found their workplaces hot, humid, stagnant, and filled with noxious fumes. Thread may have spun well and plants may have thrived in such a close atmosphere; but human beings had a more difficult time. Josephine Baker noted in an essay on a Lowell woolen mill that in certain rooms there were "occasionally, *fogs* and *clouds*" due to the dampness; "and not only fogs and clouds, but sometimes plentiful showers." The attics of woolen mills were often used for spinning jacks because there were no pillars to hamper the arrangement of machinery. These attics were filled with hot, humid air, and the spinners worked barefoot and wore very light clothing.[35]

An operative from Manchester, New Hampshire, also observed that "those who are shut up within the 'Prison walls of a Factory'" were "continually inhaling cotton-dust, lamp smoke, and away from wholesome, pure air." And a sympathetic overseer wrote to the *Voice of Industry* that he had seen "girls faint in the morning, in consequence of the air being so impure in the mill. This is quite a common thing. Especially when girls have worked in the factory for considerable length of time." Weavers may have been particularly susceptible to respiratory problems because they had to suck the thread through their shuttles. These "kiss-of-death" shuttles forced workers to constantly ingest lint, sizing, and dyes from the thread. Since shuttles passed throughout the mill, there was also the risk of transmitting communicable diseases, such as tuberculosis.[36]

The question of clean air in the factories was often linked with the issue of physical cleanliness in general. Many operatives in Lowell struggled constantly to keep their persons and clothes free from lint, dust, and oil stains. They sometimes wore "over-skirts and sleeves"; but as it was "not *fashionable* to wear masks," they often found their faces covered with dirt and grime. In some mills, the same water system used to extinguish fires also supplied sinks in the various rooms. Some proprietors provided soap so that workers could scrub their faces and hands before meals.[37]

John Rogers, after a hard day's work in the Amoskeag Machine Shop of Manchester, New Hampshire, wrote home about the continual challenge of keeping his hands clean.

> My hands get almost black before I have been in the shop five minutes but they keep growing blacker and blacker till at last they get a regular shining black polish like a new air tight stove and you may imagine what a job it is to wash them three times a day before eating. . . . I have almost used my nail brush up for I am bound to have them clean once a day.

Rogers was certainly not ashamed of his black hands, for they were a sign of his daily labors. But neither were they something to be displayed as a badge of honor; so cleaning them became another chore in the daily routine.[38]

There was also a concerted effort made by many mill girls to ask the corporations to install bathing facilities. Harriet Farley supported the idea as necessary for "cleanliness, health, and comfort." And in a rare instance where the *Lowell Offering* and the *Voice of Industry* openly met on common ground, the *Voice* praised the bathhouses in Manchester (where there never seemed to be a shortage of help), and welcomed the new ones at Lowell's Suffolk and Tremont mills. Eliza Jane Cate, in one of her "advice columns" in the *New England Offering,* "Duties and Rights of Mill Girls," also commented favorably about the Stark Corporation's bathhouse in Manchester.

> . . . [E]legance is joined with convenience. The pleasant yard, the neat brick block, the green blinds without; within the papered walls, mirrors, dressing-tables, the broad Venetian screens, and, behind them, the dressing room; the bathing rooms, with their expensive, neatly-kept baths for showering, or immersion, or for both, as one chooses; and then, further on, the long cool room, where is the plunge-bath, where are plants; while, moving here and there, wherever she is needed, is the quiet, kind lady who has the rooms, and all who come hither, in charge. Does not the reader see that it is good for those young girls that all this pains is taken for them? Are they not often made grateful to the agent? . . . and is not gratitude a happy, purifying emotion? Are they not more critical of themselves, of their health, their morals, and their manners, from seeing how in this they are cared for by others?

Cate readily acknowledged that these amenities would promote the development of a more tractable labor force, and that workers would obviously feel grateful to the owners for such benefits. Some owners probably believed that these bathhouses, like the mill gardens, could become part of a total working environment designed to pacify their employees. They were all part of an attempt to make the factory seem like a home away from home. They tried to appeal to women's concepts of domesticity and to reassure them that they did not have to fear sacrificing their femininity by going to work in the mills. Other operatives, however, saw the bathhouses, not as a way to reinforce the image of the respectable mill girl, but as a token of respect from the companies. It was the workers themselves who usually asked for these facilities as necessary for their physical health and self-esteem.[39]

Some factory proprietors thought that washrooms would help cleanse workers of their discontent. Yet personal cleanliness was never easy to maintain in the factories. Two factory-girl songs popular in the antebellum era showed how the workers had to take on the burden of keeping the workplace neat. The operatives were required to oil the picker rods, brush the looms, and scour the dirty floors, "All in the Weaving room." When workers tried to take time to keep themselves clean, however, they were admonished by their overseers for leaving their work unattended.

> No more will I take the towel and soap
> To go to the sink and wash;
> No more will the overseer say
> "You're making a terrible splosh!"

No more will I take the comb and go
To the glass to comb my hair;
No more the overseer will say
"Oh! what are you doing there?"

Finally, the very act of washing oneself was seen as the worker's last gesture before leaving the mill permanently.

Come all you little doffers
That work in the Spinning room;
Go wash your face and comb your hair,
Prepare to leave the room.

These protest songs urged operatives to cleanse themselves of the factory, to wash off the physical dirt and the psychological stains, to step out into the world and let the filth of the factory go down the drain.[40]

One of the major reasons factories were said to be so grimy and the air so foul was the large number of candles and oil lamps used to light the interiors for work before sunrise and after sunset. The Poignand and Plant mill of Lancaster, Massachusetts, used both "naked Lamps" and "Lamps in Glass lanthorns" to illuminate its carding, spinning, and weaving rooms. The Cocheco Company's upper factory in Dover, New Hampshire, used small lamps of whale oil burned at each end of a loom to assist weavers in seeing after dark. These lamps gave off only "a very dim light . . . but it was regarded as a great improvement over the candle, and especially the 'slut,' which was whale oil in a saucer and burned by placing a woolen rag in the oil, with the end over the side of the saucer." Lard oil was also sometimes used in the tin "petticoat lamps," but the light produced was so meager that a new "burning fluid" made out of alcohol and turpentine was subsequently employed. (It was not until about 1850 that gas lighting was finally introduced in some factories.)[41]

Eliza Hemmingway, in her testimony before the Massachusetts legislative committee investigating factory conditions in 1845, stated that there were "293 small lamps and 61 large lamps lighted in the room in which she worked [as a weaver in the Middlesex woolen mills of Lowell], when evening work is required. These lamps are also lighted sometimes in the morning." The sight of all these lights in a large mill was rather impressive, at least from the outside. Ann Appleton wrote to her sister about the Manchester mills: "The mills are all lighted up, they look splendid, counting room and all. They lighted up Monday eve the first time this year, will continue till next spring. I admire to go in the evening, I never saw a more splendid sight. . . ." Harriet Farley was even more effusive in her praise:

> One of the most beautiful sights, we have ever witnessed, was . . . all these factories . . . lighted up for the evening's labor. The uniform and brilliant illumination, with the lights again gleaming up from the calm Merrimack, the brightness of the city beyond, the clear blue sky above, from which the sparkling stars were sending down their glittering beams into the glassy waters of the river, all combined to form a spectacle, which might almost lead an observer to believe that our hard-working, matter-of-fact city had been transformed to fairy land.

Farley saw the lights of the factory and the lights of nature reflecting each other and shedding a kind of mystic glow on Lowell. Even inside the factories, some workers saw the lamps as an aid to their continued labor and steady wages in the midst of winter darkness or stormy weather. One of the mill-girl poets from Hopkinton, Rhode Island, rhymed approvingly: "The walls all o'er are nice and white, / Which makes the help look clever; / They love to see the glowing light, / In dark and rainy weather."[42]

Other operatives were not so pleased with their interior lighting. John Rogers wrote to his sister that "the time we are lighted up seems as long as all the rest of the afternoon." Mary Metcalf was so worried that her eyes would not "stand it to light up this winter" (of 1847) that she decided to change jobs from the spinning room to the winding room "in the attic [where] we shall not have to light up much if any." Even Harriet Farley, when she looked inside the factories, admitted that the "dark dull dreary desolate winter month[s], eked out at either end by the yellow stifling light of lamps," were very tiresome to workers.[43]

Some operatives eventually reached a point where they refused to work under these lamps. In the fall of 1846, while a labor convention was meeting in Nashua, New Hampshire, machinists attached to a local textile mill walked off their jobs when the lights were first lit for the season. On the following Monday, women in two rooms of the mill also decided that they would not work by candlelight. They moved down to the mill yard, but the overseers locked the gates and refused to open them until the evening bell. While the women were waiting to be let out, a procession of nearly 1,000 people—including the convention delegates—marched to the factory and offered the women encouragement. The town authorities sent the constable to read the Riot Act and call on the crowd to disperse, but no one paid any attention to him.

The result of this demonstration, however, was not very promising for the workers. The handful of women who protested at the Jackson Corporation were dismissed, while the large number of protesters at the Nashua Corporation were allowed to remain at work only because of the difficulty of replacing so many workers on such short notice. The machinists were the one group of workers given the privilege of not working by artificial light, but they also had their wages cut by ten percent.

There was at least one group of workmen, in another town during this same fall of 1846, who did fare better in their battle with the factory lamps. It was reported that the men of the Mechanics' and Manufacturers' Steam Shop had a procession, complete with band and illuminated banner, to celebrate the fact that they had succeeded in establishing a "NEW MACHINE SHOP" with "NO LIGHTING UP!" The mill girls of New Hampshire did not give up their fight either, but carried on their crusade into the next year. On September 21, 1847, the day of the year when lighting up traditionally began, John Haines noted in his diary: "shall not Light up at present the girls turned out at Dover & refused to Light up also at Nashua, N.H."[44]

Most operatives were not as bold as these New Hampshire residents, but they still managed to make their feelings known about working long hours under lamplight. They chose to express their attitudes through an intriguing custom known as "the lighting-up and blowing-out balls." As their names imply, these celebrations took place when the factories first lit up for winter (September 21) and blew out their lamps with the coming of spring (March 21). Actually, there are very few detailed references to lighting-up festivities. But this is not surprising, since there would have been little reason for the workers to celebrate, knowing that they were going to have to spend the fall and winter months working next to hot, smoky lamps. If any such lighting-up balls did occur, they were probably organized by managers in an effort to placate workers and turn the dreaded lighting of the lamps into a more pleasant occasion.

Blowing-out balls, however, were an entirely different matter. These were often authentic working-class celebrations to mark the onset of spring, for spring meant more daylight hours and no more work by artificial light. In Pawtucket, Rhode Island, the children from the mills filled the streets on the last night of lighting up. They carried torchlights, literally bearing light in their own hands and under their own control, and shouted at the top of their voices. During the years of Thomas Dorr's controversial campaign for the reform of Rhode Island politics, the youngsters were known to give three cheers for the slogan "Liberation." This might have been a demand for the release of Dorr from prison, or it might have meant their own release from evening work under lamplight.[45]

Lowell was, not surprisingly, also a site for many of these festivities. Some reports say that they were held in the corporations' cloth rooms. This may be significant in that these rooms had less machinery than any other department, yet they were still under the companies' purview. The management may have wanted to remove most workers from any reminders of mechanized labor, yet still retain their authority over the celebrations. Another account states that the balls were held at a modest inn, the Stone House. This may indicate that the Lowell festivities were more exclusive and less public than in other factory communities. This may also be further proof that the Lowell corporations were exerting their influence to keep the demonstrations under their control.[46]

If Lowell's blowing-out balls were inclined to be on the sedate side, then they were the exception, not the rule, for the rest of New England. The employees of Reed and Barton, for example, in 1849 had their "grand blow-out" on a hill with fireworks and a tar-barrel bonfire. Like the youth of Pawtucket, these workers may have been symbolically reclaiming the light for their own use. In Biddeford, Maine, a great ball began every year at 8:30 on the evening of March 19 in the town's largest hall. The celebration paused at midnight for refreshments and then continued until the first mill bell rang just before sunrise. Then the dancing finally ended and the day's work began. There were also concurrent parties in private homes and mill boarding-houses. This town may also have had a regular lighting-up ball in September to inaugurate the social season.[47]

There was one final gesture at the Biddeford ball, and in other celebrations as far-flung as Chicopee, Massachusetts, that was particularly poignant. Operatives draped the extinguished lamps with wreaths and flowers, and spread garlands throughout the factories in honor of the blowing out. This deliberate injection of nature directly into the factory's inner workings meant something different from growing a plant in a mill. Perhaps these garlands were intended to be funeral wreaths for the extinguished lamps. Or perhaps they were a way for the workers to bring the natural world into the factory on their own terms, as a welcome to the spring season of growth and renewal. The blowing-out balls, and their garlands in the mills, were probably not usually planned as protests against working conditions. Workers with a variety of opinions probably joined in the merriment. But these celebrations did touch a deep chord in many operatives—the need for physical pleasure and release, social interaction, and the expression of human creativity.[48]

Underlying much of the debate over working conditions inside factories was also a deep concern about health, disease, and mortality itself.[49] The key questions were: how healthy were the workers in the midst of these factories? and if the workers' health was compromised, who or what was to blame for the problems? Harriet Hanson Robinson recalled that most mill girls were healthy. They came from their rural homes with "sound bodies and a fair share of endurance. Fevers and similar diseases were rare among them, and they had no time to pet small ailments." Harriet Farley acknowledged the presence of sickness in Lowell, even in the midst of a generally healthy population, but she put the blame for most illnesses on the operatives and their careless personal habits. She firmly believed that "with proper care health need not be lost." But "this proper care" was "taken by very few of the girls." The reasons for such carelessness were many. Farley pointed out that most mill girls were "at that age when their constitutions are maturing, when girls are always most careless, and when mothers think they need most care." She also observed that some operatives were "too ambitious, some too covetous, some too thoughtless, [and] some too ignorant" to buy the proper clothing for cold and rainy weather. Yet Farley had to admit that other workers may have been "too poor to purchase all they need to preserve them from wet and cold—too poor because parents, children, and other relatives may be dependent upon their wages for support." Farley believed, however, that most operatives were not financially strapped; they had the time and money to take better care of themselves.

Farley also attributed ill health to excessive recreation. She and many other workers praised the wealth of leisure-time activities available in an industrial city such as Lowell. But Farley asserted that an operative's first priority was to maintain her physical strength for her work, even if that meant giving up many of the cultural and social advantages of the community—the very things that made work in Lowell worthwhile for many operatives.

> "But," they will ask, "are we to give up meetings, and concerts, and Sabbath schools." "Yes," we reply, "if your health is failing, and you wish to preserve it." "But we had rather die than live but to work, and work but to live." "Well, then, go on, and lose your health, but do not say that you could not have preserved it." We well know that sacrifice and self-denial are demanded, when we ask that in the prime of life they should debar themselves of so much which gives to life its zest and gladness. But there can be, with moderate labor in the factory, moderate amusements and pleasures out of it.[50]

Eliza Jane Cate concurred with Farley that "*all* the diseases and inconveniences of factory communities do not spring from the inherent corruptions of the factory system . . . on the contrary, a greater part of them proceed directly or indirectly from a neglect on the part of the operatives themselves of those means of health which are still left to them." The road to better health lay not so much in improved working conditions as in more wholesome habits outside the factories. Cate knew that most workers were not deliberately negligent about their health; they usually were simply uninformed about the necessity of proper exercise, diet, and hygiene. The results of such ignorance and inattention, however, were "not a light thing" to witness. A young girl could leave her homestead for a factory town

> a plump, rosy-cheeked, strong, and laughing girl, and in one year comes back to them—better clad, t'is true, and with refined manners, and money for the discharge of their little debts, and for the supply of their wants,—but alas, how changed! She loves them, it may be, with a new fervor, but her hand is weak when it would minister to them; and the mother transfers the care she once enjoyed as an invalid, to her weary child; and, old and feeble as she is, she takes again on herself "the burden and heat of the day."
>
> This is a dark picture; but there are even darker realities, and there is no inconsiderable number.

Cate presented a very sobering portrait of the human costs of factory labor for the operative and her family. Yet she continued to hold the system virtually blameless; the worker had to assume full responsibility for her physical debility.[51]

Other workers insisted that the blame did rest on the factories themselves for the declining health of their employees. One correspondent wrote the *Voice of Industry* that the "lamp smoke, cotton dust, the nauseaus of miserable oil, . . . wet walls from the affects of steam, . . . and badly ventilated rooms" combined to rob the workers of their health. She facetiously urged that anyone who thought otherwise "on the first indication of ill health, place his own children within the walls of one of these Hospitals where they may have their health *perfected*." The truth of the matter was, she said, that

> so far as the health of the operatives is concerned, any one blest with common observation cannot be ignorant of the fact, that the operatives are obliged to go into the country almost universally, to improve their health, and that with a few weeks stay, they return much better than when they leave. If they are improved by working in the mills, it is strange that they should be under the necessity of going into the country for such a purpose.

The workers who remained in the mills, Sarah Bagley observed, discovered "that the laws of health are *necessarily* and *unavoidably* violated by them every day." But Bagley argued that this was not a situation the workers brought on themselves; it was imposed on them by the constraints of factory labor.[52]

Some individuals did try to take charge of their own health, as Harriet Farley and Eliza Jane Cate urged. These workers often came to the conclusion, however, that the best thing they could do for themselves was to leave factory work. These were not hasty decisions, but carefully calculated ones that weighed all the costs and benefits of industrial labor and physical health. Sally Rice wrote her father during the winter of 1845 when she began working in the Masonville, Connecticut, textile mill: "if it does not agree with my health I shall give it up at once." By autumn of the same year, Rice had shown that she was as good as her word. She returned to work on a farm in Millbury, Massachusetts, and wrote to her family explaining her reasons for leaving the mill.

> You surely cannot blame me for leaving the factory so long as I realized that it was killing me to work in it. I went to the factory because I expected to earn more than I can at housework. To be sure I might if I had my health. Could you have seen me att the time or a week before I cam away you would advised me as many others did to leave immediately. I realise that if I lose my health which is all I possess on earth or have eny reason to expect to posess that I shall be in a sad condition.[53]

Sally Rice's conclusions were echoed by workers in other mechanized industries. One employee of the Crane paper mill in Dalton, Massachusetts, requested a transfer from an especially damp machine room, where the water from paper in the process of drying condensed on the cooler walls and ceilings. The worker stated his case simply: "My object in leaving this place is on account of the Room in which I work, it is verry wet and it is ingering my health." He knew that his wages were "good," but he decided to leave his lucrative job for the fundamental reason that "money will not purches health."[54]

The physical condition of workers who remained in the factories, either from choice or necessity, was the subject of numerous articles in the operatives' magazines of the 1840s. These essays, and even poetry, were often filled with the specter of human dissolution and death. One operative from Manchester wrote how those in the mills were " 'dying off' by inches." Another Manchester correspondent added: "I have seen operatives that have labored three or four years in the Mills, that looked more like skeletons than like living mortals." At a labor-reform conference in 1847, an angry operative responded to a physician's apology for the factory system. Her statement is similar to Eliza Jane Cate's portrait of a debilitated operative, but there is a crucial difference. In this reply there is no mention of any fault in the worker's conduct. The result may be the same, but it is the factory system in this case that forced the operatives to work until their health collapsed:

> They entered them with healthy, hopeful countenances; they left them with visages whose toil-worn, care-worn expression showed too plainly that they had no hope but to be invalids forever. How many such have I known, who left their employment but to go home to die. They had worked months after their gradually decreasing strength had admonished them of failing health . . . they must toil on as long as they could, knowing that they were hastening their death, which was already fast approaching.[55]

The powerful and frightening image of a human being working herself to death also found its way into a 1845 petition from Lowell to the Massachusetts legislature. The specter of death was not a romantic literary convention for these workers; they believed that it was an inherent danger in their daily labor. The "peaceful, industrious, hard-working men and women of Lowell . . . [were] confined in unhealthy apartments, exposed to the poisonous contagion of air, vegetable, animal and mineral properties, debarred from proper *Physical* exercise . . . and thereby hastening us on through pain, disease and privation, down to a premature grave."[56]

The warning was clear to those operatives who would (or could) heed it—"nature cannot be cheated." This was not the nature that gently floated into the mills; it was the world of immutable physical laws. Workers who violated these laws, either by compulsion or through carelessness, were facing the possibility of death. One poem from a worker in Hookset, New Hampshire, to the *Voice of Industry* spoke of those who were pushed beyond endurance as "The Early Called."

It was morning, and the factory bell
Had sent forth its early call,
And many a weary one was there,
Within the dull factory wall.

And amidst the clashing noise and din
Of the ever beating loom:
Stood a fair young girl with throbbing brow,
Working her way to the tomb.

O, wearily had she risen that morn,
Wearily gone to the mill;
And she felt that in her aching heart
Life's warm pulse would soon grow still.

Days, weeks, and months, on their rounds went by,
Still the young girl toiled on,
And brighter grew the light in her eye,
Though hope from her heart had gone.

The closing lines of the poem spoke of the young woman's death and burial as a release from further arduous work and a return to nature.

How dreamless then was the young girl's sleep
No light could her spirit wake,
No work, no noise, no loud chiming bell
Could that deep, death-slumber brake . . .

And they laid her softly down to sleep
Beneath the tall forest trees
Where the earliest violets weep
And the wild birds warble free.

Death was treated here with a touch of sentimentality, but it was also confronted as a distinct danger in factory labor. In the end, this pathetic, poetic operative found rest only in a grave covered with flowers; and not the kind grown in a factory.[57]

— III —

Antebellum New England operatives had yet another fundamental question in their minds when they considered the factory building. They were concerned, not only with the factory's relationship to nature, but also with its physical and psychological place in the community. Would the new industrial structures become the center of communal life, thereby displacing the church from its traditional role? Would the factory serve the needs of the community, or would the community become a handmaiden to the factory?

The physical shape of the factory buildings often reflected this struggle to find a proper place in the social environment. In certain aspects, many factories bore a resemblance to churches. On the roof, for example, many industrial buildings had special windows to allow the maximum amount of light into their attics. The earliest of these windows in America were called "trap-door" or "eyebrow" monitors. By the second decade of the nineteenth century, these windows were redesigned to let in even more light and provide more headroom. A whole segment of the roof was, in effect, sliced off and raised to create space for another wall of windows. These openings were set back from the main wall, much like the clerestory in a Gothic cathedral—hence the name "clerestory" monitors. Some factories went even further than cathedral windows; their stair towers and bell cupolas looked very much like church steeples. These factories tried to imitate the churches around them, even as they were displacing these buildings from the center of communal life. When mills were built to look like churches, the owners could cover their ventures into industrial capitalism with the physical and symbolic veneer of a religious presence and purpose. The factory would physically embody its pledge to be a moral benefit to workers and the community.[58]

There were also some towns where the corporations took it upon themselves to build churches. The first priority, however, was to build the factories; then the management turned its attention to their other construction projects. The need for religious institutions in the community was often recognized, but the churches were constructed according to the dictates of the manufacturers. S. V. S. Wilder was induced to take charge of the Ware (Massachusetts) Manufacturing Company in 1826 only when the directors voted money for the erection of a church and invested Wilder with full power to oversee construction and settle a pastor. There was a debate over where to place the meetinghouse. Some townspeople wanted it on the hill, and others wanted it in the valley, nearer to the village center. Wilder never revealed his preference—whether a church on the hill would overshadow the factory or whether a church near the town would regain its status as the community's focal point—and he let the villagers decide by the power of the purse. Instead of putting the matter to a vote, he said that whichever group first raised an additional five hundred dollars would get to choose the site. The "hill party" came forward with the requisite amount and the church was built on the hill.[59]

Lucy Larcom found this linkage between company and church in Lowell reassuring. She remembered that "St. Anne's church . . . arose close to the oldest corporation ('the Merrimack'), and seemed a part of it, and a part, also, of the original idea of the place itself, which was always a city of worshipers." The church and the factory grew together and reinforced the traditional notion that work and worship were inextricably united. Larcom never mentioned the fact that St. Anne's was not such an inspiring ediface to all the workers in Lowell. This church was founded by Kirk Boott as an Episcopal congregation. The operatives, regardless of their own religious affiliations, were taxed thirty-seven and one-half cents each quarter for its support, and they were required to be in attendance there every Sunday. Even after new churches were built, St. Anne's stood as a troubling reminder to some workers of the dangers inherent in a company church.[60]

In order to further explore this relationship between the factory and the community, it is necessary to distinguish between two distinct forms of manufacturing communities—the factory village and the industrial city. Each one had its own particular physical and spatial arrangements, and each one meant something unique (or many unique things) to the men and women working there. The industrial cities have always received a large amount of attention—both from contemporary observers and from historians. But the factory village was probably the commonest site of industrial activity in antebellum New England. In 1840, for example, Lowell was already a city of 20,000 inhabitants; but most of the seven hundred cotton mills in New England were located in small rural townships. Some of these townships had more than one factory village within their borders.[61]

Factory villages stood somewhere in the middle of the transition from an agricultural to an industrial society. Some rural factories were simply extensions of earlier gristmill and sawmill sites. The new operations did not so much intrude on their physical surroundings as evolve out of them. Other villages sprang up along isolated streams where there was substantial waterpower but few other facilities. These hamlets were usually separated from each other by expanses of green countryside, which heightened their rural character and increased their detachment. Factory owners often filled in the gaps by building houses, schools, stores, and churches. These institutions gave stability to the community—they helped control the high labor-turnover rate, attract new workers, and offset the isolation of the country factory. Many of these facilities also served as instruments of social control and enhanced their owners' public image.[62]

The particular placement of the factory and these other structures revealed the conscious effort of some owners to re-create a kind of idealized colonial, agrarian community surrounding the new industry. Two of Samuel Slater's villages—Webster, Massachusetts, and Slatersville, Rhode Island—used linear street plans and open-field land patterns to maintain a supposedly old-fashioned New England character. Yet these antebellum factory villages were not re-creations of what colonial towns actually looked like. Rather, they were built on idealized myths of past colonial communities, blended with an antebellum rural industrial economy that was becoming more centralized in closely settled villages. Thus, factory owners probably saw utilitarian as well as symbolic advantages to such spatial arrangements—combining factories with town commons could lead to a more rationally ordered industrial operation that did not seem to disturb the rural structure of the community. It was a way to reconcile a new mode of production with what people thought were traditional physical and social patterns. Change could be grafted onto the seemingly familiar, and workers would feel less threatened by the whole process.

Slatersville, for example, was built around a wide road that ran through the village center. Stores, the church, and the school were located along this road. Slater even put the church in the geographic center of the community and surrounded it with a broad common. He was apparently more interested in presenting his workers with a reassuring, seemingly familiar environment than he was in making his factory the physical center of the village. In fact, the factory was built a short distance from the village and was surrounded by the company's own fenced and cultivated fields. The mill, therefore, did not physically intrude on the community; it was placed in the midst of an ongoing farming operation. The entire scene was supposed to put industry and agriculture in harmonious balance. The mill village would be uplifting because of its rural character and because of the owner's deliberate effort to carefully lay out all its wholesome institutions. No one would deny that the new factory system defined the social and economic framework of the village, but Slater tried to make sure that the framework also retained a physical sense of the rural past.[63]

Slater designed his villages as a kind of planned pastoral landscape—a middle ground between traditional agrarian culture and the new industrial society where both might coexist. But what about the workers? Did they see these factory villages in the same light? Some operatives did respond favorably to these rural communities; they found the villages to be more hospitable working environments than the industrial cities. Sarah Maria Cornell was one operative who spent many years working in a number of different factory villages and industrial cities. The reasons for her frequent moves may have been related to the controversy that surrounded her personal conduct. She was often accused both of stealing and of promiscuous sexual behavior, and she may have repeatedly left various towns to avoid discovery and public condemnation. Nevertheless, her years of traveling gave her an unparalleled opportunity to see many different industrial communities. In 1822, she was working in a Killingly, Connecticut, factory and reassuring her sister that she was still keeping "good company." Three years later she was working in Slatersville, and she was very enthusiastic about living in that factory village. The sense of religious community was especially strong for her there—probably a combination of the physical environment itself and an active Methodist congregation. She wrote again to her sister: "Sometimes when I think of leaving Slatersville, it strikes a dread upon me. Can I ever leave this delightful spot, where I have enjoyed so many delightful reasons and privileges, it seems to be a place highly favored by God."[64]

Shortly after she wrote these lines, the factory burned down, and Cornell had to leave Slatersville in search of work. She eventually ended up at Mendon Mills, which she herself noted was only one mile from Slatersville. Cornell wanted to stay as close to her previous residence as possible; her bonds to that particular factory village were strong. "I anticipate much in returning to that delightful village," she wrote to her mother, "and seeing it assume once more that lustre that shone so brilliantly." By 1829, when Cornell was working in Lowell and saw another factory fire, it was she who said, "I am a stranger in a strange land, exposed to sickness and death." She did admit to her sister, four months later, that she had made friends in Lowell and continued her religious affiliations. But she still longed for the villages and townspeople of Connecticut and Rhode Island. Cornell was a woman with a rebellious streak, but also a yearning for friendship and community. At one point, she had been dismissed from the Methodist congregation in Slatersville for lewdness. Yet she also found the social contact and stability she craved in the carefully planned factory village.[65]

Some factory villages were not deliberately designed in their entirety by any single proprietor, but these less-structured small towns were also attractive to some workers. Caroline and Rebecca Ford each left their jobs in a Middlebury, Vermont, woolen mill, on separate occasions, to work for a stint in Lowell during the early 1840s. Both sisters, however, returned to the rural woolen factory within a year. In their letters, they never revealed the exact reasons for their returning. But it is quite possible that the town of Middlebury was a middle ground for them also. It stood, physically and psychologically, between their rural homestead and the new industrial order. These women wanted to participate in the factory system, but they did not want to put their family farm (in Granville, Vermont) completely out of reach. They wanted to be able to visit their hometown, but not live in it. They wanted the opportunities of factory work, but not in a distant industrial city.[66]

Other workers took a much dimmer view of rural industrial communities. They saw that many mill villages were laid out far more haphazardly than Slatersville. Slatersville, in fact, may have been more the exception than the rule for factory villages. Industrial plants were almost always carefully situated to get the most out of the available power sources; sometimes houses and shops and churches had to be scattered along a riverbank or perched on a steep hillside. Even in the structured community of Webster, the spatial arrangements could fragment workers. By building family cottages for most workers, Slater not only paid allegiance to traditional notions of kinship, but also physically isolated the operatives from their fellow townspeople and from each other. Customary gathering places, such as taverns, were opposed by the management, while the church and school were both under corporate control. Many a factory village may have looked like an idealized colonial New England town on the surface, but its structure and institutions often undercut the traditional village spirit of independence, integrity, and community. These villages were supposed to reassure workers that nothing was fundamentally altered with the appearance of the factory. While some operatives did find security in these locales, others remained troubled.[67]

Some workers saw the factory village, not as a middle ground embracing the best of both the agrarian and the industrial worlds, but as the worst of both these spheres. Pawtucket, in the early days of its factory development, was said to be a rowdy and vulgar place; it earned the nicknames of "Hard-scrabble," "Bungtown," and "Pilfershire." The factory village was too industrialized to be fully immersed in the beauties and rhythms of the rural life, yet it was too isolated to be part of an urban culture. It might have all the pettiness and narrowmindedness of some small towns, but the dictates of the factory destroyed any real feeling of warmth and mutual obligation. Julia Dutton put the matter bluntly when she wrote to her mother in Vermont about the factory at Lancaster, Massachusetts. "It is not a very pleasant [place,] there is nothing to make any one contented but the money." Seth Luther, an itinerant mill worker and a leading labor pamphleteer, summed up much of the antagonism toward factory communities—especially cotton mills—when he wrote: "The great body of the inhabitants of New England, look upon employment in a cotton mill with horror and detestation, and would think it as great a misfortune as could possibly befall them, to be driven by any circumstances, to labor in these 'palaces of the poor.'"[68]

Workers who were discontented with the smaller communities sometimes moved to larger industrial cities in the hope of finding conditions more to their liking. (Others probably hoped to return to an agricultural way of life.) The agent of the Dover mills reported in 1827 that workers often left for other locales such as Lowell after only two or three months on the job at Dover. But not all this traffic was moving in one direction toward the cities; the Ford sisters made a return trip back to work in their rural mill. They did not go to Lowell fresh off the farm, but had previous factory-work experience. When they left, they did not retreat to the homestead; they went back to their familiar place of employment. They, and Sarah

Cornell, demonstrated that not every newcomer to Lowell was unfamiliar with factory work. Some operatives had served a kind of apprenticeship in factory villages before embarking for industrial cities.[69]

Lowell was the best-known of the new industrial cities, and it drew the most criticism and praise. Daniel Knapp recalled that in the late 1820s the legends about Lowell were often strange and disconcerting.

> I was told by those who believed it, that the help was driven into and out of the yard the same as cattle are into a pound, and that they could not communicate with their friends except through the counting-room . . . and the growth of Lowell under such circumstances was thought to be a great calamity in a New England community.

Other rumors also flew through the countryside—the mills were reported to be more than half full with the human refuse from county jails, and many a factory girl was said to have fallen quickly into a life of prostitution.[70]

Most workers dismissed these outrageous bits of gossip, but beneath these accusations there remained a troubling side to the industrial city. Many newcomers' first impression was one of confusion amidst the "brick forest" of city buildings—a forest unlike any they had seen back in their rural homes. Sarah Bagley captured this feeling quite clearly in her story, "The Orphan Sisters."

> . . . [W]hat a great contrast from the quiet country-home in the neighborhood of the White Mountains, was the City of Spindles, to the sisters! They had been accustomed to listen only to
>
> "Nature's wild, unconscious song,
> O'er thousand hills that floats along"—
>
> But here was confusion in all its forms, and truly said Catherine, "I should like to find myself alone for a brief space, that I might hold communion with my own heart undisturbed."

The confusion and crowding of the city was, for these fictitious representatives of rural New England, an assault on their ideals of natural order and personal integrity. These qualms about urban life were shared by many city residents, whether they worked in industrial cities or not. But the conjunction of the factory and the city often heightened the feeling of dislocation and anomie.[71]

Most operatives who remained in the industrial cities grew accustomed to the cacophony of new sights and sounds. But many never believed that these cities could ever become real, organic communities. John Quincy Adams Thayer's critique of Lowell turned the problem of industrial cities inside-out. Thayer, a machinist in the Locks and Canals shops, was most troubled, not by the confusion of the city, but by its very deliberate attempt at planning. The Lowell corporations were trying to carefully construct a physically coherent community—but only as defined by these companies for their own needs.

> This external order and appearance is not without design . . . [and] not without deception. It closes the eye of the observer, and flatters the mind to believe that all is well within, and again the distant stranger reads, and by quotation is reminded

> of the land of song, and the days of young romance, and not only wishes to be in Lowell, but comes; and soon is found a dictated rhyming slave.
>
> This external appearance reminds me again, of a costly temple, the designer of which, after having completed the external gilding and beauty, at the expense of others, fortunately died; leaving the beautiful covering a fit shelter for wild beasts, and birds of prey, who there secured a home.

Thayer saw Lowell's carefully laid out streets and mill yards as a mere façade covering up the exploitative conditions of factory labor. The Lowell corporations, in his eyes, were perverting the ideals of the community to create a docile labor force.[72]

Other operatives found in Lowell something far more substantial than a hollow exterior. They welcomed the precisely defined sense of space in the city—broad, treelined streets, freshly painted boardinghouses, substantial blocks of stores, and of course the mills themselves. The whole scheme reaffirmed the stability and order of the factory buildings. Thayer saw all this as a kind of interlocking conspiracy to completely control the operatives' lives. But other workers were not threatened by this overall sense of precision and control; they felt secure in such an environment.[73]

Harriet Farley did not see the creation of Lowell as an assault on nature or on the notion of community. She believed that the industrial city represented the pinnacle of human endeavor in harmony with the physical world. When men set their hands to creating a new city, they reshaped nature and the rural world to give each of them more meaning. When rivers were channeled, dams erected, factories built, and entire communities constructed around them—then "Nature and Art in lines of grandeur are here parallel with each other; and, in the construction of the latter could we behold humanity of every grade, each efficient in its place." The harmony in Lowell between nature, industry, and community would be reflected in harmonious social relations as well. Farley saw nothing conspiratorial in this; only a healthy example for all to emulate.

> And here we have, not precisely a broad field before us, but a broad platform, divided and edged with placid canals, and running streams, covered with mighty buildings which vibrate to the fall of powerful torrents; and which are built with durability, convenience and good taste; ornamented with parterres, and trees; approached by pavement and gravelled paths . . . and brought into close neighborhood with churches, school houses, lecture rooms, and assembly halls.[74]

Harriet Farley was not the only operative who found such beauty and balance in an industrial city. Ann Appleton wrote to her sister in January of 1847 about her first impressions of Manchester: "I can say that I think Manchester is a beautiful place. The houses are mostly of brick and there are some very handsome streets." Lucy Larcom remembered that in Lowell the "long stretches of open land between the corporation buildings and the street made the town seem country-like." The mills at Great Falls also tried to create a kind of village green on land between the factories and the town's main street. The area was kept as an open common ground for the townspeople to use as a park, bleaching-field, or pasture. Though Great Falls was certainly not as urban as Lowell, this policy may have been another conscious effort to retain a portion of agricultural village life in the midst of a factory community.[75]

It probably seemed absurd to some people for a place like Lowell to pretend that it was still a quaint rural town. Yet many operatives continued to see in Lowell that middle ground where industry, nature, and community could meet as distinct yet interrelated forces. They knew that cities like Lowell were more than a mill by a forest stream. But they believed that the factory, the city, and the natural landscape could coexist, providing beneficial counterpoints to each other. Harriet Hanson Robinson clung to this memory of antebellum Lowell as a "lost Eden," and asserted that "in 1832, Lowell was little more than a factory village." Throughout the 1840s, as Lowell grew in physical size and population, Harriet Farley and others continued to argue that this industrial city retained all the human dimensions of a factory village along with the social and economic opportunities of a growing metropolis. They praised the factory and the city as positive examples of human achievement and national progress. Yet they also believed that these forces were conservative in their own right; they opened the way to the future while embracing the best of the past. The new buildings, and the new communities, did not rob workers of their rural heritage. They enhanced the bounty and beauty of nature, and gave new meaning to the ideals of communal work and life.[76]

This enthusiastic support of industrial cities was precisely what factory owners hoped to achieve through their efforts at urban planning. They wanted to create an environment that would reassure workers, and the general public, that rural values and the industrial order could coexist harmoniously. Yet it would be wrong to assume that workers were merely responding dutifully to the overt and hidden signals of factory managers. Workers strove to find a balanced way of life, not necessarily to please their employers, but because they wanted such a life for themselves. And those who said that they had already found such a balance cannot be dismissed as corporate dupes. They had their eyes open to the community around them, and they honestly believed that it held the promise of a better life.

Thus, many workers were striving for ways to reconcile the factory with nature and community. And with all these workers looking for some form of middle ground, it is not surprising that this concept took on so many different meanings. It had a quasi-religious character for Sarah Maria Cornell; it was a geographic location for the Ford sisters; and it was a sense of ordered urban space for Lowell mill workers like Harriet Farley. And with so many meanings embedded in the concept of a middle ground, it is not surprising that there were tensions and ambiguities in these meanings as well.

One of the most graphic portrayals (in every sense of the word) of the ambiguous nature of this middle landscape is found on the cover of the *Lowell Offering* (Figure 1). The women who wrote and edited this magazine set out to present an image of a mill girl and her surroundings that was beyond reproach. Whether they were aware of it or not, however, they ended up creating a study of a young woman caught between two worlds.

The *Offering* cover first appeared in January of 1845, and reappeared on the front of every subsequent issue until the magazine ceased publication in December of 1845. It showed a factory girl in the foreground "near her cottage home" and surrounded by lush vegetation. "In the background," Harriet Robinson explained, "as if to shut them from her thoughts, was a row of factories." Also in the background

Figure 1. Cover of the *Lowell Offering*
(State Historical Society of Wisconsin)

were a church and a schoolhouse, the basic institutions of a proper village. Looking at the picture as a whole, there seems to be a balance between the elements of the agricultural and industrial sectors.[77]

In describing this scene, however, Harriet Farley began to reveal some of the dualities under the surface. The agrarian vision figured prominently in the foreground of the composition. Yet Farley said that it was the "quiet country home" on which "almost every factory girl looks back." At the same time, the physical presence of the factory—which shaped so much of the operatives' daily lives—was pushed into the background as merely one of a triad of buildings. Thus, the factory was portrayed as being in close proximity to the surrounding rural culture, but it remained in the background, behind the country homestead.[78]

As for the female figure in this engraving, she stood in an ambiguous position between the factory and the country home, making no definite commitment to either the agricultural or the industrial world. Her clothing was distinctly unfashionable and out of place for a Lowell mill girl; it was even nostalgic and out of date for rural women in the 1840s. Her facial expression was also quite uncertain—was it shy and demure, or pensive? Was she bidding a sad farewell to her country home and with trepidation pondering her future in the mill? Or was she thinking back on fond memories of factory labor as she returned to her rural cottage? The very position of her head gave no clear indication whether she was looking behind her to the factory or more directly at her immediate rural surroundings. To put it simply, one did not know whether this young woman was coming away from or going back to the mills. She seemed to embody both the potential, and the tensions, of the middle ground.

Thus, for a magazine that presented so many essays and stories promoting the virtues of the Lowell mills and the operatives therein, the *Offering*'s cover presented an image in conflict with itself and at odds with the magazine's content. The whole scene bore little resemblance to the actual physical appearance of Lowell. The cover showed no sweeping panoramas of Lowell as a city, nor of the throngs of mill girls. Instead, there was a nostalgic portrait of a mill village, a country cottage, and a young woman poised between them. It was essentially a pictorial homage to rural life, character, and values. But why, then, put it on the cover of a Lowell mill girls' magazine? Was it supposed to show the typical Lowell operative in her natural country surroundings? Was it supposed to reassure these women—and their families and the surrounding public—that all their wholesome rural roots would survive and even flourish in the industrial city of Lowell?

The message may have been that while the cover was not an actual representation of Lowell and its workers, it was a portrait of the city and its work force's higher qualities; that is, the essentially rural character that transcended physical appearances. But even as the *Offering*'s cover tried, on one level, to reconcile the agricultural and industrial realms in a portrait of a harmoniously balanced world, and even as it painted a reassuring picture of the rural roots of the factory work force, it did not answer all the questions. This image was also one that, on other levels, whether consciously intending to or not, captured the very tensions between factory, nature, and community that it tried to gloss over.

Comparing the *Offering*'s cover with the masthead of its archrival, the *Voice of Industry* (Figure 2), produces some startling parallels and more insights into the

Figure 2. Masthead of the *Voice of Industry* (American Antiquarian Society)

multidimensional meaning of the middle ground. For, whether they realized it or not, the workers who criticized the factory system often shared a similar quest for the idea of a middle ground with those who supported the factories. The factory critics did not want to destroy all the industrial plants; they wanted to integrate them into a harmonious natural and social order. Their vision of this new order was portrayed on the *Voice*'s masthead, which appeared first on February 12, 1847, when the paper was published by the mechanic William Young and the operative Mehitable Eastman. This masthead appeared on every weekly issue of the newspaper until November 19, 1847.[79]

The overall composition of this masthead was similar in many ways to the *Lowell Offering*'s cover. The agricultural motifs were again placed in the foreground, but in this image, there were industrial and commercial scenes of factories, railroads, and ships (and perhaps even a city) in the background. Near the center of this composition were three figures, all looking virtually directly at the reader. The man on the left provided a classic example of the popular image of the honest, hard-working, and intelligent workman. The women were essentially allegorical in their appearance, even more so than the ideal mill girl of the *Offering*. The female figure in the center was the traditional representation of justice—but with her eyes open in this case—seated on a world created "for all." The other woman was a Muse-like figure on the right surrounded by books and musical instruments. The total structure of the masthead was another attempt at portraying a balance between nature and industry. The farmer tilled his fields in front of the factory somewhere in the middle of the scene. Trees and flowers bloomed profusely, practically spilling over the very name of the newspaper. And the factory reposed deep in the distance, not threatening to overrun the land or the sea.

The *Voice*'s masthead was denser in its illustrations than the *Offering*'s cover; broader in its scope as it strived to encompass factory, city, seacoast, and farm; and more allegorical, yet less ambiguous, with the figures in the foreground. All of these figures were firm in their posture and gaze—they were looking directly out of the page, out into the future, and out at the viewer. Thus, while there were fascinating similarities in the basic compositions of the newspaper masthead and the magazine cover, they conveyed distinctly different messages to antebellum operatives. In effect, while both images captured the struggle of workers to balance the competing claims of the agricultural way of life and the new industrial order, they also showed how many divergent forms that struggle took for these early factory workers.

The *Voice*'s banner was not drawn to represent the wholesome rural mill girl and her heritage. The masthead was a combination of an allegorical and a futuristic vision of what the ideal society would look like after the present one was reformed. If the *Offering*'s cover had elements of retrospective pastoralism in it, the *Voice*'s masthead was an expression of futuristic utopianism. It was a call to all factory operatives, and other working men and women, to unite and strive for a balanced political economy—a world of economic diversity, material abundance, and cultural richness. The real sense of community would be found, not merely in buildings, but in the principles of equality and justice. But this newspaper's readers and contributors also feared that the ideal of harmony between man, nature, industry, and community might prove to be an elusive dream. The factory was still threatening to overrun the garden, undermine all of rural society, and erode any possible remaining middle ground.

The *Lowell Offering*'s supporters, on the other hand, saw that magazine's cover as the embodiment of an ideal that was part of nearly every factory worker's rural background. They saw the goal of a balanced life and economy as within the grasp of every operative in every factory village and industrial city in New England. Yet they may not have realized how many questions were also raised by their portrait of the model mill girl.

Contributors to the *Offering,* and their counterparts at the *Voice of Industry,* also may not have realized that most of them shared the quest for a middle ground. But with so many working women and men searching for the physical and psychological balance between agriculture and industry and nature and community, there remained a great deal of disagreement over how and where to find that balance. Some workers insisted that the middle ground was already a part of their daily lives. Others argued that the middle ground was a place and time in the future when the factory system would be reshaped to serve the needs of the working people. Clearly, the struggle for the soul of the factory system and the factory worker would go on; and it would be fought over, not only machines and buildings, but the social relations of production as well.

CHAPTER 3

Harmony and Antagonism: Workers, Managers, and the Social Relations of Production

Charles and Sarah Metcalf traveled to Lowell, Massachusetts, in the spring of 1841. Soon after their arrival, Charles wrote to their parents in Winthrop, Maine, about their prospects for working and living in the "city of spindles." He also advised them about sending another sibling, Mary, in search of employment.

> I should be glad to have her come but I wish her to know what to expect should she come. I wish not to discourage *her* or *you.* She would probably find some place to work if not immediately, soon but whether she would like it or not I dont know. In the 1st place she would find theres no place like *Home,* every one here is wrapped up in self and looks out for No.1. She would find her patience taxed to the utmost. I was going to say she would find few very few to care for her in her troubles except relations and none to sympathize like *parents.* There can be no *I cants* here. If she has fortitude, patience, and perseverance . . . and wishes very much to come and you think it best *I say come* and we will do the best we can for her. She must leave home . . . sometime, and perhaps this is as good as any and the lesson though a hard one will be a good [one].[1]

The Metcalfs, like so many of their fellow operatives, had come from a small rural community. They had probably never seen anything like the sheer mass of humanity that filled a city such as Lowell. Within the factories and on the streets outside, the burgeoning industrial population was indeed a force to be reckoned with. Charles Metcalf's astute observations captured the anomie many operatives felt in their new industrial and urban environments. One of the authors of the Lowell Female Labor Reform Association's "Factory Tracts" painted an even more disturbing picture of the factory labor force.

> . . . [T]hrown into company with all sorts and descriptions of mind, dispositions and intellects, without counselor or friend to advise—far away from a watchful mother's tender care, or father's kind instruction—surrounded on all sides with the vain ostentation of fashion, vanity and light frivolity—beset with temptations without, and the carnal prosperities of nature within, what *must,* what will be the natural, rational result?

A contributor to the *Voice of Industry* provided an equally haunting answer: "... their manners are in danger of becoming rude, their language vulgar, their habits unrefined, and their minds and hearts (in the rude struggle they have now to encounter,) must, in at least nine cases in ten, become contaminated with the cold treachery and heartlessness of a selfish world." Just as the physical conditions within the factory endangered workers' bodily health, these critics argued, the chaotic social environment led to intellectual and moral degradation. Newcomers to the factory might find a scene of mechanical confusion and social pandemonium as well. Everything was in constant motion: the machines, the various levels of supervisors moving about and watching and giving orders, the workers scurrying about their tasks.[2]

Even Lucy Larcom, generally known for her positive appraisal of life in antebellum Lowell, admitted that "the congregation of very great numbers of people at any occupation cannot be considered as altogether favorable to personal development." The individual in a large factory was always in danger of being overwhelmed, physically and mentally, by the "promiscuous throng" of employees. "To hold faithfully to one's own distinct thought and purpose amid the confusions of a mixed multitude," Larcom wrote, "is no easy thing." Operatives had to constantly use their own willpower and character to maintain their personal identities. The greatest problem for workers in these new, densely populated working environments, according to Larcom, was not the temptation to retreat entirely into self-absorption, but the pressure to lose oneself in the mass. Larcom never saw any easy way out of this dilemma, and she concluded: "the necessity for close and indiscriminate contact must, perhaps, always be one of the unmanageable difficulties in the way of factory toilers."[3]

Eliza Jane Cate saw the myriad social contacts within the factory in a more positive light. The newcomers from the hinterlands were not losing their identity, they were experiencing a kind of liberation and finding new opportunities to expand their horizons.

> ... [W]hat a sublime sight are those factories, and those factory girls! Do you not see passing off from them, in every possible direction, the mystic wires of sympathetic influence, spiritual intercourse with the companions that are near and friends that are afar? And through them are borne hopes of every degree of bouyancy, fears of every shade of darkness, wishes of every grade of purity and intenseness, and holy thoughts of resignation and contentment. . . .

Some operatives felt adrift without the familiar people, places, and standards of their hometowns; others relished the sense of release and boundlessness in the crowds of the industrial city. In a place filled with strangers, one could feel very alone or very adventurous. Some workers welcomed the chance to meet new people, see new sights, even learn about new political and religious ideas that might not have been discussed much in rural villages.[4]

Many workers sensed that factories could be places of both growing social opportunities and profound social dislocations. Many factories, particularly the larger enterprises, tried to create highly organized and centralized social systems of production, even as the work forces they tried to manage became larger and more difficult to control. The focal point for much of this social control and conflict was the relationship between managers and workers—a relationship that was a new experience for many factory operatives. Quite simply, the presence of people with titles like "agent" and "superintendent" and "overseer" was a new phenomenon to many workers. Those who had previous work experience often came from farms or shops where job categories and tasks were not always precisely demarcated. Inside the mechanized factories, these operatives entered a world of officially defined and hierarchically ordered jobs.

Workers quickly discovered that factories assembled a large congregation of employees into one collective endeavor, then separated them into specialized tasks and various levels of authority. It was just as important for a worker to understand the social dynamics of the factory as it was to learn how to tend her assigned machines. Operatives realized that, when they scrutinized their relationships with their managers, they once again confronted fundamental questions of power, control, and authority. Some workers proclaimed their optimistic faith in their managers and their confidence that they would be treated fairly. Other workers saw an inherently inequitable distribution of power and resources in these factories, and they were disturbed by a managerial hierarchy that seemed intent on controlling workers for the maximum profit.

— I —

In some industries, a basic harmony was said to prevail between management and labor. Armories and machine shops were often particularly known for good working relationships between managers and workers. These industrial sites were often modest in size; thus there was a greater chance for personal contact between employers and employees. Many of the workers in these factories were also skilled men; therefore, managers may have deliberately cultivated more friendly man-to-man exchanges in order to retain their skilled work force. Many managers in these shops and armories had risen from the ranks of these skilled workers, so the social distance between worker and supervisor was not always so great.

Stories circulated throughout New England about particular armories and their benevolent owners. Simeon North would make the rounds of his Middletown, Connecticut, factory whenever he returned from his frequent business trips to Washington, D.C. He would greet each worker by name, shake his hand, and ask about his family. He also often invited employees into his home on winter evenings to sit around the kitchen fire and talk. Eli Whitney often loaned money to his workmen, perhaps because he himself had often known the difficulty of obtaining such loans. Armory workers often responded to these gestures with a dignified sense of loyalty to their employers. When Samuel Colt tried to recruit Chester Bradley from the Springfield Armory, Bradley responded: "I consulted with the Master Armorer who was willing to give me every satisfaction that I could wish and under such encouragement here it would be ungentleman like for me to leave." Generous management policies thus helped to overcome any restlessness in the labor force.[5]

Particular machine shops were also said to be places where managers and workers often developed very productive relationships. John Rogers, working in the Amoskeag Machine Shop in 1850, wrote proudly to his family: "Mr. Buxton seems to have taken a wonderful fancy to me lately. He told me the other day he would part with every hand he had before he would with me if I would stay with him & as I gain much in being with a man who takes an interest in me, I shall probably keep with him for the present." Rogers added in a subsequent letter that the shop's superintendent, C. P. Crane, gave him "as good jobs as any of his hands & better than some & I learn something new every day."[6]

William Mason's shops in Taunton, Massachusetts, were renowned for the quality of their work, and Mason's employees admired him for his talents and his fair dealings with them. Mason's office was always open to any worker with a problem; he was familiar with their difficulties from his own work experience, and he was never afraid to take off his coat and help out on the shop floor. Even when conflict loomed between him and his workers, Mason's legendary sense of humor could often defuse the situation. The machinists once voted that the workday should be reduced from ten and a half to ten hours. Their spokesman cautiously approached Mason and stated: "Mr. Mason, we are going to work 10 hours." Mason replied: "I'm glad of that . . . you never have yet." The mixture of caustic wit and stern warning served to dampen any further agitation, without leaving the workers embittered.[7]

Textile mills were often much larger and more hierarchically organized than armories or machine shops. Yet even in some of the largest mills, management went to great lengths to reassure workers about the positive nature of their working relationships—and some workers responded quite enthusiastically to these overtures. Companies in Dover, New Hampshire, and Lowell added special paragraphs to their regulation papers that stressed the ideal of harmony in the factory. The mill agents, who had responsibility for supervising entire factories and who signed their approval to these regulations, tried to convince operatives that the rules would be for everyone's benefit and enforced in an equitable manner.

The 1829 regulations for the mill in Dover stated:

> The agent is desirous of cultivating the most friendly feeling among all the members of this establishment, and while on the one hand a rigid attention to duty and observance of these regulations and any other that may be found necessary to establish, which do not affect their rights as citizens, will be required, he assures the individuals under his charge that it will give him pleasure to be of service to them.

Four years later, William Austin, agent for the Lawrence Manufacturing Company in Lowell, went even further in his solicitous concern for the workers' well-being.

> Persons in the employ of the Company will reflect, that it is their voluntary agreement to serve, and consequent mutual relations of the parties, which render it proper on their part to conform to regulations or that warrant the Agent in promulgating rules for their observance, and which govern him as well as themselves. They will perceive that where objects are to be obtained, by the united efforts and labor of many individuals, that some must direct and many be directed. That their religious and political opinions need not however be influenced, nor their personal

> independence, or self respect, or conscious equality lost sight of or abandoned . . . and it is no less desirable that all should be expert and cheerful at their business. . . . They may apply with confidence to the Agent for advice, and such aid and counsel as he can afford them will be cheerfully granted, especially to those who may be far from their parents and friends. It remains to encourage and cherish mutual respect, kindness and conciliation towards each other, and that peculiar instances of industrious and honest merit be rewarded, and which the Agent will reciprocate and aspire to accomplish.[8]

Austin was attempting to put a human face on the official requirements of his factory. He was trying to incorporate the entire work force and its managerial hierarchy into an ideal productive community. His statement was a curious blend of paternalistic sentiment for the newcomers to industrial labor, a call for "mutual respect" between workers and managers, and a pledge of political and religious freedom. All of these ideas were promulgated, however, in the very legal document that Austin was trying to humanize in theory and enforce in practice. By having operatives, and frequently overseers and higher officers, sign contracts and regulation papers, the new industrial companies were trying to codify and objectify social relations in the workplace. The role of custom and dialogue in the workshop was supposed to yield to the order and hierarchy of the manufactory. Yet Austin still believed that the worker and manager could meet on friendly terms, though not necessarily as equals, within the regulated framework of the new system.

Some operatives agreed with Austin that the traditional face-to-face relationship between employer and employee was not lost in the factory. These textile workers believed that management–labor relations on the factory floor were rooted in a sense of common identity and purpose, particularly between overseers and operatives. These workers realized that in many mills the most important authority figure in their daily lives was that immediate supervisor—the overseer. Yet these overseers did not have to be feared as omnipotent and distant figures. After all, both workers and most of the supervisory personnel were wage-earning employees of the corporations; they all had to answer to even higher authorities. Moreover, some workers pointed out that many of these supervisors had risen from the ranks of machine-tenders and repairmen. Harriet Hanson Robinson even argued that "the majority" of operatives "were as well born as their overlookers, if not better: and they were also far better educated."[9]

Harriet Farley also saw a common heritage binding the operatives and overseers. She wrote that the young women of Lowell "found cousins, friends, and acquaintances among the different grades of overseers; men who were here as good as they had been at home, and sometimes even better." The character of these managers, Farley asserted, was almost always beyond reproach. They were usually married, faithful church members, temperate, and public spirited. Consequently, "the tone of intercourse between the girls and overseers" was generally "very good—pleasant, yet respectful." Since both operatives and overseers held to such high personal standards, Farley was confident that these managers would be sympathetic to the workers' needs and interests.[10]

Other workers also cited numerous examples of supervisors who went out of their way to help operatives. Some overseers were especially willing to help out a worker having difficulty tending a machine. Others, having had previous experience in repair shops, were ready to fix a broken piece of equipment. John Wilson, a recent British immigrant to Lowell in the late 1840s, reported that his "Boss," Mr. Milne, and Milne's wife helped members of Wilson's family when they arrived in Lowell sick from their transatlantic voyage. Milne also found work for these newcomers when they were well enough to enter the mills.[11]

Harriet Farley also observed that the higher-level superintendents, though perhaps more distant from the mill workers in the course of daily labor, were also judicious in their conduct. She noted that "their duties, to those above them, require that they should not make themselves obnoxious to those beneath them; and their policy is to harmonize the interests of capitalists and operatives." There were other similar reports about higher-level factory managers who went far beyond their official duties in assisting operatives. E. A. Straw, agent of the Amoskeag Mills in Manchester, New Hampshire, encouraged workers to come directly to him with any grievances. He often personally investigated these complaints and intervened where necessary. In one instance, the fellow workers of an old woman named Mary reported that she had been fired by her overseer because her age had slowed her down. Straw visited Mary, brought her back to the mill, promised her permanent employment, and publicly reprimanded the overseer. At the Eddy Satinet Factory in Fall River, Massachusetts, the proprietors often sat around the finishing-room stove during the long Saturday evenings of the winter months, and discussed current events with their workers. And one operative remembered that Warren Colburn, superintendent of the Merrimack Company in Lowell, taught him how to read and write when he came to the mill as an illiterate immigrant. Then Colburn went on to instruct him in mathematics. In all these accounts, the employers emerge as benevolent patrons rather than adversaries.[12]

Most workers realized that these individual acts of managerial kindness and these modest adjustments in the factory's daily regimen did not radically alter the basic social structure in the mills. But such friendly interaction did add an element of flexibility and humanity to the workers' daily lives. It showed how official rules did not always govern social relations in the factories. Some workers took comfort in the fact that dialogue and compromise was still possible between labor and management. They saw no need to challenge the factory hierarchy because they believed that the higher managerial authorities were exercising their power with great restraint and openness.

Eliza Jane Cate, in one of her advice columns for operatives, specifically urged her readers to return the courtesies of their overseer with gratitude and obedience. Harmonious social relations could flourish in a factory, if both management and labor recognized their respective positions of supervision and subordination and assumed the best of intentions in each other's actions.

> Your overseer is a better judge of what he can, and what he cannot, do in the way of repairing your disordered machinery, giving you the looms or frames you desire, allowing you to go when you wish to, and furnishing you with good work, and "a spare hand," if you need help. It is your part to respectfully state your wishes in these and all matters; and there are few overseers in our New England factories who will not comply with your reasonable demands, when it is in their power, unless

> you have forfeited your just title to their favor and respect, by ill humor, want of faithfulness, or some fault which deserves the punishment of ungratified wishes.
>
> Accept any favor your overseer may grant you, in the gratefulness due to all kindness, from what source soever it may come to us.[13]

Perhaps the most important dimension of labor–management relations in many textile mills was the basic fact that all supervisory positions were held by men, while many operatives were women. Thus, the issue of employer–employee relations in many factories has to be understood predominantly in terms of male–female relationships. Gender, class, and the social relations of production all intersected when male managers supervised female workers.

Many manufacturers preferred to hire female operatives because they seemed more obedient to regulations and less likely to organize resistance against their managers. A female operative's obedience to a male overseer was seen by managers as an easy transition from the accepted practice of a young woman's obeying her father. In fact, it might have seemed quite natural for male managers to strike a paternalistic pose with their female employees. Older men saw younger women as essentially docile and willing to accept fatherly attention and authority, without feeling that their female identity was being threatened. Male workers, on the other hand, may have been more likely to resent paternalism as a challenge to their masculinity.[14]

Female operatives had their own ideas about corporate paternalism. But even those who saw advantages in the system did not always accept paternalism on management's terms. Harriet Hanson Robinson argued, for example, that the large population of women workers helped to temper the stringency of managerial actions. "If these early agents, or overseers, had been disposed to exercise undue authority, the moral strength of the operatives, and the fact that so many of them were women, would have prevented it." Robinson recalled that one Lowell agent, a former sea captain, said: " 'I should like to rule my help as I used to rule my sailors, but so many of them are women I dare not do it.' "[15]

With so many male managers interacting with so many female operatives, paternalism quickly became a prominent theme in workers' discussions of social relations. Harriet Farley stated that many overseers were "fatherly sort of men, and the girls frequently resort to them for advice and assistance about affairs other than work." Farley saw this paternalistic concern, both in and out of the factory, as one of the advantages of working in Lowell. Corporate paternalism, for Farley, did not mean female dependence or inferiority; rather, paternalistic gestures were tokens of respect and friendship from management.[16]

An operative from Chicopee, Massachusetts, in correspondence with Farley, described the Cabot Company's agent as "a kind-hearted and intelligent man," and the Dwight Company's agent was said to be a "*perfect gentleman.*" The writer added that,

> in regard to the overseers too much cannot be said in their favor; they are ever-willing to accommodate their help, and in cases of sickness and death they are like parents to those who have left the paternal roof, to seek a livelihood in our midst; and, as a general thing, perfect harmony exists between them and their help.

Obviously, this worker was also quite comfortable with the notion of corporate paternalism. She saw nothing insulting in the idea that these companies and their management were exercising a paternal interest in the workers' lives on and off the job. She believed that many operatives, often far from their homes and removed from any paternal control, welcomed the fatherly concern of their overseers. These young women were reassured by the presence of older men watching over them. But, again, this worker was not arguing for complete female submission and dependence. She saw corporate paternalism as a means of supporting women who were working on their own.[17]

Many operatives believed that good working relations in the factory were rooted, not only in management's paternal regard for the workers, but also in the idea that labor was participating in a shared enterprise with management. These workers insisted that their efforts were respected by their employers and that operatives and bosses alike were all industrial pioneers pushing the nation forward. Harriet Hanson Robinson noted that this feeling of "mutual interest . . . between employers and employed" made for a productive work force. "The feeling that the agents and overseers took an interest in their welfare caused the girls, in turn, to feel an interest in the work for which their employers were responsible. The conscientious among them took as much pride in spinning a smooth thread, drawing in a perfect web, or in making good cloth, as they would have done if the material had been for their own wearing." Robinson argued that many workers internalized a sense of loyalty and obligation to their employers—which was one of the ultimate goals of management—and these workers wanted to produce more and better goods. They subsumed whatever remaining pride they had in their skill and craft into this bond with the company. They became what managers wanted them to be; obedient, but also responsible and profitable workers. They were just as likely to forge alliances with their employers as they were with their fellow workers.

Robinson also stressed, however, that workers were not unwittingly co-opted or bribed by management favors into allowing themselves to be exploited. Rather, "there was a feeling of respectful equality between" all the parties; "the line of social division was not rigidly maintained." Everyone acknowledged their mutual interdependence and worked together for "the growing prosperity of the city"—prosperity that, Robinson believed, would touch the lives of all working men and women.[18]

Other workers concurred with Robinson's assessment; many operatives saw industrial communities as true embodiments of the American democratic ideal. "I believe there is no place," wrote one contributor to the *Lowell Offering,* "where there is so much equality, so few aristocratic distinctions, and such good fellowship, as may be found in this community." This writer also argued that, even in the midst of large-scale economic development, the criteria for personal worth in Lowell had little to do with material wealth. "A person has only to be honest, industrious, and moral, to secure the respect of the virtuous and good, though he may not be worth a dollar; while on the other hand, an immoral person, though he should possess wealth, is not respected."[19]

Eliza Jane Cate also remembered that the Lowell of 1840 was more than a physical community—it was a vibrant social entity where "mill people were on the same ground with the clergyman, the lawyer, the merchant, the landlord, and the artisan . . . we were understood and respected; thus we respected ourselves, and lived a good and pleasant life. . . . We met our agent, superintendent, and overseers at church, in the Bible-class, in society, and everywhere. They were considerate and kind, like brothers." She did not emphasize paternalism here, but a basic fraternal equality pervading the city. Cate insisted that the operatives were not treated as outsiders in the Lowell community. Quite the contrary; the workers considered themselves an integral part of the city's social structure, and they were recognized by others as equal members of the community. "We are, in fact," wrote one essayist in the *Operatives' Magazine,* "a truely republican community, or rather we have among us the only aristocracy which an intelligent people should sanction—an aristocracy of worth."[20]

Operatives who praised the democratic character of their factory republics, in effect, clearly denied the presence of classes or class-consciousness in the factory system. Lucy Larcom argued that the operatives were too diverse in background, too steeped in agrarian egalitarianism, and too friendly with each other, to think of themselves as a class or to classify those around them. "They met, with sincere sympathy, on a common ground of toil and aspiration." These workers saw their lives shaped by their own individual background and temperament more than by their occupational status. One contributor to the *Lowell Offering* remarked: "I never think of factory life as distinct from other life, and of factory operatives as distinct from other laborers. We are just like others. . . . Our hopes, fears, joys and sorrows are those to which all are subject." The sense of social and communal solidarity was more real to these workers than class solidarity. They firmly believed in the ideal that labor and capital were working together for the good of the society as a whole. They had no notion of having "fallen into another and lower class"; rather, they insisted on their equal standing with any other worker or manager.[21]

Beneath all these professions of equality, however, some workers recognized that the constant daily contact between operatives and overseers could sometimes pull loyalties in diverse directions. Overseers may have felt torn between their sympathy for operatives (some of whom they might have worked with previously), and their need to enforce the edicts of factory owners. Harriet Farley recognized this difficult situation, and she was especially sympathetic to the plight of overseers and their supervisors. She wrote, in "Letters from Susan,"

> [y]ou think I have too high an opinion of our superintendents. I hope not. I do think that many of them are chosen as combining, in their characters, many excellent qualities. Some of them may be as selfish as you suppose. But we must remember that they owe a duty to their employers, as well as those they employ. They are agents of the companies, as well as superintendents of us. Where those duties conflict I hope the sympathies of the man will always be with the more dependent party.

Farley understood that although operatives and supervisors shared something of a common identity when they were both employees of a corporation, they did not all occupy the same rung on the corporate ladder. She was concerned with managers who were torn between obligations to their subordinates and to the corporate owners. Yet Farley remained hopeful that managers would always look out for the interests of the "more dependent" workers as much as for the profits of the wealthy corporate shareholders (many of whom lived away from the mills, in places like Boston).[22]

In cases where conflicting loyalties could not be easily reconciled, Farley reminded operatives to look closely at the entire situation before placing the blame on any one party. Both workers and managers had their faults; neither side had a monopoly on vice or virtue. There were overseers who were overbearing; they did not know that "as much pain [could] be caused here by a hasty or unjust word, as could have resulted from a blow." Yet Farley believed that these men were unfortunate exceptions. "And where an absolute quarrel arises between an overseer and one of his help—a quarrel in which the girl is not favored by the superintendent, we believe herself to be in fault. Girls with unregulated feelings are more common here than men who would be unjust and unkind to females under their care." Farley's argument paralleled the one she made regarding workers' health in the factories: she blamed operatives for their problems. The fault was not with management, nor with the overall social structure in the mills; it lay with operatives who did not know their place and could not regulate their own behavior.[23]

Eliza Jane Cate took Farley's admonishments one step further. She advised operatives, even when their overseers were at fault and lost their tempers, to maintain their own decorum. Even if management could not control workers, or if overseers lost control of themselves, the employees were still supposed to behave properly and deferentially. One reason for this advice was the simple fact that any worker who talked back, no matter what the cause, ran the risk of being fired. But women were especially urged to maintain their polite carriage, as it was incumbent upon them to continue to promote social harmony within the factory.

> If he is *cross* occasionally, as it is to be feared overseers *sometimes* are; if he does slam your machinery and his tools, every moment frowning deeper and deeper, if he even lose sight of his dignity so far as causelessly to wound you with harsh words, yet let your feeling and your manner be regulated, through it all, by the respect due to him as your overseer. . . . Cry, if you are so grieved that you must; but do not for one moment forget what you owe to yourself and to others, so far as to pout, or slam, or scold in return.

If women workers lost their tempers, Cate believed, they would lose their dignity, offend the sensibilities of the male overseers, and rend the factory's social fabric. True harmony of interests in the factory rested on acceptance of the existing social hierarchy.[24]

— II —

While Eliza Jane Cate was counseling women to remain demure in the face of unfair treatment, other operatives were encouraging their fellow workers to speak out against the fundamental social inequities in the factory system. These working-class critics thought that all the ideas about social harmony within the factories were naïve and absurd. They were convinced that industrial relations had lost their human dimension; all personal contact between operatives and managers was strained through a screen of regulations and edicts. "Of what advantage is it to the employed," asked an anonymous contributor to the *Voice of Industry,* "that their employers have '*kind*' feelings for them if the '*nature*' of the 'business' forbids any expression of these feelings. The overseer who fulfills all the regulations he is hired to fulfill, can no more be kind than the task-masters of Egypt could be kind in fulfilling the commands of Pharaoh." The *Factory Girl* defined an overseer as: "A servile tool in the hands of a Agent; who will resort to the lowest, meanest and most grovelling measures, to please his Master, and to fill the coffers of a soulless Corporation." These operatives saw their supervisors, not as sympathetic figures caught between their managerial responsibilities and their interest in the workers' welfare, but as men who would often bend over backwards to demonstrate their allegiance to factory policies, no matter what the consequences for labor. All managerial personnel (including overseers), no matter how kindly they may have appeared, were a separate and distinct group from the workers—their interest was in controlling the operatives so as to maximize profit.[25]

Just as some workers cited examples of understanding overseers and generous agents, other operatives responded with their own reports about abusive and insensitive managers. One Lowell mill agent was said to have cared more for his team of horses than for the operatives under his authority. In the summer of 1843 he told an overseer to make the weavers tend three looms instead of two. The overseer insisted that the current workload was already physically taxing, and any additional looms "would use them [the operatives] up." The agent responded, "Oh well . . . you can get enough more." That same week another employee whipped one of the agent's horses and was discharged for using excessive force. "The horse had preference," wrote the operative who reported the incident to the *Voice of Industry,* "because the agent would not suffer *him* to be 'used up.'"[26]

An operative in Manchester, known only by her first name, Mary, was so angered by her harsh treatment at the hands of her overseer and the corporate agent that she publicly denounced the Amoskeag Corporation's harassment of her. As she recounted her story, she said that she had properly notified her overseer, B. F. Osgood, that she needed to leave work immediately because of ill health. Osgood was infuriated by her failure to give the two weeks' notice required in the regulations. Mary recalled that Osgood did give her "a bill of my time"; but only "after abusing me with such language as ever polluted the lips of a gentleman," and then ordering her to leave the factory.

When Osgood informed the corporation's agent, David Burnham, of Mary's transgression, the pressure on her increased. Burnham warned the family that was to take the young woman in, a family from her hometown, that the father might lose his job as an overseer if they sheltered the former mill girl. Having violated company policy, Mary found herself out of work, out of her boardinghouse, and excluded from the friendly family who were supposed to assist her. Mary, however, was not defeated. She publicized her plight as an indictment of the mill's management and a warning to workers to steer clear of these insulting supervisors.

> Burnham's mad and Osgood's sad,
> Because I left the mill.
> But how can they (so spruce and gay)

> Always have their will?
> Now be it known throughout this town
> That Burnham is a Hog,*
> And Osgood too, a perfect spew,
> Strut Burnham's barking dog.
>
> *I beg pardon of the poor four legged
> rooters for this comparison.

Mary's poem—with images of the agent as a "Hog" and the overseer as "a perfect spew" and "barking dog"—clearly conveyed her outrage at the indignities and abuses she suffered at the hands of the Amoskeag Corporation's management. These supervisors went out of their way, not to help an operative in trouble, but to inflict punishment on a woman who violated one of their rules.[27]

Some factories had a practice of paying premiums to overseers who kept production up and expenses down in their departments—and this policy was condemned by some workers as being especially poisonous to labor–management relations. An operative from Manchester declared: "This 'premium system' is a curse to us—it ought not to be tolerated. . . . I have worked under this plan, and know too well the base treatment of overseers in many instances." Many overseers, desirous of driving their workers for the maximum output to increase their premium, became quite insensitive to their employees. Some operatives were so afraid of the "Old Man" that they would not ask permission to leave even if they were sick. They worried that he might say, " 'The work must not be stopped, and if you are not able to work you better stay out all the time.'" Operatives who were not able to keep up with the pace often faced ridicule and contempt from their overseers. "No overseer ever dared use the whip, but they give looks and words, sometimes quite as severe." Even when the Stark Corporation in Manchester threw a "jubilee" to celebrate their productive and profitable enterprise, the city's Female Labor Reform Association dismissed the celebration as a distraction from the issue of exploitation under the premium system. The Association viewed

> the Premium System party with indignation, deeply regretting the participation of so many who must have been entirely thoughtless what they were encouraging by partaking of an entertainment bought with the sacrifice of health of hundreds of our associates in factory life . . . we will not tolerate these things; if we do, we shall soon find ourselves working all year round under the Premium System. . . .[28]

Even Harriet Farley had mixed emotions about the premium system. She did say that the system could be beneficial "so far as it makes the overseers faithful in their attendance, and ready always to repair a loom, mend a break-out, change a beam, or sew a band, with as little delay as possible." But Farley also acknowledged that the system could have a darker side to it—overseers could become reluctant to help workers in trouble and instead devote all their energies to pushing along the strongest operatives. Farley warned that when the system "leads to impatient or unkind feelings towards the slow or sickly girl, and makes favorites of the strong and dextrous, the other operatives have cause to regret the premium system. We have known tears to be caused by the sharp look of an overseer, who told a girl to 'fly round, and mind her work,' when she was doing the best she could with an aching head or hand."[29]

While some workers continued to insist that most factory managers were kindhearted and generous, others urged operatives to look behind the friendly façade. Working-class critics of the factory hierarchy believed that any act of purported managerial kindness always had an ulterior motive. Managers knew that any minor favors they granted to workers would help deflect any strong impulses to directly challenge their managerial authority. Critics believed that all such concessions from management were actually deliberate attempts to manipulate the labor force. They gave workers a false impression of their real standing in the factory. In reality, management was constantly trying to consolidate its own authority and protect the factory's hierarchy.

Even in those exceptional cases where an individual manager might try to act more humane, the critics warned, he was still powerless to change the basic social and physical structure of the factory system. There always remained the hierarchical order of managerial control, and operatives were always at the bottom. The factory system distorted human nature and social relations—it forced men and women, no matter how good their intentions may have seemed, into a work environment based on antagonism. The bottom line, these critics argued, was that operatives would always face hardships because of the inherent inequities and injustices of the factory system as it was organized. A friendly manager—if one could be found—might ameliorate some of the worst excesses in the system, and a particularly cruel supervisor might make a bad situation worse and expose more of the system's harsh realities. But the system of managerial power and hierarchy did not change with individual managers; workers always found themselves in the subordinate position.

These operatives argued that management actually cared very little for their welfare, especially inside the factories. Most proprietors wanted to control their work force without forging any real bonds of social responsibility. Factory owners wanted all the traditional prerogatives of authority and hierarchy that were due a master of labor, but they wanted to shed all the older notions of reciprocity toward their subordinate employees. They wanted their employees to be dependent on them, but only so that the workers would be more tractable. In the long run, these owners were ready to renounce any obligations if it was to their advantage to do so. In effect, owners exercised great power over their workers' lives with few obligations or restraints on the use of that power. Workers, on the other hand, labored under many restraints and obligations without the full power to control their own affairs.

The workers who saw the factory as a breeding ground for social antagonism were particularly skeptical of the concept of paternalism. (In fact, some women—working and living away from their parents for the first time—may have found corporate paternalism not at all reassuring, but an unwanted imposition of the very male authority they were trying to escape from.) A paternalistic managerial structure gave the appearance of being approachable by and respectful of the women under its charge, but the supervisors never had to cede any real power to the workers. As in so many families of the antebellum period, the father-manager figure had a kindly visage, but he retained kingly prerogatives. Paternalism promised harmony, but demanded deference. Moreover, by presenting the entire corporation as a family—with attentive father-managers and dutiful daughter-operatives—paternalism played on the anxiety many workers felt about their working lives and offered a way out of their dislocation through granting them a place in the company's hierarchical family.

Critics kept warning their co-workers about the dangers in the paternalistic system. These workers insisted that "corporate paternalism" was an oxymoron; it was a cover for corporate efforts to control workers' lives in and out of the factories. Mechanized manufacturing enterprises could not nurture parental relations; their power rested in the basic economic functions of hiring and firing labor. And such absolute managerial control of labor was essential to the continuation of corporate power and profits. Any pretentions about caring for the operatives were sheer hypocrisy, as one poet wrote:

> There's spirit abroad, where the swift shuttle flies
> Where the lamp lends a light which the broad sun denies
> "Accursed be the heart," grown so callous and cold,
> That can barter the lives of our maidens for gold;
> For the arm which doth boast of out-stretching to aid,
> Is the same that is dark with the blood of the betrayed;
> And the stain is less deep in the hands of the "Dyer,"
> Than the guilt of that heart which defraudeth of hire.

For this poet, there was no truth behind management's pious claims about mutual interests and paternal concern for their employees. Such pronouncements were all a ruse designed to cultivate in the public eye a favorable image of the company as a benevolent employer, a façade that tried to hide the real conditions of work and exploitation. In reality, this poet saw the factory system as based on a fundamentally antagonistic relationship where labor and capital were bound together solely by competition over production, profits, and wages.[30]

This poet's phrase "barter the lives of our maidens for gold" also demonstrated how the economic power of male management could be entwined with sexual power over female workers. Even operatives such as Harriet Hanson Robinson admitted that relations between male managers and female workers could involve an element of sexual tension. She once confronted one of her overseers, a church deacon, because of "his familiar manner with some of the girls, who did not like it any better than I did." Robinson pointed out to him his hypocrisy in preaching church doctrine while making "offensive" overtures to women workers. Soon after, she was transferred out of that room.[31]

Sarah Maria Cornell also faced the sexual and economic power of male owners in one of the mills where she worked. The owners of the establishment, two brothers, heard rumors about her reputation for loose morals and decided to test their veracity. Each brother, though both were married men, made advances to Cornell, and she refused them all. The owners then felt compromised by their conduct, and they decided to fire Cornell to get rid of any possible embarrassment. When Cornell inquired into the cause of her dismissal, she was told that " 'she was rather too fond of young men.'" But a fellow employee who overheard the conversation quipped: " 'he did not know what proof they had of her being fond of *young men,* except that she did not like *old ones.*'" Cornell was caught in a no-win situation—when she engaged in illicit sexual conduct she ruined her reputation, but when she refused immoral advances from her employers, they dredged up her past conduct and used it as a pretext for firing her out of spite.[32]

The Labor Reform Association in Manchester looked even farther into the social dynamics of the factory system and saw more than exploitation. The association warned of

> a diabolical Conspiracy, on the part of the Corporation Directors or Agents—a conspiracy of the strong against the weak—of the rich against the poor—of the employers against the employed—of monopoly against labor—a Conspiracy so infamous and criminal, in the eyes of true Republicanism, that the perpetrators of the deed of darkness should meet the indignation of an outraged community, and be punished to the extent of the law.

The Lowell Fourier Society, composed mostly of operatives and mechanics, saw the corporations reaching beyond the factory and influencing affairs throughout the city. The society's officers reported: "We have to contend with the almost omnipotent and omnipresent power of Corporate Monopoly. This controls the city government, the Pulpit, the Press—every thing."[33]

Workers who criticized the factory's social structure often integrated ideas about class and class-consciousness in their critiques. This sense of class identity was not confined to any single group of workers in any one community. Among female textile operatives in cities such as Lowell, for example, there was at least a vocal minority who spoke forcefully on the subject of class. Sarah Bagley, in her brief term as editor of the *Voice of Industry,* wrote that such class distinctions were inherent in the factory system of antebellum New England. "The great evil that accrues from the introduction of machinery, and division of labor, is the *caste* it gives to society." Bagley saw that classes were based on the economic structure of society, particularly on labor and capital's relationship to the means of production. But workers like Bagley also seemed to argue that class-consciousness was more than an objective economic fact: it was a subjective understanding of class as a real force in daily life shaping workers' own identities.[34]

Thus, these workers thought of themselves as a distinct socioeconomic group, with their own particular needs and goals, often in opposition to other groups around them. They saw how the factory system not only classified people, but also consistently denigrated the position of labor and placed it in the lower orders. Operatives found themselves required to obey their overseers in accordance with regulations, and subjected to those same managers' trying to assert their notions of social supremacy. One poet observed: "The overseers need not think, / Because they higher stand, / That they are better than the girls / That work at their command." Many operatives knew that they were as well bred and as well educated as their supervisors, if not more so. Yet many managers considered themselves superior to the operatives. Many workers believed that these class distinctions and snobbishness permeated industrial communities.[35]

Other workers extended their class-conscious critique of the factory system to include the owners and their families, wherever they lived, as well as their paid managers. Whereas some operatives praised their overseers and superintendents and hardly mentioned the wealth and power of the corporate stockholders, these working-class critics argued that the owners were just as guilty as their agents and overseers of mistreating their employees. These workers insisted that the social problems of the factory did not stop with overzealous and manipulative managers, though these men deserved the criticism directed at them. The inequitable social structure of the factory system went beyond the managers; it was rooted in the exploitative relationship between the rich owners of private industry and their poor employees.

One Lowell operative recalled that she confronted the harsh realities of class in 1849 when she was

> thrown into the society of several young women who were daughters of mill owners; and the contrast between their condition and that of the operatives was so great that it led me to serious reflection on the injustice of society. These girls had an abundance of leisure, could attend school when and where they pleased, were fashionably dressed, were not obliged to work any except when they pleased; . . . I could never see the justice of one set of girls working all the time in order that another set should live in ease and idleness. . . . But many of our people in Massachusetts are quite willing to make fat dividends on the labor of anybody they can hire, widows and orphans, boys and girls of tender age. . . .

This worker saw profound inequities and injustices in a system where the rich produced nothing of tangible value yet had everything material they wanted. Meanwhile, the workers produced all the real wealth of society, yet retained virtually none of the value of their labor because it all went back to the wealthy owners of capital. Furthermore, these rich owners had no legitimate right to claim for themselves all the wealth the workers produced. Factory owners reveled in freedom and luxury at the expense of the operatives—this was a class-based system of exploitation, pure and simple.[36]

Many operatives were particularly angered by the fact that not only were they exploited in the workplace to support a class of idle rich owners and their families, but these same usurpers of their hard work disdained the very people who provided for their luxurious lifestyle. Many factory proprietors and their families avoided personal contact with the employees. In cities such as Lowell, factories were often controlled by wealthy corporate investors from other cities such as Boston. Absentee owners had virtually no contact with work in the factories, nor with the social relations of production in the workplace. They relied on their superintendents, agents, and overseers to manage the factories, control the workers, and ensure steady profits. Instead of owners' preserving traditional face-to-face relations in the factory and the community, many operatives saw a deliberate "difference in caste which the employers create between their sons and daughters and the sons and daughters whom they employ to increase their wealth." The owners' children were often taught that it would be beneath their dignity to associate with working people. Working-class critics argued that, although they built the very economic and physical structures of the community, they were treated as outsiders and inferiors and denied access to any of the social power or prestige of the wealthy. Even though the wealthy oppressed the laboring people in the course of daily life, however, these workers insisted that they remained morally superior to the idle rich.[37]

Huldah J. Stone, in "Dialogue Between Two Young Ladies" for the *Voice of Industry,* conveyed clearly what one such wealthy young woman might have said about socializing with factory workers.

> . . . [Y]ou mistake my character much if you suppose I intend to disgrace myself by associating with the lower classes who labor in our . . . factories for a livelihood. Nothing can be further from my ideas of respectability than this. Let them be a class by themselves, and not presume to mingle in the higher circles of the wealthy and refined. Only think of our condescending to visit and associate with the *common people*—the illiterate and uncultivated who throng our city at the present day! Why we should lose our caste in society at once.

This young lady's friend responded with an impassioned defense of working people's social standing, and a plea for harmony between labor and capital.

> One would suppose that you thought yourself better than they, merely because a kind Providence had placed you in more prosperous circumstances, whereas the reverse of that is true, for all real goodness consists in active usefulness. And in our republican land it should be *merit,* not station that makes any distinction. . . . Thank heaven, there is enough of the patriotic blood of my brave *ancestors* coursing through my veins, to enable me to spurn this mean, this contemptible, aristocratic spirit and custom . . . which threatens to destroy all harmony and good feeling. . . . What can be more ridiculously absurd than the feeling of prejudice which exists against the laboring classes—those classes, too, which supply us with all the comforts and luxuries of life . . . they are the only people under heaven that deserve the esteem and respect of the entire community.—And if . . . they are illiterate and uncultivated, the more need have we to mingle with, and seek to improve and enlighten with our superior wisdom and refinement.

Stone's fictional dialogue contained the kernel of an ideal "republican" industrial community, where each individual was valued according to his or her "usefulness" and "merit." Workers would earn the "respect of the entire community"; and they would be on an equal, if not higher, social plateau with every other citizen.[38]

Stone's vision was a compelling one for the future, but other workers continued to wrestle with the contemporary social problems in the factory system. One theme that continually emerged in operatives' critiques was that of factory "tyranny." These workers saw the hierarchical system of authority as a threat to the American republican ideals of justice and equity. From the time of Samuel Slater's first mill in 1790, the factory was often criticized as a dangerous intruder from overseas bringing with it the corruption of the Old World. Slater himself was also an object of suspicion because of his background as an English factory manager. By the early nineteenth century, this criticism of factory tyranny became linked with post-revolutionary fears of a social and political aristocracy emerging in America. Kirk Boott, the man most responsible for establishing the mills at Lowell in the 1820s, was another English immigrant manager who proved to be unpopular with many workers. His riding crop and his Union Jack became infamous symbols of his Old World style of dominating workers.[39]

Factory workers throughout antebellum New England condemned overbearing managers for their arbitrary and tyrannical use of authority. Such ungoverned use of power was clearly anti-republican and smacked of the Old World elitism that Americans rejected in the Revolution. Workers continually played on this classically liberal fear of concentrated power to criticize management's monopolization of authority within the factory. The phrase "factory tyranny" appeared with great frequency in the 1820s and 1830s, when memories of the American revolution against British tyranny were particularly vivid in many workers' minds.

One worker at the first fully integrated textile mill in Waltham, Massachusetts, condemned the tyrannical practices of his managers as early as 1821. Isaac Markham, a machinist at the Boston Manufacturing Company, observed that management had "all the lordly & tyrannical feelings that were ever felt by the greatest despots in the world . . . they are determined their word shall be law & shall be obeyed." Jabez Hollingworth, writing from South Leicester, Massachusetts, in 1827, drew on his personal knowledge of England and America to warn about the dangerous social consequences of an industrial economy. "This state is better calculated for manufacturing than farming. This causes it to be more like England, because where manufacturing flourishes Tyrany, Oppression, and Slavery will follow." Another member of the Hollingworth clan, Joseph, wrote a poem one year later that painted a very bleak picture of American factories—exploitation, slavery, and tyranny were all part of his portrait.

> I hate to see a Factory stand
> In any part of the k[n]own land
> To me it talks of wickedness
> Of Families that's in distress
> Of Tyranny and much extortion
> And of slavery, a portion
> I wish that I no more might see
> Another woolen Factory.

The message in the Hollingworth family letters was clear: America was in danger of becoming like the England they had left behind. The rise of the factory system would bring with it the attendant evils of class distinctions, poverty, and repression; neither rural mills nor industrial cities were immune to this infection.[40]

The Lowell strikes of 1834 and 1836 prompted more public statements on the issue of factory tyranny. In 1834, the protesting operatives drew a sharp distinction between themselves, the "daughters of freemen"—and management, "Tories in disguise." They simultaneously claimed for themselves the revolutionary inheritance of independence and excluded their managers from this national heritage by condemning them as new incarnations of British tyranny.

> Let oppression shrug her shoulders,
> And a haughty tyrant frown,
> And little upstart Ignorance
> In mockery look down.
> Yet I value not the feeble threats
> Of Tories in disguise,
> While the flag of Independence
> O'er our noble nation flies.

The turn-out of 1836 prompted a restatement of this theme of restoring freedom in the face of factory oppression. The operatives declared: "As our fathers resisted unto blood the lordly avarice of the British ministry, so we, their daughters, never will wear the yoke which has been prepared for us." This image of the "yoke of tyranny"—a burden "which has crushed and is crushing its millions in the old world to earth; yea to starvation and death"—echoed throughout Lowell, even into the 1840s. And the warning was constantly reiterated; that same yoke would drag American workers down. The New World could not tame the forces of the factory as it was then organized. The factory would instead corrupt the republic; inside the corporations, and throughout the nation as a whole.[41]

Even as images of factory tyranny filled operatives' private correspondence and public pronouncements, another parallel image began to take shape as well—the specter of factory "slavery." As early as the late 1820s, and with increasing intensity on into the 1840s as the abolitionist movement and discussion of the sectional conflict gained momentum, operatives characterized their social relations with managers as slavery. The rhetorical image of slavery was also used in criticizing other facets of the factory system, such as mechanization and wages, but it was utilized with particular vehemence in condemning the factory's social structure. These workers were troubled by something more than the capricious, arbitrary, and even chaotic way that management imposed its will on workers. They saw themselves locked into a system that was designed to extract maximum obedience and destroy all resistance. When critics of the factory system likened industrial labor to slavery, they launched a direct challenge to the basic legitimacy of managerial authority. They called into question the economic rationality and moral foundation of the factory hierarchy. This was more than a disagreement over particular overseers' policies; it was a protest against the very power of management to control the industrial order for its own ends.

The Hollingworth family, those English immigrants working in the woolen mills of central Massachusetts and Connecticut, used the term "factory slavery" in their correspondence from the late 1820s onward. Joseph Hollingworth referred to a superintendent as a "Slave driver," and warned that "Manufactoring breeds lords and Aristocrats, Poor men and slaves." Thinking about his future, he reflected, "I cannot bear the idea, that I, or my children (if I should ever have any) should be shut up 16 or 18 hours every day all our life time like Slaves and that too for a bare subsistence." Joseph also reported that another immigrant family, the Haighs, left one job because they did not like "the Confinement, Slavery, and oppression of the Yankee Factorys." It is not certain why these early immigrant letters are filled with allusions to factory slavery. Perhaps the Hollingworths were drawing on their own memories of antislavery sentiment in England. Or perhaps they found the institution of chattel slavery to be a particularly disturbing aspect of their new country, and they thought that it made a fitting parallel to the problems they encountered in the New England woolen mills.[42]

More than a decade later, an 1844 letter to the *Manchester Operative* once again likened factory labor to slavery, but the analogy had more depth than any in the Hollingworth letters. At the Amoskeag mills, the bell was "like a slave driver's whip" hurrying operatives to their tasks. The workers toiled "like the slave himself in the dusty mill until late at night, while our employers sit in their parlors feasting on the luxuries of this life—purchased by the hard earnings of others." Under the system of factory slavery, owners derived all the economic advantages of a chattel slaveowner without all the expenses or social stigma. Another New Hampshire worker, from Nashua, declared that corporate regulations were often worse than Southern "black codes." This operative argued that slave owners frequently protected their human investments from overzealous drivers. But there were "thousands of unprotected white females of Lowell slaves to the overseers of a dozen or two cotton mills, who hold not only the bread, but the character of those girls, in the palms of their hands, and can do with them as any passion may dictate or any caprice suggest, with perfect impunity of the law, and safety from all consequences to themselves."[43]

The thrust of these arguments was not to minimize the horrors of black chattel slavery, but to make known the disturbing presence of white factory slavery. Factory slavery, like all forms of slavery, was decried as a system of arbitrary and illegitimate power. But factory slavery, in particular, was also said to be integral to the class relationship where industrial capital exploited and oppressed labor. Workers were denied the fruits of their labor and the chance to improve their condition. Moreover, female operatives may have seen a connection between sexual discrimination and slavery as well. Factory slavery denied these women any hope of advancement or independence; they were forced back into the lowly, dependent stereotypes of women and workers. One contributor to the *Voice of Industry* summed up the uneven balance of power in factory slavery whereby managers could maintain control by threatening to impoverish workers: "The voice of hungry capital cries, 'Slaves! you are mine! work, work, work.' And if, prompted by an honorable spirit of independence, the operative refuses to obey, he or she is expelled with a look of haughty scorn, which says, not in words, but in meaning, 'go, starve, and be forgotten!'"[44]

The antebellum New England operatives' efforts to denounce factory slavery may well have reached a pinnacle in the poem "Cash and Lash" by the pseudonymous "Sally Shuttle." This poem appears in the only extant copy of a Lowell operatives' paper called *The Protest,* dated November 25, 1848. The poem linked Southern chattel slavery with Northern factory-labor exploitation as interrelated components of the nation's capitalist economy. Both the slave owner and the factory owner were nonproductive, parasitic members of society who fattened themselves on the labor of others. The emphasis was not on proclaiming which system was worse, but on demonstrating that they were intertwined, especially the cotton plantations and the cotton mills. Those who tolerated black slavery would have no compunctions about exploiting operatives, and vice versa; in fact, they might even encourage each other.

> But Northern *cash* and southern *lash,*
> Both offsprings of the devil,
> Said "man and maid were stock in trade,"
> With *gins* they'd make them level.
>
> So Northern cash Southward did dash,
> Our ancestors forgotton,

A bargain made that stock in trade,
Were negroes, galls, and cotton.

Then brick and plank on river bank,
Flew into mills and houses:
Girls came from town in russet gown,
And boys in striped trousers.

And now old lash looking north to cash,
Said "pay them for a season,
For if at first we do our worst,
They'll cry aloud, 'tis treason.'"

But time and reel and water wheel,
Moved on and kept together,
And now says cash "put on your lash,
We'll cut and skin forever."

"The times," say cash, "are hard," says lash,
"Our stock divides but fifty,
There's russet gown first cut her down,
Then striped pants, we'll fix ye."

Then lash did swear the pants he'd spare,
While girl's they were enslaving;
Like fly on wheel pants cried with zeal,
"Oh, What a dust we're raising." . . .

"Cut down the pay 'till 'lection day,
For girls are not protected;"
Except from dear to her overseer,
To keep the rest subjected.

Should overseers grow rich mid tears,
And keep their pay advancing,
While girls cut low must dance the bow
To keep the donkeys dancing?

But still tis cash cut, work and lash,
From Agents, dupes and lackeys,
Girls without pay must work all day,
Then lashed like southern blackies. . . .[45]

The concept of factory slavery may actually have been particularly poignant to cotton textile operatives. The raw materials they processed usually came from Southern slave plantations, and the product they produced was often sold down South as "negro cloth." Many residents of manufacturing cities, such as Lowell, nevertheless tried to avoid discussing the slavery issue. Managers, and even some workers, were fearful of disrupting the flow of Southern cotton by criticizing the practice of slaveholding. On the other side of the issue, the Lowell Female Anti-Slavery Society was formed in 1832 by women who probably did feel a sense of guilt working with slave-grown cotton. This society sponsored petition campaigns and picnics to support the abolitionist cause, despite threats from Southern suppliers to cut off orders to Northern mills harboring such antislavery operatives. Another such society sprang up in Fall River, Massachusetts.[46]

Lucy Larcom recalled that some operatives even contemplated leaving their jobs because of the tainted raw materials. They may have felt, as Larcom wrote in her poetical reminiscence, "An Idyl of Work," that they were " 'spinning against light, to stay / And turn the accursed fibre into cloth / For human wearing. . . . Am I not enslaved / In finishing what slavery has begun?' " Some operatives saw chattel slavery and factory slavery as tied together with cotton thread. Even if conditions in the mills were improved, the link would still remain with the Southern system of human bondage.[47]

Other workers saw how the entire nation was engulfed in the byproducts of the slave economy, not just the cotton textile operatives. These workers concluded that a fight against any form of slavery should be a battle against all forms of slavery. Their condemnations of factory slavery were clear warnings that workers would not tolerate such injustice—"factory slaves" were opening their eyes to the truth about their status, and they were searching constantly for the means to break their chains.

What workers often discovered, however, was that the web of social relations in the factories bound them not only to their managers but also to a wide variety of their fellow operatives. And the relationships between workers—men and women, children and adults, immigrants and natives—were sources of both strength and conflict for operatives in the factory system.

CHAPTER 4

Solidarity and Fragmentation: Workers' Social Dynamics on the Shop Floor

Relationships between workers, as well as between labor and management, were the foundation of social dynamics in the industrial order. These relationships were shaped by a variety of factors: occupation, experience, skill, age, gender, and ethnicity all affected how operatives worked with one another on the factory floor. Even the most seemingly homogeneous labor force was usually divided into a wide variety of specialized jobs. And every factory work force was filled with cross-currents of mutuality, deference, tension, friendship, self-interest, and other emotions which coursed through individual operatives.[1]

Workers, even as they saw themselves growing increasingly distinct from their employers, also saw themselves becoming increasingly differentiated within their own ranks. Although a sense of class-consciousness was emerging among some workers, there was also the possibility that many different working groups would form without any real unifying concept of class solidarity. Workers often found that class was not the single dominant focal point in their lives. Their sense of personal and group identity could be based on their occupation, age, gender, or ethnicity just as readily as on their understanding of their class position in the factory system. Each particular group of workers could nurture a sense of belonging and solidarity within its own ranks. Yet forging links across divisions created by differences in age or gender or ethnicity was often more difficult, though certainly not impossible.

— I —

One of the primary social divisions in any work force was between newcomers to the factory regime and experienced operatives. Most factories saw a constant influx of new workers struggling to make sense of an unfamiliar environment and its social dynamics. At the same time, veteran employees had to deal with the impact of these new workers on their established social order. Recent arrivals often presented a strange appearance to their more established co-workers. For example, in the late summer of 1847, John MacDonald, an eighteen-year-old apprentice metalworker, arrived at the Reed and Barton britannia works in Taunton, Massachusetts, wearing a black broadcloth frock coat, tight-fitting pants, and a tall silk hat.[2]

Many newcomers to the textile industry were far more homespun in their dress, Harriet Hanson Robinson recalled:

> A very curious sight these country girls presented to young eyes accustomed to a more modern style of things. When the large covered baggage wagon arrived in front of a "block on the corporation" they would descend from it, dressed in various and outlandish fashions (some of the dresses, perhaps, having served for *best* during two generations) and with their arms brimful of bandboxes containing all their worldly goods. These country girls, as they were called, had queer names, which added to the singularity of their appearance.

Female operatives encouraged each other to reach out and welcome these strangers streaming into the industrial communities, no matter how funny they may have looked. One contributor to *Operatives' Magazine* wrote that "could we see the yearnings of that heart, as she looks onward toward that busy throng, unable to discover any familiar countenance, how readily should we lay aside the cold reserve which will not stoop to commune with a stranger . . . it would send a thrill of joy through the heart to know, that there are many in this 'city of strangers' ready to extend the hand of welcome."[3]

Eliza Jane Cate also emphasized that mill girls should go out of their way to be polite to new workers. Such conduct was only fitting for young ladies, and it prevented any hard feelings from forming between veterans and newcomers.

> Let it be urged upon the young ladies of the mills, to avoid ridicule, especially to avoid ridiculing any singularity that may appear in the dress, language, or manner of the stranger in their midst. . . . The high-minded, good-hearted factory girl will certainly be superior to degrading herself and wounding another. . . . It is not long before the stranger learns and adopts the usages of factory communities, in dress and such matters; and then the least evil in the consequences of the unkind treatment she received in her novitiate, is a vivid remembrance of this treatment, and a merited contempt for those who inflicted it.[4]

Unfortunately, not every operative followed Cate's advice. In fact, in one of Cate's own fictional stories about factory life, she described the unfriendly reception accorded one new worker. The protagonist of the story, Emma Hale, discovered that "the girl who was chosen to teach her to weave, had forgotten her own feelings when a learner. . . . She received Emma with a very bad grace, spoke to her only once for several hours, and then it was so roughly that it brought tears to Emma's eyes." After lunch the situation deteriorated even further. The work progressed poorly; Emma always seemed to be in the way, "and, at last, [her teacher Miss Conner] bluntly told Emma that she wished she would sit down, out of her way, until she put her work in order." Instead of giving Emma the necessary information about how to run the machines and be a productive partner, Conner vented her frustration on Emma. She did not want to train another worker, and she was mad at her overseer for giving her another pupil. She was

> inwardly determined that neither he nor Emma should be at all benefitted by her services . . . she wished her overseer and Emma to understand how much it trou-

bled her to teach her. So she slammed her loom, threw her shuttle into a box with tremendous force, loosened her cloth very much, drew it from the temples, and tore it down an inch or two farther than was necessary, to give it an appearance as ruinous as possible.

To poor Emma's alarmed inquiries as to the mischief she had wrought, she vouchsafed no reply. Emma was already worn out with the excitement of the day, and, retiring to a window, she burst into tears.

Miss Conner not only abused the new worker, Emma, she also damaged her work when she lost her temper. She violated all the rules for proper conduct Cate had delineated in her advice columns.[5]

This fictional Miss Conner was not alone in her objections to training new workers. Other experienced operatives voiced their real-life complaints about teaching newcomers. The basic problem was that instructing a new arrival took time away from an operative's own work, and could consequently mean a loss in wages for the instructor. Julia Dutton spoke directly to this point when she wrote to her sister from the mill in Clintonville, Massachusetts: "I have one of the girls that came from Canada on my work 5 weeks and hindered me so I have not earnt anything hardly and then she did not learn."[6]

Some veteran male workers subjected new arrivals to a kind of an initiation rite, or hazing, rather than a cold and hostile reception. Daniel Knapp remembered that the day he commenced work for the Appleton Corporation in Lowell in 1829, he was asked by other men working there to pay his "entrance." Knapp spurned these requests because he did not know what they entailed. He finally asked his brother, who worked in the same mill, what was going on. His brother told him to give these men all the money in his pockets, "or they would be likely to trouble [him] about it." Knapp gave them the fifty cents he had; the men went out, bought liquor, and drank it back in the mill. Knapp added, however, "I resolved then and there that if ever I found the place where I could have any influence I would stop that practice. So when I took charge of No. 1 Card Room, on the Lawrence Corporation, I told my men if ever I knew them doing anything of the kind, our connection would be dissolved at once. From that day it has not been practised unless by individuals out of the mills."[7]

Managers also often greeted new workers with mixed emotions, because they knew that recent arrivals were usually not very efficient or productive. Experienced workers could run their machines faster and with less spoilage; they also were accustomed to keeping up output throughout the long work day. Managers therefore tried to retain their veteran operatives, and these employees learned quickly that they sometimes had a certain amount of bargaining power with their employers, which they used whenever they could. One Boston machinist succinctly summed up his status by stating, "his employers needed him more than he needed them and he could make his own terms." Even textile operatives, if they were experienced enough and their labor in enough demand, could occasionally flex some real muscle in the workplace. In one instance, the Lawrence Company was unable to transfer workers from one mill to another, though this was usually a common practice for the company. In this particular case, however, the company was operating with a labor shortage. The operatives knew that they were in short supply, knew that their labor was more valuable than ever, and demanded to be left in their present positions.[8]

An overseer in Saxonville, Massachusetts, discovered that his powers were also sometimes limited when dealing with experienced operatives. He discharged five women because they would not work overtime. However, a correspondent writing to the *Voice of Industry* reported that

> the poor insignificant fellow was made to repent of it, for they were some of the best girls they had in their employ, and he was made willing to do most anything in order to get them back, so the poor fellow had to crawl out of the small hole he entered, without much honor to himself, or credit to the place he occupies . . . this *gentleman* (as he styles himself,) by begging and promising better fashions, settled the matter for the present; not, however, until the girls had gained their day, for their terms are: no more night work.

This correspondent was clearly pleased that the operatives had used their experience and bargaining power to humble an overzealous overseer. This story about women's readjusting the balance of power in the mill could also serve as an example to other factory workers. The writer closed his account with the following words of encouragement: "I hope other girls will take the same course, when they are oppressed, and thus teach those, who are favored with the like petty tyranny over them, that their rights are not so easily trampled on."[9]

Many managers wanted experienced workers because they were efficient and productive, yet management was also troubled by the efforts of these veteran operatives to increase their individual and collective power in the workplace. The gunmakers of the Springfield Armory stood out as an exceptional example of a work force that combined experience and skill with a sense of their individual prerogatives and collective rights. Throughout the antebellum period, as their craft became increasingly subdivided and mechanized, they strove to maintain their traditional methods of production and cooperation in the midst of the machines. In 1841, a War Department board reported that the armorers still had ways to control their individual and collective output, even as more machines filled the armory. Workers turned in extra work for absent shopmates, exchanged work, and even held back production at the end of the month. All of these practices helped ensure that everyone had an adequate monthly output and income, and no one made too much or too little.[10]

Even among operatives themselves, there was some disagreement about the proper status and role of veteran workers. Harriet Farley saw seasoned employees as an essential resource for new arrivals. She wrote that "no parent should ever permit a young girl to come to [Lowell] without placing her in charge of some one of more experience, who will watch over her and counsel her." But experienced workers could also seem cliquish to their fellow workers. Operatives working in lower-paid jobs sometimes felt that their better-paid colleagues were condescending to them. One textile-mill poet wrote, "the Dress-room girls, they needn't think / Because they higher go, / That they are better than the girls / That work in the rooms below." Some operatives were physically moving up in the factory buildings as well as up the wage scale, and forgetting those they left behind. It is interesting to note that in another version of this poem, the theme is reversed. The more proficient workers are not criticized for their snobbery; rather, they are praised for their sense of equality. "The best of weavers do not think, / Because the higher they go, / That they are better than their friends, / That work in the rooms below." The closing lines of this version reiterated the theme of harmony in the factory for the good of the whole enterprise. "This corporation now is good, / It's rising with some others, / May friendship reign throughout the whole, / And all unite as brothers."[11]

— II —

Another key factor that shaped social relations among factory operatives was age, particularly with children in the work force. Young girls and boys were an accepted feature in many factories, especially in many rural textile mills. Children worked on farms, and they were apprenticed in craft shops, so many people did not object to their employment in factories. In some factories where adult workers were reluctant to enter, children became an absolutely essential component of the labor force. A few factories, including some machine shops, had apprentice programs for training young people over a period of several years. Most companies, however, chose not to become involved in the legal obligations of apprenticeship; they preferred to hire children on contractual terms similar to those of adults. Many contracts for children's labor in the factories were signed by fathers, but were nevertheless binding on the children.[12]

Child labor was less common in large textile centers, yet Lucy Larcom's work in Lowell began when she was between eleven and twelve years old. She entered the factory with a vague sense of pride that she was old enough to contribute to her family's welfare.

> That children should be set to toil for their daily bread is always a pity; but in the case of my little work-mates and myself there were imperative reasons, and we were not too young to understand them. And the regret with which those who loved us best consented to such an arrangement only made us more anxious to show that we really were capable of doing something for them and for ourselves. The novelty of trying to "earn our own living" took our childish fancy.

Child labor, at least in the Lowell mills, was not very taxing physically. There were many moments for younger operatives to play together and socialize with the older workers. Nevertheless, Larcom also recalled that there was something disturbing about children's working in a mill—she was never permanently scarred by her work, but she also did not recommend it as the ideal place for youngsters.

> It did not often occur to us that we were having a hard time; but confinement within brick walls and the constant mingling with many people is not good for children, however willing they may be to assume grownup cares. Childhood is short enough, at best; and any abridgement of its freedom is always to be regretted. Still . . . we were never unkindly treated. We had homes and careful guardianship; none of us knew what real poverty meant; and everything about us was educating us to become true children of the republic.[13]

Hiram Munger, who achieved a modest amount of fame as an itinerant evangelist in antebellum New England, remembered his days as a small child in a cotton mill with little fondness. Munger was the eldest son of a large and poor family, so he was placed in Benjamin Jenks' mill in Ludlow, Massachusetts, when he was only about five or six years old. "Here was where I was first made acquainted," Munger later wrote, "with American slavery in the *second degree.* The treatment of the help in those days was cruel, especially to poor children, of whom I was one. Although I was young, I recollect of thinking that life must be a burden if I was obliged to work in a factory under such tyrants as the Jenks were *then,* and they never improved." A contributor to the *Voice of Industry* urged parents to put themselves in the place of their children in the mills. These youngsters were often "too small to go to school," and they grew up "acquainted with but little, save the chimes of bells and the thunderings of machinery." If parents realized how factory labor stunted the development of young children, then they might keep their sons and daughters under the more wholesome influence of the home and school.[14]

Some parents, in their contracts for children's labor, did retain the right to send their youngsters to school for a portion of each year. But that privilege was sometimes curtailed by the factory owners' demands for a reliable supply of operatives. Hence children could be withdrawn from the mill only when the management could "best spare them," and sometimes a replacement would also have to be found. The agreement between the Jewett City Company and Gould Brown provided for Brown to send one of his sons to school, if he sent two of his other boys into the mill to take their brother's place. In some factories, parents had to petition for the right to send their youngsters to school, because it was never actually written into their contracts. There was also the problem of some families' being so destitute that they could not afford to lose a child's wages by placing him in school. A committee of the New England Association of Farmers, Mechanics and Other Working Men reported in 1831 that many families were forced by their employers to choose between education and economic survival.

> [I]n general, no child can be taken from a Cotton Mill, to be placed at school, for any term of time, however short, without certain loss of employ. . . . Nor are parents, having a number of children in a mill, allowed to withdraw one or more, without withdrawing the whole; and for which reason, as such children are generally the offspring of parents, whose poverty has made them entirely dependent on the will of their employers, any are seldom taken from the mills, to be placed at school.

Poor families desperately needed the meager earnings their children made in the factories, so these youngsters often had little chance to go to school or to learn a trade. Thus the children and the parents were often locked into a cycle of lower-skilled, lower-paying jobs, which continued from one generation to the next.[15]

Some children found themselves to be regular members of the factory labor force; their presence, in turn, shaped the daily work of older operatives. At one point, Lucy Larcom worked in the spinning room beside "a sober, mature person, who scarcely thought it worth her while to speak often to a child like me." In her poem "An Idyl of Work," Larcom wrote further about some of the problems young workers may have faced in dealing with older co-workers. One of the young characters in the poem spoke of older workers who " 'are cross, / And some say dreadful words; if mother knew, / She would not let us work there. But we must, / And so we do not tell her.' " Other young factory operatives may have been caught in a similar dilemma. They may have been frightened or perhaps even abused by older workers. They may have wanted to tell their parents about their treatment and get out of factory work. Some parents, if they heard such stories, may have demanded to take their children out of the mill. But these children also knew how much their families depended on their earnings; so they may have kept silent about their problems so they would not lose their jobs.[16]

Larcom also remembered, however, that she and her young co-workers often had good working relations with many older operatives. She said that the youngsters "were always rather petted by the older ones, who had not forgotten their own little sisters at home." Some of the more mature workers would even steal a moment to play with the younger ones. "And we, in turn," Larcom added, "had usually each of us some chosen divinity among them, whom we worshipped from afar for her real or imagined gifts."[17]

The relationship between managers and child workers was also, in some ways, distinct from the relationship between adult operatives and supervisors. Some factories had special arrangements and requirements for supervising young workers. The 1828 memorandum of the Poignand and Plant mill to its overseers stated that the "overlooker" was to make sure that "the young persons who have the care of the Drawing [frame] keep it constantly in motion . . . the Overlooker will have to use his best judgment in keeping the young Persons under his care at all times alive and attentive to the work. . . . Talking to be . . . Discouraged as much as possible & all running about from one part of the Room to another to the neglect of the work." These guidelines tried to control the playful and social nature of child workers, the very characteristics Larcom said made her work as a young girl most agreeable.[18]

Other managers cast a more sympathetic eye on their young charges. Wilbur Kelly, agent of the Lonsdale Company's mills in Rhode Island, wrote a very reassuring letter to one boy's guardian. "Our superintendent at the mills takes an interest in his welfare," Kelly said, "and will give him good advice and will watch over his morals." The publisher of the *Factory Girl's Garland* also noted a very attentive overseer on one of his visits to the Lowell mills. This overseer had two young sisters working in his room, both of whom were sent into the mill to help support their poor widowed mother and the rest of their siblings. When their mother became terminally ill, the overseer was always willing to give one or both of the sisters permission to go home. If one of them remained in the factory to try to tend both sisters' machines, he often helped out to ease the increased workload. Children, sometimes forced to work under difficult circumstances, usually welcomed such paternal attention from their overseers. In fact, younger operatives were usually very adaptable to the entire factory hierarchy. They followed the orders of their male managers just as they were trained to obey their fathers. Thus, employers often found child laborers to be both cheaper and more docile than adult workers. Children could certainly be rambunctious, but they usually did not organize and challenge managerial authority.[19]

Patrick Donley, however, was one boy who did resent his own misfortune and the industrial regime. Donley was placed by the Massachusetts House of Industry in the employ of the Plymouth Cordage Company until he was twenty-one years old. It is not certain whether Donley was an orphan or a juvenile offender. But, regardless of his status, the company's agent, Bourne Spooner, saw him as an incorrigible child. In 1839, Spooner wrote the directors of the House of Industry that Donley failed to exhibit the "self-respect" or the steady work habits of other boys from the same institution. "Patrick Donley is yet a riddle," Spooner observed, ". . . whether a rogue, fool or mean Irish, time only can develop."

Spooner reported three years later that time had proven Donley to be "a very idle boy." Donley was also the last youngster from the institution still working at the ropewalk, and Spooner was especially happy about that fact. The company had lost interest in taking on such public charges as long-term apprentices, and Spooner's second letter to the directors gives some of the reasons why.

> Vexed at the continual complaints coming to me of his [Donley's] worthlessness I said to him about a fortnight ago, that he was not worth whistling for, or calling back when he turned away, or something tantamount thereto. I soon after saw that he was missing. After being absent a day or two he came & asked me if he might engage work with Mr. Robbins. I told him no—that he had no right to leave my employ and that I had no right to release him . . . & concluded by requiring him to go to and mind his work. He replyed saying that he would soon cut his throat than do another day's work here and walked off. . . . He came from Boston last Thursday . . . has been attentive to his work since his return. He told me that the Directors were coming here this week to see about him & he appears very cheerful. Patrick is the last of the Mohicans and the end will be very welcome to me.[20]

Bourne Spooner thought he had good cause to be exasperated with Patrick Donley's conduct at the Plymouth ropewalk. But there were also many young workers at the Plymouth Cordage Company who thought they had legitimate complaints against the factory system. Some other youngsters legally apprenticed to the Plymouth Cordage Company also ran away; one even persuaded his family to pay fifty dollars to break his indenture. And many, after they had served out their contracts, left the company for other pursuits.[21]

The children who remained in the factories sometimes ran the risk of physical abuse by overzealous overseers. Corporal punishment of children was an accepted practice in antebellum New England, and it was easily wedded to the notion of industrial discipline. But the resulting combination could have brutal consequences. Seth Luther reported that an eleven-year-old girl had had her leg broken with a piece of wood, and another had had a board split over her head "by a heartless monster in the shape of an overseer of a cotton mill 'paradise.'" A young boy was thrown over a bobbin box because he had removed it in the presence of the manufacturer. And, in 1837, an eight-year-old girl died in a Woonsocket, Rhode Island, mill under especially cruel circumstances. One of the overseers punished the child, for some unknown infraction, by tying her feet together and suspending her upside down from one of the factory windows. The girl died a few days later, and the overseer fled town because he feared retribution from the indignant citizens. Some managers tried to explain their rough physical treatment of children by citing the need for these young workers to stay alert and attentive during their long hours of labor. But stories continually circulated of wanton floggings and kickings of children, mills with specially designed "whipping rooms," and even immoral advances made against young girls.[22]

Some cases of child abuse in factories reached the local courts, but the results were a mixed blessing for aggrieved workers. A justice of the peace in 1823 found a Pawtucket, Rhode Island, overseer guilty of assault and battery on a young girl. The judge refused to accept either of the overseer's explanations: that the overseer had the same rights as a parent or teacher to inflict proper punishment to preserve order in the mill, and that the parent had assigned the authority to punish to the overseer. An appeals court, however, quickly reversed the decision. Ten years later, an overseer from Slatersville, Rhode Island, was tried for his excessive punishment of a fourteen-year-old girl. The overseer had disciplined the girl for carelessness by having her stand on a stove for one hour, then he proceeded to beat and choke her. One court awarded only ten cents in damages, but this time the father appealed and won a judgement of twenty dollars.[23]

These Rhode Island cases may have been particularly noteworthy because that state's political and judicial systems made it difficult for low-paid and disenfranchised operatives to swear out complaints. Seth Luther said that even if a child "had been beaten black and blue, from the head to the heels, in a '*whipping room of a large cotton manufactory,*'" his parents would still have to ask a voting freeholder to take up their accusation. In fact, "a deaf and dumb boy who was thus mauled by an overseer at Central Falls" had to go and show his injuries to a freeholder before he could bring his case before the court. When a case reached trial, it meant that the workers had been fortunate enough to find a sympathetic voter willing to support their criminal complaint.[24]

In some instances, however, it was the parents themselves who remained unsympathetic to the plight of their own children. Seth Luther reported that one set of parents was seen "before sunrise, each with a stick, driving their children from the house to the mill." Though the children found their factory labor to be "detestable," their parents were determined to force them into work. Luther also wrote of a "child taken from his bed at four in the morning, and plunged into cold water to drive away his slumbers and prepare him for labors in the mill."[25]

In some factories, parents accompanied their children inside to work and formed a family of operatives. Paper-mill workers often labored with their spouses, children, siblings, and other extended family, such as aunts, uncles, and cousins. Families would often travel together in search of work, and sometimes older relatives would arrange employment opportunities for younger newcomers to the mills. One mother wrote to the Crane Company in 1848 that she wanted to come with her two daughters and put one to work in the finishing room and one to work with her in the rag room. Even wives of skilled and well-paid machine-tenders and engineers often worked in the same mill as their husbands. Most of these married women began their mill work after completing their families, usually after the age of forty. Some mothers, however, worked intermittently throughout their childbearing years.[26]

Families also labored together in many of the metalworking industries. The men and women who manufactured britannia ware in Taunton were closely linked by blood and marriage. And among the English cutlers who emigrated from Sheffield to Waterbury, Connecticut, it was an accepted practice for wives to work in the factories. These families did not regret the situation, nor did they express any hope that someday it would not be necessary for their wives to work. They realized that sometimes women were able to find employment more readily than men, and sometimes the additional wages women earned enabled the family to have a modicum of economic security. James Roberts wrote to his remaining family in Sheffield: "Mary will get work at the works to wet knives & then we shal be all in work & in good circumstances."[27]

Many textile mills also employed numerous family members in their operations. The family labor system was most prevalent in southern New England, but there were mills scattered throughout the northern countryside that also used this system. Many families (or as many family members as possible) entered the mills because they could not make a living from farming; and they were searching for some other way to keep their households intact and economically viable. Gardner Plimpton moved his family to Whitinsville, Massachusetts, in 1847 and wrote back to friends in Fayettesville, Vermont, about the advantages of family labor in the mills.

> I do not know how you are situated, but I think you can live here easer and make more money here then up thare. You take some Borders, the children work in the mill, you can have stady work all the time and good wages if you are all well. You incum will bee six hundred Dollars a year. . . . I wish you to come down this winter and see me and look around and see if it is not best. Fore it is hard business for a poor man up thare. . . . I would not go back to vermont and live as I did the last two or three years.[28]

In some families, the fathers were skilled textile workers and specifically asked to work with their children. James Gorton signed an agreement with the Greene Manufacturing Company of Warwick, Rhode Island, in 1815, that provided for his own labor as a mule spinner; his son Archibald was to "tend two sides of a spinning frame and keep his ends up well." As late as 1849, another mule spinner recently arrived from England wrote to the Slater Company that he could find his own help from within his family. For skilled workers like these mule spinners, the family labor system offered them the chance to train their sons in their craft and pass on a sense of occupational status to the next generation. The tradition of a family's working together was linked with these workers' craft pride.[29]

Other families signed agreements for both the father and the children to work in the mills, but at separate tasks. The contract between the Jewett City Cotton Manufacturing Company and Jenks Mason, signed in 1815, specified that Mason was to be hired as an overseer. But final authority over his children's conduct in the mill rested with the agent.

> Mason to be in the Mill at the Ringing of the first Bell & his Children to be in at the Tolling of the Bell so as to take there places ready for work at the starting of the wheel, Said Children to be kept in the mill at all times except they are sick, or by the permission of the agent or the principle overseer superintending the business in said mill. Said Mason's business to be the overseeing of the old drawing in the Carding Room, & if he complains that he cannot stand to work there then he is to find his own employment, unless he can do such work as said *com.* has for him to do.[30]

Some workers saw the family labor system as a way to preserve paternal authority at home and at work. Fathers often believed that they retained their position as head of the household—they signed the contracts and they frequently collected all the wages. But there were other facets of the family labor system that undermined more than sustained the authority of parents. Fathers could ask to work with their children, but they had no control over such basic working conditions as the hours of labor. Parents probably felt especially concerned about the issue of disciplining children during the workday. The labor contracts usually subordinated the parent's will to that of the manager. If the father happened to hold a managerial position, he was put in a different room from his children, probably to avoid any friction or favoritism. Even when a parent worked alongside his child, they both had to obey the factory's regulations before all other obligations. One parent's agreement with the Greene Manufacturing Company stated: "I agree not to make any complaint of the Overseers for reasonable correction, if I think my children are corrected beyond reason I am to take them out of the mill." This parent had to either accept the overseer's authority, or lose the opportunity for his children to work. Another parent, at the Slater mill in Webster, Massachusetts, in 1827, tried "to controul his family whilst [it was] under charge of the Overseers." He was dismissed for his efforts to reassert his paternal authority in the presence of factory managers.[31]

One way for managers to avoid conflicts with parents was to exclude them from direct employment in the mills. Hence the term "family labor" was sometimes a misnomer when applied to work inside factories. Fathers were sometimes still retained by the companies, but often in occupations outside the factories. Company farms not only preserved the rural appearance of many factory villages, they also provided traditional agrarian employment for many men. Others worked as teamsters or day laborers for the company. Married women were rarely found in the mills; they spent their days caring for their families and taking in handicraft work.

This division of family labor also reassured some heads of households that their status and power was preserved in a quasi-agrarian way of life. But this practice actually shunted these men away from the dominant economic institution in the community. In the long run, they found their labor increasingly marginalized and themselves increasingly alienated from the currents of change around them. Many of them were only too willing to avoid the constraints of factory labor, even as they sent their children into the mills to tend machinery. Yet their children learned about the working world of the future, for better or worse, and left many of their parents' ideas behind. And the more these heads of households struggled to retain their preindustrial patriarchal privileges, the further they lagged behind the rapidly changing world.[32]

Many mills (the most famous ones being those at Lowell) developed a labor system based, not on children and families, but predominantly on individual adult workers. These mills were established in the 1820s, and had more power machinery installed right from the beginning than most rural mills. Power looms and dressers, in particular, were difficult for children to manage. Young women—with more strength and stamina than children, and often with some previous domestic experience in textile production—were thus a logical choice to work in these factories.

Thousands of these "mill girls" were recruited over the antebellum decades to run these machines.[33]

Yet even in cities such as Lowell, there was always a small population of child workers and a significant system of kin networks present in the factories. Many Lowell corporations, as a general rule, did not employ children under fifteen years old. Managers would grant exceptions only in cases of extreme economic hardship where the entire family had to work. Yet two of the best-known writers on the Lowell mill-girl experience—Lucy Larcom and Harriet Hanson Robinson—began their mill careers before the age of fifteen. Robinson started to work at age ten, and Larcom commenced her labor between the ages of eleven and twelve. They both worked as bobbin doffers to supplement the earnings of their widowed mothers, who both kept boardinghouses. Both Larcom and Robinson had other siblings working in the mills.[34]

Kinship groups often flourished in the Lowell mills. These groups usually revolved around sisters and cousins; it was extremely rare for parents and children to work together in these factories. The presence of family, and sometimes hometown friends, eased the transition of newcomers into the factory routine. These networks prevented operatives from becoming isolated individuals alienated from work and co-workers. Relatives helped each other find jobs, learn new skills, and adjust to life in an industrial city while retaining a sense of traditional family loyalty. Many pairs of sisters worked in the same room, with an older sibling giving guidance to a younger one. Parents, often living great distances from Lowell, usually took comfort in the fact that when their children worked together they could look after each other. These family networks were also often encouraged by managers who helped secure advantageous positions for their employees' relatives, even though the Lowell system was not based on family labor. The operatives who were linked with kinship groups tended to remain in their jobs longer; they had enough support in Lowell to dissuade them from returning quickly to their homes. Experienced workers were usually more productive and profitable for the corporations; they also earned higher wages for themselves. Everyone seemed to benefit from a stable labor force rooted in some kind of familial context.[35]

In an industrial city like Lowell, the presence of a relative could make a significant difference in an operative's outlook. In fact, that relative did not even have to work in the same factory to preserve the sense of close kinship. Just having family in the same city could make the community seem more hospitable. Mary Cowles wrote to her sister in 1847:

> I like Lowell very much now at first I thought I could not ever get to like it for I was so homesick I was all the time wishing I was back in Hartford. but now I feel quite different as Cousin Laura is here with me she arrived here a week from last Saturday she thought as I liked the work here she should like to come too and so it makes it very pleasant to me for it seams almost like home to me now she is here, we do not work in the same mill together as she did not like spining but chose rather to work in the Weave room she likes it very much so far I hope she will be contented here.

For some young women, working in a city like Lowell in the company of some family and hometown friends was the best of both worlds. These women may have begun to chafe under the paternal restrictions of the family homestead; yet they did not want to abandon all the emotional warmth they connected with their kin. Kinship networks in Lowell seemed to be a way to distill out all the oppressive elements of paternal authority, while retaining all the support structures built particularly (though not exclusively) around female relatives and friends.[36]

— III —

Many Lowell operatives shared Mary Cowles' love of family, but they also valued their newfound independence in the industrial city. Women workers especially welcomed the opportunity to live away from home and manage their own affairs. Lucy Larcom recalled that the mill girls'

> independence was as marked as their generosity. While they were ready with sisterly help for one another whenever it was needed, nothing would have been more intolerable to most of them than the pauper spirit into which women who look to relatives or friends for support so easily subside. Perhaps they erred in the direction of a too resolute self-reliance. That trait, however, is a part of the common New England inheritance.

Larcom recognized that "independence," "generosity," and "sisterly help" were all part of the female operatives' experience in Lowell. These women did not believe that autonomy meant isolation: they came together as individuals united by their gender and their shared working experiences. Larcom was always looking for that balance between self-interest and a sense of duty to others. An operative had to be careful not to lose herself in the factory masses, but she also had to guard against withdrawing totally from the surrounding society.

> One great advantage which came to these many stranger girls through being brought together, away from their own homes, was that it taught them to go out of themselves, and enter into the lives of others. . . . To me, it was an incalculable help to find myself among so many working-girls, all of us thrown upon our own resources, but thrown much more upon each other's sympathies.[37]

Many female operatives put great emphasis on the friendships forged in their workplaces. Friends, as well as family, were a crucial form of support throughout an operative's career. One Rhode Island mill girl wrote: "If one should get disheartened, / Or feel a little ill, / Another speaks a cheering word, / Which goes quite through the mill." Female operatives, through these networks of family and friends and co-workers, created an organic community among themselves. One woman worker succinctly conveyed this sense of female solidarity: "We are a band of sisters—we must have sympathy for each other's woes." And these bonds of interdependence were strengthened, without compromising each woman's integrity, as these female operatives continued to live and work together. As Harriet Robinson said, "they stood by each other in the mills." Experienced workers trained new arrivals, helped tend the machines of absent co-workers, and often kept up a steady stream of conversation over the factory's noise.[38]

Of course, the large congregation of women in many factories, especially in cotton textile mills, did not preclude the presence of men in these workplaces. In most factories, however, specific jobs were linked by the management with each sex. In Lowell, machinists and carding-room employees were usually male, while spinners and weavers were usually female. Some operatives ridiculed men who worked as weavers for holding a "woman's job." And the few women who tried to tend mule frames were subject to "unpleasant remarks" from the male mule spinners. Operatives of each sex were usually separated into different rooms of the factory; this was supposed to protect women from the corrupting influence of unprincipled workmen. It also served to inhibit the development of strong cross-gender networks among the workers. Men's work, by tradition, emphasized skill and strength and the supervision of women. Female operatives were never promoted to positions of managerial authority. The hierarchy of the factory reaffirmed the subordination of workers in general and women in particular.[39]

Despite efforts to keep female operatives in a subordinate position because of their gender and class, these women's sense of community often reached from factory to factory throughout entire cities. Particularly in places such as Lowell, as workers in mill after mill were subjected to the same work standards and managerial practices (an attempt by the corporations to regulate the city's entire work force), their shared experiences and labor problems actually led to an increased feeling of community. Crucial questions remained, however, about how to express this solidarity and where these ideas about unity would lead. Some workers saw their shared identity as part of the total social harmony within the factories—the operatives tolerated no petty distinctions among themselves, nor did they recognize class differences in the community as a whole. These workers often spoke of the solidarity of young women—bonds that were formed by the common experiences of their gender and not by any adversarial relations with their managers. Others saw the ideal of sisterhood as the foundation for a united labor movement. These women spoke more frequently of a workers' solidarity rooted in labor itself, and emerging when workers felt threatened by management's unbridled power.

The community of female operatives also faced particular moral questions relating to their status both as women and as workers. Every female operative rejected emphatically any assertion that only immoral women would enter a factory in the first place, or that proper women would immediately compromise their moral standing once they entered a factory. Factory women tried to refute these glib and crude assumptions by guarding their moral standards with great care and vigor. The entire community of women workers often tried to enforce a strict code of morality among themselves. The community was used as a means to protect each woman's virtue and thereby affirm the operative's legitimate standing in the surrounding society as a woman and a worker.

The moral code of the factory women was rooted in some basic assumptions and even stereotypes about female conduct in antebellum America. Virtually everyone started from the premise that women should be chaste and pure and above reproach in all their personal actions. The crucial question for all female operatives, therefore, was what happened to their moral reputations while they were working. What steps did women have to take to remain "virtuous and pure" in the factory? No one questioned the absolute importance of female virtue to a working woman's status, dignity, and future prospects (particularly in regard to marriage). No one doubted that factory work could pose risks to a woman's reputation. But where did those dangers arise from—other workers? managers? the factory system itself?—and how was the female operative to protect herself?

Here was where the female operatives split among themselves. The women could all agree that they had to work hard to preserve their character against the moral dangers of the outside world. But they could not agree on the source of those dangers, or how to enforce a moral code that would uphold the purity of individuals and the community as a whole. The campaign to preserve female virtue in the factory led some women to reemphasize stereotypes of female docility, while others saw this struggle as part of the larger battle for working women's rights. Thus, a bifurcation occurred in the moral code of these female operatives. Two moral subcodes emerged: one spoke of preserving virtue through vigilance and critical judgement against any immodest women, for corruption was due to individual weakness; the other called for action in reaching out to troubled women who were victimized, for corruption came from the factory system as a whole.[40]

Many working women who placed great value on their personal reputations demanded that their workplaces be free of any employees of questionable character. These workers believed that the factory system itself posed no great risk to their morals; it was contact with unscrupulous people that would contaminate them. One tainted operative could cast aspersions on the conduct of everyone in a factory. A Lowell mill agent told of two women who applied for work, but "before they had taken off their bonnets, they were recognized by those already at work . . . [as] persons of doubtful reputation . . . the overseer was informed and the ladies had the pleasure of calling somewhere else for employment." A carding-room overseer reported that he took similar uncompromising steps to keep his department free of women of questionable character, probably in response to the demands of his employers and employees. "No licentious or immoral person would be allowed to work in the room; but I do not recollect a single instance in which a girl has been dismissed from my room for this cause. I have sometimes suspected girls, and in such cases have contrived to get rid of them as quietly as possible." Similar practices were reported in Rhode Island mills where large numbers of women were employed. Even an experienced employee, "how expert soever she may be in her business, or profitable to her employers," would not be permitted to remain in a factory if her fellow workers suspected her moral standing and demanded her removal. No owner would risk losing a large percentage of his work force to keep one operative.[41]

Women workers who scrutinized themselves and ostracized any suspicious fellow workers clung to the idea that women had to bear the full burden of preserving their reputation. These women believed that they had to restrain themselves because female chastity was the foundation of all public virtue. Young women living on their own, even with family or friends working alongside them, had to be solely responsible for their relationships. Any woman who crossed the bounds of propriety would feel the sting of public condemnation, regardless of whether she was seduced by an unprincipled man. If a woman fell from grace, many female workers insisted that she had only herself to blame.

Even as many young women—living on their own, for the first time away from their parents and their hometown—accepted this doctrine of individual responsibility for their moral conduct; they also drew on a sense of collective female morality to watch over and guide each other's conduct. Thus, every young woman had the final obligation to regulate her own affairs, but that did not preclude all women from trying to keep each other on the moral high ground.

Some women workers welcomed this practice of carefully observing each other's conduct. One contributor to the *Lowell Offering* wrote: "We should look upon one another something as a band of orphans should do. We are fatherless and motherless: we are alone and surrounded by temptation. Let us caution each other; let us watch over and endeavor to improve each other . . . in the mill, let us strive to promote each other's comfort and happiness." Managers also welcomed this system of workers' policing themselves—in fact, the operatives often proved to be more effective than management in articulating and enforcing standards of orderly and disciplined behavior.[42]

Some workers believed that they were acting as good neighbors when they watched each other's behavior. They were doing what women often did in rural New England—carrying on the concept of a female community where women upheld the ideals of industry, modesty, and charity. These female factory workers, like rural women, formed a sisterhood that was often supportive but was essentially conservative. There was always the danger, however, that such close scrutiny could devolve into rumormongering. Even Harriet Farley admitted that "in no place is an evil report more quickly circulated, and apparently believed, than in a factory. One fiendish-minded girl can start a calumny which will soon ruin the good name of another." Such spiteful talk in such close quarters could be even more poisonous than the archetypal village gossip. The victims of unproven accusations sometimes found themselves ostracized from the very sisterhood they so desperately needed in their time of trouble.[43]

Sarah Bagley acknowledged this same impulse among the women of Lowell to guard their morals. But she hoped that workers would not use their high standards to spy on each other and do the corporations' dirty work. Bagley wanted women to watch each other, not as a means of enforcing conformity through peer pressure, but as a way to reinforce women workers' individual and collective rights. Bagley wanted operatives to maintain unimpeachable personal standards, but also to apply those same high standards to the factory itself. The cause of labor reform was dependent on women whose reputations were spotless, who could not be maligned by their fellow workers or the corporations, and who campaigned tirelessly to make factory work truly virtuous.

Bagley believed that moral action and class action by women workers were bound together. When women truly worked together to uphold their dignity and rights (rather than merely spying on and condemning each other's conduct), they appropriated conventional middle-class moral standards and used them to support workers' ideals of cooperation and respect.

> The standard of virtue in Lowell, is far above that of any city of its size within the Union, pray God it may remain. How can I find language to warn all my sisters, of the sacredness, the high charge devolving upon us in this respect? With us and us

> alone, rests the great responsibility of *the standard of female virtue in Lowell.* This must be preserved at all and every hazard, or all of our labors are as sounding brass.

Bagley urged that all female operatives work together to defend every woman's moral standing. Helping each other, not punishing each other, was the key to both individual self-esteem and collective dignity.

Bagley wanted the operatives to look after each other, not condemn each other for their human frailties. "The lone girl in Lowell, driven by poverty or misfortune, from her mother's home, to seek shelter under the task master's rod," she wrote, needed to "find sympathy" in association with other workers. The best way to promote proper conduct was through assisting those who had accidentally gone astray, not through public humiliation. Willful immorality was not to be condoned; those who fell prey to "the *fiend* in human form," however, needed to be understood and forgiven. It was vitally important to find out why a young woman was morally compromised. In many cases, it was unfair to blame the female operative, since she was the victim. It was far more just to place the blame on the victimizer himself, who took advantage of an unsuspecting woman far from home; or to look for deeper causes of corruption in the factory system as a whole. Whether the guilty party was a male manager or a seducer from the city streets, he was the one who deserved to be condemned, instead of the victimized woman. Operatives who turned their backs on their fallen co-workers were dooming the less fortunate to a life of continual misery.[44]

The Lowell Female Industrial Reform and Mutual Aid Society was one organization devoted to the idea of reaching out to those in danger of falling into despondency, or worse. The society saw itself as

> the means of saving from ruin, disgrace and an untimely grave, hundreds, nay, thousands of young, unsuspecting females, who are thrown upon the charities of a cold, unfriendly world, in helpless childhood, and compelled to earn their daily bread somewhere or perish in the streets! They would then know that there were true and sympathetic hearts to whom they could turn for council and assistance in the day of trial and want. Oh! how many have fallen and perished by the wayside in life's great thoroughfare for lack of sympathy and encouragement from the virtuous and good! How many in our own loved city of Lowell have sunk in ignorance and vice through that feeling of hopeless despondency which poverty and lack of sympathy ever engender in the human heart. They felt that no kind heart was interested in their well being—no one loved or cared for them in the *wide* world, and they would seek sympathy somewhere, (for that is the undying craving of every human being's soul,) and if denied the companionship and sympathy of the good, the true and noble of the earth, they *will,* they *must* find it among the low and the degraded in the community.[45]

The organizers of this society blamed the systemic evils of factory work, not the individual worker's acts of misconduct, for threatening the standards of female morality. They turned their energy away from judging each other harshly, and focused their critical gaze on their working conditions. They argued that long hours, low wages, and monotonous toil posed a greater threat to their health and moral vigor than any contact with other working people. Female operatives were physically and mentally debilitated by their work; therefore, having little self-esteem, they were left vulnerable to temptation. Mutual aid was not something reserved for those with unblemished reputations; it had to be extended from the virtuous to those struggling in the new industrial environment. The best way to preserve one's moral standing was not to be isolated from all possible contagion, according to the society's leaders, but to link hands with those less fortunate for the improvement of all. Helping a co-worker in trouble was both an expression of individual morality and decency and a demonstration of workers' collective identity and support. The Mutual Aid Society was only as morally strong as each of its members, and vice versa.

This mutual aid society of Lowell workers seemed to recognize that young female operatives lived in a world of difficult moral choices. The members believed in decency and dignity as much as their more judgemental co-workers. They also believed, however, that women alone could not bear all the burdens of society's moral standards. The group sought to counsel women who had nowhere else to turn, and to support those who had fallen by the wayside for lack of guidance. Banishing women would not eliminate the problems facing female operatives; women had to come together to uphold their moral standards. The Lowell society was an attempt by women workers to take responsibility for their own less fortunate sisters, rather than relying on the money and admonitions of outside moralists. This organization was trying to link conventional ideas of female modesty and respectability with a working-class ideology of collective action and the dignity of labor. The goals were not radical, but they were designed by female operatives to help themselves.

Perhaps the most basic questions surrounding this debate over the moral code of factory women are: why did young female operatives move away from their patriarchal homes, pursue their independence, and then refashion strict moral guidelines for themselves? When so many women talked about the need to maintain high moral standards, regardless of whether they were supporters or critics of the factory system, were they revealing their uncertainty over leaving the traditional social restraints of their hometowns and the need to reconstruct similar mores for themselves in the new industrial communities? Or were the female operatives' ideas about morality a kind of workers' control over sexuality and gender relations? Were working women trying to maintain some authority over their lives in spite of male economic and sexual power in the factories?

In particular, were activists like Sarah Bagley arguing that just as the entire working class was engaged in an economic struggle for its rights, so were working women engaged in a social and sexual struggle for their dignity? Female operative activists may have advocated moral restraint for the same reasons that male activists often supported temperance. Workers had to exert some control over their personal lives in order to retain some power over their labor and their future prospects. A worker who was compromised morally was particularly vulnerable to exploitation by her employers (and men in general). All workers were subject to the power of managers; but women workers in trouble were even more vulnerable to the sexual threats implicit in the power of male managers.

This debate over the moral standards of factory women was most intense in the 1840s. The shifting working conditions in the mechanized factory system as a whole during that decade—the growing concern with the speedup, the stretch-out, the hours of labor, and piece rates—may have been linked with this discussion of working women's morality. As many female operatives saw a decline in their wages and working conditions, they may have sensed that they were reaching a crisis in their struggle to uphold proper standards for their labor and their personal conduct. They may have believed that their livelihood and their moral values were both being threatened by the deteriorating situation in the factories. Women had to act decisively to preserve and defend their honor if they were to have any chance of improving their status in the factory.

Sarah Maria Cornell's controversial life and death was a particularly grim example of the dilemma of female morality for a young operative in the factories of antebellum New England. Her life revealed the darker side of a mill girl's experience. Cornell, far away from her family and with little or no access to charitable or working-class support groups (except for her church), trudged about the industrial communities of New England looking for acceptance and respectability as a mill worker. She sought protection and support in various small towns and evangelical churches, and she often did recall with fondness some of those communities she lived in. Unfortunately, in the end, what she really found was hardship, rumors and social ostracism, venereal disease, an unwanted pregnancy, and a violent death at the hands of an unknown assailant. Cornell was the kind of woman mill girls would warn each other about, and perhaps the kind of victim Sarah Bagley wanted to rescue. Her tragic fate was a reminder to all working women of the dangers surrounding the loss of respectability in antebellum New England.[46]

— IV —

There was one other major axis for social interaction among antebellum New England factory operatives—the relationship between native-born and immigrant workers. The first immigrant industrial workers were often highly skilled men whose knowledge was essential to the successful operation of many mechanized factories. As early as the 1820s, when fully integrated manufacturing was first being developed in many industries, skilled workers were coming to America (usually from the British Isles) to help install and operate the new mechanized technology. The number of these skilled immigrants, however, was always modest in comparison with the thousands of less skilled, native-born operatives in these antebellum manufactories. Moreover, there were always some less-skilled immigrant operatives in the New England factories, even before the large influx of Irish immigrants into the textile mills.

Thus, the foreign-born skilled factory workers made up only a small part of the growing industrial labor force in antebellum New England, and only a portion of the emerging immigrant work force as well. Yet these foreign-born men were sometimes a crucial source of information on new productive techniques developed overseas, and indispensable for operating machinery that was often crudely constructed and subject to frequent breakdowns. These workers could exercise a substantial amount of power on the factory floor. They used their positions of power and skill in conjunction with ideas brought over from the Old World to develop penetrating critiques of the American factory system. Yet they also found themselves subject to a growing chorus of criticism from native-born Americans who were suspicious of their role in the industrial labor force. To make their situation even more difficult, these skilled immigrants sometimes saw their positions near the top of the factory labor force threatened by improvements in machinery and new managerial strategies.

The brass-workers of the Naugatuck Valley in Connecticut were one group of predominantly English immigrants who retained a high level of skill in operating their specialized machinery, and jealously guarded their trade secrets. Wire-drawers refused to permit apprentices near any machine in operation. In Torrington, Connecticut, kettlemakers were given a separate building that was off limits to Americans. By the mid-1830s, however, local workers had learned many of the requisite skills, and production was no longer absolutely dependent on the English workers. But many of the skilled workers continued to value their specialized knowledge as the foundation of their remaining power in the workplace.[47]

Some immigrant workers were suspicious even of their own countrymen. Any newcomer could be seen as a threat to the job security of established employees. When the Scovill Company solicited recommendations for a skilled brass-roller in 1835, other English rollers remained tightlipped because they feared that the new man would be hired to replace one of them. And, in 1839, the company had to go to great lengths to reassure a die-sinker they wanted to employ that he would be welcome in Waterbury. J.M.L. Scovill wrote to his brother: "I have seen Mr. Gardner the Die Sinker . . . he will not go unless Mr. Eaves was perfectly satisfyd with his working in the room with him & that he does not come to supplant him, but to be a coworker with him . . . he will not however engage with us if there is to be any jealously and not a willingness on the part of Mr. Eaves to go hand in hand." The Scovills were finally able to convince Mr. Eaves that his position, as both toolmaker and die-sinker, was secure. J.M.L. Scovill remarked that Eaves might actually "be pleased with the acquisition of such a man as it will lighten his burdens and not his salary." With Eaves thereby appeased, Gardner was satisfied, and he signed his contract.[48]

The English immigrants who helped establish the textile printing industry in New England were also known for their secretiveness and independence. The immigrant workers at the Dover Manufacturing Company challenged their employers on a variety of issues—wages, hours of labor, contracts. They also organized a union and engaged in walkouts. John Williams, agent for the company, bitterly summed up his view of labor relations with the printers in a letter to the company's treasurer, William Shimmin. "The plain English of the whole is as it strikes me that if the Company will delegate their whole authority—& the controul of all their property to these fellows, they will do the favour to work in their shop when they please, & consult their own convenience at other times." Williams feared that these highly skilled workers were trying to control, not only their own labor, but the operations of the entire company. Williams was also distressed that immigrant supervisors were sympathetic to their countrymen and could not be relied on to enforce company policy. Company officials realized, however, that these English printers had crucial knowledge about how to set up and operate the new cylinder machines for printing. Thus they could not be fired easily, and managers and workers were locked into a contest of wills.[49]

Immigrant workers were also known to clash with their native-born co-workers. Even though so many of these early industrial immigrants were English and thus closely bound by language and culture with Americans, friction sometimes developed between the immigrants and the Americans. In industries where immigrants filled better-paid skilled positions, and Americans were employed in less lucrative, more mundane jobs, the potential for conflict was often exacerbated. At the Dover Manufacturing Company, the English printers emerged victorious after their long-running battle with American managers and apprentices. John Williams had originally devised a plan to hire American apprentices who would learn from the English printers. Williams hoped that the Americans would be a more tractable labor force and eventually replace all the English. When the Cocheco Manufacturing Company bought the printworks in 1829, they reversed this policy and returned to a complete reliance on English workers in the interests of commercial success. There was also a dose of reverse discrimination coming from the British. Samuel Dunster, one of the Americans who lost his job when the English returned, was told by the company's agent, James F. Curtis, "I was driven to part with you for the new folks (printers) will not have an American on the works." These immigrants displayed an open contempt for the less-skilled American workers. The less-knowledgeable Americans were seen as a threat to the status and wages of the English printers.[50]

Other immigrants found themselves on the losing end of such controversies. The Hollingworth family learned, through years of experience in American woolen mills, that their skills as weavers were relentlessly undermined by the growing use of power looms. Though they had more craft knowledge than many American workers, they were far less indispensable to their employees than the printers of Dover. There was an ever-growing population of workers who were perfectly capable of tending power looms; printing machines remained far more difficult to master, and continued to be mostly the province of skilled immigrants. American factory owners might have had to yield sometimes to the demands of men like the printers, or risk having their businesses grind to a halt. But the Hollingworths discovered that their bosses were far less vulnerable to pressure from a family of immigrants whose skills seemed less essential with the passage of time. The family felt the sting of prejudice from American managers and workers as economic competition aggravated the growing strains of working-class and middle-class nativism.

George Hollingworth worried that if new owners took over the mill in South Leicester, Massachusetts, where he worked, "it is . . . surmised . . . that they will apoint a Yankee Superintendent who will show neither mercy nor favour to Old Country men." Just as native-born workers often resented their immigrant managers—such as Samuel Slater and Kirk Boott—so these immigrant workers resented their American supervisors. Joseph Hollingworth took the familiar strains of "Yankee Doodle Dandy" and rewrote them as a lampoon of Yankee exploitation of foreign labor. "Yankee doodle dandy, / The Yankeys they are handy, / To rogue and cheat, / And make folks sweat— / To smoke sigars,—and drink a glass of Brandy." These English immigrants discovered that, although they shared a common language and heritage with Americans, they were still often viewed with suspicion as foreigners.[51]

Managers saw that some skilled immigrants were growing more vulnerable to displacement by mechanization, and these managers often took advantage of opportunities to rid themselves of the more independent-minded immigrants. American workers, conversely, still may have been troubled by the possibility that foreign workers would gain more jobs and leverage in the workplace. Thus immigrant workers were caught between pressure from managers and co-workers. And the growing prejudice against these foreign-born workers could be triggered by either their strength or their eroding power in the workplace. No matter what position these immigrants held, they were liable to be criticized by Americans in the factories. Skilled immigrants found themselves being either cajoled or squeezed out by management. At the same time, American workers were either resentful of the immigrants' skill and power, capitalizing on their increased vulnerability to displacement, or harboring new fears about de-skilled immigrants' competing for more American jobs.

The city of Lowell was no stranger to immigrants working in the factories. As early as 1825, the Merrimack Manufacturing Company's print works was employing printers from Lancashire in England. These printers and their descendents filled many departments for many decades. In 1837, a group of Gloucestershire woolen workers—recently thrown out of work with the failure of their local mill—came to the Middlesex Company. Other Gloucestershire families, hearing favorable reports from these first arrivals, also emigrated to Lowell in the following years. There is no evidence that these immigrant colonies provoked any controversy among the large native-born operative population. When immigrants, especially the Irish, began to appear in the cotton mills, the situation became more tense.[52]

Irish immigrants had actually begun to enter New England textile mills in the early decades of the nineteenth century. Their numbers were relatively small at that time. The great influx of Irish mill workers commenced with the famine years of 1845 and 1846 and lasted into the 1850s. But Irish workers were found in many mill towns along the Blackstone and Pawtucket rivers in southeastern New England during the earlier antebellum decades. They usually worked at the most arduous, lowest-paid tasks, and even then, they were not hired in every mill.[53]

Irish operatives began to work in large numbers in the Lowell mills during the latter part of the 1840s. Most companies channeled them into the lowest-paid, most difficult jobs, while reserving the more advantageous positions for native-born workers. The recently arriving immigrant workers were clearly excluded from most of the paternalistic policies of the Lowell corporations. They were not considered part of the family of native-born workers and managers. This was a deliberate (although unwritten) policy of discrimination against the Irish. It was probably done to ease the discontent of American women workers, who were concerned about the growing Irish presence and were leaving the mills in increasing numbers. Nativist anxiety about the Irish, ideas of racial purity, and hopes for job security converged in the corporations' new policies. Native-born workers were reassured that they were still part of the superior American family, as long as they remained subservient to management's paternal authority. In effect, American workers were still told to keep to their proper place, but their place was not with the immigrant operatives. Ethnic tensions usually undermined any attempts to create a unified workers' community.

Managers wanted to keep experienced American operatives in the better job categories: they thought that higher wages, better working conditions, and insulation from contact with immigrants would keep them at work. At the same time, the departments that were filled with Irish immigrants often had harsher regulations and working conditions. The Irish had no homes to flee to in protest, and they desperately needed steady work and wages, so they accepted the grueling regimen with few complaints. Their native-born co-workers were less tolerant of such high-handed treatment for themselves, but they showed little sympathy for the plight of the Irish. Although in reality both immigrant and native-born female operatives were usually found somewhere in the ranks of the semiskilled, they rarely recognized their common occupational status or interests. Ethnic antagonism undermined most efforts to forge any sense of workers' unity along the lines of either skill level or gender.

Nativist prejudice against the Irish became a convenient way to blame the immigrants, not the factory system, for problems in the workplace. The Irish became the scapegoats for all the resentments and dislocations caused by rapid industrialization. In particular, the American workers often condemned the Irish for taking their jobs, and for the deteriorating working conditions and wages. One operative wrote that "if the Irish and low class New England girls only remain, wages may come down. They will, on account of their comparative unprofitableness to their employers. And *they* will submit, since they have little energy, few aspirations to be ministered unto by their gains, and having poor homes, or little of the home sentiment, they will stay and the wages may be reduced again and again." The actual causes for the decline in the operatives' status were far more complex than the simple presence of the Irish, and the process began before the large influx of immigrants. But the Irish aggravated the situation by providing a pool of cheap, unskilled labor ready to accept such poor conditions. Thus, immigrants were blamed for the exploitation they were subjected to by management, excluded from alliances with native-born workers, and then condemned for ignoring those American workers and working only for themselves.[54]

Eliza Jane Cate took note of the changing labor force in the *New England Offering* of July 1849. Cate's observations reveal a divided feeling about this transformation. She condemned overt discrimination against the Irish, yet she also held them in rather low esteem. She had serious doubts about their suitability for industrial employment.

> . . . [M]any of the vacancies left by these substantial, well-educated, upright-minded girls, will be filled by the Irish; and much as I admire some traits of their national character, sincerely as I pity them and beseech for them kind treatment and room in our country, I should regret their coming into this branch of labor . . . both because they are never found to be so efficient as the New England girls, and because the pride, or self-respect, or both, makes the latter step back from the field that the former enter, and leave it entirely to them . . . thus it will be in the factories,

> if the Irish are employed in any considerable numbers; because, as a general thing, they are untidy, ignorant, passionate; and on this account, although it may be understood that they are needy, that they have a right to live and breathe as well as ourselves, that their impulses are at least half of them as noble and generous as light, the better class, even the middle class of our New England girls, will not be seen in the street with them, will not room with them, cannot find them in the least degree companionable. One can see then that it is incalculably better that the native girls fill the mills. How much better for the future!

Cate's disdainful appraisal of the Irish, and her plea for native-born workers to stay in the mills, brought a rejoinder from the editor, Harriet Farley. Farley feared that Cate's words might

> minister to an unwarrantable prejudice. Are not many of them avoided, not because they are ignorant, untidy, and passionate, but *because they are foreigners?* We have seen the emigrant shunned by those more ignorant, untidy, and undisciplined than herself, because she was a foreigner, and we have heard her ask, "From whence came your ancestors, but from that Great Britain which I left for this country?" . . . Let those who are our patrons not turn away from an unwelcome truth, but resolve that if they are avoided by the more respectable American girls, it shall not be because they are untidy, ignorant, and passionate, but because of a prejudice which only injures her who may unjustly foster it in her heart.[55]

At least one Lowell operative, Adelia Gates, did reach across the ethnic chasm and try to befriend some Irish workers. When Gates first arrived in Lowell, the woman who trained her remarked: " 'If the overseer had brought me an Irish girl to teach, I should have left the mill on the spot.' " Gates found such prejudice prevalent among the native-born operatives, and she pitied the two Irish girls in her room who caught the brunt of such hostility. Gates taught these two girls to read and write; though many claimed that they were too slow because they struggled to tend three instead of four looms. They also did not clean under their looms, and there was said to be a distinct "Irish smell" surrounding them. Yet they also worked steadier than the Americans, and Gates was one of the few American operatives to respect their rights as people and as workers.[56]

Irish men who found employment in the textile mills also faced their share of discrimination. They were usually placed in low-paid unskilled jobs, and even those who worked diligently at these unfulfilling tasks for years rarely were promoted to any position of authority. When Irish men tried to advance into the skilled work of the machine shops in Lowell and Biddeford, Maine, it was reported that the American employees nearly rioted. The Americans resented the Irish, whom they suspected of having few skills to offer the machinist's trade. Nevertheless, by the 1840s, a few Irish men were moving up from laborer to semiskilled or skilled machine-shop employee.[57]

Some metalworkers retained their suspicion of all immigrants right on up through 1850. The presence of English workers remained a controversial issue for the employees of the Reed and Barton tableware factory. On June 28, 1850, a "knock down" between two English brothers, Tom and Ed Furniss, prompted the following remarks.

> We go out from the shop as soon as we hear what is going on, & put a stop to it without ceremony. They claimed that was the way Englishmen settled their disputes. We told them, "we would *not allow* such work on *Yankee soil,* and *don't you forget it.*"
>
> The workmen of Reed & Barton considered they had been *highly insulted* by the transaction, and *told them so.* They never tried it again.[58]

Even such an enlightened labor activist as Seth Luther was very critical of all immigrant labor (skilled and unskilled). He called on the government to stop these foreigners from entering the country.

> [W]e insist, that if Congress have power to protect the owners against foreign competition in the shape of goods, they have the same right to protect the operative from foreign competition in the shape of importation of foreign mechanics and laborers. . . . We call upon manufacturers to do justice to the operative, and warn them to remember that working men, the farmer, mechanic, and laborer are the majority, and are determined to be gulled no longer by the specious and deceptive cry of American Industry, while they are ground down into the dust by importation of foreign machinery, foreign workmen, and foreign wool; and deprived of improvements for themselves and an opportunity to educate their children, merely to enable "the rich to take care of themselves". . . .

It would be many decades before Congress enacted any such stringent immigration laws. Even then, the laws were not passed primarily for the benefit of working people. But the xenophobia in Luther's demands—the tension between native-born and immigrant—would constantly plague workers as they wrestled with the American industrial order. And the roots of that tension were in the emerging factories of antebellum New England, where operatives first struggled to make sense of the new mode of production and of the new workers in their midst.[59]

CHAPTER 5

Rules, Schools, and Prisons: Workers and Factory Regulations

Antebellum factory regulations were the means by which manufacturers tried to reconcile their progressive ideas about new technology and increased productivity with their conservative ideas about social hierarchy and order. Owners were trying to promote industrial work habits while controlling any social excesses among the new industrial workers—thereby creating change and trying to control its repercussions at the same time. Factory rules were used to mold the industrial labor force into an efficient unit of production that would follow the traditional guidelines of deference, obedience, and virtue, as well as the modern requirements of punctuality, precision, and sobriety. Workers were told to follow a set of work rules and moral standards that would both prepare them to succeed in the new industrial order and still keep them in a subservient and docile position as hired labor.

As for the workers themselves, some of them readily accepted these regulations and became dutiful disciples of their factory masters. They agreed that these regulations were for their own good and would teach them valuable lessons for future success. They found that by cooperating with management in creating a regulated work force, they often received favors and flexibility from their supervisors as rewards for their proper behavior. The workers who were willing to follow the rules sometimes found that the regulations were actually enforced with a generous and magnanimous spirit. These workers did not feel manipulated by the system of rules and regulations; they felt they were incorporating good work habits into their own personalities. Other workers remained skeptical of these rules, and still saw the virtual monopoly of power and authority that lay behind the promulgation and enforcement of corporate labor policies. These operatives saw factory regulations as more threads in the web of corporate control, another step towards management's goal of total domination of the factory system—a goal some of the workers struggled to resist.

— I —

The details of particular rules varied from factory to factory, but clear patterns did emerge from these regulations. Many companies would not put a new employee to work until he or she had read the official regulations and signed a certificate agreeing to abide by them. Nearly every regulation paper emphasized basic requirements like punctuality and obedience. Even overseers were expected to be punctual and to demand the same from the workers; no worker could leave a room without good cause and permission from the supervisor, and no outsider could enter the factory without obtaining permission. Overseers could grant leaves of absence when there were "spare hands in the Rooms to supply their places: otherwise, they [were] not to grant leave of absence, except in cases of great necessity." The workers were "not to be absent from their work without consent, except in case of sickness, and then they [were] to send the Overseer word of the cause of their absence." In addition, many companies required that "all persons intending to leave the employment of the company . . . give two weeks' notice of their intention to the overseer." Many of these regulations served to stabilize the work force, reinforce the authority of management, and maintain the subservient position of the workers.[1]

Some factories went far beyond the bare necessities of punctuality and regularity in their rules. One mill in Brunswick, Maine, made it especially clear that in the factory a worker's time and energy belonged to the company. One part of its rules stated: "as it is obvious that during working hours the time of the persons employed in the mill should be at the service of the proprietors, no one will be permitted to bring work of any kind into the mill." Workers were also usually prohibited from taking any goods home from the factories for their own use. The Chicopee [Massachusetts] Manufacturing Company, in a copy of its regulations from the 1840s, specified that "any one who shall take goods from the Mills, or Yard, any yarn, cloth, or other articles belonging to the Company, will be considered guilty of *stealing,* and prosecuted accordingly." Workers were given a clear and unequivocal message through these rules—the factory was a place where diligent effort was required, but only at tasks that were assigned by the company. Workers could not bring any work into or out of the factory because labor for the company was to be done specifically within the regulated confines of the buildings.[2]

The 1828 regulations for the cotton mills in Dover, New Hampshire, specifically prohibited a number of activities that might impede the factories' efficient operations or compromise the moral standards of the work force.

> No talking can be permitted while at work, except on business. Spiritous liquor, smoking, nor any kind of amusement will be allowed in the workshops, yards, or factories.
>
> . . . To preserve the present high character of our profession and give the enemies of domestic manufacturers no cause of exhaltation, a strictly moral conduct is required from everyone. Gambling, drinking, or any other debaucheries will procure the immediate and disgraceful dismissal of the individual.
>
> . . . Self-respect, it is expected, will induce everyone to be as constant in attendance on some place of divine worship as circumstances will permit.

These numerous requirements reflected management's belief that factory rules could inject moral precepts in the work force when it was both on and off the job. The company proclaimed that the work of an operative was actually a "profession" of "high character," and each employee was expected to abide by the company's standards of obedience and propriety so that the work would proceed correctly, the workers would preserve their reputations, and "the enemies of domestic manufacturers" would have "no cause of exhaltation." The proper public image of a factory work force, in effect, would be a living advertisement for the promotion of American manufactures.[3]

The Lawrence Manufacturing Company in Lowell, Massachusetts, issued its own elaborate set of rules during the spring of 1833. These regulations also prohibited drinking, smoking, and gambling on the company premises, and even went farther in carefully delineating the character of a good operative.

> *1st.* All persons in the employ of the Company, are required to attend assiduously to their various duties, or labor, during working hours: are expected to be fully competent, or to aspire to the utmost efficiency, in the work or business they may engage to perform, and to evince on all occasions, in their deportment or conversation, a laudable regard for temperance, virtue, and their moral and social obligations. . . . No person can be employed by the Company, whose known habits are or shall be dissolute, indolent, dishonest, or intemperate, or who habitually absent themselves from public worship, and violate the Sabbath, or who may be addicted to gambling of any kind.

These company work rules further echoed traditional New England values of hard work and upright living in a new industrial setting. Managers believed that the foundation of a harmonious and productive factory was a well-behaved work force. These regulations were not designed solely to meet the technical demands of mechanized manufacturing; they were consciously shaped by manufacturers to keep workers under control. Both labor control and social control were united in the web of factory rules. Discipline, deference, and dependence were the watchwords for operatives under the system of industrial regulations.[4]

One regulation, common in many factories, excited an exceptional amount of controversy—the injunction against operatives' drinking alcohol. The problem of drunkenness in mechanized manufactories was probably less prevalent than in many other antebellum workplaces. Most women and children were not known to be consumers of liquor, and a drunken operative was a menace to himself and others around moving machinery. Nevertheless, alcoholic beverages were found in some factories, or at least drunk during the workdays. Up until the 1830s, the Slater Company followed a common custom of giving each "head of a household" a daily ration of liquor or wine as a portion of his pay. Samuel Dunster recalled that the machinists and other male workers at the Cocheco Manufacturing Company in Dover had two daily rum breaks. They did not drink in the factory, but they took time out of each day for consuming alcohol.

> [A]t 11 o'clock A.M., and at 4 o'clock P.M., when the "outer gate" was opened, nearly the whole of the machinists and employees (men) made a pilgrimage (not in a religious sense) to the store opposite, on Main Street, where "West India goods" were kept for sale; here they were allowed to spend a half hour in partaking of liquid

> refreshments. They spent a half dime each time for what they liked better than money, New Rum. Allow me to say that the half hour was considered not paid for by the Company. This "pilgrimage" across the bridge was discontinued when Captain Moses Paul was made Agent, in 1834... at the same hour the machinists made their visit across the river to the store on Main Street, the ponderous gate of that mill... the Printery... swung open and the head used to tell the boys, "if Jonathan (Fiske) comes in and asks for me, tell him I am somewhere about; if Parker comes inn tell him I have gone out to Sewell's to get a nip."

Similar drinking practices were found at the Springfield Armory. Superintendent Lee tried to ban liquor in 1833, but the armorers had their own "shop Laws," which required each man to treat the entire group he worked with on a given day (a practice called "dubbing"). Lee did succeed in keeping alcohol out of the shops; but he turned a blind eye and allowed the men to drink near a spring during the warmer months and in one of the coalhouses during the winter. Lee's successor also allowed such traditional practices to continue.[5]

Immigrant male workers were often particularly noted for their fondness for drink. One of the managers at the Reed and Barton britannia works in Taunton, Massachusetts, complained that an English solderer, who was capable of doing excellent work, was often so drunk with beer that he could barely do a passable job in the morning. Some brass-casters argued that alcohol helped prevent "brass-founder's ague," which was a fever caused by zinc fumes' poisoning the workers. Managers at the textile mills in Dover also complained that recent arrivals in the carding and spinning departments were frequently drunk. English immigrant mule spinners often failed to come to work on Mondays—thereby keeping the tradition of "Blue Mondays"—after drinking all day on Sundays. In at least two cases in Dover, fellow immigrants paid for the passage of problem drinkers back to England. Money was provided to ensure a comfortable journey, but no additional cash was given, for fear that it would be spent on liquor.[6]

William Mason took a somewhat more humorous approach to his employees' daily drinking habits on the job. When his new factory opened in 1845, drinking water had to be brought in from the nearby Mill River. The workers disliked the bad-tasting stream water, so they went across the street for a beer when they were thirsty. One day the men bet a machinist that he could not bring two beers back into the factory past Mason's watchful gaze. The man returned and demanded payment because the two beers were safely ensconced in his stomach. Mason, who had been observing the whole scene, grabbed a shovel and started to walk outside. When the men asked where he was going, Mason said simply, "To dig a well."[7]

Working men often tried to retain the privilege of taking a drink during the workday: if not in the factory, then somewhere nearby. Taking the time for a drink was a way to assert some control over the workday, as well as providing a brief escape from the monotony of mechanized work. Drinking itself was seen as both a masculine social practice and a source of needed refreshment from the long hours of toil in tedious and unhealthy conditions.

Most owners, however, eventually abandoned the practice of providing liquor or permitting its use during the workday, because they believed that drinking had become detrimental to the maintenance of a productive labor force. Managers concluded that workers who drank were far less punctual or obedient to other regulations. Management's temperance crusade was greeted with a significant amount of opposition from workers accustomed to their traditional prerogatives. Benjamin Wilbur recalled that Fall River mill workers "were treated to New England rum at 11 A.M." In 1827, however, "considerable excitement was created when a foreman refused to carry rum around among the operatives, saying he was hired to oversee the carding room, not to pass out liquor." In the 1830s, the Slater Company also abandoned its policy of providing daily liquor rations and prohibited liquor on company property. The Slaters also emphasized that temperance would be a significant criterion in hiring help. Some workers, when writing to request employment, made a point of emphasizing their temperate habits. The Lowell mills were also very strict in hiring only people who could vouch for their freedom from alcohol addiction.[8]

The temperance movement spread to more operatives; sometimes workers picked up the cause voluntarily and sometimes they did so out of necessity. Some workers embraced the temperance crusade on their employers' terms and became sober, industrious employees. Other operatives saw temperance as a necessary step for working people to regain some control over their own lives; those who let themselves be dominated by drink were vulnerable to further exploitation by the factory system itself.[9]

B. Blackburn wrote a very repentant letter to the Stevens Company, pledging sobriety in return for being rehired. He said, "If you will Employ me again Either as a carder or spinner, I will come back again, and try to Pay up my Debts in A honerable way I will leave off my Dissolute Conduct and promise not to use Ardent Spirits while in your Employ." Blackburn seemed to accept temperance and the principles of the new industrial morality as a way to regain his job. James Metcalf joined the Sons of Temperance and wrote enthusiastically to his mother about this organization's crusade. Metcalf saw temperance as a fundamental reform for workers and all of society—it was truly a battle of heroic proportions, couched in the language of labor and military might.

> We are trying to do something in the cause of Temperance in this place. Division No 34 Sons of T hold regular weekly social meetings and are endeavoring to have weekly Lectures. . . . May this great and blessed cause roll on till victory perch on our hammers and may one long, loud and universal shout be heard from combined humanity and striking out against natu[re's] great sounding board . . . reverberate throughout earths wide domains: "Temperance now and Temperance forever."[10]

Metcalf may have seen sobriety as one of the essential virtues of a self-respecting citizen and an autonomous worker. The campaign for temperance was a battle in itself, but sobriety was also part of the new code of discipline for soldiers in the army of labor. Temperance meant self-control and personal stability. Standing up for sobriety, like standing up for the rights of labor, was a true mark of manliness. Giving in to drunkenness could lead only to dependency, emasculation, and enslavement. Women obviously did not see the temperance movement in such masculine terms, and they were not often directly concerned with the question of drinking privileges in the workplace. Nevertheless, mill women in cities such as Dover also became involved in various female temperance auxiliaries, including the Daughters of Rechab.[11]

Underlying the elaborate system of rules and regulations in most factories, including the provisions against drinking, was the power of management to enforce these requirements. Some companies instituted fines to punish those who acted in violation of policies. For example, employees who did not follow the dictates of punctuality could find themselves the poorer for it. The Dover mills, in 1828, fined any tardy worker twelve and one-half cents. Another mill subtracted one-quarter of a day's wages from "Any Person being absent 15 Minutes after the Wheel is started." Amasa Whitney posted regulations in his Winchendon, Massachusetts, factory that specified monetary penalties for a variety of contractual infractions. By spelling out such penalties in precise detail, Whitney made sure that operatives knew the cost of disobeying the rules.

> *3rd.* Hands are not allowed to leave the factory in working hours without the consent of their Overseer; if they do, they will be liable to have their time set off.
>
> *4th.* Any one who by negligence or misconduct causes damage to the machinery, or impedes the progress of the work, will be liable to make good the damage for the same.
>
> *5th.* Any one employed for a certain length of time, will be expected to make up their lost time, if required before they will be entitled to their pay.
>
> *6th.* Any person employed for no certain length of time, will be required to give at least four weeks notice of their intention to leave, (sickness excepted) or forfeit 4 weeks pay, unless by particular agreement. . . .
>
> *8th.* Any one who have leave of absence for any length of time, will be expected to return in that time; and in case they do not return in that time, and do not give satisfactory reason, they will be liable to forfeit one week's work or less if they commence work again. If they do not, they will be considered as one who leaves without giving notice.[12]

The Slater Company often made individual contracts which contained penalties for poor work by operatives. William Frim signed an agreement in 1838 that stipulated that he "recommend[ed] himself as a first rate workman—which provided he shall not manifest to the satisfaction of the said Slater he the said Frim agrees to forfeit and pay to the said Slater the sum of Fifty Dollars as damages." And the dresser-tender William Smith's agreement specified that "in case he does not do his work well or any Looms stop for want of Yarn—he is to pay for the Yarn to the satisfaction of the said Slater—and if the Looms stop—at the Rate of One Dollar per Loom per Week." In some cases, these fines may have functioned as a substitute for direct management supervision at every point of production. If managers could not spot every problem immediately, they could impose their fines for poor work later on when the defects were detected. Thus the message would get through to the workers that management's standards had to be obeyed, even when the boss was not looking, or workers would be punished for their infractions.[13]

When fines were not enough to keep workers in line, management could resort to dismissing operatives. The power to fire and hire often rested directly in the hands of overseers or with higher-level superintendents and managers. The Brunswick Company's regulations carefully delineated how the power of dismissal was a strong force for controlling operatives.

> [W]henever any hand is found disorderly, disobedient, refractory, indolent, incompetent, or of a reputed bad character, it is the duty of the overseer, under whom such hand may be placed, to discharge such hand from his room: and no hand so discharged will be taken into the employ of the proprietors without the approbation of the overseer.

Workers obviously realized that whereas fines took away a portion of their earnings, a dismissal took away the job itself.[14]

Sometimes the mere threat of being dismissed was enough to bend employees to the owner's will. Joseph Hollingworth wrote about his fears for his own job, and those of his entire family, if any of them took time off or refused to work nights. He told his uncle on two separate occasions: "had I refused . . . to work a good deal of overtime at Nights . . . the whole family might have lost their work." Some owners used the threat of dismissal to enforce their moral code in and out of the factory. Amasa Sprague ordered his employees to stay out of Nicholas Gordon's store, where workers were reported to be drinking during the day, or risk being fired. Some operatives said that they were afraid to buy even a needle and thread in that store for fear of being reported and dismissed. The battle between Gordon and Sprague exploded when Gordon's brother John, an employee in Sprague's print works, was convicted and executed for murdering the manufacturer. But the company's power over its workers did not end with Sprague's death. Hundreds of mourners at John Gordon's funeral refrained from joining the procession for fear of losing their jobs, but they did line the streets as spectators. On a somewhat lighter note, though certainly not frivolous, a mill in Waltham posted a notice during the 1830s that any young woman who attended dancing school would be discharged. The overseer argued that if the operatives spent part of their evenings running about, they would become either ill or too tired on the job.[15]

Actual dismissals for work-related and non–work-related reasons were common in the Lowell mills. Drunkenness was cause for immediate discharge; so was leaving one's work "irregularly," "reading in the mill," "profanity," "altering her looms and thinning her cloth," disregarding "the advice of their overseer," "spreading false stories," dancing in a spinning room, pretending "sickness to go to meeting," having "too many trustee writs" attached to wages, hysteria, "religious frenzy," forging and tampering with accounts, scuffling, stealing, disobedience, impudence, and being a "devil in petticoats." Managers tried to justify these myriad dismissals by claiming that unacceptable behavior made for bad work and bad reputations. A well-regulated labor force would be more productive, better paid, and free from the stigma of disreputable characters. For example, the operative dismissed for "hysteria" was let go because the overseer was afraid she would get caught in the gearing. Although management professed interest in the workers' health and welfare, they used their power of dismissal mainly to ensure that the employees did nothing—in or out of the factory—that contravened the owners' regulations and orders. These rules were not to be questioned, they were to be obeyed—the authority of the manufacturer had to be recognized or workers would suffer the consequences.[16]

Some managers took further steps to ensure labor discipline and the acceptance of their stringent rules. Superintendent Roswell Lee arranged with other armory owners not to hire each other's employees without a recommendation from their last place of work. Armorers now faced, not only dismissal for disobeying the managers' orders, but also the possibility that they would be barred from practicing their trade elsewhere. It is not surprising that most workers eventually yielded to regulations or faced the threat of long-term unemployment. As late as 1847, an official in Springfield wrote to Samuel Colt with a warning about a soon-to-be-dismissed worker.

> I have taken the liberty of writing to inform you that I am going to discharge one of my hands, the one which has made my flask bodies, he will most likely come to you and ask for work, I will give you his carracter, he is one of the greatest scoundrels out . . . he has robbed and cheated, almost every one he has to do with; he owes about $150 in town now. . . . I thought I would caution you against him . . . the mans name which I speak of is George Hayden he can make and buff your flasks at 5 cents each and make $1.75 per day, but he is a very slovenly workman he will make a few of the first well for you to see, and then slip the rest, you must inspect his work as he goes on.[17]

This system of recommending workers who had satisfactorily completed their contracts and blacklisting those who violated management's rules was also found in other industries. Bourne Spooner proposed the idea to a fellow rope manufacturer after he fired one employee and saw another one leave in sympathy. He believed that using such letters of warning or recommendation was a way to regulate the labor market as well as discipline fractious employees.

> The conduct of Elizabeth Exnor has been so disorderly that I was reluctantly compelled to discharge her on Saturday Evg. last & she has induced Clarissa Bishop to leave also. I would suggest to you the propriety of requiring a letter of recommendation or of release from all persons Male and Female who leave either your place or our place for the other, previous to giving them employ.[18]

The underlying reason for many of these regulations and penalties was management's insistence that good discipline and good morals made for good workers and good work. Controlling workers on and off the job created a predictable and manageable labor force for the factories. This connection was made explicit in a contract between Anson Atwood and the clockmaking firm of Brewster and Ingrahams in Bristol, Connecticut, during the early spring of 1848. Atwood agreed to make quality clock parts and to ensure that his workers were respectable, all in the same paragraph.

> It is expressly understood that the general appearance of the movements shall be good, and that the movements shall be thoroughly finished, and warranted to perform well. The said Atwood further agrees to keep good order in the establishment, and allow no gambling, nor wrestling, or scuffling, or profane language, have regular hours for business, and not allow the factory to be opened on the Sabbath,

> except in the morning before church, and this only for the purpose of washing, shaving, and preparing for church. He and his hands shall be regular attendants at church on the Sabbath.

One of the crucial provisions in this contract, as in so many factory regulations, was the requirement that all employees observe the sabbath and attend church. Religious practice, even if it had to be enforced by official rules, was considered the bedrock of a well-regulated factory and a tractable work force on and off the job.[19]

Factory owners insisted that company-supervised religion was the foundation of all proper conduct at work and in the community. The Amoskeag Manufacturing Company regulations stated, "a regular attendance on public worship on the Sabbath is necessary for the preservation of good order." Some manufacturers built churches and supported ministers to instill in the operatives the principles of hard work, thrift, sobriety, and obedience—all characteristic of a dutiful employee. Managers often were teachers in "Sabbath Schools" where they instructed the same workers they supervised the other six days of the week. Some owners even shut down their factories so that workers could attend revivals, camp meetings, or special church quarterly sessions. The Slater mill in Webster, Massachusetts, closed for several days in the summer of 1839 to allow operatives to participate in a local Methodist revival. And S.V.S. Wilder dismissed all the employees at the Ware Manufacturing Company at noon one day to celebrate the groundbreaking for a new church.[20]

There were even reports that some revival meetings were held right in the factories themselves as the machines were shut down for prayer sessions. Revivalists saw factory buildings as ideal places for assembling hundreds of potential converts under one roof. Jacob Knapp, a leader of Baptist revivals, visited Lowell in 1842 and remembered that his work "assumed such vast proportions that in one of the cotton mills the superintendent, who was a Universalist, found it necessary to stop operations. The operatives were nearly all on their knees, in prayer for themselves, or for their unconverted associates. In fact, the entire factory was an anxious-room."[21]

The goal of all this company-sponsored (or at least company-tolerated) religious activity was to mold employees who would take work regulations and religious precepts to heart—not to be coerced into proper working behavior, but to be guided by conscience. Self-control and social control were to be merged as one seamless whole within the factory's disciplinary system; workers would internalize the regulations as part of their daily behavior. Each worker was supposed to become his own manager and instinctively follow the company's rules—to be a good worker was to be a moral Christian.

One official from the Dover Manufacturing Company wrote frankly about why religion made sound business sense: "we all consider the morals and religious principles of those employed in our service as worthy of great attention, and in fact without reference to any feelings of philanthropy, self interest, in the protection of our property would dictate a watchfulness on our part." This manager believed that a churchgoing population would pose less of a threat to the factory itself; rowdiness and defiance were associated with the unchurched. Samuel Spalding observed that the operatives who attended Sunday school helped police the rest of the workers. These "Scholars . . . certainly exercis[ed] a restraining influence over the less morally disposed. This high tone of morality not only renders our population more stable but also brings to us a better class of people—persons of more intelligence and better education." This "better class" of workers was thought to be more productive and cooperative than less-educated operatives. One agent wrote to Amos Lawrence that the presence of four religious groups in a factory community made "this place desirable for business for those of as many denominations—a matter of importance in a business light—to say nothing of the higher considerations." Many manufacturers, therefore, believed that a strict moral environment was good for their businesses: a well-controlled work force would be a productive and profitable work force.[22]

Yet the issue of religion among workers—particularly evangelical religion and religious enthusiasm—remained a subject of some contention. Some manufacturers continued to welcome revivals and preachers because of their probusiness sermons; other managers resented these interruptions of the workday. Some managers encouraged religious revivals, as they did almost all religious activity, because they believed that all such practices underscored the importance of social control and industrial morality for factory workers. Other managers became concerned that certain sects were encouraging ideas of independence and causing social disruption among the operatives.

In Ware, Massachusetts, the factory agent S.V.S. Wilder was criticized by some nonevangelical Universalist overseers in the late 1820s for sacrificing "the interests of the corporation by allowing many of the hands to attend the religious meetings during the regular work hours." Religious conflict and contention between various levels of management swirled throughout the factory. Lewis Tappan, treasurer of the corporation, investigated the situation thoroughly. Tappan recalled the results of his examination:

> I found to my surprise that the work actually accomplished during that year, when religious meetings were so abundant, considerably exceeded the quantity produced by the same number of hands the year previous. I stated this to the overseers and to the agent; the former being more surprised at the result than I had been, while the agent expressed no surprise at all, it being about what he proposed . . . the directors were well satisfied, mysterious as the result was, that the agent had not been wanting in his duty to the corporation, while he promoted the religious interests of the work-people, who had made up loss of time by greater diligence and faithfulness.[23]

As for the operatives themselves, they used religion in a variety of ways in their daily working lives. Some did become the self-disciplined, hard-working employees that their bosses expected. But many workers used their religious beliefs as part of their criticism of the factory system. Even local church buildings could, in some cases, be places where workers gathered to discuss common problems and organize protests. Sometimes these criticisms were not verbalized, but expressed in overt actions. In Webster, Massachusetts, many mill workers did not become stable residents after participating in revivals. Rather, transiency rates increased among the working population after revivals in the 1830s. Workers often remained long enough to join the church, but they did not necessarily stay afterwards to be taught by their managers the ways of proper work and personal conduct.[24]

Some operatives probably found in religion a source of both independence and working-class community; they were more willing to question their work and search for new opportunities. Sarah Maria Cornell, after she converted to Methodism, found that as she traveled from town to town, she could usually count on being welcomed by the local Methodist congregation. (Once her controversial reputation caught up with her, however, Cornell often found herself at odds with the church, and she had to set off again in search of another community willing to accept her.) This knowledge that she could always hope to find another viable community gave her the strength to move, whenever she had to, without fear of being alone. While in Lowell, in the spring of 1829, Cornell wrote a letter to her sister stating that Methodism justified transiency and gave comfort to those constant travelers.

> I received a letter from mother about four months since in which she mentioned she thought I was a moving planet, . . . tell mother she must remember that I am connected with a people that do not believe in tarrying in any one place longer than a year or two years at most at any one time—and I am with them in sentiment believing with the Apostole that we should be as strangers and pilgrims having here no continuing city or abiding place, but seek one to come.

The Methodists were also known for their emotionally and physically charged religious practices. Their services could be seen as expressions of workers' pent-up energy and frustration; but the potential for meaningful demonstrations of discontent was also channeled away from the employers and institutions and towards spiritual ideas.[25]

Of course, not every worker was caught up in the religious fervor of revivals—either inside or outside the factories. One character in Lucy Larcom's "Idyl of Work" may have spoken for many operatives who were skeptical of such evangelical enthusiasm.

> "Your sect!" said Isabel, breaking in, with heat.
> "I wish it were a little more polite,
> Less noisy, too. What right has Sister Sterne
> To quiz me all about my 'state of mind,'
> Ask if I read my Bible, if I pray,
> If I am fit for heaven?—no! not for hers,
> Nor would be, if I could! The other day
> She held a meeting, when the looms were still,
> Just before bell-time, in the window-seat.
> O, how they sung and shouted! I cried out,—
> I had a dreadful headache,—'Do, do be
> A little quieter!' Then Sister Sterne
> Groaned, 'Isabel! If you ever get to heaven,
> You'll have to hear a much worse noise than this!'"

The friction between various sects, or between skeptics and believers, was probably common in many factories. Some workers, therefore, saw religion as a source of contention and disunity, not stability and discipline. But for many other workers, the growing evangelical sects struck a responsive chord when they spoke of individual salvation and opportunity in a religious community. Ironically, some of these same denominations also appealed to factory managers when they spoke of self-control, obedience, and discipline. But the question remained—obedience to whom? to factory supervisors or to the workers' own sense of right and wrong?[26]

— II —

When operatives stepped back from the debate over religion and considered factory discipline as a whole, they were still divided about the benefits and costs of all the regulations. Some workers found little to complain about in the disciplinary system; they went through their workdays giving little thought to regulations or reasons for possible dismissal. Harriet Farley argued that factory rules were "not strictly enforced, for it is not considered necessary to treat the operatives as eye-servants, and the majority never think of their regulation paper after they have read it once."[27]

Other workers pointed out that the system of rules and regulations depended far more on the human element of interpretation and enforcement than on what was written in the official documents. And these operatives insisted that most managers were quite flexible and understanding when it came time to enforce company regulations. An operative from Waltham, Massachusetts, wrote that the rule requiring two weeks' notice before leaving the factory was not strictly enforced. "It sometimes happens that a girl becomes uneasy, or dissatisfied, and when pay-day arrives, receives her pay, and takes 'French leave'—but without fear of being pursued, or advertised as a runaway." The Hamilton Company in Lowell, throughout the 1830s, even rehired operatives who did not work the full year stipulated in their contracts or who left without giving their two weeks' notice. This rehiring policy, however, may have been due more to the need for experienced workers than to any particular friendliness on management's part. As Harriet Hanson Robinson said, "*Help was too valuable to be ill-treated.*"[28]

In regard to fines and firings, there were also numerous reports of lenient and cooperative managers. For example, factory officials at the Slater companies in Oxford and Dudley, Massachusetts, tried to avoid imposing fines and other punishments on their workers. Though punctuality was stressed and time was measured meticulously, tardy workers were not fined. Obedience to managers was required, but workers were rarely dismissed for misconduct. Zenas Crane did immediately fire any workers at his paper mill when he discovered that they were drunk. But Crane's policy combined strictness with concern for the individual. He would wait a few days for the employee to sober up; then he would lecture the miscreant on temperance, and rehire the worker with some extra money to make up for the lost wages.[29]

Some workers also denied reports that operatives, once they were fired, were prohibited from obtaining work in any other factory. An operative from Waltham very specifically stated: "it is one of the factory rules that a laborer, dismissed by one overseer, will not be employed by another, if the first forbids it; but an overseer seldom exercises his authority in the particular. . . ." And while Harriet Farley acknowledged that overseers did indeed have the power to dismiss workers from their jobs, she vehemently denied reports of harassment and corporal punishment. "To strike a female," she declared, "would cost any overseer his place. If the superintendents did not take the affair into consideration, the girls would turn out" in protest and leave the mills.[30]

Harriet Hanson Robinson recalled that most operatives never had any trouble obeying factory regulations, and they were "quite proud" of the "honorable discharges" they received when they fulfilled all their obligations to one mill and sought employment in another factory. This simple slip of paper was given to any worker who left at the end of her contract after giving proper notice. Workers who presented such a recommendation usually had little trouble obtaining work at another establishment.[31]

Some workers argued that factory regulations were not always so pliable, but strict obedience to rules could also be beneficial. Lucy Larcom, looking back on her years in the Lowell mills, admitted that the disciplined character of factory work was a healthy influence on her personal development.

> Even the long hours, the early rising, and the regularity enforced by the clangor of the bell were good discipline for one who was naturally inclined to dally and dream, and who loved her own personal liberty with a willful rebellion against control. Perhaps I could have brought myself into the limitations of order and method in no other way.

Larcom saw that her factory experience broke her youthful, headstrong attitudes, but she was happy with the lessons she learned in self-control. She became the kind of worker the management wanted—not only was she transformed into an obedient operative, but she was never resentful of how the changes were imposed on her.[32]

Harriet Farley also praised the "regularity" of factory work: "rising, sleeping, and eating, at the same hours on each consecutive day; the necessity of taking a few draughts of fresh air in their walks to and from work; and the lightness of the labor." Another contributor to the *Lowell Offering* also wrote about the salutary effects of a daily work regimen in a factory. "They rise early, take their meals regularly, both of which are conducive to health. Their work is also steady—the same one day as before." Thus the very constancy of mechanized labor, its unchanging character and carefully regulated conditions, was not always resented as a cause of drudgery. Some workers welcomed this pattern because its consistency made them into more self-controlled people, and they were comfortable with the sense of order in their lives.[33]

Harriet Hanson Robinson decided, like Lucy Larcom, that her youth was not wasted in the Lowell mills. She learned so many valuable lessons about work itself (not merely her mechanical tasks) that the factory became a kind of school to her. Both institutions emphasized the basic themes of regularity and order.

> The discipline our work brought us was of great value. We were obliged to be in the mill at just such a minute, at every hour, in order to doff our full bobbins and replace them with empty ones. We went to our meals and returned at the same hour every day. We worked and played at regular intervals, and thus our hands became deft, our fingers nimble, our feet swift, and we were taught daily habits of regularity and of industry; it was, in fact, a sort of manual training or industrial school.

Robinson also saw how the lessons of the "factory school" remained with operatives even after they left the mills.

> They went forth from their *Alma Mater*, the Lowell factory, carrying with them the independence, the self-reliance taught in that hard school, and they have done their little part towards performing the useful labor of life. Into whatever vocation they entered they made practical use of the habits of industry and perseverance learned during those early years. Skilled labor teaches something not to be found in books or in colleges.

The workers who remained in factories and found new positions in the system could think of themselves as graduating to better jobs as they matured. Varnam Lincoln began his career as a bobbin boy and then "graduated from the Lawrence Mills to the large machine shop of the Locks and Canals Company. Fortunately, this change also proved a school and favorable to the acquisition of knowledge and mental development. It brought me into the society of a class of intelligent young men, who, while they toiled over the engine or the lathe, had higher aims."[34]

The idea of the factory as school and the operative as student is expressed vividly on the cover of the *Lowell Offering*. The young woman holds a book in her right hand and contemplates a nearby beehive, which was regarded as a symbol of "industry and intelligence." The bell towers of the factory, school, and church are all visible in the background. These structures stand together as institutions promoting the virtues of hard work, discipline, and obedience. John Rogers saw many of these parallels when he worked at the Amoskeag Company's machine shop in 1850. He wrote to his father that each day's schedule in the factory "rather reminds me of Mr. Hyde's school when we had to go in when the bell rang and study hard when we got there."[35]

Critics of the factory disciplinary system also noted that there were very important human factors embedded in all the rules and regulations. But these workers argued that managers were actually quite inflexible and unyielding in their enforcement of company policies. Operatives cited numerous cases of "impassioned overseerdom" where managers went to great extremes to prove that they were not sympathetic toward workers. Overseers and agents were determined to follow the letter of the law, regardless of the consequences for labor.

One excerpt from "Factory Tracts," by the Lowell Female Labor Reform Association, told of operatives from the Lawrence Corporation being forced to take positions in the company's new mill. Their old factory was shut down, but the operatives were required to serve out their contracts in the new facilities.

> Now as they did not voluntarily leave their situation, but were discharged therefrom on account of suspension of operations by the company; they had an undoubted right to choose their own place of labor; and as the work in the new mill

> is vastly more laborious, and the wages less than can be obtained in many parts of the city, they signified their wish to go elsewhere, but are insolently told that they shall labor there or not at all; and will not be released until their year has expired.[36]

Agent Gillis in Nashua, New Hampshire, was also reported to be a man who engaged "in mean personal attacks upon the freedom of the operatives." In one instance, an operative "was a little behind 'bell-time'" and she had to pass through the counting room on her way to work. Gillis slammed the door behind her and caught her dress. He then decided to hold her there as punishment for her tardiness. While Gillis was forcing all his weight against the door, the operative quietly took a pair of scissors from her pocket and cut herself free from the door so that she could go on to her work. Some fifteen minutes later an overseer went to the counting house door, forced it open, and found the agent on the other side still trying to keep it closed with all his strength. This account in the *Voice of Industry* showed admiration for the operative's outsmarting the cruel agent, and it concluded fittingly that the agent "sneaked away" in embarrassment and defeat.[37]

On the subject of fines, workers were often angered by the prospect of paying these penalties, which cut into the wages they had already earned. Seth Luther spoke out against the injustice of fines, which he thought were grossly out of proportion to the minor infractions involved. If a "woman or child should lose five minutes time out of 13 hours, she is docked a quarter of a day. In one mill, we learn that a little girl was cut off in time, one and a quarter days for 25 minutes, that is, one quarter for five minutes for five days in succession. We believe this is a part of what is called 'judicious management.'" Weavers at the Hamilton Manufacturing Company were frequently fined for work that managers judged to be of poor quality. In April 1835, forty weavers were penalized, probably because of a managerial decision to enforce higher standards of work. Mary Johnson, fined fifteen cents, and Delia Noyes, docked ten cents, both left the company because they were angry with their punishments, which added up to pay for two and three hours' worth of work.[38]

Many workers were also disturbed by management's unalterable authority to fire workers. It is true that most dismissals occurred within the first year of an operative's career, often within the first two or three months. This was usually the case because veteran employees were familiar with the many written and unwritten regulations, and they generally avoided any infractions. Nevertheless, all employees were always on a kind of permanent probation, and the company could dismiss them at any time for any reason. No matter how trivial or unjust the reason, workers rarely had any recourse to appealing a manager's decision to fire them. In one weave room of the Merrimack Corporation in Lowell, one operative was dismissed merely for leaving her looms to go wash her hands. This was the first fault found in her work, but she made the mistake of talking back to her overseer, and she was given her notice to leave. At the Suffolk Corporation, in the same city, a young woman told her overseer that she had to leave her job on account of ill health. The overseer told her that if she left, she would not be paid for any work she had already done. The operative insisted that her health would not permit her to work any longer, so she was sent off without any money to pay for her board or her passage home. Here, again, workers decried managers who were absolutely unyielding in their enforcement of company regulations—no matter what the rule and no matter what its impact on the workers.[39]

The armorers in Springfield carried on a long-standing debate with their managers over what constituted proper behavior in the workplace and proper grounds for dismissal. As with so many other issues at Springfield, the armorers tried to retain more prerogatives than most operatives because of their relatively skilled occupations, and the management tried to dilute the skill and power of the workers. Superintendent Lee, around 1815, dismissed two men for wrestling on the shop floor. This decision was part of a broader effort to root out undisciplined and inefficient work habits, such as the careless handling of tools and supplies, and informal gambling arrangements. But the workers insisted that their tradition prescribed that the two ex-operatives, before leaving, had to buy everyone else a drink around the flagstaff or "liberty pole." Once there, some suggested cutting down the pole since their freedom to wrestle was now taken away from them. Lee told his clerk to order the men back to work; they refused; and the superintendent and master armorer had to intervene personally to save the flagpole. Lee was enraged because the superintendent of the Harpers Ferry Armory was visiting and saw the whole affair. Lee subsequently fired eleven more workers for various infractions as a followup to the incident. He also issued new regulations banning such customs as ball playing and conversation, all in the name of improving the quality and quantity of work.[40]

Some workers also took issue with the practice of not only summarily dismissing workers, but sending names of approved and disapproved workers to other companies. This procedure was condemned, quite simply, as a "blacklist." The blacklist followed Huldah Stone, one of the leaders of the female labor reform associations, beyond the factory. In 1847, when the new mills were opening in Lawrence, Massachusetts, Samuel Lawrence sent the following note to an official at the Essex Company: "Huldah J. Stone, a Radical of the worst sort & late Editoress of the Voice of Industry intends to get a Boarding House at the New City. I write this to warn you 'to keep hands off of her.'" Once again, managers tried to defend this practice as a way to weed out unsavory characters and preserve the reputation of their employees.[41]

Workers, especially in the *Voice of Industry,* spoke out vehemently against the blacklist. One woman wrote a very stark description about how a simple infraction turned into a grave personal crisis for her.

> I must tell you I am a Factory Girl, tired enough of this slave like life, seeing no prospect of a reduction in the hours of labor. My education is better than that of factory girls in general,—am very fond of books, and must tell you I am turned out of the mill, for reading in the mill, and my name has gone to all the Black Lists kept at the counting rooms. I have no home, and know not what to do.

An operative from the Nashua Corporation reported that a worker tried to change jobs in Lowell, but was refused at every mill because of a bad report from her overseer. She sued her manager for slander, "but was defeated in her suit for damages because the mill owners had established amongst themselves a rule, which custom had made law, making the ill-report of the overseer of one mill imperative cause of rejection by all mills of the place . . . and it stands by itself unexplained, final and imperative." What angered this worker most was the potential for arbitrariness and abuse in the blacklist. Operatives had to obey all the factory rules, but managers could make their own laws without any concern for their employees.

> It is of no consequence what induces [the overseer's] opinion—bad temper, immoral conduct, or nothing, on the part of the girl, or private pique, the gratification of an envious favorite, revenge for disappointed lechery, or any other cause, no matter how trivial or wicked on the part of the overseer—it may and does result in hunting and driving a girl out of the city if the overseer chooses to exercise his power over her destiny and her reputation.[42]

One contributor to the *Voice,* writing under the pseudonym "Veritas," condemned the blacklist as a conspiracy of the corporations against the workers—a conspiracy of evil men, dark deeds, and the abuse of power.

> The Corporation Conspirators against the rights of the people manage to "*libel*" the characters of the best girls of our factories, to fix upon them the stigma of "irregularity," to deprive them of the privilege of earning their bread, and do their worst to force them into crime, as their only means of support. In the estimation of a quack overseer, the character of an operative is of less importance to preserve than two threads of warp.

This operative saw the blacklist as merely a tool for labor control—owners had no interest in preserving the character of their employees, only in compelling workers to labor on the manufacturers' terms.[43]

The growing criticism of the blacklist even reached the Massachusetts legislature in 1843, with a petition from a group of seventeen workers at Lowell's Middlesex Corporation. These operatives were also frustrated by the fact that the blacklist seemed to be a law unto itself, and they asked for some kind of legislative relief.

> We, the undersigned, Females, dependent upon the labour of our hands for a subsistance: having left the employment of the Middlesex Manufacturing Company on account of a violation on their part, of the agreement existing between the undersigned and said Company; are now suffering persecution from said Company, and are hunted from place to place that we may find no employment by which to earn a living.
>
> Not being able to contend against our rich persecutors by bringing a suit at law for satisfaction, we are compelled to seek redress, or protection, from the powers which created said Company. . . .
>
> We . . . quit working for said Company and the consequence to us is as follows. Some of us went to work for other companies, but these Companies soon received our names and we were immediately turned off. Some of us applied for work where hands were wanted; but were informed that they could employ none of "The turnouts from the Middlesex," and many who laboured with us have been obliged to leave Lowell and seek their bread, they know not where on account of the persecution carried on against them by the Middlesex Company; our names are upon all the Corporations in Lowell; that we may find no employment; we therefore pray, that you will, if consistent with your constitutional powers, Stay the hands of our persecutors; and if not, that some law may be enacted, which will prevent our Brothers, Sisters and Friends, suffering as we suffer, if ever they should resist injustice from Manufacturing Companies.

There is no evidence that the legislature took any action on this petition, and the practice of blacklisting continued unabated.[44]

In 1846 and 1850, more requests were drafted for governmental action and attached to numerous ten-hour petitions. The blacklist was cited as "the cause of much injustice and oppression on the part of the corporations." Its "effects" were "becoming every day more grievous, giving to the manufacturer great power over the operative, and leading to monopoly and wrong. Your memorialists firmly believe that this combination is entered into to destroy the independence of the operatives, and place their labor within the control of the manufacturers." Some workers appeared before a legislative committee in 1850 to give personal testimony regarding the detrimental effects of the blacklist. But, as with the hearings into the hours of labor in 1845 and the continuing petition campaign, these efforts failed to produce any legislation.[45]

Many workers, in surveying the entire system of factory discipline, saw far more parallels with a prison than with a school. They did not believe that they were learning any beneficial lessons for later life and work, nor did they see any flexibility in the system. The factory was a place where men and women were locked into a maze of arbitrary and unjust regulations, enforced by a cadre of rigid managers with little or no human sympathy. These workers were not against rational order, but they saw little rationality or order in most factory rules and the way they were enforced. They did not believe that the factory was helping workers in their own search for order and self-control. These operatives strove for control in their jobs, rather than letting the manufacturing system control them.

These workers compared the factory to a prison because, where others saw regularity, they saw repetition and regimentation. When Abigail Mussey went to work in a cotton mill in 1827, she quickly became disillusioned with her daily regimen.

> Little did I think I was going into a prison, and could not have my liberty when I pleased. In a few weeks I began to find it was not so pleasant as I had anticipated. The confinement affected my health. I could no longer walk out in the open fields, and my opportunities to visit my brother's family were few. I had scarcely time to eat my dinner, before the bell would call me again to my loom.

An operative from Maine, writing in *Factory Girl's Album,* looked at the young men in machine shops and asked "if *gold can* pay for toiling fourteen hours a day, in this airless, pent-up grave of youth and health—like the mine where the unpitied criminal drags out his guilty existence." Seth Luther turned his attention to the young children in factories and claimed that he could show "in some of the prisons in New England, called cotton mills, instead of rosy cheeks, the *pale,* sickly *haggard* countenance of the ragged child, haggard from the *worse* than *slavish* confinement in the cotton mill." Luther's rhetoric linked the image of the factory as a prison with the concept of industrial slavery as he painted a bleak portrait of child labor.[46]

Amelia Sargent echoed the theme of slavery in her criticism of factory regulations. She saw workers being oppressed, not only by the actions of management or by any one particular requirement, but by the entire body of rules governing the factory system. Sargent described how the operative received a

> [r]egulation paper, containing the rules by which she must be governed while in their employ; and lo! here is the beginning of mischief; for in addition to the tyrannous and oppressive rules which meet her astonished eyes, she finds herself com-

pelled to remain for the space of twelve months in the very place she then occupies, however reasonable and just cause of complaint might be hers, or however strong the wish for dismission; thus, in fact, constituting herself a slave, a very slave to the caprices of him for whom she labors.

Sargent saw the specter of factory slavery lurking not only in the relationship between worker and manager, but in the entire regulatory structure that undergirded the industrial order. Rules and regulations did not ensure justice; rather, they propped up the system that oppressed workers.[47]

When managers countered that workers were always free to leave the system of factory labor, many operatives were unimpressed. They knew that any worker who tried to assert her independence and leave according to her own wishes could be denied an "honorable discharge." And workers who could not present such a document, specifying how long they had worked at the last company, would immediately find themselves under a cloud of suspicion as someone not to be employed. One worker condemned these documents as merely another facet of factory prisons and industrial bondage. Corporations, she wrote,

may deign to bestow upon [their operatives] what is in common parlance termed, "a regular discharge," thus enabling them to pass from one prison house to another. Concerning this precious document, it is only necessary to say, that it very precisely reminds one of that which the dealers in human flesh at the South are wont to give and receive as the transfers of one piece of property from one owner to another.[48]

Another operative acknowledged the need for order in factories, but she returned to the image of people becoming like machines when they were forced to labor under an unfair system of rules.

I would not be understood as contending against system, or good regulations. I believe them to be for the good of all concerned—but when they conflict with our rights as rational beings, and we are regarded as living machines, and all the rules made subservient to the interest of the employer; then it would seem that we have a right to call them in question, and regard them as arbitrary, and call for a reform.[49]

All of these critics were challenging management's claims that the existing system of regulations was necessary to maintain the high moral standards of the work force and the proper public image of the employers. These workers argued that management's ideas about discipline and rules were intended only to secure high profits and complete control over the labor force. The regulations were designed only with management's interests in mind; and what was orderly and rational to managers could be confusing and arbitrary to workers. Workers were usually not opposed to standards for what they saw as good moral conduct. They objected to managers' imposing their personal whims on every detail of a worker's behavior, and then sanctimoniously justifying such rules as beneficial to the operatives.

CHAPTER 6

Paying the Price: Workers, Contracts, and Wage Labor

The mechanized factory system in antebellum New England was more than a collection of machines, buildings, people, and rules. This system was also shaped by the fundamental need to hire labor and pay wages. Workers often found themselves in an unfamiliar network of labor markets, contracts, and wage rates. They quickly learned that contracts were more than pieces of paper, and wages were more than dollars and cents. Contracts were often instruments of social control, and wages lay at the heart of what it meant to be a factory worker. Thus, when workers examined how they were recruited into the industrial labor force and how they were paid once they were in the factories, crucial issues about economic independence and social identity often came to the fore. Some workers saw contracts and wage labor as their entrée into the emerging commercial cash-based economy as autonomous actors. Others saw contracts and wage labor as one of the most dangerous threats to whatever was left of the freedom and independence of the worker.

— I —

The basic requirements of recruiting a factory work force, both written and unwritten, shaped the lives of operatives, sometimes even before they entered the workplace. The process of recruiting factory workers was a combination of informal networks and official structures that framed the competing demands of employees and owners for control of the labor market.

Many factories had to recruit workers from a wide geographic area. Small rural manufactories, in particular, may have had trouble recruiting local workers to meet their modest needs because of their isolation and uncertain reputations. In the years preceding 1830, for example, only one-quarter of all the worker households at the Slater Company mills in Webster, Massachusetts, were from the local area. The majority of workers came from communities scattered throughout southern New England. The larger factories had greater personnel needs, which also often outstripped the local supply of workers. But because the reputations of the large factories were wider spread, they attracted potential workers in greater numbers from both near and far. In 1841, the agent of the Boott Mill in Lowell, Massachusetts, reported that his employees came from an average of seventy miles away. He also stated that less than nine percent of these workers had permanent homes in Lowell. At the Hamilton mills in the same city, nearly one-half of the operatives during the 1830s and 1840s came from the northern New England states.[1]

The precise means of recruiting new workers were numerous and varied. In many factories, families served as primary agents for labor recruitment. Some families rounded up their own members, and even outsiders, for work in the factories. In other places, an individual operative might help his relations find work. Charles Metcalf, working in Lowell in the spring of 1844, assured his parents that he would do his best to find a job in the mills for his sister Mary. There were no immediate prospects when Mary arrived, but Charles wrote that "she seems to be willing to go into the spinning room and do the best she can. I intend to encourage her and help her along as much as I can." Rebecca Ford, writing from a Middlebury, Vermont, woolen mill, was more specific about the assistance she would provide her sister Caroline. Rebecca, using her knowledge of the mill and the town, was able to secure a good job, a place to live, and a seat in church for her sister. Most operatives coming to a factory town without such assistance would probably not have secured so many advantages so quickly.

> Caroline sent word that she wanted to come I spoke to Mr. Flower about it he said might write to have her come as soon as I was amine to she can have her looms in the alley with me can board with at Mr. Stows a seat in Huldah Murray pew where I set I feeling quite anxious to have her come if she wont be home sick I want should count the cost think whether she will be contented or not our month is out a week from next thursday I think she had better come a week from wednesday so to begin the month if she is ready if not come when she is ready. . . .[2]

The network for recruiting new workers encompassed friends as well as family. When Mary Paul first arrived in Lowell in November of 1845, a friend helped her find work almost immediately. She wrote to her father: "On Saturday after I got here Luthera Griffith went round with me to find a place but we were unsuccessful. On Monday we started again and were more successful. We found a place in a spinning room and the next morning I went to work." Julia Dutton told her mother that she had secured a position in advance at the mill in Lancaster, Massachusetts, for one of her friends. "I have engaged a place for Martha Coffren the first of Nov. the overseers sayed she might come at that and if she is large enough for a weaver he will take her if not she can go into some other room there is no doubt but she will work a plenty."[3]

The process of looking for a factory job was not something confined to new arrivals. Experienced workers often sought new positions when they were dissatisfied or laid off from their previous jobs. And the friendships these veterans formed with each other affected their own patterns of labor recruitment. Sometimes a group of friends tried to move together from one factory to another, just as a group of newcomers from the same hometown might all try to find work in the same company. Albert Conant wrote to the Cheney Company about the prospects of hiring his sister and her companions for work in their silk mills.

I have seen my sister and have had a talk with her about going to Manchester [Connecticut] to work in the factory for you. She concluded or would go provided Susan Lyon would go with her. Miss Lyon has formerly work in Mr Atwood silk factory but left of late . . . those two Girls will come unless we heare to the contrary. . . . Miss Susan Lyon has a sister thinks some of coming . . . all those I have spoken of were called good hands. . . . My sister will give in her notice to Mr Atwood to day she will have two weeks more to work before she leaves.

Workers in other industries (for example, young women in the paper mills) also pursued job opportunities collectively in small groups of friends.[4]

Some workers had to rely only on their own initiative, and they took it upon themselves to write letters to factory owners, requesting employment. These letters were more often from experienced operatives than from people looking for their first factory job, and some of these individuals referred to the theme of family connections. Sarah Slater wrote to Samuel Slater requesting employment, and hoping that their common surname might work to her advantage. Although she had no firm family ties to rely on, Sarah Slater tried to play on the possibility of a shared ancestry to help her find a new job in March of 1818.

I am now residing here [in Union, Massachusetts] & till lately have found employment in the Cotton Factory in this town. It is not now in operation & therefore does not afford me further employment. My object in now writing to you is to obtain a place in your factory. I can produce recommendations from the managers of this Cotton Factory which will be satisfactory to you. I am acquainted with penciling calico & other branches of a factory. You would confer an obligation either by giving me employment in yours or by informing me if I could get encouragement in any neighboring factory. This section of the country does not now afford me the means of my subsistance. I am the daughter of Mark Slater of Keithler, England & I have now addressed with an impression that an application to one who bears the name of my father would be more likely to listen to my request.

Joseph France wrote a letter to Nathan Slater, Samuel's son, in late 1840, requesting employment. France's letter also touched on the theme of family; in this case, his long history of service to the Slaters' company. He pointed out that he "[b]egan to work for Almy and Brown and Slaters in 1810 and was in their Employ about 20 years." France also mentioned his own family of three sons, each skilled in some aspect of the textile trade.[5]

Some skilled workers sought new job opportunities, not out of necessity or desperation, but out of a desire to improve themselves. S. P. Bryant, an employee of the Eli Whitney armory, was one of the workers Samuel Colt tried to hire for his new gun factory in Hartford, Connecticut. Bryant responded to Colt's offer in September 1847 with some sharp questions of his own—he was secure enough in his current position to drive a hard bargain with Colt. Bryant was in no hurry to leave his job in Whitneyville, unless Colt could assure him that the new post would be more advantageous.

As you intimated a wish to Employ me, when I should be through here. I—take this method of asking you a few—questions first Should you employ me, how long must I wait for my pay, how much—will you give me per hour. (and as it—would not be worth while for me to move for three or four months work,) how long will

> you probably have work for me either by the piece or the hour. not that I wish to engage for any particular length of time. but because I wish to be certain of bettering my-self before I make any move, I have—and can work at all kinds of machinery or gun-work—that is well known to all who work—here. but it is all humbug for a person to tell what they have or can do the proof of a Pudding is in the eating of it. I have written this because I do not wish any one here to—know that I think of leaving until I am ready to be off.

Bryant's letter was more than a typical request for work or information about wages. It was a methodical inquiry into the potential for advancement in a new job, a very rational and forward-looking investigation.[6]

Many factory owners and agents also actively engaged in recruiting workers, instead of relying solely on operatives to come in search of employment. Small rural mills frequently advertised in newspapers to attract more employees. These advertisements were aimed usually at large families; they were intended to assure these families that there would be enough work for all of them, and to enable the factories to secure a substantial labor force. Large factories, especially those in industrial cities, rarely published such advertisements. They usually had less trouble attracting workers because they were better known, and they did not seek out large families. The textile-machine building shops in Saco, Maine, however, found it necessary to distribute handbills in an effort to recruit more skilled workers during a labor shortage in 1847. The superintendent of the shops even made a trip throughout the surrounding region as part of the recruiting drive. Other proprietors also traveled in search of workers for their establishments. Shubal Wilder, who had worked as a young man in a nail factory at Wareham, Massachusetts, in 1826, recalled more than fifty years later how new technologies led to a widespread search for experienced machine-tenders. He wrote: "From 1825 to 1835 there was a great increase in the number of nail machines and factories in New England . . . consequently there was a great demand for men to run nail machines. Almost all the time men kept coming to Massachusetts . . . on the hunt for nailers. . . ."[7]

Some companies used paid labor-recruiters to help supply their personnel needs. Some labor procurers maintained offices, others traveled around various circuits on behalf of one or more factories. These circuits often grew in geographic scope as the demand increased for workers in the developing industries. The cotton mills in Chicopee, Massachusetts, for example, drew most of their first operatives from nearby towns. Some were the daughters of armorers at the federal armory in Springfield, Massachusetts. Soon, however, the mills sent labor agents farther to the north and west, into Vermont and New Hampshire, in search of more young women for the expanding mills. The labor recruiter, often traveling in remote areas away from the early railroad lines, used a wagon to transport the new employees back to the company. He was also usually paid on a per capita basis. And some companies, when they paid for the transportation expenses, later deducted these costs from the newcomers' first paychecks. Some companies may have also realized that there were certain advantages to recruiting workers from long distances, advantages that could outweigh the added expense in searching out these new employees. For example, workers who came from far away could not return home so frequently on their modest earnings. Thus they were more likely to stay in the mills; the distance, in effect, thereby lessened turnover.[8]

Sarah Bagley, in her brief tenure as editor of the *Voice of Industry,* spoke out forcefully against the deceptive practices of some labor agents working for the Lowell mills. Her editorial of May 22, 1846, observed that "it is a notorious fact that the Corporations here have been in the habit of sending out agents to procure help ever since 1836." The first recruiting foray by the Middlesex Corporation took place in England, but most Lowell companies followed the commoner routes into northern New England. Bagley did not object to all such recruiting drives, but she was troubled with the false promises made by unscrupulous agents. Bagley then proceeded to detail some particularly unsavory recruiting practices.

One agent "went out and hired all that could count one, without respect to age or condition." He even hired one girl under the age of fifteen, without informing her or her parents that she could not work in the mills without violating Massachusetts laws regulating the education of factory children. Once in Lowell, he told the girl to lie about her age and say that she was sixteen so that she could get a job. The girl discovered, after five weeks' work, that she was earning only a fraction of what the agent had promised. A friend of hers was able to get the company to send her back home so as to avoid being fined for employing a child without the proper school certificates. In another instance, an agent provided five young women from Canada with just enough advance money to buy their ticket to Lowell and nothing more for food or lodging. When reporting such incidents, Bagley argued: "That the company is responsible for violation of the truth is quite evident, from the fact, that the same man is kept out, most of the time, and if they did not approve of his course, they most assuredly would not employ him."[9]

The image of the labor agent as a conniving man taking particular advantage of unsuspecting young women appeared frequently in operatives' publications. The aura of sexual exploitation was almost palpable in some accounts. Many workers saw the recruiter as a corrupt figure who quickly enmeshed workers in the further corruptions of the factory system. One contributor to the *Voice of Industry* warned "those girls who are now at home" not to be "cajoled to come here [Lowell] by the hirelings that go about the country, seeking to flatter them from their happy homes." In 1848, a group of Lowell operatives tried to urge prospective workers not to come to their city because the newcomers would be used to replace protesting employees. Their public appeal, in *The Protest,* warned people throughout New England not to let themselves be taken in by labor agents.

> It must at once be perceived that our success will be greatly impeded, if not wholly destroyed, so long as hired agents are travelling the country in all directions, and can by fair words and false promises decoy numbers from their peaceful homes—to fill their ranks soon to be made vacant by desertion.
>
> We would urge you therefore by the mutual interest of all concerned by your own self-respect—by the future interest of these who shall live after you, at present to remain by your paternal firesides, and continue deaf to the persuasions of those who are paid to deceive you . . . sturdy and independent yeomanry of the hills and valleys of New England, we would say to you, that when one of these liberally paid

> human jackalls intrudes himself among you, regard and treat him as an enemy to your community, with the merited contempt due to his office—an office which even corporate assurance would hardly dare offer an *honest* man.

Criticism of labor recruiters reached even into the pages of the *Lowell Offering.* Josephine Baker, in surveying working conditions in the mills, remarked that "the practice of sending agents through the country to decoy girls away from their homes with the promise of high wages, when the market is already stocked to overflowing . . . is certainly wrong, for it lessens the value of labor."[10]

Eliza Jane Cate, writing in the July 1849 issue of the *New England Offering,* disagreed with all these criticisms of the corporations' recruiting policies. She claimed that workers were not deceived or driven into factories, but were voluntarily drawn by their many advantages. "If the girls are lured from their homes," she argued, "it is of themselves, of their own anticipations of gain, for the sake of seeing new places, persons, and things, not of any corporation Circe or Siren that sings, and enchants, and draws them hither . . . it was good for them that they were taken into the immediate receipt of wages, without loss of time, without disheartening search for employment, when among strangers, and nearly destitute of funds." Cate's argument seemed to raise more questions than it answered. If she was right in asserting that young women decided for themselves to enter factory work, why did the Lowell corporations feel the need to continue employing labor recruiters? Part of the explanation may be that at the same time that Cate was writing this essay (at the end of the 1840s), the Lowell mills were actually finding that native-born women were becoming more reluctant to enter mills that were gradually filling up with Irish immigrants. Mill owners who accepted the foreign workers had fewer problems in recruiting and retaining these employees, who were desperate for jobs. Those owners who still wanted a wholly native-born work force found it necessary to continue sending labor recruiters farther into the countryside, despite Cate's claims about the supposed enthusiasm of New England girls for mill work.[11]

Many proprietors made serious efforts, not only to recruit workers, but to control the labor market as a whole. Owners, acting alone or in cooperation with each other, tried to ensure that operatives did not leave unexpectedly for other factories and that other companies did not suddenly hire away their employees. Factory owners frequently wrote to prospective employees about the importance of fulfilling their previous commitments before seeking new jobs. Samuel Plant, at the Poignand and Plant mill in Lancaster, Massachusetts, wrote to Moses Smith, who was inquiring about job prospects on behalf of three young women operatives from Chesterfield, Massachusetts: "We wish you to distinctly understand that we should not approve of these young persons coming to work for us except their engagements at Chesterfield are honorably fulfilled for we have [no intention] to give employment to any one who has not given satisfaction to the person they had last worked for." Oliver Dean, agent of the Amoskeag Manufacturing Company in Manchester, New Hampshire, sent a similar message to a young man seeking employment in the company's machine shop. Dean told this Mr. Fisher: "I wish to have it understood that I do not wish to hire anyone from Maj Mann unless it is perfectly agreeable to him."[12]

It is quite probable that not all owners and operatives were so scrupulous about honoring their employment commitments. Companies could try to entice workers away from other establishments, or workers could try to leave a job without giving any notice. Just as some manufacturers would hire only those who had completed previous commitments, however, other owners made sure that their employees fulfilled every day of their agreements before leaving to take any new job. Such strict adherence to the terms of employment may have been another attempt to control a fluid labor force, or it may have been a way for an owner to make life a little more difficult for an employee who decided to leave. John Nichol found his employer in Millbury, Massachusetts, to be inflexible about letting him assume a new position a few days early with the Merino/Dudley Woolen Company. Nichol wrote to his new employers on March 27, 1833, to explain his delay: "It has been my intention ever since I was engaged with you to have quit work at this place two or three days before the first of April so that I might be with you a day or two before that Mr. Chamberlane left you, and to accomplish this I have made several efforts without success. Mr. Sheperd seems quite unwilling to let me go a day before my time expires."[13]

William Hood encountered even more difficulties when he tried to move his whole family into new jobs at the Cheney brothers' silk mill. Hood told the Cheneys that his current employer would not let the entire family leave at the same time, and the expense of the move was becoming prohibitive.

> I have made application to Mr. Bradstreet our Superintendant respecting leaving his service but he does not seem very willing, but says, that if I and my Son can better ourselves he will not hinder us from doing so when the Quarter is expired and says that my Daughter must stay out her month, likewise another of the Girls which I have spoken to about coming must stay out the month—as for myself and the rest of my Family we would wish to come to Manchester the 1st of January if it is so convenient to you and *if I possibly can* bring the Girls with me I will so that it entirely remains with you Gentlemen whether we come or not as I shall not be able to move from here without your assistance not having the means myself at present—what expenses more that you are willing to allow me I will pay from my wages. . . .[14]

Owners often backed up their claims on workers with written contracts. These legal contracts were one of the commonest devices used for controlling the labor market and assimilating workers into the factory system. The earliest fully mechanized factory, the Boston Manufacturing Company in Waltham, Massachusetts, required workers to sign contracts pledging their labor for one or two years. Some two-year contracts provided wage increases and bonuses for those who stayed their full term. Thus the company seemed to acknowledge that contracts alone would not always bind operatives to their legal length of service; some additional incentive was needed. Most manufacturers followed in the Boston Manufacturing Company's footsteps and developed their own system of contracts.[15]

Some skilled immigrant workers, brought to New England at great expense, were told to sign long-term contracts. The Scovill Company, for example, was anxious to retain its English brass-workers for as long as possible once they arrived in Connecticut. It negotiated five- and six-year contracts that gave both parties the advantages of long-term employment—the company would not quickly lose the services of an experienced worker, and the worker could not be readily turned out in the event of a business slowdown. The Scovills, however, realized that these long-term contracts sometimes forced them to keep employees on the payroll when there was no work to do. They wanted to redraft the agreements so that they would be binding on workers, but leave the company some way out. Workers, of course, were very reluctant to sign such lopsided contracts. They demanded job security in return for making multiyear commitments. Other immigrants were placed in a somewhat less advantageous position because they were in debt to their employers for their overseas passage. Many cutlery workers from England and Germany made implicit agreements with American companies to work until they had paid off their travel advances. While there was usually no formal indenture, employers saw to it that workers paid off their debts through service. Any cutlery worker leaving before his debt was paid would have trouble collecting any other back wages or finding new work.[16]

Most factory operatives did not have valuable skills to use as bargaining chips. Therefore, the contracts they signed usually gave the owners a tremendous amount of legal power and authority over the workplace. The Slater companies were even able to insert an escape clause in many of their agreements; something many other owners, such as the Scovills, sought in vain. This provision stipulated that the Slaters reserved "to themselves the right of stopping their mill and discontinuing the contract if anything should occur which may cause manufacturing to become a loosing business in which case the said [operative] agrees to relinquish the contract without claim for damage." The Slaters thus claimed the right, not only to dictate the terms of their contracts, but to abrogate those agreements unilaterally without fear of any legal repercussions. These contracts were expected to be binding on workers, but in effect only at the pleasure of the owners. In one agreement, with a mule spinner, the company did modify this clause to provide "that if either of the parties becomes dissatisfied with this agreement & wish to relinquish the same thay are to give 4 weeks notice of their intentions to do so." This provision was exceptional, however, and again reflected the power of such skilled workers to negotiate terms of employment far more favorable than the average operative could command.[17]

When a factory owner chose to exercise his power and rescind a job offer under contract, the result could mean disaster for the suddenly displaced worker. One family, promised jobs at one of the Slater mills, gave proper notice to their current employer and prepared to take on their new positions. When the offer was then withdrawn, the family found themselves in an untenable position—they had already been replaced by their previous employer and they had nowhere else to go. Their former employer was so troubled by the situation that he took it upon himself to write to the Slater Company hoping to clear up any misunderstandings that may have caused the offer to be canceled.

> [I]n consequence of Mrs. Olive Lamphere informing us you had hired her family for the year insuing we immediately engaged another family to supply their place and your note since received . . . informing them you did not want them, has caused

them considerable trouble as they will be out of employ the 1*st* April in consequence of that contract they supposed they had made with you. Our opperator of the Factory where they reside informs us they are good help; & he does not know nor has not heard of any improper conduct. Supposing you might be misinformed respecting them; we have took the liberty to trouble you; knowing you would render them such encouragement as they had reason to expect from you.[18]

Samuel Dunster was one worker who took matters into his own hands and tried to hold the Cocheco Manufacturing Company in Dover, New Hampshire, responsible for breaching its own contract. He was dismissed from the company's print works in October 1829 to make way for the return of immigrant printers. Dunster recalled:

> The Agent then was James F. Curtis, a retired naval officer, and a very austeer and domineering man. I had a contract with the company to work a certain number of years. Mr. Curtis smashed that scrap of paper, to let in some English printers, who said they would not work with Americans. By the application of a little "legal suasion", through my friend James Bartlett, Esq., the agent paid my whole claim, then turning to the book-keeper said "charge that to the Print Works' general expense account;" then turning to me he said: "Mr. Dunster," (he never called me "Mr." before that) "I thank you for the calm and candid way in which you have managed this matter . . . and now if a word of recommendation from me will be of any use to you, it is cheerfully at your disposal."

Dunster's successful challenge of management's power to unilaterally break a contract, and his ability to collect his whole pecuniary claim, was probably an exception to the rule in antebellum New England. Most workers did not have Dunster's ready access to legal advice, so they were at a distinct disadvantage in questioning the contractual authority of their employers.[19]

Most cases of breach of contract involved operatives who were accused of leaving their jobs before their contractual obligations had been fulfilled. The Collins Axe Company in Collinsville, Connecticut, was another firm that tried to sign multiyear contracts with its employees. The company claimed that it took a long time to properly train competent axemakers, so the firm needed to recoup its investment in human capital over an extended period of time (usually three to five years). Samuel Collins argued that "the trouble with them [the axemakers] arose after they got to be good workmen and could get higher wages elsewhere. Some run off. . . ." In a letter of August 27, 1830, Collins spelled out some of the particular problems with individual workers, and the strong measures he proposed to deal with such wayward employees.

> Marvin Gages has applied for a discharge, says Hunts of Douglass has offered him $600 per year and the privilege of forging axes c. 1/- each—This is a kind of game that is likely to make us a great deal of trouble. Cornwall stays away unaccountably, he went home convalescent, and I have strong suspicions that he is off. M Gages got leave of absence for a fortnight before he applied for a discharge. I assured him that I wd. prosecute him for damage as long as he lived if he broke his contract & he said he should not think of leaving unless we agreed to it, sd. I had found much fault with his work & thot I might be willing to part with him. I told I shd. continue to find fault unless his work is done well.

Eli Whitney was another manufacturer who did more than make threats about suing workers for breach of contract. In late December 1817, he informed another armory owner, Nathan Starr, that he had served legal papers on a Whitney armory employee, Benjamin Smith, who was already en route to Starr's factory in Middletown, Connecticut. Whitney also indicated that he would hold Starr liable for additional damages if Starr proceeded to employ Smith.[20]

Some factories combined their contracts with a schedule of delayed wage payments to increase their control over a footloose working population. The Collins Company's "terms with workmen" for 1834 stipulated that wages would be paid only after three months on the job. If an employee left before he had worked three months, he still had to wait those three months before he could claim whatever was owed to him. In 1835, another revised system of wage payments was introduced. Workers were still paid after three months' labor, but the company retained twenty dollars from their wages until they earned an equivalent amount in the second three-month pay period. The previously owed twenty dollars was then paid out, while the company kept its advantage over the workers' present earnings by maintaining this delayed payment schedule. All accounts were settled at the end of the contract, but any worker leaving before his contract expired forfeited the twenty dollars, which the company retained in its ledgers. Only one set of agreements, signed in 1836 with men skilled in the craft of tempering axes, specified that these workers were to receive their full pay each quarter. All other employees, no matter what their abilities, had a portion of their wages held on account by the company.[21]

The Slater companies used one-year contracts, which usually ran from April to the end of the next March, and often stipulated that final settlements would be made only at the end of the contracts. Some contracts allowed for partial payments or expenses during the work year, but all final accountings were timed to coincide in the spring so that the whole process of labor turnover could be regulated. The owners wanted the workers to change jobs no more than once a year, and even then at a predictable season each year. Neither employers nor employees, however, consistently upheld their contracts and wage schedules. But the concept of wage labor did become embedded in the mechanized factory system. Of course, wage labor was not unique to these factories; yet many new operatives held their first full-time wage-paying jobs in these mechanized industries.[22]

— II —

Wages quickly became a major focus of attention, and contention, in many factories. Workers and managers constantly argued over every part of the wage system: would payment be in kind or in cash? would wages be set by the day or the piece? when and how often would wages be paid? how much bargaining power would workers have in the wage agreements? who would decide if wages were to be cut or raised? and what exactly did it mean to earn a wage in a factory? Essentially, workers and managers were battling to determine how much was a day's work worth in jobs that had never been done before. And what did the money earned through industrial wages represent—was it payment for labor time or labor power or the finished product?[23]

To begin with, in some antebellum factories, the term "wage labor" was somewhat of a misnomer because workers rarely received cash payments. Their earnings were often kept for months as credits in the company's financial records. Many clock manufacturers used a system of allowing their employees to run accounts with local merchants, and then settling these debts with clocks for the merchants to subsequently sell. The workers' wages were thus paid in goods; their rent was also deducted, and if any balance remained it could usually be met with a small cash payment. Some clock manufacturers also paid their workers directly with food or furniture from their own resources. When cash and credit became exceedingly scarce in the depression of the early 1840s, clock factory employees began to take more clocks as direct payment because merchants would still accept these tangible assets as a form of money. The employees of the Scovill Brass Company, including the most demanding immigrant experts, were also often paid in orders for food, clothing, or furniture at the company store. The company tried the idea of paying cash wages in the late 1820s, but the hard times at the end of the next decade forced the abandonment of this scheme.[24]

Hannah Borden, when she was forced to keep her wages on account with the Yellow Mill in Fall River, revolted against this practice. Each month, when payday arrived, Borden always found that she was in debt to the company store. When her charges became suspiciously large, she asked to see the account books, and the clerks refused. The manager eventually allowed her to review her charges, and she discovered that she was billed for many purchases she never made. After her first inspection, Borden checked the books every month, even though the clerks complained that she should not have such a privilege if other workers did not have it. It is not known how prevalent such abuses of company accounts and nonwage payments were. But Borden did not care if other workers allowed themselves to be fleeced by false charges that might eat up more than their monthly wages—she would not tolerate being cheated any longer. Finally she grew tired of keeping an eye on the store (so to speak), and she asked for cash wages from the manager. He dismissed her request by complaining: "Why if I give it to you all the rest of 'em will want money and I can't stand that. It would ruin me." Borden, by then an experienced weaver, responded to his refusal by threatening to quit. The manager then agreed to her demand for ten dollars, on the condition that she tell no one else about her arrangement. Borden was thus able to obtain cash wages for herself, but she did not change the company's general policy of paying on account. And this policy of not paying cash wages continued in smaller textile mills for years to come.[25]

Another basic question concerning the wage system was whether workers' earnings would be calculated by a daily rate or by a piece rate. Piecework began as early as 1806 at the Springfield Armory, and was linked to both the division of labor and the introduction of machinery. In 1818, the armory's wage structure was revised to give more emphasis to piece-rate payments as managers more carefully calculated how much to pay for each identical unit produced by the increasing number of machine-tenders. The following year James Dalliba reported that most armory workers, each making a discrete part of a gun, were paid by the piece.[26]

The Collins Company paid its axemakers by both the piece and the day, depending on their particular task. Samuel Collins observed in 1830 that this practice led to friction between the workers paid a daily wage and those paid for each individual piece of work. He wrote on August 12, 1830:

> these $1 a day men do not accomplish as much work as our piece workmen and yet get as much or more wages, which makes others dissatisfied—If I did not fear competition I shd. discharge Marble Brainerd and Spencer—these men tell the others that they work too hard, that we do not give enough by the piece. . . . If I was rid of all my dollar per day men I never wd. have another unless he earnt it by the piece—indeed I think I shall never renew with Brainerd or Spencer unless it is at our own piece prices. . . .

Collins was bothered by day-rate workers' telling the other employees paid by the piece that they were working too hard for too little money. In effect, "the $1 a day men" were stirring up both jealousy and discontent among the pieceworkers by the simple fact that those paid a daily wage were not forced to work any harder to keep earning that dollar a day. Collins was determined to eliminate this friction by putting everyone on piece rates, so that a worker could earn a dollar a day only at the set rates per axe. And that rate, in turn, could be lowered if the company wanted to pressure workers into producing more, simply to maintain their current earnings.[27]

Other skilled workers, such as machinists, were also often paid with a combination of day and piece rates. Here again, sometimes the mixture was shifted to mostly piece rates. In the machinists' case, this was an effort to break the autonomy of skilled workers and get more output from them. Highly trained brass-workers were put on a system of payment by the pound so they would teach apprentices, yield some of their monopoly on technical knowledge, and make more brass. Horace Hotchkiss observed the same process of using piece rates to dilute the skill and power of wire-drawers.

> Our orders increased faster than our men were able or willing to execute them, but they would not allow anyone to be employed who had not served seven years apprenticeship, and of course, no such men were to be found. This difficulty was overcome by contracting with them to do the work by the pound, they employing men of their own selection. In time, these assistants equalled in skill our first workmen, and placed us beyond the necessity of submitting to dictation.[28]

The form of wage rates—either by the day or the piece—was also known to change over time in the textile industry as more machinery was introduced and workers became more proficient at tending these machines. The first weavers in Fall River, Massachusetts, for example, were paid by the week because they were mastering slow and clumsy looms that never produced enough cloth for them to make a living wage by the piece. When the looms were adapted to run more swiftly and reliably and the weavers became experienced enough to tend two looms, they began to be paid by the yard.[29]

Some operatives favored the introduction of piece rates. Samuel Moores, an operative looking back at almost fifty years' experience in English and American mills, recalled in testimony before the Massachusetts Bureau of Statistics of Labor: "Years ago, spinners preferred to work by the job, because they imagined that they escaped tyrannical driving." Some workers believed that piece rates gave them more freedom to set their own pace and more control over their total earnings.[30]

Other operatives felt pressured by the fact that their livelihood depended on their total output and not on the hours they worked. Piece rates were sometimes said to bring out competitiveness between individual workers, thus increasing the pressure, antagonism and fragmentation among operatives. In the Lowell mills, for example, the weekly output of each operative in every room was posted on a board for everyone in that room to see. The reason for this public posting, according to the corporations, was for workers to know in advance how much they would earn and to have the opportunity to appeal any questionable figures. But such public tallies also could have triggered competitiveness and resentment between operatives of varying strengths and talents.[31]

There was also a disturbing sense of uncertainty with piece rates. There was no concept of an assured or even a constantly predictable wage. Workers, upon entering a factory running on a piece-rate system, had to learn what the wage rates were, what they could expect to produce by themselves, and then try to estimate their total earnings. Operatives on piece rates often found themselves working harder and faster than they ever would on a day rate. Piece rates often did more to discipline and push a work force than any single machine or regulation. One textile mill worker expressed his dissatisfaction with piece rates in no uncertain terms. Emanuel Corey declared bluntly: "Mr. John Bacon Commander of the Pachog factory you are here notifyed that I shall not work but three weeks longer by the yeard. and if we then cannot agree we will settle and trouble each other no more."[32]

Even if a factory agreed to pay wages in cash rather than in kind or on credit, and even if wage rates were clearly established, workers encountered still other problems with the wage labor system. Promises of cash payments, for example, were often left unfulfilled because of chronic shortages of cash in the antebellum industrial economy. The Springfield Armory, being a government establishment, was especially susceptible to problems resulting from delays in appropriations from Washington. As early as January 1816, Superintendent Roswell Lee reported:

> Our workmen have almost seven months pay due. Many of them have large families to support and no other way but their daily labor, to obtain the means to carry them through this inclement season. Many of them have been compelled to sell their orders [probably some form of promissory note issued by the armory] at a discount of from six to 20%. By making this sacrifice they have sustained themselves and families to present time, with expectations that funds would soon arrive to pay their orders. The holders of them being disappointed in this: Orders will now hardly sell at any price. The armorers cannot subsist in this way, many of them must abandon the works and seek relief from their respective towns or find employment elsewhere for the purpose of obtaining immediate support.

Wage payments were so overdue that merchants stopped extending credit and refused to buy promissory notes. The armorers who were determined to remain sent a petition to Washington, which Lee vigorously endorsed. Lee also sold off arms and supplies as quickly as possible to raise the desperately needed cash for wages.[33]

Delayed payment from employers was not confined to government armories. The Slater mills, which tried to synchronize contract settlements around April 1 to regulate their labor force, sometimes found that they did not have the requisite cash on hand to hold up their end of all those simultaneous bargains. In 1839, the company delayed annual settlements for over six weeks. Charles Waite, agent for the Phoenix Thread Mill, warned: "Delay in paying off the help beyond the time it is due engenders a bad state of feeling. They think it is done by their employers to save interest." What might have particularly annoyed some workers was the fact that if they ran short of cash during the year, they often had to pay interest on any advance. But any company that witheld payment was, in effect, getting an advance from all of its employees without paying any interest.[34]

During the depression of the late 1830s, the clock manufacturer Eli Terry, Jr., also had trouble settling his annual accounts with workers. Terry realized that the whole complex web of credit between manufacturers, merchants, and workers was in grave danger when there was no possibility of paying off debts. In the early spring of 1838, Terry wrote to one of his chief peddlers to impress upon this salesman the need to send all available cash as quickly as possible. Terry explained his situation bluntly: "We are in debt to our workmen and they have got in debt to others for provisions & the necessities of life, & they must be paid or they cannot work, we have put them off as long as it will do & now they must be paid. They cannot get trusted unless they pay up once in about a year, & the time has come." Terry's employees, without some eventual cash settlement, would find themselves absolutely destitute, with no money and no further credit.[35]

Some workers not only encountered difficulties in getting their pay, they also quickly discovered that their freedom of movement was severely restricted because of their shortage of funds. Seth Luther reported that some companies delayed two weeks in paying off any worker who quit or was discharged. This delay often locked the worker into the factory system she was trying to leave, or forced her to return and apologize for her breach of the rules. Luther explained: "if she has two or three dollars due, and is 100 or more miles from home, she must wait on that MAMMOTH COMPANY a fortnight for her pay; by this time, she is in debt for her board, and she must either go to the agent, and *humbly* ask him to give her employment, or starve."[36]

Some factories did not even make an effort to settle with certain workers, but resorted to various forms of subterfuge in avoiding payment. Joseph Hollingworth wrote a letter to his uncle, William Rawcliff, describing how one company refused to pay for his first weeks at work, under the pretext that he was learning a new trade.

> [W]hen I come to Southbriggde at first there was no work for me at my old business, so Mr Sayles set me to work with my Father at the warping macheen. I worked 5 weeks when I thought it time to ask what wages I should have. The reply was NOTHING! that having the chance to learn a fresh trade was thought a Just compensation for my verry valuable services. The result of which was, that I got into a Jackass fit. Father then took the warping and spooling by the Job. He and Edwin worked at spooling and I at warping untill I got weary of the work. I then came here to work, when Mr Sayles sent for me back, as he wished to hire me to work in the fulling Room for a few days. I went back and worked 21 days for 12 dollars. And finally I came here again, And am going to do the Napping, Shearing and pressing, when the work is ready.

Hollingworth's anger at the Southbridge mill manager, Mr. Sayles, was rather short-lived; for despite his outrage at being cheated out of wages he thought were due to him, the letter also indicates that Joseph returned at Mr. Sayles' request to take another paying job.[37]

There were a few instances where workers were not so willing to forget past injustices; instead, they took legal action to recover their back wages. In 1833, Eber Eager sued Samuel Plant in the Worcester Court of Common Pleas "for not paying him the balance of his account against you." An operative in Lowell was bolder in her demands. She went to a local lawyer—Benjamin Butler, who later earned fame as a Union general and United States senator—and demanded that he "attach the great wheel and stop the mill." The woman was indignant because she had worked for the same corporation for five years, and they refused to settle her wages when she wanted to leave. The corporation said that their policy was to wait until the next payday to close her account. Butler admitted in his autobiography that he took no such dramatic legal action. He merely used his friendly relations with many of the local mill managers to informally arrange for himself to advance the woman her wages due, and for the mill to then reimburse him at payday. The operative—"a snappy-eyed old maid from Vermont" according to Butler—always believed that Butler had followed her instructions, and the legend grew about the courageous young lawyer taking on the corporations. Butler himself gained great political mileage out of such apocryphal stories. This incident also revealed how some workers refused to admit that the mills controlled their wages. This woman saw her earnings as something due to her upon her demand. She believed that she had a right to take on the entire corporation and shut down its operations to obtain her individual wages.[38]

Given all these problems in determining and collecting their wages, it is not surprising that workers looked at paydays (when cash was available) as a time of much-deserved reckoning and celebration. Some companies kept such paydays, and therefore such celebrations, to a bare minimum. The Chicopee Manufacturing Company, up until 1836, paid its workers only twice a year. But the workers compensated by treating these two paydays like real holidays. The Slater companies also had their policy of annual settlements on their contracts. Yet some individual mills within the company, by around 1830, started to have quarterly, monthly, or even bimonthly paydays. Other companies also eventually began to yield to their operatives' demands for more regular paydays.[39]

Some factories even advertised the fact that they paid wages promptly and in cash, as a way to make themselves look more attractive to prospective employees. Particularly in times of depression or a shortage of specie, a company that could continue to pay its employees regularly with an increasingly scarce and valuable supply of cash would be seen as an advantageous place to work.[40]

As for the large textile corporations, most of the mills in Lowell and Manchester had a policy of paying their workers once every month (far different from the mills in Chicopee, which supposedly patterned themselves after the Lowell companies), and always in cash. Yet, in Lowell, practice did not always precisely follow policy—there were sometimes delays of a week or more in the monthly pay cycle. Needless to say, paydays there were also greeted with great joy when there was cash paid out.

One contributor to the *Lowell Offering* wrote that "pay-days are the landmarks which cheer all hearts." Another story in the *Offering,* entitled "Evening Before Pay-Day," captured the sense of anticipation and high spirits as workers waited for the proceeds of their labor. One piece of dialogue conveyed how even management could take on a positive glow during that day.

> "Well, Lizzy, you know that 'tomorrow is pay-day,' do you not?"
>
> "Oh yes, and the beautiful pay-master will come in, rattling his coppers so nicely."
>
> "Beautiful!" exclaimed Lucy; "do you call our pay-master *beautiful?*"
>
> "Why, I do not know that he would look beautiful, if he was coming to cut my head off; but really, that money-box makes him look delightfully."
>
> "Well, Lizzy, it *does* make a great difference in his appearance, I know. . . ."[41]

The manager of a mill in Ware, Massachusetts, however, tried to resist the practice of settling his payroll accounts frequently with his employees. As late as 1842, he wrote:

> We find that most, if not all, of your neighboring manufacturers pay but quarterly, and if you once commence paying monthly you will be obliged to continue to do so, as you cannot alter back, and quarterly payments seem to us reasonable and often enough. We supposed when we altered from half yearly to three months that it would have been satisfactory to the operatives and if they now require monthly payments they will soon want weekly, and on the whole we all think you had better continue to make up your payroll and pay off your operatives once a quarter.[42]

Even after payday, some workers—particularly those who lived and worked with their families—could find that the battle over wages was not over. Members of the same family could be put in extremely tense situations when it came to managing their factory wages. Another letter from Joseph Hollingworth to his uncle William Rawcliff captured some of the competing claims of a young man and his family on his earnings. In this case, the family took some of Joseph's overtime wages to add to the household budget. The entire family worked in the factory and contributed to their collective support, but Joseph felt that he was being overtaxed.

> Last winter, I had to work a good deal of overtime at Nights; . . . so I calculated to have my overtime wages for myself. It amounted to nearly five Dollars. I have succeeded in getting 2 dolrs. ONLY! which is all the pocket money I have had in the country! . . . Nor can I bear all their frumps and scornings, to be called a selfish Devil when I asked for the money which I earned while they sleeped in their beds. . . .

Such a tense situation, when individuals tried to assert some control over their wages in the face of family obligations, was exacerbated when companies utilizing family labor stopped paying all wages to the head of the household.[43]

This family-wage policy was abandoned at many companies by the 1840s. The Slater mills actually first began to pay wages directly to each worker in 1836; but many parents complained, and the old system of the head of household's collecting all wages was reinstated. By 1845, however, the new policy of each worker's receiving his or her own wages was firmly in place. Children thereby gained a foundation for their own economic independence and the power to dispose of their own earnings. Fathers, in turn, had to negotiate constantly with their children over the distribution of these wages if any of that income was to be kept in the family economy. Over time, more young people probably came to share some of Joseph Hollingworth's complaints. Families could be seen as another potential source of coercion and control—economically and socially: they became adjuncts to the power of management rather than a refuge from and a bulwark against such authority.[44]

— III —

The most important question about the wage labor system—beyond the form and rate of payment, the timing of the payment, or the collector of the payment—was, quite simply, the bottom line. The amount inside the envelope on payday was still the bone of most contention in the wage system. The basic problem of the wage system, above any other consideration, was that operatives were selling their labor to someone else for money; and the factory owner who bought the workers' labor had the power to meddle with the wage system whenever he wanted to. Working for yourself was certainly no guarantee of steady earnings in antebellum New England. But the self-employed artisan, while not divorced from the cash economy, controlled his own wage standards within the confines of what the trade and the market would bear.

Male workers may have been particularly troubled by the factory wage system because it undermined the traditional masculine realm of the independent craftsman. Factory wages may have looked attractive to some women who had few other opportunities for wage-earning labor, but many men saw these wages as distinctly lower than the earnings of tradesmen and mechanics. For other men, it was not merely the lower wages themselves that were troubling. The very idea of being an industrial wage-worker—no matter what the pay—may have struck them as being an inherently inferior prospect. Working for someone else, someone who set your wages, smacked of dependency and emasculation.[45]

The Springfield armorers were one group of relatively skilled male factory workers engaged in a constant struggle over their wages. As early as 1819, when mechanization was first beginning to transform the skill and power of these men, the armorers faced a series of wage cuts. The armorers saw that, as employees of a government installation, they were subject to federal, military, and managerial power over their wages. James Dalliba reported that "[t]he prices paid to the workmen, on the whole, are not high. 'The times are hard,' and the wages of mechanics are now generally high in every part of the Northern States. . . . So that by comparison, considering the mechanics at Springfield are generally first rate workmen and respectable citizens, the prices now given appear to be rather under those ordinarily paid to mechanics in this part of the United States."[46]

In 1820, Superintendent Lee made the wage situation even more precarious by ordering a twenty-five percent wage cut because he saw prices falling nationwide. He wrote to the armorers: "The great reduction which has already taken place in the necessaries of life, occasioned by a diminution of the circulating Medium requires some Reduction in the wages of the workmen at the National Armories. The fact is, that a Dollar purchases as much as a Dollar and a half was two or three years ago; And the prices of everything, labor among the rest, must be accommodated to the actual state of the Currency."[47]

Within two years, however, the armorers became increasingly aware of how low their wages actually were in relation to other comparably skilled workers. They began to look to other industries—especially the growing textile machinery trade—for more lucrative employment. After enduring a series of wage reductions, the armorers showed a real sense of their power and determination to try to get some control over their own wages. Superintendent Lee was torn between keeping labor costs down and raising wages above the competition. He was finally pressed by "circumstances" to recommend a wage increase in 1822.

> I find the rage for manufacturing cotton prevails to such a degree and there is so great a call for first rate workmen, that I am apprehensive I shall lose some of our most valuable workmen except I am authorized to raise their wages according to circumstances. . . . They are sending for our machinists from Rhode Island and other places, and I have a few choice hands that are of great service to the establishment and such as I should be very sorry to part with, I am sure they cannot be retained without more wages; the additional pay will probably cost the government 250 or 300 dollars a year, but I believe this course will be the means of saving as many thousand.[48]

Nearly two decades later, in 1841, a government investigator came to the startling conclusion that as the armory became more mechanized, the workers' power to control their wages seemed stronger than ever. This report provided a detailed account of the constant pressure workers still exerted to raise their wages. G. Talcott stated that the armorers were virtually dictating their own prices. Management seemed to be yielding constantly to the workers' demands for higher wages.

> What would be the fate of a *private* manufactory where the operatives were allowed to fix their own wages and privileges? Yet this has been the case, in substance, at Springfield. I am the last man in the world who would take from an honest, industrious mechanic one mill of his just dues. I would endeavor to sustain him, by steady employment at fair wages, and act impartially between him and the Government. With the best disposition toward the operatives at this place, I cannot shut my eyes to what is passing before them. . . . The fact is they earn all the money they want, or all that they dare suffer to appear on the payroll, by working only a moderate portion of each day. . . . A change in the form or models of parts affords a favorable opportunity for the operatives to press an increase of their wages. The late change of model has been thus used to some extent. There are likewise periods in the general business of the country when labor and provisions advance in price. Such times are always seized on to increase their wages. When a revulsion takes place and prices elsewhere sink to their former level, it is no easy matter to reduce the wages of armorers. We have witnessed this state of things several times during the last twenty-five years. . . . The natural progress of things has brought the armory to its present condition, which consists in its having a superabundance of operatives who receive much higher wages than mechanics of equal or greater skill at private establishments.

A board of inquiry looking into the armory at the same time was also troubled by the wage system there.

> In looking into the prices of labor, the board became satisfied that the workmen on the different parts of the musket are very unequally paid. This results, in part, from the introduction of very expensive and perfect machinery, partly from the change in the model of the musket, partly from an undue control which the workmen have exercised in the establishment of prices, and partly from the unfaithfulness of some of the inspectors. . . . The last change [in wage rates] appears to have been made during the past winter, on the authority of the superintendent. It is understood to have been made at the suggestion of the workmen, and it is believed that the prices were mainly fixed by them. It was done in the absence of the master armorer, and without his concurrence or knowledge. Prices thus established would be likely to be exorbitant, and, when the present cost of the musket is compared with that of previous years, they are proved to be so.

These reports may have been issued before the severe wage reductions in 1841, and these investigators may have overstated the control that workers exercised over their piece rates. But the wage system at the Springfield Armory was a constant battle of wills between management and a work force trying to retain its leverage to set higher wages. If the management refused to grant an increase in wage rates, the armorers still had an ace in the hole. They could increase their output just enough to maintain their standard of living without overexerting themselves or encouraging managers to reduce piece rates still further.[49]

The axemakers at the Collins Company discovered that what they thought of as their power to set wage rates could be used against them when the company tried to confine that power within the factory wage system. Samuel Collins posted a notice in January 1843 that announced that workers would have to compete with one another in setting the price of certain labor. The company had

> frequent applications for work, and some offers to work for *less* than we now pay, we have concluded to receive proposals for forging bits of Axes and also for hammering off the heads for the year ensuing—As we are not willing to contract for a larger quantity than we are now making, those who are now at work will do well to put in proposals unless they are willing to lose their places.

Collins gave the initiative for setting wage rates back to the workers, but his decision was hardly a victory for workers' control. He knew that the labor market was still glutted with unemployed workers during that time of economic depression, and that these operatives would fight to underbid each other and secure any available job. Collins was now less interested in securing workers over the long term with favorable wages; he wanted short-term wage agreements that would be free to fluctuate with rates on the open market.[50]

Workers in other industries also tried, with varying degrees of success, to discuss their wages with management. Those with the most bargaining power tended to be the most skilled or experienced. In the textile mills of Waltham and Lowell, the male employees often bargained individually for their wages with reference to the locally accepted wage for their trade. The women industrial workers, however, could not refer to such wage standards, for they were frequently newcomers to the world of full-time work. Manufacturers took the lead in setting wages that were high enough to entice women away from the farm or teaching or domestic service, but low enough to preserve the advantage of hiring women.[51]

Some male workers took notice of these lower wages paid to women; not so much out of a sense of social justice as from a fear that their own wages were declining to the level of those paid for women's work. One carpet weaver from Thompsonville, Connecticut, wrote about the coming of the Bigelow power looms in 1846 and their impact on the skilled men's work and wages. The machine, the presence of women in the workplace, and deterioration of earnings all seemed to be linked in this man's mind. Once the new looms were installed, this weaver warned, "if we are allowed to work with them at all, we shall have to work at very low wages, probably at the same rate as girls." The mechanized carpet mill would put men and women in competition for jobs; and the women, who were accustomed to working for lower wages, would undermine the men's wage scale. It is not certain whether this man resented or felt threatened by the arrival of women weavers, or saw both male and female workers' being set against each other by management.[52]

It was the female mill workers, however, who usually voiced the most vehement criticism (as they often did) of what they saw as their own meager and declining wages. The threat of wage cuts was decried by operatives throughout antebellum New England. Maria Grout, working in Three Rivers, Massachusetts, wrote about the demoralizing effect of lower wages: "I am not to work in the factory now. The wages have been reduced more than twenty five sents on a hundred. Poor encouragement to work. Cannot tell whether I shall go on here to work again or not. . . ." Workers were often especially disturbed by what they saw as a trend toward lower wages in spite of higher corporate profits. Although real wages adjusted for the cost of living and corporate dividends both fluctuated during the 1830s and 1840s, many workers believed that their earnings were being undermined to subsidize corporate profits. This perception of the inequities of the wage-labor system, regardless of the actual wage rates, underlay much of the workers' criticism and concern about their earnings.[53]

Operatives in Lowell may not have been aware of long-term trends or regional averages for the textile industry, but many of them were convinced that their wages were being cut during a prosperous time for the corporations in the 1840s. Managers were obsessed with maintaining high dividends, and the easiest place to cut costs was in the labor column, so there was increased pressure to drive wages down. One Lowell factory operative wrote to a Fall River labor newspaper in the summer of 1842 and vented her rage at the inequities she saw in the continuing wage cuts.

> The pay of the operatives in Lowell factories has been considerably reduced, for the reason, as declared, that the depression of trade is so great and the sale of goods consequently so limited, *they are running them at a loss!* If this be a fact, (though nobody believes it,) why do they not cut down the fat salaries of their Agents, who roll about this city in their carriages, living at ease in fine houses, with servants of both sexes to do their bidding? But this is never done. The poor *laborers* must bear all the *burthens.* If there are any losses to be sustained, or any diminution of profits likely to affect the *dividends,* the difference must always be made up by the hard working female operatives, who are occasionally very *pathetically* told that the factories are only kept running at all from motive of *pure charity towards them.* Let

> us see a little more equality—a little more sincerity in this matter, and then perhaps we may have a little more charity.[54]

One year later, a group of Lowell workers sent a petition to the Massachusetts legislature that also criticized wage cuts and asked for more equitable treatment. The authors of this petition acknowledged wage labor to be part of their legal contracts, but they wanted all the parties to be equally responsible to those contracts. They defined wage cuts as a violation of their contracts, since they had agreed to work only for certain piece rates; and they felt entitled to abrogate their contracts in response to management's violations. The Lowell mills did not concur with the idea that a wage cut dissolved the existing contract. These mills tried to hold their employees to their agreements, and the aggrieved women appealed to the government for protection.

> Not being able to contend against our rich persecutors by bringing a suit at law for satisfaction, we are compelled to seek redress, or protection, from the powers which created said Company.
>
> The Regulations Paper . . . reads as follows. "All persons entering into the employment of this Company are considered as engaged for twelve months, and those who leave sooner will not receive a regular discharge." We did not imply by agreeing to this, that our wages were to be subject to any reduction which the Company might see fit to make; and when they gave us official notice that they were going to cut our wages down about Twenty Five per cent, we considered it a violation of the agreement which existed between us, and therefore did not feel bound by an agreement which they had a right to break; for if they could reduce our wages Twenty-five per cent, why not Fifty and still hold us to work twelve months![55]

In the same year, 1843, even the *Lowell Offering* editorialized "that Lowell girls will not work for wages much lower than they are at present." Josephine Baker's "Second Peep at Factory Life" in the May 1845 issue of the *Offering* contained a revealing discussion between two characters about the prospect of further wage cuts. Most contributors to this magazine avoided criticism of the factory system, but the problem of declining wages prompted at least a few to take a more outspoken position. Baker's story dared to question the sincerity of corporate promises that wages would eventually rise with the return of profitable times.

> "This cutting down of wages *is not* what they cry it up to be. I wonder how they'd like to work as hard as we do, digging and drudging day after day, from morning till night, and then, every two or three years, have their wages reduced. I rather guess it wouldn't set very well."
>
> "And, besides this, who ever heard, of such a thing as their being raised again. . . . I confess that I never did, so long as I've worked in the mill, and that's been these ten years."[56]

Mary Paul, returning to Lowell in the fall of 1848, also voiced her skepticism about the corporations' reasons for cutting wages. She could not reconcile the companies' claims about losing money with all the industrial activity going on around her. She wrote to her father:

> I presume you have heard before this that the wages are to be reduced on the 20th of this month. It is *true* and there seems to be a good deal of excitement on the

> subject but I can not tell what will be the consequence. The companies pretend they are losing immense sums every *day* and therefore they are obliged to lessen their wages, but this seems perfectly absurd to me for they are constantly making *repairs* and it seems to me that this would not be if there were really any danger of their being obliged to *stop* the mills.

Other operatives must have concurred with Mary Paul's critical assessment, because the newspaper *The Protest* was issued in this same month to voice opposition to these wage cuts.[57]

At the same time that some workers were raising their voices to criticize the wage reductions in Lowell, there were, as usual, others who were singing the praises of high wages. The defenders of the Lowell wage system frequently mentioned the savings accounts of the operatives as proof of their ample earnings. One corporation's records on women leaving its employ in the mid-1840s contain numerous references to the substantial savings of these operatives. One young woman saved thirty dollars in one year, although she had "lost considerable time" due to poor health. Another employee worked steadily for the same period of time and left with seventy-five dollars saved up. And on October 14, 1844, the following impressive entry was made about a departing worker.

> Mary *** worked nine years, discharged to go on Lowell Corporation. She and her sister, who left a short time since to be married, and who had worked for us over ten years, have never lost so much time as they have made up by extra work. They are Irish. Their father died nine years ago. They have since entirely supported their mother, having built her a house, costing six hundred dollars, in which they have kept house together. They own a pew, which cost them one hundred and twenty-five dollars, and they have from one hundred to two hundred dollars each at interest.

Harriet Hanson Robinson remembered that such examples of "industrious" and "frugal" operatives were not exceptional, but commonplace. "It was their custom the first of every month, after paying their board bill . . . to put their wages in the savings bank. There the money stayed, on interest, until they withdrew it, to carry home or to use for a special purpose. In 1843 over one-half of the depositors in the Lowell Institution for Savings were mill-girls, and over one-third of the whole sum deposited belonged to them. . . ." Harriet Farley also claimed that other operatives sent their savings to their families or to banks near their hometowns, thus increasing the number of worker depositors.[58]

Other operatives were skeptical of these glowing accounts about workers' ability to save money on their mill wages. Some suspected that these stories were fabricated by the owners to entice more prospective workers to the factories, create a surplus of labor, and thus keep actual wages down through competition. One popular report told of a woman who spent nearly twenty years working in the Lowell mills and saved over 3,000 dollars for a farm and for her poor family. Sarah Bagley discounted this story because she knew the woman in question. Bagley discovered that the woman had not worked steadily all those years, she had paid much less for her farm, and she had never been able to send large sums of money to her family. Moreover, there were intimations that some of her earnings were actually hush money paid to her for a child born out of wedlock. And what she was able to save on her own, Bagley asserted, was accumulated only because she never spent any money on books, church, or any other improvements. This woman was proclaimed by the corporations to be a shining example of the industrious worker readily saving a generous portion of her wages. Bagley saw her as a woman of questionable character and standards, an exception to the mass of hard-working, upright operatives who found little opportunity to save any money, no matter how hard they tried.[59]

Other workers also voiced their frustration with subsistence wages that afforded operatives little chance to accumulate capital. Jabez Hollingworth wrote: "when we are in work at what we may call decent wages they have so many ways to get it all back again that it is impossible to save any thing." Another operative, from Amesbury, Massachusetts, recalled her years of factory wages in testimony before the Massachusetts Bureau of Statistics of Labor. She said: "I have been a working-woman in the mill about twenty-five years, or more, and have never seen the time that I could save money enough from my wages to enable me to obtain books, or avail myself of the advantages of lectures, or pleasure trips."[60]

John Quincy Adams Thayer argued that even when operatives could save some money, they lost control of their savings when they put them in a bank. Thayer saw corporate control of factories and banks as a kind of interlocking conspiracy to cheat operatives—he was a machinist deeply imbued with hostility towards financial institutions and monopolies.

> [T]he "round numbers," owned by the operatives, and deposited in the Savings Bank, for which is paid about four dollars on a hundred per annum, becomes antagonizing to their interest and happiness, as well as that of the great mass of the people, and may well be compared to its multiplied numbers in round hot cannon-balls, directed against a peaceful, industrious, intelligent, and useful City. It falls immediately into the ignorant, speculating, and monopolizing hand of injustice, and is employed to enforce the rigid laws by which the owners are governed.

Thayer failed to acknowledge that any bank depositor, worker or not, could withdraw money from an account if she did not approve of the institution's policies. Nevertheless, Thayer was a perceptive observer who saw that whatever money workers could manage to save in a bank was controlled by the bank's owners and managers as long as it remained on deposit.[61]

Seth Luther also warned all operatives, men and women, to beware of false stories about high wages. These tales, like the accounts of workers' savings, were designed to deceive workers and bring them into the factories. Luther wrote: "If *one girl* in a mill earns, by extra exertion, $4 per week, it is blazed abroad, from Maine to Mexico, that the *girls* in that mill earn from one to four dollars per week. . . . These factory owners are very fond of using the rule of AVERAGE, and they prove everything by that rule." Some managers emphasized the gross wages of their employees, and not the net income after board and other expenses. In factories where wages were kept on account, as the case of Hannah Borden demonstrates, workers could even find themselves in debt at the conclusion of their contracts, either through their own carelessness or by the deliberate deception of management. And, even if some factories did offer relatively high wages, many workers saw little benevolence in the gesture. Such wages were paid only out of necessity, in order to entice operatives into a system based on long hours of monotonous labor under harsh regulations and unhealthy conditions.[62]

Nevertheless, in some factories, the promises of higher wages were not all deceptive and grandiose claims, particularly for the experienced operative. The Poignand and Plant mills discovered back in 1815 that the novelty of factory labor was not always enough of an attraction to keep up a steady supply of labor. One of their managers wrote: "It is very difficult to procure steady, faithful Men. . . . To get people to go into a factory at present is almost out of the question—Peace has raised their expectations too high." The company was forced to pay substantial monthly wages; one contract from 1820 even contained a provision for a monthly bonus as a reward for good work. The Merino/Dudley woolen mill also discovered that retaining an experienced labor force often required a willingness to bargain with workers. One correspondent assured the Dudley company: "I think you are correct in compromising with our hands, as it is bad policy to exchange good workmen at fair wages & hazard obtaining others who may injure our business." Even Samuel Slater, who tried to avoid yielding to workers' demands on negotiating wages and often endeavored to extract wage concessions at contract renewals, sometimes compromised in an effort to retain valuable operatives.[63]

Some contracts with new workers provided for wage increases later on during the term of the agreement. Once the operatives learned their tasks and showed that they would remain on the job, then their piece rates might be increased. The Ware Manufacturing Company instituted a related policy of paying workers an annual premium of one dollar for each full year that they had continuously worked for the company. The factory's management hoped to attract and retain experienced and productive employees through such added incentives. If wage increases were not forthcoming, workers sometimes took it upon themselves to seek such benefits. George Hollingworth wrote that his son Joseph had taken a job as a cloth finisher at a low monthly wage. "As the Job was a new one to him and one I wished him to learn I was not particular about wages at first, but now as he has got an expert hand I am thinking of asking for more wages." Hollingworth probably knew that his son's growing mastery resulted in a higher output of finished cloth. But since Joseph was not paid by the piece, he was not making any more money for his increased productivity, so his father saw the necessity of demanding a higher monthly wage to reflect his increased value as a workman. Harriet Farley pointed out that higher wages boosted workers' morale, and that the benefits of high wages spread throughout a company. She wrote: "it is much easier to instil a feeling of self-respect, of desire for excellence, among a well-paid, than an ill-paid, class of operatives." Farley believed that if workers were satisfied with their earnings, they would make a much more productive and efficient work force.[64]

In some cases, employers could not grant wage increases in the midst of a slow economy. Yet one manager did resist the temptation to cut wage rates, and proclaimed that his financial interests were in harmony with his employees'. A Boston manufacturer remarked about his woolen business in the spring of 1822: "As to the combers I do not want to cut them down—they are reasonable men and must do what is right. The fact is wool is higher and worsted lower & they can't get business or combers without they do it at such rates as to make a profit for their employers—their interest is mine, & mine theirs. . . ." Some twenty years later, as the economy remained sluggish in the wake of the 1837 depression, the Cheney family worked overtime for reduced pay at their silk mill so that they could pay higher wages to their employees.[65]

— IV —

The debate over wages and savings, particularly for factory women, often revolved around two fundamental points—were factory wages higher than those of other occupations open to women? and was the wage system a path toward independence for female workers? Harriet Farley, in one of her earliest defenses of Lowell and its operatives, argued that women's factory wages were comparatively high to compensate for the hard work and to attract a respectable labor force.

> [W]e are collected . . . to get money, as much of it and as fast as we can; and it is because our toil is so unremitting, that the wages of factory girls are higher than those of females engaged in most other occupations. It is these wages which, in spite of toil, restraint, discomfort, and prejudice, have drawn so many worthy, virtuous, intelligent, and well-educated girls to Lowell, and other factories; and it is wages which are in a great degree to decide the characters of the factory girls as a class . . . the avails of factory labor are now greater than those of many domestics, seamstresses, and school-teachers; and strange would it be, if in money-loving New England, one of the most lucrative employments should be rejected because it is toilsome, or because some people are prejudiced against it. Yankee girls have too much *independence* for *that*.[66]

Other female factory workers agreed with Farley's views on comparative wages. Factory girls often contrasted their earnings and working conditions with those of female teachers, one of the commoner occupations open to women in antebellum New England. Although the available data indicates that teachers' monthly earnings were higher in the 1840s than textile operatives', another contributor to the *Lowell Offering* drew attention to the fact that operatives usually worked more months in a year than teachers. This writer believed that factory work was steadier, more manageable, and more lucrative than teaching. In her story, entitled "Ann and Myself," the narrator says: "I found my task to be less perplexing as a factory girl than as a school teacher, and my pay was much more satisfactory . . . for instead of three months in a year, as teachers, we then had constant employment [in the factory]." Many female factory workers took comfort in the idea that their wages were relatively high compared to many other women workers', although these same wages were low in comparison to those of the male labor force.[67]

The women workers who saw the factory as a place of new opportunities for better pay also often viewed the entire wage system as a fair bargain made between free and equal parties. Harriet Hanson Robinson remembered how the wage system was based on trust between employer and employee. She wrote that "the mill-girls . . . were subject to no extortion, and if they did extra work they were always paid in full. Their own account of labor done by the piece was always accepted. They kept the figures, and were paid accordingly." Another operative, writing in the *Lowell Offering,* spoke of the spirit of mutuality in this system. Though owners set the wage rates and paid the workers, both groups were linked in the running of the factory.

"Those who have wealth are not more independent of us," she asserted, "than we are of them. If they wish for the benefit of our industry and strength, they must give us, in exchange for it, a living, even if it be at the cost of a few of their luxuries." This operative believed that experienced workers were a valuable resource, and that owners would recognize them as essential to the success of the enterprise and always pay them a fair wage. Harriet Farley thought that everyone could retain her dignity in such as system; no one was "prostrated by any consciousness of personal indebtedness to any one."[68]

Harriet Hanson Robinson saw the wage system as a real source of independence for women. Though female operatives were dependent on the owners for their wages, the earnings themselves gave many women their first sense that their labor was worth something in the outside world—something of value they could manage. Wage work gave new dignity to women whose labor had been taken for granted for so long in the domestic sphere. These women often came from homes where their labor might raise some cash, but was also just as likely to be unpaid domestic chores; and they went into jobs that frequently paid regular cash wages to each individual. Female operatives asserted their legitimacy, as women workers and as wage earners, by proclaiming the very value of the money they made. Robinson observed that textile mills were an especially "great opening" for

> lonely and dependent women. From a condition approaching pauperism they were at once placed above want; they could earn money, and spend it as they pleased; and could gratify their tastes and desires without restraint, and without rendering an account to anybody. . . . For the first time in this country a woman's labor had a money value. She had become not only an earner and a producer, but also a spender of money, a recognized factor in the political economy of her time.[69]

Robinson saw particular significance in the fact that women were working and earning their own money and spending that money as they saw fit. Women workers were participating in the growing cash economy as earners and consumers. Their work acquired public meaning because it now earned wages that could be spent in the marketplace. And women's emerging economic power and autonomy enhanced their feelings of security and control over their lives. Clearly, then, many female operatives saw wage labor, not as a threat to their independence (as many male workers did), but as an opportunity to gain some real autonomy. These women did not fear a descent into the ranks of wage labor; they welcomed the chance to earn their own living.

Other women workers did not accept the idea that wage labor meant freedom for them. Instead, these female operatives argued that the wage-labor system was exploiting working women in the factories. The *Factory Girl* defined an operative as "a person who is employed in a Factory, and who generally earns three times as much as he or she receives." An operative named Sarah wrote to the *Factory Girl's Album* about how owners cheated workers out of the full value of their labor.

> Her industry is to be commended—she toils from morning until night at the loom, or on some portion of the work which goes to make up the Whole. But does she receive an adequate reward for her services? Not so. Her pay is too little in comparison to the profits derived from the work, it must be acknowledged that the employer receives too much, the operative too little.

This operative saw the wage system as an inherently unequal bargain between wealthy and powerful owners and the underpaid workers. She saw no bonds of mutuality, only a proprietor interested in keeping labor costs down and dividends up. This operative, and others like her, argued that working for wages was not a sign of free labor in a land of liberty. Rather, there were both implicit and explicit elements of coercion in the labor market and in the wage relationship itself. The basic inequities in wealth and power between individual workers and incorporated capital meant that the supposedly free market, and the supposedly freely made wage-bargain between an employer and an employee, were always weighted in the owners' favor. Workers had the stark choice of either selling their labor wherever possible at whatever price capital dictated, or going hungry.[70]

The older operative from Amesbury, Massachusetts, who testified before the state's Bureau of Statistics of Labor in 1872, added her criticism of the exploitation of wage labor. Looking back on her more than twenty-five years of mill work, she asserted that from the time she started working in the 1840s, new technology and new managerial strategies merely made the owners richer and the workers poorer.

> I am now growing old and wearing out. Poverty is and has been, the price of my laborious life. There seem to have been many improvements, reducing the cost of manufactures by the invention of machinery. Yet the wages of the work women have not advanced thereby. Larger dividends have blessed capital, while labor remains the same.[71]

Other workers also argued that techniques such as the speedup and stretch-out exacerbated the exploitation inherent in the system of wage labor. The *Factory Girl* defined industrial conditions as "oppressive" because they were designed "to make two men do the work of three, without making any addition to their wages." Many operatives were convinced that the manufacturers' profits were keeping pace with the faster machines, but the workers' earnings were lagging behind. The labor force was being driven faster to maintain those high rates of return, but the working men and women were seeing only a fraction of the value of their increased production. In Waltham, operatives' wages rose eight percent from 1840 to 1845; but output per worker increased by twenty-five percent, and profit per yard of cloth jumped from one cent to over two cents.[72]

Another worker spoke of how the wage system was particularly hard on female operatives because of the sexual discrimination in industrial wage rates. Women workers were robbed of their independence both because they were wage workers, and because their wages were even less, due to their being women. In some factories, men could earn an average wage nearly triple that of women. Wage comparisons were often a difficult issue to sort out because men and women were frequently assigned different jobs. But this contributor to the *Voice of Industry,* writing under the pseudonym "Pro Bono," confronted the problem of comparable worth head-on.

> It is well known that labor performed by females commands but little when compared with that what is paid to men—though the work may be of the same character. . . . A female generally receives but about one-half as much as is paid to a man for doing the same amount of labor. It has been urged that they are the weaker sex, and are dependent upon us for assistance, and per consequence this difference in

> the price of labor should be made. But this very dependence is the result of inequality, and would not exist were the proper remedy applied. . . . If a certain amount of labor is performed, it can make no difference by any manner of rational reasoning, by whom that labor is done. It is folly to argue that labor by females is not in every respect done as well as by men; and there is no earthly reason why they should not receive as much. When it is considered that it requires ten and twelve hours a day, and the most strict regard to economy and industry on the part of laboring men and our mechanics to acquire a comfortable living—so low are the wages of labor—is it not a wonder how our female laborers can succeed as well as they do with such a meagre and miserable pittance? It cannot be done but by the greatest deprivation of the common wants of nature.

These glaring pay inequities based on gender, or other personal characteristics, could be used to the advantage of management. If these differentials were introduced on capital's own terms, they could redirect workers away from any sense of class identity or solidarity and toward increasing individual competitiveness and personal gain. Pay discrepancies could create grievances between men and women, or skilled and unskilled workers, or native-born operatives and immigrants. These wage differentials could also lead to the development of significant status distinctions within the working class; distinctions that management could cultivate and exacerbate.[73]

A group of women in Dover, during the strike of 1834, painted an even bleaker portrait of wage labor declining into wage slavery. These women saw working for factory wages as the very antithesis of independence. The money itself offered no freedom if the purse strings were controlled by management; because when wages were cut, the economic foundations of independence were undermined. These women could not focus merely on the money; they felt it necessary to look at the relations behind the payroll. They publicly stated: "We view this attempt to reduce our wages as part of the general plan of the proprietors of the different manufacturing establishments to reduce the Females in their employ to that state of dependence on them in which they openly, as they do now secretly, abuse and insult them by calling them their 'slaves.'" For these women, it was not the money itself that made wage labor like slavery. It was the operatives' dependence on those wages for their livelihood, and owners' exploiting those women's dependence on wage labor.[74]

Other factory workers, both men and women, spoke out against wage labor because it seemed to turn people and their labor into mere commodities in the marketplace. Operatives were forced to sell their labor—some would say, a portion of themselves—to whoever would buy it. One poem, "The Price of Weavers in Greenville," by the pseudonymous "Rambler," captured this sense of a market in humanity—not quite a chattel-slave market, but still a degrading experience that smacked of wage slavery.

> All ye that have got woolen weavers for sale,
> Can sell them in Greenville wholesale or retail;
> That great man of trafic, that deals in the fleece,
> Will readily buy them at ninepence apiece.

A famed speculator is this Mr. Steere,
When wool is so cheap, and cloth is so dear,
And knowing that laborers always were geese,
He thinks he can buy them at ninepence apiece.

He gave a commission, tis plain to be seen,
To a great man of mutton, they call Mr. Greene;
He told him bid ninepence, and not be affraid
To add something more, if they'd take in trade. . . .[75]

A correspondent to the *Voice of Industry,* writing from Fall River in the spring of 1848, talked about the commodification of labor in harsher terms. Operatives were being dehumanized and transformed into merely another factor of production. John Adams told the newspaper's editor: "we use up human flesh here for labor, about as fast as we use oxen and other animals for the purpose of gratifying our carnivorous apetites. In fact, we think nothing of working up the . . . factory help . . . here without stint or measure. They are a commodity in the market not to be reckoned among humans." For this worker, the ultimate danger of the factory wage system went beyond even the specter of human bondage. Workers, when they sold their labor to the factory owners, lost their very humanity; they became mere objects of trade to be bartered without any considerations of morality or dignity.[76]

Surely something had to be done to stop this dehumanizing process—but what could the workers do to make their grievances known, and to make some changes in the factory system? The answer is that workers were always doing something. Throughout the antebellum decades, even many years before such haunting letters were written, operatives turned to the power of protest—in deeds as well as words—to challenge the power of the factory system.

PART II

CHAPTER 7

To the Streets and the Halls: Workers, Protest, and Organizing

Working-class protest in the mechanized factories of antebellum New England took a variety of forms—from verbal and written criticisms of factories, to defiance of company regulations, to work stoppages, to the formation of labor organizations. Sometimes the expression of workers' discontent was spontaneous and not intended to be a conscious critique of industrial labor. In other instances, simple statements and acts resonated with a deeper feeling of opposition to the factory system.[1]

Working-class protest was also quite rich and dynamic as it evolved in the antebellum decades. Operatives often experimented with new forms of protest and adapted their tactics to changing conditions in the factories and among the workers. Sometimes the changing character of protest also had rather ironic consequences. Workers often found themselves taking bold action in defense of rather modest goals, or laboring hard to build mass organizations that launched scathing critiques of the factory system but rarely directly confronted the power of the corporations.

— I —

Some workers engaged in anonymous and surreptitious protest against particular authority figures rather than publicly challenging the factory system as a whole. John Rogers observed how machinists in the Amoskeag shops of Manchester, New Hampshire, displayed their displeasure with the superintendent, C. P. Crane. He told his father: "Mr. Crane is *not* a popular man in the shop. . . . There are chalk sketches, all about, in the shape of a bird's body with a man's head & he is nicknamed the 'old bird.'" Such caricatures were a way for workers to vent their grievances without directly confronting the manager and risking dismissal. These practices of mocking management were also found in the poem "The Price of Weavers in Greenville." The author noted that the rather suggestive name "Cock-sparrow" was "given by an ingenious yankee to the Boss weaver." And some workers in one of the Bristol, Connecticut, clock factories hanged their overseer, Levi McKee, in effigy. Perhaps this was a variation on the practice of tying puppets to moving machinery, but here the clockworkers were putting themselves more in the role of puppeteer. The employees succeeded in upsetting McKee so much that he soon moved out of town.[2]

Other workers chose to express their discontent with the factory system through direct, instead of symbolic, action. One common practice was for workers to pilfer small amounts of goods and sneak them out of the factories. Operatives knew that they could be fired if they were caught, yet stealing factory goods may have served as a way for them to even the score with a manufacturer who was paying low wages. The operatives took in kind what they could not earn in cash; if they were denied what they saw as the full value of their labor, they would find a way to get what they thought was due them.[3]

There were also rumors that some operatives were settling scores by setting fires. Throughout antebellum New England, the flames of a burning factory often signaled the possibility of arson. The cause of a suspicious fire was extremely difficult to prove, but it was a sobering event for factory owners. Even the hint of such a deliberate incendiary act could give management cause for reflection. The Scovill brothers, for instance, had wanted to dismiss certain English workers from their brass factory in 1835. Nevertheless, "fearful of having the mill burned or something else happen," they waited a "long time" before carrying out their intentions.[4]

When suspicious fires actually did occur, they were often linked to strikes and economic hard times. There was a rash of suspicious fires reported during the depression years of 1828 and 1829. Some workers probably looked on these fires as acts of individual, anonymous protest and as a form of redress for their collective grievances. When William Harris' mill at Valley Falls, Rhode Island, burned, the workers were said to have stood by and cheered on the destruction. There were also suspicious fires at the Springfield Armory in 1842, and at that time even the surrounding community was reluctant to help in extinguishing the flames. The same apathy was noted in Manchester, New Hampshire, when the Steam Mill burned down in 1844. Arson was suspected at the time; and the public made so little effort to assist in fighting the flames that the company's paymaster had to put out the blaze almost singlehandedly. There was no cooperation between factory owners, workers, and neighbors in meeting this emergency. In Springfield and Manchester, the workers and townspeople were willing to watch the factories burn to the ground.[5]

Yet other workers chose to make their grievances known, not through any dramatic acts of destruction, but through simply taking their own time away from the factory. Absenteeism was a means to exert some control over the workday and a basic form of personal protest—a kind of individual strike, an implicit challenge to the factory management. Samuel Collins saw, in the fall of 1830, that his "grinders fell cross and take this opportunity to be sick many of them and the rest dont do as much. . . ." At the Slater mills, overall punctuality increased as the years progressed, but many operatives still tried to take a few hours or days off as a way to reassert their autonomy without quitting their jobs. This tactic was not without its risks, however, because unexcused absences could be cause for dismissal.[6]

Some workers turned their brief respites into definite decisions to permanently leave a particular company or factory work in general. These individual decisions were based on a variety of considerations, and sometimes they appeared to be more spontaneous than calculated. But they often sprang from a kernel of protest driving the worker away from his job. Workers knew that owners were always trying to hold their work forces together for the sake of productivity and profit. When an operative quit his job, he asserted his power to remove himself from that work force and disrupt (even in a small way) the factory's productivity.

Wage cuts often prompted workers to consider leaving the factory to look for other opportunities. One poem said simply: "Then since they've cut my wages down, / To nine shillings per week, / If I cannot better wages make, / Some other place I'll seek." Jabez Hollingworth probably captured the thoughts of many young men in factories when he wrote about moving westward in 1827: "I expect if things go on as they do I shall either have to work for less wages or quit, and if I have to quit I expect I shall go to the west." In fact, the very act of leaving may have been a way for workers to say—without words—that their jobs were virtually meaningless. It was not worth the operatives' time and effort to stay and fight for better conditions in a job that had so little value to begin with.[7]

Workers who continually left jobs and became part of a transient labor force were also repeatedly expressing their footloose discontent with factory work. But their instability undercut their chances to get together with other like-minded workers and collectively protest. Transients rarely remained long enough in any one factory to help build any means for social change. They usually avoided agitating for any changes in the system, because any improvements would be lost when they moved on to the next job. All that transients usually gained was a vague sense of release; yet there were workers who thought that they could sustain real personal freedom by moving to new jobs frequently. These workers believed that quitting or changing jobs was still the most effective way of leaving behind personal grievances with managers, rules, wages, or job routines. Workers, who had no job security or realistic chance for advancement, had few incentives to keep them loyal to any one company. They may have formed a few friendships or had a certain familiarity with their work (which could easily lead to boredom), but that often was not enough to make them stay and fight for better conditions.[8]

The individual act of leaving factory work might therefore have undermined other forms of protest. To quit one's job was to make some kind of statement, but it was often a personal gesture that did little to change the factory system. These individual acts of protest may have been an indication that the work force as a whole was divided against itself. Workers may not have been able to coalesce and protest as a group. This did not mean that all protest ceased—it took forms that were less collective and less overt. Workers' solidarity was not always a prerequisite for protest, but it did shape protest in particular ways.[9]

— II —

Even while many individual workers were engaging in their own private acts of defiance, other operatives in communities across the region did come together to engage in collective job actions. There is no doubt that strikes were the most dramatic form of collective protest activity in the factories of antebellum New England. This was agitation based on some sense of community, common interests, and shared identity among the workers. When workers struck, they withdrew their labor from the factory as a group, with the hope of returning to work once their grievances were resolved. More than any one individual's quitting, a strike was a bolder assertion of the workers' power to disrupt the factory's operations, to challenge the power of management, and perhaps to question the future development of the industrial order.

Strikes were not a fact of daily life for most operatives, but a number of noteworthy turn-outs did occur in antebellum New England factories. There are no precise figures on the number of these strikes; some turn-outs may have been so brief or small or isolated that they slipped by unnoticed. Yet over fifteen strikes lasted long enough (from one day to several weeks), and engulfed enough workers (from a few dozen to several thousand) to leave a lasting impression on antebellum labor relations.

The earliest strike at a large manufacturing company was at Waltham, Massachusetts, in 1821. Isaac Markham, a machinist at the mill, wrote to his brother on May 30: "a few weeks since they cut down every unmarried mans wages (except mine) that they employ & without giving them the least notice until the day came for payment the same trick was played off on all the girls but they as one revolted & the works stopped 2 days in consequence." Markham's letter is the only existing account of this first strike in a New England mechanized factory. Although Markham's report is rather brief, the strike he described did follow a pattern that would be repeated frequently. First, the strike was directed at the textile industry; second, it focused on a large mill in a more urban setting; third, it revolved around the female operatives; and fourth, it was called to protest a reduction in wages.[10]

Three years later, in May of 1824, the female weavers in Pawtucket, Rhode Island, led a strike against longer working hours (i.e., decreasing meal breaks) and lower piece rates. Workers gathered at mill gates when the bells rang to try to prevent, without force, other operatives from working the extra hours. The women weavers, who were severely affected by the twenty-percent reduction in piece rates, gathered in their own meeting and agreed not to tend their looms unless the old piece rates were restored. One evening, soon after the strike began, a crowd of townspeople—not all of them operatives—traveled through the town shouting at the houses of the mill owners and even breaking windows in one factory. This kind of crowd action echoed some of the practices prevalent in the revolutionary period, and it demonstrated that at least some of the Pawtucket community supported the workers.

The strikers and their allies rejected the owners' arguments that the austerity measures were necessary in order to keep the mills in business. The protesters publicly chided the manufacturers for exploiting their employees while living in their well-appointed homes. These houses stood as physical symbols of the owners' wealth and power, and as rallying points for the operatives' discontent. The following day, the mill owners—perhaps concerned that any further demonstrations would be more destructive—closed their gates and shut down operations until a settlement could be reached.

The strike dragged on into a second week with continued reports of unrest and even an attempt to set fire to a portion of one mill. Seven bales of cotton were ignited near a window in Edward Walcott's mill, but the flames were discovered soon enough to prevent major damage. The circumstantial evidence pointed to arson, either as an act of anger or as a warning regarding the strike. Perhaps it was intended that the mill not be completely consumed, only that a strong statement be made. And perhaps the message was heard, for the strike was settled soon afterwards in the early days of June with a compromise between the two sides.

The workers could not roll back all the changes in wages and hours, but the owners also discovered that they could not completely dominate a population of operatives supported by other townspeople. After the strike was settled, it was the owners who issued a statement defending their decisions, even though the workers' use of the strike was the bolder and more controversial act. The owners decided not to stir up any more animosity by attacking the operatives' tactics, and instead concentrated on shoring up their factories' reputations to attract more workers and protect their growing power in the community.[11]

Cotton mill operatives walked off their jobs in Dover, New Hampshire, in December 1828. Their strike was somewhat unusual in that it was called not to protest wage cuts, but to resist the imposition of new working regulations. Three or four hundred women marched out of the factory in a procession with flags and placards, and they fired off gunpowder to demonstrate their opposition to the "obnoxious regulations" that strictly governed their conduct and fined them for infractions. The women turned out on a Friday afternoon, and managers promptly advertised for "better behaved women" to take their places. By the following Monday, all those who had not been fired for their participation in the protest went back to work. The operatives had certainly vented their anger, but they had failed to change any of the company's policies.[12]

On another Friday, four months later, the morning of April 30, 1829, women mill workers in Taunton, Massachusetts, walked out because of the familiar problem of wage cuts. Once again, it was the female weavers who pledged themselves not to go back into the mills unless wages were raised back to their previous levels. These women marched through the streets of Taunton, gathering nearly a hundred weavers from the various mills, and walked to the green in front of the courthouse. This procession was more sedate than the one in Dover; there was no music or shouts or banners.

The women, however, had designed a uniform for themselves in advance of their walkout, indicating that their strike was a planned event. They were attired in black silk dresses with red shawls and green bonnets. The black dresses may have been worn as traditional mourning clothing—the women may have been publicly mourning their loss of wages, status, and respect. The use of silk and colorful shawls and bonnets gave the women the appearance of coming out in public in their best clothes. The strikers thereby paid homage to themselves and their protest by dressing in such a refined yet serious manner. They displayed their femininity, dignity, and respectability in the face of low wages and criticism for their conduct. And, by all dressing alike, the women made a personal and public statement of their common identity and solidarity with each other.

The women then met in a nearby hall where an operative named Salome Lincoln addressed them. Lincoln's emergence as a leader of the strike is noteworthy because she was also an itinerant Baptist preacher. Lincoln frequently left her job as a weaver to preach throughout southeastern Massachusetts. She used those same oratorical skills, cultivated in Baptist meetings, to exhort her fellow workers to stand firm against the company. Lincoln could be seen as the embodiment of workers' hopes, and managers' fears, about religious activism. Her Baptist faith did not make her a docile employee; instead, it gave her the strength to break away from social conventions of female deference, and to speak in public about religious matters and the rights of labor.

Many workers eventually returned to their jobs at the lower wages, but Lincoln's convictions prompted her to leave the Taunton factory rather than go back on her pledge not to work at the reduced rates. Lincoln was never blacklisted for her actions, however, and within a few weeks she had secured a new weaving position in another mill about ten miles from Taunton. Although the strike she led was a challenge to the factory system, Lincoln still considered factory work to be a worthwhile occupation.[13]

The decade of the 1830s saw the establishment of regional labor organizations such as the New England Association of Farmers, Mechanics, and Other Working Men. But these working-class groups rarely developed any significant contacts with factory operatives, particularly with working women. This lack of institutional support may be one reason why female operatives continued to turn to strikes in the 1830s as a crucial form of protest in their fight for better wages and working conditions.

The year 1834 saw strikes in Lowell, Massachusetts, and another in Dover, which attracted wide attention. The Lowell operatives walked out in February when the corporations announced a fifteen-percent pay cut to take effect on March 1. The strike began on yet another Friday morning (February 14) when a woman who had spoken up at meetings and urged her fellow workers to give their notice and withdraw their savings was dismissed. She waved her bonnet in the air as a signal to other workers who were looking in the office windows as she was being discharged, and they immediately left work and gathered around her. A procession of nearly 800 workers soon formed and marched around the city, drawing workers out of all the factories.

On Saturday, February 15, the second day of the strike, the protesters (their numbers now estimated at up to 2,000) issued a proclamation that rooted their actions in the tradition of the American Revolution and pledged them all to the ideal of mutual assistance. They saw the issue as more than money; it was imperative for workers to band together and protect their dignity.

> UNION IS POWER.—Our present object is to have union and exertion, and we remain in possession of our own unquestionable rights. We circulate this paper, wishing to obtain the names of all who imbibe the spirit of our patriotic ancestors, who preferred privation to bondage and parted with all that renders life desireable—and even life itself—to produce independence for their children. The oppressive hand of avarice would enslave us, and to gain their object they very gravely tell us of the pressure of the times; this we are already sensible of and deplore it. If any are in want of assistance, the ladies will be compassionate and assist them, but we prefer to have the disposing of our charities in our own hands, and, as we are free,

we would remain in possession of what kind Providence has bestowed upon us, and remain daughters of freemen still.

All who patronize the effort we wish to have discontinue their labor until terms of reconciliation are made.

Resolved, That we will not go back into the mills unless our wages are continued to us as they have been.

Resolved, That none of us will go back unless they receive us all as one.

Resolved, That if any have not money enough to carry them home that they shall be supplied.

One worker reiterated the point that the wage cuts undermined more than the workers' economic position: the imposition of such policies on the operatives, without any opportunity for discussion or negotiation, was an expression of the owners' growing power over the community. This young woman argued: "We do not estimate our liberty by dollars and cents, consequently it was not the reduction of wages alone which caused the excitement, but that haughty, overbearing disposition, that purse-proud insolence, which was becoming more and more apparent. We beseech them not to asperse our characters or stigmatize us as disorderly persons."

Despite the operatives' proclamations of unity and their appeal for respect, their fervor cooled rapidly during the traditional day of rest on Sunday. The overall economic climate was sluggish, and some workers may have realized that the corporations were in no hurry to resolve the disruption of production. It was the operatives who would have to move quickly if they wanted to protect their jobs.

By Monday, another familiar pattern had set in—new workers began inquiring about the jobs of the striking workers; some of the leaders were fired; many others returned to work at reduced wages. But life in Lowell did not return immediately to the status quo. Some strikers had rented their own quarters, others forced the banks into paying out their accounts in cash, and they hired wagons to take them to their rural homes. One former overseer recalled nearly fifty years later that in some mills the "looms stood idle a long time. . . . As late as September, '35, some of the looms were still idle."[14]

The factory owners in Dover also decided to cut wage rates in late February 1834, and many operatives once again walked out in protest. It was reported that 800 women formed a union for mutual support, while the company advertised for 500 new employees. The strikers issued their own public appeals, saying that they were willing to work if the wage cuts were rescinded, and warning newcomers to beware of low wages. They also refrained from boisterous demonstrations during this strike, probably because they were criticized for their noisy conduct in 1828. The strikers left work on a Friday morning and kept mostly to their boardinghouses. But over 600 of them gathered for a meeting in the local courthouse on Saturday afternoon and unanimously adopted a series of resolutions.

These resolutions (as was much of this strike in Dover) were influenced by the confrontation in Lowell. Operatives in both communities were probably aware of their shared struggle against corporate encroachment on their wages and self-respect.

> . . . [W]e will never consent to work for the Cochaco Manufacturing Company at their reduced "*Tariff of Wages*" . . . we believe the "*unusual pressure of the times,*" which is so much complained of, to have been caused by artful and designing men to subserve party purposes, or more wickedly still, to promote their own private ends . . . we view with feelings of indignation the attempt made to throw upon us, who are least able to bear it, the effect of this "pressure," by reducing our wages, while those of our overseers and Agent are continued to them at their former high rate. That we think our wages are already low enough when the peculiar circumstances of our situation are considered; that we are, many of us, far from our homes, parents and friends, and that it is only by strict economy and untiring industry that any of us have been able to lay up any thing. That we view, with feelings of scorn, the attempt made by those, who would be glad to see us bond slaves for life, to magnify the small amount of our earnings into fortunes, that their oppressive measures may wear the appearance of justice. . . . That while we feel our independence, we will neither be cajoled by flattery nor intimidated by threats, from using all the means in our power to prevent the accomplishment of a purpose so much to be deprecated . . . we view both the ungenerous accusation of our effecting "*riotous combination*" and the poor compliment of our being "*otherwise respectable*" with like feelings of contempt: and consider them both as the last degree insulting to the daughters of freemen . . . however freely the epithet of "Factory Slaves" may be bestowed upon us, we will never deserve it, by a base and cringing submission to proud wealth or *haughty insolence.*

The mass meeting urged workers not to renege on their determination to stay out of the mills until the wage rates were restored to their previous levels. The strikers also voted that a committee of correspondence "communicate the proceedings of this meeting to the girls employed in the Factories at Great Falls, Newmarket, and Lowell"; and "that a fund be raised and appropriated to defray the expenses of those, in returning to their homes who may not have the means at their command." Like their fellow workers in Lowell, the operatives of Dover organized themselves around the principle of mutual support and solidarity in protest. Yet they also failed to secure any concessions from management, and many of them returned to work the following Monday at the lower wage rates—another, more painful, parallel with the strike in Lowell.[15]

The strikes of 1834 in Lowell and Dover seemed to be more sophisticated than previous turn-outs. Women workers in Lowell had signed pledges in advance to leave the mills when the wage rates were cut and to pay a five-dollar fine if they went back on their word. The use of savings accounts as strike funds and the correspondence with other industrial communities also demonstrate that these protesters were planning in advance for the struggle. But all of their plans were no match for the wealth and power of the corporations: those who needed or wanted to retain their jobs had to come back on the company's terms.[16]

Yet the written legacy of these protests—the strike declarations from both Lowell and Dover—are documents rich in the symbols and rhetoric of workers' early struggles against the factory system. These operatives saw themselves as equal in all fundamental rights and standing with their employers, since they had all originated at some point from the same middling Yankee stock. Their protests were directed against all attempts to undermine the basic social and economic foundations of that equality and dignity. A reduction in wages not only threatened the operatives' daily earnings, it cut at the heart of the material basis of their independence and autonomy. If the workers were forced to take lower wages, their future prospects for new opportunities through hard work would be severely curtailed. Higher wages held the promise of real female power in the marketplace; lower wages reduced the operatives to the status of factory slave.[17]

The workers demanded their independence back because they saw it as a right due all honest American workers, not a favor to be bestowed or removed at management's discretion. Moreover, these women saw a clear connection between asserting their claim to their independent status as workers and American citizens, and preserving their respectability as women. For only an independent female operative could be free from all potentially contaminating influences in the factory.[18]

The women of both Lowell and Dover protested as workers, as women, and particularly as "daughters of freemen." They demanded their rights as the inheritors of their forefathers' republican status. Since these women usually did not have personal artisanal traditions to draw on, they tapped the revolutionary background of their parents and grandparents. The strikers, living on their own away from their families, still invoked strong feelings about their personal heritage in defense of their bold actions. These women, in their rhetoric and their strikes, showed themselves to be both progressive and traditional. Even as they declared their allegiance to middle-class status as daughters of freemen, they organized themselves as workers to defend that status.

The women appealed to their patriarchal legacy, not to deny their own identity as operatives and as autonomous females, but to morally and politically justify their public claims to independence and integrity as women and as workers. The strikers were demanding that the traditional ideals of respect, justice, and equity be honored within the new factory system. By invoking these memories and ideals of the Revolution, the strikers were creating a link between the fathers who bore the burdens of fighting and dying for the nation's freedom, and their descendents who were the bearing the burden of working for the nation's prosperity. Both fathers and daughters deserved to be recognized for the sacrifices they made at onerous tasks: they were the lifeblood of the country.

The women protesters were challenging the male managerial power structure to recognize them as workers and as fellow citizens of the republic (albeit nonvoters): workers with legitimate rights to a fair and just wage for their labor, and citizens with legitimate rights to respectful treatment in the factory and the surrounding community. By calling themselves the daughters of freemen, these women were clearly saying that they were not going to play the role of dutiful daughters to their substitute father–managers in any scheme of corporate paternalism.

The stirring phrase "daughters of freemen" was also a warning about dangers of factory slavery and a clear rejection of bondage. These working women were forcefully stating that they were the descendents of free workers and citizens; they were not the slave children of slave parents. Therefore, they were entitled to have the same rights and privileges as their ancestors and to be treated as free laborers in their own right.

These women's strike declarations were also an open appeal to the community's sense of public morality to condemn male employers who were taking advantage of female operatives. The women were arguing that their demands involved more than money; they were resisting tyranny, and fighting for dignity and justice. They urged the public to stand up for the women who were struggling for the rights of all citizens to respect and decent work. Thus, their strikes were justified by blending the ideology of citizenship, republican rights, and self-determination (all patriotic and mainstream democratic themes) with the language of class- and gender-consciousness and solidarity in support of working women's rights.

In the fall of 1836, operatives in Lowell again turned out over the issue of falling wages. Actually, in this instance, their boarding charges were increased without any corresponding raise in pay, and the result was a net decrease in earnings. Harriet Hanson Robinson recalled that "as many as twelve or fifteen hundred girls turned out, and walked in procession through the streets. They had neither flags nor music, but sang songs. . . ." Despite her later reputation as a defender of the factory system, Robinson was an active participant in this protest. She was eleven years old at the time, working as a doffer in a spinning room; nevertheless, Robinson said that she prodded many of her older co-workers into action.

> I had heard the proposed strike fully, if not vehemently, discussed; I had been an ardent listener to what was said against this attempt at "oppression" on the part of the corporation, and naturally I took sides with the strikers. When the day came on which the girls were to turn out, those in the upper rooms started first, and so many of them left that our mill was at once shut down. Then, when the girls in my room stood irresolute, uncertain what to do, asking each other, "Would you?" or "Shall we turn out?" and not one of them having the courage to lead off, I, who began to think they would not go off, after all their talk, became impatient, and started on ahead, saying, with childish bravado, "I don't care what you do, *I* am going to turn out, whether any one else does or not;" and I marched out, and was followed by the others.
>
> As I looked back at the long line that followed me, I was more proud than I have been since at any success I may have achieved. . . .

Robinson's sense of accomplishment was short-lived, however, because the corporations soon took action against her for her role in the strike. She was left to conclude that such protest accomplished little in the way of permanent change.

> The agent of the corporation where I then worked took some small revenges on the supposed ringleaders; on the principle of sending the weaker to the wall, my mother was turned away from her boarding-house, that functionary saying, "Mrs. Hanson, you could not prevent the older girls from turning out, but your daughter is a child, and *her* you could control."
>
> It is hardly necessary to say that so far as results were concerned this strike did no good.[19]

Despite Robinson's pessimistic conclusions about this strike, it was a harder-fought battle than the turn-out of 1834. Once again, thousands of women assembled to hear speeches on their rights as daughters of revolutionary patriots. The Lowell turn-out of 1836 became a kind of progressive protest. The strikers made a concerted effort to close down the mills by focusing on the rooms that were central to production: if those departments shut down, the entire factory would have to stop. These workers knew more than their managers suspected about how the whole factory ran, and they tried to find the vulnerable spots on the production line. The weavers, though they were relatively well paid and felt the increase in boarding costs less, were well organized and led the walkout. They probably knew that their department was one of the most central in the mill, and they urged other workers to leave their rooms and thereby close down the entire mill. If enough workers joined the protest, though they might not be a majority, they could stop the factory's operations.[20]

Many operatives held out for more than two weeks, and it was reported that a "Factory Girls' Association" was organized with 2,500 members. This organization demanded that the manufacturers communicate with its officers and that no sanctions be taken against any members. Robinson's account, however, demonstrates that some strikers were punished. After a month of agitation, the strike concluded much as the one in 1834 had. Some workers left mill work altogether and returned to their families; others straggled back to their jobs under the new rates. But one observer reported that the corporations had actually rescinded the board increase for workers paid by the day. Thus, about forty percent of the women workers (those paid a daily wage) did win their basic demand. The corporations, faced with thousands of strikers and mills shut down for weeks in the midst of a sales boom, were rather anxious to settle this dispute.[21]

Another strike was also reported in Dover in 1836 to protest wage cuts. The turnout lasted only three or four days, although it was reported that during that brief period the women managed to cover the mill fences and the door of the company office with placards supporting their cause. The first strike in Chicopee, Massachusetts, also occurred in 1836 to protest the same practice of raising boarding fees without increasing wages. Operatives in Amesbury, Massachusetts, staged a brief walkout during that same year; their grievances, however, revolved around the institution of the stretch-out. This strike had something to do with money, but also with the intensification of labor. The weavers were ordered to tend two looms for the same pay they received for tending one. They immediately stopped work, proceeded to the local Baptist church, and pledged not to work under the new system or pay a five-dollar fine. The agent sent a written notice to the strikers telling them to come back, under the old system. Rarely was a dispute settled so quickly, or so favorably for operatives, in antebellum factories.[22]

In the early 1840s, women workers in a variety of industrial communities also continued to walk off their jobs when they felt that their basic rights were at stake. Over 300 operatives in Saco, Maine, left the mills during the early spring of 1841 to protest new regulations requiring them to live in company housing or face dismissal. There were also rumors of a wage cut, but it was the boarding rule that stirred up the most discontent.

Although the cause of this strike was unusual, the protest followed a familiar pattern. The workers marched through the streets to the strains of the village band. The strikers then met at the Baptist church and voted on resolutions to restore more lenient boarding rules and condemn the proposed wage cut as "severely reprehensible and calculated to enrich the few at the expense of the many." They also proclaimed, in language reminiscent of the republican rhetoric of Lowell strikers in the 1830s: "We are not slaves!—We scorn the name! / We ask nor friends or foeman's favor; / We're freemen's daughters—and we claim / The Rights that woman's father gave her."

The regulations affected all the employees, but it was the women who publicly denounced them. Some said it was particularly the employees raised in the contentious atmosphere of Dover who led this strike. Others claimed that it was the older workers—better paid, more experienced, with influence over the new arrivals—who resented being pushed back into the restrictive atmosphere of the boardinghouses and organized the protest. A committee of townspeople investigated the workers' grievances (an unusual gesture of community interest), but found only minor points in need of rectification. The strike was over quickly, with most workers returning to the jobs under their new regulations, or looking for new positions elsewhere.[23]

The women who turned out in Chicopee during the closing days of April 1843, were able to organize yet another procession in support of their cause. They marched through the streets to the music of fife and drum, dressed in their best clothes, and waved their handkerchiefs to women in other mills as a signal to join the parade against wage cuts and speedups. In this case, however, workers in other factories were slow to join the strike, so the women returned to their jobs and were, apparently, permitted back in to work. They took to the streets again a few days later, but still met with little success. To add to their problems, when they tried to go back to work for a second time, their managers dismissed them. The Chicopee mill owners were apparently lenient enough to let their workers blow off some steam once, but two strike processions were one too many.[24]

Two years later, some spinners at the Dwight Corporation in Chicopee refused to tend their machines when they were started one Monday morning, because of a reported wage reduction. They remained off the job until Tuesday afternoon, when management persuaded them to return for a fifty-cent per week raise. This walkout was very limited in scope, without any accompanying public displays. But these women maintained their ranks, and the managers quickly realized that even a small turn-out could adversely affect their company, so they settled the matter. Why this modest turn-out succeeded where larger protests failed is not certain. Perhaps the Dwight Corporation was caught at a vulnerable moment in its production schedule and needed those spinners at work no matter what the cost.[25]

Most of the strikes in the mechanized factories of antebellum New England, from the early 1820s to the mid-1840s, confirmed the patterns set by the first walkout at Waltham. Most strikes took place at large textile mills; they were often led by women (frequently weavers); and they usually revolved around a dispute over wages. There are many possible explanations for this basic pattern of protest. First, the predominance of strikes in textile mills may be a historical artifact. Protests at large mills usually involved a substantial number of workers, and women often spoke out publicly for the first time at these turn-outs. These strikes were therefore bound to attract attention because of their unusual character. It is possible that other protests occurred at smaller, more isolated factories, but no one bothered to record these walkouts for posterity.

Rural factory villages may also have been particularly unconducive to organizing labor protests because there were fewer workers to draw on, fewer public meeting places to congregate at, and more power concentrated in the hands of the owners. The large textile mills, on the other hand, brought together unprecedented numbers of workers in a single factory complex. Many of these operatives, especially the women, were living and working away from home for the first time. As a community of female operatives formed, with its own moral standards and its own forms of peer pressure, that emerging network could have been a powerful source of protest and resistance. The workers who participated in strikes were reappropriating the sense of discipline and interdependence they learned in the mills and using those principles to organize themselves in united protest. Weavers were often particularly known for their willingness to assist each other on the job, and perhaps on strike as well. Weavers also had more skill and earned higher wages than many other operatives—hence, they had higher working status and more economic resources. These weavers may have thought, therefore, that they had more to fight for, and more to fight with, than their co-workers.[26]

In some mills, women ran the entire strike when their male co-workers failed to offer much assistance. Male operatives, often paid on a daily basis, were usually less affected by the wage cuts, which were based on piece rate reductions. Managers may have deliberately aimed at women's piece rates because such cuts produced the most savings and seemed to divide the work force along gender lines. But manufacturers who assumed that women would accept these cuts more readily than men were often gravely mistaken. Female operatives showed clearly that, in many cases, they were ready and willing to organize in defense of their rights. They were saying that if men would not ally with them—whether out of fear of economic competition or social stereotypes about the supposedly weaker sex—then the women would help themselves.[27]

The close connection between strikes and wage reductions is also an intriguing phenomenon. Workers would occasionally walk off their jobs in protest against long working hours, factory and boardinghouse regulations, stretch-outs and speed-ups. But the main bone of contention was usually a cut in piece rates leading to a reduction in earnings. Why did so many strikes focus on the restoration of wages? It is possible that wage cuts actually became a lightning rod for workers' discontent with other aspects of the mechanized factory system. Operatives may have had long-standing grievances with their work and their employers, and wage reductions were the last straw. Wages were, after all, the result workers saw after all their labor—they had very little contact with any finished products. If their bottom line was cut, or their livelihood tampered with, then immediate action was called for to rectify this problem, which would show up in their next pay envelope.

Many operatives may have believed that they could not influence the basic structures and operations of the factory; they refused to believe, though, that they had no control over the value of their labor. Wage cuts jeopardized the operatives' standard of living immediately. They also undermined whatever future prospects for upward economic mobility were available to workers. Many workers believed that they had to challenge these decisions, and they remained hopeful that wages were an issue they could really negotiate about. To protest wage cuts may have been a way to vent frustration with the entire factory system on an issue where workers might still make a difference.

Other patterns also emerged in many of these strikes, which were often quite complex in their form and context. Turn-outs were frequently accompanied by processions and rallies, and the strikes became public displays of indignation as much as deliberate attempts to withhold labor. They were more than spontaneous outbursts of pent-up anger; they also had a core of organized collective action, a kind of choreographed protest.

Women strikers in particular knew that when they complained and struggled and fought, they were often condemned for being unruly and unnatural and unfeminine. So they often tried to orchestrate their strikes to present as dignified, restrained, and "feminine" an image as possible. The numerous street demonstrations that often accompanied strikes—with women dressed in their best clothes, bands playing, banners flying, songs being sung—indicated that these women also had a very sophisticated political consciousness. They took the idea of using public space for political activity and applied it directly to themselves and their demands.

These demonstrations at times almost took on a festive atmosphere. But they were not joyous celebrations; they were deliberate efforts to capture people's attention and address crucial problems. The protesters engaged in a kind of public theater to make their grievances known without appearing to be threatening. Thus, violent confrontation was rarely seen in these strikes; rather, the women often based their own protest marches on the political and religious parades they saw all around them.[28]

Factory operatives learned about elaborate processions from their own participation in such gala occasions as the visit of a president or foreign potentate to an industrial community. As early as July 1817, President James Monroe began a tradition of presidential visits to notable new manufacturing sites. He visited the mills at Waltham and was especially impressed by the double line of female operatives he passed through on his way out. When General Lafayette visited the factories at Dover in 1825, he entered the mill yard through a double column of 200 women dressed in white with blue sashes. By 1833, when President Andrew Jackson came to Nashua, New Hampshire, 1,000 operatives greeted him in row after row of white dresses and red ribbons.[29]

Jackson also visited Lowell at this time, just one year before the first strike there, and the parallels between the great parade in his honor and many of the antebellum protest processions are clear. Nearly every mill girl in the city, all of them wearing white dresses with sashes and parasols, marched in the parade along with many other townspeople. The women marched by corporation and department, each company going in order, from the first incorporated to the most recent, with a banner at the head of each division.[30]

In some industrial communities, such as Nashua, women textile operatives became a regular feature in other public celebrations like militia musters and election day rallies and the Fourth of July. The proceedings on July 4 were often an especially significant moment for the operatives to immerse themselves in rallies. The women of Lowell marched in a "temperance procession" during one Independence Day, and the Hamilton Mill threw a picnic for operatives. Political and religious rallies were also often commingled on this day, and these combined fêtes, again, bear a strong resemblance to labor protests. Mary Hall's description of July 4, 1834, speaks of a day of rallies and speeches not unlike the strikes of the preceding February and the fall of 1836. Hall wrote in her diary:

> This morning at the hour of eight many assembled at the Lawrence printing house where we heard some very important remarks addressed to those present by their Agent Capt. Wm. Austin. At the hour of ten went with others to the Unitarian Church where a highly interesting Oration was delivered. . . . At four joined my Sabbath School Class and walked in procession to Chapel Hill from where the audience were addressed by different Clergymen belonging in town.[31]

Caroline Ford wrote about a similar march in Middlebury, Vermont, during the summer of 1841. Although there were no strikes in Middlebury, those who lived and worked there may have taken the memory of such demonstrations with them when they moved on to new jobs and relied on these models for their own protest parades. In making their strike processions like July 4th processions, workers may have been proclaiming their protests to be public demonstrations of their own ideas about independence and freedom. Ford wrote to her brother with details about the Sunday school march.

> [W]e had selebration here the 6 of July the four Sabbath schools met at the congregation meeting house thare was sone whare abou four of hundred scholers besides a grate number spectators they had four addresses delivered at the white meeting house . . . and they had four hymns sung by the scholers And then we marcht out Before the Hotell two by two and every teacher to the head of their class and each school had A banar that was cared by four boys. . . . And thare we was before the hotell side by side thare till we had orders to march the congregational school went forward the episecle school went next and then the Methodist school went next and then the Baptist school fecht up the rear we marcht acrost the S Bridge and up the walk over and went threw the coledge and up to the Ecademy . . . then they formed the prosesion and marcht down to the coledge green and thare they formed into a square and thare the banors met in the token friendship and love they sung the doxology and then eachschool returned to its own home.[32]

The organized marching units, the waving of banners, and the final convocation, were all similar to labor rallies of the period. But protesters did not simply copy these parades, they took the basic structures and redesigned them for their own needs. For example, women usually wore white dresses in religious processions, but the strikers at Taunton wore black. And managers often marched with their workers in political parades, but they were never found in the streets with strikers. Workers had taken these public displays of civic pride (which were often used to celebrate the prosperity of manufacturing communities) and turned them on their heads as demonstrations of workers' grievances with the factory system. Those who protested chose not to march dutifully in a procession organized by the manufacturers: they took to the streets under their own direction.

The public political image of many strikers was also filled with allusions to their revolutionary heritage and republican values. The spirit of independence and resistance to tyranny, and the ideal of equality, were very real to antebellum operatives. Many of them had fathers and grandfathers who had fought in the war against Britain—they really were the "daughters of freemen." They deliberately invoked these images of the Revolution to show the world that they had legitimate rights as citizens of their community and the nation.

Therefore, when women protested, their rhetoric bristled with classical republican notions of citizenship and justice, even though they were automatically disenfranchised because of their sex. Yet these women clung tenaciously to their rights as descendents of the patriots. The spirit of the Revolution, for the strikers, was not merely a memory but an ongoing social process. Republicanism was not a conservative or moderating doctrine of civic virtue or social order, but a call to reform and action in the name of justice and equal rights. Workers' republicanism was the ideal of freedom from all exploitation and oppression, of individual liberty, and of social solidarity—respect, decency, and dignity were the watchwords of the workers' republic. To struggle for the rights of labor was to fulfill the promise of freedom and equality proclaimed in 1776. Those who took to the streets in the industrial communities were the new patriots; they drew on their traditional values of Yankee independence and used them to justify their new strike tactics. Protest was a necessary tool to restore the balance of power and fundamental rights when the inequities of the factory system undermined the revolutionary heritage of equality.[33]

Strikers often put a great deal of energy into public displays and rhetoric as a means of rallying more workers to their cause and developing a common identification with the strike. Most operatives probably had little previous experience with labor protest, and many may have viewed the strikes with uncertainty and fear. Strike leaders knew they had to mobilize as many workers as possible if they were to have any chance of success in meeting their demands. Thus, although most walkouts were not directed by established unions, their internal organization was frequently quite sophisticated. Strike actions were often discussed in advance, although they also retained a certain amount of spontaneous energy. And workers often formed various associations (albeit usually short-lived ones) during the course of their strikes to support their efforts. Organization did not always have to precede agitation, but coordination of public protest could strengthen the strikers' resolve.

In some strikes, public agitation helped spread the protest throughout a factory, or throughout many factories in a particular community, without regard to occupational distinctions. Workers from a variety of specialized mechanized departments, from one factory to another, took to the streets when manufacturers combined to institute simultaneously a new policy or a wage cut. Antebellum New England factory operatives did not stage general strikes to shut down entire cities or national strikes against an entire industry. But female textile workers in particular made deliberate efforts to unite operatives with varying skills and interests under their protest banners. Even when male workers did not join the strikes, the women redoubled their efforts to recruit more mill girls to the cause.[34]

Strikers also used their public demonstrations in an attempt to mobilize (rather than polarize) community support for their protests. The protesters wanted their communities to see them as fellow residents with legitimate grievances, not as outside agitators intent on stirring up negative reactions. The strikers therefore tried to make both a class-conscious appeal to their fellow operatives and a call beyond their own class interests to the larger public's sense of justice and fairness. They did not shy away from criticizing the factory system, but they did not articulate an ideology of open class conflict. The protesters saw themselves both as workers fighting for their own immediate goals and as citizens—part of the larger community—fighting to preserve the shared republican heritage of equal rights. That sense of citizenship and political community is why they thought that they could gather support from other townsfolk.[35]

Protesters believed that other townspeople shared some of their concerns about the manufacturers and were not content to remain servile members of company towns. The calls to strike were frequently couched as public appeals to support workers who saw themselves as the underdogs engaged in a fight for equality with the powerful corporations. Occasionally, some support was offered, as in the 1824 strike in Pawtucket; and this support seemed to give the workers more bargaining power. These endorsements, though, were more likely to emerge when the operatives were connected to the industrial community by ties of kinship or marriage. Many of the striking weavers in Pawtucket were the daughters of local artisans and laborers.[36]

Many workers in other factories, however, did not have such personal connections with the surrounding townsfolk. They were recruited from a broad geographic area and their roots were in distant rural villages. The women of Lowell, for example, learned to form bonds with each other for support, because they received little sympathy from the strangers in the city itself. Many townspeople were especially disturbed by the sight of women engaged in public protest. This distance between the strikers and the local community may have been one of the reasons why the Lowell strikes failed. In general, when protesters had little or no political and economic support from the surrounding community, they found it much more difficult to wage a prolonged strike. The lack of such a prolabor alliance did not preclude the emergence of protest, but it could severely restrict the long-term viability of a strike movement.

Another cause for the failure of many strikes was the pressure manufacturers exerted to force the protesters back to work or out of the factories permanently. The owners rarely resorted to lockouts or invoking conspiracy laws, because they did not believe that the strikers posed that great a threat to their companies. Manufacturers did regularly fire and blacklist workers for their participation in any form of protest, and even the threat of such action often persuaded workers to go back into the factories.[37]

Perhaps the most powerful force against the strikers was the reluctance of so many of their fellow workers to join in the protests. Some workers were reluctant to participate in strikes because of their personal reservations about the propriety of such actions. Many women were uncomfortable with the idea of challenging social norms about female modesty by protesting in public. One character in Lucy

Larcom's "Idyl of Work" may have spoken for many female operatives in her opposition to strikes. She advocated the idea that workers should simply exercise their individual option to retreat from any form of disagreeable labor, rather than confront their employers with demands for improvements.

> [Ruth was] quiet, 'mid continual stir
> Of work-and-wages questions. There had been
> Meetings, conventions; now and then a girl
> Spoke on the rostrum for herself, and such
> As felt aggrieved. Ruth did not like that course,
> Nor "strikes," that ever threatened. "Why should we,
> Battling oppression, tyrants be ourselves,
> Forcing mere brief concessions to our wish?
> Are not employers human as employed?
> Are not our interests common? If they grind
> And cheat as brethren should not, let us go
> Back to the music of the spinning-wheel,
> And clothe ourselves at hand-looms of our own,
> As did our grandmothers. The very name
> Of "strike" has so unwomanly a sound,
> If not inhuman, savoring of old feuds
> And savage conflicts! If indeed there is
> Injustice,—if the rule of selfishness
> Must be, invariably, mill-owners' law,
> As the dissatisfied say,—if evermore
> The laborer's hire tends downward, then we all
> Must elsewhere turn; for nobody shall moil
> Just to add wealth to men already rich.
> Only a drudge will toil on, with no hope
> Widening from well-paid labor."

Many other women may also have associated protest with a kind of intense passion and conflict that defied social control and jeopardized the social order—there could even be the implication of sexual impropriety. For these women, protest and disorderly behavior was far more dangerous to female operatives than any possible problems in the factories. There was no need for public demonstrations; the streets were for tramps and harlots, not for respectable workers.[38]

Other operatives opposed strikes on more pragmatic grounds—most resulted in defeat for the operatives. Harriet Hanson Robinson said simply: "strikes . . . usually end, as the first Lowell one did, for the time being at least, in the success of the employer, rather than of the employee." Available figures do indicate that by the 1840s, many of the strikes that did occur were smaller than earlier turn-outs. This is one indication that fewer workers in that decade were willing to participate in such risky activities.[39]

The sum total of many of these strikes for female operatives in antebellum New England was a certain degree of tension in their lives. Many women were, for the first time, assuming stances openly antagonistic toward their managers, which were also defensive postures designed to protect what workers thought were basic rights.

They were forming new networks to reassert traditional ideas about equality, even as their real economic status was being eroded. In many cases, protest erupted precisely because workers were told that their position was subordinate to management's directives, and that sense of inferiority came into direct conflict with the workers' belief that they should be treated as equals in the factory system. Therefore, the strikers concluded that they had to band together and create new forms of solidarity to defend each individual's freedom and equality. They lashed out in anger because they thought that management was destroying the economic and social foundation for the proper relationship between labor and capital, and they demanded that those equitable relations be restored.[40]

A profound tension also was at the heart of these strikers' means and ends. Operatives walked out as a public expression of their grievances and a demonstration of their determination to right the wrongs they saw in the workplace. They used protest and militancy as bold tactics to reassert their respectability and their rights. Their specific demands, however, usually did not entail any major restructuring of the factory system. Strikers rarely challenged the rights of private property or capital itself. Their protests were rooted in a classically liberal critique that respected private property but feared concentrated power. In particular, most workers wanted to stop management's power from encroaching on accepted wage standards and working conditions. Operatives rarely staged offensive campaigns for wage increases; they usually fought to roll back a cut in wage rates. These protests did strike a blow at management's position atop the factory hierarchy and the imperious use of managerial power. But most workers did not use the strikes as an aggressive crusade to overthrow the entire factory system.[41]

Strikers were trying to prove to their co-workers, their employers, and the public that they were responsible citizens standing up for their rights. They considered themselves respectable and patriotic people; but their patriotism was linked with the idea of fighting for justice, not conservative obedience to political authority. Yet they were not trying to destroy the factory or the community, they simply wanted a fair deal from the company. There was no talk of seizing the means of production, only disagreements over the standards for a fair day's pay and decent working conditions. These disagreements certainly produced sharp words from workers about factories and managers and owners, but rarely was there a call for drastic change. Workers usually used their most vehement rhetoric to justify modest demands, such as restoring wages to former levels.

In the end, most of these strikes were defensive struggles for limited goals. Workers' activism was rarely translated into radical social visions—militance was not the equivalent of radicalism; militance was a tool for fighting against greedy owners. Strikers fought for decent wages, decent working conditions, and some status in the workplace—it was more than a matter of money, but far less than a workers' revolution. Yet they were quite capable of acting with real determination and forcefulness—in words and deeds—in pursuit of what were essentially moderate demands. And the more often they saw these modest requests rejected, the more often they heard themselves being condemned as the radicals they decidedly were not, the more they strove to protect their rights and preserve their status.

— III —

Although most strikes by operatives in antebellum New England involved female workers, there were also several significant turn-outs by male factory workers. None of these working men's factory strikes attracted the same kind of public notoriety as the women's protests in cities such as Lowell and Dover. Even though these strikes were less frequent and more obscure, however, they provide an important counterpoint to the more prevalent and more famous working women's strikes.

The skilled immigrant textile printers at the Dover Manufacturing Company engaged in a series of job actions to try to secure favorable contracts, wages, hours, and the right to unionize. Management resisted the printers' efforts to dictate their own working conditions because it undermined corporate authority and ran the risk of fomenting discontent among other workers. (It is possible, in fact, that the 1828 strike of female mill workers in Dover was triggered by the protests of the immigrant male printers that were going on around the same time.)

In early April 1827, the printers first voted not to allow new workers into the printery who were hired at lower wage rates. The printers even decided to "furnish a purse sufficient to meet all" of the company's "pecuniary claims" on the new employees "and demand their discharge, but after further consideration, they had voted the Saturday previous, that they might go to work." By Tuesday, however, the printers changed their minds again. It was reported that they had "all quit their work . . . and have been engaged in Gunning & drunkenness and other diversions. . . ." The company agent, John Williams, wrote to the treasurer:

> *all* the printers are engaged in the difficulty & they boast that they have such rules and such an understanding throughout the *world,* that we cannot get any men from England, or any where else untill we come to their terms. . . . The printers have notified all their brother printers in this country, of the course they have pursued & future determinations. They say decidedly and peremtorily that the contracts . . . shall not be complied with, if they do not conform to the prices they receive here.

The following day, Williams again wrote to the treasurer, William Shimmin, about the printers' "*determinations* to control the printing establishments in this Country and their *belief* that they can do so . . . these men calculate to stop both Lowell & Taunton" print works as well. The agent stated "that the whole body of them had determined to erect a printery for themselves." About ten days later, the workers agreed to go back to printing, but different groups of workmen straggled back over the course of several days.[42]

The printers at Lowell were also known for their fierce independence and combative nature. Harriet Hanson Robinson remembered that when the English workers arrived at the Merrimack Corporation, "they were not satisfied with the wages, which were not according to the agreement, and they would not go to work, but left the town with their families in a large wagon with a band of music." Kirk Boott himself was said to have ridden out after them and agreed to their demands for higher wages; and they returned to Lowell playing an even livelier tune. Robinson did not say when this dispute occurred. But correspondence among the Dover Manufacturing Company managers indicates that they were aware of labor unrest in

Lowell (perhaps the same incident Robinson recounted) at the same time that they were wrangling with their own employees. On May 9, 1827, another letter to William Shimmin stated:

> I have this morning been informed Lowell printers, cutters, designers, color mixers, &c &c, "*turned out* when English prices were offered to them" this applies to both old and newly imported men and comes to me through one of our overseers in the *business*—It remains to be seen whether they or the owners of works shall manage them—I apprehend that if the printers now dictate prices at this time they can by the same rule increase or modify them when they feel so disposed—.

Robinson saw the printers' action as a celebration of workers' spirit and autonomy. The Dover managers, on the other hand, saw such walkouts as a threat to the hierarchy of the factory system and the principle of owners' control. Such diametrically opposed visions of working-class protest lay at the root of many such conflicts with these skilled immigrants.[43]

The immigrant printers fought tenaciously against encroachments on what they saw as their craft privileges. Their resistance seemed to be based on both Old World ideas of work and collective struggle they brought over from England, and a healthy dose of American working-class republicanism with its demands for justice and equity. These workers were trying to retain traditional English craft prerogatives over wages and working conditions in American factories, and at the same time claim their newfound American ideals about freedom and liberty for their own use. These workers' constant efforts to organize and protest were probably due both to their experience with such activism in England and to the examples of working-class agitation they saw in America.

These immigrant printers also seemed concerned that if managers were allowed to usurp the rights of English printers and American workers, then the factories of New England would descend to an even lower depth than the factories of Old England. By fighting to preserve, in New England, the power and status they had previously held in the Old World, these immigrant workers tried to carve out a niche for themselves in the American factory system. But they also wanted to make sure that, if or when they returned to England, they would have kept their craft knowledge intact and broken no union rules, which would jeopardize their acceptance back into the circle of English workers.

Although most antebellum factory strikes were marked by a distinct lack of violence, the one known instance when managers did try to physically break up a labor protest involved a group of striking male mule spinners. (It should be noted that company agents often tried to disrupt labor reform meetings in any way possible, but they seemed to shy away from directly taking on strikers.) This altercation occurred in a Valley Falls, Rhode Island, mill during the spring of 1829, when a group of mule spinners decided one Monday morning to leave work after lunch because of a cut in their wage rates. The spinners later returned to the mill, found other workers at their mules, and tried to force the new employees to leave by tampering with their machines. The factory agent eventually arrived on the scene and ordered the strikers to leave. The spinners now refused to be forced back out, and the agent drove them from the mill with a stick. The workers charged him with assault and battery, but a court found the agent within his rights in forcing the strikers from the mill.[44]

Male operatives in Salisbury, Massachusetts, turned out to protest the elimination of their customary morning and afternoon recesses. Management had eliminated these breaks, when men usually gathered to talk with each other or attend to personal matters, because workers were leaving their posts for up to an hour. But when the new rule barring such breaks was supposed to take effect, the overseers reported that

> many of the operatives, in direct violation of the above rule, left their work in an UNUSUAL MAN[NER]. . . . The result was that the public mind became very much excited. Public Meetings have been held by the Operatives, and others, denouncing the proceedings of Mr. Derby [John Derby, agent of the Salisbury Manufacturing Company], in the most unqualified terms. Flags have been suspended near his Counting Room, on which were inscribed insulting mottoes, he has been in various ways insulted while quietly passing through our streets. Great efforts have been made to induce the remaining help to leave the employ of the Company. A Band of Music has paraded our streets for the purpose of collecting a crowd, and indignities in various ways have been heaped upon him.

The male factory workers of Salisbury, like women strikers elsewhere, tried to broaden their base of support throughout the labor force and in the community at large through public meetings and musical bands and flags. Yet the overseers' report also contains numerous references to the company agent's being "insulted" by the strikers. If the overseers are to be believed, the male strikers appear to have been even more forceful in their denunciations of the company, and particularly of the agent, than most female protesters. The men were not constrained by the need to pay any allegiance to social conventions about female modesty, so they directed their anger personally against the agent wherever he appeared in town.[45]

No clear patterns emerge from these strikes of factory men, probably because these turn-outs were few in number. These particular protests, however, do have certain similarities with and differences from the more prevalent strikes by factory women. Both male and female strikers made use of public demonstrations—especially bands and music—to attract attention to their cause and rally support from more workers and townspeople. Both the men and the women who protested also saw their cause as more than a matter of money and regulations; it was a struggle for the right of the workers to be treated with respect and dignity.

When male workers struck, though, reports of drunkenness, insults, and violence also accompanied their protests. Strike activity became linked with the traditional masculine realm of alcohol and guns and physical tests of strength. (At least that is what management reported during these strikes. Since the male strikers issued no proclamations justifying their actions, as women strikers often did, these reports provide many of the details of these strikes.) Perhaps most important, management also seemed to fear a stronger challenge to their authority, and to the entire factory system, when male factory workers—especially the skilled immigrants—walked out in protest. The sight of women marching in protest was disconcerting to male managers, but it seemed to threaten the rules of social propriety more than it did the corporate control of the factories. After all, more women could always be found to replace the strikers, even if it took a while to recruit and train them. But when men like printers or mule spinners walked off their jobs, then managers worried that the workers were doing more than protesting particular policies. Male strikers were feared because they seemed determined "to control" the factories for themselves, to create their own workplaces, free from corporate power. And managers would be hard pressed to replace the skilled men who did leave. In the end, male strikers never achieved such dramatic results, though the more skilled among them often gained more concessions than most female strikers. But for at least a few days, in cities such as Dover, male strikers raised their own challenge to authority, hierarchy, and control in the factory system.

— IV —

The substantial number and size of the strikes by female and male factory operatives in the 1820s, 1830s, and early 1840s clearly indicates that the early decades of the mechanized factory system in New England were not a golden age that subsequently fell into decline. There were always voices raised in concern and protest over the emerging industrial order in antebellum America. By the middle of the 1840s, workers' voices became louder and their concern more widespread; even as the expressions of discontent changed in form and character. The moments of protest from past decades coalesced into a far broader movement, which launched a more extensive critique of the harsher working conditions in the mid-1840s. Labor newspapers and operatives' organizations flourished as never before, but strike activity decreased significantly. Even where walkouts did not end, it is important to note that the emerging labor organizations rarely led such protests. For a few crucial years in the middle of the 1840s, labor reform associations eclipsed strikes as the dominant form of labor protest in the factories.

More and more workers concluded that strikes were not only unlikely to win concessions on immediate issues from manufacturers, they also usually failed as foundations for building any lasting labor organizations for future agitation. Yet the activists of the mid-1840s did learn from the struggles of those who preceded them; they knew that they were not coming onto the scene after decades of pure contentment in the factories. They drew on many years of operatives' agitation, but refocused it on the idea of building workers' institutions for long-term change.

Factory workers, who had shown little organizational activity on their own during the 1820s and 1830s, and who had been left out of numerous other working-class groups that sprang up in those decades, finally turned to organizing themselves with a vengeance in the mid-1840s. They finally began to build on an understanding of the social relations of production in the mechanized factory system. If operatives worked as a collective unit within the factory, then they had the potential not only to strike as a group but also to create organizations for the whole work force.

This impulse to create stable organizations may have been felt particularly strongly in the wake of the depression of 1837, and it grew in strength on into the middle of the next decade. Many workers felt that they were being pushed into the factories, more than ever, out of necessity rather than choice. Once inside the factories, they found that manufacturers were pushing them harder (through tactics like the speedup and the stretch-out) to cut costs in the face of increased competition. The forces of labor and capital seemed to be moving farther into opposition; the workers decided to try to channel the conflict through labor organizations rather than brief strikes, hoping for more success in securing their rights. Many workers believed that there was a connection between deteriorating working conditions and the rise of labor organizations in the 1840s. While strikes usually lasted only a few days or weeks at the most, the labor organizations of the mid-1840s often endured for several years, and gave workers hope that sustained and collective effort would bring about change in the long run.[46]

The workers of Lowell are a prime example of the shifting focus of protest in the mid-1840s. Where thousands of female operatives had walked off their jobs twice in the 1830s, Lowell in the 1840s saw only one brief (and completely unsuccessful) textile workers' strike. Over 100 women went on strike at the Middlesex Company's woolen mill in December 1842 to oppose a twenty-percent cut in piece rates. The company justified the cut by the speed of the new, more efficient Crompton looms. The strikers never specified whether they were really angry about the new machines or the lower piece rates. The protesters never had large enough numbers to seriously challenge the mill's operations. They were fired immediately, blacklisted, and quickly replaced by new workers who were said to earn almost as much on the new machines.[47]

By the middle of the 1840s, Lowell operatives who had complaints about the factory system turned their energies toward forming labor organizations for long-term agitation rather than engaging in brief outbursts of strike activities. The Lowell Female Labor Reform Association (LFLRA) was formed in the winter of 1845, with thirteen officers and two additional members. The association's ranks swelled into the hundreds by the spring of 1845, under the dual mottos of "Try Again" and "Union, for Power." Sarah Bagley, the association's president, stated that the organization's purpose was to "arouse the minds of men and women to a sense of their own individual rights, and cause them to think for themselves, then will they begin to act for themselves!" The goal was for workers to regain a sense of autonomy in their lives, in place of the absolute and arbitrary authority of managers to control them. Bagley believed that, in the midst of collective activity, each operative would find the strength to better her own condition and contribute to the common good of all workers. "Union and action" were the watchwords for workers who saw themselves losing control of their lives. Yes, workers needed to speak out against the inequities of the factory system; but they could not let the matter rest there. Collective, organized criticism of the factory would go further than individual complaints. They needed to mobilize to fight those injustices and take back control over their own labor.[48]

Organized labor was also better equipped to take a defensive stand, when necessary, against the abuses of management. "In the strength of our united influence," proclaimed Amelia Sargent in the Lowell association's "Factory Tracts," "we will show these *drivelling* cotton lords, this mushroom aristocracy of New England, who so arrogantly aspire to lord it over God's heritage, that our rights cannot be trampled upon with impunity; that we will no longer submit to that arbitrary power which has for the last ten years been so abundantly exercised over us." The phrase "mushroom aristocracy" clearly conveyed Sargent's contempt for the authority of the factory owners—a group that seemed to spring up quickly in the damp of night and feed off the labor of others without any legitimate basis for their power. Sargent made no attempt to conceal her belief that workers needed to organize as a direct challenge to that corporate power, which had been expanding unchecked and unchallenged for far too long.[49]

The LFLRA was part of a broad working-class movement that swept through New England industrial communities in the mid-1840s. More important, the LFLRA was one of the first stable organizations of female operatives in the nation. These women, who had been excluded from so many working men's groups for so long, focused their own organizational energies on the female labor reform associations. The LFLRA was deeply involved in publishing the *Voice of Industry,* and a widely circulated series, "Factory Tracts." The association sponsored an industrial reform lyceum and various fairs and rallies to publicize its message and raise money. The organization also quickly became a leading force in coordinating the campaign for a ten-hour workday.[50]

The LFLRA, with Bagley as president, tried to steer a middle course between agitation and restraint in the campaign for labor reform. The association's constitution called for strikes only as a last resort. The organization did not want to renounce this ultimate weapon, but there seemed to be a general agreement among most Lowell workers in the 1840s that strikes were not the most effective means of change in the workplace. Therefore, the Labor Reform Association did not direct any major walkouts. The mid-1840s were years of intense discussion and activism by organized operatives in Lowell, but in the midst of all this activity, there were fewer calls for strikes. Many workers seemed to see their organizations as a way to secure their rights without confrontation, through strong and steady action on a variety of fronts, rather than as a staging ground for future labor conflict. Yet in theory the LFLRA did reserve the right to call a strike, as is specified in its constitution: "The members of this Association disapprove of all hostile measures, strikes and turn outs until all pacific measures prove abortive, and then it is the imperious duty of every one to assert and maintain that independence which our brave ancestors bequeathed us and sealed with their blood."[51]

Interest in labor reform associations spread to female operatives in other industrial cities. Larger factory communities may have been particularly conducive to organizing such groups because the sheer number of workers present made the possibility of long-term collective action seem more realistic. The workers of Manchester formed their own Female Labor Reform Association, as did operatives in Fall River and Dover. Meetings were held in Manchester boardinghouses to discuss labor reform issues and a constitution for the association. One operative, called home by the death of her brother, wrote an encouraging letter to be read at the Manchester association's meeting in December 1846.

> May every one present have something to say, and above all be sure to say it, even if to yourselves it may not seem to be "quite so bright." Encourage each other by words, acts, and looks. Let your light shine that those who are fearful may come forward in the mighty work of Reform. This subject is now discussed almost every-

> where. Don't get to sleep just as everybody is wakening up. . . . Don't be afraid to speak to the "Old man," "second hand," and "Bobbin Boy," and I venture to say they will become converted to our faith and be with us. Union is power, knowledge is the same and both we can possess. . . . At our next meeting I hope to be present and enjoy the hearty co-operation of every member of our Association, and a host of the sisterhood, who will go heart and hand in ameliorating our condition.[52]

This letter was a clear call for workers to overcome their fears through the very process of organizing. Those who were afraid for themselves and their jobs or for their friends and family had to rise above those fears. Organizing labor reform associations was the only meaningful way to protect the workers' interests and rights. There was no tension between workers' solidarity and security for an individual worker and her family. Those who refused to unite would remain trapped by their fears in a no-win situation—they would continue to be frightened by the powers of management arrayed against them as isolated individuals, and they would have nowhere to turn for support in protecting themselves.

The association in Manchester also received support from their fellow organized operatives in Lowell. One worker cautioned her co-workers in Manchester not to be taken in by corporate promises that " '[c]apital will take good care of labor.' " Such offers were merely an attempt to deceive the public and distract the workers. The operatives needed their organizations to "let the proud aristocrat who has tyrannized over your rights with oppressive severity, see that there is ambition and enterprise among the 'spindles.' " This operative also advised the Manchester workers to take that "ambition and enterprise," forged through union, yet part of each individual, and "act independently and no longer be a slave to petty tyrants, who, if they have an opportunity will encroach upon your privileges." The well-developed labor organization was seen as an organic whole striving to be as self-reliant as any individual.[53]

Huldah J. Stone, secretary of the Lowell association, also sent encouraging words to the Manchester organization. She urged the group to "persevere united, faithfully, triumphantly . . . hundreds more are ready to join your ranks . . . if you prove active and vigilant,—true to yourselves and faithful to the noble enterprise in which you are now engaged." It was especially important, Stone advised, that meetings be fully attended. Each member had to share in the association's responsibilities; it was not up to a "spirited and zealous" few to do all the work. Shared labor within the organization was crucial to promoting real solidarity. Stone also gladly offered to continue her correspondence with the Manchester workers and to attend their meetings whenever possible.

Stone had a vision of solidarity among operatives that transcended any one location, occupation, or industry. "Let us seek to encourage and strengthen each other in every good word and work," she wrote.

> . . . To effect this glorious work of reform we believe a complete *union* among all the worthy toilers and spinners of our nation so as to have a concert of action, is all that is requisite. By organizing associations and keeping up a correspondence throughout the country, and arousing the public mind to a just sense of the claims of humanity, we hope to roll on the great tide of reformation until from every fertile

> vale and towering hill the response shall be echoed and re-echoed:—*Freedom—freedom for all!*

Stone's ultimate goal was for each operative to find personal independence through united action with other workers; true liberty for every individual could only be realized and nourished through collective struggle. To be free was not to be alone, but to be a part of a free labor movement.[54]

Workers who joined unions were not sacrificing their freedom. Quite the contrary: they were gaining real freedom to work with others to improve their lives, rather than the meaningless freedom of an individual operative—with no power or money—forced to find work in a so-called free market dominated by capital. Collective action and labor unity were essential for workers to better themselves as individuals and as a group or class. Ironically, operatives could restore the ideal of individual freedom of advancement only through organization and collective action to uphold the rights of all the workers. Operatives had to organize, not only for their own individual security and advancement, thereby using collective means for personal ends; they also had to build organizations that would embody a more collective and social vision of cooperation over competition. Unions would protect workers' immediate needs; moreover, they would be a vital step in the transformation of society.

The labor movement among antebellum factory operatives was a way for them to respond to what they saw as a loss of autonomy in the industrial system. Yet these workers responded in a way that both accepted and challenged the growing collectivization of labor in the factory system. Operatives, by joining unions and associations, recognized the value of collective action in a system where independent craft workers were few and large groups of semiskilled operatives were often the rule. But these workers insisted that the goal of their collective action was more than to forward the interests of labor as a group—or a class: it was also to preserve each worker's independence as a person.

The operatives who built the labor organizations of the 1840s, like the strikers before them, based much of their agitation on the premise that they were the equal of any other man or woman, regardless of wealth or position. But these workers (again like the strikers) also believed, with just as much conviction, that the factory system was undermining that principle of equality. They did not welcome the sense of inferiority that was inflicted on them, yet they could not deny its presence. In fact, one of the fundamental reasons for workers to band together was to reassert that idea of equal worth among themselves, and to demand that respect from their employers. Labor organizers argued that, since the workers and managers usually came from the same republican roots, then all operatives deserved respect from their managers. The elaborate hierarchies of managerial authority had to be torn down if employers and employees were really to work productively together.

These demands for mutual rights and respect were exemplified by a representative of the Manchester association when she wrote: "we Factory Girls must be vigilant, we must act for ourselves and push these matters along. No Reform . . . can progress without your co-operation. Remember, you are entitled to 'Equal Rights and Equal privileges' with those whom you give fat Dividends." Other Manchester operatives adopted their own set of resolutions, which spoke not only of equality, but of "justice to ourselves and to our employers," which was "clearly right" and which they were "willing to give and receive."[55]

Mutual rights and respect also needed to be forged between female and male operatives in order to build the strongest possible labor organizations. Even back in the 1830s, Seth Luther realized that such cross-gender solidarity was essential for any successful effort at labor reform. He stated that "it is quite certain that unless we have the female sex on our side, we cannot hope to accomplish any object we have in view." Luther saw that bringing more women into labor organizations would strengthen unions in terms of sheer numbers and in their sense of solidarity. Moreover, organizing women workers would prevent unorganized women from being used by management to undermine the unions.[56]

In some trades, working men labored long and hard at keeping all women out of workshops because of fears that women lowered wages, skills, and status. But in the textile industry, and in other manufactories where women were firmly established, some men (though certainly not all) encouraged women to organize for better working conditions for themselves. These men not only supported women's efforts, but hoped that improved standards for female operatives would translate into better working conditions for themselves as well.[57]

Female workers, who were usually to be found in the more homogeneous ranks of the semiskilled, tended to favor industrial unions of all operatives. These women believed that all factory workers, regardless of their particular jobs, had to come together to meet the challenges of the changing industrial workplace. They may have sensed that workers' organizations, if confined to a small group, might reinforce bonds within that group, but would also incur resentment among those left out of the fold. It was crucial to form associations that were both supportive and inclusive.

The Manchester Labor Reform Association reported in 1846 that its female and male branches had begun to meet together. "We find this the best way as we can devise plans together, to better advantage," Sarah Rumrill and Mehitable Eastman wrote to the *Voice of Industry,* "seeing men can do nothing without us, and we cannot do much without them." These women added that "so many of our sisterhood" were afraid of their overseers—" 'The old man' "—and many men were reluctant to "move in our cause, for fear of being 'discharged.' " But there was strength in numbers and in the unity of men and women. It was essential to mobilize and unite men and women so that they could not be pulled apart when managers tried to divide the work force along the lines of gender. Mehitable Eastman, in her capacity as a subscription agent for the *Voice,* also submitted a report that testified to the support she received from many men working in factories. " 'This Voice of Industry Girl,' " she wrote, "is exceedingly grateful to the gentlemanly working men, . . . from whom so much encouragement has been received not only in pecuniary point of view, but by kind treatment which made the task more agreeable and easy."[58]

Male workers were sometimes still uneasy about the activism of their female coworkers, and the women sometimes were concerned that men would dominate any unified organization. There was always the danger that gender distinctions would erode any emerging class solidarity among the workers. Working women and men might form alternative, or even opposing, work cultures, apart from each other. In general, however, the mutual respect that flowed between these men and women showed a kind of equality between the sexes rarely seen in antebellum America. At least some male workers had come to see female operatives as fellow laborers. These men abandoned whatever previous hostility they may have had toward women in favor of a respect rooted in a common working-class experience. For these workers, there were no separate spheres of female and male working-class consciousness. This is not to say that these men and women abandoned all ideas about gender differences. But they were able to merge those ideas into a sense of a common class experience and recognize the need for working women and men to unite at the workplace.

As female operatives became deeply involved in local labor reform associations, and in regional organizations (an opportunity that had usually been denied them before the mid-1840s), they faced new challenges in arguing their case for labor activism. Sarah Bagley, when she addressed the New England Workingmen's Association in May of 1845, defended the right of women to speak for themselves even as she assured her largely male audience that female activists would not threaten the men's sphere of power and politics. Bagley was a strong advocate for the rights of working women, but she did not want to jeopardize the support of working men by making her demands seem too strident. Her crusade for working women's rights was wedded to more traditional concepts of female nurturing and morality. Bagley's speech about women and protest, before a crowd filled with many men, took public political acts and associated them with gestures of personal benevolence.

> For the last half a century, it has been deemed a violation of woman's sphere to appear before the public as a speaker; but when our rights are trampled upon and we appeal in vain to legislators, what shall we do but appeal to the people? Shall not our voice be heard, and our rights acknowledged here; shall it be said again to the daughters of New England, that they have no political rights and are not subject to legislative action? It is for the workingmen of this country to answer these questions—what shall we expect at your hands in future? . . . We do not expect to enter the field as soldiers in this great warfare; but we would like the heroines of the Revolution, be permitted to furnish the soldiers with a blanket or replenish their knapsacks from our pantry.
>
> We claim no exalted place in your deliberations, nor do we expect to be instrumental of any great revolutions, yet we would not sit idly down and fold our hands and refuse to do the little that we may and ought to.[59]

Bagley saw the fight for labor reform, whether women acted on their own or in support of men, as essential to the protection of women's health and dignity. Those who protested were not violating the ideals of female modesty, they were defending the virtue of women from the encroachments of greedy owners. If women were said to be the guardians of higher moral values against the corruptions of the commercial industrial culture, then women had to use those values in an active effort for labor reform. Women best fulfilled their obligations as moral guardians, not in isolation from the outside world, but in helping each other and their male co-workers in the battle for workers' rights. Crusading for labor reform could be seen as a particularly important calling for women and as an expression of their natural maternal and benevolent instincts. But women had to remember that sometimes they had to cast off the stereotypes of female docility and false refinement in order to take action to defend their real respectability. Women had a moral obligation to organize and fight against the injustices of the factory system.

Bagley also wanted to reassure male workers, outside observers, and even female operatives themselves, that public agitation would not destroy the femininity of women or the basic sexual divisions in society at large. Bagley argued that working women would come together and take on the corporations, in the factories, the press, the legislature, and even the streets if they had to; but always in the name of preserving women's decency and dignity. Bagley never envisioned a revolution of fire and blood; she wanted a reassertion of workers' fundamental rights. Public protest did not compromise dignity and morality, it preserved the workers' status and respect.

Working-class leaders like Bagley, and their emerging organizations, devoted most of their energy and rhetoric to mobilizing operatives for collective action. Although these groups fired off many penetrating critiques of the factory system, they rarely made specific demands on particular companies. Since they were struggling to gather support and to make some sense out of the industrial order itself and were never recognized in any meaningful way by management, demands for collective bargaining or specific contract clauses seemed to be very premature. Unlike many antebellum craft unions, the operatives' organizations rarely made detailed demands for particular work rules to enhance their control over the production process. Nor did these operatives' organizations try to exert any control over the labor recruitment process through apprenticeship or union hiring procedures. Neither did they propose any standard lists of wages or piece rates for bargaining with management. These associations were filled mostly with semiskilled operatives with little or no organizational experience or bargaining power who were trying to lay the groundwork for their critique of the factory system and their initial campaign for labor reform.[60]

Operatives in the mid-1840s worked hard to form and solidify their organizations. Ironically, as workers became better organized and perhaps better able to protest more forcefully than ever before, they became more cautious and moderate in their direct actions. Workers in previous decades had tended to come together and strike out at immediate issues; many operatives feeling that they had few institutions to rely on. They seemed willing to act boldly for those immediate goals, without worrying about protecting any established organizations. By the mid-1840s, labor organizations had become forceful critics of the factory with a breadth of vision rarely seen before. Their activities, however, tended to focus on more moderate tactics of petition campaigns and publishing labor newspapers. They usually avoided strikes, perhaps because they were afraid to jeopardize the organizations they had now established.[61]

The labor movement of the mid-1840s was therefore broader and more outspoken in its campaign for significant reforms in the factory system, but less physically militant than previous strikers. What the labor agitation of the 1840s gained in breadth, it may have lost in intensity, compared with the more limited strikes. The message of the labor reform associations was heard, to some extent, throughout

New England. But the power of that message may have been diluted by its very diffusion throughout the region. The previous strikes had been discrete bursts of workers' anger, which certainly disrupted particular factories' daily schedules. But these walkouts did little to directly challenge, or propose alternatives to, the factory system as a whole. The labor reform movement was a broader-based effort that engulfed literally thousands of operatives throughout New England and launched far stronger criticisms of the industrial order. Yet on a day-to-day basis this movement rarely physically confronted the power of the corporations in a direct way.[62]

The early strikers had often proved themselves to be militant, but they were not radical. The strikes were quickly revealed to be limited in scope and power. Yet despite these limitations, they were often charged with a high degree of human emotion and energy. The labor organizations, on the other hand, were more powerful in their critique and in the potential strength of their membership. Yet these groups proved to be more moderate and less confrontational in their actions, despite their size and breadth. Strikers were more likely to take on managers and owners, though less likely to criticize the factory system as a whole. Labor organizers were more likely to speak out about restructuring the factories themselves, but less likely to directly confront the factory owners.

— V —

Despite their relatively moderate stance, factory workers' organizations—and their demands for equality and justice—were usually not welcomed by factory managers. Management wanted sole authority to determine how to organize the labor force; it did not want workers to have the power to organize themselves.

Management's battle against labor organizations did not begin in the 1840s. As early as 1816, the Springfield Armory issued one of the earliest known "yellow dog" contracts—documents that prohibited workers from attempting to organize, under penalty of fines or dismissal. The armory's regulations stated:

> It is enjoined upon every workman in this est. not to begin, excite or join in any Mutinous, riotous or Seditious Conduct against the Regulations of the Armory, nor to oppose the officers when in the execution of their Duty, nor wilfully refuse to observe the lawfull direction of the officers of the Armory, nor enter into any combination against them.

The regulations added that "all combinations against the officers or regulations of the Armory will be noticed by an immediate reduction of the wages of all concerned." In 1834, another regulation was issued with stronger penalties: "all combinations formed for the purpose of disparaging . . . any . . . officer or impeding the progress of the work will subject the delinquents to dismission from the armory." The Cocheco Manufacturing Company's regulations were among the most explicit in terms of interdicting workers' organizations. This factory expressly forbade "any combination, whereby the work may be impeded, or the Company's interest in any work injured." Operatives who engaged in any such "combination" lost any wages due to them.[63]

By the 1840s, the crusade to stamp out labor organizing often concentrated on blocking the distribution of labor newspapers—at least an implicit acknowledgement by management of the growing presence and power of the labor press in this decade. Some factories, such as the Great Falls Manufacturing Company in New Hampshire, were not completely sure of themselves when first dealing with the growing workers' associations and the labor press. Management at the company was divided on whether to stop the distribution of literature as an organizing tool. Mehitable Eastman, a subscription agent for the *Voice of Industry,* reported that the factory agent did not object to her entering the mills. No one else made her "afraid by looks or words" until she "came to enter a lower weave room there was a lord who molested me, but could not make me afraid, though his appearance was very much like the feline species. He ordered me out of his room, but 'Bill' could not extend his authority any further and I went on with my business and was well treated throughout the premises." The North Chelmsford (Massachusetts) Machine Shop was firmer in its ban on the local *Voice* agent. The management said that it did not allow any publications to be circulated on its premises. Yet, a year previously, the same female agent was granted permission to sell temperance newspapers on the shop floor.[64]

Distributing the *Voice* was especially difficult in Dover. The subscription agent there encountered opposition from the overseers and found the operatives "afraid to express their true sentiments." The watchman, upon hearing that subscriptions were being solicited for the *Voice,* rushed in and ordered the subscription agent out of the mill yard, "using the most abusive language which [she had] ever heard." The watchman added "with an important air: 'we do not want our help hindered by your presence; we want you to go to work about your business, and not be idle with other peoples.'" The subscription agent, after being threatened with jail, later returned to the factory in disguise and succeeded in obtaining many orders for the newspaper.[65]

Obviously managers were selective about the kind of literature they wanted their employees to read. The *New England Offering,* for example, was welcomed by many factory agents because of its procorporation sentiments. Harriet Farley wrote that, during her travels to Manchester and Nashua, the managers of many mills were more than willing "to give every girl an opportunity to subscribe, without taxing [my] own time too heavily." But when an unsanctioned newspaper made its appearance in a factory, it was usually confiscated under the pretext that regulations prohibited reading on the job. One New Hampshire overseer was said to have frequently seized such papers and then told his fellow overseers that "it costs me nothing for papers." After looking over the entire issue, he would conclude: "there's nothing in it worth reading. . . . [I] wouldn't *take* such a paper!" He never revealed whether he derived any real insights into the sources of workers' discontent or any information about future labor organizing schemes.[66]

Many companies also made strenuous efforts to inhibit organized meetings and lectures among their workers. In factory villages, it was often especially difficult for operatives to find a meeting place that was not owned by the company or under its control. The mill owners of Woonsocket, Rhode Island, used their political influence on the town's school committee to prevent workers from assembling in the schoolhouse. Local ministers, if sympathetic to the cause of labor reform, would sometimes make their church buildings available for workers' meetings (as they did during several strikes). But these clergymen proved to be exceptions to the rule for most ministers, who avoided such labor organizations or opposed them outright. If operatives were able to find a suitable hall, many were still reluctant to participate in organized activities. Some probably saw no need for such gatherings; others were intimidated by the possibility of company reprisals. N. W. Brown reported that in Blackstone, Rhode Island, the operatives were so afraid of the corporations that no one would act as chairman at a lecture on labor reform.[67]

John Cluer, an English labor activist immigrant who spoke to textile workers throughout New England in the 1840s, was frequently harassed in his efforts. He once went to Fitchburg, Massachusetts, had himself introduced as an English manufacturer, and was invited to look around the Stone Mill. When Cluer started asking the operatives about their wages and hours, the agent caught on to the real purpose of his visit. The agent "told some of the girls that he only gave him leave to look at the work, but did not give him leave to speak to the help. . . . But that did not prevent them from going to hear Mr. Cluer that night." More than twenty women walked over half a mile after work in bad weather to hear Cluer speak and to voice their own support for labor reform.

In Manchester during the winter of 1846, Cluer was greeted by newspaper stories containing lurid rumors about his personal life. One overseer even showed his female employees all the published details in a effort to shock their sensibilities. Nevertheless, many people turned out to hear Cluer's lecture, and he did speak, despite written threats of violence and imprisonment. Cluer even read part of the menacing communication to the audience, and he remarked that he "pitied the *wretch*" who wrote it "and his *employers.*" Cluer then proceeded to Peterborough, New Hampshire, where another of his lectures was disrupted by a lawyer who wanted the meeting to vote on resolutions regarding Cluer's character. The issue was put to a vote, and not a single person supported the attorney's proposals. Cluer knew perfectly well that all these tactics were aimed not solely at him, but at the cause he espoused. He wrote: "The capitalists and *their* press aided by British villains, hunt me like blood-hounds—they have money, and at present they do not spare it, in order to crush me; but it is not *me,* they care about, it is the cause I am engaged in; they will be foiled, let them do their worst, I defy them!"[68]

Other labor organizers had faced an even more hostile reception in Manchester during the fall of 1846. Their first meeting was held in a lumberyard because all the public buildings were closed to the speakers. Corporation agents then called on the local constable to stop the proceedings, but hundreds of listeners simply moved into the streets to hear the speeches on labor reform. After a week of torchlight rallies, the corporations sent out thugs to intimidate the organizers and to pelt the crowds with rotten eggs. Yet hundreds of workers continued to gather every evening, on into a second week, and raise their voices in condemnation of the corporations' and the city's harassment.[69]

The simplest and most direct way to stop workers from organizing was for individual managers to put personal pressure on individual operatives to desist from such activity. This technique also provoked some of the most stinging rebukes of managers. Sarah Bagley recounted one example of a Lowell agent's reprimanding one of his female employees for using "her leisure hours in assisting in the organization of our 'Labor Reform Association.'" The agent offered to excuse any "past offences," but he also threatened to punish the woman if she persisted in her organizational activities. Bagley, in her brief tenure as editor of the *Voice of Industry,* used her position to blast the agent's conduct and to proclaim her newspaper's power to put its own pressure on managers.

> What! deprive us after working thirteen hours, the poor privilege of finding fault—of saying our lot is a hard one. Intentionally turn away a girl unjustly—persecute her as men have been persecuted, to our knowledge, for free expression of honest political opinions! We will make the name of he who dares the act, stink with every wind, from all points of the compass. His name shall be a byword among all laboring men, and he shall be hissed in the streets, and in all the cities in this widespread republic; for our name is legion though our oppression be great. . . . We war with oppression in every form—with rank, save that which merit gives.[70]

Bagley always stood ready to champion the rights of operatives to organize and defend themselves against management's threats. But what Bagley did not recognize, or at least did not admit publicly, was that managerial pressure did not unilaterally undermine the workers' solidarity. The physical nature of mechanized factory labor and the workers' own personal biases also often weakened group consciousness. Factory work was not always an asocial experience, but it frequently was more atomizing than other forms of labor. The sheer size of some factories made it difficult for workers to get to know one another. The presence of machinery—with its noise and its demands on the workers' attention—when combined with work rules prohibiting talking, made social contact among operatives increasingly difficult. Moreover, factory populations were divided by age, sex, and skill. Many workers were also transients; they had little sense of belonging to any one place or group. And those who worked with their families often felt that their domestic life was their primary concern. Thus, mechanized factories brought large numbers of workers into close physical proximity with each other, even while creating and fostering many distinctions among them. With a frequently heterogeneous factory population, it was almost impossible to avoid certain points of social conflict among the workers. Such conflict often eroded any organizational consciousness among them.[71]

By January of 1847, just two years after its founding, the LFLRA was transformed into the Lowell Female Industrial Reform and Mutual Aid Society (LFIRMAS). The organization's name change was more than cosmetic; it reflected a deeper shift from a group centered on working women's own agenda for labor reform, to an organization based on applying middle-class notions of "moral uplift" to working women. The new society was certainly not a wholesale capitulation to pressure from managers or to possible divisions in the ranks of female operatives. But this new group was even more moderate in its direct actions than its predecessor, and often limited in its overall vision.

The LFIRMAS was rooted in the ideals of female friendship and shared obligation. The concept of solidarity was firmly linked with women's traditional nurturing roles. Huldah J. Stone, in introducing the society's constitution, wrote: "Let us unite together and protect each other. In health and prosperity we can enjoy each other's society from week to week—in sickness and despondency share in and kindly relieve each other's distress. The young and defenceless female, far away from home and loving heart, can here find true sympathy and aid." The constitution's preamble went on to link the society's relief programs with the larger goals of labor reform. "We feel that by our mutual, *united* action . . . we can accomplish much, which shall tell for the progress of Industrial Reform—the elevation and cultivation of mind and morals, in our midst—the comfort and relief of destitute and friendless females in this busy city." This society saw itself as essential to providing a sense of social identity and value in the midst of rapid change and growing anonymity at work. The goal was to connect middle-class ideals of pure womanhood and respectability with a working-class ideology of collective action and the dignity of labor. Yet the society never was clear about how it was going to reconcile those divergent ideas into one unifying organizational philosophy.[72]

— VI —

By 1848, most factory labor organizations were in eclipse, if not outright collapse, and another round of wage reductions went through the Lowell mills, prompting more female operatives to consider their response. The avenue many chose was neither a strike nor a new association. Instead, a group of women published a newspaper, *The Protest,* in November to try to coordinate a mass exodus from the mills. The object was not to have each operative decide on her own whether to quit, and thereby fracture any collective response; but to organize all the disgruntled operatives so that each individual decision to leave could become a part of an effective collective exodus to shut down the mills because of low wages. If the women coordinated their movements and left the mills in large numbers to return to their rural homes, then they could strike a blow at the corporations themselves. The plan was not to remain in Lowell and picket, but to leave the city *en masse.*

> To our homes then we will go,—not individually, isolated and alone, but as a host of united sisters. Together we will pledge a new devotedness, to the cause of liberty and boldly assert our independence . . . we give our head and heart to the work of equal rights, and to stay the oppressor's hand. It is of no use to lop off a branch here and there; the axe must be laid at the root of the tree, and no more effectual way can we do this than by *leaving.*

Leaving *en masse* may not have been the perfect solution; but it may have been the one response, in a world of low wages and no unions, that gave workers hope of achieving some kind of unity.

With this bold scheme in mind, the following resolutions were published:

> That on account of the reduction of wages in the several mills in Lowell, it becomes a duty, in justice to ourselves, to the country, and to the world as laborers, to leave "this city of spindles" and seek our livelihood elsewhere. . . .
>
> That as ours is a common cause and what interests us, should interest every female operative in Lowell, therefore it becomes us, to act *unitedly,* and to suffer no root of bitterness to spring up that might hinder the furtherance of our pro-

ject. . . . That as there are many, who would gladly leave but for want of means, it is therefore our duty to lend them a helping hand and assist them on their way.

The last resolution was significant because it recognized that leaving the factory was not always a simple step for every operative. Some workers felt tied to their jobs, even though they may have had their grievances, because they had neither the money nor the skills to seek out other opportunities. This resolution urged those with more resources to help out the less fortunate, so that all who wanted to free themselves from the system of falling wages could do so.

The women who wrote *The Protest* also included an eloquent (if unsuccessful) plea for workers to rebuild their organizations in support of continuing agitation for better wages. There was an open letter to "the female Operatives throughout New England" urging them to oppose corporate policies on wage cuts. This letter clearly acknowledged that the key to the companies' power was their ability to organize and act in concert. The workers needed to create a similar organization to secure their rights from this corporate combination. The authors of this letter, writing after the heyday of organizing in the mid-1840s, still mustered some important arguments about the necessity for collective action.

Workers were told that owners might preach the virtues of competition to their employees, but all the while, they were forming legal confederations. Therefore, workers had to ensure that they did not fall for all this talk of competition. They had to organize themselves to be as tough and disciplined as the corporations they faced. Only organized labor could deal on equal terms with organized capital. Quite simply, if capitalists had the right to combine and form corporations, then workers had the right to combine and form unions.

> In order to render our resolutions effectual, combinations among ourselves are indispensable for our mutual protection—protection against a power before which even legislation has shown itself weak and inefficient; a power from which the liberal institutions of our country, have more to dread than from internal traitors or foreign foe: namely, chartered corporations. It is by a system of combination alone; admirably adapted to secure its object that these oppressors are able to carry their measures into execution. Therefore, the only alternative remaining to us, is to resort to the same means of resistance and resolve by united effort, to foil them by their own weapons . . . in union and determination alone, lies our strength—that united we stand divided we fall.

The corporations were clearly portrayed as the threat, not only to good working relations in the factories, but to the nation's basic "liberal institutions." The workers' organizations, on the other hand, were seen as a means of defending the operatives' and the country's best interests.[73]

Organizing individual workers for a mass exodus was not an easy task; many operatives seemed to pick up on the opposite idea of leaving on their own as an alternative to any protest or collective demonstrations. Harriet Farley, in an editorial written for the *New England Offering,* also in 1848, advised her readers:

> A continual grumbling and whining are, to say the least, in shocking bad taste; and a constant abuse of those from whom one is voluntarily receiving the means of subsistance, seems also to be something more than bad taste. But the eye may be

> open to every evil, and the mind active to devise remedies and ameliorations, without the whine of discontent, or the clamor of sedition . . . one of the methods by which a factory girl may improve her condition. She may leave the mill. What girls have done, girls may do. She may become a teacher, to say nothing now of less influential positions.

Farley assumed that a variety of employment opportunities was available to operatives who chose to leave the factories. She argued that workers were not permanently bound to their factory labor. Thus there was no need to remain in a mill and argue about the terms of employment when there were other jobs to be done. One of the characters in Lucy Larcom's "An Idyl of Work" also urged a friend to leave the mill and avoid becoming embroiled in an impending strike. "They talk of strikes,—they say that half the looms / Must stop, or wages be reduced. A muss / Of some kind must be stirring. So get leave / To come, and, till it settles, rest with me."[74]

Eliza Jane Cate, writing in the summer of 1849, also saw the logic behind many young women's leaving the mills when faced with low wages.

> [T]hus comes a reduction of wages through the works. Ha! it is as if an earthquake came. The electricity goes out of the girls, their hands lie heavily in their laps, and their eyes are dull. What shall be done? . . . Shall they stay there away from home and friends, shut up day after day within those brick walls, for the pittance of two dollars . . . a week? Suddenly, as their thoughts go out, they alight upon England, with the miserable wages, the vice, ignorance, and starvation of her factory people. . . . Will they . . . *they,* the daughters of New England, the indomitable, . . . of Yankees, the Midas of these modern times . . . will they submit to—in short, to anything? Will they work on "like the sheep that is dumb before its shearers," and let English wages, English prices of labor, English misery come home here into our pleasant places? No, no! They will go home and breathe the fresh air, and course it through the fields and woods up there. . . . In the self same hour their notices are given; in a fortnight they are on their way home, with hearts alternating between joy over the meetings that are to come, and sorrow over the late partings with the friends of their factory life. . . .
>
> Others are poor; their parents are poor; but they will find a home, and loving hearts made glad by their return. And they have no fear. They have always been above want; they are quite sure they always will be; and they will go home where the broad blue sky will be above them, and the green turf beneath them . . . they cannot stay and work at reduced wages. They cannot lend their aid to perpetuating English rates of compensation. If it can do them little harm, it will affect hundreds and thousands, who are as needy as they are. They must go home. And if the time comes that good wages are restored, they will be rested; they will have seen their friends, and they will come back.

Cate added that the result of this flight from the mills was counterproductive for the companies that cut wages.

> A thousand, it is said, left that one manufacturing city, Lowell, in a few months. This is bad every way; bad for the proprietors, their works being stopped, or managed so imperfectly by the new help coming in to take the place of the old; bad for overseers, on account of parting with so many of his best and best-liked girls, and

> on account of things going so crazy through their rooms; and bad for the girls; for while multitudes go away with quiet dignity, and multitudes stay in very friendliness for agent and overseers, and in pity for their troubles, yet other multitudes lose their tempers, and scold, and behave most unbecomingly; sometimes, although not in this case, getting up "a turnout," "a strike," for higher wages.

Cate's observations also raised the possibility that some workers left their jobs, not as an act of protest, but as a way to avoid any kind of confrontation. She knew that many operatives left because they were discontent, but she believed that such individual decisions were more dignified than organized work stoppages.[75]

In the closing years of the 1840s, as the women of Lowell saw their labor organizations disappear and as they endeavored to make some alternative response to deteriorating wages and working conditions, Fall River became a new focal point for labor unrest and renewed interest in strike activity. Strikes, therefore, did return to the antebellum New England industrial scene, but in new locations and in somewhat altered forms. The most important changes were that native-born and immigrant workers were beginning to come together in common protests (in Fall River, if not in Lowell), perhaps reflecting the growing presence of these foreign-born workers in the factories. Also, more men and women were participating in the same strikes, although they sometimes chose to create separate groups for coordinating protest activity.

Wages were cut in the Fall River mills during the winter of 1848, and workers began to hold meetings to organize a strike. At first the protesters asked the manufacturers to meet with them to show why the wages were reduced. When the manufacturers spurned these requests, some workers left their jobs and tried to lobby those still in the mills to come out and join the strike. In the midst of the protest, tensions amongst the workers flared up as some native-born operatives began to blame immigrants for the decline in wages. John Norris, a leader of the strike, tried to resolve these disputes by having natives and immigrants each visit their own countrymen to gain support from both groups for the walkout. Norris, however, soon found himself arrested on criminal charges in an effort to break the strike. He was held on 300 dollars' bail, and he wrote to the *Voice of Industry:* "no larger sum would be demanded by this same court had one man stabbed another. I guess a man raising his voice against the encroachments of the corporations is a greater criminal, for he is then stabbing at the selfish hearts of a many." After three weeks, the strike ended, and most of the 800 workers who had left their jobs (and closed down four mills) went back to work at reduced wages.[76]

Operatives at many Fall River mills struck again in November 1850 to protest wage cuts. These workers walked off their jobs suddenly, without giving any notice; unlike operatives in nearby New Bedford, Massachusetts, who paid a high price for their courtesy to management. The New Bedford workers told their employers in advance that they would leave their jobs rather than work at the reduced rates. The mill owners immediately hired replacements and fired all those who threatened to walk out. The Fall River operatives did not give any warning to their employers; they simply left work on the day they chose. Both mule spinners and weavers met to form unions for mutual support. The strikers also pointed out that the reductions were made in the fall when work was especially hard to find and money had already been spent on winter provisions. Many of the Fall River workers in 1850 were immigrants, and they were left with few resources to return to their homeland; so they had to stay in Fall River and fight on as long as they could hold out. But they also had with them many traditions of union solidarity which they brought over from the old country, and such memories helped them to hold tenaciously to their strike demands.

The mill owners tried to point out to their mule spinners that the companies hired additional help to lighten each worker's load and bought new machines to increase productivity and earnings. The mule spinners countered that their labor was actually becoming more arduous: some men were even forced to clean their own mules on Sundays. The strike lasted about six months, into 1851, and created great hardship for many protesters during the winter. Thousands of dollars were raised throughout the country for the 1,300 strikers in need. But by the middle of 1851, most of the best spinners had left the city, and the mills were filling up again with new workers at the lower rates. As with so many other factory strikes in the antebellum period, no matter how skilled the workers or how long they stayed off the job, the companies emerged victorious.[77]

Thus, the legacy of protest for many workers—from Waltham in 1821, to the surge of labor organizations in 1845 and 1846, to Fall River in 1850—was a mixed one. Operatives could take some pride in their displays of courage and power, knowing that they could stand up and fight for their rights if they had to. But the failure of so many strikes and labor organizations also left many workers with lingering frustration and bitterness toward their managers and the entire factory system. Some operatives wanted to avoid any more agitation in the future for fear of further losses. For other workers, the smoldering resentments lay scattered around the factory waiting for the next spark—a wage cut or a new regulation—to ignite them again in another confrontation with corporate power.[78]

CHAPTER 8

A Time to Labor: Workers, the Workday, and the Ten-Hour Movement

The labor reform movement of the 1840s voiced many criticisms of the factory system and many ideas for correcting these problems. One issue, however, became a focal point for many workers' organizations—the problem was the long hours of factory labor, and the solution was the campaign for a ten-hour law. This early crusade for labor legislation underlay much of the organizational activity among factory operatives in the mid-1840s, and brought to the forefront a long-standing debate about the hours of labor. The ten-hour movement also raised new and crucial questions about the meaning of politics and citizenship for factory operatives.

Just as with wage labor, workers knew that the hours of labor were more than a matter of minutes and time on a clock. The struggle to regulate the workday was yet another test of power and control in the workplace. Some workers felt that they already had all the freedom they needed to work as long as they needed to make as much money as they needed. Other workers felt that it was imperative for workers to demand an absolute limit on the length of their workday; and, in the campaign for a ten-hour day, these workers introduced another factor into the factory system. The government and the political process became part of the debate over the mechanized factory. Most state legislatures quickly sidestepped any permanent involvement in such delicate matters as labor–management relations, but politics and the workers' fight for some leverage on the shop floor would never be the same as before.

— I —

The fundamental question of just how long a workday should be had always been a bone of contention among antebellum factory operatives, and between them and their managers. Many new operatives had to adjust to a factory system wherein work was usually regulated by precise measures of time. This emphasis on time was not unique to mechanized factories; many antebellum workplaces were trying to regularize their employees' hours of labor. This desire for a clearly defined workday, however, was especially keen in many mechanized industries where management thought it most economical to keep all machinery running and all operatives at work throughout the day. Although operatives were often paid by the piece, employers wanted to regulate the hours of labor so that production would be precise and predictable. Owners usually demanded that all their employees labor together as a unit within the factories for the same number of hours and at the same time.

The actual hours in a workday varied from factory to factory, but they were almost always longer than modern standards. New England textile mills in the 1820s and 1830s reported anywhere from eleven- to fifteen-hour workdays. "A Committee of Factory Girls" stated in the June 26, 1845, issue of the *Voice of Industry:* "the operatives work on an average of the whole year, more than twelve and a half hours per day, exclusive of going to and from their work. . . . A woman in a Factory in New England, works an hour and some minutes longer, every day in the year, than a woman in a British Factory. . . ." The precise length of each workday often varied with the seasons, but in Lowell during the mid-1840s, it always fell between eleven and a half and thirteen and a half hours of actual labor.[1]

Many workers complained that they spent more than half of every full day, excluding Sundays, inside a factory. The winter months, when daylight was so precious, were especially hard on operatives. Joseph Hollingworth commented caustically on the beginning of evening work by lamplight: "We have begun waking . . . the Factory tonight & shall have to continue till about 1*st* of March. May God Blast the Factory System altogether for what I care about it. We leave work at night by Moon Light & returns in the morn' by the same." A young factory girl shared this frustration at being trapped in a kind of perpetual darkness. "I go to work before daylight in the morning," she wrote, "and never leave till it is dark and don't make enough to support mother and baby." Sarah Bagley discovered on a visit to the New Hampshire state prison that convicts at "hard work" labored about two hours less than most factory operatives and never by lamplight in the evenings.[2]

Some workers linked the long hours of labor with their concerns about occupational health. One contributor to the *Voice of Industry,* a veteran of nearly two decades in the factories and a one-time overseer, stated that the excessive working hours were unhealthy in and of themselves.

> The time we are required to labor is altogether too long. It is more than our constitutions can bear. If any one doubts it, let them come into our mills of a summer's day, at four or five o'clock, in the afternoon, and see the drooping, weary persons moving about, as though their legs were hardly able to support their bodies. . . . In fact there is nothing more common amongst operatives, than the remark that "their legs ache so, it seems as though they would drop off." Now if they desired to work so long, they would not complain in this way.

If working conditions inside a factory were particularly onerous—for example, if there were overheated and poorly ventilated rooms—then long periods of confinement under these conditions made the debilitating effects even worse. Workers fatigued by the extended workdays also probably ran a greater risk of being injured by machinery.[3]

Operatives spoke of being, not only physically debilitated by their toil, but also mentally stunted by their many hours of work. Those workers who saw machine-tending as a monotonous occupation to begin with, often saw their long workdays aggravating that boredom. A spinner in a woolen mill recalled that he worked thirteen hours a day in the late 1840s, slept very little, and became physically and mentally depressed. A Manchester operative wrote glumly: "mill labor has no attraction, the scenery is always the same, 'tis work, work fourteen hours per day, the year in and out, we are tired of the same routine and duties and singing the song of the fourteen hour system, worn out and cast down by the long hours of labor in the mills, which . . . seem tedious and longer than elsewhere." Many workers probably wondered why they had to work such long hours, when management was praising machinery that supposedly saved so much arduous and time-consuming labor. Whose time and effort were being spared? certainly not that of the operatives working fourteen-hour days.[4]

Many workers had a thirst for intellectual pursuits beyond the factories, but it was a constant battle to find the time and energy after work for exercises in self-improvement. One former Lowell operative remembered her own futile efforts to find the strength for serious learning after finishing her day in the mill. She wrote: "After one has worked from ten to fourteen hours at manual labor, it is impossible to study History, Philosophy, or Science. . . . I am sure few possessed a more ardent desire for knowledge than I did, but such was the effect of the long hour system, that my chief delight was, after the evening meal, to place my aching feet in an easy position, and read a novel." She added, however, that she "was never too tired . . . to listen to the lectures given by the friends of Labor Reform, such as John Allen, John C. Cluer or Mike Walsh." Overworked operatives—like this woman—often felt caught in a trap. Most of their time was monopolized by their employers to maximize corporate production and profit, and they were left with few physical or mental resources for their own advancement.[5]

Workers in industrial cities often felt particularly frustrated because they did not have the time to participate fully in the community around them. Factory supporters constantly reminded workers in these urban locales that they were fortunate to have access to a wealth of cultural and commercial opportunities. Some said that the shops and lyceums and libraries were the real benefit of working in a place like Lowell. An essay in the *Voice of Industry,* however, pointed out that many operatives were so worn out by their work that they could not avail themselves of these advantages. Many workers, in their desperate search for a fast dose of relaxation, gravitated toward the more risqué side of urban life, where corruption and danger lurked.

> Those who recollect the fable of *Tantalus* in the old Mythology, will be able to appreciate the position of a large portion of the population with respect to these exalted privileges. They are all around them, on every side, but they cannot grasp them. . . . Do you ask why they cannot partake? Simply from physical and metal exhaustion. The unremitted toil of thirteen long hours, drains off the vital energy and unfits for study or reflection. They need amusement, relaxation, *rest,* and not mental exertion of any kind. A really sound and instructive lecture cannot, under such circumstances, be appreciated, and the lecturer fails, to a great extent, in making an impression.—"Jim Crow" performances are much better patronized than scientific lectures. . . .[6]

Many workers saw the system of long hours, and its physical and mental burdens, embodied in the factory bells and gates and clocks. These structural components defined the workday precisely and publicly; their measurements of time were beyond workers' control; and they synchronized the labor force's movements in and out of the factories. The factory bell was usually placed on top of the building in a cupola or stair tower. The belfry could be in the center of the factory or on the side, but it usually stood atop the highest point where it could be seen and heard by all. The bells in Lowell woke the operatives up, called them into the mills, rang them out for breakfast and back in again, did the same thing at lunchtime, pealed out at closing time, and finally at evening curfew. The sound of the factory bells was a constant refrain in the workers' lives and a common figure in their writings. The bells symbolized the unyielding rigidity of the factory schedule. Operatives had to respond or risk losing their jobs.[7]

The song "The Lowell Factory Girl," popular in the 1830s, conveyed this sense of bondage to the sound of the bell.

> But now I am in Lowell,
> And summon'd by the bell,
> I think less of the factory
> Than of my native dell
>
> The factory bell begins to ring,
> And we must all obey,
> And to our old employment go,
> Or else be turned away.

A poem from the 1840s, "The Factory Bell" follows the sound of the bell throughout an entire workday. The bell overrules the sun and all other standards of time. Yet its sound seems to change throughout the day—it is both a stern taskmaster calling the workers to their jobs and a friendly voice reminding them of their brief respites.

> Sisters, haste, the bell is tolling,
> Soon will close the dreadful gate;
> Then, alas! we must go strolling,
> Through the counting room, too late.
>
> Now the sun is upward climbing,
> And the breakfast hour has come;
> Ding, dong ding, the bell is chiming,
> Hasten, sisters, hasten home.
>
> Quickly now we take our ration,
> For the bell will babble soon;
> Each must hurry to her station,
> There to toil till weary noon.
>
> Mid-day sun in heaven is shining,
> Merrily now the clear bell rings,
> And the grateful hour of dining
> To us weary sisters brings.

Now we give a welcome greeting
To these viands cooked so well;
Horror! oh! not half done eating—
Rattle, rattle goes the bell!

Sol behind the hills descended,
Upward throws his ruby light;
Ding dong ding,—our toil is ended,
Joyous bell, good night, good night.[8]

Poetry about the factory bell was also found in the *Lowell Offering*, and even here the image was sometimes bleak. One stanza, said to be sung by mill girls upon awakening, was rather mournful: "Morning bells I hate to hear, / Ring dolefully, loud, and drear. . . ." In another story, "The Spirit of Discontent," a young woman revolts against being enslaved by the bells.

> "I am going home, where I shall not be obliged to rise so early in the morning, nor be dragged about by the ringing of a bell. . . . I object to the constant hurrying of everything. We cannot have time to eat, drink, or sleep. . . . Up before day, at the clang of the bell—and out of the mill by the clang of the bell—into the mill, and at work, in obedience to that ding dong of a bell—just as though we were so many living machines. I will give my notice to-morrow: go, I will—I won't stay here and be a white slave."

As with so many other *Offering* stories, which ran the risk of criticizing the factory system, this one quickly glossed over these complaints and concluded with the indignant operative's being persuaded to stay in the mill. Her friends pointed out that working without bells was no guarantee of an easy job. But her rhetoric about workers' becoming machines and slaves to the factory bells remains quite striking.[9]

Factory clocks were closely linked with bells and the precise measurement of time, but these clocks were not always put in towers for public display. The official timepiece was often literally in the hands of managers, and many operatives could not afford their own watches. Thus factory owners frequently had the power, not only to set the hours of labor, but to measure those hours. They could abuse their position by tampering with the clocks, and then having the bells rung at their command. "Factory time" and "bell hours" could be significantly longer than "real time." It was a customary practice for some companies to add up to half an hour to the workday. Workers who already saw their hours as excessive were quick to condemn such insidious efforts to keep them at work even longer. Seth Luther declared that workers were "*robbed*, yes, *robbed* of a part of [their] time allowed for meals, by moving the hands of the clock backwards, or forwards, as would best accomplish that purpose." Luther added that there was "*patent lever 'clockwork'* of the *first quality* running on *diamonds*, which never was *guilty* of keeping the *true* time while in the atmosphere of a manufacturing village, or in the pocket of an agent, overseer, or owner of a cotton mill."[10]

Luther's complaints were echoed throughout antebellum New England. Women workers in Exeter, New Hampshire, walked off their jobs in 1834, and secured a promise from the agent that the foreman's watch would be regulated by solar time. This victory of the sun over the clock and bell was not a return to untimed preindustrial labor, but it was a way to get managers to be accurate in their measurement of time. The operatives of Pawtucket, Rhode Island, benefited from the construction of a town clock that broke the factory owners' monopoly over the measurement of time. The clock was intended to be an accurate display of the real time of day, and an important arbiter of the real hours of labor. Yet the public timepiece was also an indication that clock-time was now an accepted measure of labor for all parties. There was no turning back to preindustrial work rhythms. The issue was not whether labor would be measured in hours and minutes, but who would make the measurements and decide when the day was done.[11]

Operatives in Lowell were also concerned about the manipulation of their working hours in the 1840s. One veteran worker wrote:

> from November till March our time is from twenty minutes to half an hour too slow. So you see instead of getting out of the factory at half past seven o'clock in the evening, it is *really* eight. And more than this some of the clocks are so fixed as to lose ten minutes during the day and gain ten minutes during the night, thereby getting us into the mill five minutes before five in the morning and working us five minutes after seven at night.

Another operative spoke eloquently of how tinkering with factory clocks and gates for just a few extra minutes each day could add up over the years of a worker's career.

> You are laboring hard to show the injustice of compelling the operatives to labor the unreasonable number of hours which they now do . . . but . . . there are Minutes also to be looked after. I know sir, it will be said we are dabbling in "small matters," but when I reflect that many littles make a great whole, and that these littles are daily being wrenched from the operative, particle by particle, I am constrained to speak out, that this ever grasping, tyrannizing spirit may be rebuked and receive the contempt which it so richly deserves. Perhaps those who are accustomed to reflect and mourn over the fact that thousands of hard working females are allowed but thirty minutes to lave themselves, go down three flights of stairs, travel one fourth of a mile to their boarding house, eat their meal and return the same distance to their work . . . are not aware that it is even worse; *it is so.* On some of the Corporations in this city . . . it is, and has been since 1841, an established rule to hoist the gate twenty-eight minutes from the time it shuts down for meals, and on commencing in the morning it is to be hoisted eight minutes from the time that the Merrimack bell strikes, which is two minutes early at each time of hoisting, than is practised on that Corporation. Thus you see by tightening the screws in this way, the operatives lose from four to six minutes per day, under the pretense of allowing them thirty minutes for meals. A little calculation will show how it would stand at the end of five years; and it will be recollected that many of the operatives have worked in the same mill more than five years. Four to six minutes per day, say average five minutes—thirty minutes per week, two hours per month, two days of thirteen hours per year, and ten days for five years. This is the practical effect of this irresponsible, over-working oppressive system.[12]

The corporations' practice of shaving a few minutes each workday, particularly at mealtimes, made the entire issue of dinner hours another grievance for many workers. Management's goal was to keep the operatives at their machines for the maximum amount of time with minimal breaks for meals. Manchester operatives, in turn, frequently complained of insufficient time to eat and digest enough food to sustain them through the long workday. Workers had to drop their forks and run to beat the bell back into the factories. Another worker in Lowell also reported that a few minutes were always cut off from the half hour usually allotted for meals by ringing the bells ahead of schedule. This practice was condemned in no uncertain terms.

> This is corporation work truly, for no man can so far lose sight of his honor, as to compel his fellow laborers to return to their toil by ringing the bell before the time, unless ordered so to do by the corporation. One agent seems not to be satisfied even with this, as he often stands in front of the mills under his charge, with watch in hand, evidently to frighten them to work a few minutes before the time, and then trundles home in his carriage to spend his dinner time, in aristocratic luxury, as one of the privileged of the earth.[13]

Seth Luther pointed out that it was more hard work, not a welcomed respite, for an operative to go home for her meal and get back to the factory in thirty minutes. He observed, with a caustic touch of humor, "while on a visit to that pink of perfection, Waltham, I remarked that the females moved with a very light step, and well they might, for the bell rung for them to return to the mill from their homes in 19 minutes after it had rung for them to go to breakfast: some of these females boarded the largest part of half a mile from the mill." Even stories in the *Lowell Offering* described crowds of operatives hurrying to their boardinghouses for a hasty meal and running back to work. "And if, as is sometimes the case, the rules of politeness are not punctiliously observed by all, the excuse of some lively country girl would be, 'They don't give us time for *manners.*'" Perhaps the owners did not want their employees to have a free moment for socializing during the workday. But most workers yearned for longer mealtimes as a way to promote better health and friendlier social relations.[14]

In some factories the hours of labor were not extended by tinkering with clocks or mealtimes. Instead, operatives would have to work extra evening hours or on Sundays. In Lowell, managers said that evening work was done only infrequently in a few departments, only up to nine or ten o'clock in the evening, and always by volunteers. Joseph Hollingworth reported that the mill in South Leicester, Massachusetts, made more forceful demands on his time. In February 1829, he wrote: "I am now a Shearer and we have to run the Shears Night and Day. Of course I wanted to rest on Sundays." The next fall, Hollingworth revealed the pressure he had been under to work those late hours. "Last winter, I had to work a good deal of overtime at Nights; had I refused the whole family might have lost their work." Hollingworth also spoke of the demands put on the family for Sunday work. Managers were issuing orders, not looking for volunteers, and some of the Hollingworths took the risk of disobeying those orders and guarding their free time on Sundays.

> 'Tis true that they work on Sundays here. Bro. Jbz. has to work every 2 or 3 sundays in the factory repairing macheniry and doing such work as can not be conveniently done on other days. Bro. James is a spiner and he odered by the Bos spiner one sunday afternoon in the church while attending devine Service to go spin that eve-

> ning soon as the church service ended, but he neither woad nor did obey. I had to go tenter the second sunday after I began work and was ordered to go again but I did not obey and I have not been on a sunday since. The Factory system is the caus of this.

Families, like the Hollingworths, may have been particularly resentful of Sunday and overtime work. When the hours of labor were stretched out to such an extent, members of the same household could find themselves working different shifts, and it could become increasingly difficult for them to gather all their members together for meals or any other social occasion.[15]

The Collins Axe Company also used night work on occasion when departments fell behind in their production schedules. In 1830, Samuel Collins reported that grinders were working at night. These extra hours of labor, however, often created more production problems than they solved. Collins wrote: "I am hiring men to grind nights . . . *raw hands* . . . it is very difficult to get men to grind nights and they cannot do as much nor do it as well." Experienced workers seemed reluctant to put in time on the night shift, and the constant stream of newcomers at night made for slow work of poor quality. When veteran axemakers were compelled to work at night, they evaded the distasteful task by claiming sickness or working only half the late shift.[16]

The company's agreement with workmen in 1836 tried to address these problems with night work. The terms specified that workers' "bell hours will not exceed an average of ten hours per day through the year." But these terms also included this provision: "Any branch of the business that gets behind the rest will work evenings untill 9 o'clock, to catchup, if requested." The grinders' nighttime duties and pay were further detailed:

> in case of a scarcity of water in the river, the press grinders agree to work nights instead of days during such deficiency of water for which they are to be paid on each common axe three quarters of a cent more than the day prices . . . also in case there is not water enough during the day for the rest of the wheels the finish grinders agree to work during the nights instead of the days, for which they are to receive ⅜ of a cent on each axe above the day price, & the same on broad axes & hatchets.

The company recognized the need to pay nighttime wages that were above the day rates in order to get their employees to work steadily on a nightly schedule. The idea of more pay for overtime or nighttime work was therefore known to at least some antebellum factory workers.[17]

Many workers remained reluctant to work night shifts, and their resistance was one of the reasons antebellum manufacturers rarely ran their plants twenty-four hours a day. Some paper mill owners were exceptions to this rule. They tried to get the most out of their expensive machines by running constantly in two twelve-hour shifts from noon to midnight and then from midnight to noon. Sometimes these shifts were rotated from week to week because these workers also did not like working nights all the time. Most other factory owners, however, did not think it economical to hire two sets of workers or to run their plants all through the night by lamplight. They believed that they received the best return on their investments by keeping one set of workers on the job for an extended workday.[18]

One anonymous poem in the *Voice of Industry* summed up many of the sentiments against the long hours of factory labor. The workers' sense of time was shaped by mechanical and managerial forces beyond their control. Every day, it was "Get Up Early" and work by someone else's standards.

Get up early! Bells are ringing,
Calling you from bed;
Get up early! Steam is singing,
Water gains a head.
Get up early! Ere the red Sun
First lights up the skies;
Get up early! Well nigh dead one,
Ope your heavy eyes.

Get up early! Or a "quarter"
Minus, counts your time,
Get up early! Each pale daughter,
Hark! the "last bell's" chime.
Get up early! Tho' no flowers,
Blush upon *your* sod;
Get up early! With your powers
Win your master's God!

Get up early! Tho' before ye,
Lies the long day's toil;
Get up early! Tho' set o'er ye,
Agents reap the spoil.
Get up early! If a rhymlet,
Be your task to write;
Get up early! And if time let
Pen it for your Right.

It is only in the poem's closing lines that a ray of hope emerges that workers can retain at least some moment in the day for their own thoughts and goals. And it was to save those precious few moments of time for oneself and to ensure that every worker had those moments that so many operatives joined in the struggle for a ten-hour workday.[19]

— II —

In the 1840s, a growing number of factory workers fought to gain some control over their hours of labor through a mass legislative petition campaign for a legal ten-hour workday. Of course, workers' discontent with their long hours of labor did not suddenly emerge with the ten-hour movement. In previous decades, workers had also voiced their concerns with the problems of overwork. But these criticisms became sharper and the search for a solution to these problems seemed more imperative in the 1840s. Working men and women insisted that too many operatives had little or no chance on their own of ameliorating their long hours of toil. Moreover, the corporations showed little inclination to voluntarily accede to the workers' call for a shorter workday. Therefore, it was now necessary for the government to step in and pass a law mandating more reasonable hours of labor. The way to gain this legislation, however, was to shift the action from the picket line to the political arena. The movement would have to become active in political lobbying campaigns because the cost of strikes had become too high.

The first of these efforts to restrict the hours of labor focused on legislation for child workers. One former operative recalled that youngsters were often subject to the same work schedule as adults. He said that he was in the mill sixteen hours a day, including the one hour for meals (which he ate in the factory because he did not have time to go home), during his childhood in the 1830s and 1840s. He remembered that it was not until 1848 that this particular mill reduced its hours to fourteen a day. Other reports also stated that children in textile mills often worked more than thirteen hours a day, and they could be kept at work longer by manipulating the clocks and bells. Harriet Hanson Robinson stated that, as a child, she and her fellow doffers "were forced to be on duty nearly fourteen hours a day. This was the greatest hardship in the lives of these children." And Seth Luther claimed that "children born in slavery do not work *one half* the hours, nor perform one *quarter* of the labor, that white children do in cotton mills, in free New England." The outcry against the practice of employing children for long hours eventually produced an 1842 law in Massachusetts prohibiting youngsters under the age of twelve from working more than ten hours a day. In the same year, Connecticut passed a ten-hour law for children under fourteen.[20]

These new laws spurred other operatives to agitate for a ten-hour day for all adult workers. Throughout the mid-1840s, especially in Massachusetts, operatives circulated petitions to state legislatures calling for a reduction in the hours of labor. The ten-hour movement brought working men and women together under a common banner. Male and female operatives found a shared cause to struggle for; they were more united in this movement than in any previous protests at specific factories or in particular towns. In many industrial cities, women took a leading role in organizing the petition drives and often outnumbered men in the rank and file as well. A contributor from Maine to the *Factory Girl's Album* especially urged women to speak up, and not let social conventions of female modesty get in the way of their crusade for a shorter workday.

> Brethren and sisters in the cause of human rights—of *female* rights—ye who have espoused the glorious "ten hour system,"—and *ye* fellow sisters in *factory slavery,*—I ask you "is it not *time!*" "Is it not time" there was a law for the protection of *females,* as well as *males?* Shall not *woman's* voice be heard—be *heeded?* . . . Doth not the blood of the Operative cry from the ground, whither she has been thrust by excess of toil! . . . Operatives, let your motto be "liberty or death!" The broken, crushed, the maddened *heart* echoes "liberty or death!" Shall your *lives* be silent? God forbid! Peal forth the pass word of America's second *independence,* "*The ten hour system, or death!*"

Other workers also encouraged each other to continue agitating for this new law. They often chanted: "We will have the Ten Hour Bill— / That we will—that we will; / Else the land shall ne'er be still— / Never still—never still."[21]

Thousands of operatives took up this call to political action and signed petitions to the Massachusetts legislature (making sure not to address them to any one party). Nearly sixteen hundred Lowell "operatives and other citizens" signed a document in 1843 that clearly stated what they thought were the advantages of a ten-hour workday.

> WE . . . pray that a Law may be enacted, in such a manner as to affect all the *Manufacturing Corporations* of this State, so that they shall not employ persons to *work more than ten hours a day.* The tendency of such a law would be good. It would, in the first place, *serve to lengthen the lives of those employed,* by giving them a greater opportunity to breathe the pure atmosphere of heaven, rather than the *heated* air of the mills. In the second place, *they would have more time for mental and moral cultivation,* which, no one can deny, is necessary for them in future life—(it ought not be supposed those who work in the mills will do so as long as life lasts.) In the third place, *they will have more time to attend to their own personal affairs,* thereby saving considerable in their expenditures.

This early petition laid out many of the basic themes of the ten-hour movement—legislation limiting the hours of labor would give workers more time for healthful activity outside the factories, more time for improving their minds and their future prospects, and more time to attend to their daily necessities.[22]

Workers needed more time for themselves—this was a constant refrain in the ten-hour petition campaign. The petitions revealed the strong desire of many operatives to balance their work with the rest of their daily lives. Workers saw labor as a part of human existence, but only a part. Working men and women both proclaimed that they had real intellectual needs; they had to live for something more than work. They wanted to nurture their higher spiritual values and have some joy in life. Specifically, workers said that they needed more time to attend to their health, families, education, religion, culture, and the duties of citizenship. Therefore, the ten-hour advocates wanted a law that recognized the workers' right to regulate how much of their time they would have to sell to their employers and how much they would be able to keep for themselves.[23]

This yearning for a life that balanced thought and action, labor and knowledge, was echoed in other places as well. Mehitable Eastman, when she became one of the publishers of the *Voice of Industry,* wrote to the readers: "How are we to get information and keep knowledge? Give us time to read, for social intercourse, for amusement. Let us work less hours. Let us have the hearty cooperation of the many, and there will great good done to the toiling sons and daughters of New England—to the country, for knowledge is more powerful and important than dollars and cents." At a spring picnic in Dover, toasts were offered by various operatives on this same theme of a balanced life. One worker praised "*The Mind as well as the Body*—Both should be cared for—both should labor and be improved and supported; and the hours of labor of the body should not exceed those of the mind." Another operative toasted "*Ten Hours*—Fully sufficient for actual labor of either sex, and fully sufficient and long enough for all 'useful purposes,' and thereby leave the mind proper time for study and improvement."[24]

The need for workers to find some time for themselves and their personal needs was felt particularly acutely by young people. Ten-hour advocates often spoke about how important their movement was for the future of young workers. One woman focused her attention on the young men working in machine shops—"that noble youth at the forge, with bared breast"—and told the "Overseers and Agents . . . [to] ask thy *heart,* (if thou *hast* that scarse commodity,) if he deserves not a few hours to labor at the forge of the mind, that he might light a flame by which the midnight of other minds may become sunshine. . . ." A contributor to the *Voice of Industry* also developed this theme of how the ten-hour system would be especially beneficial to the younger workers; it would create a legacy of hope and opportunity for their future and that of the nation.

> [I]t is not for our sakes alone that we would labor—no, but for the rising generation; what, I ask, will they, or what can they be good for who are brought up amidst the whirl of spindles fourteen hours out of the twenty-four, with no time for improving the mind? Look with me through the dark vista of future years, and devise if you can what fathers, mothers, citizens or statesmen they will make when they come onto the stage with broken down constitutions and unimproved intellects; yes, it is for their good as well as for our own, that we would labor. . . . Perhaps some Agent may say, "Oh we give them a chance to go to school three months in a year," very well, but still they must have time to improve upon what they learn in that three months, or else it will prove almost useless to them. . . . We must have a reduction in the hours of labor, so that the young as well as the older ones, can have time for improvement; for how can it be expected they will make any progress in learning while they are tied both mind and body to their work, until they almost become a part of the machinery itself.[25]

Supporters of the ten-hour movement hammered home the advantages of a shorter workday; benefits that, they asserted, clearly outweighed any potential loss of earnings from working fewer hours at piece rates. A Manchester operative argued that a reduction in earnings was a small price to pay for better working hours. She wrote: "My present employment is under the ten hour system by a corporation—health has improved, spirits restored, and knowing the great number of applications by mill girls for situations in this branch of business, tells plainly they would rather work less hours, even if they must have less money." John Quincy Adams Thayer also raised the possibility that factories could run two ten-hour shifts each day. This practice would increase production and the demand for labor; wages could go up and so could profits. Thayer believed that the ten-hour system would then lead to better working relations in every industry. "Give the producing classes time for mental action," he urged, "and preserve their physical condition, and the employed will no longer stand in fear of the employer; they will harmonize and reason together." Thayer felt that the ten-hour movement would help workers achieve the basic material security and self-respect they needed in order to become full participants in the nation's social and economic systems.[26]

The ten-hour petition campaign reached a fever pitch in 1845 when the Massachusetts legislature appointed a committee to investigate the hours of labor in factories. The committee heard testimony from operatives on the difficult conditions inside Lowell mills, but decided not to recommend any legislation. Nevertheless, the reluctant committee received a plethora of petitions that year, which testified to workers' continuing uproar over the question of working hours. Yet, in the midst of trying to put increasing public pressure on the legislature, the petitioners found their voices muffled by various legal technicalities.

A petition from another 301 Lowell workers, for example, contained a harsh criticism of how capital had come to dominate labor. But this document was not as clear as previous ones in delineating the kind of remedial legislation needed. The earlier petitions had asked specifically for a law prohibiting corporations from employing workers, or running their machinery, more than ten hours a day. The 1845 petition requested only that ten hours be declared a legal day's work if there were no other contracts outstanding.

> [I]n view of the disparity between Capital and Labor, the latter almost entirely within the control of the former, thereby subjecting the honest laborer to the will of the capitalist, or to customs established by his avaricious disposition, . . . which if not intercepted by judicious Legislation, will, in the opinion of your petitioners, produce speedily, such a state of moral turpitude, ignorance and degradation, amongst the laborers, (the true source from which must spring the wealth and prosperity of a nation,) as no humane or wise Legislator could witness without regret; and believing that to establish by law the time which shall constitute a day's labor, in such a way as to afford the laborer some time for mental culture and moral improvement, without an exorbitant tax upon his physical constitution, would tend greatly to the advancement of the *whole* community.
>
> We therefore respectfully request that your Honorable Body will enact a law making ten hours a *day's work*—where no specific agreement is entered into between the parties interested. . . .

This proposed law would have been ineffectual in regulating the many factories that had already signed contracts with workers giving the companies the right to set the hours of labor.[27]

This watered-down request for a legal ten-hour day appeared in other petitions written in 1845. There were 500 signatures on a petition from Andover, which also spoke poignantly about the physical and intellectual costs of working long hours, yet asked only for a declaration of a ten-hour day in corporations.

> Your petitioners . . . believing that you have the power to regulate all corporate bodies which you have created, and realizing that to work more than ten hours per day, *especially in factories,* is injurious to the Physical and Mental powers of man—thus debasing his intellect—that it deprives him of the opportunity of cultivating his mind, and of raising himself to that high rank and station in society for which God designed him—do respectfully petition your Honorable body to pass a law constituting Ten Hours a day work in all corporations, created by the Legislature of this State. . . .[28]

One other 1845 petition from Lowell seemed to recognize the problems and loopholes in the other documents. This petition not only asked for a legal ten-hour day, it added the following provision: "that no incorporated body, or any individual or individuals, either private or associated, shall be allowed, except in cases of emergency, to employ one set of hands more than ten hours per day." The Lowell workers who drew up this petition wanted to make sure that the ten-hour day was not only legislated, but applied to every employer.[29]

While the Massachusetts legislature received all these petitions and then declined to act on them, some workers began to consider alternative strategies for the ten-hour movement. John Cluer became deeply involved in the campaign to rally support among operatives for the legislative drive. But Cluer also elaborated a strategy that combined a number of different stages into a total plan to mobilize operatives throughout the region. He called first for a convention of operatives and managers to work out a plan for reducing working hours. If the convention failed, then he urged a renewed petition drive in the legislature; and if that campaign did not produce results, then he advocated a general strike for the Fourth of July—a second Independence Day. (Cluer set the date for July 4, 1846.)[30]

The general strike was seen as a last resort: Cluer's plan favored arbitration, if at all possible, to win the ten-hour day. But Cluer also believed that launching the strike on July 4, if it was necessary to do so, would give his campaign more strength. The ten-hour movement and the general strike of workers across the region would both be infused with the patriotic colors of the Fourth of July. The campaign would be seen as a struggle for American workers' rights, not a crusade with overtones of radicalism and violence.

Cluer's plan was a fascinating mixture of the British Chartists' concept of a general strike wedded to the Americans' ideal of the Fourth of July as a celebration of their revolutionary legacy. Cluer was trying to use Old World patterns of resistance and independence as a powerful force for labor organizing in the New World by merging these patterns with the concepts of citizenship and self-determination at the core of American republicanism. Cluer's critique of the American factory system combined English and American ideas of public display and protest—factory workers would proclaim their revolutionary rights through mass action.

When Cluer addressed a gathering of operatives in Manchester during the winter of 1845, they heartily endorsed his plan with the following resolution:

> In view of the alarming increase of the evils of factory labor, as it now exists, the tendency of which is to gradually subvert the republican institutions of our country and fill the land with a dependent, overworked and much oppressed populace, and spread disease and poverty among our people, therefore *Resolved,* That we, the operatives of Manchester, do fully and heartily concur with the plan . . . that the Fourth of July 1846, shall be the day fixed upon by the operatives of America, to declare their INDEPENDENCE of the oppressive Manufacturing power, which has been imported from Old monarchical England, and now being engrafted upon the business institutions of our country; provided the manufacturers shall *practically* signify an unwillingness to mutually adopt the Ten Hour System.

This resolution, like the strike proclamations of the 1830s, resonated with memories of the American Revolution. Workers vowed to "declare their INDEPENDENCE of the oppressive Manufacturing power, which has been imported from Old monarchical England"; thereby rekindling the fires of their patriotic ancestors and sealing the promise of freedom and equality inherent in the nation's republican heritage. Yet, despite this moving rhetoric, neither the workers in Manchester nor any other operatives in the ten-hour campaign ever followed up on Cluer's ideas. The Fourth of July, 1846, passed without any ten-hour laws and without any further action on the plan for a general strike.[31]

Most leaders of the ten-hour movement, perhaps chastened by the legal confusion and legislative inaction of 1845 or perhaps seeking to head off any more agitation for a general strike, circulated copies of a standardized printed petition throughout Massachusetts in 1846. This statewide form was one way to reduce the chances that disagreements or conflicting proposals would emerge from among the ranks of the movement. The preprinted petition returned to the earlier demand for a law prohibiting corporations from working any "one set of hands more than ten hours per day."

This document also reached new rhetorical heights by invoking the Declaration of Independence in the ongoing political crusade for shorter working hours. (Republican ideology was thereby used to justify the petition campaign itself, as well as more activist ideas about a general strike.) It declared that there was a fundamental social need for reducing the hours of labor, and that this social need had to be embodied in legislation. Workers were the very fabric and future of society; if they were oppressed, then the whole republic was in peril.

> [B]elieving this system of tedious and protracted toil to exist, in a great degree, by virtue of legislative enactments, in opposition to the great principles of justice, equality and republicanism, laid down in the Declaration of Rights, so essential to the moral, mental and physical well-being of society, and the existence of a free and virtuous people; therefore, in justice to ourselves, to our fellow workers, and to posterity, we anxiously and hopefully invoke your aid and assistance in removing this oppressive burden, by enacting such a law, as will prohibit all incorporated companies from employing one set of hands more than ten hours per day.
>
> That the present hours of labor are too long, and tend to aggrandize the capitalist and depress the laborer, is admitted by the good, the wise and philanthropic of the world; and we trust by every consideration of duty to your highly revered State, and the prosperity of her industrious population, and as just and righteous legislators, you will be induced to grant this reasonable petition; thereby saving our country from many of the calamities which have visited all people who suffer wealth and monopoly to feed upon the natural rights of the working classes.

Despite this renewed attempt to create a united movement for a strong and unambiguous ten-hour law, no such legislation was ever enacted in Massachusetts during the antebellum period.[32]

In April 1847, however, perhaps responding to pressure generated by the ten-hour movement, the Lowell corporations acted by themselves to reduce their operatives' workdays. They trimmed fifteen minutes off each day for eight months in the year, and thirty minutes a day for the remaining four months, through extending the meal breaks. Many of the New Hampshire mills soon followed suit. But this reduction in hours, which even Harriet Farley had recommended, did not seem to produce many beneficial results. One contributor to the *Voice of Industry* accused both the corporations and individual operatives of violating the spirit and substance of this new regulation.

> It came to pass in the month of April 1847, that there went forth a new decree from the Cotton Lords of Lowell, that their living machinery should have forty-five minutes in which to leave their work, partake of their meals, and return back again. Now this decree was well pleasing to the friends of Humanity who had been striving for a long time to obtain a reduction in the hours of toil in the pestilential air of the cotton mills. For they understood well how for many years the girls had been shut up thirteen hours per day to the destruction of health and life, while the Cotton Lords had been waxing fat upon their blood and sinews! It came to pass in these days that when this decree took effect the great gates were all shut until the ringing of the second bell, (which took place just *thirty-five* minutes from the time they were closed, instead of *forty-five* as *was decreed,*) that many *foolish* girls were seen standing at the gates *waiting* for admittance. . . . Why is this! Have they common sense, or any *minds* at all? If so, why are they seen wasting their precious moments, standing by hundreds before the gates? Have they been so long accustomed to watching machinery that they have actually become dwarfs in intellect . . . instead of being seen waiting at the gates for the bell to strike, the *gates* should wait for *them* after the bell gives the summons. . . .

Some workers also claimed that this small reduction in the workday led manufacturers to increase the speed of the machinery to make up for lost time. Such tactics, however, only strengthened these workers' resolve to gain a legally enforceable ten-hour day.[33]

A few weeks after the reports on the failure of the new work schedule, the editors of the *Voice* wrote that it was a small cadre of experienced workers who were scurrying back early, and not the overly anxious new arrivals, as originally expected. These veterans were apparently hardened to the long hours, and wanted to push their wages higher regardless of what their fellow workers did. A Manchester operative had a more succinct explanation for why "the girls come to the gate before 'tis open," no matter what the hours of labor and even if they did not want to "work so many long hours." The pressure came, she said, not from the workers' quest for more money, but from the overseers' desire to earn bonuses under the premium system. "The premium is offered, the girls drove up, and they want to keep the 'old man' good natured if possible. No overseer ever dared use the whip, but they give looks and words, sometimes, quite as severe."[34]

Also in 1847, the state legislature of New Hampshire passed a ten-hour law; but this law was riddled with legal loopholes, which manufacturers used to dash the high hopes of workers. The law specified that "in all contracts for or relating to labor, Ten Hours of actual labor shall be taken to be a day's work, unless otherwise agreed by the parties, and no person shall be required or holden to perform more than ten hours labor in any one day, except in pursuance of an express contract requiring a greater time." This law had the same weaknesses as many of the proposals in various Massachusetts petitions—it merely declared ten hours to be a legal day's work in the absence of any contract requiring more hours. Most factories circumvented this law by pressuring their workers into signing contracts specifying longer hours of labor. The Nashua Manufacturing Company, for example, had its employees sign a regulation paper that contained the following provision: "All persons entering into the employment of this Company are to work as many hours as the mills run, which will be the same as heretofore, and that time will be considered a day's work."[35]

Harriet Putnam, a Manchester operative, wrote to a local newspaper with details of how the corporations deceived workers (including herself) into signing new contracts nullifying the law.

> . . . [I]n that act there has been a provision made for the capitalist, allowing him to hire those who will agree to work the same number of hours as heretofore, provided they will voluntarily enter into such contracts . . . during the few weeks past that the subject of reduction of the hours of labor has been agitated, some of the operatives have been away, and consequently have been ignorant of what was being done for the amelioration of their condition. On their return, they call on their overseer to secure a place in the mill, take a new regulation paper, being urged to do so under pretense that the name of the corporation has been changed, or that some new arrangements have been made, which render it necessary to have new regulations.
>
> Many have done so, and others continue to place their names upon these documents without reading them, thereby signifying their willingness to work fourteen instead of ten hours. Their names are now upon the records of the corporations, purporting to signify an agreement to a contract they had nothing to do in making, against which nature and reason would have remonstrated, had they but glanced at that detestable paragraph in that article.
>
> I know not what others may do, but for myself, my resolution is fixed. Justice to myself and fellow operatives, with whom I would cooperate by yielding my influence toward breaking off the shackles with which we are bound, compels me to make a public retraction of the agreement I so thoughtlessly put my name to. I am fearless of the result. . . . If I am discharged, be it known, that it is not because I have not performed my duties faithfully to my employers. . . . I respect them, and have ever been treated kindly by them, and am sorry that necessity obliges me to assume a position hostile to their expressed wishes; but it will be simply for asserting my right to think, speak, and act, according to the dictates of an enlightened and reluctant mind . . . shall we not rather come up in one mighty phalanx, and with one voice say we will be free—that the ten hour system shall prevail?. . . the law requires that this contract be entered into by us voluntarily. It does not compel us to sign this document, but takes the power and places it in our own hands, to choose liberty or bondage, and invests every individual with the free use of their thinking and reasoning faculties, enabling them to act according to the dictates of reason and common sense.[36]

Many other Manchester operatives shared Putnam's spirit of resistance, and mass rallies were held in the summer of 1847 to gather support for the ten-hour law and against the corporation contracts. The machinists in the Amoskeag shop petitioned the corporation's stockholders to join them in enforcing the new law, "believing . . . that it would be for the interest of all concerned in the labor of this establishment,—the employers, as well as the employed—that this principle should prevail." The petitioners asked the company agent if they could circulate their petition in the shop, but he refused their request. Working men and women from all over Manchester filled the city hall in late August, and unanimously adopted a series of resolutions reemphasizing their determination to work only the legal ten-hour day. These resolutions, prepared by a committee of male and female operatives, returned to the Declaration of Independence as the foundation of the workers' rights to uphold the new law.

> *Resolved,* That we hold these truths self-evident,—that man is endowed by his creator with certain inalienable rights; among which is life, liberty, the pursuit of happiness, a home on the earth, a right to labor, and the power to limit for himself, his hours of labor.
>
> *Resolved,* That agreeable to the laws of New Hampshire, Ten Hours constitutes a legal day's work.
>
> *Resolved,* That ten hours' labor in each day is all that a man's constitution is able to bear.
>
> *Resolved,* That on and after the 15th of September next, we will not work more than the legal number of hours in each day. . . .
>
> *Resolved,* That to the support of the Resolutions we pledge our lives and our sacred honor.

Two days later, the operatives met again to consider the crucial resolution: "that we will sign no contracts to work more than ten hours per day." They also unanimously adopted more resolutions expressing their determination to work only ten hours a day, even if it meant a loss in production and pay.

> *Resolved,* That justice, reason, and law, demand that we should not be constrained by promise of place, or by fear of discharge from place, to work more than ten hours in one day.
>
> *Resolved,* That if ten hours of daily work fail to produce as much as is now produced by the long hour system, we ask only corresponding pay. . . .
>
> *Resolved,* That the ten hour system is a system better adapted to carry out the principles of equal rights to all men, than any system that has ever been promulgated in any time or in any country . . . knowing our cause to be just, our motto shall be "*onward and upward*"—less labor and more intellectual culture—less toil and more leisure—less confinement and more air. . . .[37]

When the ten-hour law went into effect on September 15, 1847, many workers continued to refuse the special contracts offered to them. Those who did not sign these new agreements were fired. It was reported that over half the operatives at the Nashua Corporation were dismissed. The workers also planned demonstrations outside the mills on the fifteenth, with music and banners, to show their united opposition to the special contracts that emasculated the law. A Manchester correspondent to the *Voice of Industry* claimed that some workers would gladly leave New Hampshire to find jobs in other states, even if they still had to work longer hours, rather than give in to their employers' undermining of the law.

> To leave this place we are fully determined, and leave their old dingy Factory walls to echo if they will to the hootings of the owl, and the screams of the jackall, a monument of oppression and wrong, which shall become a hissing and a by-word to the nations of the earth, as being a specimen of the fate of tyrants, when a free people shall breathe the breath of indignation upon them.

Some Manchester operatives discovered, however, that when they sought employment in Lowell they were refused because their names had already been sent down from New Hampshire as people not to be employed. Over the fall and winter months, most New Hampshire mills were once again filled with workers who signed the required papers and worked over ten hours each day.[38]

It is unclear whether or not workers in New Hampshire ever succeeded in fully organizing complete strikes against the undermining of their state's ten-hour law. But their refusal to sign new contracts, their resolutions, and their rallies all testify to their struggles to make the law a working reality in the factories. And their actions demonstrate that, while the ten-hour movement's emphasis remained on moderate political petition campaigns, operatives were capable of using more dynamic tactics when they felt it was necessary. Strikes and protest rallies outside of mills were the hallmarks of earlier activists. Leaders of the ten-hour movement usually did not advocate such aggressive tactics in their political plan (with the exception of John Cluer). Yet the workers of New Hampshire showed that even within this more moderate movement, the sparks of militance could be ignited when a matter of rights and law was at stake. Workers rarely used direct protest at the point of production when they focused on lobbying the legislature for a ten-hour law. Once such a law was enacted, however, operatives were more willing to take to the streets and fight for the legitimate enforcement of that law.

The results of the ten-hour movement were not very encouraging for antebellum New England workers. State legislatures either refused to enact any laws governing the hours of labor or approved legislation that was easily undermined by the manufacturing corporations. Yet, despite these defeats, workers throughout the 1840s continued their campaign for the ten-hour day. Why did so many workers fight against such great political and economic odds in their crusade for a shorter workday? For some, the ten-hour movement was an expression of their faith in working people's future. For others, agitation for the ten-hour day was the desperate appeal for government protection of an overworked population.

Some workers believed that the ten-hour movement had a broad base of support and a large amount of untapped potential for social change. Although workers usually downplayed their ideas about large-scale social reform in their petitions, they sometimes admitted to each other that the ten-hour movement was part of a greater scheme for transforming society. The Lowell Female Labor Reform Association reported that they did "not regard this measure, (the reduction of the hours of labor) as an end, but only as one step, towards the great end to be obtained. They deeply feel, that their work will never be accomplished, until slavery and oppression, mental, physical and religious, shall be done away with." If workers had more time to educate themselves, they would learn why it was necessary to redesign the factory system and the social structure. For these women, the ten-hour movement was more than an adjustment of the timing of the workday; it was a challenge to the legislature and the corporations to recognize the rights of workers to shape the conditions of their own labor. Workers wanted to secure their own ideas of control and order in their daily work schedules, rather than being controlled by the edicts of management. The more optimistic operatives in the ten-hour movement believed that if the legislature investigated working conditions in the factories, such an inquiry would inevitably lead to more legal leverage and power for labor. Through all the legislative setbacks and loopholes, some workers held to this vision of the movement's unrealized potential.[39]

Other workers rallied around the ten-hour banner more out of desperation than a belief in the possibility of substantive change. For these workers, the reason why all this conflict about the hours of labor took place in the 1840s was that so many factories were pushing their employees harder during that decade than ever before. Some operatives felt that they had a better chance of controlling the hours they worked than the precise conditions they worked under. If they could not stop the speedup and stretch-out, they could try to minimize the debilitating effects by decreasing the number of hours they labored under such intense pressure.[40]

The ten-hour movement can be seen as a way workers accepted the basic premise of timed labor, yet tried to shape that system to meet their own needs. They did not fight against having set hours; they did try to control how much of each day they would spend in the factory. Thus, the ten-hour movement, in some ways, was an expression of some workers' pessimism as well as their activism. Workers were at least implicitly saying that, at that moment, they could not change the workplace as a whole; so they would focus their efforts on regulating their hours of labor. The operatives hoped that they could at least gain a sense of control over their hours, with some help from the government.

Although some workers fought for the ten-hour day as a rear-guard defense against the intensification of factory labor, and others hoped to carry the crusade farther into the realm of social change, the movement was held together along an axis of political action. The petitions themselves were an exercise in mass political expression—even for women, who could not vote—and a call for public support to back the workers' own campaign. Workers often spoke of their petitions for a ten-hour law as a request for simple "justice" from their legislators. Many petitions argued that if corporations received legal protection from the legislature, then the government had the power to grant equal protection to workers. An 1844 petition from Lowell asked that "protection . . . may be as generously extended toward the *employed* as toward the *employer.*" This request focused on the idea that governments granted corporations their charters, and therefore the legislature could "modify all charters . . . as to forbid the running of machinery for the manufacture of yarn or cloth more than ten hours per day."[41]

Operatives asserted that political activity was a fundamental right of every individual. They saw themselves as citizens, regardless of whether they could vote or not; and they believed that the government would respond to their needs. These operatives believed that, as workers and as citizens, they were the vital center of the nation's political economy, deserving of respect and a fair share of power in the workplace and the legislature.

Workers tried to bring together the demands they made on employers with their requests for legislative relief—they wanted to enact a law that would require the owners to treat them fairly. The operatives believed that the corporations were neither respecting the workers, nor even acknowledging the operatives' grievances; so they turned to the government out of need and out of a belief in their right to do so. The "daughters of freemen," and the sons as well, were now demanding justice, not directly from the corporations as they had done in previous protests—they were now demanding their rights from the government, to keep manufacturers in line. Though they often saw themselves arrayed against the manufacturers, they still believed that the legislative process could resolve the differences. They believed that they could air their grievances and get a fair hearing in the political forum.

The ten-hour movement therefore often reflected a heightened class consciousness, but most workers hoped to avoid the specter of class conflict through the mediation of political action. The movement was decidedly less confrontational than the strikes of the 1820s and the 1830s. Again, the goal was not to take on the corporations directly, but to mobilize a mass political movement that would stir the government to restrain corporate excesses. Operatives conceived of their movement as a patriotic fight for the rights of American workers, not as an expression of violent struggle. Some workers hoped to pave the way for broader changes through their campaign, but the roots of the movement remained in peaceful political action. Workers were convinced that the exploitation of labor by capital was far likelier to stir up conflict than labor's own battle for legislation.

The workers reaffirmed the basic structures of the industrial economy and American politics, whether they all intended to or not, by continuing to present petitions concerning the hours of labor instead of taking more direct action against the factory system. Their petitions often contained sharp criticism of the inequities and hardships of mechanized labor, but the authors rarely backed up their words with anything more militant than another round of speeches, testimony, and editorials. (Both the ten-hour movement and the labor organizations involved usually adhered to this moderate stance.) New Hampshire workers took a more aggressive stance in 1847, but that was after they saw the law—which they, too, had patiently lobbied for—immediately emasculated by legislative loopholes and corporate pressure tactics.

In the end, the ten-hour legislative campaign both mobilized female and male operatives as a political force in their own right and deflected their political activism away from a radical, class-based agenda. The movement became an expression of the workers' own political strengths and weaknesses. When the workers petitioned their legislatures *en masse,* they were asserting their political equality with capitalists and their demands that government recognize their equal rights. But they were also acknowledging their socioeconomic disadvantages in relation to capital, and their need for government protection. The ideal of equality and the phantom of dependence both seemed to hang over the ten-hour movement.

— III —

The question of the hours of labor, as was true of every other major issue regarding the factory system, did have more than one side to it. There were many defenders of the factories who argued that their workdays were less onerous than those in other occupations. In Biddeford, Maine, retail clerks were reported to be working fifteen-hour days in 1845, while the mill workers spent only eleven hours at their machines. In the *Lowell Offering,* one author took up the accusation that being regulated by factory bells was concomitant with slavery and refuted the charge. She set up a dialogue, "Factory Labor," wherein one character stated: "to be called and to be dismissed by the ringing of a bell, savors of compulsion and slavery, and cannot cease to produce mortification, without having been destructive to self respect." Her companion responded with the winning argument: "In all kinds of employment it is necessary to keep regular established hours. . . . Because we are reminded of those hours by the ringing of a bell, it is no argument against our employment, any more than it would be against going to church or to school." The factory bell was thus placed in context with the school bell and the church bell—all were justified as symbols of proper social order and good personal conduct.[42]

Other operatives told their fellow workers that no matter how long they worked every day, there was always time for self-improvement. Elizabeth Rowe, in her testimony before the Massachusetts legislative committee investigating factory labor in 1845, stated that her overseer allowed workers to leave before the final bell on Saturdays and to attend lectures. A contributor to the *Olive Leaf and Factory Girl's Repository* stated: "The time allowed us for mental improvement, it is true, is extremely limited, but if we are zealous to redeem each moment as it flies, there are but few, we trust, but will have something to offer on the side of virtue and morality." Another correspondent to the same newspaper testified that "all the learning I now have has been gained without instruction, having obtained it alone, and that too, after I had labored in the mill twelve hours a day on the average through the year."[43]

Although many workers did not leave the factories until seven or eight o'clock in the evening and had only an hour or two of leisure time at night, those free moments were especially precious to young people living on their own for the first time. Ann Appleton said simply: "I leave my work at seven o'clock then I come home and I do what I please." Lucy Larcom recalled: "Country girls were naturally independent, and the feeling that at this new work the few hours they had of everyday leisure were entirely their own was a satisfaction to them." Appleton, Larcom, and other operatives welcomed the precise hours of factory work because they were assured of a definite end to the day's labor and a period of time for themselves—precious commodities that could not always be found working on a farm.[44]

Other workers, through their actions if not their words, demonstrated their ability to carve out some time each day for themselves. The Springfield armorers probably exercised more control over their hours of labor (as they tried to do with so many aspects of their work) than most other operatives. In 1819, James Dalliba reported that day workers at the armory usually put in ten hours, while piece workers came and went as they pleased, as the shops often remained open from sunrise to sunset. By 1841, the situation seemed to be even more advantageous for most armorers. G. Talcott wrote: "In one branch of labor, every man finishes his work by *ten o'clock* in the morning. In others, they complete it in the first half of the day. A very limited number work over *five* hours, and probably not so long a time as *seven* hours a day when engaged in 'piece-work.'" A board of examiners basically confirmed Talcott's observations when they reported: "no class of workmen have averaged ten hours per day. Those employed in the finishing shops have, perhaps, averaged between nine and ten hours; those employed in forging at the hill shops, between seven and eight; while the workmen at the water-shops average from four to seven hours per day." The board recommended that barrel-welders and bayonet-forgers work seven hours a day, and all other employees (regardless of whether they were paid by the piece or the day) should work a ten-hour day. The board was essentially calling on the armory to enforce already existing regulations, and the superintendent apparently did try to follow their recommendation, regardless of any opposition from the workers.[45]

At the Collins Axe Company, the management also felt it necessary to strengthen their enforcement of regular working hours. Samuel Collins posted a notice on July 28, 1832, which stated:

> great numbers of our men have gone home to haying, and harvesting without leave, and we have not men enough left to carry on our business. Some men commence work fifteen or twenty minutes, and even half an hour after bell ringing; and some leave their work during bell hours for that length of time, and even leave the shops and go up to the houses and stores. We do therefore give notice to all men in our employment, that none of these things will hereafter be tolerated. No man in our employment will have credit for a day's work, unless he goes to work at bell ringing, or calls on the overseer of the shop where he works and gives a satisfactory excuse, and every man who washes up before bell ringing without leave, and leaves the shop during working hours without leave, will be considered as breaking our rules, and will be treated accordingly in our settlement with him.

These new regulations could not have been entirely successful, because, four years later, Collins was still disturbed by the short working hours inside the factory. When the workmen asked for a wage increase in 1836, he responded in part that they did not work hard enough to justify higher pay. "Many of our men quit work in the shops by half past two or by three o'clock," he wrote to his employees, "and they have plenty of time and strength left for a game of ball, and I am glad to see it, but they ought not to expect us to pay for time spent at play."[46]

It was not only the more skilled male workers who were sometimes able to bend the workday to meet their own schedules. Even textile mill managers often compained of their workers' tardiness and irregular hours. N. B. Gordon's work diary is filled with references to workers' not being at their jobs during the prescribed working hours. On March 24, 1829, for example, he noted how the employees' social life could overshadow their responsibilities in the mill: "Mr Thayers party last night broke up 3 oclock morning hands in consequence come in late & one, No 6 weaver not untill noon." Gordon's work diary also contains notations of workers' being absent for part or all of a day due to elections, town meetings, weddings, and musters. Gordon's patience wore thin with these repeated interruptions, but workers continued to take the time off. On May 26, 1830, he wrote: "Election day, Factory stoped—Oatis and myself jobing ½ the day.—I hereby enter my dissent to this day, being one spent in a useless & worse than useless manner.—I could not peaceably work the mill as all hands seemed determined to have the whole day."[47]

Some operatives even found opportunities to leave the factory for days or weeks at a time. Many factories were plagued by frequent shutdowns due to high or low water, or mechanical breakdowns. These spontaneous vacations could be a source of both welcome relief and concern for factory workers. Rebecca Ford wrote in the summer of 1839, "we factory girls have a resting spell this afternoon the big shafts wants fixing so they sent us home." But, in the spring of 1843, she was more troubled when the mill stopped for an extended period of time due to high water. "The factory business is rather dull now," she said; "the snow is melting off from the mountain the water is so high we have not worked any since a week a go last Saturday I dont know how soon we shall go to work I hope we shall be fore long for I have got most tired of doing nothing and paying my board in the bargain." Ford saw a brief shutdown as a pleasant respite from work, but if the factory closed for weeks, the loss in wages could put the operatives in strained financial circumstances.[48]

Overall, the Ford sisters found that the daily patterns of working time in a rural woolen mill were not always radically different from patterns in agriculture and artisanal labor. Periods of intense activity were often interspersed with stretches of no work at all. In fact, the time book of the late 1840s from the mill in which they worked indicates that both sisters were away from work up to fifteen times in a single year. Sometimes the entire factory was stopped for part of a day; sometimes only the women were given a day off; and sometimes the Fords took extended leaves of absence for themselves, probably to visit their family.[49]

Many other female textile operatives also left the mills for regular vacations, if they could afford to do so. One Waltham worker said:

> I do not think there is an American female, employed here, who does not leave the mills for a few weeks, or months, every year; [the change] of air and diet are conducive to health. Many of the girls go home to spend their summer, and are succeeded in their labors by others, who have remained at home through the winter. There are others who leave for a few weeks to visit their relatives and friends in different places.

This worker praised the factory system for permitting operatives to sojourn away from the mills, but she also implied that such excursions helped restore the workers who were worn out by their labors. Lucy Larcom also remembered how visits to her birthplace in Beverly, Massachusetts, were a tonic after her work in Lowell. One of her married sisters sent for her, she recalled, "just when the close air and long days were beginning to tell upon my health, and it was decided that I had better go. The salt wind soon restored my health, and those months of quiet family life were very good for me." The factory owners were sometimes annoyed by summertime labor shortages, but they also seemed to recognize that workers returned from their vacations well rested from the long hours of labor. The corporations made no official provisions for such vacations, and most contracts specified a working period of one year. Yet managers were usually willing to rehire women in the fall who had left the mills in the summer.[50]

In fact, many of these workers probably assumed that they would return to their previous positions when they came back to the mills. Mary Metcalf was quite surprised when she returned to Lowell only to find that her overseer had given her place to someone else. She wrote to her mother:

> Went in to see Gage . . . he said *Well* you've got back. Said he had not wanted me. . . . Mr Gage gave away my frame while I was gone but I have another one

> about as good the girl teased him for it or he would not let her had it. He is so ashamed of it he has not spoken to me since I went in to work, nor I to him for I shall not speak to him till he does to me and them I shall give him a piece of my mind for he knows he had no business to give it away.

In her letter, Metcalf pointedly wrote of how her overseer had given away "my frame" and "he had no business to give it away." Clearly Metcalf believed that she had a personal connection with, and a proprietary interest in, that particular machine; and she fully expected to tend that same machine when she returned to the mill. Metcalf's outspoken criticism of the overseer and the manager's own embarrassment indicate that both sides realized a customary practice had been violated. Workers who returned from their time off, at least in Lowell, expected to get their old jobs back—that may have been one reason why some felt at ease about taking time away from the mill—and they felt aggrieved if their machines were offered to another employee.[51]

For workers who could not afford to take time off, there was often pressure to work even longer hours rather than campaign for shorter workdays. Many factory workers were paid by the piece, and they often felt the need to work more hours to increase their daily output and earnings. Eliza Hemmingway, in her testimony before the Massachusetts legislative committee investigating the hours of labor in factories, reported that there was "always a large number of girls at the gate wishing to get in before the bell rings. On the Middlesex Corporation one fourth part of the females go into the mill before they are obliged to. They do this to make more wages." Other operatives also voiced their concern that any reduction in hours would also entail a decrease in wages. Clementine Averill asserted that "the majority" of Lowell mill workers "would not be willing to work less, if their earnings were less."[52]

Harriet Farley also noticed that many workers pushed themselves to get in additional work time because of their pride in hard work and their desire to earn more money. She expressed some concern for the ill effects of such extended labor, but she also argued that it was the individual operative's responsibility to regulate her extra efforts.

> Many, who are not able to do it, will have extra work, and scarsely any are satisfied that they do enough while in the mill. They eke out the hours of labor by every possible contrivance, and work as though work were the chief end of woman. We have known girls to rise before the first bell on a summer's morning—do, from choice, their own chamber work, be at work in mill, brushing oiling, etc., ten minutes before "the gate was hoisted"—stay, after "the gate was shut down," till the watchman sent them out to their breakfast—then trot home as fast as possible—eat about five or six minutes . . . then back to the mill as soon as the gate is opened—and so on through the day.[53]

Farley returned to this issue of operatives' working extra hours when she discussed the published testimony before the Massachusetts legislature. In an April 1845 editorial in the *Lowell Offering,* she took particular notice of Eliza Hemmingway's reports about women waiting at the mill gates to get into work before the bell rang. Her new explanation for this phenomenon rested on notions of group psychology and competition.

> . . . [T]he remarks of the first witness—"There is always a large number of girls at the gate, wishing to get in before the bell rings" . . . is frequently spoken of as evidence of a general desire to work even more hours than at present. It is not generally known how much the feeling of emulation is appealed to among the operatives. The desire to be "the smartest girl in the room," or among the smartest, and to get off so many "*sets*" or "*pieces*" often stimulates to exertions which no love of money would ever prompt. One girl goes to the mill, and waits until the gate is opened, that she may rush in first, and have her machine oiled and cleaned, and ready to start the moment the works are put in motion; not so much because she wishes for the few additional cents, which she will thus obtain, as because she is ambitious to have her name at the head of the list. The rest follow her—either in hopes of successful competition, or of ranking next in order . . . those who are behind them in time and "*honors*" . . . a word or two should be spoken in their behalf. They feel that they are unable to work all these hours, and "work upon the stretch," as they say. They are older, or weaker, or more heavily moulded, or unwilling, if not unable. Therefore, they are not favorites with the overseer. They are not so "profitable servants," and the kind look and word, or obliging act, is not often bestowed upon them.

Farley tried to portray the overly ambitious operative as a young woman eagerly seeking recognition for a job well done, not a mercenary counting her added pennies. Farley was also clearly concerned with the less able-bodied operatives left behind, and the scorn they may have received from their managers. Yet she specifically suggested only that the meal breaks be expanded to require even the most assiduous workers to leave their machines for a respite of at least three quarters of an hour. Farley continued to believe that most workers "consider it a blessing that they may labor long, and diligently," for themselves and whoever was dependent on them.[54]

Farley, therefore, was reluctant to call for a ten-hour day because she did not think that a majority of the workers supported the idea. "Could we know," she editorialized, "or believe, that it would gratify the majority of female factory operatives—we mean those, and they are almost the whole, who 'work by the job,' who have worked several years, or expect to work several years—to adopt the '*Ten Hour System*,' we would make its establishment a definite aim of our magazine." Farley was probably correct in arguing that many piece workers feared that a ten-hour day would mean less time to produce as many goods, and thus a reduction in their pay. These operatives believed that the reduced wages caused by a ten-hour law would result in more hardship than the supposedly harsh working conditions the law was designed to ameliorate. Some operatives thought that they could work longer hours for as much time as they needed to make the money they wanted. They saw the ten-hour day as something needed only by a permanent class of factory workers, and many operatives did not think of themselves in those terms.[55]

What about the minority of workers who might spend many years in the mills? Were they more likely to favor a reduction in the hours of labor, given the possibility that they were going to be working in the factories for many more years? One supporter of the ten-hour movement argued that, quite to the contrary, veteran employees often were the most concerned with the impact of a reduction in working hours on wages. Even those workers who faced the prospect of remaining permanently in factories were often reluctant to tamper with the hours of labor.

> Of the many obstacles that prevent the operation of the Ten Hour System, there is no greater than that presented by some of the operatives who have been employed in the mills for a number of years. Possessing a strong constitution, and a parsimonious disposition, they would prefer the continuance of the present oppressive system, and advocate that it would be preferable for the operatives generally to work on the present plan, than it would on the ten hour system, notwithstanding it is yearly sending hundreds who possess a less vigorous constitution than themselves, to a premature grave. It is the love of money that leads them to make this assertion. . . . Hence the operatives take it for granted that those that have worked the longest, are better qualified to judge.

Experienced operatives were often seen as leaders in their workplaces. And both supporters and opponents of the ten-hour movement hoped that if these workers could be swayed to one side or the other in the campaign, then they might influence those around them to also take their stand.[56]

Thus the battle for the hearts and minds of the operatives on the question of the ten-hour day raged on. The workers active in the ten-hour movement saw their campaign as a way for operatives to regain some control over a workplace that was becoming ever more frenetic and debilitating. Other workers saw no need for such legislative action, because they believed that they were already participating fully in shaping the workplace and the workday to suit their needs. Time and again, when workers argued about what constituted a fair day's work in a new industrial setting, they raised the fundamental questions of power and control in the workplace. For the ten-hour movement was more than a matter of time: it was a struggle over who would have the authority to define the terms of labor in the factory system.

CHAPTER 9

Means and Ends: Workers and the Value of Work

The debate over the mechanized factory system in antebellum New England cannot be reduced to simple biographical, chronological, or demographic categories. Workers did not criticize or praise the factories simply on the basis of their age, sex, occupation, location, or any other single factor. Nor were they always likely to paint the factories in stark black-and-white terms—the debate spread over a broad spectrum of attitudes, ranging from outright condemnation, to profound ambivalence, to enthusiastic support. Workers from similar backgrounds could stand on opposite ends of this spectrum, and a single worker could pass through various emotional stages in the course of years working in the factories. Some workers, struggling to make sense of the changes taking place on the shop floor, could find themselves—whether they realized it or not—trying to hold contradictory ideas within their own world view of the factories.

What this dialogue on technological and socioeconomic change does reveal is deeper differences among operatives about the fundamental economic and ethical value of labor itself in a period of flux and uncertainty. Workers were trying to place their experience with factory labor in a broader intellectual context—they looked back on their own past, examined their present circumstances, and peered ahead into their future in an effort to try to define the significance of the new mode of industrial production. Workers disagreed about the factory system because they differed among themselves as to how they saw previous forms of labor, how they defined the role of work in daily life, and how they saw the future promises or perils of the factory. To put the matter in simple terms: workers were debating not only the factory itself, but the history of work in America, its present value, and its future possibilities.

— I —

When workers compared industrial labor with their previous work experiences, they often measured the factory against the farm. Some of the earliest male factory workers never saw their factory jobs in stark contrast to agricultural work because they were able to integrate the two forms of work. These workers may have seen the combination of agricultural and industrial labor, on a personal level, as the key to independence and advancement. Some of the Springfield, Massachusetts, armorers, before 1830, owned farms; and one of the reasons they worked irregular hours was so that they could tend to their fields. By the 1830s, the practice of combining armory work with farming was sharply curtailed, and barely one-tenth of the armory employees still performed additional farm work. Mixing farming and factory labor was also a common practice on into the 1830s at the Collins Axe Company in Collinsville, Connecticut. Samuel Collins, when he issued his new work rules in the summer of 1832, noted that "great numbers of our men have gone home to haying, and harvesting without leave, and we have not men enough to carry on our business." Collins wanted his employees to put their manufacturing responsibilities before their farming chores. Many operatives in the paper mills of western Massachusetts also took time away from the mills during the September harvest season so they could tend to their gardens.[1]

Rural textile mills were also not always divorced from the agricultural economy. Farmers might occasionally spend a few winter months in a mill's machine shop to earn extra money. More often, however, operatives kept a garden plot and possibly a few animals for a steady food supply. Some of the contracts with the Slater mills made specific provisions for such agricultural practices. The agreement with Rufus Bennet stipulated that he was to have "the Garden & Barn Privilege during the time his family shall remain in the employ of said Slater—The said Bennet is however not to have barn privilege unless he keeps a cow during the winter months—The said Bennet is not to sell any manure—and he is not to keep any hens—he is also to keep his cow yarded nights." These small-scale agricultural operations may have been a way to keep parents occupied while their children worked in the mills. In some cases, the Slater companies rented enough land for a father to have a modest farm of his own while his children were employed in the factories; or the father was sent to work on one of the larger factory-owned farms. Sometimes children left their factory work to help their fathers run the farms they had rented from the companies. Manufacturers probably did not intend for such tenant farms to attract workers back out of the factories, but they could not stop the practice if all contracts and leases were obeyed.[2]

Other factories also ran their own farms rather than (or perhaps in addition to) parceling out garden plots to individual workers. The Scovill brassworks in Waterbury, Connecticut, had a farm and sometimes assigned some of its unskilled workers to various chores there. Dividing up the work force could produce delays in the factory's production schedule, but the company did not abandon its in-house source of food. The Pomfret (Connecticut) Manufacturing Company even assigned a skilled worker to its company farm at harvest time. On July 22, 1824, it was noted that "Francis Pierce began to work at haying this morning and is to have two shillings per day in addition to his yearly wages. J. H. Morris is to tend mule at 4/ per day while Pierce works out." The mill must have been desperate for help if it sent a mule spinner into the fields, but it was expected that he would return to mule spinning once the harvesting was completed.[3]

Factory farms may have been a more efficient and economical way to grow food for operatives' tables. Owners may also have thought that mingling agricultural and industrial labor would ease the transition of an agrarian work force into an industrial regimen. These farms, too, might have been an indication that the "industrial revolution" proceeded at a less than revolutionary pace in many rural areas. The factory was making inroads, but manufacturers still had to accommodate themselves to the rural community. Some workers probably welcomed the mix of agricultural and industrial labor. Combining farm and factory work may have ameliorated the incessant rhythm of mechanized labor and made the factory seem a less threatening place. But the constant movement between jobs could also frustrate workers and prevent them from becoming comfortable in either environment.

In larger industrial cities, many of the operatives who had left their rural homes and moved to these urban areas still maintained contact with family and friends back home and in the mills. Yet there was also a greater physical gap between farms and factories in these cities, as workers were usually no longer laboring within the agrarian family economy. Furthermore, many large urban manufacturers took steps to remove certain agricultural privileges from their operatives. Seth Luther reported that at Dover, New Hampshire, "no operative is allowed to keep a pig or a cow, because it would take a few minutes time to feed a pig or cow. We learn also it is now, or has been the case, that the 'Republican Institution' even monopolized the *milk business,* kept cows themselves, and compelled their 'help' to buy milk of them." This regulation not only prevented workers from spending time tending livestock, it denied them the right to hold these animals as a source of capital. If operatives could not raise money by selling their cattle, they would have less independent income and become more dependent on their employers.[4]

This feeling of separation between an agricultural way of life and working in a factory underlay many critiques of industrial labor. One of the major reasons some workers were troubled by the factory system was that they saw it as distinctly inferior to the agrarian way of life. These operatives retained a very positive, almost sentimental, attitude towards the farm. It was the repository of all that was good and virtuous, as opposed to the corruptions of the factory. The farmstead, unlike the factory, was more than a work site; it was a place to call home. Joseph Hollingworth, though a recent immigrant from England, argued in good Jeffersonian fashion that agriculture was the foundation of American independence.

> [D]ont you think farming the best, and surest way of getting a living? Manufacturing is a very unsteady business, sometimes up, and sometimes down, some few gets Rich, and thousands are ruined by it. Rogues, Rascals, Knaves and vagabonds are connected with it. Some persons you trade with will cheat you in spite of your teeth, and must cheat others in return to make ends meet and tie. In short no honest man can live by it. A Factory too, is liable to be burnt down, but a Farm cannot be easily burnt up . . . the Farmer the American farmer, he, and he alone can be independent, he can be industrious, Healthy, and Happy. I am for Agriculture. . . . If I had the chance to morrow of either a Factory worth 10000 dollars, or a farm worth 5000, I would take the Farm.[5]

A contributor to the *Voice of Industry* asserted that the strength of body and mind that was noted in so many Lowell, Massachusetts, operatives was due to their upbringing in the countryside, not to their labor in the mills. The factories undermined the wholesome influences of the farms. When this operative looked to life on the farm, she did not dwell on the possibility of poverty or limited horizons; she saw it as a benchmark of human dignity, wholeness, and self-respect.

> They see the graceful form, the bright and speaking eye, the blushing cheek and the elastic motions of "Industry's Angel daughters," but they fail to see that these belong not to Lowell Cotton Mills, but to New England's country Homes.—There the fair cheek kissed by the sunlight and the breeze, grew fresh and healthful. There the eye borrowed its brightness from stream and lake and sky, and there too the intellect received the culture which enabled the "Factory girls" to astonish Europe and America. . . .

As for industrial labor and factory operatives, they both literally paled in comparison with life and work on the farm. Huldah Stone echoed this idea that in their country homes, where nature truly resided, the operatives had learned all their valuable lessons about life. Rural life, for Stone, was always bucolic and wholesome.

> Grant there is intelligence among the spindles; how it came there? Was it acquired by bending in unnatural positions thirteen hours per day over machinery, whose clatter is sufficient to confuse the clearest head, and cause the whole intellectual machinery to run out of gear? No, far from this! They gathered their intellectual treasures among the green hills and fertile vales of their own loved mountain homes, where the pure air of heaven, gave life and animation to the whole being—where earth's variegated beauties and harmonies, all combined to fill the soul with rapture and peace!

Working and living on a farm was not necessarily easy, but no one was forced to perform the same monotonous task every day of the year. A woman might spin thread for a season, but she also might tend the house, the garden, or the livestock.[6]

H. E. Back, a friend of Harriet Hanson Robinson's, captured perhaps best of all the joy some young women felt in the freedom and space of the countryside. "One must be happy," she wrote to Robinson while the latter was sojourning in Wentworth, New Hampshire, "while they are free to rove when and where they will among the green fields, by the running streams, in the depth of the forest, and in the pleasant valley with none to molest or make them afraid, so different from a city life . . . do not think I am unhappy because I cannot wish you here; far from it, but I think you are happier *there*."[7]

Some female operatives compared factory work with another traditional woman's occupation—domestic service—and they found the latter to have more advantages. Abigail Mussey at one time "thought the noise of a factory would be preferable to that of crying children." After a brief stint as a weaver in a mill, Mussey concluded that her "former work" as a housekeeper "was far more healthy, and offered me greater privileges, and I began to think the crying of children, with the sound of their little voices, is melody to a factory bell. . . . I commenced my labors again as housemaid with a pleasant mistress and an agreeable family of children; and if they did cry occasionally, it was much better than the life of toil and bondage in a factory."[8]

Sally Rice also carefully evaluated all the costs and benefits of factory work, domestic service, and agricultural labor. She saw her job in the mill as a short-term option for more money, but her long-term goals were rooted in the home and farm. She wrote to her father in the winter of 1845, after she had started working as a weaver:

> I like quite as well as I expected but not as well as I do house work. To be sure it is a noisy [pla]ce and we are confined more than I like to be but I do not wear out my clothes and shoes as I do when I do house work. If I can make 2 dollars per week beside my board and save my clothes and shoes I think that it will be better than to do housework for nine shillings I mean for a year or two. I should not like to spend my days in a mill not by a good deal unless they are short because I like a Farm to well for that.

Sally Rice's stay in the mill actually lasted only a few months, and she then returned to her previous work helping to keep a farmhouse in Millbury, Massachusetts. She, too, decided that tending a household was healthier than tending looms in a mill.[9]

Operatives who criticized the factory and praised the farm were striving to uphold the agrarian way of life. Their ideas and memories about their farms were not simply nostalgic reflections of some mythic golden age. These workers believed that agriculture did not lie solely in the nation's past; it was an essential part of the present and the future. They were looking for ways to keep young people on their homesteads and to help operatives in factories return to the land. Yet most of these workers were not reactionaries; they were not trying to retreat to the farm and stop all progress. Workers who preferred farm labor saw the agricultural community as the real source of independence and self-respect. They thought it far better to work the land with family and neighbors than to depend on corporations for cash wages that rarely fulfilled their promises of economic independence. Many operatives who supported agriculture rather than industry did not see the issue as an all-or-nothing proposition. They were searching for a balanced economy—the factories did not have to be destroyed; they had to be reformed so that they would harmonize with other facets of society. To support the farm was in the best progressive spirit of land reform, labor reform, and even women's rights. In a balanced economy, both men and women would have opportunities for improving themselves.[10]

Some workers found their own personal balance by working winters in factories and spending summers back on family farms. Marie Currier, another friend of Harriet Hanson Robinson's, wrote about how her perceptions of the country and the industrial city changed with the seasons.

> . . . I suppose you have by this time become naturalized to Lowell and become accustomed to the din and clatter of machinery. Is the sight of brick walls and side-walks, in the place of the quiet and stillness, the green trees and grass covered walks of the country. Doubtless you sometimes cast a wistful glance to your country home when the bright sun is shining cheerily forth and nature is alive with beauties, but in a few weeks you will be thankful that you are not buried up in impenitrable snowbanks and obliged to make your own paths through drifts of snow. Give me the country in the summer, but I would prefer when winter comes to be situated in some place where all the avenues to enjoyment do not seem to be frozen up.[11]

For other workers, such as Harriet Farley, the scales tipped decidedly in favor of factory labor. After looking back to their rural homes and the world of their mothers, Farley and some other female textile operatives concluded that industrial work held out better advantages. Farley was raised in rural New Hampshire, and she recalled that, "at fourteen years of age, I commenced exertions to assist in my own maintenance, and have at different times followed the various avocations of New England girls. I have plaited palm-leaf and straw, bound shoes, taught school, and worked at tailoring, besides my labours as a weaver in the factory, which suited me better than any other." Farley consistently argued that factory work was a better option than most other employment available to women in antebellum America. She respected the values of rural New England, but she cast a critical eye on the reality of agricultural labor. Life on a farm was not always a frolic with nature: it meant long hours of strenuous work for men and women, with few opportunities for amusement. Men may have derived some ultimate satisfaction from working the land if they owned their farms and believed in the ideal of the independent yeoman. But women's farm labor was often done in an environment that offered little in the way of ownership or independence. Nearly all the other traditional female occupations also subjected women to working conditions that were far less healthy than a factory's. Farley's support of the factory system was therefore grounded in her own experience with rural handicraft work and her belief that industrial labor was superior to these other unsatisfying tasks.

> . . . [S]empstresses, shoe-binders, straw-braiders, have been accustomed to labor, sitting in nearly the same position, a greater number of hours than those employed in the mill, and in an atmosphere quite as warm, confined, and impure; unless it is contended that the smoke of a cooking stove is less impure than the dust of a cotton mill . . . notwithstanding the complaints which have been lately made, the work allotted to one [in the factory] is light—were it not so there would not be so many hurrying from their country homes to get rid of milking cows, washing floors, and other such healthy employments. It is light work—otherwise so many could not work here, who cannot do any thing requiring much strength.[12]

Farley painted an especially stark portrait of textile production before the advent of mechanization. She believed that those who criticized the mills wanted to return to some mythic preindustrial past where every worker was a craftsman and all labor was pleasant and beautiful. She realized that even some stories in the *Lowell Offering* tended to romanticize the agrarian life. But she saw a much harsher reality in the farmhouse—the world before the coming of the factory was not one of perfect harmony and balance.

> In old ballads, and romantic tales, the imagination of the writer can throw a halo around the spinner, with her distaff in hand, but strip it of the ideal, and what a picture is here . . . a woman in a rickety chair, with her feet resting upon a cold, stone floor; she is watching the boiling pot with one eye, while the other follows her thread drawn, by a painfully slow process, from the tuft upon the stick, then to be wound upon the quill: at her right hand is a crock, but *not* "of gold"; . . . Through the casement she can look upon the hills and vales, but necessity, by its iron law, chains her to her seat. Peg-warping, done by a lad is tedious to look upon. Hand-carding, roving and spinning by hand-wheel, are equally unattractive to look upon. . . . And, outwardly, the scene may be as repulsive. . . . Poverty and discomfit were doubtless then the lot of the operative.

Some would have argued that the cottage spinner at least was free to set her own pace without being pushed to keep up with power-driven machinery. But Farley saw such hand labor as far more difficult and burdensome than tending machines, and she believed that these handicraft workers were driven even harder by their own desperate circumstances. Labor without the aid of machinery could lead workers into an ignorant, brutish, and depraved existence.[13]

Farley clearly never set out to condemn rural life as a whole; it was still home to many operatives, and the foundation of what they saw as their high moral standards and dignity. Up to a point, factory supporters and factory critics agreed on the wholesome character of the country homestead itself. But Farley parted company with the critics on the question of agricultural work, particularly for women, which she saw as a far heavier burden than factory labor. Farley argued that industrial labor was superior to agricultural and handicraft work precisely because the factory made labor so steady, consistent, and predictable. In her opinion, factory work usually did not whipsaw the operative from one burst of intense activity to the next.

One contributor to the *Lowell Offering* set out her own critical comparison of the farm and factory in a fictitious dialogue between a woman unhappy with life in Lowell and her friend who reminded her of the dreary side of rural life.

> "I think you thought differently while you were at home, on a visit, last summer—for you were glad to come back to the mill, in less than four weeks. Tell me, now—why were you so glad to return to the ringing of the bell, the clatter of the machinery, the early rising, the half hour dinner, and so on? . . . You are fully aware, then, that a country life does not exclude people from labor— . . ."
>
> "We have no bell, with its everlasting ding-dong."
>
> "What difference does it make . . . whether you shall be awakened by a bell, or the noisy bustle of a farmhouse? For, you know, farmers are generally up as early in the morning as we are obliged to rise."
>
> "But then . . . country people have none of the clattering of machinery constantly dinning in their ears."
>
> "True . . . but they have what is worse—and that is a dull, lifeless silence all around them. The hens may cackle sometimes, and the geese gabble, and the pigs squeal"—.

The author, as the narrator, concluded her story by saying that

> Ellen's hearty laugh interrupted my description—and presently we proceeded, very pleasantly, to compare a country life with a city life in Lowell. Her scowl of discontent had departed, and she was prepared to consider the subject candidly. We agreed, that since we must work for a living, the mill, all things considered, is the most pleasant, and best calculated to promote our welfare. . . .[14]

Some women workers also favored factory labor over domestic service. They reversed the arguments of factory critics and claimed that it was industrial labor that offered more freedom than housekeeping. Lucy Larcom took issue with those who said that "it would be better for all of us mill-girls to be working in families, at domestic service, than to be where we were." She believed that factory work was more suited to the temperament of New England women, and "they preferred it to going out as 'hired help.'"[15]

For some workers, especially many young women in the industrial cities, the opportunity to work in a factory was the first step on the road leading permanently away from the rural homestead. Some of these workers may have gone into industrial labor as a conscious rejection of agrarian life, and a deliberate move to other opportunities and away from what they saw as the lonely and arduous life of a farmer and his wife. Many of these women remained in the mills for only a few years, but some of them subsequently married and made new homes in these cities. The economic and social opportunities in an urban environment proved more attractive than returning to the family farm. Even the operatives who did go home again often had a new perspective on rural life and a desire to chart a new course away from the farm and into other occupations. For every worker who yearned to return to the land, there was another who sought new opportunities in the industrial economy.[16]

— II —

This debate over the factory system cannot be completely explained by the simple—and inaccurate—statement that all workers who loved farms hated factories, and all workers who loved factories hated farms. There are other reasons that help explain why some operatives cast a critical eye on industrial labor, while their co-workers continued to view the system in a more positive light. These other explanations depend more on workers' ideas about the role of labor in everyday life. Workers continued to disagree about the impact of the factory on their lives because they also disagreed about the value of labor itself.

From their first days in the factories, different operatives had different reasons for entering these mechanized workplaces and for staying there. Many operatives believed that their work was an obligation to others and themselves. Yet it was a duty they were willing to assume because it gave their labor more meaning. Female operatives often wrote essays and stories about the value of serving others through industrial labor, perhaps because this motif of female selflessness helped make their personal interests in factory work more socially acceptable. Harriet Farley wrote in an autobiographical sketch that she devoted "all my spare earnings to them [her family] and their interests. I made good wages; I dressed economically; I assisted in the liberal education of one brother; and endeavoured to be the guardian angel to a lovely sister. . . ."[17]

Farley believed that there were many other working women also laboring for the support of their families. In her early essay, "A Defense of Factory Girls," she wrote about "widows earning money for the maintenance and education of their children . . . daughters providing for their aged and destitute parents . . . widows, single women, and girls, endeavoring to obtain the wherewithal to furnish some other home than a factory boarding-house." Elizabeth Turner, another contributor to the *Lowell Offering,* wrote that "many a factory girl . . . has the sweet consciousness of having assisted others, and added to their happiness. And are they not rewarded? Yes—the smiles of an approving conscience are theirs . . . they rise at the early dawn, to attend to their daily avocation, with as light and bouyant hearts, and as pleasing expectations of the future—as those who do nothing but spend money and misspend time."[18]

Harriet Hanson Robinson remembered that when she was about ten years old, her mother needed "the money which I could earn, [and] allowed me, at my urgent request (for I wanted to earn *money* like the other little girls), to go to work in the mill." Robinson also believed that her motivation for entering the factory—to help support her family—was similar to that of many of her co-workers (even though most female operatives in Lowell were older than Robinson and not living with their parents). She painted a portrait of a work force in which everyone seemed to labor for a noble cause, and no one thought of her own needs.

> Some of these were daughters of professional men or teachers, whose mothers, left widows, were struggling to maintain the younger children. A few were the daughters of persons in reduced circumstances, who had left home "on a visit" to send their wages surrepticiously in aid of the family purse. And some were the granddaughters of patriots who had fought at Bunker Hill, and had lost the family means in the war for independence. . . . Some of the mill-girls helped maintain widowed mothers or drunken, incompetent, or invalid fathers. . . . It is easy to see how much good [their earnings] . . . would do in a rural community where money, as a means of exchange, had been scarce. Into the barren homes many of them had left, it went like a quiet stream, carrying with it beauty and refreshment. The mortgage was lifted from the homestead; the farmhouse was painted; the barn rebuilt. . . . Many of them educated the younger children of the family and young men were sent to college with the money furnished by the untiring industry of the women relatives.
>
> The most prevailing incentive to labor was to secure the means of education for some *male* member of the family. To make a *gentleman* of a brother or a son, to give him a college education, was the dominant thought in the minds of a great many of the better class of mill-girls. I have known more than one to give every cent of her wages, month after month, to her brother, that he might get the education necessary to enter some profession. I have known women to educate young men by their earnings, who were not sons or relatives. There are many men now living who were helped to an education by the wages of these early mill-girls.[19]

Robinson, in an article in the *Journal of Social Science,* repeated this argument about female operatives' working to educate men and added an interesting commentary on this phenomenon. Women workers, when they used their wages to pay for men's education, were giving their own work a significance beyond the factory, while keeping themselves in their traditional role as helpmate.

> The average woman of forty years ago was very humble in her notions of the sphere of women. What if she did hunger and thirst after knowledge? She could do nothing with it even if she could get it. So she made a *fetich* of some male relative, and gave him the mental food for which she was starving; and devoted all her energies towards helping him to become what she felt, under better conditions, she herself might have been. It was enough in those early days, to be the *mother* or *sister* of somebody.[20]

These portraits of the self-sacrificing operative were often a way for young women to reconcile their desires to work on their own, independent from their families, with the image they wanted to maintain of female duty to family. Through these images, women workers showed themselves to be progressive and traditional at the same time—earning their own money and managing their own affairs, while still laboring for the good of their families. They carried their economic role beyond the physical confines of the home, and they lived away from their parents, but they still adhered to the concept of women's work as service to the family. When women claimed that they were going away to the factories to work for their families, they were trying to bridge the gap between the new opportunities for social and economic independence offered by the mills, and the enduring values of kin and home, which were felt keenly by so many operatives.

In reality, many workers in Lowell and other industrial communities were not toiling away for the lofty goals Farley and Robinson enumerated. Many young women worked in factories for the opportunity to earn and spend their own money, free from any other obligations. These operatives came from families of modest means who were glad to see their children earn their own keep, but not in desperate need for them to send home all their earnings. Some workers, such as Martha Russell, sent small amounts now and then, more as gifts than as regular payments. Russell wrote to her parents: "I here inclose three dollars for you to by any little necessities you need most." She added, in a magnanimous gesture, "write if there is any thing that I can help you to I shall do it with pleasure while I have my health. . . ." Russell was certainly more than willing to send some of her wages home to aid her family, but there was no desperate necessity for her to scrimp every available penny to rescue the homestead. Russell probably earned personal satisfaction and social approval from sharing a modest portion of her savings with her family.[21]

Some operatives did admit that the public image of the completely unselfish laborer was not an entirely accurate picture. Workers did have personal reasons for working in factories, but they were often phrased in very modest terms. An operative from Waltham, Massachusetts, explained that many mill girls came from all over New England to earn money for something more than the bare essentials, not to rescue their families from destitution. "There may be several daughters in one family, and each is desirous of promoting the general welfare; and, though they may have all the necessities of life, yet they desire more of its comforts and conveniences than they have the means of procuring at home."[22]

Many women clung tightly to their factory jobs, not because they had to support their families: quite to the contrary, because they saw their work as the foundation of their personal freedom. Beneath their proclamations of sacrifice and the ethic of hard work, they believed that industrial labor afforded them an independent living. "Song of the Spinners" reassured workers: "Despite of toil we all agree, / Or out of the mills, or in, / Dependent on others we ne'er will be, / So long as we're able to spin." Elizabeth Turner, even as she was praising the generosity of those who worked to help others, also recognized that many operatives felt "a spirit of honest independence, as they . . . realize that they can support themselves by their own efforts." Factory work was liberating women from the myths of female inferiority and dependence; female operatives were fulfilling their needs and rights to women's independence. When these women argued that their work and their wages were the foundation of their independence, they were not saying that they necessarily had to labor for their very survival; but neither were they dismissing their own efforts as mere diversion for pin money.[23]

Lucy Larcom saw how the spirit of independence in female factory workers gave them a sense of their own potential they had never known before. "It was like a young man's pleasure in entering upon business for himself. Girls had never tried that experiment before and they liked it. It brought out in them a dominant strength of character which the world did not previously see, but now fully acknowledges. Of course they had a right to continue at that freer kind of work as long as they chose. . . ." The editors of the *Operatives' Magazine,* veterans of the Lowell mills, saw factory workers as the epitome of the honorable producer who made all of America independent. They wrote: "we have not with some, been accustomed to look upon the Operatives of our country as a low degraded class; but as those who, by their industry, energy, and enterprizes, are the producers of all that is around, which render us more independent and happier, than the other nations of the earth; and, hence, the most honorable class, and those of us who are of the greatest benefit to the world." Working women were encouraged to have pride in their being independent workers and respectable women.[24]

Many women workers believed in their independence because they earned their own cash wages and managed their own finances. They were still subject to the authority of their male managers, but they were not living in the family household, where their work was likely to be owned, in a sense, by their fathers or husbands. They were responsible for their own standard of living much more than they were contributing to their family's daily welfare.

These women did not seem to recognize that their two models—the selfless female worker and the independent female worker, each eagerly embracing factory labor—might come into conflict with each other. After all, if women were laboring for others, how could they say that their work was a crucial step toward their independence? Or if women wanted to live and work for themselves, how long would they remain a key component of the family economy? Tensions arose when women tried to retain genteel notions of femininity, propriety, sacrifice, and refinement, while also defining new realms of women's self-reliance, respect, intelligence, and dignity in the workplace.

Yet, many operatives argued that the more women worked in the factories, the more successful they were in uniting their high moral standards with their newfound autonomy. Nearly every worker agreed that they started out from their country homes with strong ethical constitutions—but the question remained as to whether the factory system complemented or compromised those moral principles. Lucy Larcom saw the mill girls rising above any possible detrimental effects of factory labor and preserving their rural inheritance of honesty and hard work. "Their vigor of character was a natural development. The New Hampshire girls who came to Lowell were descendents of the sturdy backwoodsmen who settled that State. . . . They were earnest and capable; ready to undertake anything that was worth doing. My dreamy, indolent nature was shamed into activity among them." Larcom knew that industrial labor was not always inspiring; it could sometimes be quite confining, but it did not necessarily jeopardize the high standards bred into most operatives. She concluded that "the girls who toiled together at Lowell . . . practically said, by numbering themselves among factory girls, that in our country no real odium can be attached to any honest toil that any self-respecting woman might undertake."[25]

Other operatives were even more enthusiastic in their defense of the factory system. They argued that the factory did not merely protect the workers' reputations; factories could actually exert a wholesome influence to improve the operatives' character. One worker from North Adams, Massachusetts, wrote: "Intelligent, healthy and happy;—respected at home, and admired abroad. . . . As a whole, the Mill Girls of Adams think, that good manners can flourish in and around a factory." Harriet Robinson recalled: "It was the good fortune of these early mill-girls to teach the people that this sort of labor is not degrading; that the operative is not only 'capable of virtue,' but also capable of self-cultivation."[26]

The *Lowell Offering* was also filled with stories and editorials about the moral development of women in the factories. Each issue seemed to proclaim the intelligence and imagination of the work force that was raised in rural New England and nurtured further in the Lowell community. Contributors asserted their respectability by avoiding most discussions of class and conflict and criticism of the factory system. There was no need to protest or crusade for reforms because the factory posed no threat to the workers. These workers saw themselves as conservatives intent upon promoting the orderly development and continuation of the factory system as it then existed.

The female operatives who wrote for the *Offering* saw nothing disingenuous in defending the factory system and denying that problems existed. Many of them went on their own offensive and actively promoted the virtues of industrial labor, rather than merely fending off criticisms. They believed that they could be both pro-factory and pro-worker. They supported the factory system and the basic rights and dignity of workers within that system, because they thought that the factory and the workers supported each other.

One contributor to the *Offering* stated her case boldly:

> We have abundant proof that unremitted toil is not always derogatory to improvement. A factory girl's work is neither hard nor complicated; she can go on with perfect regularity in her duties, while her mind may be actively employed on any other subject. There can be no better place for reflection, when there must be toil, than the factory . . . factory operatives find leisure to use the means for improvement both in mind and heart.

Harriet Farley clearly summed up her own views on how factory labor was compatible with women's high moral status in one of her final editorials: "the 'factory girl' feels that . . . she has not fallen into another and lower class. She takes much pains to inform herself, and 'keep up her respectability,' . . . so long as she retains her self-respect and upright character, she has neither degraded herself, nor those connected with her."[27]

Many of these arguments about women's moral improvement in the factory were premised on these operatives' faith that their industrial work was only a voluntary and temporary stage in their lives. These workers insisted that their brief sojourn in the factories did not relegate them to a permanently lower status. They came in with what could be called a "middle-class identity," and they left with that status intact and their character improved. They arrived as the daughters of rural families, spent a few years in wage labor, and then left to become wives and mothers with no fear that their social position had ever changed for the worse, and often with a modest dowry to show for their efforts.

Those who said that they were voluntarily taking up factory work as a short-term option and could leave it whenever they chose to, were also likely to retain their optimistic view of the mechanized workplace as a whole. Those workers embraced the factory system with confidence; confident, however, that they would not remain in the arms of the factory for the rest of their lives. The factory was good because it offered workers the chance to get out. It was ironic that workers praised factory labor because they did not think that they would be factory laborers for a long period of time. Factory work retained its positive glow as long as it was done for only a relatively short period.

Lucy Larcom observed how "this feeling that they were at work in the mills for a little while, only to accomplish some special purpose," gave these mill girls a feeling of "contentment, without any sacrifice of independence." These workers believed that they could control the duration and terms of their labor. If there were any problems in the workplace, they could be glossed over, because these operatives thought they would have to endure them for only a brief time. While many men may have considered factory work to be a long-term occupation, many women, especially those who were working only for their own maintenance, believed that industrial labor was "not the business of our lives"; it was one relatively brief stage in their lifecycle, an opportunity to be seized and then left behind when it had served its purpose. They believed that they always had the option to explore new opportunities beyond the factories.[28]

It is quite probable that the mill girls in cities like Lowell were more likely to see factory work as a temporary option than workers in rural mill villages where industrial labor seemed to be a permanent way of life for many poorer families. Many women in Lowell remained confident that they were leaving the confines of the family homestead, and even the family economy itself, for a few years of financial independence and personal savings. The ultimate goal in life for these mill women, however, was usually to return to the familial bonds as a wife and mother, though perhaps not back in the old rural community.

The idea that factory labor was a temporary and voluntary option persuaded many workers to dismiss—completely and finally—all the recurring charges of factory enslavement. Workers were not enslaved to their machines, nor to their managers, nor to the factory regulations, nor to the wage labor system. These workers argued that the wealth of new social and economic opportunities, the allegiance to traditional notions of personal worth and integrity, and the fundamental faith in equality all precluded the possibility of exploitation or enslavement. While the work could be tedious and the hours long and rigidly measured, the operatives were not legally bound for life to their employers. Once their contracts were fulfilled, they could move wherever they wanted to. And this ability to pick up and leave—sheer physical mobility—was the foundation of an operative's freedom and power over herself and her destiny. The workers still owned their own persons, and many believed that such personal integrity was the basis of all freedom. A Maine operative penned the following poem to proclaim that spirit of freedom in the midst of the mill.

Though to this noisy, tiresome room,
At early dawn, I take my way,
Where sterner fate has fixed my doom
To labor the live-long day—
Ye proudly great, sigh not for me,
For still my thoughts and will are free . . .
I am not rich nor wish to be
For now my love, my acts, are free.[29]

Workers who spoke of free, voluntary, temporary labor also saw the chance for real mobility for operatives. In textile mills, women could move up from the spinning room to better-paying jobs in the weaving or dressing departments. In metalworking shops, women could rise from washing and packing britannia ware to soldering and polishing. Operatives could also move from one factory to another to try to secure a better job. Sometimes even the threat of making such a move would prompt managers into promoting an experienced worker to avoid losing her services. The very act of physically moving was said to be an assertion of a laborer's autonomy, as well as a means of promoting occupational advancement. Some workers saw physical and occupational mobility as a clear indication that they had job choices both inside and outside of the factory system.[30]

Male factory workers could also consider the possibility of working their way up into the ranks of overseers and agents. Isaac Parker was a carder at a spinning mill in Keene, New Hampshire, then an overseer at Waltham, and finally owned his own mill. Charles Furber apprenticed as a carpenter, eventually became a machinist, and then a carding room overseer at the Middlesex Corporation in Lowell, and in 1848 he helped establish the woolen machinery manufacturing concern of Davis and Furber. Numerous workers in the clock industry of Bristol, Connecticut, also started their own businesses. Some of the new clock factories were modest in size, others grew to be substantial companies. These rags-to-riches stories were not common. But some workers thought that there were enough upwardly mobile men to support the idea that factory labor could be a steppingstone to more powerful and more lucrative positions for the operative with ambition. In the factory system, these operatives argued, there was both an equality and a freedom of opportunity for men of talent and energy to move upward. Every man had a fair chance in the race for wealth and success.[31]

The root cause of this drive for mobility, and this optimistic faith in the factory system, was a particular conception of the value of labor itself. Operatives who retained their positive outlook on factory work saw labor as having an instrumental value. There was a direct correlation between this instrumental view of labor and support for the factory system—the same workers who wrote in praise of factory work often wrote about the instrumental view of labor.

These workers saw labor, quite simply, as a means to other ends. Factory supporters did not usually praise mechanized labor for its inherent creativity and craftsmanship. They argued that the factory system made labor easier on the operatives' minds and bodies, paid high wages, and taught useful lessons in discipline and obedience. Even if industrial work was not always inherently fulfilling, the benefits derived from it would help workers reach their economic and social goals.

These workers seemed less concerned with deriving intrinsic satisfaction from their factory jobs, as long as the extrinsic benefits—particularly the monetary ones—were readily available.

One contributor to the *Lowell Offering* noted that many women workers linked their ideas about mill work as a temporary occupation with this conception of instrumental labor. "There are few who look upon factory labor as a pursuit for life. It is but a temporary vocation; and most of the girls resolve to quit the mill when some favorite design is accomplished. Money is their object—not for itself, but for what it can perform. . . ." There was a certain risk, however, in women's arguing that they did not have to work in the factories, and that their labor was only a temporary option to earn enough money for some pet project. This argument could lead to all women's work, and all women workers, being dismissed as unnecessary and frivolous. How could women reconcile such a seemingly casual attitude toward their jobs with their other claims that they and their labor should be treated with dignity? How could these same women say that they were working as a sacrifice for their families, and as a temporary means of earning money for themselves?[32]

Harriet Farley continued to defend the right of women to work in the mills for whatever reasons they chose. She also saw that underlying much support for the factory system was the simple truth that many people went into the mills to make money for the things that were far removed from their work. While factory critics often focused their attention on the nature of labor and working conditions, factory supporters like Farley talked more about the money they made for themselves and their families. Farley wrote: "This, was their reasoning respecting the mills. Here is work offered, and high wages. Of this we are sure. This money, though it comes from factory labor, is as good as any money; and will perform all the good offices of any money." Farley sold factory labor to her readers as basically routine, mechanized tasks that paid relatively high wages to women. The work had little creative meaning in itself, so operatives were encouraged to work for money and for the goods that money could buy.

Farley was quick to add, however, that workers would not sell their souls for a few dollars. She summed up her confidence in the factory system and the factory operatives by asserting that "to work in Lowell, cannot make *us* ignorant and degraded. We will go, and get all the good there; and see that we do not become contaminated by the evil influences." Farley argued that female operatives saw their labor as their own resource to be sold to the highest bidder, but they were also sure that their employers would not treat them as merely another factor of production. The women's efforts to uphold and improve their status sent a clear message to their male bosses that they thought of themselves as respectable people first and operatives second.[33]

Farley believed that, in the final accounting, industrial labor was what workers made of it. Operatives had the opportunity to help themselves through their work and their wages. They remained free men and women with the final responsibility for their own conduct. Those who criticized the factories were wrong to blame the system—the fault for any worker's problems lay with herself. Poverty and corruption were due solely to personal weaknesses in the operatives, not to any larger social injustice.

— III —

Workers who criticized the factory system had a very different vision of the role of labor in everyday life. They quickly took issue with the idea that workers entered factories willingly and happily, as a matter of free choice. Sarah Bagley faced head-on the question of what brought workers into the factories and what kept them at their jobs.

> Whenever I raise the point that it is immoral to shut us up in a close room twelve hours a day in the most monotonous and tedious employment, I am told that we have come to the mills voluntarily and we can leave when we will. Voluntarily! Let us look a little at this remarkable form of human freedom. Do we from mere choice leave our father's dwellings, the firesides where all of our friends, where too our earliest and fondest recollections cluster, for the factory? . . . By what charm do these great companies immerse human creatures in the bloom of youth and first glow of life within the mills, away from their homes and kindred? . . . The whip which brings us to Lowell is NECESSITY. We must have money; a father's debts are to be paid, an aged mother to be supported, a brother's ambition to be aided, and so factories are supplied. Is this to act from free will? . . . Is any one such a fool as to suppose that out of six thousand factory girls of Lowell, sixty would be there if they could help it?

Bagley's concluding figures were certainly rhetorical; but other workers agreed with the basic fact that factories were preying on needy migrants from declining hill towns and old seaports to fill their requirements.[34]

Ironically, Bagley listed some of the same reasons for working in factories that Harriet Farley and Harriet Hanson Robinson did: paying off family debts, supporting aged parents, helping a brother get an education. Workers like Farley and Robinson argued that laboring for others was a noble calling that workers often assumed in a spirit of generosity. The "whip" of necessity was found only in the dim recesses of the pre-industrial cottages, where women were forced to toil at arduous tasks. Factory labor, according to Farley and Robinson, was a welcome opportunity for these women to help themselves and others. Bagley certainly did not begrudge helping family and friends, but she also argued that such bonds of need could be exploited by the manufacturers to lock their employees into the factory system. Farley and Robinson believed that most workers could eventually leave the mills when their family obligations were fulfilled. Bagley, however, feared that some families were so destitute that their children would have to spend their entire working lives in the factories. Thus, when Bagley saw operatives working for others, she did not see independent women covering their labor with a glowing veneer of self-sacrifice. She saw workers forced into an industrial regimen due to sheer economic necessity, and held there out of fear of destitution for themselves and their families.

Bagley also, once again, raised the specter of slavery when she argued that dire economic circumstances in many middling New England homes stripped factory labor of its voluntary character. The liberty to not work in a factory could easily become a license to go hungry. Thus, to say that factory workers had fundamental power over their own persons and that they always had the option to leave their jobs were empty phrases to Bagley.

> Every body knows that it is necessity alone, in some form or other, that takes us to Lowell and keeps us there. Is this freedom? To my mind it is slavery quite as real as any in Turkey or Carolina. It matters little as to the fact of slavery, whether the slave be compelled to his task by the overseer or the wages of the Lowell Corporation. In either case it is not free will, leading the laborer to work, but an outward necessity that puts free will out of the question.[35]

The workers who felt trapped by economic necessity in the factory also worried about the results of long-term exposure to industrial labor. What would happen to those who were forced into the factories when they did not want to go in the first place, and kept at their tasks long after they wanted to move on to other opportunities? Some workers feared that the result would be a factory system that pulled workers deeper and deeper into a descending spiral of dependence and deterioration. For these workers, there was no escaping the conclusion that industrial labor corrupted the operatives. The Lowell Female Labor Reform Association stated in its constitution that "the Laborer . . . is a slave to a false and debasing state of society. . . . It is evident, that with the present system of labor, the minds of the mass *must* remain uncultivated their morals unimproved, and our country be flooded with vice and misery!" The industrial economy was destroying the system of free labor in America; factories were creating their own forms of slavery and tyranny. As workers became alienated from their labor, as they saw their independence and creativity ripped from their grasp, they also became alienated from society and the bonds of communal obligation.[36]

A Manchester, New Hampshire, worker wrote a poem for a local newspaper, which painted a stark portrait of the industrial city dragging the operatives down into a life of degradation. The poem was titled simply, "Manchester As It Is":

> This place is large of great dimensions,
> Where demons dwell with bad intention,
> Females, incarnate upon its surface crawl,
> Steep'd in Hell's dyes and hardened by its laws.
> This place is known to the whole nation,
> Where devils seek for higher stations,
> Fiends, inhuman make its laws.
> Beings created for a more noble cause,
> This place has sunk into degradation,
> Its victims fallen in confrication,
> Burn on, burn up, ye poisonous vipers, burn,
> God's name be honored, virtue to its elay return.
> This place is meaner in my estimation,
> Than the smallest link in animal creation,
> And could I but paint the lowest gradations,
> I would Manchester lower than the lowest detestation.[37]

John Quincy Adams Thayer agreed with most other workers, factory critics and supporters alike, that the operatives were not an inherently morally flawed group. But where workers such as Harriet Farley argued that the operatives' strong rural moral inheritance was enhanced by factory labor, Thayer countered that workers—no matter how righteous their upbringing—were victims of a cruel labor system.

Mill girls "do leave their homes and take their way to Lowell, in possession of the most choice treasures, valued only for their virtue, intelligence, health, morals, and industry." Once in the factory, Thayer said, "these same individuals [were] cast into chains and supported by the same innocent priceless blood." Thayer summed up the connection between factory work and the deteriorating quality of life for operatives by stating: "We wish the world to know that the operatives in Lowell are poor, because they are poor, less and less intelligent year after year, their burdens and monopolized machinery increasing on the one hand, their health and intelligence decreasing on the other, leaving slavery and starvation to the many." The factory system was eroding the very moral standards it claimed to be upholding, Thayer asserted; workers were dissipated and weakened instead of disciplined and productive. Workers never had the opportunity to improve their skills or to learn a new and useful trade under the system of industrial labor; they were always exploited as mere factory drudges.[38]

Of course, the workers who painted this bleak picture were not pleased with what they saw. Yet they did not think that the situation was entirely hopeless; workers were being physically and mentally debased in the factories, but they were not beyond redemption. It was important to remember that workers were not inherently inferior and depraved; rather, it was the oppression of the corporation that was degrading the operatives. Critics were trying to draw a careful line between condemning the factory system for corrupting the operatives and yet upholding the inherent dignity of labor and the laborer. The two arguments may have seemed contradictory on the surface, but they were actually mutually reinforcing components of a single appeal to operatives to recognize the dangers of the factory even as they strove to overcome them.

Workers who criticized the factory system tried not to get caught in a bind between the need to recognize the constraints in their lives and the desire to obtain some power over their lives. Workers needed to be honest about what the factory was doing to them, but they also had to avoid becoming completely discouraged about their situation. They needed to keep hope alive and assert their ability to take action to change their lives.

The first step on the road back to dignity was to recognize the problem itself. Operatives had to realize that they did not have to defend the factory system in order to defend their own honor, virtue, and status as factory workers. Rather, the best defense was an offense—workers had to be willing to criticize the factories and what the system was doing to labor, as the only way to protect their position and interests. Those who denied that workers were suffering and declining and who proclaimed a positive image of workers untainted by their harsh labor were actually defending the exploitative manufacturers. Those who blithely continued to sing the praises of the factory system decade after decade, even through the turbulent 1840s, were engaging in mere self-delusion. They were trying to uphold some façade of false gentility in the face of declining working conditions. Sarah Bagley responded that she did not "*want* . . . oppression and abuse . . . to exist, but because they *do* exist [they] should not go unrebuked."[39]

Mehitable Eastman, speaking before the Manchester Industrial Reform Association, also declared that although operatives were under siege in the factories, they could still stand up for themselves. The task for operatives was to defend themselves against the abuses of the factory system, rather than apologize for the system in a backhanded attempt to defend their honor. Some outside observers were ready to dismiss the operatives as a lowly and depraved class. But the operatives knew that they still had a core of self-respect that had not been destroyed, and they were determined to stop the downward spiral by facing the truth about factory work.

> [N]ever while we have hearts to feel and tongues to speak will we silently and passively witness so much that is opposed to justice and benevolence,—never, while a wretched being is crying to us for succor, from the allies and dens of our cities—from our crammed manufactories and work-shops, from poverty stricken garrets and cellars,—never, with the awful facts of female degradation, under our present system of industry, staring us in the face; never, while we are conscious of powers undeveloped, affections hemmed in, energies paralyzed, privileges forfeited, and destiny thwarted. No, never shall we hold ourselves exempt from responsibility, never shall we cease our efforts in the warfare against evil.[40]

The longer some operatives stayed in the factories, the more they felt trapped by economic necessity and degraded by the exploitation of their labor, and locked into a system that turned workers into transitory and easily expendable factors of production. Where some spoke of the freedom of temporary labor, others saw the uncertainty of an unstable transient labor market.

In theory, transiency could be a primitive form of protest, a fundamental assertion that people would not work under dehumanizing conditions. Transiency could also be an expression of workers' desires to find some variety in labor, to resist being locked into the same factory job day-in and day-out. Some workers may even have hoped that by staying on the move constantly, they could hold open the possibility of real occupational mobility.

The reality of the transient worker's life, however, was often much bleaker. Workers might leave on their own in search of a better workplace, but just as frequently they were forced to move on due to dismissals or factory closings. Yet these workers often found themselves returning again and again to factory jobs for lack of other opportunities. Even if workers were not locked into work at one particular site, they often felt that they were still trapped in the factory system as a whole.[41]

Jabez Hollingworth noted that he and his father were forced to travel throughout southern New England in search of work in woolen mills. He wrote to his uncle: "Mr. Denny the Agent told Father that they wanted some hands at Southbridge 12 miles from here. Father and I went to see about it but did not make a final agreement. They wished us not to make Application any where else and they would write in a few days. Now you see the Fruits of Large Factorys. . . . Here we are driven from one Factory to another seeking rest and finding none. . . ." The Hollingworths realized that their own high rate of geographic mobility did not always translate into occupational mobility. Their constant search for new jobs was more often a threat to family stability than an opportunity to improve their situation. As workers traveled around looking for jobs to keep their families together, they often found themselves isolated and at a disadvantage in a society that also placed great value on neighbors and community.[42]

Workers who felt compelled to stay in factories were particularly fearful of the prospect of unemployment. Operatives with no land, no skills, no other occupation to fall back on, and hence no alternatives, saw the loss of work as a real crisis. As much as they disliked the factory system, even a bad job was better than no job for someone in dire need of money. Therefore, while some workers took to the road with the optimistic notion of finding a better line of work, many others were engaged in a more desperate quest to escape the problem of unemployment.

Unskilled workers were often especially vulnerable to layoffs, which could be the result of a nationwide depression or slack times in a particular industry or a single factory. Even though their wages were lower than the skilled workers', there were more unskilled laborers to be dispensed with and they were easier to replace when business revived. The Scovill brassworks laid off the unskilled men, the women, and the children first when sales were slow in 1832. Paper manufacturers also usually laid off more women than men, and often only reduced the hours for heads of households rather than laying them off in bad times. Paper-workers took in boarders, sold produce from their gardens, or labored around the owners' farms to earn money during slack times. Some male managers even took over jobs traditionally held by women in order to keep working while the paper mills were cutting back on staff.[43]

The Whitin Machine Company in Whitinsville, Massachusetts, on the other hand, made extraordinary efforts to protect its employees from losing their jobs even in the worst of depressions. The company wanted to retain its skilled work force and prevent the entire local economy from suffering, so it maintained a policy that no worker with dependents would lose his job, even when there were no orders to fill. The company would cut back on everyone's hours so that any existing work could be passed around. When that work ran out, the company would pay its employees for maintenance projects around the factory and the town so that everyone would still earn enough for food and shelter. The Waltham machine shops, at least in the early years of their operation, were not so intent on keeping all their machinists at work. They would lay off men during slow periods rather than keep everyone on a part-time basis.[44]

Textile mills also occasionally made provisions for unemployed workers. Some Slater mills tried to retain at least one member of each family on the payroll, even during large-scale layoffs, and they saw to it that the rest of the family was rehired as soon as possible. When Lowell mills had to shut down because of high water levels, they still paid for their employees' boarding costs.[45]

Other mills made few efforts to ameliorate the hardships caused by their decisions to lay off workers. Many companies would let workers go at any time of year, with only a brief notice, even though these same firms often insisted that their employees always serve out their contracts. Many operatives had to set out on their own in search of new jobs. Sally White wrote to the Poignand and Plant mill in Lancaster, Massachusetts, during the late summer of 1816, hoping to find a job there. The factory in Fitchburg, Massachusetts, where she worked was shutting down—the owners had other interests to pursue, and the workers had to fend for themselves.

> I have converst with those Gentlemen which now imploy me they think they have as much yarn now in hand as they can dispose of this winter to advantage they have

> come to A determination that they will stop the Factory till the Market is better they have so many other branches of bisness which is proffitable to attend to they do not want the perplexity of it.[46]

When layoffs were announced near the onset of winter, the problems could become particularly acute for operatives who had to scramble to find work and shelter from the cold. Zachariah Allen noted in his diary for October 1 and 2, 1833: "I have been out to my mill and given notice that I shall dismiss one half of the workmen at the mill, which appears to have caused some sorrowful faces there among those who had calculated on snug winter quarters & constant employment."[47]

The Hollingworth family also confronted the problem of unemployment, which helps explain why their labor was so transient. George Hollingworth wrote to his brother-in-law William Rawcliff about how bad business practices among the mill owners meant hard times for the workers. Maintaining a place in the local factory was

> a matter of doubt for things here are in a very curious and precarious state . . . Mr. Anderton has cut and run from South Leicester and left his Wife and all his personal debts unpaid. . . . It is expected that the factory will have to stop when we have worked up the present Stock which will only last us about 3 Weeks or a Month. Some are of the opinion that it will not stop long, only while a new Company takes hold but this to us who know nothing about it is doubtful.

George's son Joseph confirmed his father's gloomy assessment—the opportunities for work seemed to be slipping further from the operatives' grasp. "The Factory will stop as soon as the stock is worked up. Some of the spinners has already done and cleared; all our folks expects to have done this this month. It is said that all Englishmen will have to leave this place; work is very scarce in this part, and when a man gets out of employ tis hard for him to get in again." Joseph saw a clear connection between nationality and unemployment—his experience in American mills convinced him that immigrants were the first fired in hard times, and the last rehired when business picked up again.[48]

Joseph's brother Jabez tried to fall back on his carpentry skills when he lost his job in the mill repair shop, but the enduring prejudice against immigrants made even that task difficult. Jabez wrote to his uncle: "I have had no work since I left you only what I have done in our own house. I have made a bench to work on which hass [cost] me about 6 dollars. I have made a broad loom for Brother John and . . . wheelbarrow and some Winterhedges for Sale but I cannot sell them. There is no encouragement for such business here. I am an Englishman amongst Yankees. They want to give me half what they are worth." Jabez and other skilled workers discovered that their talents might make them attractive during periods of high demand for labor; but, if in spite of all management's efforts to keep them at work, they finally lost their jobs during hard economic times, it would be far more difficult for them to secure work of comparable skill, status, and wages. If they were immigrant skilled workers, they were likely to find the hard times even harder; native-born workers and managers tried to first look after their fellow "Yankees" with whatever limited resources were available.[49]

Some workers, realizing that industrial employment was unstable, began to place more emphasis on job security than on high wages. W. Patton wrote to the Scovill

Company that "he would be glad to go to waterbury again if you could give him permanent employment as permanency is more an object with him than large wages." The workers at the Springfield Armory struggled to secure their own jobs when they were threatened by cuts in government appropriations. The armory tried to be fair in setting procedures for layoffs; younger and unmarried men were let go before the veterans and those with families. The management also tried to find new jobs for the unemployed with other armories. Despite these efforts to ease the impact of unemployment, the armorers fought an attempt to lay off fifty workers at the end of 1832. The superintendent refused to grant leave to the bayonet-forger who wanted to go to Washington and contest the austerity measure. But this employee used his political influence to get the leave, and the layoff order was delayed until the spring of 1833, so that the armorers would not be out of work through the winter.[50]

Unemployed workers often found it hard to secure new jobs because they were laid off in the midst of a sluggish economy. Some operatives, however, began to suspect that manufacturers were taking advantage of labor surpluses, which made the plight of the unemployed difficult even when the economy improved. P. T. Jackson, one of the managers of the Boston Manufacturing Company's mills in Waltham, wrote to the Poignand and Plant Company: "we have seldom less than 40 hands on our list more than we can employ & are more puzzled to get rid of hands than to get them." Some companies may have actively recruited a large pool of labor and kept a number of "spare hands" on the job so they could readily replace any recalcitrant workers. A surplus of workers eager for employment could keep both discontent and wages down. Samuel Collins noted this effect when he wrote: "I want very much to see more applicants for employment in every department that I may make some changes for I think it wd. have a salutory influence on some. . . ." The line between laying off someone for economic reasons and dismissing someone as a means of enforcing labor discipline sometimes became blurred. If a company's sales stagnated, managers could seize that opportunity to release any "troublemakers" in the name of fiscal responsibility, without stirring up the animosity that might be generated by other disciplinary actions. Even Eliza Jane Cate explained once that a "surplus of help" was hired "because there are in the [mill] some unproductive girls; some ill-natured, turbulent girls, who always will be ill-natured and turbulent girls, and they wish to be rid of both one class and the other, as soon as they are provided with good substitutes."[51]

Underlying much of this fear of industrial unemployment was a growing sense, for many workers, that they were becoming part of a permanent factory proletariat. Industrial labor was not a temporary option for these workers, a welcome opportunity to be taken before moving on to new adventures. Factory work was instead a permanent fact of life in these workers' eyes; there were no other realistic options or greater opportunities.

Some said that a landless, permanent factory population was more likely to be found in rural mills than in cities such as Lowell. Whole families, lacking a homestead to rely on, had always come to these country factories in search of a living wage. In the wake of the Panic of 1837, when many farms and small businesses were lost, this emerging industrial proletariat probably grew in size.[52]

Sarah Bagley and other factory critics feared that more and more mill girls in cities like Lowell were also becoming part of the permanent factory population. Necessity was not just driving workers into the factories, it was holding them there for the rest of their lives. The wake of the depression of 1837 swept landless laborers into the isolated rural mills, and it sent more women scurrying to Lowell as well, because they had to find jobs that paid cash wages. Ironically, it was Bagley who believed all those stories about operatives toiling to rescue their families from foreclosure. But she felt that the underlying tone in these accounts was not one of glorious self-sacrifice, but a dirge of desperation.

Throughout the 1840s, Bagley and Harriet Farley continued to debate the question of whether the Lowell mill girls were becoming a permanent factory labor force. Farley always insisted that even when these women were working to help their families, they did so willingly, confident in the knowledge that they would have to labor for only a few years. These women always took comfort from the fact that they came from stable rural homes. "The majority of the operatives are country girls. These have always the preference, because, in the fluctuations to which manufacturers are liable, there would be much less distress among a population which could resort to other homes, than if their entire interest was in the city."[53]

Bagley and other critics were concerned that many operatives felt they had to stay in the mills either because they could no longer afford to go back to their rural homesteads, or because there were no longer any farms left to return to. These operatives may have felt more dependent on the manufacturers, more vulnerable to the hardships of unemployment, and less willing to fight for their rights. Some owners, in turn, may have decided to increase workloads and decrease wage rates when they sensed that they had a captive labor force. Yet the growth of a permanent industrial proletariat could also lead workers to consider a more activist stance. The growth of labor organizations and the campaign for the ten-hour day in the 1840s could be linked to the increasing number of workers who looked at their factory jobs as a long-term necessity and decided to endeavor to improve their working conditions. These workers concluded that problems could not be left behind; they had to be addressed.[54]

One Lowell operative painted an especially grim portrait of factory workers in the mid-1840s (before the large influx of unskilled immigrants into the mills). This woman was convinced that all manufacturing communities were deteriorating and that more operatives were becoming part of a permanent industrial working class struggling for survival.

> . . . [H]ear the "factory bell" calling thousands of our sisters out on the frosty morning, through sleet and snow, to their task before the curtain of heaven has been raised, that day with its rosy light, might cheer and warm the sons and daughters of toil, as they hie their way to their labors, there to remain, till long after night with her sable veil, has shut out the last glimmering ray of the sun . . . see (as may be seen in large manufacturing cities and towns) hundred of half-clad, meagre, dwarfish children, flocking at this early hour, into those prison-houses, with eyes half shut . . . see them, as they creep along to this twelve and fourteen-hour task, almost decriped with the fatigue of the previous day's labor, which the short hours of rest, have failed to throw off, I know that they thus suffer, and that their natures are out-

> raged by the present cruel factory system . . . in Lowell, and other thickly populated places, many fathers, yes, mothers too, struggling and toiling to obtain a mere pittance of food, fuel and clothing for themselves and their babes; and even this they are unable to accomplish in many cases with all their labor; and they are care-worn and sad, borne down with sorrow, for the helpless condition of their helpless offspring. Their lot is indeed a hard one; if they are blessed with health; but if sickness grasps them with her paralyzing hand, Oh, how wretched is their condition.

By 1850, as many poor Irish immigrants began to enter many factories, this picture of an emerging industrial proletariat became even more of a reality in industrial communities throughout New England. Workers' fears of industrial wage labor as the ultimate form of degradation were fueled by this image of thousands of starving Irish immigrants descending on the mills. These immigrants had far less of a chance than even the poorer native-born operatives to escape from the factory system. Some operatives warned that a downward spiral of progress would continue; the factory proletariat would multiply, and, if they were left exploited and unenlightened, they would undermine the nation's political and economic structures.[55]

The operatives who opposed the factory system—who decried the necessity of industrial labor, warned of the corruption inherent in factory work as it was presently organized, and feared for the emerging proletariat filling the mechanized manufactories—rooted their critique in their own particular definition of the value of labor. As with the factory supporters, there was a definite correlation between what the critics said about the factory system and what they said about labor itself. Where supporters based their optimism on the instrumental value of labor, however, critics anchored their concerns in the intrinsic value of work. The same workers who criticized the factory system were the ones who were likely to enunciate this concept of the intrinsic value of labor.

Factory critics believed that labor should have an inherent meaning and should be an end in itself, above any material gain. They wanted their work to give them some satisfaction through physical and mental effort. These workers upheld a kind of craft ideal that saw work as more than a mere job, more than the hours put in at the factory, even something different from middle-class notions of a career. They wanted labor to be an extension of a person's life and values all the time, not just during the workday. Work should be an expression of life itself—creative and joyful—as well as a means of making a living.

These workers were not saying, however, that labor was the only goal in life. Many of them also advocated a ten-hour day so that everyone would have time to pursue other interests besides work. They wanted their work to mean something, but it was not the only thing in life for them. The problem with factory work, in their eyes, was that it stripped labor of any inherent meaning even as it monopolized all of the operatives' time. Workers were spending more and more hours at mechanized tasks that offered less and less stimulation to their creative faculties. Factory labor compromised both people's economic status and their human creativity; it was impoverishing their bodies and their minds.

One Lowell contributor to the *Voice of Industry* wrote a poem, entitled "The Toiler's Lament," about her yearning to continue working for something more than money, even though the manufacturers scorned the laborers. This operative asserted that those who took pride in being workers were not without their own ambitions and ideals, but their goal was not to escape from the realm of manual labor.

> How vain it is, to seek a happy life,
> Where there's naught but contention and strife,
> To get and to gain—aye, a name to obtain
> By oppression's iron heel, or the toiler's pain.
> Was it Heaven's design that human beings
> Should live, void of all those better feelings,
> That seeks to elevate the human race,
> And thinks, to love equals, is no disgrace!
> Is the toilers lot, such a degraded one,
> That so many were born, its pollution to shun?
> Or was it nature's just and great design,
> That others should bask in a sunnier clime.
> Oh, Labor! may I ever cling to thee,
> 'Till heaven sees fit to set me free,
> From the cares of life, and the scenes of strife
> That fills the heart, and strews the path of life.
> Then give me my hood and my calico dress,
> And to the looms and spindles I'll press,
> For to labor, is the life I love best,
> And I'll pity those, who its blessings detest.[56]

Another poet urged workers:

> Then ply the spindle, ply the horn,
> Though tyrants take the cloth;
> Your happy limbs they cannot doom
> To feel the pains of sloth.
>
> While life is left that can't destroy
> Your blissful muscle-play;
> That glorious spark, creative joy,
> They cannot take away.

This operative affirmed her fundamental belief in the goodness of hard work, particularly when workers made their labor part of themselves by infusing it with creative energy.[57]

Many workers wanted to toil for something more than wages. Their goal was to live by a higher standard of pride in their work and solidarity with others, rather than a higher material standard of living for each individual. Operatives in Manchester, while they were agitating in support of the ten-hour law in 1847, adopted a resolution that stated: "money is not our only object in our pilgrimage on this earth, but the welfare of the rising generation is worthy of our regard." These workers certainly did not deny that hard work should have a just and fair material reward, but they also believed that work had to be worth something more to the operatives than money alone. If work had an intrinsic meaning, it meant that labor itself was more real and tangible and significant than capital or money.[58]

A Lowell operative, writing under the name "Juliana," pleaded with her fellow workers to be guided by a higher principle than dollars and cents.

> Let it not be said of us here in this land of boasted liberty and equal rights, that thousands are bound down in *ignorance* and worshipping at the altar of the god of mammon! Awake! daughters of America to a realization of the evils which follow on the train of ignorance and selfishness! Awake and arise from the low grovelling charms of *dollars* and *cents,* to a knowledge of your own high and holy duties and destinies! Awake and resolve from this time forth to *live,* not merely to gain a bare subsistence, but to live for nobler, worthier objects. *Live,* not to wear out and exhaust your physical energies in obtaining a few more paltry shillings, but to adorn and beautify the minds and intellects. . . .

By proclaiming that work should have a higher intrinsic worth than mere monetary gain, Juliana was positing an alternative morality for factory operatives, one beyond acquisitive individualism. She was warning workers not to be sold on the idea that money was justification enough for work that was stripped of its skill and pride.[59]

A former employee of the Ames Company in Chicopee, Massachusetts, who moved to Springfield, wanted to return to the Ames metalworking factory because he also realized that there was more to work and life than making money. This unidentified worker wrote to N. P. Ames: "This living in Springfield is not what it is cracked up to be. I can make some money here, but what is the use of living where we cannot enjoy ourselves. I consider it a poor bargain when I sacrifice my own happiness and that of my family for money. . . ." And Sarah Maria Cornell summed up her attitude toward work, money, and higher values in a letter to her mother. Cornell wrote: "I don't want great riches nor honors—but a humble, plain, decent, and comfortable living will suit me best." In that one sentence, Cornell staked her claim to what many workers called a "competence"—a standard of living sufficient for basic material comfort.[60]

Many workers shared Cornell's hopes for such a modest standard of living: that was all they wanted, in material terms, from their jobs. What these operatives really wanted from their work was something money could not buy—a sense of pride and satisfaction in a job well done. These workers were not looking for jobs that would merely be an avenue to other positions. They wanted work that would pay them a decent wage and, more important, give them an opportunity to display their talents and skills. Factory supporters kept insisting that such a competence, and perhaps many more opportunities, were already available to any hardworking operative. Factory critics were convinced that even a modest competence could not be attained in the existing factory system, and the possibility for a truly satisfying factory job was virtually nil.

Even Lucy Larcom reevaluated her attitudes about work, money, and time in the factory when she moved into the cloth room and away from the machinery. Her new job paid less than tending machines, but Larcom recalled that it was "far more satisfactory, as it would give me the openings of leisure which I craved." When the paymaster asked if she was " 'going where you can earn more money?' " Larcom responded that she was "going where I can have more time." The paymaster then pointed out that in the factory " 'time is money.' " But Larcom wrote: "that was not my thought about it. 'Time is education,' I said to myself; for that was what I meant it should be to me." Larcom decided that if she "could earn enough to furnish . . . food and raiment . . . and have time to study besides . . . it seemed to me a sufficiency. . . . Those who were earning much more, and were carefully 'laying it up,' did not appear to be any happier than I was. . . . Freedom to live one's life truly is surely more desirable than any earthly acquisition or possession; and at my new work I had hours of freedom every day." Larcom learned that time, when the worker had some control over it, was far more valuable than money.

> [M]any of our best friends were still . . . in the mills . . . preferring their work because it brought them more money than we could earn.
>
> For myself, no amount of money would have been a temptation, compared with my precious daytime freedom. Whole hours of sunshine for reading, for walking, for studying, for writing, for anything that I wanted to do! The days were so lovely and so long! and yet how fast they slipped away! I had not given up my dream of a better education, and as I could not go to school, I began to study by myself.[61]

Many workers thus argued that money was not the only thing they wanted from work. They also wanted some control over their work so that their labor did not physically and mentally overwhelm them, and they wanted a workplace where they could all stand by each other. Their goals were to make work both materially productive and personally rewarding; for many workers, these two goals were inextricably linked. They wanted jobs in which they could feel pride and satisfaction, and exercise initiative, as well as make a living. Work was more than a finished product for sale, or the labor time and wages accrued. Work was the total process of making something tangible, of a worker's seeing the task through from start to finish. Therefore a job that supposedly promised higher wages was not automatically attractive, for that reason alone, to workers who wanted something more than money from their labors.

Those workers who criticized the factory and espoused the intrinsic worth of labor envisioned a world where everyone would earn a decent living, without the wealthy's exploiting the less fortunate. They saw a world where people worked together to make sure that everyone was provided for, and everyone helped each other to do the best job possible. They spoke for a world of individual freedom and achievement without destructive competition: a world where work was part of a life balanced with family and community. These workers were not opposed to bettering themselves or their children's future, but they did not want to do it at the expense of higher values, such as pride in their work and their duty to fellow workers.

These workers wanted something more than a materialistic society wherein people's worth was measured only by what they accumulated; they wanted a real workers' republic where a person's worth was measured by her honesty and her diligence. This was not merely some fuzzy, nostalgic dream of a golden age of craft labor that had never really existed for the majority of workers. Although tinged with a romantic view of artisanal work, these operatives' vision was one in which the rights of labor and the rights of people were far more sacred than the rights of money. It was much more important to work hard and cooperate with others than it was to compete for the selfish accumulation of wealth. Work would both improve an individual's personal and financial worth and contribute to the advancement of the community as a whole.

— IV —

The debate over the factory system involved more than a series of disagreements over the history and the value of work. Operatives also had divergent views on the future of industrial labor in America. Not surprisingly, those who spoke about factory labor as a means to more important ends were confident that their chances for upward mobility would improve even more in the future. Many female operatives, in particular, developed their own ideas about mobility and their own guideposts for future plans. Since they could not rise into the managerial ranks in the factories, they looked for new opportunities beyond the factory walls. They were quite confident that the factories themselves would help open up these opportunities. Once again, they asserted that industrial labor was only a temporary stage for them, one stop on the road to economic and social improvement. The future promised more chances for advancement for any diligent operative. They saw no fixed class relations in industrial New England; they believed that everyone had the opportunity to advance socially and economically as far as their talents allowed. Operatives could take the money, experience, and discipline they gained in the mills and use them to improve their future prospects wherever they went.

Since women's previous work experiences were often limited by social prejudices, many female operatives saw an expansive future for themselves in and beyond the factories. Those who saw their factory jobs as distinct advances in their occupational status and earnings—gaining access to new workplaces, even though their work itself usually remained less skilled and lower paid than men's—were often confident that the economic trends were pointing farther upward beyond the factories.

One Waltham worker wrote, in surveying the prospects of factory operatives: "No one who enters the factory thinks of remaining there his whole life-time. True, some remain until they are too old to work in a factory; they then retire to comfortable homes, purchased by themselves, with the wages of factory labor. Others remain until they have accumulated sufficient to enable them to engage in other pursuits," such as a trade or farming. Harriet Hanson Robinson also pointed out the fact that working men as well as women were looking for opportunities outside the factories as well as inside. Some men tried to work their way up the manufacturing hierarchy; others had different plans for their futures. "Young men and women who had spent their two or three years of probation in the Lowell mills, often returned to the old place, bought land, built their modest houses, and became new and prosperous heads of families." Robinson sketched a pattern whereby people were leaving the farms and going to the factories, but with the ultimate goal of earning enough money to buy a farm and return to their agrarian life. The workers who saved their factory wages to buy a farm were, in effect, appropriating the proceeds of the industrial system for their own agrarian ends. Factory work was a temporary requirement on the road back to the rural homestead. Purchasing a home of one's own or a farm was a vital symbol of a male worker's achieving an autonomous status, the linchpin of his independence and respectability. Nearly every worker could agree on the crucial importance of a home of one's own, but not everyone was as sure as Robinson that factory labor was the key to that home.[62]

Robinson's observations also raise some interesting problems with the arguments supporting the factory system. Factory supporters praised industry for being in harmony with nature; they also said that factory labor was better than farm labor—and yet they asserted that operatives often saved enough of their earnings to buy the farm they wanted in the first place! If factory labor was superior to agricultural work, why did it matter if the factories were in harmony with nature, and why would operatives want to save their money to buy a farm? If factory supporters wanted to get back to the land as much as the factory critics, why did they support the factory in the first place? On the other hand, if all these workers wanted to save their factory wages and buy a farm, why did so many workers actually leave the factories but stay in the cities? These inconsistencies reveal that here was another struggle, in many operatives' minds, to reconcile divergent ideas about their roots in agricultural labor and their interest in industrial work.

Lucy Larcom noted that many women with her in the mills saw their labor as primarily a means to earn money for an education. The work itself was not always educational—at times it was mentally deadening—but the wages one earned would pay for the opportunity to expand one's mind at school. Moreover, women who worked in the larger cities often saw educational opportunities surrounding them in the many cultural institutions outside the mills. Larcom also saw how the notion of upward mobility was passed on from former mill girls to their children. Many operatives saw no disgrace in their hard work, but they had hopes that their daughters would have more promising careers. They worked in the mills so that their children would never have to. Larcom recalled in an essay written in 1882:

> A mill-girl among her spindles or shuttles, thirty or forty years ago, had not the slightest idea of remaining there. When she went back to her country life and saw her daughters growing up around her in homes of their own, she did not expect them to go and toil in a mill as she had done. She had higher ambitions for them. She expected them to teach, or to take some other useful position in society; and she used the money she had earned in the factory to give them an education; or, if she was a woman of humbler desires, she laid it by for their dowry, against the time when they also should be mistress of their own households.
>
> It would have been . . . unreasonable to think of New England women spending their whole lives at factory labor. . . . Their work was not its own end; it was pursued for a purpose beyond itself; for an opening into freer life.[63]

The Hollingworths are a fascinating case study of how the possibilities of planning for future advancement could have problematic consequences for a family of skilled immigrant working men. Even as this family criticized the factory system, they held onto their goal of owning their own mill. What they really resented was the dependent status of being employees, not the business of making textiles. The roots of factory slavery, according to the Hollingworths, did not necessarily lie in the machinery or the buildings. They believed factory slavery was the result of a wealthy few owning the manufactories and taking unfair advantage of the workers. The way to break the chains of such bondage was in the factory itself, not in its destruction. If a hardworking family could buy their own mill, they could demonstrate how such factories could work to the advantage of labor itself. This was not some theoretical vision; it was a plan for small-scale proprietorship by a working family. The plan was not to smash the factory system, but make the system work for the family who owned and ran it themselves.

George Hollingworth, after considering the uncertainty of factory employment, concluded in the fall of 1829, "If the Factory should Stop or any other unpleasant thing should happen so as we should have to Quit, we think to try if possible to do something for ourselves." One of the reasons the Hollingworth family became so interested in owning a factory may have been their desire to control the conditions of their own employment and avoid being dependent on or dismissed by other factory owners.[64]

A few months later, George described his plans in somewhat more detail, as he advocated a policy of cautious investment.

> If we intend ever to rescue ourselves from Factory Thraldom . . . I think it would be much better when we are able to buy cheap a small Manufacturing Establishment susceptable of emprovement and connected with some land. If this cannot be done that is bought cheap then to try to buy a Farm with a Water privilege thereon suitably situated for Market and then build or Erect thereon by degrees whatever we wanted always being mindful not to try to fly til our Wings are grown.

Just one week later, George again wrote to his brother-in-law William Rawcliff about a plan to join forces with another "Industerouse Family" named Shaw and buy a factory.

> We are aware the greatest difficulty will be to begin or make a start. This over we have not the least doubt of success if we be blessed with Health, for we by our united Families could do all the work and have no wages to pay which is of vital Intrest to the success of a Manufactury Besides Jas. Shaw . . . is sober steady Industerous and a good workman, I believe an excellent Carder . . . he is a man that has a good share of Courage Fortitude and Confidence (viz. what the Yankees call SPUNK) which are necessary requisites for as Trade's-mans &c. James Shaw and me has agreed and I hope you will concur, that you and he and me form a Co-partnership on equal Shares and engage Richmond's Factory and use our United efforts to sett it a going, for we can perceive no other mode of extercating ourselves from poverty and thraldom.[65]

The purchase of Richmond's factory was never completed, but the Hollingworths did rent a mill in Woodstock, Connecticut, and tried to eventually purchase that factory. Even Joseph Hollingworth, who did not conceal his own preference for agriculture over industry, was not entirely opposed to the idea of being a manufacturer. He admitted that "A small Factory with a quantum suficit of land along with it might do pretty well if well managed." Yet Joseph balked at the specific requirements for buying the Woodstock mill. He was concerned that the cost of moving up in the factory system might eventually drag him further down.

> In my last letter I said that I was one of the Company here; It was so proposed, and at first I accepted the proposal; but when I thought more deliberately about it, I again declined . . . 1st Because I did not wish to becom rich suddenly. 2nd Because I did not want to *get into debt.* I am poor enough already, but then I owe nobody anything . . . 3rd When I settle down on a place I should want to have some land, at any rate enough to make sure of a living.

The rest of the Hollingworth family was more confident that they could make the transition from workers to owners, while retaining the family as the central economic and social unit. They were willing to set aside their criticisms if they could have the chance to use the factory system on their own terms.[66]

The Hollingworths, as a family of higher-skilled textile workers, retained pride in their craft knowledge and in being skilled workers. But they also had this impulse to use their skilled positions as a springboard to becoming independent tradesmen, an impulse shared by many other skilled workers. What would happen, however, if their pride in being workers—their own form of working-class consciousness—came into conflict with their desire to purchase their own factory—their own brand of middle-class upward mobility? Would their competition for promotion and advancement undermine their loyalty to other workers or even to the family itself? The Hollingworths never answered these questions directly, since they never reached their goal of free and clear title to their own factory. But these questions must have lurked in many workers' minds as they contemplated their prospects in and beyond the factories.

The hopes of female operatives, as explained by Harriet Hanson Robinson and Lucy Larcom, and the plans of male factory workers like the Hollingworths, demonstrate that gender exerted a significant influence on how labor saw the promises and perils of the industrial order. Most women wanted factory work to be merely a brief stage in their life's course, but they disagreed about whether, in reality, such work would remain a temporary option. Most women also accepted the idea that they should not have to remain permanently in the wage labor force, particularly after marriage. Factory supporters then used that idea to help explain why they did not stay in the factories very long, and why factory labor easily permitted women to move on to other opportunities. Factory critics used the same idea to argue that it was dangerous to force women to stay within the confines of the factory on a long-term basis.

Most working women also said that they were proud to be both women and workers, but they did not want to be thought of as a permanent working class. Yet here again the basic question was debated: would the factory force women into such a working-class status? Factory supporters always asserted that they were not degraded, nor did they think of themselves as a working class in any definitive or permanent sense, because the factory system never forced the women into such a position. The female factory critics countered that they had become a degraded working class, and that the factory itself was to blame for making them so. But the critics were quick to add that workers had to struggle to break out of their degradation and their lowly status.

Virtually every working woman agreed that they had a right to earn their own money and hold their own job, that there was dignity and virtue in hard work, and that being a worker ought to be seen as an honest and noble calling. Many of these women also believed, however, in the nobility of being a wife and mother, and insisted that women should engage in factory work only as a stage in their development before marriage. They argued with each other, though, about whether the factory system served as just such a stage in a young woman's life. Was it a sojourn in a realm of full-time wage labor before most of these women returned to a middle-class domestic sphere where men earned most of the money so that their wives would not have to work for wages? Or were female operatives becoming locked into a permanent cycle of wage dependence and working-class exploitation? Were these operatives drifting away from a future of middle-class domesticity, and toward a working-class lifestyle where mothers were rarely removed from wage labor? Would these women, instead, see their entire family struggling for a living wage?

Many female factory operatives approached their work from the perspective of their identity as young rural women. That is, they believed that working hard outside the home for wages was a perfectly acceptable thing for them to do. But they also felt that wives and mothers should not be forced to continue such employment when it was expected that they would devote their energies to their homes and children. The key difference was that women who supported the factory system were convinced that their perspective on their work was recognized and honored—they were treated as respectable young women spending just a few years of their lives in that full-time employment. Critics of the factory system argued that young women often entered the mills with just such middle-class assumptions about a brief sojourn in wage labor, but they soon realized that they were being exploited as an industrial proletariat. Female operatives were increasingly being seen as permanent working women of the laboring class, and these women had to fight the factory system if they were to reclaim their hopes and ideals about industrial labor's being a positive stage in their development.

Most men looked at their labor from a different perspective. They acknowledged that they would have to work for a living, and that such work was going to be a permanent fixture in their lives. Many of them were also concerned, however, that if they worked in a factory, they would get locked into a permanent status of operative. These men often agreed with the female factory critics that they had become degraded workers and the factory system had made them so. They also believed in the fight to break the bonds of degradation and to regain their pride and recognition as productive workers in society.

Many workers remained very skeptical of any optimistic reports about the prospects for factory labor. They were troubled by the factory system and fearful of the future for working men and women. They warned that a growing population of unskilled, underemployed, low-paid operatives was filling the factories of New England, and that these people were the future of the region. John Quincy Adams Thayer feared that America's factory population was becoming as impoverished as England's. "They will stand in relation to each other, the same as two portions of poison alike in their nature. . . . Then will come a time when we too can boast of a 'manufacturing population in the strict sense of the word'—we too can boast of 'the whole family going into the mills as soon as they have sufficient bodily strength to earn a penny,' and 'never come out until they die.'" The Lowell operative who wrote under the name "Juliana" asked the poignant question: "what are we to expect . . . will be the mental and intellectual character of the future generations of New England? What but a race weak, sickly, imbecile, both mental and physical? A race fit only for corporation tools and timeserving slaves?" "Progress," in these workers' eyes, meant only an acceleration of the process by which a permanent industrial proletariat was being chained to the factory system.[67]

Many operatives believed that the handwriting was clearly on the factory walls—their economic and social status was going to decline; their only mobility would be downward. They would have to work harder just to earn a subsistence wage; their chances for accumulating capital would decrease, while the cost of starting a business would increase. No one would be able to rise from the shop floor to buy his own business. The factory system would close off more and more opportunities for workers. Even the simple opportunity for women to marry and raise a family would be shut off if they remained locked into permanent factory labor. The factory system would become increasingly characterized by a surplus of labor, frequent layoffs, low wages, and declining skills—all the ingredients for maintaining a permanent industrial proletariat.[68]

The prospect of being permanently dependent on factory work may have been especially disturbing to male operatives, because it ran counter to the American mythology of the manly, independent producer. Here again, dependency would have smacked of enslavement and emasculation. Since male factory operatives sometimes came from a background of craft labor, they may have seen an especially bleak future lurking in the factory system. In fact, they may have seen the threat to their skills, status, and earnings coming particularly from those women who were entering the factories by the thousands. But women workers would also have been troubled by the prospect of permanent dependency in the factories, for they would be locked into another system of male dominance and exploitation. They would be exchanging their subordination in the male-headed household for another, perhaps even more inequitable, position in the male-headed factory.

The workers who had family homesteads would leave quickly, or never come to the factories in the first place. The landless operatives would not have the choice to go back to the farm; they would have to keep on working. They would be left with the narrow options of staying at one company as long as the work lasted, traveling from factory to factory looking for a marginally better job, or finding some other occupation where they would most likely still have to be an employee. Given such bleak prospects, the notion of just picking up and moving could become more attractive to some workers. Transiency could be the last expression of freedom for these people, even if, in the long run, they ended up coming back to the same factory.[69]

This grim prognosis—of a labor force composed of essentially forced labor—was not something the factory critics took pride in. They were as adamant as any worker in insisting that factory work deserved respect, but they felt that the system robbed them of their dignity. These operatives, however, never gave up hope that they could break this cycle of misery. Although they saw the factory system becoming more stratified and solidified every day, it was still in its formative stages. And operatives, if they could mobilize enough of their own strength, could push the system in a more favorable direction before it became completely entrenched. What, then, was to be done in order to shape a new future for factory operatives?

Many critics of the factory system argued that the problem lay in the existing institutions, and not necessarily in the basic idea of mechanized production. The problem was not the technology itself, but the management of that technology by owners who used it to exploit workers. Workers could see that the technical changes of mechanization were only part of the total mechanized factory system. That system, in turn, was only one aspect of the broader changes sweeping across the American economy with the advent of industrial capitalism. Workers were concerned with the new machines, and even more with new economic and social relationships. The question became one of control—who would control the machines and the pace of work, who would control the factory floor and determine the working conditions, and perhaps most important, who would control the economy of the factory and the profits produced. Workers realized that all these questions were linked—in order for them to regulate the terms of their labor, they would have to exert some control over the factory system itself. This was not a prescription for workers to seize the means of production, but it was an assertion that workers should have the power to prevent overwork and exploitation. Workers knew that control over the basic processes of production was the key to power in the workplace.

The workers did not intend to smash all the machines and burn all the buildings. They wanted to reorganize the productive process and the managerial system so that they would get the just value of their labor and some control over their livelihood. The goal was to secure economic advantages and social mobility, and not merely for a few isolated individuals; to create a reformed system that would ensure stability and improvement for the entire community of workers. These workers' ideas about progress encompassed individual security and competence, and a sense of collective good as well. A reformed factory system would allow women the chance to work for their own independence, and then go forth uncompromised into marriage and family. Working men would be respected and rewarded for their efforts and given the opportunity to improve their craft or become proprietors if they chose to.

These reformers wanted to take the productive power of the machine and the economic power of industrial capitalism and use them for the benefit of the workers. Only a reformed factory system would uphold the ideals of free labor in America. Sarah Bagley laid out two basic principles for channeling all the potential energy of the factory away from destroying itself.

> The division of labor consequent upon the introduction of machinery, while it has enhanced the general stock of human production, and thereby benefitted the general weal, has at the same time entailed terrible calamity—unutterable woe. . . . Two great principles must be introduced as a basis for the organization of the factory system in this country, or the same results are to flow in here that have caused such crying anguish in the old world. *Capital must not be permitted to demand so much of labor. Education of the mass, must be made to possess an individual certainty, past escape.*

Bagley believed that educating the workers would give them some security and real hope for advancement in the developing industrial order, and that establishing some restraints on the power of capital would further ensure that workers' opportunities were not closed off.[70]

Bagley did not see her ideas about labor and capital and education as a radical overthrow of the social order. She saw the greatest threat to society coming from the unregulated growth of the factory system. It was the owners who were the agents of undesirable change; they weakened social cohesion with unchecked competition and greed, even as they claimed to be staunch defenders of the nation's best interests. Bagley's idea of a new world was one where basic values of labor, dignity, and knowledge were upheld over the force of mindless change and growth in private riches.

Activists like Bagley saw themselves as the true conservatives in the purest sense of the word—not simply guardians of the status quo, but conservators of America's fundamental ideals of justice and equity. Yet embedded in her plan was also a classically liberal critique that respected the basic value of private property, but warned of the dangers of concentrated power in industrial capitalism. The factory system did have to be changed substantially, but that was in order to preserve the American republic's essential values. For if the degradation of labor continued unchecked, the foundation of all republican institutions and society itself would be undermined. Therefore, Bagley and her supporters did envision a new factory system and a new social order, but one that would restore—not destroy—their belief in an American heritage of equal rights and justice for all working people.

Thus, the labels of "conservative" or "liberal" or "radical" do not stick easily to factory critics like Bagley. The workers who denounced the factory system and advocated a transformation of that system often did so in the guise of traditionalists calling for a restoration of the principles and values of workers' rights in a reformed economic order. They strove to stop the course of ungoverned change, which they thought was destroying the basic moral and social fabric they had known growing up in rural New England—and, here again, they spoke like conservatives. Yet their activism and their efforts to root out the corruption they saw in industrial capitalism gave them a radical cast. Their ideals of a just factory system in which workers' rights and dignity would take precedence over the financial machinations of owners and managers were clearly the work of real dissidents.[71]

Most operatives probably realized that factories could not be argued away, and that the nation might be worse off without any mechanized manufacturing. The answer was not to destroy the factories, but somehow to master them. At least some workers even discussed owning the factories themselves. Of course, most operatives had little or no money to start their own manufacturing cooperatives. But one group of Boston machinists did consider such a scheme in 1847. They urged their employers to meet with them to discuss the ten-hour system, but if no agreement was reached, the machinists thought about a bolder course of action—establishing a producers' cooperative. They discussed appointing "a committee to procure the names of one hundred Machinists who will invest $100 each in a fund and solicit the cooperation of capitalists if necessary,—immediately procure a location for business and then employ their own capital, perform their own labor, establish their own hours, manufacture their own machinery and put the proceeds thereof into their own pockets." These machinists were searching for a way to become independent of corporate control and the wage system, while recognizing the legitimate benefits of property and the factory itself. Like the Hollingworth family, they were not opposed to mechanized manufacturing, if workers could control the terms of their own labor. There is no record of this resolution's ever getting beyond the discussion stage. But it is clear that these workers were not urging some retreat into a mythic past; rather, these skilled men were arguing that the workers should redirect the course of socioeconomic change and democratize relations in the emerging industrial order.[72]

Workers who criticized the factory system, as it then existed in antebellum New England, were usually not opposed to technological progress per se. They wanted to change the economic system so that a few wealthy individuals would not control all the means of production and exploit the thousands of operatives who labored under their dictation. Workers did not want to strip the gears out of the nation's industrial engine. They were tired of getting their fingers caught; they wanted some say in the direction of the machine. These operatives were trying to regain control over what had belonged to them before they entered the factory system—some autonomy in the pace of their life and labor and some freedom to choose their daily activities on and off the job. Workers were not looking for some mythical place where there was absolute freedom from labor. They wanted a workplace where they still had the freedom to control the terms of their labor.

Factory reformers also recognized that their campaign could be part of a larger attempt at socioeconomic reorganization. Some workers became interested in the utopian designs of Robert Owen and Charles Fourier. They believed that only a collective crusade to reform society as a whole would ensure an equitable factory system and justice for each operative. The Hollingworth family, being articulate and perceptive critics of the factory system, thought a great deal about alternatives to the industrial order. When they first emigrated from England in 1827, before they even discussed buying a factory, they were deeply interested in starting a farm (and possibly a future factory) along the principles of Owenite socialism. John Hollingworth explained the family's original goals in America:

> we are doing all that lays in our power to accomplish the objects that induced us to leave Old England to brave the dangers of the Atlantic Ocean and to come to America that is to provide an happy asylum for our kindred our friends and ourselves into a system after the manner of Robert Owen's plan, that is to form ourselves into a society in common to help and assist each other and to have one common stock for it is the unnatural ideas of thine and mine that produces all the evils of tyranny slavery poverty and oppression of the present day.

The family soon concluded that such Owenite joint-stock plans were not feasible, and they then turned their attention to buying a mill—they decided not to escape from the factory system but to master it.[73]

By the 1840s, the elaborate social theories of Charles Fourier were popular with intellectuals and reformers. The experimental community at Brook Farm outside of Boston adopted a Fourierist constitution in 1844 and sent speakers throughout New England preaching the ideas of "phalansteries" and "attractive industry." Harriet Hanson Robinson recalled some of the objections raised by Lowell operatives to the Fourierist plans for independent communities based on agriculture and domestic industry.

> Lectures on the doctrine of Fourier were read and listened to, but none of them were "carried away" with the idea of spending their lives in large "phalansteries," as they seemed too much like cotton-factories to be models for their own future house-keeping.

> The Brook Farm experiment was familiar to some of them; but the fault of this scheme was apparent to the practical ones who foresaw that a few would have to do all the manual labor and that an undue share would naturally fall to those who had already contracted the working-habit.[74]

Other workers, however, were not so quick to dismiss Fourierism as a scheme for social and economic change. A new strain of working-class utopian thought emerged as Fourierist organizations—such as the Lowell Union of Associationists, which elected Sarah Bagley as its vice-president in 1846—sprang up in many industrial locales. These groups discussed plans for redesigning work to suit people's interests and talents, and breaking down the artificial social divisions based on class and gender. Some workers believed that Fourierism addressed their own need to find meaning in their labor and a sense of community with their fellow workers. Fourierism, with its ideas of a mixed economy and close-knit communities, may have looked to some workers like the middle ground they were striving for between tradition and innovation. Instead of following the plans laid out by factory owners, these workers put forth their own plans for preserving their heritage of freedom by radically reshaping society.[75]

The impulse for reform was not confined to the critics of the factory system. Even staunch supporters of industrial labor, such as Harriet Farley, insisted that the operatives were not complacent about their work.

> The girls here are not contented; and there is no disadvantage in their situation which they do not perceive as quickly, and lament as loudly, as the sternest opponents of the factory system do. They would scorn to say they were contented, if asked the question; for it would compromise their Yankee spirit—their pride, penetration, independence, and love of "freedom and equality" to say that they were *contented* with such a life as this. Yet, withal, they are cheerful. I never saw a happier set of beings.

Farley praised workers who kept a watchful eye out for problems and potential improvements in the factories. But her concept of reform remained a very restrained one—workers had to reform themselves before they could restructure the factory. Meaningful change would come through moral improvement and economic progress, not confrontation and protest.

> The wearisome hours, the monotonous toil, the separation from friends, and the seclusion from the accustomed healthful and bouyant influences of nature, were spoken of in terms—it might be regret and sadness, but not of captious discontent. And we are rejoiced at this. We thank them that they have presented themselves to their readers with cheerfulness and self-respect. They have thus done honor to their heads and their hearts. They have shown that their first and absorbing thought was not for an advance of wages or a reduction of labor hours. . . . They have implied that it was quite as important to be good, as to have good. They have striven for improvement of head and heart before that of situation. They have attended more to self-reformation, than to the reformation of society. . . . If they have, in one or two cases, acted upon the defensive, yet they have never been the aggressors.

Farley adhered to the prevailing middle-class moral standards, preferring individualism and self-improvement to any ideal of a cooperative society where right was derived from a concept of the common good and the dignity of labor.[76]

The one major reform Farley proposed in any detail was a program by which women in the mills could combine factory work with education in a manual labor school. She believed that such a scheme would benefit the workers and the corporations, but she also knew that any change was usually opposed by management.

> [T]he dislike of the capitalist to any change is insuperable. This extreme conservativism is the fault of manufacturers—this dislike to change, and love of having all things go on as they have always done. . . . But reforms must come—some changes must be. . . . Man was not made to be a mere beast of burden—far less woman . . . factory labor is with most of them task work—something is to be suddenly achieved, and then will come repose. But as the manufacturing population becomes more stable, if so it will ever be, and it is more generally considered a means of obtaining a livelihood, the wish for a pleasanter life will become stronger. But something might now be done which would be gratifying to a part, and, perhaps, eventually benefit all.

This was one of the few times Farley considered the possibility that a permanent factory population might emerge. But her plans for addressing this potential problem were framed so that reform became another means of preserving deference in the mills. The manual labor school would ensure that operatives continued to learn their proper place inside and outside the factories.

> Well educated girls are not more fond of insult and oppression than are the ignorant, but they are less under the dominion of passion, and more guided by reason. They would not easily be made the tools of aristocrats or demagogues. They would not be so influenced by prejudice, or so easily led by the designing to disgrace themselves by "showing their spirit." They would not surround the City Hall in a mob, but if wronged, would seek redress in some less exceptional manner.[77]

Harriet Farley thus left her readers with the impression that the factory system needed only a few readjustments to continue operating efficiently and equitably. Farley, and the operatives who shared her overall approval of the factory system, saw mechanized factories as part of a total positive vision of technological progress and social change. The factory was a liberating force, freeing workers from past constraints. These workers saw the factories as a kind of engine—an engine of constructive change moving society toward a future of material abundance, yet also a tool serving the workers' best interests for personal advancement. Farley's opponents saw factories as a fundamental reason why progress in antebellum America was on a dangerously steep downward slope. The factory, to them, was an enslaving force stripping away workers' rights and freedoms. These workers also can be said to have seen the factory as an engine—but an engine of great destructive potential that was breaking down workers and compromising the very meaning of work itself as an exercise in human expression. The future of the operatives seemed to be mortgaged for the gain of factory owners and their visions of progress.

Workers, in debating the future of factory labor, were once again endeavoring to understand their own roles in the important changes taking place in their working lives. Those who saw the factory as part of a positive trajectory of social change tended to be more confident about their own immediate opportunities in the new system. Their factory work was a means to other ends beyond the industrial system, and they felt sure that there would always be a place for them above mere factory labor. These operatives shared their employers' faith in the promises of entrepreneurial success and upward mobility through industrial capitalism. They looked on working for others as merely one stage in their lives, not as a permanent condition. They saw themselves as working in a society filled with honest laborers like themselves, but without a distinct laboring class. Progress, for these workers, meant the obliteration of any class tensions between labor and capital.

Those who criticized the factory for being the foundation of a regressive system tended to be more concerned about the long-range consequences of factory work, for themselves, and for all operatives as a distinct social group. These were the working men and women who began to think in terms of a working class, and who began to understand that the future of the factory system would be even more difficult for workers than its first challenges. These workers, quite simply, did not readily accept the optimistic American myth of national progress for everyone. They saw that the progress of the factory was creating growing social distinctions and class conflict between labor and capital.

Other operatives tried to steer a middle course between criticism of and support for the factory system. The debate over industrial labor was not always one with clearly drawn sides; it often became a discussion encompassing far more than two schools of thought. One contributor to the *Lowell Offering* saw both a bright and a dark side to factory work.

> Much has been said of the factory girl and her employment. By some she has been represented as dwelling in a sort of brick-and-mortar paradise, having little to occupy thought save the weaving of gay and romantic fancies, while the spindle or the wheel flies obediently beneath her glance. Others have deemed her a mere servile drudge, chained to her labor by almost as strong a power as that which holds a bondman in his fetters; and, indeed, some have already given her the title of "*the white slave of the north.*" Her real situation approaches neither one nor the other of these extremes. Her occupation is as laborious as that of almost any female who earns her own living, while it also has sunny spots and its cheerful intervals, which make her hard labor seem comparatively pleasant and easy . . . there is very little variety in an operative's life, and little difference between it and any other life of labor. It lies half in sunlight—half in shade. Few would wish to spend a whole life in a factory, and few are discontented who do thus seek a subsistence for a term of months or years.

Another operative made a kind of balance sheet on factory labor. On the debit side, she put long hours, short meal breaks, low wages, "and the feeling too, that comes over us (there is no use in denying it) when we hear the bell calling us . . . the feeling that we are *obliged to go.*" On the credit side, the side tipped in favor of working in the mills, was the fact that the operatives had at least some time for themselves every day, cash wages paid promptly, and work that was regular and predictable. Many workers seemed to agree with this accounting. Factory work was not perfect; it was a mixed proposition, but it was still worth the effort.[78]

While the debate over the factory system raged, more and more operatives probably found themselves somewhere in the middle of the argument. But were these workers really the average operatives with mixed emotions? Or was this a more disturbing phenomenon—were more workers finding themselves lost somewhere between the farm and the factory? Julia Dutton conveyed such a sense of confusion in one of her letters to her mother: "I feel pretty well contented here now but I have been rather discontented some but like better now though I do not feel quite as contented as I did before I went home." Harriet Farley also noted the problem of some workers' becoming discontented with both agrarian and industrial work. "Many, who are dissatisfied here, have also acquired a dissatisfaction for their homes, so that they cannot be contented any where, and they wish they had never seen Lowell." Some workers might have moved continuously between farms and factories, not to refresh themselves with a change of scenery, but in a futile attempt to overcome a profound feeling of dislocation and to reestablish roots somewhere.[79]

There was also the more encouraging possibility that the operatives who stood in the middle of the debate, weighing both the positive and negative sides of factory labor, might find a common ground on which most workers could stand. Many factory critics and supporters shared a rural heritage. Most of these workers believed that their roots in the countryside endowed them with a clear sense of personal honor and dignity. Thus both groups based many of their arguments on the virtue of hard work and the nobility of the worker. Every worker wanted her labor to be recognized, respected, and rewarded with the means sufficient to promote physical and mental development. Female operatives were especially insistent that work itself did not automatically rob them of their femininity, and that it was as worthy as any labor a man performed.

Apart from these common assumptions, however, the workers remained divided in their appraisal of the factory system. Factory supporters asserted that the industrial system already respected the workers and opened up a wealth of new opportunities for upward mobility. Critics countered that the system needed to be reformed in order to restore pride in their work to those who were estranged from their labor. Supporters steadfastly maintained that industrial labor was already an improvement over the past and compatible with the goals of continuing individual improvement and social advancement. The critics warned that factory work was undermining the promise of prosperity and improvement for all workers. The system had to be restructured if the workers were to have a chance at bettering themselves and society as a whole.

Thus the common ground between operatives—their heritage and their ideals about their worth as workers—was constantly eroded, and the debate continued. Some workers were confident that their status and values were nurtured in the factories. Others warned that their ideals would never be realized in a system that denigrated the social standing and moral standards of the workers.

The debate among factory workers in antebellum New England proved to be more than a disagreement over machinery and managers, or wages and hours, or even power and control; although each of these issues was important in its own right. The richness of the workers' dialogue over the decades, and their continuing disagreements with each other about the factory system, reveal a profound conflict among these first operatives trying to make sense of the emerging industrial order. These working men and women were also seeking to define themselves as workers and to determine the economic value and ethical meaning of work itself, in the midst of a changing economy. Workers on all sides of this debate about the mechanized factory system discovered some crucial, and often surprising, commonalities in their experiences and world views. Yet there were also many important and enduring differences in how they saw America as an emerging industrial nation. Some warned their fellow operatives about the unavoidable and unaffordable costs of a factory system controlled by private capital. Other workers cited the benefits of technological and economic change for every operative willing to participate fully and loyally in that same factory system. With the passage of time, as the mechanized factory system came to dominate many sectors of the American economy, more and more operatives realized that the warnings and costs clearly outweighed the hopes and promised benefits for labor.

Notes

Chapter 1

1. Mrs. Ephrain Holt, "Reminiscence," (written in the winter of 1888–1889), Peterborough Historical Society, Peterborough, New Hampshire (copy in the New Hampshire Historical Society, Concord, N.H.). All quotations in this study from nineteenth-century sources, whether published or in manuscript form, have been left in their original spelling, punctuation, and grammar. The rhetoric and voices of the workers have been preserved without imposing modern usage on them.
2. Abigail Mussey, *Life Sketches and Experiences* (Cambridge, Mass.: Dakin and Metcalf, 1866), pp. 12–14, 16.
3. Letter of L[ucy] M Davis to Sabrina Bennett, September 25, 1846, in Gary Kulik, Roger Parks, and Theodore Penn, eds., *The New England Factory Village, 1790–1860,* in *Documents in American Industrial History,* v. 2, ed. Michael Folsom (Cambridge, Mass.: MIT Press, 1982), p. 399.
4. Letter of Mary Cowles, Lowell, [Mass.], to her sister, December 6, 1847, Museum of American Textile History (hereafter, MATH), North Andover, Massachusetts; Lucy Larcom, *A New England Girlhood* (1889; reprint, Gloucester, Mass.: Peter Smith, 1973), pp. 153–154.
5. *Lowell Offering,* v. 1, August 1841, pp. 169–170.
6. Letter of Mary Paul, Lowell [Mass.], to her father, Bela Paul, December 21, 1845, in Thomas Dublin, ed., *Farm to Factory: Women's Letters, 1830–1860* (New York: Columbia University Press, 1981), p. 104.
7. *Lowell Offering,* v. 1, August 1841, pp. 169–170.
8. Lucy Larcom, "An Idyl of Work" (Boston: Osgood, 1875), p. 49.
9. Memorandum, May 1828 (doc. 293), Poignand and Plant Papers, Town Library, Lancaster, Massachusetts; Brooke Hindle and Steven Lubar, *Engines of Change: The American Industrial Revolution, 1790–1860* (Washington, D.C.: Smithsonian Institution Press, 1986), p. 199.
10. *Olive Leaf and New England Operative,* September 2, 1843; Larcom, "Idyl," pp. 173–174.
11. Letter of H. E. Back, Lowell, [Mass.], to Harriet Hanson, Wentworth, New Hampshire, September 7, 1846, in Philip S. Foner, ed., *The Factory Girls* (Urbana: University of Illinois Press, 1977), p. 334.
12. *Lowell Offering,* v. 1, November 1841, p. 273.
13. Harriet H. Robinson, "Early Factory Labor," in *Fourteenth Annual Report of the Massachusetts Bureau of Statistics of Labor* (Boston: Wright and Potter, State Printers, 1883), p. 393.
14. Lucy Larcom, "Among Lowell Mill-Girls: A Reminiscence," *Atlantic Monthly,* v. 48 (1881), p. 601; Larcom, *Girlhood,* p. 154; Claudia L. Bushman, *"A Good Poor Man's Wife": Being a Chronicle of Harriet Hanson Robinson and Her Family in Nineteenth-Century New England* (Hanover, N.H.: University Press of New England, 1981), p. 14.
15. Robinson, "Early Factory Labor," p. 383.

16. "A Factory Girl" [pseud.], "Lights and Shadows of Factory Life in New England," *The New World,* February 13, 1843 (the author was Eliza Jane Cate). The fact that the overseer permitted such amusements in the workplace raises interesting questions about managerial authority and factory regulations, which are discussed further in Chapters 3 and 5.
17. *Boston Daily Evening Voice,* February 23, 1867, in Foner, *Factory Girls,* p. 341.
18. *Lowell Offering,* v. 1, July 1841, pp. 117–118; *Lowell Offering,* v. 2, July 1842, pp. 318–319. The theme of nature in many of these writings is explored more fully in Chapter 2.
19. Robinson, "Early Factory Labor," p. 393; Harriet H. Robinson, *Loom and Spindle; or, Life Among the Early Mill Girls* (New York: Thomas Y. Crowell, 1898), p. 98.
20. Larcom, "Among Lowell Mill-Girls," pp. 602–603, 605; Larcom, *Girlhood,* pp. 180–181, 227. This controversy over reading in the mills is linked not only with mechanization but with the authority of managers and the enforcement of regulations. See Chapters 3 and 5 for a further discussion of these issues.
21. *Lowell Offering,* December 1840, p. 25 (there is no volume number for this issue).
22. Letter of Julia Dutton, Grafton, [Mass.], to her mother, Lucretia Dutton, May 4, 1847, Lucretia W. Dutton Papers, Bailey/Howe Library, University of Vermont, Burlington; Larcom, *Girlhood,* pp. 154–155.
23. Hindle and Lubar (1986), p. 182.
24. The manager's testimony is found in the *Fourth Annual Report of the Massachusetts Bureau of Statistics of Labor* (Boston: Wright and Potter, State Printers, 1873), p. 497; Thomas R. Navin, *The Whitin Machine Works Since 1831: A Textile Machinery Company in an Industrial Village* (Cambridge, Mass.: Harvard University Press, 1950), p. 109.
25. *Voice of Industry,* February 11, 1848. The *Voice of Industry* was the premier labor newspaper in antebellum New England. As such, it served a wide readership, which included factory operatives and artisans and other laborers as well. While the *Voice* was not exclusively a mill girls' newspaper, it does contain a wealth of material written by and for factory workers. It should be kept in mind that sources from the *Voice* used in this book are the letters, reports, and essays that shed direct light on the experience of operatives. Unsigned correspondence or editorials, which cannot be traced to factory workers, have not been used.
26. *Voice of Industry,* April 24, 1846, in Foner, *Factory Girls,* p. 162; Norman Ware, *The Industrial Worker, 1840–1860* (1924; reprint, Chicago: Quadrangle, 1964), p. 111; Hannah Josephson, *The Golden Threads: New England's Mill Girls and Magnates* (New York: Duell, Sloan and Pearce, 1949), p. 78; Caroline F. Ware, *The Early New England Cotton Manufacture: A Study in Industrial Beginnings* (Boston: Houghton Mifflin, 1931), p. 272.
27. *Voice of Industry,* May 15, 1846, in Foner, *Factory Girls,* p. 104. It is clear that the debate over the speedup and the stretch-out involved more than machinery: workers were also often angry that their wages were being cut in the process of increasing production. See Chapter 6 for a more extensive discussion of workers' attitudes toward piece rates, wage cuts, and the idea that they were being exploited by the tampering with production and wage rates. Also, the intense debate over the speedup and the stretch-out was often part of the argument in the 1840s that working conditions overall were deteriorating in the factories. This belief that the conditions of labor were becoming steadily worse was linked with the rise of labor organizations and the ten-hour movement in the mid-1840s. See Chapter 7 for more on labor organizing, and Chapter 8 for more on the ten-hour movement.
28. Letter from a "Lowell Factory Girl" to a Boston newspaper, November 9, 1844, in William Scoresby, *American Factories and their Female Operatives* (1845; reprint, New York: Burt Franklin, 1968), pp. 33–34.
29. *New England Offering,* November 1849, p. 263; *Olive Leaf and New England Operative,* September 2, 1843; *Voice of Industry,* March 5, 1847, in Foner, *Factory Girls,* p. 315.
30. *Lowell Offering,* v. 4, June 1844, p. 170; *New England Offering,* November 1849, p. 265; Elfrieda McCauley, "The New England Mill Girls: Feminine Influence in the Development of Public Libraries in New England, 1820–1860" (Ph.D. diss., Columbia University, 1971), pp. 46–47.
31. Larcom, *Girlhood,* pp. 182–183, 193; Larcom, "Among Lowell Mill-Girls," pp. 602, 608.
32. Hindle and Lubar (1986), p. 198.

33. Robert B. Zevin, *The Growth of Manufacturing in Early Nineteenth-Century New England* (New York: Arno Press, 1975), sec. 1, p. 8; Caroline F. Ware (1931), p. 83; Holmes Ammidown, *Historical Collections* (New York: the author, 1874), v. 1, p. 493; and v. 2, p. 371.
34. Letter of Joseph and Jabez Hollingworth, South Leicester, [Mass.], to William Rawcliff, Wadsworth Factory, Poughkeepsie, New York, March 14, 1830, in Thomas W. Leavitt, ed., *The Hollingworth Letters: Technical Change in the Textile Industry, 1826–1837* (Cambridge, Mass.: MIT Press, 1969), p. 66.
35. *Fall River Daily Globe*, February 27, 1889, in Stephen Victor et al., eds., *The Fall River Sourcebook: A Documentary History of Fall River, Massachusetts* (American History Workshop, 1981), pp. 37–39.
36. John W. Lozier, "Taunton and Mason: Cotton Machinery and Locomotive Manufacture in Taunton, Massachusetts, 1811–1861" (Ph.D. diss., Ohio State University, 1978), p. 62; *Lowell Offering*, v. 5, May 1845, p. 98.
37. Gary Kulik, "The Beginnings of the Industrial Revolution in America, Pawtucket, Rhode Island, 1672–1829" (Ph.D. diss., Brown University, 1980), p. 351; David Jeremy, *Transatlantic Industrial Revolution: The Diffusion of Textile Technology Between Britain and America, 1790–1830s* (Cambridge, Mass.: MIT Press, 1981), p. 198.
38. John L. Hayes, *American Textile Machinery* (Cambridge, Mass.: University Press, J. Wilson and Son, 1879), p. 43.
39. Larcom, "Idyl," p. 80; Thomas Dublin, *Women at Work: The Transformation of Work and Community in Lowell, Massachusetts, 1826–1860* (New York: Columbia University Press, 1979), pp. 67, 70–72. See Chapter 4 for a further discussion of the social relations among women textile workers.
40. *Lowell Offering*, v. 4, August 1844, p. 238.
41. Dublin, *Women at Work*, p. 67; Letter of Mary Cowles (Dec. 6, 1847); Larcom, *Girlhood*, p. 181.
42. *Lowell Offering*, v. 5, May 1845, p. 98.
43. Dublin, *Women at Work*, p. 68.
44. Letter of S.V.S. Wilder, Ware, Massachusetts, to Lewis Tappan, June 6, 1827, in Jeremy (1981), p. 196; *Lowell Offering*, v. 4, June 1844, p. 169. In Rhode Island mills, most dresser-tenders were men, because manufacturers thought that men could run the machines more efficiently.
45. Larcom, *Girlhood*, pp. 154, 226; Larcom, "Among the Lowell Mill-Girls," p. 602.
46. Larcom, *Girlhood*, pp. 227–233. Larcom's comments about the cloth room imply that she believed that the presence of machines in a factory necessitated a faster pace of labor and a more disciplined industrial regimen. What Larcom never discussed was the fact that regulations were made by managers, not by the machines. Manufacturers decided how fast to run machines, how long the operatives would work, and what behavior would be permitted in the factories. Mechanized labor involved certain technical requirements—there were minimum speeds to be maintained and certain tasks to be performed—but much of the daily working experience was shaped by conscious decisions of managers and workers.
47. *Boston Daily Evening Voice*, February 23, 1867, in Foner, *Factory Girls*, pp. 342–343; *Lowell Offering*, v. 4, June 1844, p. 170.
48. Letter of Aaron Jewett, Jr., Lowell, [Mass.], to his father, Aaron Jewett, September 25, 1840, MATH; Letter of Julia Dutton, Grafton, [Mass.], to her mother, Lucretia Dutton, May 4, 1847, Dutton Papers; Letter of Joseph Hollingworth, Muddy Brook Pond Factory, Woodstock, Connecticut, to William Rawcliff, September 5, 1830, in Leavitt (1969), p. 88.
49. *Voice of Industry*, November 13, 1846; this operative's testimony is found in *Third Annual Report of the Massachusetts Bureau of Statistics of Labor* (Boston: Wright and Potter, 1872), pp. 430–431.
50. *New England Offering*, November 1849, p. 263.
51. *Voice of Industry*, April 17, 1846; *Voice of Industry*, June 26, 1846; and *Voice of Industry*, January 8, 1847. See Chapter 2 for a related discussion on how the operatives' health was affected by conditions inside the factories, besides disabilities directly related to accidents and machinery.

52. Ware Manufacturing Company Records, MATH (a manuscript copy of the vote recorded in the Board of Directors Records).
53. Kulik et al. (1982), pp. 429–430; *Manchester Operative*, February 10, 1844; *Voice of Industry*, August 14, 1845. The term "industrial accident" could also be used to describe injuries occurring inside the factories that were not due directly to machinery. There were reports of workers slipping on floors or falling down stairs, thereby breaking arms and legs. The January 8, 1847, issue of the *Voice of Industry* reported that a man named Henry Kirk Wight was killed by falling through the "elevator hole" in the Prescott mill. It was said to be the second such death in Lowell in two weeks. Also, factories powered by steam engines ran the risk of explosions and fatalities.
54. Factory Tracts #1, in Foner, *Factory Girls*, p. 133; *Voice of Industry*, August 14, 1845.
55. *Voice of Industry*, January 9, 1846, in Foner, *Factory Girls*, p. 243; *Voice of Industry*, November 14, 1845, in Foner, *Factory Girls*, p. 140; *Manchester* [N.H.] *Democrat*, September 1, 1847, in Foner, *Factory Girls*, p. 264.
56. *Voice of Industry*, July 17, 1845, in Foner, *Factory Girls*, p. 62; *Voice of Industry*, June 19, 1846; *Voice of Industry*, April 2, 1847.
57. Larcom, *Girlhood*, pp. 182–183; Lucy Larcom, "American Factory Life—Past, Present, and Future," *Journal of Social Science*, v. 16 (1882), p. 144; Larcom, "Idyl," pp. 141–142.
58. N. B. Gordon, work diary, June 8–9, 1829, in Kulik et al. (1982), pp. 288–289.
59. *Pawtucket Chronicle*, April 15, 1829, in Kulik et al. (1982), p. 492. This incident also raised important questions about the character of protest. See Chapter 7 for further discussion.
60. Letter of A. & J. Spaulding, Greenfield, [Mass.], to Maj. Brown, June 12, 1825, Merino/Dudley Wool Companies Records, Research Library, Old Sturbridge Village, Sturbridge, Massachusetts.
61. Letter of George Hollingworth, South Leicester, [Mass.], to William Rawcliff, January 24, 1830, in Leavitt (1969), p. 61; Day Book, 1849–1860s, p. 103, Kellogg and Company Account Books, Stowe-Day Library, Hartford, Connecticut; George Howe, "The Minister and the Mill Girl," *American Heritage*, v. 12, no. 6, (1961), p. 83; Barbara M. Tucker, "The Family and Industrial Discipline in Antebellum New England," *Labor History*, v. 21 (1979–1980), p. 72. See Chapter 5 for an extensive discussion of how fines and dismissals were used to enforce a variety of working regulations.
62. Robinson, *Loom and Spindle*, pp. 3–4.
63. Harriet Farley, *Operatives' Reply to the Hon. Jere Clemens* . . . (Lowell, Mass.: S. J. Varney, 1850), pp. 5, 9.
64. *Lowell Offering*, v. 3, November 1842, p. 48; *Lowell Offering*, v. 5, August 1845, p. 184.
65. C. Upham, "The Factory Song" (found in a mill girl's autograph book from the 1830s), Nashua Public Library, Nashua, New Hampshire; Hindle and Lubar (1986), p. 199.
66. William G. Lathrop, *The Brass Industry in the United States* (Mt. Carmel, Conn.: 1926), pp. 56–57; reminiscences by William J. Clark, in W. R. Wilbur, *History of the Bolt and Nut Industry of America* (Cleveland, Ohio: Ward and Shaw, 1905), pp. 358–359.
67. Letter of James Roberts and family, Waterville [Waterbury], Connecticut, to John and Mary Loxley, Sheffield, England, September 30, 1849, in Charlotte Erickson, *Invisible Immigrants: The Adaptation of English and Scottish Immigrants in Nineteenth-Century America* (London: Weidenfeld and Nicolson, 1972), p. 322.
68. *Greenfield Gazette & Courier*, December 9, 1850, in Robert Merriam et al., *The History of the John Russell Cutlery Company, 1833–1936* (Greenfield, Mass.: Bete Press, 1976), p. 74; *Voice of Industry*, May 28, 1847.
69. Samuel Collins, "Early History of the Collins Co." (1866: typed copy at the Canton Historical Museum, Collinsville, Connecticut), pp. 24–25; Donald R. Hoke, "Ingenious Yankees: The Rise of the American System of Manufactures in the Private Sector" (Ph.D. diss., University of Wisconsin, Madison, 1984), pp. 163–164, 169; Paul Uselding, "Elisha K. Root, Forging, and the 'American System,'" *Technology and Culture*, v. 15 (1974), p. 562.
70. Report of James Dalliba, October 1819, "Communicated to the House of Representatives by the Committee on Military Affairs, March 3, 1823," 17th Congress, 2nd session, no. 246, in

Walter Lowrie and William Franklin, eds., *American State Papers. Class V. Military Affairs* (Washington, D.C.: Gales and Seaton, 1834), v. 2, p. 543.

71. "Notes on the Springfield Armory," in Letter of G. Talcott, Springfield [Mass.] Armory, to the Hon. John Bell, Secretary of War, August 6, 1841, in Steven V. Benét, comp., *A Collection of Annual Reports and Other Important Papers Relating to the Ordnance Department* (Washington, D.C.: Government Printing Office, 1878), v. 1, pp. 395–397. Talcott's letter also points out that, at the armory, mechanization and the division of labor were not always linked. Certain departments, such as the manufacture of locks, depended on hand labor, yet divided the process into a multitude of steps. This division of handicraft labor was linked to the introduction of piece-rate wage payments, a procedure that is discussed further in Chapter 6.

72. "Report of the Board Convened at Springfield, Mass. August 30, 1841, to Examine into the Condition and Management of Springfield Armory," [Exec. Docs., House of Representatives, 27th Congress, 2nd session, v. 4, Doc. No. 207], in Benét, *Ordnance Department,* v. 1, pp. 401–402. See Chapter 4 for a further discussion of the social relations among armory workers and their efforts to work together to control output.

73. Henry Howe, *Memoirs of the Most Eminent American Mechanics* (New York: Alexander V. Blake, 1841), pp. 201–202; Asa H. Waters, *Biographical Sketch of Thomas Blanchard and His Inventions* (Worcester, Mass.: Lucius Goddard, 1878), pp. 6–8; D. Hamilton Hurd, *History of Worcester County, Massachusetts* (Philadelphia: J. W. Lewis and Company, 1889), v. 2, p. 1122; Felicia Deyrup, *Arms Makers of the Connecticut Valley: A Regional Study of the Economic Development of the Small Arms Industry, 1798–1870,* in *Smith College Studies in History,* v. 33, ed. by Vera Holmes and Hans Kohn (Northampton, Mass., 1948), pp. 97–98; Derwent Whittlesey, "The Springfield Armory: A Study in Institutional Development" (Ph.D. diss., University of Chicago, 1920), n.p.; Hindle and Lubar (1986), p. 229; Letters of Thomas Blanchard to Roswell Lee, February 19, 1821, and April 13, 1821 (Springfield Armory, letters received, National Archives, Washington, D.C.), in Carolyn C. Cooper, " 'A Whole Battalion of Stockers': Thomas Blanchard's Production Line and Hand Labor at Springfield Armory," *IA: The Journal of the Society for Industrial Archeology,* v. 14 (1988), p. 40; Cooper (1988), pp. 40, 43, 48, 52, 53. Howe's account of the Springfield armorers and Blanchard's machinery appears to be the most comprehensive of all the many reports. Other authors, such as Hurd, say that the encounter occurred at Asa Water's armory in Millbury, Massachusetts. But nearly all the various versions of this event convey the same general conversation, regardless of where it took place.

74. Deyrup (1948), pp. 100, 171; Paul Uselding, "An Early Chapter in the Evolution of American Industrial Management," in *Business Enterprise and Economic Change,* ed. by Louis Cain and Paul Uselding (Kent, Ohio: Kent State University Press, 1973), p. 77; Otto Mayr and Robert Post, introduction to *Yankee Enterprise: The Rise of the American System of Manufactures,* ed. by Otto Mayr and Robert Post (Washington, D.C.: Smithsonian Institution Press, 1981), pp. xii, xvii; David A. Hounshell, *From the American System to Mass Production, 1800–1932: The Development of Manufacturing Technology in the United States* (Baltimore: Johns Hopkins University Press, 1984), p. 27; Robert B. Gordon, "Who Turned the Mechanical Ideal into Mechanical Reality," *Technology and Culture,* v. 29 (1988), pp. 744–778.

75. Letter of Nathan Starr, Middletown, [Conn.], to Col. George Bomford, July 30, 1827, in James E. Hicks, *Nathan Starr: The First Official Sword Maker* (Mt. Vernon, N.Y.: the author, 1940), p. 128; Deyrup (1948), pp. 131–132, 174.

76. William Worthen's recollections are in Robert Allison, "The Old and the New," *Transactions of the American Society of Mechanical Engineers,* v. 16 (1895), p. 747; Hindle and Lubar (1986), p. 173.

77. Hindle and Lubar (1986), p. 173.

78. See Chapters 3 and 4 for more on the gender relations between male managers, male workers, and female workers.

79. W. Paul Strassman, *Risk and Technological Innovation: American Manufacturing Methods During the Nineteenth Century* (Ithaca, N.Y.: Cornell University Press, 1959), p. 147; Hindle and Lubar (1986), p. 181; George S. Gibbs, *The Saco-Lowell Shops: Textile Machinery Build-*

ing in New England, 1813–1949 (Cambridge, Mass.: Harvard University Press, 1950), p. 146; Kulik, "Beginnings of the Industrial Revolution," p. 254.

80. Kulik, "Beginnings of the Industrial Revolution," p. 304; Letter of George Hollingworth, South Leicester, [Mass.], to William Rawcliff, October 21, 1829, in Leavitt (1969), p. 50; also ibid., p. xxi.
81. Hindle and Lubar (1986), p. 181.
82. Letter of Charles Metcalf[?], Lowell, [Mass.], to his parents, April 27, 1844; Letter of S[hubal] Adams, Lowell, [Mass.], to "Cousin Chloe" [Metcalf], April 29, 1844; Letter of Charles A. Metcalf, Lowell, [Mass.], to Mrs. Chloe F. Metcalf, Winthrop, Maine, July 10, 1844: all in the Adams-Metcalf Papers, MATH.
83. Gibbs, *Saco-Lowell,* pp. 88–89; Lozier, "Taunton and Mason," p. 474; Kulik, "Beginnings of the Industrial Revolution," p. 296.
84. Letters of John Rogers, Manchester, [N.H.], to his father, July 16 and 19, 1850; to his mother, July 28, 1850; to his father, September 1 and November 9, 1850; to his mother, November 17, 1850: Amoskeag Manufacturing Company Papers, MATH (excerpts from the John Rogers Papers at the New-York Historical Society); Lozier, "Taunton and Mason," p. 474.
85. Gene S. Cesari, "American Arms-Making Machine-Tool Development, 1798–1855" (Ph.D. diss., University of Pennsylvania, 1970), pp. 162–163, 368.

Chapter 2

1. *New England Offering,* April 1848, p. 24; *Hand-Book for the Visiter to Lowell* (Lowell, Mass.: A. Watson, 1848), p. 15; John Ewing and Nancy P. Norton, *Broadlooms and Businessmen: A History of the Bigelow-Sanford Carpet Company* (Cambridge, Mass.: Harvard University Press, 1955), pp. 21–22.
2. Orra L. Stone, *History of Massachusetts Industries* (Boston: S. J. Clarke Publishing Co., 1930), v. 2, p. 1,967; Mary Feldblum, "The Formation of the First Factory Labor Force in the New England Cotton Textile Industry, 1800–1848" (Ph.D. diss., New School for Social Research, N.Y., 1977), p. 268.
3. Steve Dunwell, *The Run of the Mill* (Boston: David R. Godine, 1978), p. 24; William H. Pierson, Jr., "Industrial Architecture in the Berkshires" (Ph.D. diss., Yale University, 1949), pp. 271–272.
4. Theodore Sande, "The Textile Factory in Pre–Civil War Rhode Island," *Old-Time New England,* v. 66, nos. 1–2 (1975), pp. 18–19; Pierson, "Industrial Architecture," p. 69; William H. Pierson, Jr., "Harrisville, N.H.: A Nineteenth-Century Industrial Town," *Antiques,* v. 102 (1972), p. 637.
5. Thomas Dublin, *Women at Work: The Transformation of Work and Community in Lowell, Massachusetts, 1826–1860* (New York: Columbia University Press, 1979), p. 61; Henry A. Miles, *Lowell, As It Was, And As It Is* (Lowell, Mass.: Powers and Bagley, 1845), pp. 64–65; Brooke Hindle and Stephen Lubar, *Engines of Change: The American Industrial Revolution, 1790–1860* (Washington, D.C.: Smithsonian Institution Press, 1986), p. 205.
6. Theodore Sande, "Architecture of the Rhode Island Textile Industry, 1790–1860" (Ph.D. diss., University of Pennsylvania, 1972), pp. 219, 223, 225–226.
7. *New England Offering,* May 1849; *New England Offering,* July 1849, p. 161.
8. Letter from Lucy Larcom, in *Proceedings in the City of Lowell at the Semi-Centennial Celebrations of the Incorporation of the Town of Lowell, March 1st, 1876* (Lowell, Mass.: Penhollow Printing, 1876), p. 94; Lucy Larcom, *A New England Girlhood* (1889; reprint, Gloucester, Mass.: Peter Smith, 1973), pp. 163–164; Harriet H. Robinson, *Loom and Spindle; or, Life Among the Early Mill Girls* (New York: Thomas Y. Crowell, 1898), p. 37.
9. John Coolidge, *Mill and Mansion: A Study of Architecture and Society in Lowell, Massachusetts, 1820–1865* (New York: Columbia University Press, 1942), p. 31; Larcom, *Girlhood,* pp. 163–164; James Montgomery, *A Practical Detail of the Cotton Manufacture of the United States of America . . . Contrasted and Compared with that of Great Britain* (1840; reprint, New York: Johnson Reprint Corp., 1968), p. 197; Mrs. Ephrain Holt, "Reminiscence," (written in

the winter of 1888–1889), Peterborough Historical Society, Peterborough, New Hampshire (copy in the New Hampshire Historical Society, Concord, N.H.).

10. *Lowell Offering,* v. 3, December 1842, p. 57; *Lowell Offering,* v. 5, May 1845, p. 97; Lucy Larcom, "Among Lowell Mill-Girls: A Reminiscence," *Atlantic Monthly,* v. 48 (1881), p. 611.
11. Lucy Larcom, "An Idyl of Work" (Boston: Osgood, 1875), p. 12; *New England Offering,* November 1849, p. 263; *Lowell Offering,* v. 4, September 1844, p. 237.
12. Larcom, *Girlhood,* p. 216.
13. Larcom, "Among Lowell Mill-Girls," p. 593; Larcom, *Girlhood,* pp. 163, 216; *Lowell Offering,* v. 5, December 1845, p. 272.
14. *Proceedings . . . of Lowell . . . Semi-Centennial,* pp. 94–95; Larcom, "Idyl," pp. viii, 127.
15. *New England Offering,* December 1848, pp. 215–216.
16. Pierson, "Industrial Architecture," p. 68; Hannah Josephson, *The Golden Threads: New England's Mill Girls and Magnates* (New York: Duell, Sloan and Pearce, 1949), p. 218; Dunwell (1978), p. 68.
17. *Lowell Offering,* v. 5, December 1845, pp. 265–267.
18. *Factory Girl's Album,* February 14, 1846, in Philip S. Foner, ed., *The Factory Girls* (Urbana: University of Illinois Press, 1977), p. 79; *Voice of Industry,* December 3, 1847, in Foner, *Factory Girls,* p. 92; *Factory Girl's Garland,* May 25, 1844, in Philip S. Foner, ed., *American Labor Songs of the Nineteenth Century* (Urbana: University of Illinois Press, 1975), p. 67.
19. *Lowell Offering,* December 1840, p. 20 (there is no volume number for this issue).
20. *Lowell Offering,* v. 1, August 1841, pp. 188–189.
21. Bryant F. Tolles, "Textile Mill Architecture in East-Central New England: An Analysis of Pre–Civil War Design," *Essex Institute Historical Collections,* v. 107 (1971), pp. 230–231; Pierson, "Industrial Architecture," pp. 51, 142; Coolidge (1942), p. 32.
22. Sande, "Textile Factory," pp. 19–20; John Haines, diary, November 18 and 25, and December 27, 1845, MATH.
23. Letter of Maria Cornell, Lowell, [Mass.], to Mrs. Cornell, January 11, 1829, in [Catherine Williams], *Fall River An Authentic Narrative* (Boston: Lilly, Wait and Company, 1834), pp. 133–134.
24. *New England Offering,* May 1849, p. 119.
25. George S. Gibbs, *The Saco-Lowell Machine Shops: Textile Machinery Building in New England, 1813–1949* (Cambridge, Mass.: Harvard University Press, 1950), p. 746; Pierson, "Industrial Architecture," pp. 177–179.
26. Pierson, "Industrial Architecture," p. 180; Judith McGaw, "The Sources and Impact of Mechanization: The Berkshire County, Massachusetts, Paper Industry, 1801–1885, As a Case Study," (Ph.D. diss., New York University, 1977), p. 224; J. Montgomery (1840; reprint, 1968), p. 17; Steven Victor et al., eds., *The Fall River Source Book: A Documentary History of Fall River, Massachusetts* (American History Workshop, 1981), p. 663.
27. Victor et al. (1981), pp. 663–664; Ewing and Norton (1955), p. 19.
28. J. Montgomery (1840; reprint, 1968), p. 16; Tolles (1971), p. 235.
29. *Lowell Offering,* v. 4, June 1844, p. 169; Larcom, "Idyl," pp. 77–78; Larcom, *Girlhood,* p. 226.
30. *New England Offering,* July 1848, p. 92; *Lowell Offering,* v. 4, June 1844, p. 169; *Lowell Offering,* v. 4, August 1844, pp. 237–238; Josephson (1949), p. 43; J. Montgomery (1840; reprint, 1968), p. 101; Harriet Farley, *Operatives' Reply to the Hon. Jere Clemens . . .* (Lowell, Mass.: S. J. Varney, 1850), p. 17.
31. *Lowell Offering,* v. 3, May 1843, p. 192; *Lowell Offering,* v. 4, August 1844, p. 237; Robinson, *Loom and Spindle,* pp. 208–209.
32. Factory Tracts #1, in Foner, *Factory Girls,* p. 135; Susan Forbes, diary, May 20, 1843, American Antiquarian Society, Worcester, Massachusetts; Letter of Caroline Ford, Middlebury, [Vt.], to William R. Ford, Orwell, Vermont, [Sept.] 15, 1845, in David A. Zonderman, "From Mill Village to Industrial City: Letters from Vermont Factory Operatives," *Labor History,* v. 27 (1986), p. 282.
33. Fall River *Daily Globe,* February 27, 1889, in Victor et al. (1981), p. 39; Feldblum (1977), p. 139.
34. George S. Gibbs, *The Whitesmiths of Taunton: A History of Reed and Barton, 1824–1943*

(Cambridge, Mass.: Harvard University Press, 1943), p. 72; Minnie Atkinson, "Old Newburyport Ropewalks—A Vanished Industry," *Essex Institute Historical Collections,* v. 82 (1946), p. 48; Samuel E. Morison, *The Ropemakers of Plymouth: A History of the Plymouth Cordage Company, 1824–1949* (Boston: Houghton Mifflin, 1950), pp. 24–25.

35. *Lowell Offering,* v. 5, May 1845, p. 97.
36. *Factory Girl's Album,* September 12, 1846, in Foner, *Factory Girls,* p. 221; *Voice of Industry,* March 26, 1847, in Foner, *Factory Girls,* p. 88; "Homespun to Factory Made: Woolen Textiles in America, 1776–1876" (North Andover, Mass.: Merrimack Valley Textile Museum, 1977), pp. 74, 78 (exhibition catalogue).
37. *Lowell Offering,* v. 5, May 1845, p. 98; J. Montgomery (1840; reprint, 1968), p. 17.
38. Letter of John Rogers, Manchester, New Hampshire, to his father, July 19, 1850, Amoskeag Manufacturing Company Papers, MATH (excerpts from the John Rogers Papers at the New-York Historical Society).
39. *Lowell Offering,* v. 3, May 1843, p. 192; *Voice of Industry,* May 23, 1846; *Voice of Industry,* September 4, 1846; *New England Offering,* June 1849, p. 135.
40. "The Lowell Factory Girl," in Foner, *Labor Songs,* p. 43; "The Factory Girl's Come-All-Ye," in Foner, *Factory Girls,* p. 338.
41. Insurance survey, November 28, 1828 (doc. 303), Poignand and Plant Papers, Town Library, Lancaster, Massachusetts; "Mrs. Burn's Story," in Cocheco Manufacturing Company Materials (manuscript of reminiscences of employees who worked during the 1820s to the 1840s), p. 19, Old Berwick Historical Society, South Berwick, Maine; George W. Browne, *The Amoskeag Manufacturing Co. of Manchester, New Hampshire* (Manchester: Amoskeag, 1915), p. 139; Vera Shlakman, *Economic History of a Factory Town: A Study of Chicopee, Massachusetts,* in *Smith College Studies in History,* v. 20, ed. by John C. Hildt, William Dodge Gray, and Harold Underwood Faulkner (Northampton, Mass., 1934–1935), p. 91.
42. Massachusetts Legislative Documents, House No. 50, March 12, 1845, p. 3; Letter of Ann Appleton, [Manchester, New Hampshire], to her sister, n.d., in "Sister Ann" (a copy of the letters edited by Priscilla Ordway in 1953), p. 26. Manuscript is at the Manchester Historic Association, Manchester, New Hampshire. *Lowell Offering,* v. 3, April 1843, p. 149; *New England Offering,* May 1849, p. 119.
43. Letter of John Rogers, Manchester, New Hampshire, to his sister, Laura, September 22, 1850, Amoskeag Manufacturing Company Papers, MATH; Letter of Mary C. Metcalf, to her mother, August 1, 1847, Adams-Metcalf Papers, MATH; *Lowell Offering,* v. 4, November 1843, p. 14, in Benita Eisler, ed., *The Lowell Offering* (New York: Harper and Row, 1977), p. 83.
44. Josephson (1949), pp. 276–277; *Voice of Industry,* October 2, 1846; *Nashua* [N.H.] *Gazette,* October 1, 1846, in Foner, *Factory Girls,* p. 260; *Factory Girl's Album,* October 3, 1846; John Haines, diary, September 21, 1847. The reports of these protests against working by lamplight are not all complete, so it is difficult to determine whether these demonstrations were organized strikes or not. It is not clear whether the operatives refused to work only those hours under lamplight or whether they walked off their jobs with the intention of staying out of work for as long as it took to abolish the use of lamps. Workers may have intended their demonstrations to be full-scale walkouts, or brief displays of their displeasure at particular times of the day. The renewed refusal of women to work by lamplight in 1847 may also have been related to the controversy about the new ten-hour law in New Hampshire at that time. The ten-hour law and worker protest are discussed in depth in subsequent chapters.
45. Gary Kulik, "The Beginnings of the Industrial Revolution in America: Pawtucket, Rhode Island, 1672–1829" (Ph.D. diss., Brown University, 1980), pp. 379–380.
46. Elfrieda McCauley, "The New England Mill Girls: Feminine Influence in the Development of Public Libraries in New England, 1820–1860" (Ph.D. diss., Columbia University, 1971), p. 39; Josephson (1949), p. 83.
47. Gibbs, *Whitesmiths,* p. 144; Dane Yorke, *The Men and Times of Pepperill* (Boston: Pepperill Manufacturing Co., 1945), pp. 20–21.
48. Yorke (1945), pp. 20–21; Shlakman (1934–1935), p. 55.
49. The issues of health, disease, and mortality were also related to the problems of industrial accidents and fires, which have already been examined. These issues were linked to the hours of

labor, as will be seen in the discussion of the ten-hour movement in Chapter 8. But it was the physical environment inside the factories—the day-to-day working conditions, regardless of accidents and long hours—that brought these questions to the forefront of workers' concerns.

50. Harriet H. Robinson, "Early Factory Labor in New England," in *Fourteenth Annual Report of the Massachusetts Bureau of Statistics of Labor* (Boston: Wright and Potter, State Printers, 1883), pp. 390–391; *Lowell Offering,* v. 3, May 1843, pp. 191–192; *Lowell Offering,* v. 5, December 1845, p. 281.
51. *New England Offering,* April 1848, pp. 3–5.
52. *Voice of Industry,* September 4, 1845; *Voice of Industry,* May 8, 1846, in Foner, *Factory Girls,* p. 164.
53. Letter of Sally Rice, Masonville, [Conn.], to her father, February 23, 1845, in Gary Kulik, Roger Parks, and Theodore Penn, eds., *The New England Mill Village, 1790–1860,* in *Documents in American Industrial History,* v. 2, ed. Michael Folsom (Cambridge, Mass.: MIT Press, 1982), p. 390; Letter of Sally Rice, Millbury, [Mass.], to her family, September 14, 1845, in Kulik et al. (1982), p. 391.
54. Unidentified letter, April 3, 1849, Crane Company employment file, 1844–1865, in McGaw (1977), p. 326.
55. *Factory Girl's Album,* September 12, 1846, in Foner, *Factory Girls,* p. 221; *Voice of Industry,* December 4, 1846; *Voice of Industry,* April 23, 1847.
56. House Unpassed Papers, 1587 (1845), Massachusetts State Archives, Boston.
57. *Voice of Industry,* May 7, 1847; *Voice of Industry,* December 3, 1847, in Foner, *Factory Girls,* p. 94.
58. Pierson, "Harrisville, N.H.," p. 637; Sande, "Textile Factory," pp. 24–26; Gary Kulik, "A Factory System of Wood: Cultural and Technological Change in the Building of the First Cotton Mills," in Brooke Hindle, ed., *Material Culture of the Wooden Age* (Tarrytown, N.Y.: Sleepy Hollow Press, 1981), pp. 316, 318.
59. *Records From the Life of S.V.S. Wilder* (New York, 1865), pp. 196–202, 208–209, in Kulik et al. (1982), pp. 243–252. Zachariah Allen went even further in his plans for the church at Allendale, Rhode Island. He put the question of church affiliation to a popular vote, and the majority of operatives chose the Freewill Baptists. Although Allen was an Episcopalian, he abided by the vote, contributed to the support of a preacher, and made other meeting places available to other denominations. See Richard E. Greenwood, "Zachariah Allen and the Architecture of Industrial Paternalism," *Rhode Island History,* v. 46 (1988), pp. 117–135. The construction of company churches is closely related to how managers and workers perceived religion in the workplace, which is examined further in Chapter 5. The discussion in this chapter is focused on the physical relationship between church, factory, and community.
60. Larcom, *Girlhood,* p. 164; Josephson (1949), pp. 46–47.
61. Kulik et al. (1982), pp. xxiii–xxiv. In using the term "industrial city," I should make it clear that I usually do not mean large commercial and manufacturing cities such as Boston. Throughout the antebellum period, most manufacturing in Boston was not performed in mechanized factories. Cities like Boston remained strongholds of shipping, retail trades, and large-scale handicraft production. I use the phrase "industrial city" to indicate places like Lowell and Manchester. These were communities with sizeable populations whose economies revolved around mechanized production. This is not to say that there were no other forms of manufacturing in these industrial cities. But these particular locales were inextricably linked to the mechanized factory system.

    It should also be noted that not every industrial community could be easily classified as an industrial city or a factory village. Many lay somewhere in between the rural manufacturing sites and the more urbanized industrial environments. Moreover, many industrial communities changed over time. When a factory prospered and expanded its operations, the surrounding community often grew around that factory and shed some of its rural characteristics. The examples of factory villages and industrial cities discussed in this section are not intended to be representative of all such communities in antebellum New England; they are used to give a sense of the diversity of industrial communities at the time. For more on the variety of industrial communities in antebellum New England, see Richard M. Candee, "New Towns of the

Early New England Textile Industry," in *Perspectives in Vernacular Architecture,* ed. Camille Wells (Vernacular Architecture Forum, 1982), pp. 31–50.

62. John W. Lozier, "Rural Textile Mill Communities and the Transition to Industrialism in America, 1800–1840," *Working Papers from the Regional Economic History Research Center,* v. 4, no. 4 (1981), ed. by Glenn Porter and William Mulligan, Jr., pp. 79, 83, 86–87; Peter J. Coleman, *The Transformation of Rhode Island, 1790–1860* (Providence: Brown University Press, 1963), p. 223.
63. Barbara M. Tucker, "The Family and Industrial Discipline in Antebellum New England," *Labor History,* v. 21 (1979–1980), p. 57. See Greenwood (1988), pp. 117–135, for details on Zachariah Allen's efforts to build a planned factory village at Allendale, Rhode Island. See also Joseph S. Wood, "Village and Community in Early Colonial New England," in Robert Blair St. George, ed., *Material Life in America, 1600–1860* (Boston: Northeastern University Press, 1988), pp. 159–169, for more details on the distinction between actual settlement patterns in colonial New England and the villages that developed in the early nineteenth century. The presence of factory-owned farms and individual garden plots attached to workers' housing raises the important issue of the relationship between agricultural and industrial labor in factory communities. This interaction will be analyzed further in subsequent chapters.
64. Letter of Sally Maria Cornell, Killingly, [Conn.], to her sister, May 12, 1822, in C. Williams (1834), pp. 119–120; Letter of Sally Maria Cornell, Slatersville, [R.I.], to her sister, September 6, 1825, in C. Williams (1834), p. 124.
65. Letter of Maria Cornell, Mendon Mills, [Mass.?], to her mother, August 6, 1826, in C. Williams (1834), p. 126; Letter of Maria Cornell, Lowell, [Mass.], to her mother, January 11, 1829, in C. Williams (1834), p. 133; Letter of Maria Cornell, Lowell, [Mass.], to her sister, May 3, 1829, in C. Williams (1834), p. 134. It should be noted that Sarah Maria Cornell also died in a controversial way. Her body was found in a Fall River hay yard under suspicious circumstances on December 21, 1832. She was pregnant, and letters she left behind implicated a Rhode Island minister, Ephraim K. Avery, as the father. Avery was tried for strangling Cornell, but the jury acquitted him and ruled the death a suicide. For more on the trial, see Luke Drury, *A Report on the Examination of Rev. Ephraim K. Avery, Charged With the Murder of Sarah Maria Cornell* (1833); *The Correct, Full and Impartial Report of the Trial of the Rev. Ephraim K. Avery, Before the Supreme Judicial Court of the State of Rhode Island, at Newport, May 6, 1833 for the Murder of Sarah M. Cornell* (Providence: Marshall and Brown, 1833); and David R. Kasserman, *Fall River Outrage: Life, Murder, and Justice in Early Industrial New England* (Philadelphia: University of Pennsylvania Press, 1986). It should also be noted that Cornell's frequent change of name, even in correspondence with her family, probably was part of her effort to conceal her controversial past as she moved from one community to another.
66. Kulik et al. (1982), p. 5; Zonderman (1986), pp. 266–268. Other workers may have preferred these country mills for reasons besides this sense of a middle ground. Some may have been drawn by the rural mills' willingness to hire entire families. Or some operatives may have had difficulty traveling to urban factories, so they settled in nearby mill villages.

    Timothy Coogan's recent study of Adams, Massachusetts, points out another example of a factory community that lay somewhere between farming hamlets and industrial cities. Coogan also notes that Adams was a middle ground between the Slater system of family labor in cottages and the Waltham system of young women in boardinghouses. See Timothy C. Coogan, "Minders of the Machines, 1825–1845," in Kenneth Fones-Wolfe and Martin Kaufman, eds., *Labor in Massachusetts: Selected Essays* (Westfield, Mass.: Institute for Massachusetts Studies, 1990), passim.
67. John S. Garner, *The Model Company Town: Urban Design Through Private Enterprise in Nineteenth-Century New England* (Amherst: University of Massachusetts Press, 1984), p. 27; Coolidge (1942), p. 164; Jonathan Prude, *The Coming of Industrial Order: Town and Factory Life in Rural Massachusetts, 1810–1860* (Cambridge, England: Cambridge University Press, 1983), pp. 96, 98.
68. Joseph Brennan, *Social Conditions in Industrial Rhode Island: 1820–1860* (Washington, D.C.: Catholic University, 1940), p. 75; Letter of Julia Dutton, Grafton, Massachusetts, to

Lucretia Dutton, May 4, 1847, Lucretia W. Dutton Papers, Bailey/Howe Library, University of Vermont, Burlington; Seth Luther, *An Address to the Working Men of New England* (New York: Office of the Workingman's Advocate, 1833), p. 35.

69. David Jeremy, *Transatlantic Industrial Revolution: The Diffusion of Textile Technologies Between Britain and America, 1790–1830s* (Cambridge, Mass.: MIT Press, 1981), p. 201; Zonderman (1986), p. 266. The decision to work in a smaller or larger industrial community was also shaped by other factors than workers' preferences. Workers had to consider wage rates, availability of jobs in particular labor markets, and other issues.
70. "Autobiography of Daniel Knapp. Read February 12, 1872," *Contributions of the Old Residents' Historical Association,* [Lowell], v. 1 (1874), p. 71; *Lowell Offering,* v. 1, August 1841, p. 164.
71. *New England Offering,* April 1849, pp. 92–93; *Lowell Offering,* v. 1, November 1841, p. 263.
72. J.Q.A. Thayer, *Review of the Report of the Special Committee of the Legislature of the Commonwealth of Massachusetts on the Petition Relating to Hours of Labor* (Boston: J. N. Bang, 1845), p. 15.
73. Josephson (1949), pp. 42–43.
74. Farley, *Operatives' Reply,* pp. 13, 19–20.
75. Letter of Ann Appleton, Manchester, [N.H.], to her sister, January 8, 1847, in "Sister Ann," p. 3; Larcom, *Girlhood,* p. 163; J. Montgomery (1840; reprint, 1968), p. 197.
76. Thomas Bender, *Toward an Urban Vision: Ideas and Institutions in Nineteenth-Century America* (1975; reprint, Baltimore: Johns Hopkins University Press, 1982), p. 79; Robinson, *Loom and Spindle,* p. 216; Robinson, "Early Factory Labor," p. 380. Bender's study demonstrates that the antebellum New England operatives were not alone in their search for a middle ground. Many middle-class residents of cities like Lowell also sought to reconcile the rural and urban environments. The operatives, however, were not merely imitating these middle-class conventions. These working men and women were the ones in closest contact with the emerging mechanized factory system; and their understanding of it was drawn directly from their working experiences.
77. Robinson, *Loom and Spindle,* p. 109; *Lowell Offering,* v. 5, March 1845, p. 72; Harriet H. Robinson, "The Life of the Early Mill-Girls," *Journal of Social Science,* v. 16 (1882), p. 137.
78. *Lowell Offering,* v. 5, March 1845, p. 72.
79. *Voice of Industry,* February 12, 1847; *Voice of Industry,* November 19, 1847. Both of these pictures are rich in symbolism, and they will be examined even further in following chapters. It is not known who designed these graphics; the editors of the *Voice* and the *Offering* both said that many people were involved in their creation. But it is quite possible that at least some operatives involved with these publications had a say in their pictorial content.

Chapter 3

1. Letter of C. A. Metcalf, Lowell, [Mass.], to Joseph A. Metcalf, Winthrop, Maine, April 5, 1841, Adams-Metcalf Papers, MATH.
2. Factory Tracts #1, in Philip S. Foner, ed., *The Factory Girls* (Urbana: University of Illinois Press, 1977), pp. 133–134 (the author of this article may be Huldah J. Stone); *Voice of Industry,* April 2, 1847. The question of whether factory labor degraded workers will be discussed further in Chapter 9.
3. Lucy Larcom, "American Factory Life—Past, Present, and Future," *Journal of Social Science,* v. 16 (1882), pp. 142–143.
4. *New England Offering,* May 1848, p. 26.
5. S.N.D. North and Ralph North, *Simeon North: First Official Pistol Maker of the United States* (Concord, N.H.: Rumford Press, 1913), p. 31; Jeannette Mirsky and Allan Nevins, *The World of Eli Whitney* (New York: Macmillan, 1952), p. 312; Letter of Chester Bradley, Springfield, [Mass.], to Mr. Colt, September 25, 1847, Colt Company Papers, State Library—Archives, Hartford, Connecticut.

6. Letters of John Rogers: to his mother, October [4], 1850; to his father, November 9, 1850; Amoskeag Manufacturing Company Papers, MATH (excerpts from the John Rogers Papers at the New-York Historical Society).
7. John W. Lozier, "Taunton and Mason: Cotton Machinery and Locomotive Manufacture in Taunton, Massachusetts, 1811–1861" (Ph.D. diss., Ohio State University, 1978), pp. 190–192, 478.
8. Cocheco Manufacturing Company Regulations, [Dover, New Hampshire, 1828–1829], in 61st Congress, 2nd session, Senate Doc. No. 645 (1910), *Report of the Condition of Women and Child Wage-Earners in the United States,* vol. 10, part 1: John B. Andrews, *History of Women in Trade Unions, 1825 Through the Knights of Labor,* p. 24; "General Regulations, to be observed by persons employed by the Lawrence Manufacturing Company, in Lowell," May 21, 1833, MATH. This discussion of regulations will be continued in Chapter 5. The focus in this chapter is on how these documents delineate social relations within the factory. In Chapter 5, I will analyze what these documents reveal about work discipline.
9. Henry A. Miles, *Lowell, As It Was, And As It Is* (Lowell, Mass.: Powers and Bagley, 1845), p. 141; Harriet H. Robinson, *Loom and Spindle; or, Life Among the Early Mill Girls* (New York: Thomas Y. Crowell, 1898), p. 72.
10. Harriet Farley, *Operatives' Reply to Hon. Jere Clemens*. . . (Lowell, Mass.: S. J. Varney, 1850), pp. 17–18; *Lowell Offering,* v. 4, August 1844, pp. 238–239.
11. *Factory Girl's Garland,* July 20, 1844; *New England Offering,* July 1849, p. 161; Letter of John Wilson, Lowell, [Mass.], to his father, April 21, 1849, Wilson Letters, MATH.
12. Farley, *Operatives' Reply,* pp. 17–18; James P. Hanlan, *The Working Population of Manchester, New Hampshire, 1840–1886* (Ann Arbor, Mich.: UMI Research Press, 1981), p. 38; Frederick M. Peck and Henry H. Earl, *Fall River and Its Industries* (Fall River, Mass.: Benjamin Earl and Son, 1877), p. 33; "Reminiscences of Warren Colburn," *Contributions of the Old Residents' Historical Association,* [Lowell], v. 4 (1889), p. 180.
13. *New England Offering,* March 1849, p. 57.
14. Mary Feldblum, "The Formation of the First Factory Labor Force in the New England Cotton Textile Industry, 1800–1848" (Ph.D. diss., New School for Social Research, 1977), p. 104. Of course, the actual behavior of female operatives was often nothing like what male managers expected. Women factory workers were as likely to organize and protest against company policies (particularly wage cuts) as they were to accept the paternalistic favors of male supervisors.
15. Harriet H. Robinson, "Early Factory Labor in New England," in *Fourteenth Annual Report of the Massachusetts Bureau of Statistics of Labor* (Boston: Wright and Potter, State Printers, 1883), pp. 382–383.
16. *Lowell Offering,* v. 4, August 1844, p. 238.
17. Letter from Chicopee, [Mass.], March 29, 1850, in Farley, *Operatives' Reply,* p. 23.
18. Robinson, "Early Factory Labor," p. 383; Robinson, *Loom and Spindle,* pp. 17–18.
19. *Lowell Offering,* v. 1, July 1841, p. 112.
20. *New England Offering,* May 1849, p. 98; *Operatives' Magazine,* June 1841, p. 37.
21. Lucy Larcom, "Among Lowell Mill-Girls: A Reminiscence," *Atlantic Monthly,* v. 48 (1881), p. 610; *Lowell Offering,* v. 5, January 1845, p. 23; *Lowell Offering,* v. 5, December 1845, p. 279.
22. Jonathan Prude, *The Coming of Industrial Order: Town and Factory Life in Rural Massachusetts, 1810–1860* (Cambridge, England: Cambridge University Press, 1983), p. 83; *Lowell Offering,* v. 4, August 1844, p. 240.
23. *Lowell Offering,* v. 3, September 1843, p. 284; *Lowell Offering,* v. 5, December 1845, p. 281.
24. *New England Offering,* March 1849, p. 57.
25. *Voice of Industry,* April 2, 1847; *The Factory Girl,* January 15, 1845, in Foner, *Factory Girls,* p. 76; Prude (1983), p. 83.
26. *Voice of Industry,* July 3, 1846.
27. *Gleaner,* June 10, 1843, in Hanlan (1981), p. 58. See Chapter 5 for an extensive discussion of whether management was lenient or overzealous in its enforcement of factory regulations.
28. *Voice of Industry,* January 8, 1847; *Voice of Industry,* February 12, 1847, in Foner, *Factory Girls,* p. 126.

29. *Lowell Offering,* v. 5, December 1845, p. 281.
30. *Voice of Industry,* February 27, 1846, in Philip S. Foner, ed., *American Labor Songs of the Nineteenth Century* (Urbana: University of Illinois Press, 1975), p. 59.
31. Robinson, *Loom and Spindle,* pp. 57–58.
32. [Catherine Williams], *Fall River An Authentic Narrative* (Boston: Lilly, Wait and Company, 1834), p. 93.
33. *Voice of Industry,* October 23, 1846; *The Harbinger,* May 29, 1847, in Foner, *Factory Girls,* p. 290.
34. *Voice of Industry,* May 15, 1846, in Foner, *Factory Girls,* p. 166.
35. "The Factory Girl's Come-All-Ye," in Foner, *Labor Songs,* p. 44.
36. *Boston Daily Evening Voice,* February 23, 1867, in Foner, *Factory Girls,* p. 342.
37. *Factory Girl's Album,* February 14, 1846, in Foner, *Factory Girls,* p. 78.
38. *Voice of Industry,* February 20, 1846, in Foner, *Factory Girls,* p. 148.
39. Gary Kulik, "Pawtucket Village and the Strike of 1824: The Origins of Class Conflict in Rhode Island," *Radical History Review,* v. 17 (1978), pp. 18–19; Robinson, *Loom and Spindle,* p. 10.
40. Letter of Isaac Markham, Waltham, Massachusetts, to his brother, David Markham, May 30, 1821, Markham Collection, Sheldon Museum, Middlebury, Vermont; Letter of Jabez Hollingworth, South Leicester, [Mass.], to William Rawcliff, [1827], in Thomas W. Leavitt, ed. *The Hollingworth Letters: Technical Change in the Textile Industry, 1826–1837* (Cambridge, Mass.: MIT Press, 1969), p. 15; Letter of Joseph Hollingworth, South Leicester, Massachusetts, to William Rawcliff, May 20, 1828, in Leavitt (1969), pp. 22–23.
41. *The Man,* February 22, 1834, and *Boston Transcript,* February 18, 1834, in *Report of the Condition of Women . . . Wage-Earners,* v. 10, part 1, p. 28; Hannah Josephson, *The Golden Threads: New England's Mill Girls and Magnates* (New York: Duell, Sloan and Pearce, 1949), p. 238; Factory Tracts #1, in Foner, *Factory Girls,* p. 134.
42. Letter of Joseph Hollingworth, Muddy-Brook-Pond Factory, Woodstock, Connecticut, to William Rawcliff, Wadsworth's Factory, Poughkeepsie, New York, November 8, 1830, in Leavitt (1969), pp. 92–93; Letter of Joseph Hollingworth, Pond Factory, Woodstock, Connecticut, to William Rawcliff, July 17, 1831, in Leavitt (1969), p. 99.
43. *Manchester Operative,* June 1, 1844; *Nashua Gazette,* October 1, 1846, in Foner, *Factory Girls,* p. 83.
44. *Voice of Industry,* November 27, 1846.
45. *The Protest,* November 25, 1848. It is not known whether any other issues of this newspaper were published.
46. Arthur L. Eno, Jr., "The Civil War: Patriotism vs. King Cotton," in *Cotton Was King: A History of Lowell, Massachusetts,* ed. by Arthur L. Eno, Jr. (Lowell, Mass.: Lowell Historical Society, 1976), pp. 127–128; Philip S. Foner, *History of the Labor Movement in the United States: From Colonial Times to the Founding of the American Federation of Labor,* v. 1 (New York: International Publishers, 1947), p. 267; Larcom, "Among Lowell Mill-Girls," p. 607.
47. Lucy Larcom, "An Idyl of Work" (Boston: Osgood, 1875), pp. 135–136.

Chapter 4

1. While this chapter focuses on the social dynamics among the workers themselves, these relationships never existed in a vacuum, removed entirely from relations between labor and management. In this chapter, the discussion will therefore sometimes return to a consideration of how certain workers interacted with each other and how particular kinds of workers related to managers.
2. George S. Gibbs, *The Whitesmiths of Taunton: A History of Reed and Barton, 1824–1943* (Cambridge, Mass.: Harvard University Press, 1943), p. 121.
3. Harriet H. Robinson, "Early Factory Labor in New England," in *Fourteenth Annual Report of the Massachusetts Bureau of Statistics of Labor* (Boston: Wright and Potter, State Printers, 1883), p. 381; *Operatives' Magazine,* November 1841, p. 119.
4. *New England Offering,* February 1849, pp. 26–27.

5. "A Factory Girl" [pseud.], "Lights and Shadows of Factory Life in New England," *The New World,* February 13, 1843, pp. 10–12 (the author was Eliza Jane Cate).
6. Letter of Julia Dutton, Clintonville, Massachusetts, to Jane Witherby, [1848], Lucretia W. Dutton Papers, Bailey/Howe Library, University of Vermont, Burlington.
7. "Autobiography of Daniel Knapp. Read February 12, 1872," *Contributions of the Old Residents' Historical Association,* [Lowell], v. 1 (1874), pp. 71–72.
8. *Voice of Industry,* May 28, 1847; Mary Feldblum, "The Formation of the First Factory Labor Force in the New England Cotton Textile Industry, 1800–1848" (Ph.D. diss., New School for Social Research, 1977), pp. 139–140.
9. *Voice of Industry,* February 27, 1846.
10. "Report of the Board Convened at Springfield, Mass., August 30, 1841, to Examine into the Conditions and Management of Springfield Armory," [Exec. Docs., House of Representatives, 27th Congress, 2nd session, v. 4, Doc. No. 207], in Steven V. Benét, comp., *A Collection of Annual Reports and Other Important Papers Relating to the Ordnance Department* (Washington, D.C.: Government Printing Office, 1878), v. 1, p. 402. This board also noted that the armorers had a great deal of control over their wages and hours of labor. This will be discussed further in Chapters 6 and 8. It should also be noted that the Springfield armorers maintained a great deal of control at the workplace, not only through their own deliberate efforts, but because the machinery in the armory required a substantial amount of skill to operate properly.
11. *Lowell Offering,* v. 5, December 1845, p. 280; "Lowell Factory Girl," in Philip S. Foner, ed., *American Labor Songs of the Nineteenth Century* (Urbana: University of Illinois Press, 1975), p. 44; C. Upham, "The Factory Song" (found in a mill girl's autograph book from the 1830s), Nashua Public Library, Nashua, New Hampshire. There was no absolute correlation between experience and skill; not all experienced operatives could be called skilled workers. Most operatives were semiskilled machine-tenders, but those with more experience were usually more proficient and earned higher wages. Only a few industries, such as machine-building itself, saw workers retain a large amount of craft skill along with increased mechanization.
12. Edith Abbott, "A Study of the Early History of Child Labor in America," *American Journal of Sociology,* v. 14 (1908), p. 37; Carl Siracusa, *A Mechanical People: Perceptions of the Industrial Order in Massachusetts, 1815–1880* (Middletown, Conn.: Wesleyan University Press, 1979), pp. 195–196.
13. Lucy Larcom, "Among Lowell Mill-Girls: A Reminiscence," *Atlantic Monthly,* v. 48 (1881), pp. 601–602.
14. Hiram Munger, *The Life and Religious Experience of Hiram Munger* (Boston: Advent Christian Publication Society, 1881), pp. 10–15; *Voice of Industry,* January 23, 1846.
15. Agreement between Christopher Lippitt Agt. and Gould Brown, February 28, 1815, Slater Company Records, Historical Manuscripts and Archives, University of Connecticut Library, Storrs, Connecticut; Jonathan Prude, *The Coming of Industrial Order: Town and Factory Life in Rural Massachusetts, 1810–1860* (Cambridge, England: Cambridge University Press, 1983), p. 125; *Proceedings of the New England Association of Farmers, Mechanics, and other Working Men* (December 1831), p. 7; W. J. Rorabaugh, *The Craft Apprentice: From Franklin to the Machine Age in America* (New York: Oxford University Press, 1986), p. 119.
16. Lucy Larcom, *A New England Girlhood* (1889; reprint, Gloucester, Mass.: Peter Smith, 1973), p. 175; Lucy Larcom, "An Idyl of Work" (Boston: Osgood, 1875), p. 49.
17. Larcom, "Among Lowell Mill-Girls," p. 601.
18. Memorandum, May 1828 (doc. 293), Poignand and Plant Papers, Town Library, Lancaster, Massachusetts.
19. Letter of Wilbur Kelly, Providence, [R.I.], to Joseph Hatch, April 18, 1843, Lonsdale Company Records, Rhode Island Historical Society, Providence; *Factory Girl's Garland,* July 20, 1844; Barbara M. Tucker, "The Family and Industrial Discipline in Antebellum New England," *Labor History,* v. 21 (1979–1980), p. 64.
20. Letters of Bourne Spooner, Plymouth, [Mass.], to the Directors of the House of Industry, February 6, 1839, and September 26, 1842, Plymouth Cordage Company Records, Baker Library, Harvard University Graduate School of Business Administration, Boston, Massachusetts.

These letters are the only known correspondence relating to New England manufacturers and their employment of orphans and public charges. It appears that this practice was much less prevalent than in England during the first half of the nineteenth century.

21. Samuel E. Morison, *The Ropemakers of Plymouth: A History of the Plymouth Cordage Company, 1824–1949* (Boston: Houghton Mifflin, 1950), p. 22.
22. Seth Luther, *An Address to the Working Men of New England* (New York: Office of the Workingman's Advocate, 1833), p. 20; *Report of the Rhode Island Commissioner of Industrial Statistics,* 1889, p. 130; Feldblum (1977), p. 112.
23. Gary Kulik, "The Beginnings of the Industrial Revolution in America: Pawtucket, Rhode Island, 1672–1829" (Ph.D. diss., Brown University, 1980), p. 355; 61st Congress, 2nd session, Senate Document No. 645 (1910), *Report on the Condition of Women and Child Wage-Earners in the United States,* v. 6: Elizabeth L. Otey, *The Beginnings of Child Labor Legislation in Certain States: A Comparative Study,* p. 65; Joseph Brennan, *Social Conditions in Industrial Rhode Island: 1820–1860* (Washington, D.C.: Catholic University, 1940), p. 42.
24. Seth Luther, *An Address on the Right of Free Suffrage* (Providence, R.I.: S. R. Weeden, 1833), p. 16.
25. Luther, *Address to the Working Men,* pp. 20, 35.
26. Judith McGaw, "The Sources and Impact of Mechanization: The Berkshire County, Massachusetts, Paper Industry, 1801–1885, As a Case Study" (Ph.D. diss., New York University, 1977), pp. 349–350, 356–358, 376, 378 (the letter is found in Crane Company employment file, 1844–1865).
27. Gibbs, *Whitesmiths of Taunton,* p. 67; Charlotte Erickson, *Invisible Immigrants: The Adaptation of English and Scottish Immigrants in Nineteenth-Century America* (London: Weidenfeld and Nicolson, 1972), p. 254; Letter of James Roberts and family, Waterville [Waterbury], Connecticut, to John and Mary Loxley, Sheffield, England, September 30, 1849, in Erickson (1972), p. 322.
28. Letter of Gardner Plimpton, Whitinsville, [Mass.], to Werden Babcock, January 10, 1847, in Thomas Dublin, *Women at Work: The Transformation of Work and Community in Lowell, Massachusetts, 1826–1860* (New York: Columbia University Press, 1979), pp. 175–176.
29. Agreement between Greene Manufacturing Company and James Gorton, Warwick, [R.I.], March 14, 1815, Contract Book, 1814–1831, Greene Manufacturing Company Records, Rhode Island Historical Society, Providence; Letter of Thomas Archer, to S. Slater and Sons, August 2, 1849, in Prude (1983), p. 222.
30. Agreement between Christopher Lippitt Agt. and Jenks Mason, May 28, 1815, Slater Company Records.
31. Barbara M. Tucker, *Samuel Slater and the Origins of the American Textile Industry, 1790–1860* (Ithaca, N.Y.: Cornell University Press, 1984), p. 160; Prude (1983), pp. 65, 125; Contract Book, 1814–1831, Greene Manufacturing Company Records; Slater and Kimball Records, v. 3, in Prude (1983), p. 136.
32. Tucker, "Family and Industrial Discipline," p. 60; Contract Book, 1833–1844, Greene Manufacturing Company Records.
33. Kulik, "Beginnings of the Industrial Revolution," p. 341.
34. Henry A. Miles, *Lowell, As It Was, And As It Is* (Lowell: Powers and Bagley, 1845), p. 184; Elfrieda McCauley, "The New England Mill Girls: Feminine Influence in the Development of Public Libraries in New England, 1820–1860" (Ph.D. diss., Columbia University, 1971), pp. 23–24.
35. Dublin, *Women at Work,* pp. 44, 46, 48–49.
36. Letter of Mary Cowles, Lowell, [Mass.], to her sister, December 6, 1847, MATH.
37. Larcom, "Among Lowell Mill-Girls," p. 600; Larcom, *Girlhood,* pp. 178–180.
38. *New England Offering,* July 1849, p. 161; *Voice of Industry,* January 8, 1847, in Philip S. Foner, ed., *The Factory Girls* (Urbana: University of Illinois Press, 1977), p. 90; Robinson, "Early Factory Labor," p. 9 (reprint edition, n.d.); Dublin, *Women at Work,* pp. 70–72, 82.
39. Dublin, *Women at Work,* pp. 64–65, 142; Edith Abbott, *Women in Industry* (1910; reprint, New York: Arno Press, 1969), pp. 92, 95.
40. This discussion of female operatives and their ideas about work and morality is linked with the

issue of whether or not the factory system itself was corrupting the work force. The question of corruption and the antebellum factory will be pursued further in Chapter 9.

41. *Operatives' Magazine,* December 1841, p. 138; the carding room overseer, Mr. Wellman, is quoted in Miles (1845), p. 189; Letter of Israel Saunder, Woonsocket, Rhode Island, to Crawford Nightengale, February 16, 1837, in *Rhode Island Commissioner of Industrial Statistics,* 1889, p. 134; *Lowell Offering,* v. 4, July 1844, p. 200.
42. *Lowell Offering,* v. 2, August 1842, p. 379; Miles (1845), pp. 144–145.
43. *Lowell Offering,* v. 4, July 1844, p. 214.
44. *Voice of Industry,* May 15, 1846, in Foner, *Factory Girls,* p. 167.
45. *Voice of Industry,* February 19, 1847, in Foner, *Factory Girls,* p. 332.
46. David R. Kasserman, *Fall River Outrage: Life, Murder, and Justice in Early Industrial New England* (Philadelphia: University of Pennsylvania Press, 1986). See Chapter 5 for a related discussion of how management tried to enforce its own ideas about morality and proper conduct in the factories.
47. Jeremy Brecher et al., eds., *Brass Valley* (Philadelphia: Temple University Press, 1982), pp. 5–6.
48. Letter of J.M.L. Scovill, to W. H. Scovill, May 7, 1839, in Theodore F. Marburg, "Management Problems and Procedures of a Manufacturing Enterprise, 1802–1852; A Case Study of the Origin of the Scovill Manufacturing Company" (Ph.D. diss., Clark University, 1945), pp. 282–284.
49. Letters of John Williams, Dover, [N.H.], to William Shimmin, April 5 and April 16, 1827, Dover Manufacturing Company Letter Books, pp. 373, 380, resp., New Hampshire Historical Society, Concord. The Dover printers' particular concerns with contracts, wages, etc., will be discussed in later chapters.
50. Caroline Sloat, "The Dover Manufacturing Company and the Integration of English and American Calico Printing Techniques, 1825–1829," *Winterthur Portfolio,* v. 10 (1975), pp. 61 and 67; Document G (originally a letter of Samuel Dunster, June 28, 1880, in Historical Memoranda III, no. 394, Public Library, Dover, N.H.), Cocheco Manufacturing Company Materials, Old Berwick Historical Society, South Berwick, Maine.
51. Letter of George Hollingworth, South Leicester, [Mass.], to William Rawcliff, October 21, 1829, in Thomas W. Leavitt, ed., *The Hollingworth Letters: Technical Change in the Textile Industry, 1826–1837* (Cambridge, Mass.: MIT Press, 1969), pp. 48–49; Letter of Joseph Hollingworth, Muddy-Brook-Pond Factory, Woodstock, Connecticut, to William Rawcliff, November 8, 1830, in Leavitt (1969), p. 92.
52. "The Foreign Colonies of Lowell, by Charles Cowley. Read February 15, 1881," *Contributions of the Old Residents' Historical Association,* [Lowell], v. 2 (1882), pp. 168–169, 172–174.
53. Brennan (1940), pp. 66, 72, 78.
54. Dublin, *Women at Work,* pp. 153–154, 156, 162; *New England Offering,* July 1849, pp. 156–157. The deterioration of wages and working conditions will be discussed in subsequent chapters.
55. *New England Offering,* July 1849, p. 156.
56. Adela E. Orpen, *The Chronicle of the Sid; or, The Life and Travels of Adelia Gates* (London: Religious Tract Society, 1893), pp. 29–30.
57. H. M. Gitelman, "No Irish Need Apply: Patterns of and Responses to Ethnic Discrimination in the Labor Market," *Labor History,* v. 14 (1973), pp. 65–66; George S. Gibbs, *The Saco-Lowell Shops: Textile Machinery Building in New England, 1813–1949* (Cambridge, Mass.: Harvard University Press, 1950), pp. 146, 178, 754–755.
58. Edmund W. Porter's notebook, in Gibbs, *Whitesmiths,* p. 137.
59. Luther, *Address to the Working Men,* p. 38.

Chapter 5

1. "Regulations To be observed by all persons in the employment of the Amoskeag Manufacturing Company, at their New Mills in Manchester," 1840s, in Daniel B. Stearns, diary, New Hampshire Historical Society, Concord; "Regulations to be observed by all persons employed

by the Chicopee Manufacturing Co.," 1840s, in John M. Cudd, *The Chicopee Manufacturing Company, 1823–1915* (Wilmington, Delaware: Scholarly Resources, 1974), p. 302; "Regulations to be observed by all persons employed in the factories of the Middlesex Company," 1840s, in House Unpassed Papers, 1215/4 (1843), Massachusetts State Archives, Boston.

2. "Mill Regulations," Brunswick Company, ca. 1840, in Caroline F. Ware, *The Early New England Cotton Manufacture: A Study in Industrial Beginnings* (Boston: Houghton Mifflin, 1931), p. 255; "Regulations . . . Chicopee Manufacturing Co.," in Cudd (1974), p. 302.
3. Cocheco Manufacturing Company Regulations, [Dover, New Hampshire, 1828–1829], in 61st Congress, 2nd session, Senate Document No. 645 (1910), *Report on the Condition of Women and Child Wage-Earners in the United States,* v. 10, part 1: John B. Andrews, *History of Women in Trade Unions, 1825 Through the Knights of Labor,* pp. 23–24.
4. "General Regulations, to be Observed by Persons Employed by the Lawrence Manufacturing Company, in Lowell," May 21, 1833, MATH. Many factory regulations touched on conduct outside the workplace. There were rules governing boardinghouses, church attendance, temperance in public places, etc. These requirements demonstrate that many manufacturers wanted to extend their efforts at discipline and control into the community. The focus of this chapter, however, remains on how these regulations shaped behavior in the factories.
5. Barbara Tucker, *Samuel Slater and the Origins of the American Textile Industry, 1790–1860* (Ithaca, N.Y.: Cornell University Press, 1984), p. 151; Document G (originally a letter of Samuel Dunster, June 28, 1880, in Historical Memoranda III, no. 394, Public Library, Dover, N.H.), Cocheco Manufacturing Company Materials, Old Berwick Historical Society, South Berwick, Maine; Derwent S. Whittlesey, "The Springfield Armory: A Study in Institutional Development" (Ph.D. diss., University of Chicago, 1920), n.p.
6. George S. Gibbs, *The Whitesmiths of Taunton: A History of Reed and Barton, 1824–1943* (Cambridge, Mass.: Harvard University Press, 1943), p. 149; Theodore Marburg, "Management Problems and Procedures of a Manufacturing Enterprise, 1802–1852; A Case Study of the Origin of the Scovill Manufacturing Company" (Ph.D. diss., Clark University, 1945), p. 279; David Jeremy, *Transatlantic Industrial Revolution: The Diffusion of Textile Technologies Between Britain and America, 1790–1830s* (Cambridge, Mass.: MIT Press, 1981), pp. 170–171; John L. Hayes, *American Textile Machinery* (Cambridge, Mass.: University Press, J. Wilson and Son, 1879), p. 31.
7. *Taunton Daily Gazette,* May 11, 1914, in John Lozier, "Taunton and Mason: Cotton Machinery and Locomotive Manufacture in Taunton, Massachusetts, 1811–1861" (Ph.D. diss., Ohio State University, 1978), p. 181.
8. "Life of Benjamin Wilbur," n.d., p. 3, Fall River Historical Society, Fall River, Massachusetts; Frederick M. Peck and Henry H. Earl, *Fall River and Its Industries* (Fall River, Mass.: Benjamin Earl and Son, 1877), p. 28; Tucker, *Samuel Slater,* p. 180; Henry A. Miles, *Lowell As It Was, And As It Is* (Lowell: Powers and Bagley, 1845), p. 131. Some companies also made efforts to close down taverns and restrict drinking outside the factories and after working hours. These campaigns were yet more attempts to make sure that the employees were under control all the time so that no problems would arise to disrupt work or the community.
9. Jill Siegal Dodd, "The Working Classes and the Temperance Movement in Ante-Bellum Boston," *Labor History,* v. 19 (1978), p. 530.
10. Letter of B. Blackburn, Walpole, [Mass.], to N. Stevens, November 19, 1841, Stevens Company Records, MATH; Letter of James Metcalf, to his mother, Adams-Metcalf Papers, MATH.
11. Elfrieda McCauley, "The New England Mill Girls: Feminine Influence in the Development of Public Libraries in New England, 1820–1860" (Ph.D. diss., Columbia University, 1971), pp. 218–219.
12. *Report on the Condition of Women . . . Wage-Earners,* v. 10, part 1, p. 23; "Unknown Mill Regulations," in Gary Kulik, Roger Parks, Theodore Penn, eds., *The New England Mill Village, 1790–1860,* in *Documents in American Industrial History,* v. 2, ed. Michael Folsom (Cambridge, Mass.: MIT Press, 1982), p. 464; "Rules and Regulations to be Observed by all Persons Employed in the Factory of Amasa Whitney," Winchendon, [Mass.], July 3, 1830, Research Library, Old Sturbridge Village, Sturbridge, Massachusetts.
13. Agreement between Venner Kimball for John Slater, and William Frim, March 11, 1838;

Agreement between V. S. Kimball for John Slater, and William Smith, August 13, 1838; both in Slater Company Records, Historical Manuscripts and Archives, University of Connecticut Library, Storrs.

14. "Mill Regulations," Brunswick Company, ca. 1840, in C. Ware (1931), p. 266.
15. Letter of Joseph Hollingworth, South Leicester, [Mass.], to William Rawcliff, September 6, 1829, in Thomas W. Leavitt, ed., *The Hollingworth Letters: Technical Change in the Textile Industry, 1826–1837* (Cambridge, Mass.: MIT Press, 1969), p. 46; Letter of Joseph Hollingworth, South Leicester, [Mass.], to William Rawcliff, November 7, 1829, in Leavitt (1969), pp. 53–54; Joseph Coccia, "The Cranston Print Works—Its Economic Significance to the City of Cranston and Its Influence on the Political, Social, and Industrial Life of the City and State of Rhode Island" (Master's thesis, Rhode Island College of Education, 1955), pp. 109–110; Hannah Josephson, *The Golden Threads: New England's Mill Girls and Magnates* (New York: Duell, Sloan and Pearce, 1949), p. 84.
16. Miles (1845), pp. 131, 138–139, 173; Carl Gersuny, " 'A Devil in Petticoats,' And Just Cause: Patterns of Punishment in Two New England Textile Factories," *Business History Review,* v. 50 (1976), pp. 137–144, 148–152; C. Ware (1931), pp. 266–267 (the primary sources are not specified). Workers could also be fired for involvement in labor disputes. This will be discussed in Chapter 7.
17. Whittlesey (1920), n.p.; Letter of Joseph Bath, Springfield, [Mass.], to Samuel Colt, Hartford, Connecticut, November 23, 1847, Colt Company Papers, State Library—Archives, Hartford.
18. Letter of Bourne Spooner, Plymouth, [Mass.], to W. Day, January 28, 1839, Plymouth Cordage Company Records, Baker Library, Harvard University Graduate School of Business Administration, Boston, Massachusetts. Owners and managers often wrote letters that not only recommended or criticized workers, but that specifically mentioned whether an operative had completed his or her contractual length of service. This network of correspondence served to reward obedient employees and punish recalcitrant workers; it was also a means of preventing workers and other companies from breaching contracts and enticing workers away from employers. The use of such letters to control the labor market will be discussed in Chapter 6.
19. Contract between Anson Atwood and Brewster & Ingraham, March 4, 1848, in John J. Murphy, "The Establishment of the American Clock Industry: A Study in Entrepreneurial History" (Ph.D. diss., Yale University, 1961), p. 305.
20. Barbara Tucker, " 'Our Good Methodists': The Church, the Factory, and the Working Class in Ante-Bellum Webster, Massachusetts," *The Maryland Historian,* v. 8, no. 2 (1977), pp. 28–31; "Regulations . . . Amoskeag Manufacturing Company," 1840s; *Records From the Life of S.V.S. Wilder* (New York, 1865), pp. 196–202, 208–209, in Kulik et al. (1982), p. 249. It is also possible that some owners closed factories during revivals, not because of their own interest in promoting religion, but because so many workers were leaving on their own to participate in the enthusiasm that the factories could not be kept operating anyway.
21. Charles C. Cole, *The Social Ideas of the Northern Evangelists, 1826–1860* (New York: Octagon, 1966), pp. 184–185; *Autobiography of Elder Jacob Knapp* (New York: Sheldon and Co., 1868), pp. 138–139. It is possible that workers led the move to shut down operations for revivals in the factories. Due to this great interest in revivals, management may have agreed to these interruptions in the production schedule.
22. Letter from Dover, [N.H.], to William Shimmin, August 2, 1826, Dover Manufacturing Company Records, New Hampshire Historical Society, Concord; Letter of Samuel G. Spalding to Amos A. Lawrence, February 26, 1849, in McCauley (1971), p. 200; Letter of T. Lawton to Amos A. Lawrence, March 9, 1849, in McCauley (1971), p. 200.
23. *Records From the Life of S.V.S. Wilder* (New York, 1865), pp. 208–209, in Kulik et al. (1982), pp. 251–252.
24. Jama Lazerow, "Religion and the New England Mill Girl: A New Perspective on an Old Theme," *New England Quarterly,* v. 60 (1987), p. 442; Jonathan Prude, *The Coming of Industrial Order: Town and Factory Life in Rural Massachusetts, 1810–1860* (Cambridge, England: Cambridge University Press, 1983), p. 154.
25. Letter of Sarah Maria Cornell, Lowell, [Mass.], to her sister, Lucretia Rawson, May 3, 1829, in [Catherine Williams], *Fall River An Authentic Narrative* (Boston: Lilly, Wait and Co.,

1834), p. 135; Theresa Murphy, "Labor, Religion, and Moral Reform in Fall River, Massachusetts, 1800–1845" (Ph.D. diss., Yale University, 1982), p. 52; Tucker, " 'Our Good Methodists,'" p. 34.

26. Lucy Larcom, "An Idyl of Work" (Boston: Osgood, 1875), pp. 70–71.
27. *Lowell Offering,* v. 4, December 1843, p. 45.
28. Letter of a Waltham, [Mass.], operative, in Harriet Farley, *Operatives' Reply to the Hon. Jere Clemens* . . . (Lowell, Mass.: S. J. Varney, 1850), pp. 11–13; Thomas Dublin, *Women at Work: The Transformation of Work and Community in Lowell, Massachusetts, 1826–1860* (New York: Columbia University Press, 1979), p. 60; Harriet H. Robinson, "Early Factory Labor in New England," in *Fourteenth Annual Report of the Massachusetts Bureau of Statistics of Labor* (Boston: Wright and Potter, State Printers, 1883), p. 382.
29. Prude (1983), pp. 155–156; Judith McGaw, "The Sources and Impact of Mechanization: The Berkshire County, Massachusetts, Paper Industry, 1801–1885, As a Case Study" (Ph.D. diss., New York University, 1977), pp. 280–281.
30. Letter of a Waltham, [Mass.], operative in Farley, *Operatives' Reply,* pp. 11–13; *Lowell Offering,* v. 4, August 1844, pp. 238–239.
31. Harriet H. Robinson, *Loom and Spindle; or, Life Among the Early Mill Girls* (New York: Thomas Y. Crowell, 1898), p. 73. Not surprisingly, many workers who had generally favorable attitudes toward management, as discussed in Chapter 3, were likely to view corporate regulations and management's enforcement of those rules in a positive light.
32. Lucy Larcom, *A New England Girlhood* (1889; reprint, Gloucester, Mass.: Peter Smith, 1973), p. 183.
33. *Lowell Offering,* v. 3, May 1843, p. 91; *Lowell Offering,* v. 5, May 1845, p. 110.
34. Robinson, *Loom and Spindle,* p. 42; Robinson, "Early Factory Labor," p. 397; "My Schools and Teachers in Lowell Sixty Years Ago, read May 3rd, 1892, by Rev. Varnum Lincoln," *Contributions of the Old Residents' Historical Association,* [Lowell], v. 5 (1894), p. 138. Mills outside the Lowell system may have also resembled schools in that a few adults directed the activities of groups of children.
35. *Lowell Offering,* v. 5, January 1845 (cover); *Lowell Offering,* v. 5, March 1845, p. 7; Harriet H. Robinson, "The Life of the Early Mill-Girls," *Journal of Social Science,* v. 16 (1882), p. 137; Letter of John Rogers, to his father, July 19, 1850, Amoskeag Manufacturing Company Papers, MATH (excerpts from the John Rogers Papers at the New-York Historical Society).
36. Factory Tracts #1, in Philip S. Foner, ed., *The Factory Girls* (Urbana: University of Illinois Press, 1977), p. 136.
37. *Voice of Industry,* October 16, 1846.
38. Seth Luther, *An Address to the Working Men of New England* (New York: Office of the Workingman's Advocate, 1833), p. 29; Gersuny (1976), pp. 139–140.
39. Gersuny (1976), pp. 149–151; *Voice of Industry,* June 19, 1846; *Voice of Industry,* September 11, 1846.
40. Whittlesey (1920), n.p.
41. Letter of Samuel Lawrence, Lowell, [Mass.], to Charles Storrow, Methuen, [Mass.], March 6, 1847, Essex Company Correspondence, MATH; Miles (1845), pp. 134, 138.
42. *Voice of Industry,* December 11, 1846; *Nashua Gazette,* October 1, 1846, in Foner, *Factory Girls,* pp. 82–83.
43. *Voice of Industry,* September 11, 1846.
44. House Unpassed Papers, 1215/4 (1843), Massachusetts State Archives. It is likely that the women who signed this petition were some of the female operatives who walked off their jobs at the Middlesex Corporation in December 1842 to protest a decrease in their piece rates. See Chapter 7 for more details on this strike.
45. Senate Unpassed Papers, 11983 (1846), Massachusetts State Archives; Massachusetts Legislative Documents, House No. 153, April 1850.
46. Abigail Mussey, *Life Sketches and Experiences* (Cambridge, Mass.: Dakin and Metcalf, 1866), pp. 14–15; *Factory Girl's Album,* April 11, 1846; Luther, *Address to the Working Men,* p. 20.
47. Factory Tracts #1, in Foner, *Factory Girls,* p. 135.
48. Ibid., p. 136.
49. *Voice of Industry,* November 14, 1845, in Foner, *Factory Girls,* p. 140.

Chapter 6

1. Jonathan Prude, *The Coming of Industrial Order: Town and Factory Life in Rural Massachusetts, 1810–1860* (Cambridge, England: Cambridge University Press, 1983), pp. 88–89, 301–302; Caroline F. Ware, *The Early New England Cotton Manufacture: A Study in Industrial Beginnings* (Boston: Houghton Mifflin, 1931), p. 219; Robert G. Layer, *Earnings of Cotton Mill Operatives, 1825–1914* (Cambridge, Mass.: Harvard University Press, 1955), p. 70.
2. Letter of Charles Metcalf, Lowell, [Mass.], to his parents, April 27, 1844, Adams-Metcalf Papers, MATH; Letter of [Rebecca Ford], Middlebury, [Vermont], to her sister, Sally Ford, Granville, Vermont, June 1, 1840, in David A. Zonderman, "From Mill Village to Industrial City: Letters from Vermont Factory Operatives," *Labor History,* v. 27 (1986), p. 274. Having family members help was no guarantee of finding a factory job. Charles Metcalf's letter mentions the fact that he spoke to a number of overseers who said that they had no openings in their departments. He finally found a manager who was more encouraging but offered no promises. When factories were full or the economy was sluggish, employment prospects dimmed for everyone, regardless of their connnections.
3. Letter of Mary Paul, Lowell, [Mass.], to her father, Bela Paul, November 20, 1845, in Thomas Dublin, ed., *Farm to Factory: Women's Letters, 1830–1860* (New York: Columbia University Press, 1981), p. 101. Letter of Julia Dutton, to her mother, September 26, 1847, Lucretia W. Dutton Papers, Bailey/Howe Library, University of Vermont, Burlington.
4. Letter of Albert Conant, Mansfield, [Conn.], to Mr. Cheney & Brothers, January 22, 1844, Cheney Family Papers, Connecticut Historical Society, Hartford; Judith McGaw, "The Sources and Impact of Mechanization: The Berkshire County, Massachusetts, Paper Industry, 1801–1885, As a Case Study" (Ph.D. diss., New York University, 1977), p. 358.
5. Letter of Sarah Slater, Union, Massachusetts, to Samuel Slater, March 21, 1818, Nelson Slater Collection, Slater Mill Historic Site, Pawtucket, Rhode Island. This letter is also concerned with how an operative responds to unemployment, and that response will be discussed further in Chapter 9. Letter of Joseph France, to H. N. Slater, November 15, 1840, in Prude (1983), p. 211.
6. Letter of S. P. Bryant, Whitneyville, [Conn.], to Samuel Colt, Esq., September 5, 1847, Colt Company Records, State Library—Archives, Hartford, Connecticut. The issue of career advancement will be discussed further in Chapter 9.
7. C. Ware (1931), p. 213; George S. Gibbs, *The Saco-Lowell Shops: Textile Machinery Building in New England, 1813–1949* (Cambridge, Mass.: Harvard University Press, 1950), p. 146; Wilder's remarks (published in 1879) are quoted in James M. Swank, *History of the Manufacture of Iron in All Ages and Particularly in the United States from Colonial Times to 1891* (1892; reprint, New York: Burt Franklin, 1965), pp. 448–449; but no further reference is given. See Chapter 1 for another discussion of how mechanization sometimes increased the immediate demand for certain skills.
8. Vera Shlakman, *Economic History of a Factory Town: A Study of Chicopee, Massachusetts,* in *Smith College Studies in History,* v. 20, ed. by John C. Hildt, William Dodge Gray, and Harold Underwood Faulkner (Northampton, Mass., 1934–1935), p. 39; Mary Feldblum, "The Formation of the First Factory Labor Force in the New England Cotton Textile Industry, 1800–1848" (Ph.D. diss., New School for Social Research, 1977), p. 129. Labor agents, or recruiters, were not the same as factory agents: factory agents supervised the operations of the factories themselves.
9. *Voice of Industry,* May 22, 1846, in Philip S. Foner, ed., *The Factory Girls* (Urbana: University of Illinois Press, 1977), pp. 168–169.
10. *Voice of Industry,* June 19, 1846; *The Protest,* November 25, 1848; *Lowell Offering,* v. 5, May 1845, p. 100.
11. *New England Offering,* July 1849, p. 159; Prude (1983), p. 336.
12. Plant's response is found in draft form, dated August 28, 1823, on the back of the letter of Moses Smith, Jr., Chesterfield, [Mass.], to the Agent of the Lancaster Cotton Manufactory, Lancaster, Massachusetts, August 11, 1823, (doc. 225), Poignand and Plant Papers, Town Library, Lancaster; Letter of Oliver Dean, Agt. for Amoskeag Manufacturing Co., Goffstown,

[N.H.], to Mr. Fisher, June 17, 1826, Letterbook, v. 1, Amoskeag Manufacturing Company Papers, Manchester Historic Association, Manchester, New Hampshire.

13. Letter of John Nicol, Millbury, [Mass.], to Mr. Claymonz, March 27, 1833, Merino/Dudley Wool Companies Records, Research Library, Old Sturbridge Village, Sturbridge, Massachusetts.
14. Letter of William Hood, Plymouth Hills, to Messrs. Cheney Brothers, December 20, 1843, Cheney Family Papers.
15. Kenneth F. Mailloux, "The Boston Manufacturing Company of Waltham, Massachusetts, 1813–1848: The First Modern Factory in America" (Ph.D. diss., Boston University, 1957), p. 201.
16. Theodore F. Marburg, "Aspects of Labor Administration in the Early Nineteenth Century," *Bulletin of the Business Historical Society,* v. 15 (1941), p. 5; Theodore F. Marburg, "Management Problems and Procedures of a Manufacturing Enterprise, 1802–1852: A Case Study of the Origin of the Scovill Manufacturing Company" (Ph.D. diss., Clark University, 1945), p. 278; Martha Taber, *A History of the Cutlery Industry in the Connecticut Valley,* in *Smith College Studies in History,* v. 41, ed. by Vera B. Holmes, Sidney R. Packard, and Leona C. Gabel (Northampton, Mass., 1955), pp. 98–99.
17. Agreement between N. S. Scott, agent for J. and W. Slater, and Billings B. Lewis, February 17, 1843; and Agreement between Nicholas S. Scott, agent for J. and W. Slater, and Calvin W. French, April 1, 1842; both in Slater Company Records, Historical Manuscripts and Archives, University of Connecticut, Storrs.
18. Letter of Duane & Treat, Voluntown, [Conn.], to S. C. Colyer, March 2, 1832, Slater Company Records.
19. Document G [originally a letter of Samuel Dunster, June 28, 1880, in Historical Memoranda III, no. 394, Public Library, Dover, N.H.], Cocheco Manufacturing Company Materials, Old Berwick Historical Society, South Berwick, Maine. See Chapter 4 for a further discussion of Dunster's case as it relates to the interaction between native-born and immigrant workers. A few workers also took legal action to recover back wages when they decided to leave rather than when they were fired; this will be discussed later in this chapter.
20. Samuel Collins, "Early History of Collins Co." (1866: typed copy at the Canton Historical Museum, Collinsville, Conn.), p. 7; Letter of S. W. Collins, South Canton, [Conn.], August 27, 1830, Collins Company Materials, Connecticut Historical Society, Hartford; Letter of Eli Whitney, New Haven, [Conn.], to Nathan Starr, December 26, 1817, Eli Whitney Papers, Manuscripts and Archives, Yale University Library, New Haven, Connecticut.
21. "Terms With Workmen," December 1, 1834, and March 2, 1835; "Terms With Axe Temperers," 1836; both in Collins Company Materials, Connecticut Historical Society.
22. Prude (1983), pp. 150–151.
23. This discussion of wage labor will focus on issues raised by the concept of working for wages in and of itself, rather than on measuring specific wage rates.
24. Bruce Clouette and Matthew Roth, *Bristol, Connecticut: A Bicentennial History, 1785–1985* (Bristol: Bristol Public Library, 1984), pp. 67–68, 86–87; Marburg, "Aspects of Labor Administration," pp. 6–7.
25. *Fall River Daily Globe,* February 27, 1889, in Stephen Victor et al., eds., *The Fall River Sourcebook: A Documentary History of Fall River, Massachusetts* (American History Workshop, 1981), pp. 40–41; C. Ware (1931), p. 245.
26. Felicia Deyrup, *Arms Makers of the Connecticut Valley: A Regional Study of the Economic Development of the Small Arms Industry, 1798–1870,* in *Smith College Studies in History,* v. 33, ed. by Vera Holmes and Hans Kohn (Northampton, Mass., 1948), p. 108; Report of James Dalliba, October 1819, "Communicated to the House of Representatives by the Committee on Military Affairs, March 23, 1823," 17th Congress, 2nd session, no. 246, in Walter Lowrie and William Franklin, eds., *American State Papers. Class V. Military Affairs* (Washington, D.C.: Gales and Seaton, 1834), v. 2, p. 542.
27. Letter of Samuel Collins, August 12, 1830, Collins Company Materials, Connecticut Historical Society.
28. Gibbs, *Saco-Lowell,* p. 53; William G. Lathrop, *The Brass Industry in the United States* (Mt.

Carmel, Conn., 1926), p. 96; Horace Hotchkiss, in the "Miller manuscripts," in Marburg, "Management Problems," p. 297.

29. Frederick M. Peck and Henry H. Earl, *Fall River and Its Industries* (Fall River, Mass.: Benjamin Earl and Son, 1877), p. 17.
30. Samuel Moore's testimony is in the *Third Annual Report of the Massachusetts Bureau of Statistics of Labor* (Boston: Wright and Potter, State Printers, 1872), p. 399.
31. Henry A. Miles, *Lowell, As It Was, And As It Is* (Lowell: Powers and Bagley, 1845), p. 80.
32. Letter of Emanuel Corey, to John Bacon, December 5, 1827, Slater Company Records.
33. Letter of Roswell Lee, to George Bomford, January 25, 1816, in Deyrup (1948), p. 103; Derwent S. Whittlesey, "The Springfield Armory: A Study in Institutional Development" (Ph.D. diss., University of Chicago, 1920), n.p.; Paul Uselding, "An Early Chapter in the Evolution of American Industrial Management," in *Business Enterprise and Economic Change,* ed. by Louis Cain and Paul Uselding (Kent, Ohio: Kent State University Press, 1973), p. 65.
34. Letter of Charles Waite, to Samuel Slater and Sons, May 17, 1839, in Barbara M. Tucker, *Samuel Slater and the Origins of the American Textile Industry, 1790–1860* (Ithaca, N.Y.: Cornell University Press, 1984), p. 156; *Factory Girl's Garland,* May 25, 1844, in Foner, *Factory Girls,* p. 78.
35. Letter of Eli Terry, Jr., to Jeptha Gillett, Pittsburgh, Pennsylvania, March 21, 1838, in Barrows Mussey, *Young Father Time: A Yankee Portrait* (New York: Newcomen Society in North America, 1950), p. 39.
36. Seth Luther, *An Address to the Working Men of New England* (New York: Office of the Workingman's Advocate, 1833), p. 23.
37. Letter of Joseph Hollingworth, Muddy Brook Pond Factory, Woodstock, Connecticut, to William Rawcliff, September 5, 1830, in Thomas W. Leavitt, ed., *The Hollingworth Letters: Technical Change in the Textile Industry, 1826–1837* (Cambridge, Mass.: MIT Press, 1969), p. 80.
38. Summons to Samuel Plant, Worcester County Court of Common Pleas, October 5, 1833, (doc. 370), Poignand and Plant Papers; Benjamin F. Butler, *Butler's Book* (Boston: A. M. Thayer and Co., 1892), pp. 1,031–1,033. Christopher Tomlins has also cited several other cases of workers' suing factories in antebellum Massachusetts over disputed wages. In these cases, the companies claimed that workers quit without giving proper notice and thereby forfeited a portion of their wages. The workers went to court in an effort to recover the earnings they thought were due them. Tomlins rigorously examines these cases for what they reveal about legal and judicial concepts of employer contractual power. These cases also speak to the ongoing contest over control of wages in antebellum factories. See Christopher Tomlins, "The Ties That Bind: Master and Servant in Massachusetts, 1800–1850," *Labor History,* v. 30 (1989), pp. 222–224.
39. Shlakman (1935), p. 57; Prude (1983), p. 152.
40. C. Ware (1931), p. 247.
41. James P. Hanlan, *The Working Population of Manchester, New Hampshire, 1840–1886* (Ann Arbor, Mich.: UMI Research Press, 1981), p. 67; C. Ware (1931), p. 247; *Lowell Offering,* v. 1, August 1841, p. 170; *Lowell Offering,* v. 1, October 1841, p. 243.
42. This letter of the Ware manager is dated December 28, 1842, found in Arthur Chase, *History of Ware, Massachusetts* (Cambridge, Mass.: 1911), p. 222, and quoted in C. Ware (1931), p. 246.
43. Letter of Joseph Hollingworth, South Leicester, [Mass.], to William Rawcliff, November 7, 1829, in Leavitt, pp. 53–54.
44. Barbara M. Tucker, "The Family and Industrial Discipline in Antebellum New England," *Labor History,* v. 21 (1979–1980), p. 70; Tucker, *Samuel Slater,* p. 225.
45. C. Ware (1931), p. 245.
46. Report of James Dalliba, October 1819, in Lowrie and Franklin (1834), v. 2, p. 542.
47. Order from Superintendent's Office to Armory, April 8, 1820, in Deyrup (1948), p. 106.
48. Letter of Roswell Lee, to George Bomford, February 18, 1822, in Deyrup (1948), p. 105.
49. Letter of G. Talcott, Springfield Armory, to John Bell, Secretary of War, August 6, 1841, in Steven V. Benét, comp., *A Collection of Annual Reports and Other Important Papers Relating to the Ordnance Department* (Washington, D.C.: Government Printing Office, 1878), v. 1, p. 395; G. Talcott, "Notes on the Springfield Armory," [1841], in Benét (1878), v. 1, pp. 396–

397; "Report of the Board Convened at Springfield, Mass., August 30, 1841, to Examine into the Condition and Management of Springfield Armory," [Exec. Docs., House of Representatives, 27th Cong., 2nd sess., v. 4, Doc. No. 207], in Benét (1878), v. 1, pp. 401–402; Deyrup (1948), p. 173.

50. Notice, January 16, 1843, Collins Company Materials, Connecticut Historical Society.
51. Foner, *Factory Girls,* p. xix.
52. *The Harbinger,* June 20, 1846, in 61st Congress, 2nd session, Senate Document No. 645 (1910), *Report of the Condition of Women and Child Wage-Earners in the United States,* v. 9: Helen L. Sumner, *History of Women in Industry in the United States,* p. 38. This letter is similar in some ways to the letter of Jabez Hollingworth discussed in Chapter 1 (note 34). Hollingworth's letter focuses even more on the machines themselves and their threat to men's jobs and the quality of work produced, but both Hollingworth and this carpet weaver see links between mechanization, feminization of the work force, and declining wages.
53. Letter of Maria L. Grout, Three Rivers, Massachusetts, to her mother, Lucy Grout, Stratton, Vermont, probably 1838 or 1839, Grout Family Papers, Russell Vermontiana Collection, Martha Canfield Memorial Free Library, Arlington, Vermont; John M. Cudd, *The Chicopee Manufacturing Company, 1823–1915* (Wilmington, Del.: Scholarly Resources, 1974), pp. 261, 263; Layer (1955), p. 46.
54. Hannah Josephson, *The Golden Threads: New England's Mill Girls and Magnates* (New York: Duell, Sloan and Pearce, 1949), pp. 214–215; *Wampanoag, and Operatives' Journal,* July 9, 1842, in Foner, *Factory Girls,* pp. 75–76.
55. House Unpassed Papers, 1215/4 (1843), Massachusetts State Archives, Boston. The women who signed this petition were probably some of the female operatives who walked off their jobs at the Middlesex Corporation in December 1842. See Chapter 7 for more discussion of this strike.

    There is only one known instance where an antebellum manufacturer actually accepted the premise that an alteration in wage rates entitled the workers to be excused from their contracts. Samuel Collins issued a revised wage schedule in 1839 and stated that, under the contracts the workers had signed, the company had the right to reduce wages. He also acknowledged, however, that such an action released workers from their contractual obligations, since the terms they had originally agreed to contained specific wage rates. Collins, by this declaration, may have been trying to recognize the bargaining power of his relatively skilled labor force, renegotiate with them at a lower wage, and avert any confrontation over the proposed changes. The company also expressed its willingness to settle with those who chose to leave their positions. But Collins warned that the same economic difficulties in 1839 that necessitated the wage cuts also dictated that any settlements of back pay might have to be held for up to three months. (Notice, November 9, 1839, Collins Company Materials, Connecticut Historical Society.)
56. *Lowell Offering,* v. 3, June 1843, p. 216; *Lowell Offering,* v. 5, May 1845, p. 98.
57. Letter of Mary Paul, Lowell, [Mass.], to her father, Bela Paul, November 5, 1848, in Dublin, *Farm to Factory,* p. 106. This discussion of wage cuts has focused on what workers thought of these reductions rather than on any actions they may have taken to challenge the cuts. In the following chapter, the connection between wage cuts and direct actions, such as strikes, will be explored. For now, it is interesting to note that these written criticisms of wage cuts were the most prevalent in the 1840s, while strikes against wage cuts were more common in the 1820s and 1830s.
58. The records of this unidentified Lowell mill are quoted in Miles (1845), pp. 114–115; Harriet H. Robinson, "Early Factory Labor in New England," in *Fourteenth Annual Report of the Massachusetts Bureau of Statistics of Labor* (Boston: Wright and Potter, State Printers, 1883), p. 386; Josephson (1949), p. 78.
59. *Voice of Industry,* April 24, 1846, in Foner, *Factory Girls,* pp. 161–162.
60. Letter of Joseph and Jabez Hollingworth, South Leicester, [Mass.], to William Rawcliff, March 13, 1830, in Leavitt (1969), p. 66; the Amesbury operative's testimony is in the *Third Annual Report of the Massachusetts Bureau of Statistics of Labor,* p. 110.
61. J.Q.A. Thayer, *Review of the Report of the Special Committee of the Legislature of the Commonwealth of Massachusetts on the Petition Relating to Hours of Labor* (Boston: J. N. Bang,

1845), pp. 21–22. The issue of workers' savings is also linked to their ideas on career mobility and future advancement, which will be discussed in Chapter 9.

62. Seth Luther, *Address to the Working Men,* pp. 22–23; Prude (1983), p. 91.
63. Letter of David Greenough, to Poignand and Plant, March 14, 1815, (doc. 96); Agreement between Charles Lewis and the Poignand and Plant Company, December 30, 1820, (doc. 175), both in Poignand and Plant Papers; Letter of S. H. Babcock and Company, Boston, [Mass.], to J. Brown and Company, Dudley, [Mass.], November 27, 1823, Merino/Dudley Wool Companies Records; Tucker, *Samuel Slater,* p. 149.
64. Letterbook, 1825–1826, John Gray and Company Papers, State Library—Archives, Hartford, Connecticut; Letter of S.V.S. Wilder, Boston, [Mass.], to S. H. Howes, January 17, 1828, Ware Manufacturing Company Records, MATH; Letter of George Hollingworth, South Leicester, [Mass.], to William Rawcliff, June 28, 1828, in Leavitt (1969), p. 27; *Lowell Offering,* v. 2, November 1842, p. 48.
65. Letter of W.H.S., Boston, [Mass.], to Moses Hey, Worsted Factory, Dedham, [Mass.], March 29, 1822, Moses Hey Papers, MATH (microfilm of originals in the Pennsylvania Historical Society); John S. Garner, *The Model Company Town: Urban Design Through Private Enterprise in Nineteenth-Century New England* (Amherst: University of Massachusetts Press, 1984), p. 55.
66. *Lowell Offering,* December 1840, pp. 17–18 (there is no volume number for this issue).
67. *Lowell Offering,* v. 1, June 1841, p. 177; Howard Gitelman, "The Waltham System and the Coming of the Irish," *Labor History,* v. 8 (1967), pp. 234, 237–238.
68. Robinson, "Early Factory Labor," p. 383; *Lowell Offering,* v. 5, January 1845, p. 19; *New England Offering,* March 1849, p. 72.
69. Harriet H. Robinson, *Loom and Spindle; or, Life Among the Early Mill Girls* (New York: Thomas Y. Crowell, 1898), p. 69. See Chapter 9 for a further discussion of how work and independence were linked.
70. *Factory Girl,* January 15, 1845, in Foner, *Factory Girls,* p. 76; *Factory Girl's Album,* February 14, 1846, in Foner, *Factory Girls,* p. 78.
71. The Amesbury operative's testimony is in the *Third Annual Report of the Massachusetts Bureau of Statistics of Labor,* p. 110.
72. *Factory Girl,* January 15, 1845, in Foner, *Factory Girls,* p. 77; Fidelia O. Brown, "Decline and Fall: The End of the Dream," in *Cotton Was King: A History of Lowell, Massachusetts,* Arthur L. Eno, Jr., ed. (Lowell: Lowell Historical Society, 1976), p. 142; Mailloux, pp. 210–211. See Chapter 1 for a further discussion of speedups and stretch-outs.
73. David Jeremy, *Transatlantic Industrial Revolution: The Diffusion of Textile Technology Between Britain and America, 1790–1830s* (Cambridge, Mass.: MIT Press, 1981), p. 198; *Voice of Industry,* April 2, 1847, in Foner, *Factory Girls,* pp. 309–310.
74. *The Man,* March 8, 1834, in Foner, *Factory Girls,* p. 11. See Chapter 7 for a further discussion of this strike.
75. "Rambler" [pseud.], "The Price of Weavers in Greenville," n.d., Mowry Family Papers, Rhode Island Historical Society, Providence.
76. *Voice of Industry,* April 7, 1848. This debate over the meaning of wage labor in the factories is also related to questions about the meaning of work itself. Were operatives laboring primarily to earn money, or were they striving for some other meaning in work beyond the wages? See Chapter 9 for an extensive discussion of the motivations behind the labor of factory operatives.

Chapter 7

1. Much of the written criticism of the factory system can be interpreted as a form of protest. The focus of this chapter, however, is mostly on more physical forms of protest—strikes and labor organizations, and more individual, spontaneous gestures as well.
2. Letter of John Rogers, to his father, November 9, 1850, Amoskeag Manufacturing Company Papers, MATH (excerpts from the John Rogers Papers at the New-York Historical Society); "Rambler" [pseud.], "The Price of Weavers in Greenville," n.d., Mowry Family Papers,

Rhode Island Historical Society, Providence; "Reminiscences of Samuel Bryan Jerome," *The Timepiece Journal,* v. 2 (1980), p. 30.

3. James P. Hanlan, *The Working Population of Manchester, New Hampshire, 1840–1886* (Ann Arbor, Mich.: UMI Research Press, 1981), p. 213; Carl Gersuny, " 'A Devil in Petticoats' and Just Cause: Patterns of Punishment in Two New England Textile Factories," *Business History Review,* v. 50 (1976), p. 144.
4. Letter of W. H. Scovill, to J.M.L. Scovill, July 24, 1835, in Theodore F. Marburg, "Aspects of Labor Administration in the Early Nineteenth Century," *Bulletin of the Business Historical Society,* v. 15 (1941), p. 5.
5. Mary Feldblum, "The Formation of the First Factory Labor Force in the New England Cotton Textile Industry, 1800–1848" (Ph.D. diss., New School for Social Research, 1977), p. 266; Gary Kulik, "The Beginnings of the Industrial Revolution in America: Pawtucket, Rhode Island, 1672–1829" (Ph.D. diss., Brown University, 1980), p. 366; Derwent S. Whittlesey, "The Springfield Armory: A Study in Institutional Development" (Ph.D. diss., University of Chicago, 1920), n.p.; *Manchester Operative,* August 10, 1844. There were also reports of an arson fire during the 1824 strike in Pawtucket, Rhode Island; this incident will be discussed later on in this chapter.
6. Letter of S. W. Collins, to Collins and Co., Hartford, [Conn.], November 15, 1830, Collins Company Materials, Canton Historical Museum, Collinsville, Connecticut; Jonathan Prude, *The Coming of Industrial Order: Town and Factory Life in Rural Massachusetts, 1810–1860* (Cambridge, England: Cambridge University Press, 1983), p. 137; Gersuny (1976), p. 141. See Chapter 8 for a further discussion of workers' taking time off from their jobs.
7. "Lowell Factory Girl," in Philip S. Foner, ed., *American Labor Songs of the Nineteenth Century* (Urbana: University of Illinois Press, 1975), p. 44; Letter of Jabez Hollingworth, 1827, in Thomas W. Leavitt, ed., *The Hollingworth Letters: Technical Change in the Textile Industry, 1826–1837* (Cambridge, Mass.: MIT Press, 1969), p. 17.
8. See Chapter 9 for a related discussion on whether operatives perceived themselves to be a transient population as a whole.
9. Barbara M. Tucker, *Samuel Slater and the Origins of the American Textile Industry, 1790–1860* (Ithaca, N.Y.: Cornell University Press, 1984), pp. 254–255. When workers engaged in frequent absenteeism, or showing up late for work, or quitting altogether, they may have been making an implicit argument that since they could not control their machines or the pace of their labor, they would try to control their hours and days on the job. Thus these actions contained elements of protest and power, as well as anger and desperation.
10. Letter of Isaac Markham, Waltham, [Mass.], to his brother, David Markham, May 30, 1821, Markham Collection, Sheldon Museum, Middlebury, Vermont.
11. *Manufacturers' and Farmers' Journal,* May 31, 1824, in Gary Kulik, Roger Parks, and Theodore Penn, eds., *The New England Mill Village, 1790–1860,* in *Documents in American Industrial History,* v. 2, ed. Michael Folsom (Cambridge, Mass.: MIT Press, 1982), pp. 485–486; Kulik, "Beginnings of the Industrial Revolution," pp. 360, 364–368. Barbara Tucker points out that Samuel Slater's mill in Pawtucket had not begun to employ women power-loom weavers in 1824. Therefore, Slater's mill was probably not deeply involved with this strike. See Tucker, *Samuel Slater,* p. 184.
12. 61st Congress, 2nd session, Senate Document No. 645 (1910), *Report on the Condition of Women and Child Wage-Earners in the United States,* v. 10, part 1: John B. Andrews, *History of Women in Trade Unions, 1825 Through the Knights of Labor,* pp. 23–24; Hannah Josephson, *The Golden Threads: New England's Mill Girls and Magnates* (New York: Duell, Sloan and Pearce, 1949), p. 231.
13. Almond Davis, *The Female Preacher or Memoir of Salome Lincoln* (Providence, R.I., 1843), pp. 49–53, in Kulik et al. (1982), pp. 513–516; William F. Hanna, *Taunton Remembered* (1982: typed copy at the Old Colony Historical Society, Taunton, Massachusetts).
14. *The Man,* February 22, 1834, and March 20, 1834, in *Report on the Condition of Women . . . Wage-Earners,* v. 10, part 1, pp. 28–29; Thomas Dublin, *Women at Work: The Transformation of Work and Community in Lowell, Massachusetts, 1826–1860* (New York: Columbia University Press, 1979), p. 97; *Boston Globe,* 1883, n.d., Scrapbook, v. 29, p. 52, Harriet Rob-

inson Papers, Arthur and Elizabeth Schlesinger Library on the History of Women in America, Radcliffe College, Cambridge, Massachusetts; Mary Hall, diary, February 14, 1834, New Hampshire Historical Society, Concord.

15. *Report on the Condition of Women . . . Wage-Earners,* v. 10, part 1, pp. 25–26; *The Man,* March 8, 1834, in Philip S. Foner, ed., *The Factory Girls* (Urbana: University of Illinois Press, 1977), pp. 10–12; Elfrieda McCauley, "The New England Mill Girls: Feminine Influence in the Development of Public Libraries in New England, 1820–1860" (Ph.D. diss., Columbia University, 1971), p. 217.
16. Dublin, *Women at Work,* pp. 90–91.
17. The following extensive analysis of these documents is based partly, though certainly not entirely, on Thomas Dublin's own careful discussion of the Lowell strikes in Chapter 6 of *Women at Work.*
18. It is important to note that the rhetoric of these strikers included both ringing assertions of their equality and warnings about the dangers of factory slavery and tyranny. Protesters often argued that their beliefs in equality were being undermined by the autocratic behavior of managers. It is also important to remember that strikers used the principle of equality as a foundation for their protest to protect their status, whereas workers who supported the factory system argued that their equal status was already respected by factory managers.
19. Harriet H. Robinson, *Loom and Spindle; or, Life Among the Early Mill Girls* (New York: Thomas Y. Crowell, 1898), pp. 84–85; Claudia L. Bushman, *"A Good Poor Man's Wife," Being a Chronicle of Harriet Hanson Robinson and Her Family in Nineteenth-Century New England* (Hanover, N.H.: University Press of New England, 1981), pp. 24–27. Bushman also argues that Robinson may have embellished her relatively minor role in this strike as a way to bolster her crusade for women's rights. The more often Robinson recounted the incident, the more attention she gave to her own conduct. But her memories of the overall course of the strike remain generally consistent and accurate.
20. Dublin, *Women at Work,* p. 101; Josephson (1949), pp. 237–238.
21. Bushman (1981), p. 25; *Report on the Condition of Women . . . Wage-Earners,* v. 10, part 1, p. 30; Foner, *Labor Songs,* p. 45; *Zion's Herald,* October 19, 1836; Dublin, *Women at Work,* pp. 99, 101–102.
22. Edith Abbott, *Women in Industry* (1910; reprint, New York: Arno Press, 1969), pp. 131–132; Vera Shlakman, *Economic History of a Factory Town: A Study of Chicopee, Massachusetts,* in *Smith College Studies in History,* v. 20, ed. by John C. Hildt, William Dodge Gray, and Harold Underwood Faulkner (Northampton, Mass. 1934–1935), p. 62; Philip S. Foner, *History of the Labor Movement in the United States: From Colonial Times to the Founding of the American Federation of Labor* (New York: International Publishers, 1947), v. 1, p. 110.
23. Roy P. Fairfield, *Sands, Spindles, and Steeples* (Portland, Me.: House of Falmouth, 1956), pp. 47–48; McCauley (1971), pp. 218, 239. (The quotations are from Fairfield (1956), p. 47, but no original sources are specified.) It should be noted that between the strikes of 1836 and the Saco turnout of 1841 was a four-year period with no reported strike activity. These years, 1837 through 1840, were a time of nationwide depression.
24. *New York State Mechanic,* May 18, 1843, in Foner, *Factory Girls,* p. 233; Josephson (1949), pp. 242–243.
25. *Voice of Industry,* November 21, 1845.
26. Kulik et al. (1982), p. 481; Dublin, *Women at Work,* pp. 85, 103–104.
27. Shlakman (1934–1935), pp. 122–123.
28. Antebellum factory operatives may also have drawn inspiration for their protests from other artisanal labor demonstrations they read or heard about. (See Dublin, *Women at Work,* p. 95.) The operatives' strikes of the mid-1830s coincided with a series of strikes by craftsmen in urban centers such as Boston. But the craft strikes usually focused on the ten-hour day, while the factory strikes usually concerned wage cuts. The connection between protest processions and political or religious parades seems to be more direct in many communities.
29. Kenneth F. Mailloux, "The Boston Manufacturing Company of Waltham, Massachusetts, 1813–1848: The First Modern Factory in America" (Ph.D. diss., Boston University, 1957), p. 105; McCauley (1971), pp. 173–174, 216.

30. "Gen. Jackson in Lowell, by Z. E. Stone, Esq., Read November 11, 1875," *Contributions of the Old Residents' Historical Association,* [Lowell], v. 1 (1875), pp. 115, 119; Josephson (1949), p. 61; Robert Dugan, "The Outsiders' View: Visitors to the Industrial Showcase," in *Cotton Was King: A History of Lowell, Massachusetts,* ed by Arthur L. Eno, Jr. (Lowell: Lowell Historical Society, 1976), p. 242.
31. McCauley (1971), pp. 173–174; *New England Offering,* August 1848; Mary Hall diary, July 4, 1834.
32. Letter of Caroline Ford, Middlebury, [Vt.], to her brother, Asa Ford, Jr., Granville, Vermont, August 1, 1841, in David A. Zonderman, "From Mill Village to Industrial City: Letters from Vermont Factory Operatives," *Labor History,* v. 27 (1986), p. 276.
33. Dublin, *Women at Work,* p. 106.
34. Fidelia O. Brown, "Decline and Fall: The End of the Dream," in Eno (1976), p. 150.
35. Howard Gitelman, "The Waltham System and the Coming of the Irish," *Labor History,* v. 8 (1967), pp. 237–238.
36. Gary Kulik, "Pawtucket Village and the Strike of 1824: The Origins of Class Conflict in Rhode Island," *Radical History Review,* v. 17 (1978), p. 19.
37. Caroline F. Ware, *The Early New England Cotton Manufacture: A Study in Industrial Beginnings* (Boston: Houghton Mifflin, 1931), pp. 276–277.
38. Lucy Larcom, "An Idyl of Work" (Boston: Osgood, 1875), pp. 118–119.
39. Robinson, *Loom and Spindle,* p. 206; Josephson (1949), p. 243.
40. Dublin, *Women at Work,* p. 95.
41. Prude (1983), p. 142.
42. Letters of John Williams, Agent, Dover Manufacturing Company, Dover, [N.H.], to William Shimmin, Treasurer, Dover Manufacturing Company, April 5, 6, and 16, 1827, Dover Manufacturing Company Records, New Hampshire Historical Society, Concord.
43. Robinson, *Loom and Spindle,* p. 11; Josephson (1949), p. 229; Letter from Dover, [N.H.], to William Shimmin, May 9, 1827, Dover Manufacturing Company Records.
44. *Pawtucket Chronicle,* April 15, 1829, in Kulik et al. (1982), pp. 492–493.
45. Salisbury Manufacturing Company, Overseers, "To the Public," broadside, (Salisbury, Mass., 1835), MATH; Barbara Tucker, "The Family and Industrial Discipline in Antebellum New England," *Labor History,* v. 21 (1979–1980), p. 70.
46. See Chapter 9 for a further discussion of why some workers felt increasingly that they were being forced by necessity into factory labor. Also, see Chapter 1 for a more detailed examination of the intensification and deterioration of working conditions in the mid-1840s under the speedup and the stretch-out.
47. *Report on the Condition of Women . . . Wage-Earners,* v. 10, part 1, p. 69; Bernice Selden, *The Mill Girls: Lucy Larcom, Harriet Hanson Robinson and Sarah G. Bagley* (New York: Atheneum, 1983), pp. 126–128; Josephson (1949), p. 242. There is some indication that the Lowell strikers of 1842 were the same women who petitioned the Massachusetts legislature in 1843 for relief from the blacklist. See Charles E. Persons, "The Early History of Factory Legislation in Massachusetts," in *Labor Laws and Their Enforcement,* ed. by Susan M. Kingsbury (New York: Longmans, Green, 1911), pp. 45–46.
48. *The Mechanic,* April 2, 1845, in Foner, *Factory Girls,* p. 108; *Voice of Industry,* April 3, 1846, in Foner, *Factory Girls,* p. 101; *Voice of Industry,* June 5, 1845, in Foner, *Factory Girls,* p. 109; *Voice of Industry,* June 12, 1845, in Foner, *Factory Girls,* p. 110.
49. Factory Tracts #1, in Foner, *Factory Girls,* p. 137.
50. Jama Lazerow, "Religion and the New England Mill Girl: A New Perspective on an Old Theme," *New England Quarterly,* v. 60 (1987), p. 433. The ten-hour movement became one of the primary issues for the labor reform associations as a whole. In fact, the peak years of labor organizing—1845 to 1847—parallel the peak years of the ten-hour movement. The fortunes of both of these crusades were intimately linked, and they rose and fell together. The ten-hour movement will be discussed in detail in Chapter 8.
51. *Voice of Industry,* February 27, 1846, in Foner, *Factory Girls,* p. 106.
52. *Voice of Industry,* December 4, 1846.
53. *Voice of Industry,* April 17, 1846, in Foner, *Factory Girls,* pp. 120–121.

54. *Manchester Democrat,* December 16, 1845, in Foner, *Factory Girls,* p. 118.
55. *Voice of Industry,* July 30, 1847, in Foner, *Factory Girls,* pp. 128–129; *Voice of Industry,* September 1, 1847, in Foner, *Factory Girls,* pp. 269–270.
56. Seth Luther, *An Address to the Working Men of New England* (New York: Office of the Workingman's Advocate, 1833), pp. 3, 5; Louis Hartz, "Seth Luther: The Story of a Working-Class Rebel," *New England Quarterly,* v. 13 (1940), p. 418.
57. *Report on the Condition of Women . . . Wage-Earners,* v. 10, part 1, pp. 45–46.
58. *Voice of Industry,* October 2, 1846, in Foner, *Factory Girls,* pp. 122–123; *Voice of Industry,* October 8, 1847, in Foner, *Factory Girls,* p. 205.
59. *Voice of Industry,* June 5, 1845, in Foner, *Factory Girls,* p. 109. The New England Workingmen's Association (N.E.W.A.) was an organization that included factory operatives, skilled artisans, laborers, and middle-class reformers. Their meetings and proceedings covered a broad range of issues—from the ten-hour movement, to land reform, to cooperatives, to utopian socialism. Since the scope and membership of this organization involved much more than factory operatives and the mechanized workplace, a comprehensive examination of the N.E.W.A. lies beyond the scope of this book.
60. Isaac Cohen, "American Management and British Labor: Lancashire Spinners in Industrial New England," *Comparative Studies in Society and History,* v. 27 (1985), p. 616.
61. Strike activity certainly appears to have declined during the peak years of the labor reform associations—1845 to 1847—but strikes did not necessarily disappear entirely. In 1846 and 1847, there was a series of protests against the lighting up of factories in New Hampshire (see Chapter 2). But it is difficult to determine whether these actions were strikes or not. Also in 1847, there was a great deal of agitation in the fall throughout New Hampshire factories to demand enforcement of the state's new ten-hour law. Again, it is not certain whether operatives in particular factories or cities actually developed strike plans and carried them out. (See Chapter 8 for a detailed discussion of these protests and the ten-hour movement.) What can be said with certainty is that leading labor organizations, such as the L.F.L.R.A., usually did not coordinate strikes in the mid-1840s.
62. Workers' responses to wage cuts in the mid-1840s, compared to their reactions earlier, are an excellent example of the changing character of protest. Wage cuts were the leading cause of strikes in the 1820s and 1830s. By the mid-1840s, workers were more likely to publish scathing critiques of such wage reductions than they were to walk off their jobs. They aired their grievances forcefully and publicly, but they were reluctant to confront the corporations directly over this issue. See Chapter 6 for more on these written critiques of wage cuts in the 1840s.
63. Springfield Armory Regulations of 1816, in Brooke Hindle and Stephen Lubar, *Engines of Change: The American Industrial Revolution, 1790–1860* (Washington, D.C.: Smithsonian Institution Press, 1986), p. 233; Springfield Armory Regulations of 1816 and 1834, in Felicia Deyrup, *Arms Makers of the Connecticut Valley: A Regional Study of the Economic Development of the Small Arms Industry, 1798–1870,* in *Smith College Studies in History,* v. 33, ed. by Vera Holmes and Hans Kohn (Northampton, Mass., 1948), pp. 104, 165; Luther, *Address to the Working Men,* p. 36.
64. *Voice of Industry,* May 14, 1847; *Voice of Industry,* July 30, 1847, in Foner, *Factory Girls,* p. 202.
65. *Voice of Industry,* May 7, 1847.
66. *New England Offering,* May 1849; *Factory Girl's Album,* October 10, 1846.
67. Peter J. Coleman, *The Transformation of Rhode Island, 1790–1860* (Providence, R.I.: Brown University Press, 1963), p. 237; Lazerow, "Religion and the New England Mill Girl," p. 442; *Voice of Industry,* January 9, 1846.
68. *Voice of Industry,* January 9, 1846; *Voice of Industry,* February 6, 1846; Ray Boston, *British Chartists in America, 1839–1900* (Manchester, England: Manchester University Press, 1971), p. 47.
69. *Voice of Industry,* October 23, 1846.
70. *Voice of Industry,* May 15, 1846, in Foner, *Factory Girls,* pp. 166–167.
71. John W. Lozier, "Rural Textile Mill Communities and the Transition to Industrialism in America, 1800–1840," *Working Papers from the Regional Economic History Research Center,*

v. 4, no. 4 (1981), ed. by Glenn Porter and William Mulligan, Jr., p. 89; Kulik, "Strike of 1824," pp. 29–30; Prude (1983), p. 96. See Chapters 3 and 4 for extensive discussions of the composition of the factory work force and the social dynamics among workers.

72. *Voice of Industry,* January 8, 1847, in Foner, *Factory Girls,* pp. 328–329.
73. *The Protest,* November 25, 1848.
74. *New England Offering,* July 1848, p. 95; Larcom, "Idyl," p. 99.
75. *New England Offering,* July 1849, pp. 154–157.
76. *Voice of Industry,* April 7, 1848; *Eleventh Annual Report of the Massachusetts Bureau of Statistics of Labor* (Boston: Wright and Potter, State Printers, 1881), p. 6.
77. *Eleventh Annual Report,* pp. 6–9.
78. One intriguing question about antebellum strikers remains, and there is no definite answer to it. Which worker was more likely to strike—an operative who felt he had to work in the factory, or one who thought that his factory work was merely a temporary option? Those who felt tied to their jobs may have been willing to strike, instead of leaving permanently, to protect basic standards at work. Yet these same workers may have also feared that they would lose their jobs if they walked out in protest. These workers may therefore have been the ones who did not leave work and accepted lower wage rates. On the other hand, those who did not feel bound to their factory jobs may have simply chosen to leave rather than strike; or those workers might have been more willing to strike since they had less fear of being fired.

Chapter 8

1. 61st Congress, 2nd session, Senate Document No. 645 (1910), *Report on the Condition of Women and Child Wage-Earners in the United States,* v. 9: Helen L. Sumner, *History of Women in Industry in the United States,* pp. 62–63; *Voice of Industry,* June 26, 1845, in Philip S. Foner, ed., *The Factory Girls* (Urbana: University of Illinois Press, 1977), pp. 218–219. The focus of this section's discussion is not on the precise hours and minutes of labor, but on workers' perceptions of their working hours. Also, some people defined the hours of labor as those spent working at the machines; others measured the workday from start to finish including the brief meal breaks. In this study, wherever possible, the hours of labor are calculated as the time spent actually at work in the factories. See Norman Ware, *The Industrial Worker, 1840–1860* (1924; reprint, Chicago: Quadrangle, 1964), p. 128, for more on differing definitions of the hours of labor.
2. Letter of Joseph Hollingworth, South Leicester, [Mass.], to William Rawcliff, September 24, 1828, in Thomas W. Leavitt, ed., *The Hollingworth Letters: Technical Change in the Textile Industry, 1826–1837* (Cambridge, Mass.: MIT Press, 1969), p. 34. See Chapter 2 for more on "lighting up" factories. *Voice of Industry,* June 19, 1845; and *Voice of Industry,* September 11, 1846, in Foner, *Factory Girls,* pp. 173–174.
3. *Voice of Industry,* March 26, 1847, in Foner, *Factory Girls,* pp. 87–88; James P. Hanlan, *The Working Population of Manchester, New Hampshire, 1840–1886* (Ann Arbor, Mich.: UMI Research Press, 1981), p. 61.
4. *First Annual Report of the Massachusetts Bureau of Statistics of Labor* (Boston: Wright and Potter, State Printers, 1870), p. 295; *Factory Girl's Album,* September 12, 1846, in Foner, *Factory Girls,* p. 221.
5. *Boston Daily Evening Voice,* February 23, 1867, in Foner, *Factory Girls,* p. 343.
6. *Voice of Industry,* December 3, 1847, in Foner, *Factory Girls,* p. 93.
7. Theodore Sande, "Architecture of the Rhode Island Textile Industry, 1790–1860" (Ph.D. diss., University of Pennsylvania, 1972), pp. 216–217; Thomas Dublin, ed., *Farm to Factory: Women's Letters, 1830–1860* (New York: Columbia University Press, 1981), p. 10.
8. "Lowell Factory Girl," in Philip S. Foner, ed., *American Labor Songs of the Nineteenth Century* (Urbana: University of Illinois Press, 1975), p. 43; *Factory Girl's Garland,* May 25, 1844, in Foner, *Labor Songs,* p. 67.
9. *Lowell Offering,* v. 1, July 1841, pp. 111–113; *Lowell Offering,* v. 4, May 1844, p. 147.
10. Mary Feldblum, "The Formation of the First Factory Labor Force in the New England Cotton

Textile Industry, 1800–1848" (Ph.D. diss., New School for Social Research, 1977), p. 86; Seth Luther, *An Address to the Working Men of New England* (New York: Office of the Workingman's Advocate, 1833), p. 20.

11. Hannah Josephson, *The Golden Threads: New England's Mill Girls and Magnates* (New York: Duell, Sloan and Pearce, 1949), p. 231; Gary Kulik, "The Beginnings of the Industrial Revolution in America: Pawtucket, Rhode Island, 1672–1829" (Ph.D. diss., Brown University, 1980), pp. 370–371; Gary Kulik, "Pawtucket Village and the Strike of 1824: The Origins of Class Conflict in Rhode Island," *Radical History Review,* v. 17 (1978), p. 28. Not every factory owner measured the workday with a clock. Some manufacturers ran their establishments from sunrise to sunset each day. The length of each workday therefore varied with the seasons, but it was still the manager who decided when to ring the bell at sunrise and sunset. Time may have been measured less precisely in these factories, but management still defined the workday and held workers accountable to it. David Brody has noted that early nineteenth-century factories were more likely to follow a sunrise-to-sunset schedule, while the larger establishments in the 1830s and 1840s developed more precise measures for the workday. See David Brody, "Time and Work During Early American Industrialism," *Labor History,* v. 30 (1989), pp. 30–39.
12. *Voice of Industry,* March 26, 1847, in Foner, *Factory Girls,* p. 88; *Voice of Industry,* January 8, 1847, in Foner, *Factory Girls,* p. 86.
13. Hanlan (1981), pp. 65–66; *Voice of Industry,* February 27, 1846.
14. Luther, *Address to Working Men,* pp. 18, 21; *Lowell Offering,* v. 5, October 1845, p. 217.
15. Henry A. Miles, *Lowell, As It Was, And As It Is* (Lowell: Powers and Bagley, 1845), p. 107; Letter of Joseph Hollingworth, South Leicester, [Mass.], to William Rawcliff, February 8, 1829, in Leavitt (1969), p. 40; Letter of Joseph Hollingworth, South Leicester, [Mass.], to William Rawcliff, November 7, 1829, in Leavitt (1969), pp. 53–54; Letter of Joseph Hollingworth, South Leicester, [Mass.], to William Rawcliff, May 20, 1828, in Leavitt (1969), pp. 22–23; Barbara M. Tucker, "The Family and Industrial Discipline in Antebellum New England," *Labor History,* v. 21 (1979–80), p. 69.
16. Letters of S. W. Collins, to Collins & Co., Hartford, [Conn.], November 11 and 15, 1830, Collins Company Materials, Canton Historical Society, Collinsville, Connecticut.
17. Terms With Workmen, January 1, 1836, Collins Company Materials, Connecticut Historical Society, Hartford.
18. Judith McGaw, "The Sources and Impact of Mechanization: The Berkshire County, Massachusetts, Paper Industry, 1801–1885, As a Case Study" (Ph.D. diss., New York University, 1977), p. 320; "The Lowell Young Ladies: Early American Cotton Manufacturing, 1833–1854," *The History Reference Bulletin,* no. 16, sec. 1, February 1934, pp. 85–86.
19. *Voice of Industry,* September 10, 1847.
20. *Second Annual Report of the Massachusetts Bureau of Statistics of Labor,* 1871, in Edith Abbott, "A Study of the Early History of Child Labor in America," *American Journal of Sociology,* v. 14 (1908), p. 33; *Proceedings of the New England Association of Farmers, Mechanics, and other Working Men* (December, 1831), p. 7; Harriet H. Robinson, "Early Factory Labor," in *Fourteenth Annual Report of the Massachusetts Bureau of Statistics of Labor* (Boston: Wright and Potter, State Printers, 1883), p. 382; Luther, *Address to Working Men,* p. 37; *Report on the Condition of Women . . . Wage-Earners,* v. 6: Elizabeth L. Otey, *The Beginnings of Child Labor Legislation in Certain States; A Comparative Study,* p. 78; Caroline Ware, *The Early New England Cotton Manufacture: A Study in Industrial Beginnings* (Boston: Houghton Mifflin, 1931), p. 289. In 1847, New Hampshire also passed a law that required written permission from parents to employ children under the age of fifteen for more than ten hours a day. As did other New Hampshire ten-hour laws, this piece of legislation had large loopholes. This law did not prohibit children from working more than ten hours a day; it merely required their parents' permission. Many poor families, dependent on every penny their children could bring into the household budget, would probably have yielded to pressure from manufacturers and signed whatever was necessary for their children to work as long as possible.
21. Thomas Dublin, *Women at Work: The Transformation of Work and Community in Lowell, Massachusetts, 1826–1860* (New York: Columbia University Press, 1979), p. 113; *Factory Girl's Album,* February 14, 1846, and April 11, 1846. The campaign for the ten-hour day prob-

ably drew on memories of past labor agitation—strike processions and proclamations, for example—as inspiration for its own political petitions and rallies. The strike was not, however, the basic tool of this protest movement in the 1840s.

22. House Unpassed Papers, 1215/3 (1843), Massachusetts State Archives, Boston.
23. Jama Lazerow, "Religion and the New England Mill Girl: A New Perspective on an Old Theme," *New England Quarterly*, v. 60 (1987), p. 449.
24. *Voice of Industry*, February 12, 1847, in Foner, *Factory Girls*, p. 196; *Voice of Industry*, April 30, 1847.
25. *Factory Girl's Album*, April 11, 1846; *Voice of Industry*, April 30, 1847.
26. *Factory Girl's Album*, September 12, 1846, in Foner, *Factory Girls*, p. 222; J.Q.A. Thayer, *Review of the Report of the Special Committee of the Legislature of the Commonwealth of Massachusetts on the Petition Relating to the Hours of Labor* (Boston: J. N. Bang, 1845), pp. 30–31.
27. House Unpassed Papers, 1587/8 (1845), Massachusetts State Archives; Charles E. Persons, "The Early History of Factory Legislation in Massachusetts," in *Labor Laws and Their Enforcement*, ed. by Susan M. Kingsbury (New York: Longmans, Green, 1911), p. 44.
28. House Unpassed Papers, 1587 (1845), Massachusetts State Archives.
29. House Unpassed Papers, 1587/10 (1845), Massachusetts State Archives.
30. Philip S. Foner, *History of the Labor Movement in the United States: From Colonial Times to the Founding of the American Federation of Labor* (New York: International Publishers, 1947), v. 1, pp. 201–202.
31. *Voice of Industry*, December 19, 1845, in Foner, *Factory Girls*, p. 254.
32. Senate Unpassed Papers, 11983 (1846), Massachusetts State Archives; Persons (1911), p. 45.
33. *Report on the Condition of Women . . . Wage Earners*, v. 9, p. 70; *Voice of Industry*, May 7, 1847, in Foner, *Factory Girls*, pp. 88–89; Hanlan (1981), p. 68.
34. *Voice of Industry*, May 28, 1847; *Voice of Industry*, January 8, 1847, in Foner, *Factory Girls*, p. 90.
35. John R. Commons et al., *History of Labour in the United States* (New York: Macmillan, 1918), v. 1, pp. 541–542; *New Hampshire Acts*, v. 39, p. 155 (manuscript in New Hampshire State Archives, Concord, N.H.); Regulations, 1848, Nashua [N.H.] Manufacturing Company Records, Baker Library, Harvard University Graduate School of Business Administration, Boston, Massachusetts.
36. *Manchester Democrat*, September 1, 1847, in Foner, *Factory Girls*, pp. 263–266.
37. *Manchester Democrat*, August 25, 1847, in Foner, *Factory Girls*, pp. 266–269; *Manchester Democrat*, September 1, 1847, in Foner, *Factory Girls*, pp. 269–270.
38. *Voice of Industry*, September 17, 1847, in Foner, *Factory Girls*, p. 270; *Voice of Industry*, September 3, 1847, and September 10, 1847. When a similar ten-hour law went into effect in Maine during the spring of 1849, the manufacturers there also had workers sign contracts for longer working days. See E. Stagg Whitin, *Factory Legislation in Maine*, in *Studies in History, Economics and Public Law*, v. 33, no. 1 (New York: Columbia University, 1908), p. 38.
39. *Voice of Industry*, January 23, 1846, in Foner, *Factory Girls*, p. 113.
40. Dublin, *Women at Work*, p. 112.
41. Massachusetts Legislative Documents, House No. 48, February 1844. The one problem with aiming the law at legally chartered corporations was that it left open the question of how to deal with unincorporated companies, which seemed to be less liable to legislative regulation.
42. Dane Yorke, *The Men and Times of Pepperill* (Boston: Pepperill Manufacturing Company, 1945), pp. 17, 19; *Lowell Offering*, v. 4, July 1844, p. 199. The rhetorical link between factories and schools was discussed further in Chapter 5.
43. Massachusetts Legislative Documents, House No. 50, March 12, 1845, p. 5; *Olive Leaf and Factory Girl's Repository*, April 25, 1843, in Foner, *Factory Girls*, p. 50; *Olive Leaf*, September 16, 1843, in Foner, *Factory Girls*, p. 51.
44. Letter of Ann Appleton, in "Sister Ann" (a copy of the letters edited by Priscilla Ordway in 1953), p. 18. Manuscript is at the Manchester Historic Association, Manchester, New Hampshire. Lucy Larcom, *A New England Girlhood* (1889; reprint, Gloucester, Mass.: Peter Smith, 1973), pp. 199–200.

45. Report of James Dalliba, October 1819, "Communicated to the House of Representatives by the Committee on Military Affairs, March 23, 1823," 17th Congress, 2nd session, no. 246, in Walter Lowrie and William Franklin, eds., *American State Papers. Class V. Military Affairs* (Washington, D.C.: Gales and Seaton, 1834), v. 2, p. 543; Letter of G. Talcott, Springfield Armory, to John Bell, Secretary of War, August 6, 1841, in Steven V. Benét, comp., *A Collection of Annual Reports and Other Important Papers Relating to the Ordnance Department* (Washington, D.C.: Government Printing Office, 1878), v. 1, p. 395; "Report of the Board Convened at Springfield, Mass., August 30, 1841, to Examine into the Conditions and Management of Springfield Armory," [Exec. Docs., House of Representatives, 27th Congress, 2nd session v. 4, Doc. No. 207] in Benét (1878), v. 1, pp. 401 and 404.
46. Notice written by Samuel Collins, July 28, 1832, Canton Historical Museum; Samuel Collins, "Early History of Collins Co.," (1866: typed copy at the Canton Historical Museum), p. 23.
47. N. B. Gordon, work diary, March 24, 1829, May 26, 1830, et passim, in Gary Kulik, Roger Park, and Theodore Penn, eds., *The New England Mill Village, 1790–1860,* in *Documents in American Industrial History,* v. 2, ed. Michael Folsom (Cambridge, Mass.: MIT Press, 1982), pp. 286–287, 288, 293, 296, 298–299. In some textile mills, carders and dressers were allowed to come in late and leave early when their departments were running ahead of schedule. Not every employee was required to work every hour that the mill was in operation, but most were told to do so.
48. Letter of Rebecca Ford, Middlebury, [Vt.], to Sally K. Ford, Granville, Vermont, August 6, 1839, in David A. Zonderman, "From Mill Village to Industrial City: Letters from Vermont Factory Operatives," *Labor History,* v. 27 (1986), p. 273; Letter of Rebecca Ford, Middlebury, [Vt.], to Asa Ford, Jr., Granville, Vermont, April 24, 1843, in Zonderman (1986), p. 277.
49. Zonderman (1986), p. 268. See Chapter 9 for more on the comparison between industrial and agricultural labor.
50. Letter of a Waltham, [Mass.], operative, in Harriet Farley, *Operatives' Reply to the Hon. Jere Clemens . . .* (Lowell, Mass.: S. J. Varney, 1850), pp. 11–13; Larcom, *Girlhood,* pp. 188–189; Josephson (1949), p. 258; Elfrieda McCauley, "The New England Mill Girls: Feminine Influence in the Development of Public Libraries in New England, 1820–1860" (Ph.D. diss., Columbia University, 1971), pp. 42–43; Feldblum (1977), p. 139.
51. Letter of Mary Metcalf, Lowell, [Mass.], to her mother, January 28, 1848, Adams-Metcalf Papers, MATH.
52. Massachusetts House Document, No. 50 (1845), p. 3.
53. *Lowell Offering,* v. 3, May 1843, pp. 191–192.
54. *Lowell Offering,* v. 3, May 1843, p. 192; *Lowell Offering,* v. 5, April 1845, p. 96.
55. *New England Offering,* April 1848, p. 3; *New England Offering,* May 1848; C. Ware (1931), p. 280. See Chapter 9 for further discussion of how operatives felt about temporary versus permanent factory labor.
56. *Factory Girl's Album,* February 28, 1846.

Chapter 9

1. Felicia Deyrup, *Arms Makers of the Connecticut Valley: A Regional Study of the Economic Development of the Small Arms Industry, 1798–1870,* in *Smith College Studies in History,* v. 33, ed. by Vera Holmes and Hans Kohn (Northampton, Mass., 1948), pp. 163, 170; Notice written by Samuel Collins, July 28, 1832, Canton Historical Museum, Collinsville, Connecticut; Judith McGaw, "The Sources and Impact of Mechanization: The Berkshire County, Massachusetts, Paper Industry, 1801–1885, As a Case Study" (Ph.D. diss., New York University, 1977), p. 325.
2. Caroline F. Ware, *The Early New England Cotton Manufacture: A Study in Industrial Beginnings* (Boston: Houghton Mifflin, 1931), p. 213; Agreement between Rufus Bennet and Venner S. Kimball for John Slater, February 5, 1838, State Library—Archives, Hartford, Connecticut; Barbara Tucker, *Samuel Slater and the Origins of the American Textile Industry, 1790–1860* (Ithaca, N.Y.: Cornell University Press, 1984), pp. 235–236.

3. Theodore F. Marburg, "Aspects of Labor Administration in the Early Nineteenth Century," *Bulletin of the Business Historical Society,* v. 15 (1941), p. 8; Memorandum Book, v. 2, July 22, 1824, Pomfret Manufacturing Company, in Gary Kulik, Roger Parks, and Theodore Penn, eds., *The New England Mill Village, 1790–1860,* in *Documents in American Industrial History,* v. 2, ed. Michael Folsom (Cambridge, Mass.: MIT Press, 1982), p. 458. Some factories, even when they did not combine agricultural and industrial labor, may have run on an erratic schedule due to problems with machinery or water supplies. The combination of bursts of activity and frequent respites resembled a traditional agricultural cycle.
4. Thomas Dublin, ed., *Farm to Factory: Women's Letters, 1830–1860* (New York: Columbia University Press, 1981), p. 30; Seth Luther, *An Address to the Working Men of New England* (New York: Office of the Workingman's Advocate, 1833), p. 37; Mary Feldblum, "The Formation of the First Factory Labor Force in the New England Cotton Textile Industry, 1800–1848" (Ph.D. diss., New School for Social Research, 1977), p. 143.
5. Letter of Joseph Hollingworth, Muddy-Brook-Pond Factory, Woodstock, Connecticut, to William Rawcliff, Wadsworth's Factory, Poughkeepsie, New York, November 8, 1830, in Thomas W. Leavitt, ed., *The Hollingworth Letters: Technical Change in the Textile Industry, 1826–1837* (Cambridge, Mass.: MIT Press, 1969), p. 93.
6. *Voice of Industry,* December 3, 1847, in Philip S. Foner, ed., *The Factory Girls* (Urbana: University of Illinois Press, 1977), p. 92; *Voice of Industry,* September 25, 1846, in Foner, *Factory Girls,* p. 189.
7. Letter of H. E. Back, Lowell, [Mass.], to Harriet Hanson, Wentworth, New Hampshire, September 7, 1846, in Foner, *Factory Girls,* p. 335.
8. Abigail Mussey, *Life Sketches and Experiences* (Cambridge, Mass.: Dakin and Metcalf, 1866), pp. 14–15.
9. Letter of Sally Rice, Masonville, [Conn.], to her father, February 23, 1845, in Kulik et al. (1982), p. 390.
10. Feldblum (1977), pp. 135–136. The issue of reforming the factory will be discussed in more detail later in this chapter.
11. Letter of Marie Currier, Wentworth, [N.H.], to Harriet Hanson, October 12, 1845, in Allis Wolfe, ed., "Letters of a Lowell Mill Girl and Friends: 1845–1846," *Labor History,* v. 17 (1976), p. 98.
12. Harriet Farley, autobiographical sketch, in Sarah J. Hale, *Woman's Record* (New York: Harper and Brothers, 1855), pp. 657–658; *Lowell Offering,* v. 3, May 1843, p. 191.
13. Harriet Farley, *Operatives' Reply to the Hon. Jere Clemens* . . . (Lowell: S. J. Varney, 1850), pp. 3–4. Some stories in the *Lowell Offering* contain a curious combination of love of factory, nature, and home. These authors remained attached to their family homestead, but not to the hardships of agricultural labor. They also yearned for the beauty of the rural countryside, yet they often said that the factory remained in harmony with nature. See Thomas Bender, *Toward an Urban Vision: Ideas and Institutions in Nineteenth-Century America* (1975; reprint, Baltimore, Md.: Johns Hopkins University Press, 1982), p. 92.
14. *Lowell Offering,* v. 1, July 1841, p. 113.
15. Lucy Larcom, *A New England Girlhood* (1889; reprint, Gloucester, Mass.: Peter Smith, 1973), pp. 199–200.
16. Dublin, *Farm to Factory,* p. 36.
17. Harriet Farley, autobiographical sketch, in Hale (1855), pp. 657–658.
18. *Lowell Offering,* December 1840, p. 18 (there is no volume number for this issue); *Lowell Offering,* v. 1, May 1841, pp. 50–51.
19. Harriet H. Robinson, *Loom and Spindle; or, Life Among the Early Mill Girls* (New York: Thomas Y. Crowell, 1898), p. 30; Harriet H. Robinson, "Early Factory Labor in New England," in *Fourteenth Annual Report of the Massachusetts Bureau of Statistics of Labor* (Boston: Wright and Potter, State Printers, 1883), pp. 380–381, 386–387.
20. Harriet H. Robinson, "The Life of the Early Mill-Girls," *Journal of Social Science,* v. 16 (1882), p. 133. Robinson knew first-hand about women's working for their brothers' education. She worked in the mills while her older brother, John, finished grammar school and two years of high school. But Robinson's work history also had an interesting twist to it. Her

brother, after completing part of his high school education, then went to work so that Harriet could attend school for a while. See Claudia L. Bushman, *"A Good Poor Man's Wife," Being a Chronicle of Harriet Hanson Robinson and Her Family in Nineteenth-Century New England* (Hanover, N.H.: University Press of New England, 1981), p. 36.

21. Letter of Martha Russell, Andover, [Mass.], to her father, Benjamin Russell, Newry, Maine, January 19, 1839, Mehitable Abbott Russell Papers, Andover Historical Society, Andover, Massachusetts; Thomas Dublin, *Women at Work: The Transformation of Work and Community in Lowell, Massachusetts, 1826–1860* (New York: Columbia University Press, 1979), p. 39.
22. Letter of a Waltham, [Mass.], operative, in Farley, *Operatives' Reply,* pp. 11–13.
23. *Lowell Offering,* v. 1, April 1841, p. 32; *Lowell Offering,* v. 1, May 1841, p. 50.
24. Larcom, *Girlhood,* pp. 199–200; *Operatives' Magazine,* July 1841, p. 64.
25. Larcom, *Girlhood,* p. 196.
26. Letter from North Adams, [Mass.], March 9, 1850, in Farley, *Operatives' Reply,* p. 25; Robinson, "Early Factory Labor," p. 380.
27. *Lowell Offering,* v. 4, July 1844, p. 200; *Lowell Offering,* v. 5, December 1845, p. 279.
28. Lucy Larcom, "Among Lowell Mill-Girls: A Reminiscence," *Atlantic Monthly,* v. 48 (1881), p. 609; Robinson, *Loom and Spindle,* pp. 177–178.
29. *Maine Farmer,* May 27, 1843, in Richard P. Horwitz, *Anthropology Toward History: Work and Culture in a 19th-Century Maine Town* (Middletown, Conn.: Wesleyan University Press, 1978), p. 85.
30. David Jeremy, *Transatlantic Industrial Revolution: The Diffusion of Textile Technologies Between Britain and America, 1790–1830s* (Cambridge, Mass.: MIT Press, 1981), p. 201; George S. Gibbs, *The Whitesmiths of Taunton: A History of Reed and Barton, 1824–1943* (Cambridge, Mass.: Harvard University Press, 1943), p. 140; Jonathan Prude, *The Coming of Industrial Order: Town and Factory Life in Rural Massachusetts, 1810–1860* (Cambridge, England: Cambridge University Press, 1983), p. 148.
31. Elfrieda McCauley, "The New England Mill Girls: Feminine Influence in the Development of Public Libraries in New England, 1820–1860" (Ph.D. diss., Columbia University, 1971), p. 207; *The Davis and Furber Machine Company and the Men Who Made It* (Davis and Furber Machine Company, 1908), n.p.; Bruce Clouette and Matthew Roth, *Bristol, Connecticut: A Bicentennial History, 1785–1985* (Bristol: Bristol Public Library, 1984), p. 69. This discussion of mobility is linked with workers' anticipations of the future, which will be analyzed in a later section of this chapter. This paragraph focuses on basic occupational and physical mobility.
32. *Lowell Offering,* v. 1, August 1841, p. 170.
33. Farley, *Operatives' Reply,* p. 17.
34. *Voice of Industry,* September 18, 1845, in Foner, *Factory Girls,* p. 160.
35. Ibid., pp. 160–161.
36. *Voice of Industry,* February 27, 1846, in Foner, *Factory Girls,* p. 105.
37. *Gleaner,* October 11, 1845, in James P. Hanlan, *The Working Population of Manchester, New Hampshire, 1840–1886* (Ann Arbor, Mich.: UMI Research Press, 1981), p. 63.
38. J.Q.A. Thayer, *Review of the Report of the Special Committee of the Legislature of the Commonwealth of Massachusetts on the Petition Relating to Hours of Labor* (Boston: J. N. Bang, 1845), pp. 21, 25.
39. *Lowell Advertiser,* July 26, 1845, in Foner, *Factory Girls,* p. 67.
40. *Voice of Industry,* September 4, 1846. When workers launched such criticisms of the factory system, they also often proposed reforms to alleviate these problems. These reform schemes will be discussed further in the next section of this chapter.
41. Gary Kulik, "The Beginnings of the Industrial Revolution in America: Pawtucket, Rhode Island, 1672–1829" (Ph.D. diss., Brown University, 1980), p. 354.
42. Letter of Jabez Hollingworth, South Leicester, [Mass.], to William Rawcliff, March 13, 1830, in Leavitt (1969), p. 66; Prude (1983), pp. 146–147.
43. Theodore Marburg, "Management Problems and Procedures of a Manufacturing Enterprise, 1802–1852; A Case Study of the Origin of the Scovill Manufacturing Company" (Ph.D. diss., Clark University, 1945), p. 316; McGaw (1977), pp. 333, 347, 348.

44. Thomas R. Navin, *The Whitin Machine Works Since 1831: A Textile Machinery Company in an Industrial Village* (Cambridge, Mass.: Harvard University Press, 1950), p. 4; George S. Gibbs, *The Saco-Lowell Shops: Textile Machinery Building in New England, 1813–1949* (Cambridge, Mass.: Harvard University Press, 1950), p. 53.
45. C. Ware (1931), p. 226; Henry A. Miles, *Lowell, As It Was, And As It Is* (Lowell, Mass.: Powers and Bagley, 1845), p. 109.
46. Prude (1983), p. 151; Letter of Sally White, Fitchburg, [Mass.], to Samuel Plant, September 1, 1816, (doc. 107), Poignand and Plant Papers, Town Library, Lancaster, Massachusetts.
47. Zachariah Allen, diary, October 1–2, 1823, Zachariah Allen Papers, Library, Rhode Island Historical Society, Providence.
48. Letter of George Hollingworth, South Leicester, [Mass.], to William Rawcliff, October 21, 1829, in Leavitt (1969), p. 48; Letter of Joseph Hollingworth, South Leicester, [Mass.], to William Rawcliff, November 7, 1829, in Leavitt (1969), pp. 53–54.
49. Letter of Jabez Hollingworth, South Leicester, [Mass.], to William Rawcliff, March 13, 1830, in Leavitt (1969), p. 65.
50. Letter of W. Patton, September 12, 1831, in Marburg, "Management Problems and Procedures," pp. 313–314; Deyrup (1948), pp. 102–103; Derwent S. Whittlesey, "The Springfield Armory: A Study in Institutional Development" (Ph.D. diss., University of Chicago, 1920), n.p.
51. Letter of P. T. Jackson, Boston, [Mass.], to Messrs. Poignand Plant & Co., Lancaster, [Mass.], June 3, 1820, (doc. 170), Poignand and Plant Papers; Letter of Samuel Collins, to Messrs. Collins & Co., September 10, 1830, Collins Company Materials, Connecticut Historical Society, Hartford; *New England Offering,* July 1849, p. 154.
52. Prude (1983), p. 93; Feldblum (1977), pp. 133, 149.
53. *Lowell Offering,* v. 4, August 1844, p. 237.
54. Hannah Josephson, *The Golden Threads: New England's Mill Girls and Magnates* (New York: Duell, Sloan and Pearce, 1949), pp. 225, 227.
55. *Voice of Industry,* March 12, 1846.
56. *Voice of Industry,* February 6, 1846.
57. *Voice of Industry,* July 9, 1845, in Philip S. Foner, ed., *American Labor Songs of the Nineteenth Century* (Urbana: University of Illinois Press, 1975), p. 60.
58. *Manchester Democrat,* September 1, 1847, in Foner, *Factory Girls,* p. 269.
59. *Voice of Industry,* May 7, 1847, in Foner, *Factory Girls,* p. 89.
60. Letter of a worker, to N. P. Ames, February 2, 1841, in Vera Shlakman, *Economic History of a Factory Town: A Study of Chicopee, Massachusetts,* in *Smith College Studies in History,* v. 20, ed. by John C. Hildt, William Dodge Gray, and Harold Underwood Faulkner (Northampton, Mass.: 1934–1935), p. 95; Letter of Sally M. Cornell, Slatersville, [R.I.], to her mother, Lucretia Cornell, December 18, 1825, in [Catherine Williams], *Fall River An Authentic Narrative* (Boston: Lilly, Wait and Co., 1834), pp. 125–126.
61. Larcom, *Girlhood,* pp. 228–229, 236.
62. Letter of a Waltham, [Mass.], operative in Farley, *Operatives' Reply,* pp. 11–13; Robinson, "Early Factory Labor," p. 387.
63. Larcom, *Girlhood,* p. 223; Lucy Larcom, "American Factory Life—Past, Present, and Future," *Journal of Social Science,* v. 16 (1882), p. 144.
64. Letter of George Hollingworth, South Leicester, [Mass.], to William Rawcliff, October 1, 1829, in Leavitt (1969), p. 49.
65. Letter of George Hollingworth, South Leicester, [Mass.], to William Rawcliff, January 17, 1830, in Leavitt (1969), pp. 57–58; Letter of George Hollingworth, South Leicester, [Mass.], to William Rawcliff, January 24, 1830, in Leavitt (1969), pp. 60–61.
66. Letter of Joseph Hollingworth, Muddy-Brook-Pond Factory, Woodstock, Connecticut, to William Rawcliff, November 8, 1830, in Leavitt (1969), p. 93; Letter of Joseph Hollingworth, Muddy-Brook-Pond Factory, Woodstock, Connecticut, to William Rawcliff, July 17, 1831, in Leavitt (1969), pp. 98—99.
67. Thayer (1845), p. 17; Factory Tracts #1, in Foner, *Factory Girls,* p. 134.
68. Hanlan (1981), p. 97.

69. Prude (1983), p. 234.
70. *Voice of Industry,* May 15, 1846, in Foner, *Factory Girls,* p. 166.
71. Jama Lazerow, "Religion and the New England Mill Girl: A New Perspective on an Old Theme," *New England Quarterly,* v. 60 (1987), p. 453.
72. *Voice of Industry,* May 28, 1847; Prude (1983), p. 138.
73. Letter of John Hollingworth, South Leicester, [Mass.], to William Rawcliff, April 1, 1827, in Leavitt (1969), pp. 5–6.
74. Robinson, *Loom and Spindle,* p. 81; Norman Ware, *The Industrial Worker, 1840–1860* (1924; reprint, Chicago: Quadrangle, 1964), pp. 172–173.
75. Foner, *Factory Girls,* p. 59.
76. *Lowell Offering,* v. 4, June 1844, pp. 170–171; *Lowell Offering,* v. 5, November 1845, p. 263.
77. *Lowell Offering,* v. 3, June 1843, pp. 214–215.
78. *Lowell Offering,* v. 5, May 1845, p. 99; *Lowell Offering,* v. 5, October 1845, pp. 217–218.
79. Letter of Julia Dutton, to her mother, Lucretia Dutton, Winooski, Vermont, August 29, 1847, Lucretia W. Dutton Papers, Bailey/Howe Library, University of Vermont, Burlington; *Lowell Offering,* v. 4, September 1844, p. 258.

Bibliography

Primary Sources—Unpublished

Adams-Metcalf Papers. Museum of American Textile History (MATH), North Andover, Massachusetts.

Allen, Zachariah. Papers, Diary, 1821–1824. Library, Rhode Island Historical Society, Providence, Rhode Island.

Amoskeag Manufacturing Company. Papers, Letter Books, vols. 1 and 2, 1826–1838, 1848. Manchester Historic Association, Manchester, New Hampshire.

———. Papers and excerpts from the John Rogers Papers at the New-York Historical Society, 1850. MATH.

Bennett, Rufus. Agreements, 1838. State Library—Archives, Hartford, Connecticut.

Cheney Family Papers. Connecticut Historical Society, Hartford, Connecticut.

Cocheco Manufacturing Company. Materials, reminiscences of employees in the mills, 1820s–1840s. Old Berwick Historical Society, South Berwick, Maine.

Collins Company. Materials. Canton Historical Museum, Collinsville, Connecticut.

———. Materials. Connecticut Historical Society, Hartford, Connecticut.

Colt Company. Papers. State Library—Archives, Hartford, Connecticut.

Cowles, Mary. Letter, 1847. MATH.

Dover Manufacturing Company. Letter Books, 1825–1828. New Hampshire Historical Society, Concord, New Hampshire.

Dutton, Lucretia W. Papers. Bailey/Howe Library, University of Vermont, Burlington, Vermont.

Essex Company. Correspondence. MATH.

Forbes, Susan. Diary, 1843. American Antiquarian Society, Worcester, Massachusetts.

Gray, John and Co. Papers. State Library—Archives, Hartford, Connecticut.

Greene Manufacturing Company. Contract Books, 1814–1831, 1833–1844. Library, Rhode Island Historical Society, Providence, Rhode Island.

Grout Family Papers. Russell Vermontiana Collection. Martha Canfield Memorial Free Library, Arlington, Vermont.

Haines, John. Diaries, 1845–1850. MATH.

Hall, Mary. Diary, 1821–1836. New Hampshire Historical Society, Concord, New Hampshire.

Hey, Moses. Papers, microfilm of originals in Pennsylvania Historical Society. MATH.

Holt, Ephrain, Mrs. Reminiscences. Peterborough Historical Society, Peterborough, New Hampshire. Copy may be found at New Hampshire Historical Society.

Jewett, Aaron. Letters, 1840–1841. MATH.

Kellogg and Company. Day Book, 1849–1860s. Stowe-Day Library, Hartford, Connecticut.

Lonsdale Company. Letter Books, v. 3, 1843. Library, Rhode Island Historical Society, Providence, Rhode Island.

Markham Collection. Sheldon Museum, Middlebury, Vermont.

Massachusetts State Archives. House Unpassed Papers, Senate Unpassed Papers. Boston, Massachusetts.

Merino/Dudley Wool Companies. Records. Research Library, Old Sturbridge Village, Sturbridge, Massachusetts.

Mowry Family. Papers. Library, Rhode Island Historical Society, Providence, Rhode Island.

Nashua Manufacturing Company. Records, Regulation Papers, 1837, 1848. Baker Library, Graduate School of Business Administration, Harvard University, Boston, Massachusetts.

New Hampshire Acts, v. 39. New Hampshire State Archives, Concord, New Hampshire.

Plymouth Cordage Company. Letter Books. Baker Library, Graduate School of Business Administration, Harvard University, Boston, Massachusetts.

Poignand and Plant Company. Papers. Town Library, Lancaster, Massachusetts.

Robinson, Harriet Hanson. Papers. Arthur and Elizabeth Schlesinger Library on the History of Women in America, Radcliffe College, Cambridge, Massachusetts.

Russell, Mehitable Abbott. Papers. Andover Historical Society, Andover, Massachusetts.

"Sister Ann." Letters by Ann Swett Appleton, 1847–1850. Edited by Priscilla Ordway, 1953. Copy at the Manchester Historic Association, Manchester, New Hampshire.

Slater, Nelson. Collection. Slater Mill Historic Site, Pawtucket, Rhode Island.

Slater Company. Records. Historical Manuscripts and Archives, University of Connecticut Library, Storrs, Connecticut.

Stearns, Daniel B. Diaries, 1841, 1848, 1849. New Hampshire Historical Society, Concord, New Hampshire.

Stevens Company. Records. MATH.

Ware Manufacturing Company. Records. MATH.

Whitney, Eli. Papers. Manuscripts and Archives, Yale University Library, New Haven, Connecticut.

Wilbur, Benjamin. "Life of Benjamin Wilbur." n.d. Fall River Historical Society, Fall River, Massachusetts.

Wilson, John. Letters, 1849. MATH.

Primary Sources—Government Documents

American State Papers. Class V. Military Affairs, 2 vols. (1819–1825). Ed. Walter Lowrie and Walter Franklin. Washington, D.C.: Gales and Seaton, 1834.

Annual Reports of the Massachusetts Bureau of Statistics of Labor. Boston: Wright and Potter, State Printers. V. 1, 1870; V. 3, 1872; V. 4, 1873; V. 11, 1881.

Documents Relative to the Manufactures in the United States. 1833; reprint, New York: Burt Franklin, 1969.

Massachusetts Legislative Documents. House No. 48, February 1844; House No. 50, March 12, 1845; House No. 153, April 1850.

Report of the Commissioner of Industrial Statistics. Rhode Island, 1889.

Sixty-first Congress, 2nd session, Senate Document No. 645, (1910). *Report on the Condition of Women and Child Wage-Earners in the U.S.* Vol. 6, *The Beginnings of Child Labor Legislation in Certain States; A Comparative Study,* Elizabeth L. Otey. Vol. 9, *History of Women in Industry in the United States,* Helen L. Sumner. Vol. 10, part 1, *History of Women in Trade Unions, 1825 Through the Knights of Labor,* John B. Andrews.

Primary Sources—Newspapers and Magazines

Factory Girl. Newmarket and Exeter, New Hampshire, 1841–1843.

Factory Girl's Album. Exeter, New Hampshire, 1846–1847.

Factory Girl's Garland. Exeter, New Hampshire, 1844–1846.
Lowell Offering. Lowell, Massachusetts, 1840–1845.
Manchester Operative. Manchester, New Hampshire, 1843–1845.
New Era of Industry. Lowell, Massachusetts, 1848.
New England Offering. Lowell, Massachusetts, 1848–1850.
Olive Leaf and Factory Girl's Repository. Cabotville, Massachusetts, 1843.
Operatives' Magazine. Lowell, Massachusetts, 1841–1842.
The Protest. Lowell, Massachusetts, 1848.
Voice of Industry. Boston, Fitchburg, and Lowell, Massachusetts, 1845–1848.
Wampanoag and Operatives' Journal. Fall River, Massachusetts, 1842.
Zion's Herald. The issues of October 5, 12, and 19, 1836.

Primary Sources—Broadsides

General Regulations, To Be Observed By Persons Employed By The Lawrence Manufacturing Company, In Lowell. 1833. Museum of American Textile History (MATH), North Andover, Massachusetts.

Regulations To Be Observed by all persons in the employment of the Amoskeag Manufacturing Company, at their New Mills in Manchester. 1840s. Found in the Daniel Stearns diary. New Hampshire Historical Society, Concord, New Hampshire.

Rules and Regulations To Be Observed By All Persons Employed in the Factory of Amasa Whitney. July 5, 1830. Winchendon, Massachusetts. Research Library, Old Sturbridge Village, Sturbridge, Massachusetts.

Salisbury Manufacturing Company, Overseers. *To The Public.* 1835. Salisbury, Massachusetts. MATH.

Primary Sources—Published

Allison, Robert. "The Old and the New." *Transactions of the American Society of Mechanical Engineers,* v. 16 (1895).

Butler, Benjamin F. *Butler's Book.* Boston: A. M. Thayer and Co., 1892.

[Cate, Eliza Jane]. "Lights and Shadows of Factory Life in New England." *The New World.* February 23, 1843.

Contributions of the Old Residents' Historical Association, 6 vols. Lowell, Massachusetts, 1874–1900.

The Correct, Full and Impartial Report of the Trial of Rev. Ephraim K. Avery, Before the Supreme Judicial Court of the State of Rhode Island, at Newport, May 6, 1833, for the Murder of Sarah M. Cornell. Providence: Marshall and Brown, 1833.

Drury, Luke. *A Report of the Examination of Rev. Ephraim K. Avery, Charged With the Murder of Sarah Maria Cornell.* 1833.

Farley, Harriet. *Operatives' Reply to the Hon. Jere Clemens . . .* Lowell, Massachusetts: S. J. Varney, 1850.

Hale, Sarah J. *Woman's Record.* New York: Harper and Brothers, 1855.

Hand-Book for the Visiter to Lowell. Lowell, Massachusetts: A. Watson, 1848.

[Knapp, Jacob]. *Autobiography of Elder Jacob Knapp.* New York: Sheldon and Co., 1868.

Larcom, Lucy. "American Factory Life—Past, Present, and Future." *Journal of Social Science,* v. 16 (1882).

———. "Among Lowell Mill-Girls: A Reminiscence." *Atlantic Monthly,* v. 46 (1881).

———. "An Idyl of Work." Boston: Osgood, 1875.

———. *A New England Girlhood.* 1889; reprint, Gloucester, Massachusetts: Peter Smith, 1973.

Luther, Seth. *An Address on the Right of Free Suffrage.* Providence: S. R. Weeden, 1833.

———. *An Address to the Working Men of New England.* New York: Office of the Workingman's Advocate, 1833.

Miles, Henry A. *Lowell, As It Was, And As It Is.* Lowell, Massachusetts: Powers and Bagley, 1845.

Montgomery, James. *A Practical Detail of the Cotton Manufacture of the United States of America . . . Contrasted and Compared with that of Great Britain.* 1840; reprint, New York: Johnson Reprint Corp., 1968.

Munger, Hiram. *The Life and Religious Experience of Hiram Munger.* Boston: Advent Christian Publication Society, 1881.

Mussey, Abigail. *Life Sketches and Experiences.* Cambridge, Massachusetts: Dakin and Metcalf, 1866.

Proceedings in the City of Lowell at the Semi-Centennial Celebration of the Incorporation of the Town of Lowell, March 1st, 1876. Lowell, Massachusetts: Penhollow Printing, 1876.

Proceedings of the New England Association of Farmers, Mechanics, and other Working Men. 1831.

Robinson, Harriet Hanson. "Early Factory Labor in New England." *Fourteenth Annual Report of the Massachusetts Bureau of Statistics of Labor.* Boston: Wright and Potter, State Printers, 1883.

———. "The Life of the Early Mill-Girls." *Journal of Social Science,* v. 16 (1882).

———. *Loom and Spindle; or, Life Among the Early Mill Girls.* New York: Thomas Y. Crowell, 1898.

Scoresby, William. *American Factories and their Female Operatives.* 1845; reprint, New York: Burt Franklin. 1968.

Thayer, J.Q.A. *Review of the Report of the Special Committee of the Legislature of the Commonwealth of Massachusetts on the Petition Relating to Hours of Labor.* Boston: J. N. Bang, 1845.

Upham, C. *The Factory Song.* Dunstable [Nashua], New Hampshire. Found in an autograph book of the 1830s, in the Nashua Public Library.

[Williams, Catherine]. *Fall River An Authentic Narrative.* Boston: Lilly, Wait and Co., 1834.

Secondary Sources

Abbott, Edith. "A Study of the Early History of Child Labor in America." *American Journal of Sociology,* v. 14 (1908).

———. *Women in Industry.* 1910; reprint, New York: Arno Press, 1969.

Ammidown, Holmes. *Historical Collections,* 2 vols. New York: the author, 1874.

Armstrong, John B. *Factory Under the Elms: A History of Harrisville, New Hampshire, 1774–1969.* Cambridge, Massachusetts: MIT Press, 1969.

Atkinson, Minnie. "Old Newburyport Ropewalks—A Vanished Industry." *Essex Institute Historical Collections,* v. 72 (1946).

Bender, Thomas. *Toward an Urban Vision: Ideas and Institutions in Nineteenth Century America.* 1975; reprint, Baltimore: Johns Hopkins University Press, 1982.

Benét, Steven V., comp. *A Collection of Annual Reports and Other Important Papers Relating to the Ordnance Department.* Washington, D.C.: Government Printing Office, 1878.

Boston, Ray. *British Chartists in America, 1839–1900.* Manchester, England: Manchester University Press, 1971.

Brecher, Jeremy, et al., eds. *Brass Valley.* Philadelphia: Temple University Press, 1982.

Brennan, Joseph. *Social Conditions in Industrial Rhode Island: 1820–1860.* Washington, D.C.: Catholic University, 1940.

Brody, David. "Time and Work During Early American Industrialism." *Labor History,* v. 30 (1989).

Browne, George W. *The Amoskeag Manufacturing Co. of Manchester, New Hampshire.* Manchester, New Hampshire: Amoskeag, 1915.

Bushman, Claudia L. *"A Good Poor Man's Wife," Being a Chronicle of Harriet Hanson Robinson and Her Family in Nineteenth-Century New England.* Hanover, New Hampshire: University Press of New England, 1981.

Candee, Richard M. "New Towns of the Early New England Textile Industry." *Perspectives in Vernacular Architecture.* Ed. Camille Wells. Vernacular Architecture Forum, 1982.

Cesari, Gene S. "American Arms-Making Machine-Tool Development, 1798–1855." Ph.D. diss., University of Pennsylvania, 1970.

Clouette, Bruce, and Matthew Roth. *Bristol, Connecticut: A Bicentennial History, 1785–1985.* Bristol: Bristol Public Library, 1984.

Coccia, Joseph. "The Cranston Print Works—Its Economic Significance to the City of Cranston and Its Influence on the Political, Social and Industrial Life of the City and the State of Rhode Island." Master's thesis, Rhode Island College of Education, 1955.

Cohen, Isaac. "American Management and British Labor: Lancashire Spinners in Industrial New England." *Comparative Studies in Society and History,* v. 27 (1985).

Cole, Charles C. *The Social Ideas of the Northern Evangelists, 1826–1860.* New York: Octagon, 1966.

Coleman, Peter J. *The Transformation of Rhode Island, 1790–1860.* Providence: Brown University Press, 1963.

Commons, John R., et al. *History of Labour in the United States,* v. 1. New York: Macmillan, 1918.

———, eds. *A Documentary History of American Industrial Society,* vols. 5–8. Cleveland: Arthur H. Clark Co., 1910.

Coogan, Timothy C. "Minders of the Machines, 1825–1845." *Labor in Massachusetts: Selected Essays.* Ed. Kenneth Fones-Wolf and Martin Kaufman. Westfield, Massachusetts: Institute for Massachusetts Studies, 1990.

Coolidge, John. *Mill and Mansion: A Study of Architecture and Society in Lowell, Massachusetts, 1820–1865.* New York: Columbia University Press, 1942.

Cooper, Carolyn C. " 'A Whole Battalion of Stockers': Thomas Blanchard's Production Line and Hand Labor at Springfield Armory." *IA: The Journal of the Society for Industrial Archeology,* v. 14 (1988).

Cudd, John M. *The Chicopee Manufacturing Company, 1823–1915.* Wilmington, Delaware: Scholarly Resources, 1974.

The Davis and Furber Machine Company and The Men Who Made It. Davis and Furber Machine Company, 1908.

Deyrup, Felicia. *Arms Makers of the Connecticut Valley: A Regional Study of the Economic Development of the Small Arms Industry, 1798–1870. Smith College Studies in History,* v. 33. Eds. Vera Holmes and Hans Kohn. Northampton, Massachusetts, 1948.

Dodd, Jill Siegel. "The Working Classes and the Temperance Movement in Ante-Bellum Boston." *Labor History,* v. 19 (1978).

Dublin, Thomas. *Women at Work: The Transformation of Work and Community in Lowell, Massachusetts, 1826–1860.* New York: Columbia University Press, 1979.

———, ed. *Farm to Factory: Women's Letters, 1830–1860.* New York: Columbia University Press, 1981.

Dunwell, Steve. *The Run of the Mill.* Boston: David R. Godine, 1978.

Early, Frances H. "A Reappraisal of the New England Labor Reform Movement of the 1840s: The Lowell Female Labor Reform Association and the New England Workingmen's Association." *Social History,* v. 13 (1980).

Eisler, Benita, ed. *The Lowell Offering.* New York: Harper and Row, 1977.

Eno, Arthur L., Jr., ed. *Cotton Was King: A History of Lowell, Massachusetts.* Lowell, Massachusetts: Lowell Historical Society, 1976.

Erickson, Charlotte. *Invisible Immigrants: The Adaptation of English and Scottish Immigrants in Nineteenth-Century America.* London: Weidenfeld and Nicolson, 1972.

Ewing, John S., and Nancy P. Norton. *Broadlooms and Businessmen: A History of the Bigelow-Sanford Carpet Company.* Cambridge, Massachusetts: Harvard University Press, 1955.

Fairfield, Roy P. *Sands, Spindles, and Steeples.* Portland, Maine: House of Falmouth, 1956.

Feldblum, Mary. "The Formation of the First Factory Labor Force in the New England Cotton Textile Industry, 1800–1848." Ph.D. diss., New School for Social Research, 1977.

Foner, Philip S. *History of the Labor Movement in the United States: From Colonial Times to the Founding of the American Federation of Labor,* v. 1. New York: International Publishers, 1947.

———, ed. *American Labor Songs of the Nineteenth Century.* Urbana: University of Illinois Press, 1975.

———, ed. *The Factory Girls.* Urbana: University of Illinois Press, 1977.

Garner, John S. *The Model Company Town: Urban Design Through Private Enterprise in Nineteenth-Century New England.* Amherst: University of Massachusetts Press, 1984.

Gersuny, Carl. " 'A Devil in Petticoats,' and Just Cause: Patterns of Punishment in Two New England Textile Factories." *Business History Review,* v. 50 (1976).

Gibbs, George S. *The Saco-Lowell Shops: Textile Machinery Building in New England, 1813–1949.* Cambridge, Massachusetts: Harvard University Press, 1950.

———. *The Whitesmiths of Taunton: A History of Reed and Barton, 1824–1943.* Cambridge, Massachusetts: Harvard University Press, 1943.

Gitelman, H. M. "No Irish Need Apply: Patterns of and Responses to Ethnic Discrimination in the Labor Market." *Labor History,* v. 14 (1973).

———. "The Waltham System and the Coming of the Irish." *Labor History,* v. 8 (1967).

Gordon, Robert B. "Who Turned the Mechanical Ideal into Mechanical Reality." *Technology and Culture,* v. 29 (1988).

Greenwood, Richard E. "Zachariah Allen and the Architecture of Industrial Paternalism." *Rhode Island History,* v. 46 (1988).

Hanlan, James P. *The Working Population of Manchester, New Hampshire, 1840–1886.* Ann Arbor, Michigan: UMI Research Press, 1981.

Hanna, William F. *Taunton Remembered.* Taunton, Massachusetts: Old Colony Historical Society, 1982.

Hartz, Louis. "Seth Luther: The Story of a Working-Class Rebel." *New England Quarterly,* v. 13 (1940).

Hayes, John L. *American Textile Machinery.* Cambridge, Massachusetts: University Press, J. Wilson and Son, 1879.

Hicks, James E. *Nathan Starr: The First Official Sword Maker.* Mt. Vernon, New York: the author, 1940.

Hindle, Brooke, and Stephen Lubar. *Engines of Change: The American Industrial Revolution, 1790–1860.* Washington, D.C.: Smithsonian Institution Press, 1986.

Hoke, Donald R. "Ingenious Yankees: The Rise of the American System of Manufactures in the Private Sector." Ph.D. diss., University of Wisconsin—Madison, 1984.

———. *Ingenious Yankees: The Rise of the American System of Manufactures in the Private Sector.* New York: Columbia University Press, 1989.

Horwitz, Richard P. *Anthropology Toward History: Culture and Work in a 19th-Century Maine Town.* Middletown, Connecticut: Wesleyan University Press, 1978.

Hounshell, David A. *From the American System to Mass Production, 1800–1932: The Development of Manufacturing Technology in the United States.* Baltimore: Johns Hopkins University Press, 1984.

Howe, George. "The Minister and the Mill Girl." *American Heritage,* v. 12, no. 6 (1961).

Howe, Henry. *Memoirs of the Most Most Eminent American Mechanics.* New York: Alexander V. Blake, 1841.

Hurd, D. Hamilton. *History of Worcester County, Massachusetts,* v. 2. Philadelphia: J. W. Lewis and Co., 1889.

Jeremy, David. *Transatlantic Industrial Revolution: The Diffusion of Textile Technologies Between Britain and America, 1790–1830s.* Cambridge, Massachusetts: MIT Press, 1981.

Josephson, Hannah. *The Golden Threads: New England's Mill Girls and Magnates.* New York: Duell, Sloan and Pearce, 1949.

Kasserman, David R. *Fall River Outrage: Life, Murder, and Justice in Early Industrial New England.* Philadelphia: University of Pennsylvania Press, 1986.

Kasson, John. *Civilizing the Machine: Technology and Republican Values in America, 1776–1900.* 1976; reprint, New York: Penguin Books, 1979.

Kulik, Gary. "The Beginnings of the Industrial Revolution in America: Pawtucket, Rhode Island, 1672–1820." Ph.D. diss., Brown University, 1980.

———. "A Factory System of Wood: Cultural and Technological Change in the Building of the First Cotton Mills." *Material Culture of the Wooden Age.* Ed. Brooke Hindle. Tarrytown, New York: Sleepy Hollow Press, 1981.

———. "Pawtucket Village and the Strike of 1824: The Origins of Class Conflict in Rhode Island." *Radical History Review,* v. 17 (1978).

Kulik, Gary, Roger Parks, and Theodore Penn, eds. *The New England Mill Village, 1790–1860. Documents in American Industrial History,* v. 2. Ed. Michael Folsom. Cambridge, Massachusetts: MIT Press, 1982.

Kull, Nell, ed. " 'I Could Never Be So Happy There Among All Those Mountains': The Letters of Sally Rice." *Vermont History,* v. 38 (1970).

Lathrop, William G. *The Brass Industry in the United States.* Mt. Carmel, Connecticut, 1926.

Layer, Robert G. *Earnings of Cotton Mill Operatives, 1825–1914.* Cambridge, Massachusetts: Harvard University Press, 1955.

Lazerow, Jama. "A Good Time Coming: Religion and the Emergence of Labor Activism in Antebellum New England." Ph.D. diss., Brandeis University, 1982.

———. "Religion and the New England Mill Girl: A New Perspective on an Old Theme." *New England Quarterly,* v. 60 (1987).

Leavitt, Thomas W., ed. *The Hollingworth Letters: Technical Change in the Textile Industry, 1826–1837.* Cambridge, Massachusetts: MIT Press, 1969.

"The Lowell Young Ladies: Early American Cotton Manufacturing, 1833–1854." *The History Reference Bulletin,* no. 16, section 1. February 1934.

Lozier, John W. "Rural Textile Mill Communities and the Transition to Industrialism in America, 1800–1840." *Working Papers from the Regional Economic History Research Center,* v. 4, no. 4. Eds. Glenn Porter and William Mulligan, Jr. (1981).

———. "Taunton and Mason: Cotton Machinery and Locomotive Manufacture in Taunton, Massachusetts, 1811–1861." Ph.D. diss., Ohio State University, 1978.

McCauley, Elfrieda. "The New England Mill Girls: Feminine Influence in the Development of Public Libraries in New England, 1820–1860." Ph.D. diss., Columbia University, 1971.

McGaw, Judith. *Most Wonderful Machine: Mechanization and Social Change in Berkshire Paper Making, 1801–1885.* Princeton, New Jersey: Princeton University Press, 1987.

———. "The Sources and Impact of Mechanization: The Berkshire County, Massachusetts, Paper Industry, 1801–1885, As a Case Study." Ph.D. diss., New York University, 1977.

Mailloux, Kenneth F. "The Boston Manufacturing Company of Waltham, Massachusetts, 1813–1848: The First Modern Factory in America." Ph.D. diss., Boston University, 1957.

Marburg, Theodore F. "Aspects of Labor Administration in the Early Nineteenth Century." *Bulletin of the Business Historical Society,* v. 15 (1941).

———. "Management Problems and Procedures of a Manufacturing Enterprise, 1802–1852: A Case Study of the Origin of the Scovill Manufacturing Company." Ph.D. diss., Clark University, 1945.

Marchalonis, Shirley. *The Worlds of Lucy Larcom, 1824–1893.* Athens: University of Georgia Press, 1989.

Mayr, Otto, and Robert Post, eds. *Yankee Enterprise: The Rise of the American System of Manufactures.* Washington, D.C.: Smithsonian Institution Press, 1981.

Merriam, Robert, et al. *The History of the John Russell Cutlery Company, 1833–1936.* Greenfield, Massachusetts: Bete Press, 1976.

Merrimack Valley Textile Museum. "Homespun to Factory Made: Woolen Textiles in America, 1776–1876." Exhibition catalogue. North Andover, Massachusetts: M.V.T.M., 1977.

Mirsky, Jeannette, and Alan Nevins. *The World of Eli Whitney.* New York: Macmillan, 1952.

Morison, Samuel E. *The Ropemakers of Plymouth: A History of the Plymouth Cordage Company, 1824–1949.* Boston: Houghton Mifflin, 1950.

Murphy, John J. "The Establishment of the American Clock Industry: A Study in Entrepreneurial History." Ph.D. diss., Yale University, 1961.

Murphy, Theresa. "Labor, Religion and Moral Reform in Fall River, Massachusetts, 1800–1845." Ph.D. diss., Yale University, 1982.

Mussey, Barrows. *Young Father Time: A Yankee Portrait.* New York: Newcomen Society in North America, 1950.

Navin, Thomas R. *The Whitin Machine Works Since 1831: A Textile Machinery Company in an Industrial Village.* Cambridge, Massachusetts: Harvard University Press, 1950.

Nisonoff, Laurie. "Bread and Roses: The Proletarianization of Women Workers in New England Textile Mills, 1827–1848." *Historical Journal of Massachusetts,* v. 9 (1981).

North, S. N. D., and Ralph North. *Simeon North: First Official Pistol Maker of the United States.* Concord, New Hampshire: Rumford Press, 1913.

Orpen, Adelia E. *The Chronicles of the Sid or The Life and Travels of Adelia Gates.* London: The Religious Tract Society, 1893.

Peck, Frederick M., and Henry H. Earl. *Fall River And Its Industries.* Fall River, Massachusetts: Benjamin Earl and Son, 1877.

Persons, Charles E. "The Early History of Factory Legislation in Massachusetts." *Labor Laws and Their Enforcement.* Ed. Susan M. Kingsbury. New York: Longmans, Green and Co., 1911.

Pierson, William. "Harrisville, N.H.: A Nineteenth-Century Industrial Town." *Antiques,* v. 102 (1972).

———. "Industrial Architecture in the Berkshires." Ph.D. diss., Yale University, 1949.

Prude, Jonathan. *The Coming of Industrial Order: Town and Factory Life in Rural Massachusetts, 1810–1860.* Cambridge, England: Cambridge University Press, 1983.

"Reminiscences of Samuel Bryan Jerome." *The Timepiece Journal,* v. 2 (1979–1980).

Roediger, David R., and Philip S. Foner. *Our Own Time: A History of American Labor and the Working Day.* New York: Greenwood Press, 1989.

Rorabaugh, W. J. *The Craft Apprentice: From Franklin to the Machine Age in America.* New York: Oxford University Press, 1986.

Sande, Theodore. "Architecture of the Rhode Island Textile Industry, 1790–1860." Ph.D. diss., University of Pennsylvania, 1972.

———. "The Textile Factory in Pre–Civil War Rhode Island." *Old Time New England,* v. 66, nos. 1–2 (1975).

Selden, Bernice. *The Mill Girls: Lucy Larcom, Harriet Hanson Robinson and Sarah G. Bagley.* New York: Atheneum, 1983.

Shlakman, Vera. *Economic History of a Factory Town: A Study of Chicopee, Massachusetts. Smith College Studies in History,* v. 20. Eds. John C. Hildt, William Dodge Gray, and Harold Underwood Faulkner. Northampton, Massachusetts, 1934–1935.

Siracusa, Carl. *A Mechanical People: Perceptions of the Industrial Order in Massachusetts, 1815–1880.* Middletown, Connecticut: Wesleyan University Press, 1979.

Sloat, Caroline. "The Dover Manufacturing Company and the Integration of English and American Calico Printing Techniques, 1825–1829." *Winterthur Portfolio,* v. 10 (1975).

Stearns, Bertha M. "Early Factory Magazines in New England: The Lowell Offering and Its Contemporaries." *Journal of Economic and Business History,* v. 2 (1930).

Stone, Orra L. *History of Massachusetts Industries.* 4 vols. Boston: S. J. Clarke Publishing Co., 1930.

Strassman, W. Paul. *Risk and Technological Innovation: American Manufacturing Methods During the Nineteenth Century.* Ithaca, New York: Cornell University Press, 1959.

Swank, James M. *History of the Manufacture of Iron in All Ages and Particularly in the United States from Colonial Times to 1891.* 1892; reprint, New York: Burt Franklin, 1965.

Taber, Martha. *A History of the Cutlery Industry in the Connecticut Valley. Smith College Studies in History,* v. 41. Eds. Vera B. Holmes, Sidney R. Packard, and Leona C. Gabel. Northampton, Massachusetts, 1955.

Tamburro, Francis. "A Tale of a Song, 'The Lowell Factory Girl.'" *Southern Exposure,* v. 2 (1974).

Thompson, E. P. "Time, Work-Discipline and Industrial Capitalism." *Past and Present,* v. 38 (1967).

Tolles, Bryant F. "Textile Mill Architecture in East-Central New England: An Analysis of Pre–Civil War Design." *Essex Institute Historical Collections,* v. 107 (1971).

Tomlins, Christopher. "The Ties That Bind: Master and Servant in Massachusetts, 1800–1850." *Labor History,* v. 30 (1989).

Tucker, Barbara M. "The Family and Industrial Discipline in Antebellum New England." *Labor History*, v. 21 (1979–1980).

———. " 'Our Good Methodists': The Church, The Factory, and the Working Class in Ante-Bellum Webster, Massachusetts." *The Maryland Historian*, v. 8, no. 2 (1977).

———. *Samuel Slater and the Origins of the American Textile Industry, 1790–1860.* Ithaca, New York: Cornell University Press, 1984.

Uselding, Paul. "An Early Chapter in the Evolution of American Industrial Management." *Business Enterprise and Economic Change.* Ed. Louis Cain and Paul Uselding. Kent, Ohio: Kent State University Press, 1973.

———. "Elisha K. Root, Forging, and the 'American System.'" *Technology and Culture*, v. 15 (1974).

Victor, Stephen, et al., eds. *The Fall River Sourcebook: A Documentary History of Fall River, Massachusetts.* American History Workshop, 1981.

Vogel, Lise. "Humorous Incidents and Sound Common Sense: More on the New England Mill Women." *Labor History*, v. 19 (1978).

Ware, Caroline F. *The Early New England Cotton Manufacture: A Study in Industrial Beginnings.* Boston: Houghton Mifflin, 1931.

Ware, Norman. *The Industrial Worker, 1840–1860.* 1924; reprint, Chicago: Quadrangle, 1964.

Waters, Asa H. *Biographical Sketch of Thomas Blanchard and His Inventions.* Worcester, Massachusetts: Lucius Goddard, 1878.

Whitin, E. Stagg. *Factory Legislation in Maine. Studies in History, Economics and Public Law*, v. 33, no. 1. New York: Columbia University Press, 1908.

Whittlesey, Derwent S. "The Springfield Armory: A Study in Institutional Development." Ph.D. diss., University of Chicago, 1920.

Wilbur, W. R. *History of the Bolt and Nut Industry of America.* Cleveland: Ward and Shaw, 1905.

Wolfe, Allis, ed. "Letters of a Lowell Mill Girl and Friends: 1845–46." *Labor History*, v. 17 (1976).

Wood, Joseph S. "Village and Community in Early Colonial New England." *Material Life in America, 1600–1860.* Ed. Robert Blair St. George. Boston: Northeastern University Press, 1988.

Wright, Helena. "Sarah G. Bagley: A Biographical Note." *Labor History*, v. 20 (1979).

Yorke, Dane. *The Men and Times of Pepperill.* Boston: Pepperill Manufacturing Company, 1945.

Zevin, Robert B. *The Growth of Manufacturing in Early Nineteenth-Century New England.* New York: Arno Press, 1975.

Zonderman, David A. "From Mill Village to Industrial City: Letters from Vermont Factory Operatives." *Labor History*, v. 27 (1986).

Index